AstroAnalysis

SUN SIGNS Compatibility Guide

The American AstroAnalysts Institute

GROSSET & DUNLAP
A FILMWAYS COMPANY
Publishers • New York

Published simultaneously in Canada
Library of Congress catalog card number: 77-77124
ISBN 0-448-14363-1 (hardcover)
ISBN 0-448-14364-X (paperback)
First printing 1977
Printed in the United States of America

CONTENTS

INTRODUCTION

No Islands in the Universe

The basis of Astrology is that the universe, like the Earth we live on, is a whole and that there is a correlation between what goes on out there and human experience. It maintains that when a massive body, such as a star like our Sun, or the planets or the Moon, changes position, it produces an effect on the rest of the system. This is not disputed by science. The effects are not all observable or measurable, though every schoolchild has heard of some that are. The phases of the Moon, for instance, control the tides in association with the position of the Sun. But some effects are liable to raise scientific eyebrows, and perhaps blood pressures, even though they are undeniable. Correlated with the movements of the Moon, the Sun and the tides are the breeding cycles and habits of fish, which, in turn, are correlated with the economics of the fishing industry and the prosperity of those engaged in it. This is an oversimplification, a generalization; there is no need to belabor it. But it does make a point: the correlations with this one fact are virtually infinite. Correlations can obviously be found for everything. There are no islands in the universe.

The scientific and astrological views of the universe diverge at the point where man enters. Astrology includes the individual in the system. Science, surprisingly, does not—except as a statistic. Astrology says without equivocation that the individual's personality and behavior are influenced by the interaction of the massive solar bodies, particularly at the moment of his or her birth. The conventional scientific mind says: "Definitely not." And then science announces the kind of brilliant discovery—which shall be discussed shortly—that *just about* reaches across the gulf to the outstretched hand of Astrology.

The polarization of the two points of view—that is, their valid existence as an indispensable pair of opposites forming a whole new system of knowledge—seems relatively near. One could go so far as to say it requires only one more scientific breakthrough. But the link can't be forged until scientists are willing to see man's needs in correct perspective to his longings.

We are not here for science, any more than we are here for Astrology. They are only means. Man longs to feel at peace in his psychological self. He does not need many possessions to achieve this. He was happy (and unhappy) in himself long before science heaped its benefits upon him. Astrology recognizes that peace and fulfillment come through understanding, for what a person understands, he can generally control. And it is the scientist's task to enlarge our understanding of the physical universe. But that is the second half of the story.

Astrology is a science of people. It is the chronology of observations of individual traits and cosmic correlations since time began. It does not depend on the experiments and observations of less than 300 years, as modern science does; Astrology has been classifying results for about 10,000 years. It has not been restricted by any lack of sophisticated instruments and technical expertise. People are people. And the solar bodies have always been there for the inquiring mind to observe and draw conclusions from. Telescopes and the like have not changed the fundamental principles of Astrology because Astrology is based on observations made from the Earth. And Earth people still live on the Earth and have the same correlations with the cosmos that they did thousands of years ago. The momentous sixteenth-century discovery that the Earth revolved around the Sun did not invalidate Astrology. On the contrary, it has never had so many serious followers, among them a large number of distinguished men and women of science. The famous psychologist C. J. Jung said: "Astrology is assured of recognition from psychology without further restrictions because astrology represents the summation of all the psychological knowledge of antiquity."

The Genetic Code Bombshell

The exciting scientific discovery that makes it possible to speak of an approaching standoff between Astrology and science is DNA—the genetic code. Most people know that the cell is nature's building block for all living things. In the nineteenth century, Gregory Mendel, an Austrian priest and botanist, proposed the first theory of heredity after experiments principally associated with the familiar sweet pea. This led to a new branch of science that established that the medium whereby hereditary features are transmitted from one cell to the next is an element called the gene. At the moment of conception, the genes in the cells of the parents mix in a wild scramble—and suddenly there is a new individual, all packed and ready to go with his or her particular hereditary baggage.

The exact nature of the genes remained pretty much a mystery for some time. But eventually geneticists found that the important material in the genes was an amazing and complex substance called deoxyribonucleic acid, or DNA. On this substance was "stamped" the hereditary data in a code form—something like the perforated cards of a computer program.

And then came the bombshell. Three brilliant biologists, J. D. Watson (U.S.), F. H. C. Crick and M. H. F. Wilkins (Britain), proposed one of the most startling theories of the age:

The fate of every individual is written at birth in the genes. Our predispositions of character, our intelligence, their varying inclinations and strengths throughout youth, maturity and old age, are all stamped there in indelible script. Not only our future physical strengths and weaknesses are written there, but also that moment in the future when our body and its organs will begin to break down and dip toward feebleness and senility.

The three scientists were awarded the Nobel Prize for chemistry. However astrologers have been saying the same thing, only in a different handwriting, for thousands of years. They call it a horoscope.

Researchers have shown that the DNA in the genes is structurally different for every human being. The parallel in Astrology is the "genetic" or natal horoscope, which records the correlated positions of the solar bodies at the moment of birth. The astrologer draws from this information about an individual in much the same way as the geneticists have begun to from the genetic code. Both types of deduction require considerable skill and experience.

The Planetary Clocks

Despite the genetic breakthrough, there is an outstanding question science has yet to answer: What activates the different stages of the genetic program? Or, who or what pushes the button?

The genetic code is an extremely recent discovery. Scientists know roughly what is in it, but they can't yet be specific. They have had only a few years to observe the phenomenon, and it may be centuries before its full significance is known. Astrology, on the other hand, has had millennia to observe "genetic" horoscopes. Therefore it offers unparalleled classifications of the basic types of people (12 Sun Signs), as well as variations and refinements of character (Planetary Aspects and Ascendants). "Human personalities," observed Jung, "coincide in the most remarkable way with traditional astrological expectations."

The astrologer, because of his greater experience, is in a much stronger position to predict character and behavior than the scientist. But Astrology is most soundly predictive when it is used by the individual to know himself. If you understand the potentialities and tendencies that were inscribed in you from your beginning, you can use or curb these to advantage and thus have a hand in your own destiny. You are a pawn only as long as you want to be. You have a free will, and you may choose to exercise it.

Earlier, reference was made to the effect that the Moon has on the Earth. Its tidal influence, through gravity acting on the fluid bulk of the oceans, is fairly well understood. But science has recently made remarkable discoveries that back up the astrologer's method of looking at and interpreting this and other influences.

An American biologist, Dr. Frank Brown of Northwestern University, transported some oysters from Long Island Sound in hermetically sealed containers to his laboratory at Evanston, Illinois, 1000 miles inland. He wanted to know how they would behave so far away from their native habitat when feeding time came. As he had suspected, the oysters at first obeyed the East Coast tidal rhythm and opened at the time they had in the Sound. But at the end of 14 days, a remarkable thing happened. Their rhythm shifted progressively until the oysters opened exactly when the tide would have come in had the laboratory been by the water. This was the moment when the Moon reached the meridian overhead. The "lunar clock," correlated to the cell cycle of the oysters, was not confused for very long by the laboratory's experiment.

The same biologist wanted to know if the fiddler crab's change of color was caused only by environmental responses. He put a number of these crabs in a dark room well sheltered from the Moon's light rays and—*presto!* They changed color according to the Moon's position.

He decided to go further. How would a water creature that had lived all its life in a dark, completely enclosed cave and had never felt the effects of the tide behave? He chose a crayfish and produced evidence that its metabolic processes responded to a rhythm related to the Earth's rotation and the position of the Moon.

Researchers have discovered that mammals—specifically, rats—are also sensitive to the Moon clock's commands. Locked inside a closed room for several months without a clue as to whether it was day or night, the rats showed peaks of activity clearly related to the Moon's positions. They also showed a behavioral rhythm that seemed to depend on the position of the Sun.

After their experiments with animals, researchers now think that conditions they once believed were constant may in reality be continuously influenced by the Sun, the Moon and possibly the other planets—a point Astrology has been making for centuries.

Stress Among the Stars

That the planets affect all living things is obvious to astrologers. But despite their own discoveries, this contention is so far unacceptable to scientists. Yet, here too, science is having to consider some extraordinary new evidence.

Most people know that sunspots affect radio reception, but when a technical director of Radio Corporation of America Communications, John H. Nelson, carried out a study over a period of years, he found evidence of an unsuspected factor: the planets. "It is very clear that other forces [than the Sun] are involved," he said. "It is therefore necessary to find a new approach. Study of the planets has revealed encouraging results and a more detailed examination is indicated. A highly developed technique of forecasting radio interference based on the motions of the planets would have the advantage of making possible long-range calculations, since the motions of the planets are well known."

So Nelson made his more detailed study and proved his point: a new approach was necessary. By bringing the planets into his figuring, he was able to predict poor radio reception days with 93 percent accuracy, a result not possible prior to this time.

One of the strange (but to astrologers not so surprising) observations made during the study was that radio interference reached a peak when the planets, in relation to the Sun, were either square to each other (90 degrees), in conjunction (0 degrees) or in opposition (180 degrees). It so happens that in Astrology these same aspects, as they are called, are regarded as causing stress and tension. Conjunctions, however, may be modified in their effect by the nature of the planet concerned—which suggests another field worthy of scientific inquiry.

The Living Sundial

The power of the Sun to affect human behavior is also receiving increasing attention from scientists. One tremendous advance in this study followed an astonishing piece of detective work by a famous Japanese doctor named Maki Takata, a professor at Toho University, Tokyo.

The Takata effect had long been used by gynecologists the world over to indicate the stage of ovarian and menstrual cycles in women patients. The effect was produced by mixing a reactive substance with a blood sample. As male blood did not react, the Takata effect was an excellent aid.

Suddenly, all over the world, blood reactions went wild, canceling out the Takata effect. At the same time, male blood was showing very unstable properties.

Takata and his international colleagues were mystified. He determined to solve the problem. Seventeen years later, he was able to announce that sunspot activity had changed the blood of every person on the planet.

His research showed that the effect on the blood occurred in particular when a group of sunspots moved to the center of the Sun's surface during their 11-year cycle, causing the Sun to shoot a maximum of waves and particles toward the Earth.

"Man is a kind of living sundial," Takata declared. "If the Sun causes irregularities of the blood serum, these must necessarily follow that star's changes of mood."

Takata made another very interesting discovery. Just at the moment when the Sun is about to rise, activity in the blood suddenly shows an enormous increase after having been calm all night. And the odd thing is, he found, the increase begins some minutes *before* sunrise as though the blood anticipated the appearance of the Sun.

The Moon's power to interfere with solar radiation next attracted Takata's attention. In tests made during three eclipses, he found that as soon as the Moon began to move across the Sun, the blood activity started to drop, reaching a minimum during full eclipse. The Moon appeared to be intercepting the solar radiation.

The results of the Takata experiments show an extraordinary resemblance to what Astrology has to say about the Sun-Moon relationship. One astrologist theorized that the Moon represents the ability to *absorb the solar currents which pulse through every nerve and tissue of the human and cosmic organism.* In other words, as Takata found, the solar currents throb through human blood and the cosmic plasma.

Russian scientists have been concerned with the effects of sunspot activity on behavior, particularly in regard to wars, revolutions and mass migrations—the last, of course, being quite common among lower animals. One significant point is that intense sunspot reaction occurred in 1938, and the following year the world plunged into the worst war in history. The outbreak of the Korean War was another case in point.

An achievement by the Italian chemist Giorgio Piccardi demonstrates in strictly scientific terms the kind of forces acting on the earth that Astrology has continually tried to draw attention to. Piccardi was asked to explain why activated water descaled boilers and pipes while normal water did not. Also, why activated water only worked sometimes.

After an immense amount of work over a period of years, Piccardi found the answers in the stars, so to speak. He discovered that the inorganic colloids in water were affected by conditions in outer space and varied with the position of the Earth in the galaxy. He found that certain cosmic forces broke down the structure of water. Activated water was structurally suited to dissolve scale, whereas normal water wasn't. But the treatment didn't always work because the *conditions in outer space prevented it. He found success depended on the year, the month, the day and even the hour!*

Since the human body is essentially made up of water and colloids, the Piccardi effect has great ramifications and these are currently the subject of considerable research.

So another striking scientific fact had emerged to confirm astrological method: the time at which experiments were conducted was often of vital importance. Cosmic factors had to be considered as contributory determinants—an obvious parallel to Astrology's concern with the date and moment of birth.

The Ten Life Stages of Man

The correlation of planetary symbolism with the facts of life is quite amazing when considered with an open mind. An interesting example is the astrological scheme of the ten life stages of man. Each stage of seven years is represented by a planet. The sequence follows the actual order of the planets, going away from the Sun. Their "natures," and therefore the particular effect each has on man during the life stage it governs, are the same as has been ascribed to the traditional planets for thousands of years.

The Moon Age (1 to 7 years)

The Moon, the nearest body to the Earth, is treated as a planet. It has always signified the mother, rhythms, water and all other life-giving liquids. It reflects the dual nature of the evolving human spirit, part conscious, part unconscious. It is itself the unconscious side of the personality, bound by instincts, involuntary responses and momentary urges. It is passively receptive to outside influences.

So the child begins its life in a psychologically fluid state, taking its early egotistical shape from the maternal mold. Although an individual with distinct characteristics that will later become conscious, the infant experiences helplessness and vulnerability, and is unable to act for itself except in blind or dim responses. Throughout these first seven years, the child registers the effects of its environment and in so doing displays the acutely impressionable nature of the Moon.

The Mercury Age (7 to 14 years)

Mercury is the intellectual force that governs speech, writing, communication and the mental functions in general. It also rules common sense. It is adaptable, versatile, quick, restless, irresponsible, logical, inquisitive and fast-moving.

The early school years are when the child learns the mechanics of communication, how to write, to speak, to express him- or herself as a mental being and not just as a collection of clamorous desires. He discovers he can contradict the voice of authority sometimes and assert his ideas so that others will listen and pay attention. He makes innumerable connections and contacts, developing a casual attitude toward responsibility and a flexible sense of morality. He moves around incessantly with inquisitive purpose, loses interest as quickly as he gains it and begins to control aspects of his environment through the advancing power of his mental processes.

The Venus Age (14 to 21 years)

Venus is the influence of love, art, culture, sympathy, social relationships, evaluation. All emotions that have a sexual or sensual basis begin here, including the love of beauty. Creative activities—poetry, acting, music, dancing—come under the Venusian force. It aims to unify.

This is the time when the mental enthusiasms of the Mercurial Age turn to love, when intense emotions come and go with brief but remarkable impact. It is the age of fads and crazes that develop in various ways into mature and admirable tastes. The adolescent learns to discriminate, to assess people and situations, to test values, to experiment with the feelings of others, to observe the power of his or her physical presence. The value of cooperation, the social advantages of popularity, the deeper meaning of friendship and the conduct that society demands are also learned. The adolescent prepares for adult life.

The Earth Age (21 to 28 years)

In geocentric (Earth-centered) Astrology, the Earth is not considered a planet, so this period of development is one of self-confrontation. Having come of age, the individual must adjust to material living and all its attendant responsibilities. As the Earth is in the center of the planetary lineup between the extremes of pliability and rigidity, so is the person during the Earth Age. The lessons of the past, ideally, have produced in him or her a sense of balance, proportion and moderation. Other factors not so easy to define may now become influential.

Normally the young adult will endeavor to establish himself in a career or particular occupation—put roots down and set about justifying his existence. The end of the Earth cycle frequently produces a crisis. This is the time when the individual realizes life is not what he thought it was, when he must decide what he is going to make of it and face the person that he really is. The talents he has uncovered (or covered up) in himself will not easily be denied self-expression. The young man or woman may have to make one or two painful decisions that will mean considerable reorientation. The end of this phase marks the return of the restrictive planet Saturn to the position it occupied in the horoscope at the time of birth, which signifies a new beginning.

The Mars Age (28 to 35 years)

Mars is the planet of energy, activity through enterprise, self-assertion and leadership.

This is a strenuous period when the individual, now stabilized in character, endeavors to make a personal imprint on his or her community. He or she becomes a dynamic influence, responding with vigor to challenges, competing for leadership and acclaim. Ambition is usually the first consideration, money the second. The need to accomplish at almost any cost is paramount. Physical strains are ignored or overcome by aggressive determination to succeed. Those who have laid sound foundations in the previous age now build their edifices with relentless energy. On these, they must now stand or fall.

The Jupiter Age (35 to 42 years)

Jupiter represents expansion—by growth, material acquisition and understanding. It signifies law, banking, philosophy, religion, moderation, reason. It also stands for foreign affairs, including distant journeys.

Now the individual begins to profit from earlier efforts and experience. He or she assumes some authority as a counselor of others, and becomes established in his or her chosen calling. This is the prime of life when the person expands financially, becomes an established citizen, a respectable and reliable member of the community. It is also a time associated with middle-age spread. The growth process reflects itself in a psychological maturity; the person develops an inner sense of law, order and morals. Religious convictions become more certain, and the mature adult reflects the type of person that has been formed through the earlier ages and anticipates future development. Since the direction of life is now probably fairly well fixed, the individual must look for ways of modifying his or her underlying attitudes and illusions in order to experience the deeper fulfillment of self-progression.

The Saturn Age (42 to 49 years)

Saturn is sometimes symbolized as Father Time, the old man with the hourglass and scythe. It represents the formative principle through restriction, discipline and rigidity. It stands for gravity, profundity, prudence, caution and organization. It is the symbol of the limitation of the physical, through which the human spirit, evolving as mind, must penetrate to go on.

This is the period when the person learns the lessons of self-discipline. The formative years, physically, are over. He or she is now a fixed and determined entity. If mistakes have been made in the creation of the self, this is the age when they are apt to be revealed and demand rectification. Here is where the habitual person finds himself heading for the abyss of decline and depression. But the individual who has fulfilled the earlier stages, it marks the way up, a different kind of path, a compensation for growing old.

This Saturn Age teaches the need for realistic, practical and responsible handling of life's affairs, as distinct from expediency and the habit of self-interest. By the end of the Saturn period, the person has almost concluded his first 50 years. He knows the difference between right and wrong. If he has had to pay, he understands the reasons why. By obeying the community's laws, he upholds these laws and is capable of performing as an authority within the social system. His own endeavors to effect order within himself can now be used to create order in his surroundings. As society once helped to shape him, so now he can help to shape society. And having learned to serve, he may now himself be served. But for the ordinary man or woman, it is difficult to withstand the constrictive and ossifying influence of the Saturn Age. It usually ends in hardening of the arteries, brittleness of the skeleton and a fixation of views that can only be dissolved by the grave.

The Uranus Age (49 to 56 years)

Uranus stands for independence, drastic change, revolt, anarchy, genius, intuition. It also represents Astrology, metaphysics, telepathy and events of a curious or wondrous nature.

This is the age of a second flowering for those who can allow the old self to die. It is the time that the young man or woman at the end of the Earth Age is unconsciously striving toward as the greatest good, but seldom attains. For here is the chance to leap forward, not with enthusiasm, but with wisdom, into a new state of consciousness. This is the age that offers the person the power to break away from the rigidly controlled norm. Here is the realization that uniqueness lies not only in being safe, sober and reliable. Within each individual is the power to be exceptional, if only he can reach it, and this is the stage where he discovers that instead of reaching up, he must reach within to unlock the spontaneous force that will free him from the cyclic rut of accepted limitations. From this renewing impulse springs originality, creative inspiration, scientific thought and inventiveness. Here men and women can produce their most valuable and original work.

The Neptune Age (56 to 63 years)

Neptune symbolizes the evolving human spirit as mind transcending the physical condition. It stands for refinement—through dissolution, subtlety and immateriality. The Neptune function, like the sea with which it is traditionally identified, has no material roots. It is a dissolver of form.

The fully developed person now begins to withdraw from inordinate attachments to the world. His values have a deepening spiritual content that goes beyond the dogma and ceremony of orthodox religions. He meditates without concepts, places less and less dependence on memories of the past and yearns to empty himself of his egotistical cravings.

By rising above the Saturnian need for psychological security and continuity, the ripe man or woman finds both, either in enlightenment or death.

The Pluto Age (63 to 70 years)

Pluto is the last known planet in the solar system. As the Sun represents the beginning of the person, so Pluto symbolizes the cyclic return through experience to that beginning. It is said to be the deliverer. As the Sun is the unexpressed potential at the center, so Pluto, as the final stage of man's progression, represents the seed—a new crystallized beginning.

The fully developed person at this stage knows himself, and in knowing that, comprehends the last mystery.

ARIES' CHARACTER

Yours is the most refreshing Sign of the Zodiac. You come with the spring, when the beleaguered winter world is waiting for a change. It is your nature to rush in, to burst upon the scene as brisk and vibrant as the new season that marks your birth. You are rash, full of life, impulsive—and spontaneous. You are always where the action starts. But you are seldom there when it's over and it's time for cleaning up.

Aries, which is Latin for *Ram,* is the first Sign of the Zodiac. It represents energy's thrust into matter, birth, new beginnings. Being first and like an infant with no history to fall back on, it knows little about restraint. Throughout his or her life, the Aries person has to battle to overcome this lack of restraint. He's always a bit bewildered by it. Why shouldn't I be me, he demands. All the other Signs with whom the Aries lives have built-in curbs, inhibitions, finely conditioned persuasions that make it almost impossible for them to appreciate the elemental nakedness of the Aries drive.

You want the world and you want it now. You can never really grow up, thank goodness. The childlike need to reach out, to grab what you want whenever you want it, is not bad. Certainly, it has to be controlled so you can live in this world. But that's what the mind is for, to bring young Aries to a stage of evaluation and discrimination. And the Aries mind is an excellent, finely tuned instrument for doing just this. But basically, you want the adventure of life. This is your reason for being. It's as simple as that. Others may want to understand life, to experience it, explain it, serve it. But not you. You are in it for the old-fashioned adventure. You want to be the first to reach out for whatever life has to offer. In that sense, you are "me first" all the way. And you are seldom bothered if others disapprove, or too distracted by who gets hurt in the process.

It's not so much that you want what you grab for. If you got all you wanted, you'd probably give most of it away. You are neither a hoarder nor a stingy person. It's just that when something is there, the sheer presence of it is a challenge for you to try to take or conquer. The person who risks death to climb mountains just because they are there embodies this peculiarly Aries drive.

So you see, it's not surprising that your type is always described as a natural leader. Nor that you have courage, energy and initiative. To be an adventurer in the audacious Aries style requires all these qualities.

You are also a loner. Unlike the proud Leo leader, you don't need a following. It's enough for you to be out in front, where the action is. If others wish to follow, good. You'll enjoy the company—and they may be valuable to clean up the mess of detail and unfinished business you leave behind when another great new idea sends you racing off.

As bold, daring and energetic as you are, sustained effort exhausts you. You like to bowl up to the challenge of the moment, grapple with it and get it over with—quickly. While the struggle is on, you can display amazing strength and determination. No one could be more resourceful, willing or active. But you tend to stop just short of the final mark. It's as though you never really wanted what you were after. Despite all the trouble you may have taken, you seldom seem to find sufficient incentive to make the last gesture. Detail and trivia appall you. Once you've accomplished the broad objectives, your interest wanes. You leave it to others to do the mopping up, the mundane organizing, the paying off of willing helpers. Sometimes you have even gone on your way before the spoils are divided. You are not really in it for the loot. You are more suited to bursts of extreme effort. Routine bores you stiff.

You will always retain the basic childlike eagerness to reach out, to try to take. It makes you extremely impulsive. You see something, an idea or an object, and you act. You'll never really control this impulse. If you do, you'll lose something of yourself. Your spontaneity will fade (let's trust this has not already happened) and you will become dull, a problem to yourself, a little more responsible, sober, reliable; a little more sophisticated, intellectually inhibited and conformist—straitjacketed.

It is because of this childlike quality that you are so open and honest. It is not in your nature to complicate. You prefer everything out in the open, simple, easy to absorb. Intrigue is something you sometimes pretend to know all about but actually it is beyond you. You are a bad liar unless it is a simple yes-or-no affair. Any attempt you make to be devious or scheming will hardly come up to schoolchild standards. You find life easier being direct. If you do what you want, why should you have to be dishonest about it? A delightful philosophy. The trouble is, Aries, it doesn't work.

You often hurt people. You might not mean to, but you do. You stride through their lives with a careless disregard for the wounding word and the reckless action. The far-reaching implications of your casual conduct rarely occur to you. You are also unwittingly selfish through your impulsiveness. You are not to blame—in a way. The Aries person, like the other Signs of the Zodiac, is an evolving personality, gradually moving toward the true character of his or her type.

The pure Aries character contains a lofty nobility. This is because the Sun—the most powerful and ennobling force in our cosmic system—is exalted or at its peak strength in this first Sign. The Sun's power is purposefulness, individuality and dignity through self-awareness. This influence allows the Aries personality to develop in a unique and integrated way. You do not need to put mental handcuffs on yourself—as other Signs do—to control with thought your wonderful, fundamental quality of spontaneity. How can you be spontaneous if you think first? It is true that you frequently express this gift as impulsiveness—that is its negative form. But mind curbs will only repress your true self, make you explosive, violent. Through self-awareness, spontaneity can become an integral part of your character and not something separate that acts unconsciously to the injury and detriment of others. A mature, developed Aries is forever young psychologically, ennobled by his or her originality.

On the surface, you can be friendly and communicative, but you don't encourage intimate relationships. Few people ever really get close to you and you rarely confide your secrets. You hold your cards close to the chest and anyone found peeping is likely to get a verbal swipe or feel the cold edge of the sword every Aries has hidden in his or her nature. For the sword, the symbol of primal force and aggression, is very much a part of the Aries personality. Your planetary ruler is Mars, the mythological god of war. Your Sign is also associated with iron, a quality of strength and an essential metal for weaponry.

In many ways, the Aries is the world's soldier. He wades in against fearful odds. He is able to fight on an empty stomach and without pay to achieve his ends. What he can vanquish he considers his. And when the battle is over and it's time for carousing, heaven help the man or woman who stands between an Aries and the bar—or the bed. This may seem an odd analogy when both Aries women and men are being discussed, but heat, energy and aggressive self-assertion are the primal impulses of both sexes.

You are kind and generous. You enjoy doing things for people, especially if it involves organizing them. The sweeping, throwaway charitable flourish is right up your alley. If someone asks you to walk a mile with him, you'll go ten, racing around, picking up this, arranging that, and meeting him at the other end with a basket of goodies he probably didn't want. You're a bit of a bossy benefactor, although you mean well. You know what is good for everyone—and you aim to see that they get it. Asking you for a favor can be a pretty exhausting business.

Despite your superpolyurethane crack-resistant veneer, you hurt easily. For one thing, you must receive recognition for favors done. Even though you may give the impression you never want the matter mentioned again, you'll be looking for the right word of thanks, the appropriate expression of gratitude. If it's not forthcoming, you'll be dejected, hurt—perhaps throw a tantrum. But you'll recover quickly and say "yes" again, unhesitatingly, if asked for help.

People are attracted by your irrepressible enthusiasm and optimism. You can always be counted on for a good idea or an exciting scheme. You never bore your audience with detail. And you don't ask many questions because you're usually talking about yourself or your projects and tend to become glassy-eyed when others try to do the same. But if their ideas are bright and catch your interest, they couldn't have a more willing or live-wire supporter. You'll work for another person's good idea as loyally as you would for your own, as long as there is no compulsion. You are an incurable idealist and there is much of the visionary in your concepts. You paint broad and sweeping mental pictures, erect magnificent imaginative enterprises and sometimes mistake your own fiction for fact. As you talk or think about a scheme, you become intense, urgent, and convince yourself that it can't wait. Rarely do you pause long enough to plan an action through from go to whoa. Much of your life is played by ear because you won't wait for the music to be written. Impatience is almost a disease with you.

The Aries Sign produces a physically distinctive type of person. Although a pure Aries is probably nonexistent because of hereditary factors and other planetary considerations, all those born between March 21 and April 20, or who have Aries as their Ascendant, embody a greater or lesser degree of the archetypal features. A common one is well-marked brows—generally bushy eyebrows that join and dip at the bridge of the nose, forming the Sign of the Ram. The Ram, of course, is an animal whose main means of defense or attack is its butting power. Like the Aries, it fixes its gaze on a target, lowers its head and charges. It's a simple and effective tactic, but it's rather hard on the head. Aries, because of their impatience and Ramlike impulsiveness, are accident-prone. Sooner or later they end up injuring their face or head. Aries children are especially vulnerable. Adults frequently carry some sort of scar commemorating an early introduction to their Ramlike nature. Burns, scalds and cuts are regular woes.

The typical Aries doesn't give his or her body much chance to accumulate fat. He often walks very slightly bent, as though leading with his head (a walking battering Ram?), and occasionally there's something pugnacious or belligerent about his mien. When he feels he is being observed, he straightens up and effects what he imagines is the most flattering stance. Usually it has a touch of haughtiness about it. In a room, the Aries can emanate an irritating irruptive presence, making some sensitive types feel an immediate dislike for them. Sexually, it can work just the opposite.

As with all zodiacal Signs, there is the developing Aries personality and the unevolved type. In other words, there is the Ram and the sheep. The unadvanced type is a caricature of his sturdy and valiant brother or sister. He is nervously restless but reluctant to act, timid and vacillating, sneaky and greedy, whining and purposeless. In place of a healthy and assertive drive, there is indecisive irritableness. Generally speaking, the positive and ennobling Aries qualities are stunted.

You are incredibly self-confident, convinced that you can do anything that appeals to you better than the next person. Experience is something you believe you were born with. If you don't know a subject or a technique, you will read up on it or ask. You are an exceptionally good listener when you want to learn. But all the time you are waiting—with good-humored impatience, mind you—for the moment when you have absorbed enough to be on your way. Enough may not be much by ordinary standards, but you can do wonders with only a tip or two. There couldn't be just one Aries who quit a course in architecture after two years, worked on provincial newspapers for a few weeks and then bluffed his way onto a big city daily as an assistant editor! Admittedly, the office didn't try to deter him when he threatened in a rash moment to resign, but the point is he held the job down for the best part of a year. You don't enjoy the student role. It's against your nature to have to acknowledge that someone else might be better equipped to handle a situation.

You learn quickly because you can't bear the thought of someone else being in a position to give you orders. Wherever you work, you'll end up making the immediate decisions. You will ably implement policy that has been laid down. This is a specialty of yours—impressing the guys at the top. You have no objection, either, to some faceless boss way up in his ivory tower handing down broad objectives. But don't let him or his sidekicks try to tell you how to go about achieving them. You'll quit first. (Actually, you wouldn't have taken such a job in the first place, unless you thought you might be able to get the sidekicks to work for you.) You'd rather starve (for a while) than have to report in for orders.

But, fortunately, you usually contrive to get your own little work number going. What impresses employers about you is your eager willingness and edge-of-the-chair get-up-and-goness. No one will ever be able to call you lazy. Perhaps silly, immature, foolish at times—but never lazy. And you don't put obstacles in the way, either. If the boss will only leave you to your own devices, you'll promise him the world, if you want it—and cope conscientiously later with the problem of delivering it. You'll find a way—or one of your own unique Aries alternatives, which you'll probably present to him all neatly tied up and organized without the benefit of any prior consultation! The unveiling of an Aries "alternative" is a moment of truth guaranteed to bring out the best or worst in anyone. You're a great one for ideas, there's no doubt about it, though some people would describe your methods as experimentation or practical amateurism.

Anyway, you go places and are remarkably successful in many fields. The secret of much of your success is that you will literally work night and day to deliver the goods—or your alternative—just as you promised you would. Naturally, you are always in danger of overreaching yourself physically. Like the adolescent, you think there is no end to your reserves of energy. And then suddenly—admittedly after most of the others have dropped around you—you're exhausted, a breakdown case, or an outright winner in the ulcer derby.

Not surprisingly, your unquenchable self-confidence often lands you in a jam. There are limits you just won't acknowledge when someone throws down a challenge. Say yes, pay later, is the Aries style. And another remarkable thing is the way you can put a story together that will convince the most hard-headed tycoon that you're just the person for the job.

You are frequently not fully qualified for the work you do. Usually you lack some credential that you have to pussy-foot around. But your manner is so persuasive and convincing that others find it impossible to believe you could be so self-assured without having all the necessary training. You're the type who in the old Wild West days would have accepted a gun duel and learned to shoot on the way to the appointment. Your education is often disjointed. You may have been sent to the best of prep schools and entered a university, but the chances of your having successfully completed an education are less than average.

Where your job is concerned, you have a knack for making important decisions when no one else is around. You assume responsibility in a shockingly irresponsible way. You'll make instant off-the-cuff decisions without the boss's authority because he is at lunch. And when the whole place goes down the drain and your superior asks why the hell you did it, you'll be astounded. Don't they recognize initiative anymore? Consequences, however, are not terribly important to you.

You are a person who generally has to learn the art of getting along with people the hard way. Diplomacy is an incomprehensible concept to Aries until they are well into their thirties or forties. They use an approach that is a pleasant enough substitute, but so phony and transparent that most people think it's some sort of joke of which they've missed the point. Usually acutely intuitive of the world about them, they seem to have a block when it comes to gauging the impact they are having on others. They develop a social conscience very slowly and mainly by default, by being repeatedly told, ticked off, confronted. Their unabashed selfishness depends on the tolerance, courtesy and good nature of others in excusing or overlooking their gaucherie and heavy-handed tactlessness. The kindly tip, the broad hint, don't work on them; they'll get the point, but it won't penetrate deep enough into the mechanism to effect a fundamental change. Only failures that touch their ambitions eventually deliver the message. The fact is, most Aries don't need people enough to be overly concerned about their opinions. But they desperately need to get on, to keep going in the direction they have set for themselves.

You are a great conversationalist. You can hold a roomful of people even when you are discussing a subject you know very little about. You are amusing, interesting and outrageously provocative. You possess refreshing insight and are a keen observer of life. You understand the doings and feelings of people, but you genuinely have enormous difficulty trying to relate yourself seriously to others. There's you and . . . who else did you say?

This trait is more easily understood and the Aries character is appreciated for its unique qualities when one considers the indomitable faith in human nature—or you could say, in life—that these people possess. The Aries trust is a wondrous thing; it never seems to fail. But people fail you time and time again. Still, you keep coming back for more. You never learn. Your trust is certainly naive by the standards of experience. But thank goodness for Aries—that refreshing sign of spring that doesn't lose its newness or sight of itself in the clamor of expediency and compromise. You might not fit in so well with all individuals, you might have trouble relating to people, but you do believe passionately in human nature, though you are continually let down. You might complain about it, hit the roof, suffer a brief but bitter depression. Then you are back again, giving spontaneously in some way or other—and being constantly disillusioned. That is the game for Aries. If you could seriously relate to people, join in their diplomatic courtesies or conduct yourself with what they regard as adult sophistication, you might see them as they really are and lose this abiding simple faith.

But that is impossible. Aries is Aries for all time. Only if you allow your mind to rule you with conventions your character rejects will you lose your artlessness and trust.

You can act with polished ease in social affairs and are a hospitable and entertaining host. You can listen attentively to the other person's point of view because in most cases you have your own apparently unshakable views that you *know* are correct. If others contribute to your opinion, okay. Otherwise you're not really concerned with what they think. So you seem to be a pretty receptive and interesting person to talk to. But when the conversation gets around to a topic you feel strongly about, you'll soon start the fur flying. You enjoy a good argument—and you're not too fussy about the truth, in the heat of the moment. You'll impulsively grab any old fact that enters your head, embellish it appropriately and toss it in as gospel. Who cares if someone does check up later? It's winning now that matters.

You have a most disarming air of sincerity, even when you are lying. Accusing you and thus evoking that look of affronted innocence is like committing a shameful act. You are a virtuoso of the expedient lie.

Although you are likely to defend your opinions with stubborn conviction and cosmetic erudition, you change them regularly because you unconsciously reject all that is repetitive. And this includes saying the same old things over and over. Life being what it is, opinions are something people trot out in company with the wearied affection of a smoker fondling his old pipe. So you change your mind. Suddenly, you discover a different point of view. This is it. What about yesterday's? Yesterday? You don't have any time for the past. You are an impulse of *now*. The fact that you may be contradicting your old stand seems irrelevant to you.

One of your favorite pastimes is to have a regular clearout around the home or office. Out goes everything that doesn't have a place in your view of the future. The worth of an object doesn't deter you from discarding it. Nor does sentiment. What you are doing on these occasions is impulsively cutting your ties with the past. Aries is the first Sign, remember. It has no history, no real yesterdays.

This is what makes you so desperately ambitious, determined to get on. You have a gulf behind you and you can't look back. It's today and where you'll be tomorrow that matter most. Born leader that you are, you often clear the way for the success of others and never quite enjoy the rewards of your own efforts. Very often you spurt ahead to grapple with some obstacle before it actually appears across your path. Sometimes you discover the effort wasn't necessary after all, that the difficulty would have passed you by.

All this is not to say that you can't be calm and collected. You can. And you can be serious and deliberative. Not for long, perhaps, but long enough to show that you are a deeper and wiser person than your drive and idealistic haste often suggest.

You are not the type to gather a great number of possessions around you. One may surmise that this is because you haven't got the time to spend looking after them—a discerning point. But it is basic to your nature to desire mainly those things that are immediately necessary. These may include artistic objects and works of art, for you have a sensitive appreciation of the aesthetic. The acquisitive need to accumulate worldly goods is something you may learn from others but will never be happy engaging in for yourself. Sometimes you get sidetracked by an acquisitive love mate, but eventually you will turn away from a cluttered nest or a cluttered person. You have a rare aloofness toward possessions that the avaricious individual will never understand.

If you acquire wealth and property, it is usually after middle age. You are the pioneer of the Zodiac, not the settler. You are the type who blazed the trail across the American West, who fought the harshest and loneliest battles with nature and pitted your strength and wits against those who may have tried to drive you back. You didn't stay to farm, to found cattle empires or to administer the law. When the others came with their wagons, families and fences, you sprang onto your pony and were off again.

Not that your home is unimportant to you. It matters, terribly. But you've got a different attitude toward it than others have. A home to an Aries is not a house, an enclosure, a little temporary hideaway from the outside world where he or she settles down. It's an ambition, a kind of abstract idea you pursue but never seem to realize. What you call your home is usually an unconscious staging place. It may be a mansion or a suburban bungalow, you may settle there to raise your family, but always you will feel either that your real home is somewhere else or that it is incomplete. The search for a home is the substance of your ambition, something yet to be attained. It is not surprising that Aries often doesn't acquire a home until quite late in life. Until the mellowing years, they tend to move around a lot and prefer to pay rent. After all, if the trailblazer succumbs to home comforts for too long, who is going to discover those new worlds for us?

As partners, the Aries woman and man are very similar; only the music has a different beat. Their particular characteristics and responses to the women and men of all the other Signs are given at length in the chapter "Aries in Love." But basically, the Aries lover of either sex likes to be in charge. For the male, this means he doesn't want to be pursued. He just wants to know the lady is interested and for her to understand that she can leave the rest to him. Woosh! He's a fast worker. The Aries woman also insists on calling the shots. She wants a real man—one who can wait, who won't grab her until she gives the okay. The caveman is not going to get anywhere at all with this girl . . . well, at least, not until she's ready. She doesn't respond to gushing, immature and premature declarations of undying love. This lady is very passionate. And she means business. No boys on men's errands, please.

They are both suckers for flattery as long as it comes from a true appreciation of their essential qualities. They know what they are; they don't mind a bit of poetic license, but don't attempt blatant insincerity. Both are extremely generous and nothing is too much trouble if they are asked a favor. The Aries idealism is clearly reflected in the attitude toward love of these people. Although they are usually highly sexed and capable of very intense physical expression, they don't get that side mixed up with their idea of romance. This is a chocolate-box image they can't erase from their minds no matter how many of their affairs end disastrously.

You, Aries, expect your man or woman to fill the ideal role. You put your lover on a pedestal and you look for the same sort of approbation in return. The fact that you are human and often fail to come up to your own expectations doesn't matter. Dreamboats are not supposed to spring leaks.

You might also tolerate an unhappy relationship for the sake of your children. You have a very developed sense of duty where offspring are concerned. If you feel it is in their interests not to split, you'll soldier on. But you won't be a very easy person to live with under these conditions. And you'll be biding your time. And how!

Home activities alone will never be enough for the Aries woman. The kids might tie her down for a while, but as soon as they're at school, she'll be looking for outside interests. Remember, home is a place for Aries to sleep, entertain and bring up children—not to settle down in forever.

As realistic as you are in everyday affairs, you revel in the illusion of romance. When it comes to bedtime, you're as practical and sexy as they come. A few loving bruises or scratches won't worry an Aries man or woman. Where you hurt most is in the mind. Here is where illusions are shattered. Here is where the man or woman who doesn't understand you begins to lose you. (It might help to leave this around for him or her to read.)

Once you love a person and are sure of his or her loyalty, you will be true. Well, you'll sincerely try. There are some considerations, though. For a start, you possess a deep sense of pride. Once you have selected a mate, you don't like anyone to think you've made an error of judgment. You might even put up with the odd case of infidelity on your partner's part (especially if you are a woman) so long as you are convinced no one else knows about it. You might suffer quite a bit of unhappiness as long as your friends and neighbors aren't aware of it. But let the facts get out and you'll cut away with an icy aloofness and do whatever you want.

ARIES IN LOVE

YOUR ARIES MAN

You like him? Love him? Just what sort of guy is he?

He's passionate. He's bold. He's full of dash and carry. He'll sweep you off your feet (as he probably has by now) and carry you off to unknown places. But you'd better keep a return ticket handy because he loses interest terribly quickly—unless, of course, you're the girl who's going to finally corral this maverick.

Corralled he can be—but only if you let him believe the slip rails are down. He's one of the most independent guys you'll ever meet. He won't stand for your trying to tell him what to do. You've got to use finesse with this one. He's direct. He's like the zodiacal Ram who symbolizes his Sign. He'll walk straight up to you first time with a jaunty arrogance and probably say something outrageously provocative. He's very sure of himself, and very likable. He thinks he does most things extremely well, and lovemaking is one of which he feels most proud.

He's flirtatious. He likes to imagine he's got his own personal flock of female admirers to impress as well as administer to. If you try to convince him that you're the only girl for him—you won't. Mr. Aries has got to make all the decisions himself. And if you want an exclusive claim on him, you'll probably have to get him in his late twenties or early thirties because this boy likes to sow a lot of wild oats before settling down and blessing the world with his offspring. Flatter him, but be sincere. Don't push him. Enjoy his manly ways. He's a real powerhouse of masculine energy, and quite a humorist in his open, boyish way. If you want him, you mustn't be too obvious. He likes his woman soft, feminine, intelligent and a bit mysterious. He doesn't really want to hear how much you love him—not yet, not before he struts his stuff. He's going to win *you,* remember. He intends to make the moves. And he doesn't want any implied proposal either! Let him do the asking. Let him set the pace. Make him come to you. Show him you know what you want in a man and that it might be him—but then again, it might not. You can tease him to death while you hold his interest—which will probably be for about 30 minutes before he pops some sort of leading question. And "leading" means he expects to be the leader and you the follower.

Underneath all this bouncing energy and self-confidence, he's a bit of a child. He's simple in his needs and can be handled quite easily by the girl who understands him. Once you've landed him, he can be extremely loyal. He won't go looking for other company if he genuinely loves you. He has a high sense of duty. If, when you're out, opportunity happens to knock on his door dressed in a negligee, he won't have the stamina for much resistance. But then, who would among the red-blooded fiery males you've known?

You'll have a much better chance of holding Mr. Aries if he's a dad. He loves his children and won't do anything to hurt them if he can help it. And if you are a good mother, he'll love you for that too.

But if he's young and proposes marriage, be very careful. He rarely knows his own mind when it comes to love and sex, apart from the fact that he has a great need for both. It's such a great big beautiful world he discovers after puberty, filled with loads of willing and pretty young bopeeps, that he's likely to get carried away and decide impulsively he wants one for keeps. Mr. Aries always wants what he wants, now. But the next day, he might want what he wants in a different package.

On the debit side, he can be bossy, impetuous and fly into a rage at the drop of a hat, although it may not last long. And although he's got the original roving eye, he just can't tolerate a flirtatious mate! How much more typically male can you get than that?

YOUR ARIES WOMAN

You like her? Love her? Just what sort of woman is she?

She's spontaneous, says what she thinks. And she'll never say die. But she'll say drop dead if you don't handle her in a very special way. This girl is extremely intelligent and instantaneous in her mental judgments. She'll see right through you the moment you meet. If you're weak, you're not for her. She's an outward-going, sexually aggressive lady. She's strong in character and has tremendous vitality. She knows she can look after herself. She's all initiative. She's a bit of a man-eater, if you haven't run into her type before.

Miss Aries has got it all together. She may seem a bit bossy, but that's the way she is. She wants a man with the strength and wit to control and handle her, so that she can look up to him. Then she's pertly feminine and a very stimulating and satisfying companion.

She is usually very attractive to men. They are a bit wary of her, though. She's something of an Amazon, a little wild, impulsive, unpredictable. You get the feeling that if you weren't around with all your masculine protectiveness and capabilities, she'd manage quite well, thank you. You've got to show this girl why she can't manage without you.

In romance, Miss Aries will sometimes take the initiative. She's a passionate lady, and she seldom thinks before she acts if the impulse is strong enough. She is rarely a dominating type. She just likes to be out in front until she finds someone who can overtake her. She is an exciting woman, filled with live-wire tension. Moderation is the great battle of her life. She can't seem to help going to extremes. She likes to play hard, work hard. And when it comes to casual love affairs, she can cover a lot of territory—fast.

Clothes are not the main thing in her life. She enjoys dressing appropriately. She's a great outdoor girl and loves sports. So jeans, shorts and lots of action garb are in her wardrobe.

Miss Aries is very adaptable to change. No matter how hard things become, she'll keep smiling and waiting for the golden opportunity just around the corner. And when she does smile, she means it. There are no back doors about this girl. She's straightforward and direct, sometimes embarrassingly so. But you'll know where you stand with her. It won't be long before she has other boyfriends if you can't convince her she's exclusively yours. She won't two-time you—she'll just tell you.

If she marries you, she'll be loyal—but only so long as you continue to come up to her expectations. She'll take her full share of marital responsibilities and you'll find she can manage most things as well as you. But she'll stick to her side of it and appreciate you for your talents. She will be a good housekeeper and will make an excellent mother.

She is a very serious person inside. She's looking for something more than is found on the surface of people. If you're a playboy, she may be your eager and lovable playmate for a while, but she'll seldom marry you. In maturity, she likes her men to be dedicated to their pursuits. She'll want you to fulfill your potential, to get the best out of life and put back all you can. If you don't, she's got a fiery temper that she'll turn on you and make you feel either all man or all worm. But no matter how petulant she may become, she doesn't hold grudges. It is just that she has to let off steam.

To be happy, Miss Aries must have plenty of change, movement, excitement. She's filled with daring and a love of the unusual. She'll drive like a stock-car enthusiast and do just about anything once, for the sheer novelty of it. She likes comfort and the good life whenever she can possibly get it.

On the debit side, she may be foolishly impulsive and prone to waste her energy on projects that never quite get finished. With her children, she may be a bit bossy.

ARIES WOMAN—ARIES MAN

Let's face it, there is no such person as a one hundred percent Aries man or woman. There are, after all, so many factors to take into consideration; for instance, the position of the various planets and the Moon at the time of birth. Everyone has a little bit of Aries in him or her, and for that matter, a little of all the other Signs that contribute to the makeup of the Zodiac. What is definitely a fact is you will find it much easier to understand a member of the opposite sex who was born pretty much around the same time of the year as you were, for you are likely to have a number of other influences in common.

Life is not going to be a bed or roses when two fire Sign playmates like Aries come together. But when arguments do erupt, it should be possible for you to understand the other person's point of view. Imagine two people who know exactly what they want, and who were obviously born to lead, living in the same house! Well, you won't be whispering sweet nothings to each other all day. Life will be exciting, though, and this alliance could give you just the stimulation you need to spark you off in the outside world.

You will make your Aries man happy by playing a supporting role—never an easy thing for you to do. Still, if you love him enough, you will be pleased to make whatever sacrifices you feel are necessary to keep him happy and contented.

On your first real contact with him, you may have a sixth-sense feeling you have run into a person of your own Sign. There is nothing shy or retiring about this guy. If you appeal to him physically, he will let you know without too many preliminary niceties. You prefer someone who is down-to-earth and speaks his mind—he may go too far in this direction even for you. It would be silly for you to rush headlong into a permanent relationship here because—let's face it—the Aries man is not the ideal husband for you. You may recognize his good qualities but, by the same token, you will also be well aware of the negative points in his makeup.

If you are a career-minded woman—someone who wishes to keep working and being successful after marriage—you are going to have a terrible time with the masculine Ram because he will feel you are competing with him. He likes his woman to be at home waiting happily for his arrival. This state of affairs is unlikely to fit in with the sort of life-style you envisage for yourself. Oh yes, you like your home and can be very handy around the garden or with a pot of paint. But outside interests are important to you as well.

In lovemaking, you should have a whale of a time. The Aries man will have no trouble satisfying you. His desire to experiment in bed will certainly excite you. Your uninhibited love of sex will certainly appeal to his nature, too.

Financially, you will find he takes his responsibilities very seriously indeed. He is, as a rule, a good provider for his dependants, and if he takes on a commitment, he will live up to his word. He will ensure that his wife and children never want for anything. You may have to guide him away from taking silly risks on the stock exchange or from gambling. He can be easily duped into backing get-rich-quick schemes.

One word of comfort for you: if you really love him and can stick it out to middle age, he will slow down a bit—though not to the point where life will ever become dull.

ARIES WOMAN—TAURUS MAN

If you are the patient type of Aries lady, you might be able to cope with slow and deliberate Taurus. He will certainly take his time deciding that you are the girl for him.

Taurus never comes to an important decision quickly. He rarely acts on impulse. Don't expect to be swept off your feet. He dislikes change and keeps his feet firmly planted on the ground. This might be rather irritating for an all-action girl like you. If you are looking for one of those whirlwind romances where your man meets you one night and proposes to you under the stars the next, you had better look elsewhere.

He is intelligent all right and can usually talk well on any subject, and he also has a great love of art and will be keen to share his appreciation of beauty with you.

The Taurus man loves a comfortable home life. You will find him a good handyman; if you have to go away to visit mother, you will discover he is perfectly capable of looking after himself and keeping the home tidy. As a cook, you might be surprised to discover he outshines you. With your talent for making your home a happy place to live in, you should find you agree very well on matters connected with domestic life. He will appreciate your drive and ambition to get on. The Taurus man is a hard worker, and what is more, this is a quality he values highly in others.

What is it that makes you fall head over heels in love with him? Well, for one thing, he is good fun. You will never encounter a dull moment. He is very fond of the good life and usually knows all the best places to go. On first acquaintance, you may find him a little full of himself. But as you get to know him better, you will understand that this is really only a cover for his shyness.

You may have some difficulty in holding on to him because he finds it impossible not to flirt—in fact, he has quite an eye for the pretty girls. When it comes to finances, you need have no worry about debtors knocking at the door. The Taurus person likes to keep on the right side of the law and hates owing money. Life will be secure from the material angle. It is on the emotional side that you will have your doubts and fears. He is a bit lighthearted as a lover. You like more high-powered emotionalism in your sex.

It is very important to Mr. Taurus to have a mate who is a friend as much as a person to enjoy a strong physical relationship with. You won't have to worry too much about the housework. Your Taurus man is very gadget conscious and will make sure that you have all the latest appliances to cut routine chores to the very minimum. As a dad, you couldn't ask for more. He's crazy about kids. This is not to say he won't keep them in line. You'll find that he can be a very strict father when he has to be.

He retains his youth pretty well and you may find it hard to keep up with him as the years roll by. If you can last the pace, he will help you to keep as young in heart as he is. You are always likely to find him intriguing; just when you feel you really know him well, he will do something you find totally surprising.

So long as you can desire the same things he does from your life together—lots of fun in the relationship—there is no reason why you should not have a very happy life.

ARIES WOMAN—GEMINI MAN

Mr. Gemini is very cuddlesome and a loving playmate guaranteed to bring out the motherly instinct—and a little more—in most Aries ladies.

Someone once said: "All men are children at heart"—these words must have been uttered with our Mercurial friend in mind. He is a bit of a Peter Pan character. This is not to say he doesn't have a good mind; he is, in fact, an excellent conversationalist. He also possesses a terrific sense of humor, although when he gets into his practical jokes, you might find him a bit of a bore. In many ways, however, you make an ideal twosome; you are bound to share many interests.

An Aries lady can be just the girl of Gemini's dreams—his better half, as it were. He will admire many of the qualities in the Ram that he does not possess himself—for instance, your ability to see a job through once you have started it. One of his faults is that he finds it difficult to concentrate on one thing for very long. He needs plenty of incentive to stick at tasks he finds routine and boring. And even then, material rewards will not tie him down for too long a time.

He will be happy for you to carry on with your career after you get married. Liking the free life himself, he won't expect you to settle for boring drudgery. You will need plenty of driving force and energy to keep up with him because he never stays in one place for very long.

Helpful person that you are, you should be able to guide him and keep him away from danger. He will usually listen to good sense and good ideas. He can also be influenced quite easily by the wrong sort of people. You will have to make sure he does not get duped into backing risky projects; if he does, he will more likely end up a loser than a winner.

Mr. Gemini, it is true to say, is attractive to many different people. You will often have a houseful of various characters to entertain. He picks his chums from all walks of life; he is as at home with royalty as with rogues. What will you find most appealing about him? Well, his sense of humor, for one thing. He will always keep you amused and come up with fresh ideas.

Don't expect to be able to boss him. You will have to give him quite a lot of freedom if you wish to keep him. Always try to share his interests, though, because if he gets into the habit of going out alone, your interests could grow wide apart. As far as children are concerned, you will have to be the one who hands out the punishment. Your Gemini mate will probably get the kids into trouble—don't forget his love of pranks and what a child he is at heart himself.

You will have to allow him his odd flirtation—even though this goes against your grain. Don't get too worried if you see him making eyes at another girl; it's likely to turn out to be quite harmless.

To sum up, everything he sees and hears sets his agile mind working. He can't sit still for a minute. You will often have to be the steadying influence in his life. If you are really gone on him, you should be able to cope with this relationship even though you are likely to be in a bit of a spin at times.

He hates having to have decisions made for him, but finds it almost impossible to make them himself. He is a mass of contradictions. A question you will have to answer for yourself is: Are you prepared to mother your husband as well as your kids?

ARIES WOMAN—CANCER MAN

Life will certainly have its ups and downs with a Cancer man. He's a moody one, there's no doubt about it.

On first meeting, you are likely to think that here is a person full of confidence who doesn't have a care in the world. You will also find him very amusing. It might take you a long time—many years—to discover what really makes him tick. Our Crablike friend is not easy to get to know well, partly because he doesn't want to expose himself to the possibility of having his feelings hurt.

Your first impression will be of a man who knows exactly what he wants and where he is going. But, in reality, he is easy to influence and even more easily hurt. If you love him, you will be able to help him find himself, though, it will take a great deal of patience and understanding on your part. Don't believe he is trying to pretend he's something he isn't. His problem is that he fears making a big outward show of his nervousness and insecurity. His hard shell hides a gentle and sensitive soul.

He will want to protect you as well, and this is where you will find the relationship particularly difficult. Being the independent woman you are, you don't like advice on what to do and what not to do. It will take a great deal of give and take on both sides to form a lifelong pairing.

It will be the Aries girl with her wits about her who will have the most chance of hitting it off with the sensitive and touchy Cancer. Once he falls for you, he will stick by you. Men born under this Sign of the Zodiac make very faithful husbands. Another favorable factor is you will be given security—he will always do his best to provide for you. Cancer people are very careful with money, mainly because they don't like to leave too much to chance.

Never think that he is slow-witted. He may appear to have lost track of what is going on, but in fact he rarely misses a trick. When the outside world mistreats him—and he does tend to blame other people for his own mistakes—you may find he comes running back to you. He needs a shoulder to cry on.

You will have to be quite tough with him at times to see that he makes the most of his talents. You who admire independence will have to give him that extra push to make him stand on his own two feet. Be very careful how you express your feelings, though, because he does not take kindly to criticism. The best way to get him to do what you want is to boost his self-confidence.

You both love your home and Mr. Cancer will be delighted with the way you run domestic affairs. He will do everything he can to make sure nothing interferes with the smooth running of family life. In bed, there will be no problems; the Cancer man makes a very intuitive lover. You will find he soon hits on what really satisfies you. He will be considerate and gentle with you, too.

You may have to watch out for a bit of competition from his mother. Your mate finds it rather difficult to cut the apron strings. However, you are a woman who knows her own mind. Aries are very much at home in the kitchen, and it should not be too long before you become the number one lady in his life. If you are prepared to take the time to pamper him, you will be able to help him forget his emotional hangups, which should belong to the past.

It will be important for you to make an effort to share his interests—otherwise you'll find him slipping off into his own little dream world. He will make a fine father for your children, though he can be a surprisingly strict parent.

ARIES WOMAN—LEO MAN

Of all the types of men, it is Mr. Leo who is for you. What makes this a perfect match is that you are also his type of woman. If ever there was such a thing as a love match, it is the pairing of the Ram and the Lion.

Here we see the bringing together of two active and proud personalities. You will admire his qualities of leadership—the way he sweeps you off your feet; head-over-heels fashion, and what is more, the right royal way that he does it. Yes, Mr. Leo is a great romantic and a great lover. He will have great respect for your independence and recognize that you are a born leader, too. It is probable that you will share many of the same ideals. As a twosome, you will be pretty unstoppable. What an impact you will make whenever you go out together!

The Lion is all heart. He will put you on a pedestal and make you feel like a woman. It could be a case of love at first sight. Mr. Leo knows his own mind. Once he has decided that you are the girl for him, there will be no half-measures. Your lovemaking will be dramatic. It is important to both of you that you give as much pleasure as you get. There will be no inhibitions holding you back. You will delight in exploring each other's minds and bodies.

There is only one slight problem in this union. Mr. Leo does like to have a great fuss made over him. Whether you are in the mood or not, he likes lots of petting and attention. When he is about, he will expect you to drop everything and give him priority. He needs lots of compliments, too. You will find he is very good with self-criticism but not so good if others find fault with him—especially his woman.

Although he is a ladies' man, he is quite

choosy about his ladies. He never goes to bed just for the fun of it. He has to feel a strong attraction before he tries to get to first base. He is definitely not a flirt. With him, sex is a pretty serious matter. Not every Leo looks like the King of the Jungle, but you don't have to be stronger than the next guy to be that.

He will expect a great deal from you, and this should be quite an exciting challenge in itself. You will have to fill the role of wife, mother, sister and homemaker. You should have no difficulty, though, in keeping your balance on the pedestal our feline friend sets you on.

You will have to be all women rolled into one. Sometimes he will want you to be his little girl—yes, he has a bit of a father complex and will like to feel that he is looking after you and protecting you from the dangers of the big, bad outside world. On other occasions, he will want you to be the perfect hostess, impressing his friends with the wonderful way you entertain. So long as you can live up to his demands, there will be no problems.

For his part, he will be prepared to accept your sudden outbursts with patience and understanding. Leos are very fond of youngsters, although you may feel at times he is a bit too strict and logical in his approach to children. However, with you on hand to give them all the love they need, the pair of you should be a perfect balance for your offspring.

ARIES WOMAN—VIRGO MAN

Quite honestly, the Virgo man could be a bit too much for Ms. Aries to take.

He is very fussy and particular. Everything has to be just right for him. His home has to be spotless—he will notice right away if there is a speck of dust on the windowsill. He is a firm believer in a place for everything and everything in its place.

He's a cool customer, completely devoid of the sweep-'em-off-the-feet attitude toward love and romance. He is not one for sentimental mush. He's also a guy who can go without sex for long spells at a time. He has so many other interests that he doesn't have time to miss physical love.

This is not to say that Virgo does not have a lot to give you. He will be devoted and faithful should you decide to try living together. The real question is: Can you accept his straightforwardness and down-to-earth approach all the time? You like to get out and about. Change is important to you. Mr. Virgo is a person of habit. You might find that he is a bit too predictable for your liking. He is a thinking man. He will work everything out from the logical point of view. To you, there is a lot more to life than the fact that two plus two equals four—sometimes you like it to add up to five just for the hell of it!

If you are going to be a happy couple, it is essential that you have a lot of mutual interests. If you both share a love of a certain type of music or enjoy travel (both Virgo and Aries people like visiting foreign countries and going on long journeys), this could be a solid foundation for you to build on.

You might be the right girl to get this old stick-in-the-mud out of his rut. It all depends on whether you feel strongly enough about him to make the effort. If he is really gone on you, he will make the supreme effort to change his ways if he feels that is what you really want. You could try to tempt him to take more of an interest in sports, or anything else for that matter that would shake him out of his complacency. He needs a girl like you to push him out into the big wide world. If left to his own devices, he will sit back in judgment of other people and their situations without once getting his feet dirty.

You will not be doing all the teaching in this relationship. Mr. Virgo will be able to show you a thing or two. For one thing, he is excellent at summing people up very quickly—he realizes their strengths and weaknesses on one meeting.

He is definitely more of a sentimental old softy than a sexual being. This is another area where you will have to arouse his instincts. Lust is a word you will think he never heard of! But don't write him off as frigid. He's not. As a matter of fact, he is probably a little bit frightened of sex. You might enjoy the challenge of opening him up and making him aware that sex is something to be enjoyed. He has a bit of a problem when it comes to expressing his feelings.

Don't make the mistake of showing your feelings for him in public. He will blush down to his little toe should you give him a big hug and a kiss in front of others. As far as he is concerned, romance is something to be shared between two people when they are alone together. He will like to get to know you really well before he offers you his love. Being a slow and methodical person, he will never jump into anything feet first. No on-off relationship will work for him. If you're going to make a go of your alliance, you must try to remain faithful—a difficult thing for you to do.

Don't forget, if you do marry a Virgo, he will

expect his kids (like everything else) to be kept spick-and-span.

ARIES WOMAN—LIBRA MAN

You should get along famously with a Libra male. The vital question is: Will this relationship be exciting enough to sustain you over a long period—say, forever after?

He will make a charming and amusing companion. You will undoubtedly be attracted by his agile mind and quick wit. Where things could go a bit wrong for you is when it comes to settling down. Libra likes a changing scene and needs to be surrounded by lots of friends. He needs constant stimulation.

You who look for consistency in romance will find his attitude to love rather puzzling. One moment he will be all over you, telling you that you are the only person in the world as far as he is concerned. The next moment, you may feel you are talking to a completely different guy. Yes, he certainly blows hot and cold, but don't mistake him for the fickle type. With him, lovemaking is a matter of mood. If you care about him deeply enough, you may get to understand what makes him tick and adapt yourself accordingly.

One thing you must never do is put pressure on him. He hates fights and can't function properly in a difficult atmosphere. In fact, he is a born peacemaker. Can you, a person to whom a good stand-up scrap comes so naturally, accept this?

He certainly knows how to pay a compliment. He will always notice if you have taken special trouble over your appearance or have made any important changes in the home. This doesn't mean he will pass out compliments indiscriminately, but he will be tactful enough not to pass comment on anything that is not agreeable to his eye.

You are one of those women who speaks her mind and likes to bring differences out into the open. It is very important to you to know exactly where you stand in your relationships with members of the opposite sex. It will be very frustrating to try to get Mr. Libra to commit himself—especially if he senses that by airing his opinion, he will be heading for a clash. He will be prepared to lie if necessary to avoid an argument. You, with your frankness and openness, will find it very difficult to understand this aspect of his personality.

He will be able to interest you in subjects that are important to him. Mr. Libra can make any topic he has a passion for sound fascinating and enthralling. His love of music, art and beautiful things is genuine. If he loves you, he will take the time to open up worlds for you that you never realized existed. He may also awaken in you a sense of justice because he is usually on the side of the underdog, and when he takes up a cause, he sees it through to the finish.

He is a very well-mannered person who always does what he can to make people feel comfortable and relaxed in his company. His sense of humor is good, if somewhat dry. You may find his attitude to life a bit too cynical at times. In moments of extreme stress, you will discover he can be as hard and cruel as the next person. When it comes to survival, he will usually come out a winner.

He finds it very difficult to stay in one spot for any length of time. He is very keen on travel and enjoys nothing more than visiting strange out-of-the-way places. Humdrum routine is a bore to him. Oh yes, he likes his domestic comforts, but he can't bear a life that is altogether too organized.

The Libra man is genuinely egalitarian. If he has a night out with his friends once a week, he will be happy to stand in for you and do the household chores if you want the same. He is very attractive to other people, with a friendly nature that is bound to draw friends from all walks of life. As a father, he will be understanding and patient with his children. You may even find him too tolerant on this score. Mr. Libra finds it very hard to be strict with youngsters.

When it comes to finance, you will have to take over. Mr. Libra finds it very difficult to save. Sweet words and gentleness will persuade him to go along with you. He can't tolerate being told what to do, and that is one thing you should well understand.

ARIES WOMAN—SCORPIO MAN

This relationship will be all action. There is never going to be a dull moment when Mr. Scorpio and Miss Aries get together.

Don't think you will be able to dominate this man. He will be just as righteous as you are when you have a fight. There will be plenty of verbal battles (nothing too serious), which should help keep you both on your toes. You and your Scorpio man could continue to strike sparks off each other for years if you decide to try to settle down to a permanent life together. You will bring out the man in him and he will bring out the woman in you.

As bed partners, you should have a great time together. This might at first seem a pretty disastrous combination, two Martian types sharing a life together, but when two passionate people really love each other and want to be together more than anything else, it is amazing how much they are capable of adapting.

He is an ardent lover and it will be very important to him that he satisfy you in bed. Lovemaking is his main way of expressing what he really feels for a person. He is much better at action than with words. He's not the romantic type who whispers sweet nothings in your ear. He's heard all the old moon, June chat before. It will be through his body that he will communicate his real feelings to you. Being a passionate woman yourself, you shouldn't have too much difficulty in getting the message.

If you set your sights on this man (many consider it a terrible fate for any woman), you will have to put up with a very jealous person. Woe betide the man who tries to flirt with you once Scorpio considers you his woman. The poor guy is more than likely to end up on his back in five seconds flat.

He won't be particularly interested in your love of beauty and art. He will consider such matters woman's domain. He's a bit of a man's man. He certainly prefers masculine company to feminine, except for the woman of his choice. He's not a women's libber! He will consider your role in life to be strictly in the home. This is where the sparks could fly. However much you love and desire him, it will be very difficult to keep that independent streak in your nature under control.

If he goes out on the town with the guys, it will appear perfectly logical to you to live it up a bit too. Not so, from Mr. Scorpio's point of view. There will be one hell of a row if he gets home in the early hours and your side of the bed hasn't been slept in.

He is, as a rule, a very good businessman and a very hard worker. He is also a man of his word. He will always make sure that you are adequately provided for. If he loves you, he will do everything he can to provide the wherewithal to buy and maintain a comfortable home. Materially, you will lack for nothing with him around.

He's a very ambitious person and will strive to get to the top in his career. Still, his home is very important to him. He needs to relax and unwind at the end of the day. He also tends to separate his business and domestic life. This tendency could place you in a pigeon hole that you find not only very monotonous but also unacceptable.

He is capable of dishing out pain as well as pleasure. Being a very strong-willed person, he can be moody for days—until he gets his own way, that is. It will be up to you to ensure that you never get to the point where arguments become serious quarrels. You should be able to recognize the danger signals and avoid trouble when you see it coming.

Scorpios are pretty honest people. He will admire you for your grit and determination. At times, you may find him very difficult to understand. He likes to be on his own when he's got problems to work out. Don't mistake silence for moodiness. He can be rather vague when he has a lot on his mind.

He's very fond of children, and is usually a better father to young kids than to teenagers. He may become a bit jealous and possessive as they grow up.

ARIES WOMAN—SAGITTARIUS MAN

Like his symbol, which is half-man and half-horse, the Sagittarius man, who shoots an arrow straight from his bow, is a strange and mysterious being.

The symbolism of this last fire Sign is one of the most interesting things about the Zodiac. We call it simply "the Archer," but traditionally Sagittarius is shown as a Centaur (half-man, half-horse). The Centaur himself is shown galloping along and trying to speed his effect on the world ahead of his physical presence by means of a well-aimed arrow. At least, the Aries girl should hope it is well aimed, because that bow looks like a mighty powerful weapon!

He is a difficult man to trap. Many would say he is marriage-shy, though he certainly isn't shy where romance is concerned. But he loves his freedom. You may find him a desirable man to have a wild fling with. Even if you spend only a short period of your life with a person born under this Sign, it will be a period you won't forget in a hurry.

He has a deep sense of fair play, and that will please you. Underneath all that wildness is a gentle and sensitive soul. He often seems to be a bit of an actor, but this is only to cover up an acute inferiority complex. If you decide you are going to be the woman in his life for keeps, you'll probably have to accept him more as a buddy than an ardent lover. But he is faithful and takes his marriage vows very seriously.

Aries and Sagittarius are compatible because they both have a wild streak and enjoy taking risks. You will probably get along with him like a house on fire, or two houses on fire, as you are both fire Signs. You will discover that you have a great deal in common. Both of you have a high regard for nature and enjoy the outdoor life. The sort of place you might meet Mr. Sagittarius is at the pool or your local sports club.

You might wonder if he can ever really settle down because he seems to be a gypsy type who is constantly looking for thrills and excitement. This is a fair summing up. Until he reaches his mid-thirties, he thinks of home as a place to take a bath, change his clothes and start out again. If you can keep up with him, well and good. He is the type who can be quite happy in a furnished room because he is not that involved with possessions as such. He is a bit of a Walter Mitty type. His idea of himself doesn't always match other people's. He has a keen imagination and is a great lover of freedom. Humdrum routine bores him.

He will keep you on your toes and interested in what is going on in the outside world. There will rarely be a dull moment when he is around. He is very proud of his woman and will enjoy showing you off to his friends. It would be fair to say that he is sensual rather than sexual. He will know how to arouse you physically and bring you to a speedy climax.

He likes a gamble, so you would be wise to look after the money. He doesn't always have a great sense of responsibility where savings are concerned because he feels money is something to have a good time with. He won't mind your working. If you are intelligent and hold down a good job, he will be very proud of you, rather than jealous. He likes company. Another thing that you have in common is that you both enjoy entertaining.

When it comes to children, you will have to cope alone. Poppa Sagittarius will be happy to tell them the odd bedtime story and give them a loving kiss good night. But it is highly unlikely you'll get him to change a diaper or give a bottle.

If you can accept that the sparks will fly between you from time to time, this can be a successful pairing.

ARIES WOMAN—CAPRICORN MAN

In Astrology, Capricorn is associated with climbing. Its symbol is the Goat, an animal that can climb to heights no other four-footed creature would dare attempt. The mind of Mr. Capricorn takes quite a lot of explaining. He certainly has plenty of drive and ambition, and material success means a great deal to him.

This third Earth Sign is a little more complicated than it would seem at first glance. This man wants power and prestige as well as earthly wealth. Looking at his virtues, it would seem that the matching of Mr. Capricorn and Ms. Aries is going to be rather interesting.

You like someone who has an independent streak and is self-reliant. You also like your man to have plenty of ambition. This is a good description of Mr. Capricorn. He will be very appreciative of many of your fine qualities, too: your stamina, your willingness to take up almost any challenge even if you only have the slimmest chance of succeeding.

Where are the drawbacks then? Well, for one thing you may have to be satisfied with taking second place to his work much of the time. Once your relationship is past the first passion stage you will find he often stays late at the office—and he really *is* at the office because he is a terrible perfectionist.

You certainly don't want a man who is an idle shirker, but he may take the hard-work bit too far even for you. Capricorn loves the struggle of life for its own sake. It excites him. On the highest level, he will work for the joy of the task and not for what he gets out of it. It's been said that the man who is in love with his job is more difficult to win over than the man who is in love with another woman—and there may be something to this as far as Capricorn is concerned.

At a lower level, this Sign can be the coldest and greediest personality imaginable, though only if he is totally in the grip of Saturn. You'd better check on his birthday in *AstroAnalysis*, Capricorn, before doing anything drastic. But assuming he's a regular Goat, so to speak, you will have to be interested in what he does for a living because he will wish to discuss all aspects of his career with you and may want your advice from time to time.

So long as you greatly admire his talents, all will be well. The crunch may come if you are hell bent on having a career of your own. The little home you build for yourselves may not be big enough to contain two great egos.

You will find him very desirable physically. The way he makes love is groovy and passionate. He is free from complications or physical hang-ups. Even if you have had an argument, this will not stop him from being sexy with you. In fact, he'll probably get quite a kick from petting you out of a bad mood.

He is very careful with money and may find you a bit too free and easy with the cash. He will certainly do all he can to make you less extravagant. He tends to take care of future financial security, so you won't have the slightest worry about whether the insurance policy is paid up. He will always make sure his family is covered where it counts.

You may be wonderful friends for some time before you realize you are in love with each other. You tend to be attracted by qualities of the mind rather than the body, first off.

When you are out together, you may feel he has little interest in other people present. You will be surprised when you get home to discover he hasn't missed a trick. He is very adroit at summing up the strengths and weaknesses of people.

You may have some trouble getting along with his side of the family. He finds it very hard to break away from old ties.

With children, you will have to be the one who provides most of the love. He knows what is good for his kids, but overdoes the heavy-handedness from time to time.

ARIES WOMAN—AQUARIUS MAN

The man born under Aquarius will be an extremely dazzling partner for you. His Sign is associated with friends, social life, hopes, fears and brotherhood. It is also connected with unexpected happenings.

You will find he is quite a thinker. If he falls head-over-heels in love with you, he will be prepared to use unorthodox methods to win you. Certainly he is a forceful communicator of his own ideas. His symbol is pouring out water; it's the same with his knowledge, although he's inclined to keep his feelings bottled up. It will be extremely important to him that you try to understand what makes him tick.

As a rule, Mr. Aquarius has a deep concern for the problems of the world—for the starving and the underprivileged wherever they may be. He might find it difficult to understand how you can be so absorbed in mundane matters such as keeping the house clean and worrying about the price of butter. Yes, in many ways you two will think very differently. Sometimes he will go further than just talking about the dreadful state of the world—he will actually get up and try to do something about it! He is a wonderful friend to the disadvantaged, going to any lengths to help.

The Age of Aquarius is supposed to bring us peace and understanding. You will find that your man has these aims very much on his mind.

How will you get on as partners? Well, he enjoys sex, though perhaps not so much on the physical plane as you because his mind has to be as committed as well as his body. Sometimes you may feel he has lost interest in lovemaking completely. But this is unlikely—probably he has just gotten involved with someone who really needs his help.

Don't ever think that he doesn't really care about you; recognizing your strength and independence, he will feel you don't need his help that much.

You will not find a jealous man here. He will be prepared to let you have your own life, just as he will expect you to give him his freedom to act as he sees fit. You may have to put up with some pretty odd-bods around the house. When you wake up in the morning, you could well find some stray nestling on your couch. You may not find it easy to accept this. After all, you are drawn to people who are able to fight for themselves and stand on their own two feet. This side of his character will not be easy to take for an Aries woman.

Routine does not appeal to this man. He may change his job a number of times and will find it very difficult to settle down. Don't get too pessimistic about this though, because in many ways you will be extremely good for each other. If you want to learn more about life, this is certainly the man for you. He will keep you on your toes both in a worldly and a spiritual sense. And you should be able to show him that an intimate relationship between two people is every bit as important as setting to world to rights.

You might not find it easy to live with each other, and you will both have to keep your wits about you to avoid losing your identities. As in your early courting days when Mr. Aquarius took so long to get around to giving you that first good night kiss, in marriage you might find that you are the one who has to do the coaxing in bed! Far from finding this humiliating or a bore, you will probably be stimulated by the challenge.

If you do decide to get married, you will find you have a faithful husband. He is unlikely to go off the rails with another woman. He is a great dad because he has a feeling and understanding for the problems children encounter growing up.

ARIES WOMAN—PISCES MAN

It will not be easy for you to understand a man born under the Sign of Pisces. Your birthdays may be close together, but you are the first Sign of the Zodiac and he is the last.

You will be poles apart in your attitudes toward life. You are a realist; he tends to be a dreamer. At first, he will probably seem rather a weak person to you, someone who doesn't have very fixed ideas about anything. This snap judgment would be less than fair. The fact is he is adaptable and can easily hold many opinions. To a woman who has her feet firmly on the ground and likes to know where she is going, this will be infuriating.

There are many traits you will admire in this man. He has great sympathy and understanding for people who have serious problems. More than just an ear someone can pour out their troubles to, he is capable of coming up with sensible solutions to their difficulties. He also has strong powers of intuition and will often know exactly what is on your mind without your having uttered a single word.

If he is serious in his feelings toward you, he will know exactly how to make a good impression. The Fish can transform himself into whatever will please you most. Pisces has the happy knack of involving the person he loves in his fantasies. If you want to retain his love, you will have to be prepared to enter into his make-believe world from time to time. But you will have to point out to him very firmly that you are an individual in your own right. He must be made to respect the space you need around you in order to function properly and you must not allow him to interfere in projects that you feel are your domain. Your verve and enthusiasm for life will make a strong impression on a Pisces man. He will admire your direct qualities, which he finds lacking in himself.

When you are feeling a bit down, he will be by your side to comfort you. It is unlikely that you could find a more sympathetic partner in the whole of the Zodiac.

If you decide you really love him and wish to settle down to a permanent relationship, you will have to forget about finding the man of your dreams. You will have to show a great deal of patience, and it will be a difficult business for both of you, fraught with emotional trauma. But if you can bring it off, it will turn out to be a very happy and lasting alliance. Still, it will need a great deal of give-and-take on both sides.

He will place you on a pedestal and it will not be easy for you to live up to it. You will be very good for him, though. You will certainly make him more of a realist, and it will be very good for his character to be continually pushed. Left to his own devices, the Pisces man may well let the roof fall in over his head!

Sexually, you will never be bored. What is more, you will never know what is coming next. You could find that all you do in bed is sleep for a couple of weeks. At other times, he won't give you the opportunity to get forty winks the whole night. Sometimes gentle in his lovemaking, sometimes rough, Mr. Pisces will be full of surprises. Sometimes his imagination in sexual matters may be a bit mind-blowing. Go along with whatever he desires; you will find it a lot of fun if you forget your inhibitions.

In marriage, you will discover that you have a guy who does not go off the rails. Once he's decided on a partner for life, he generally sticks.

He is very good with children. He prefers kids to be little individuals in their own right.

ARIES MAN—ARIES WOMAN

You will only be content with the woman born under the same zodiacal sign as yourself if she is prepared to play Ophelia to your Hamlet. You certainly will not take kindly to any upstaging. One thing you people born under the Sign of the Ram cannot tolerate is a companion who tries to steal the limelight.

Aries is the sign of the leader of the pack—so woe betide the woman who tries to set the pace with you. If your Aries partner has accepted the fact that you are the boss, there is no reason why you should not have a very fruitful relationship. All will run smoothly as long as you are the one who makes most of the important decisions. This can be an unstoppable combination, provided you make a determined effort to understand each other's needs.

This coming together of the male and female elements of the first Sign of the Zodiac makes interesting chemistry. You, with your ever-present driving force that spurs you on to continually accept greater challenges, will be pleased to discover that you have an excellent homemaker, a person who makes absolutely sure you have all the comforts close at hand when you want to relax and put your feet up. You take your love life very seriously, and you expect the same seriousness in return from the other party. It can be a very dangerous game to play with your feelings.

What you will be looking for in your Aries partner is someone who shares your interests without trying to wrest power from you, a person who will hold your hand affectionately without trying to squeeze the life out of you. In a nutshell, someone who needs your love and affection but who won't drain you emotionally.

There are, you will find, many things you have in common. For example, your love of a settled home life. As a rule, you also share a desire to have a large family. Children usually play a very important role in the relationship between Mr. and Mrs. Aries.

You will find that your woman is a wonderful lover. You need not worry that offspring will be put before you, either. You will be delighted to discover that this particular mate knows how to share her love so that no one feels left out in the cold. But you both must guard against the danger of dominating your children. Together, you can be an overpowering combination for any youngster. You must both show a greater willingness to let go when the time comes for your teenage son or daughter to get to know the outside world.

Fidelity is not the Ram's strongest point. You always find it difficult to control that old wanderlust. This is one of the dangers you will both have to face up to if you decide to settle down into a permanent relationship. You have a tendency to become very preoccupied with your personal problems and interests; your Aries woman should be the first to realize that this is not calculated selfishness but simply the way you explore your potentialities to the fullest.

You like to use other people as sounding boards, and who better to turn to than the person you feel understands you most? Your cultivated Aries woman has no difficulty in filling such a crucial role in your life.

So long as your good lady keeps the home shipshape and makes certain that life on board goes smoothly, you are not likely to run into stormy weather. Just be sure that *both* of you remember who is captain and who is first mate.

There is no reason, then, why your time together should not be one long pleasure cruise.

ARIES MAN—TAURUS WOMAN

You may be wondering whether the fire of the Aries Ram may not be like a red flag to the Taurus Bull. Far from it. One of the dangers of this linkup between the first and second Signs of the Zodiac is that the lady may lack the sparkle you look for in a woman.

In fact, contrary to popular belief, this Sign can be quite passive. This lady likes to keep her feet firmly on the ground and, as a rule, abhors change.

With your desire to jump from place to place, you may find Ms. Taurus' settled approach to life rather tame. All is not gloomy, however. If you do manage to get it together with a Taurus woman, you won't be disappointed with her sexual appetite. She has a very romantic side to her nature, too. Do not expect to make it to first base with her unless you can make her believe you have more than a passing interest. She simply will not want to know about a here-today-gone-tomorrow affair. If you do make any impulsive amorous advances in her direction, the black eye you end up with will remind you which particular Sign of the Zodiac you are dealing with. But since Venus rules her Sign and the Moon is at its strongest here, once Miss Taurus has stars in her eyes, you will know what romance is all about.

Taurus people are no-nonsense types. They go for the sturdy and substantial in their dress as much as in their political beliefs. Because you can be pretty dogmatic about what you believe in, too, you had better make sure you think along much the same lines before you contemplate any sort of permament alliance.

Taurus also signifies a nail or hook—in fact, any implement that holds down or secures something. You may find being put on a leash simply goes against your grain. And once she has taken a certain point of view, it will be very difficult to budge her.

On the other side of the coin, she's a great little lady to have pitching for you. Miss Taurus will be by your side come hell or high water if she believes in what you are doing. As a fighter for her man, she is second to none.

On the intellectual plane, it is no use trying to interest her in some new project outside her experience of life. She will pay little or no attention to subjects she finds it hard to appreciate, no matter how persuasive and enthusiastic you may be. A quality you can't fail to admire in the Taurus woman is that she is very difficult to deceive. No traveling salesman or peddler of shoddy merchandise will pull the wool over her eyes.

If you have her devotion, you will find that the moment you walk in, dinner is ready to go on the table, your drink is poured out, your slippers are warming by the fire. She won't mind a little harmless flirting on your part, either. When you're out at a party or dining in mixed company, she will accept your winking and games playing with other women. But if she catches you two-timing her for real—that's it. She'll be gone.

You could not wish for a better mother for your children. She will fight hard to get the very best that life has to offer her young. She can become a little irritable, though, when her babes turn into teenagers.

ARIES MAN—GEMINI WOMAN

The Gemini lady could turn out to be the girl of yor dreams, for in this zodiacal Sign, the head rules the heart. Ms. Gemini will certainly be sympathetic and very understanding about any problems you have difficulty in overcoming. The reason for this empathy is she is traveling much the same path as you are. Where you will find yourself branching off in different directions is in the way you go about solving life's difficulties. This lady prefers to slip into a new dress, pack her bags and roll on to pastures new rather than work through her hangups methodically. She may find your tenacity a little too much to cope with.

There are, however, many things that will appeal to you about the lively Gemini mind in that trim little figure. There will never be a dull moment when you are in her company. Miss Gemini shares your love of people and parties. Like you, she prefers to keep on the go. If you have to do any special entertaining—like having the boss over to dinner—you couldn't possibly wish for a more dazzling or charming hostess. Her inner warmth and quick wit will be apparent to all.

Do not worry if your lady flirts outrageously with men; this is such second nature to her that she will wonder what you're talking about if you bring the subject up. There is no need to be really concerned—if she's your girl. But if you're foolish enough to make too much of it, you'll be teased to distraction!

In this companion you will find you have met your match when it comes to speed of thought. In games that call for quick reflexes, you will have a lot of trouble keeping up with your Mercurial partner.

You will need to take hold of the purse-strings in this relationship because people born under the Sign of Gemini are apt to forget how much cash there is in the bank when they go on a spending spree. As a rule, she will not be the world's greatest cook, but on the other hand, it is unlikely you will ever go hungry. Just when you thought the larder was empty, a quick and tasty snack will be produced—apparently out of thin air.

When organizing holidays or trips to visit friends, leave all the arrangements to your Gemini sweetheart. She is a wonder at making exciting things happen. You will never experience a dull moment when she's around. You will find it very difficult to pin this Miss down to a settled and secure life, though. She doesn't like to become deeply involved. Always aware of the wide variety of choice open to her, she'll hold back before committing herself to any positive course of action.

The restless Twins in Ms. Gemini's zodiacal makeup prefer to take their entertainment at a social level. Nothing pleases them more than to be gadding about town, eating in different restaurants night after night and taking in plenty of movies and plays.

The woman born under this Sign makes a wonderful mother. This may be because she has so much Peter Pan in her. She will keep youngsters happy and occupied for hours on end, mainly because she is having so much fun herself. One thing that this lady does not want to know about is settling down into a dull day-after-day routine.

ARIES MAN—CANCER WOMAN

Ms. Cancer can be an ideal partner for you in more ways than one.

Women born under this Sign often have a very sound business head on their pretty little shoulders. Cancer is the Latin name for Crab—and Cancers certainly like to hold on tightly to what they've got. Do not be put off by the hard shell she may seem to wear. It is only for protection, to hide her fears and doubts from the outside world. Be careful that you are not rough with her, and above all, never, never take her for granted.

Miss Cancer will not give herself easily to a man. It could take an awful lot of candy and many bouquets of flowers before she will accept your promises of everlasting love as serious. Cancer is a feminine Sign. This woman is, as a rule, very passive—definitely a taker rather than a giver. But if you do fall head over heels for her, and she reciprocates, you will have a bundle of passion on your hands who will follow you to the ends of the Earth. Once Ms. Cancer is smitten by love, her man can do no wrong. She may not always know where she is going, but she does know she's got to go with you.

On the debit side, you could find that she is slovenly, extremely critical and ready to blame others for her own shortcomings. She can also be a dreadful nagger. You won't be able to get away with any slouching or shirking of your responsibilities. As an Aries type, you sometimes need a kick in the backside to get you going; a pinch from the claws of your Crablike friend will serve just as well.

You will have to be prepared for displays of jealousy. Once you are her man, you had better keep that roving eye of yours under control. An important problem Miss Cancer faces in dealing with the opposite sex is how to keep her hard exterior without grinding to a formless pulp the passion that lurks inside her. Alone, she can't succeed; with patience and perseverance, you may be able to help her come to terms. If you hurt this lady, she may never forgive you; you could well find that you have made an enemy for life.

This relationship could run into trouble because you may feel at times that you are being suffocated by so much attention. You have a strong resistance to anyone or anything that makes you feel you are not totally in command of your own destiny. You may get the notion you are being slowed down by your sideways-walking companion. As a rule, you don't like to be pampered. However, you are not involved with a stupid lady, and she should be perceptive enough to know your real needs.

The Cancer woman is regarded as the best homemaker of all 12 Signs. This reputation is not based on idle superstition. You will find you have a loving and devoted wife and mother for your children. Offspring will not be wanting for anything with Mrs. Cancer as their mother. One fault, though, if you can call it that: she is reluctant to let go of her kids when they reach an age to leave the nest. If you happen to have a child with a strong, independent streak, then the rows that take place in the household could have your neighbors banging on the walls. One thing is for sure: if you don't take as much interest as she does in the happiness and security of your children, her affection for you is likely to wane.

When your Cancer woman hits middle age, she will need all your affection and understanding. Life can begin at 40 for both of you, so long as you are prepared to work hard at all times to make this relationship work.

ARIES MAN—LEO WOMAN

It is said that when an irresistible force meets an immovable object, something has to give. Don't listen to those doubting Thomases who say the matching of Mr. Aries and Ms. Leo will be one long drawn out battle of superegos. You should find you understand each other's point of view perfectly.

Astrologers have often been carried away with the King of the Jungle idea, to the point where they forget that in personal relationships, Leo likes plenty of give and take. You will have to throw all those jealous fears you are capable of harboring out the window, though. Ms. Leo is an independent woman, let there be no doubt about it. You will probably find that when you two walk down the street, she will attract her fair share of wolf whistles. Plenty of heads will turn, not just because of the attractive looks these people are usually blessed with, but because of their arresting vibrations.

She will always make the very best of her lot in life. She will work very hard to make her dreams come true. If you have fallen under her spell, you are one of the Signs of the Zodiac able to win her over for keeps. You will have to allow her to retain her individuality, though—not always an easy thing for you to do.

When you are discussing this second fire Sign—yours is the first, remember—money necessarily comes up. Gold being the metal of the Sun—her planetary ruler—this elusive substance often seems to shower into her lap like raindrops. Where Leo reigns, money often flows like water—in and out.

You will find she is a very dedicated person and a very hard worker. You have here a woman who is always interested in learning something new, especially about herself.

Still waters run deep. You must allow her to have her solitude. Peace of mind is very important to Ms. Leo, and she finds it extremely difficult to function unless she is allowed her private moments. Do not try to burst her bubble to find out how she ticks. There are not many people who fail to fall for her Leonine charms, and the Ram is no exception.

You will find her very valuable as a steadying influence. If you are at all unsure about which way to go when dealing with a complicated business matter or some problem connected with your career, turn to your feline companion. You will discover that this Miss is able to unravel in a matter of minutes what has remained unsolved for days. She is also the right person to entertain influential people. It isn't so much her witty conversation or her culinary expertise; just having her on your arm will make you feel like a million dollars. You might find that your good lady needs a bit of watching when it comes to running up accounts in the big stores.

People many years her junior will ask her advice on personal matters and seek her friendship. As a mother, she deserves few, if any, criticisms. She has a strong sense of duty. This is the sort of partnership that ripens with maturity. The traits that you will come to admire most are her level-headedness and her ability to ride the storm in any emergency.

It would be inadvisable to form a casual relationship with this particular Sign. Neither of you is very good at playing games. In fact, if you are not on the level, you could end up getting your eyes scratched out, or at any rate, suffering a nasty mauling.

ARIES MAN—VIRGO WOMAN

Don't fall into the popular trap of believing that this second earth Sign has some sort of connection with the word "virgin." This is not so. Virgo is derived from the Latin, *virginis,* which correctly translated means "girl" or "damsel."

The Aries man may find that this particular maiden takes some getting to know. She is not one to wear her heart on her sleeve. Since the intellectual planet Mercury rules her Sign and is at its strongest here, her agile mind will often be one jump ahead of yours. As mentioned before, Virgo is an earth Sign: in order to reap the harvest of her love, you will have to cultivate the soil and sow the seed of true romance. Never take her for granted. You will find that she is perfectly capable of keeping things from you. She will reveal her real feelings only when she's absolutely certain you can be trusted with her love.

You may not be aware of it at the time, but during your courting days she will be watching to see how you conduct yourself in company. Good manners and sensitive feelings are very important to Ms. Virgo. When you first begin to date, you may find her a bit hard going and too down to earth. In fact, you may even wonder what it was that attracted you to her in the first place. Only when you are on your own once again will you realize that she has got you under her spell. It won't be too long before you come to understand that there is something mystical and magnetic about this particular lady.

Most men can't resist running back to try to figure her out, and the Ram is no exception. Like Gemini—which is also ruled by Mercury—Virgo, you will discover when you get to know her well, is a chatty Sign. In Ms. Cancer, we discovered a lady who tends to complain about how badly she has been treated; Ms. Virgo, on the contrary, will show much more interest in you and your problems. She will find great pleasure in taking you apart to discover what makes you tick, then putting you back together again with improvements of her own devising!

To you Aries-born people, love is very important, so you may be a bit put off by Virgo's cool ways. You will have to work hard to win her over. Still waters run deep. Underneath that cool exterior, you will discover there beats a passionate heart. When Ms. Virgo does fall in love, there are no half-measures. Once convinced that you are Mr. Right, she will have eyes for no one else.

One thing she simply can't tolerate at any price is hypocrisy. This should fit in very well with your attitude toward relationships, as you prefer to play it straight with people, too. If you are totally honest and serious in your interest, she will know it intuitively. If she does not reciprocate your love, she will lay her cards on the table.

Virgo women put much store in appearance. They can't abide sloppy dress or slovenly habits. Make sure you are always well turned out when you date her.

She can be a bit of a prude. Blue jokes will not raise any laughs, here. If you get involved with anyone else while you are going steady with her, she will break off with you immediately. She can't stand a two-timer.

Virgo people can become terribly preoccupied with matters connected with health. You will have, in fact, something of a hypochondriac on your hands. She does not put much trust in mother nature to cure her ills. She shows more faith in the doctor's pills and potions, and the surgeon's scalpel.

Ms. Virgo is sometimes thought to be a nagger. Not so—she is only trying to tell you things that she feels are for your own good. Self-discipline is very important to Virgo. She cultivates it in herself and expects it of others. As a mother, she will have a tendency to be rather strict, but this control will be exercised in a caring and loving manner.

ARIES MAN—LIBRA WOMAN

With Venus-ruled Ms. Libra you, Mr. Aries, can expect the sparks to fly! Behind the cool exterior of this lady is a burning passion. Just take a closer look at the two of you paired together—Venus in her own bright green house and Mars in his blazing red house. It's quite a bundle of passion to put under one roof.

You are going to discover fairly quickly that Ms. Libra is very much a girl after your own heart. You certainly won't find it necessary to explain the depths of your passion to her. If you hit it off on the sexual plane, actions will speak louder than any sweet nothings you could whisper in her ear.

It is also true that when a decision requiring a logical approach is called for, your Libra lady will be able to apply her mind to the problem without any trouble. She is generally a very brainy person, although you may think her a bit dizzy and vague. You would be badly underestimating her if you were to put her in the "dumb broad" category.

As a wife, it is unlikely you will find any other Sign more concerned for her man's welfare. The words of the marriage ceremony—"in sickness and in health" and "for richer, for poorer"—will be taken very seriously by her. She will go to great lengths to make you feel the master in the relationship. When you get around to thinking about it, though, you will discover that the important decisions you made were probably instigated by her ideas.

Once she has made up her mind that she loves you, there will be no holding out or playing hard to get. She does not believe in forming flirtatious relationships to while away the time. If you want to make her yours for keeps, then come straight out with a proposal. She likes a decisive man, one who knows his own mind. She also likes to feel protected by her lover. She will want you to put your arms around her and she'll snuggle up close to you in front of the fire on cold winter nights.

She's a perfectionist. When eating out, she will not hesitate to send the food straight back to the kitchen if it fails to come up to her standards, no matter who may get upset.

Burning passion and a declaration of undying love will never scare Ms. Libra away. If you decide to settle down to a permanent life together, you will find that your partner never tires of spoiling you. She will also like to plan little surprises that she knows will make you happy.

Woe betide the person who says anything bad about you within her earshot. She'll be just as strong when standing up for you as she is when protecting her own rights. Since you also like to believe totally in the individual you decide to settle down with, this desire to put you on a pedestal will only help to strengthen the admiration you feel for her.

Once Ms. Libra has made a decision about anything, she will do her level best to stick to her guns. One thing is certain: she is not quitter. It is a matter of principle with a person born under this Sign to keep her word.

As a mother, you have here a woman who will always know what is best for her offspring. She is also one of those people able to combine bringing up her family with a successful career. You can rest assured, too, that you will never play second fiddle when tiny feet are pattering around the house. You will always come first with her.

ARIES MAN—SCORPIO WOMAN

If you decide to take on this powerhouse of a woman, then good luck to you, Mr. Aries! If you settle down to a permanent relationship with a Scorpio lady, you are going to need all the help you can get. It will take a very strong person to win her over in the first place. And once you have reached first base, the fun will only have begun.

It is very difficult for any man to keep a harmonious relationship going for very long with a woman born under this Sign. But looking at your credentials, you might be the sort of person who can secure the love of this bundle of dynamite.

Scorpio has sometimes been labeled the most troublesome, bad-tempered and downright nastiest Sign in the whole Zodiac. Yet, surely, we must try a little harder to understand Ms. Scorpio before we condemn her out of hand.

The astrological meaning of the word *Scorpio* is connected with the Hebrew letter *nun*, which is also a word signifying *fish*. Water teams with life, and let us not forget that we are dealing here with the second water Sign. Scorpio signifies life endless and everlasting, and this woman will certainly give you an action-packed time of it. You will never encounter a dull moment when she is around. If she should ever lose her temper with you, you had better get out of the way quickly.

This is not a lady to cross swords with, so you had better make sure you are really compatible before you settle down to any sort of permanent union. You could discover that once your passion cools, there is not very much to keep you together. You may find it impossible to cope with her moods and tantrums.

She has a very quick mind, so don't try to fob her off with excuses like "The car's got a flat tire, darling," or "So sorry, my love, I'm afraid I've got to work late at the office tonight," just so you can go and have a couple of drinks with the boys. Always play it straight with her because she is a great respecter of truth.

Scorpio people often show a great deal of interest in the occult and matters connected with a life hereafter. It could be that this knowledge is often made available to them because they need all the help they can muster in this life. Your Scorpio mate will be good at keeping secrets—even from you! Don't get her motives wrong, though. Her main reason for withholding information will be to protect you from facts she doesn't think you can take. You see, in many ways she is a very protective person.

Don't give her any reason to be jealous. She will repay you twice over if you go off the rails while she is your woman.

On balance, it would appear unlikely that you would wish to spend your life with this person because it could be too draining on your emotions. Still, a passionate affair with Ms. Scorpio would be unforgettable.

If despite all these caveats you do decide to get hitched, you'd better forget any ideas you ever had of life being a bed of roses.

ARIES MAN—SAGITTARIUS WOMAN

If you are looking for a woman who will always try to see the positive side of things, you have found her here. No matter how depressing the future may seem, Ms. Sagittarius will always retain her sense of humor and the attitude that something good is just around the corner.

It is true that Sagittarius believe they know what is best for everybody, so Ms. Sagittarius is always surprised when people don't follow her advice. She will always try to be helpful, and though she may appear to be a bit bossy at times, her intentions are good. She is also an independent Miss. In business, she will never be satisfied until she is her own boss in charge of her own material fortune.

Your relationship will have to allow for plenty of give and take as our Sagittarius friend likes to keep control of her personal destiny. Women born under this Sign are rarely given to gossip or spreading rumors—it is simply not in their nature to do so. However, you may find yourself cringing at some of the statements she comes out with because she does have a habit of saying the wrong thing at the wrong time.

If you are a keen sports fan, she is a great partner. This lady loves the outdoor life and usually excels at any sort of game or pastime she puts her mind to. In fact, she may even beat you at some events. Keeping in good shape is very important to her. You will never be able to call her lazy. She likes to keep busy, whether around the house or in her chosen career. Whatever she takes on, she will make every effort to see through to a satisfactory conclusion.

You will find you have a gentle and very understanding partner, a woman who will go out of her way to give anyone less fortunate than herself a helping hand. She is also prepared to face up to her responsibilities and will not try to shift the blame for her own mistakes onto others.

Sagittarius women often marry with an eye to security, whether they admit it or not. They like comfort and can't stand to be in debt or to feel insecure about the future. Being a pretty steady guy, you should have no trouble in providing for most of her needs. You will not find her poking into your business affairs or interfering with the way you handle your career, though should you turn to her for help, her advice will always be practical and sound.

Once she decides on her partner, she won't dilly-dally. She'll fire Cupid's arrow and will rarely miss hitting the bull's-eye. You may think you are doing all the chasing—but, in fact, you only chase this girl until she catches you. Indeed, she is a very determined lass who does not believe in half-measures.

She will make a good housewife, though you mustn't expect her to be satisfied wearing a pretty apron and slaving over a hot stove forever and a day. She is interested in far too many aspects of life to settle for a humdrum routine. As a mother, she will give you no reason to be critical, though you may sometimes get the feeling that she puts her children before everything else. She is very protective of her young.

ARIES MAN—CAPRICORN WOMAN

Ms. Capricorn is just the sort of partner you need to complement your personality—but only if you are one of those go-ahead Aries types who is good at business and dead set on making it to the top. Capricorn is the third of the earth Signs, and earthly wealth and possessions are very important to his woman.

She craves security and needs permanence and stability in her life. You will not hold much appeal for her if you are the kind of guy who gets plenty of bright ideas but seldom follows them through. Females born where Saturn rules and Mars is exalted are strongly influenced by the urge to amass a large fortune. If you work hard, you will have her love and support all the way.

Capricorn has often been described as the Sign of ambition, and there can be no doubt about it, this Miss is tremendously ambitious—not only for herself, but for her man as well. If you are really gone on a Capricorn lady but appear to have little chance of making it to the top of your chosen career, it's unlikely that your amorous advances will arouse much response. This may sound cold, but it's true. After all, it is true to say that the Ram and the Goat—which are the symbols of your respective Signs—have much in common.

We must make a greater effort to understand this lady's complex personality. Although she is keenly interested in rising to the top, she can't be said to be aggressive about it. In fact, you will find her attitude to life quite an asset. But don't make the mistake of thinking her head rules her heart at all times. It's just that she is strong-willed enough to be selective. She feels she will save herself a lot of heartache in the future if she is very careful now about choosing a lifelong partner. And who can blame her? Marriage is a very important business, and she wants to make sure that it's going to be "for richer" and not "for poorer."

She is very quiet about her wishes. She can play a waiting game if she feels what she wants is worth waiting for. But when an opening or an opportunity does appear, you can bet she will be the first through the door to grab it.

As a lover, you are unlikely to find a more passionate mate—she has an insatiable sexual appetite. She will do all that she can to make you feel 100 percent man—when she gets to work, you will have all you can do to keep pace with her! She is extremely thorough in everything she takes on. She is also a great booster of confidence. She makes a wonderful hostess at parties or gatherings, and is always at home in any sort of company.

You have here a very capable cook. She is also a person with excellent artistic taste. Whether your Capricorn woman comes from a family high up the social scale or from a working-class background, you will always feel you are in the company of a lady.

You needn't worry about the way she handles the family budget because she is very good at recognizing a bargain when she sees one. She will save you loads on groceries and furnishings, although she may enjoy an extravagant spending spree on clothes and personal adornment from time to time. No matter what knocks she has to take in this world, she will always find a way to get back on the road to success. Like the Goat, she keeps climbing. If her love is important to you, you will be by her side every step of the way.

She does not have a jealous nature and will expect you to accept her flirtations (don't read anything more into them than that) with members of the opposite sex. You have a fine mother type here; someone who will bring up her young with a sensible and realistic attitude toward life.

ARIES MAN—AQUARIUS WOMAN

Ms. Aquarius is difficult to pin down, make no mistake about it. You could feel that you are chasing a rainbow if you decide to make her your one and only girl.

She is a very difficult person to get to know, which does not bode well for you, who like to know where you stand with people. Her independent nature will have you constantly worrying when you are not in her company. In fact, Ms. Aquarius may represent a special sort of challenge for you.

If you do decide to go a-courting, you will have little time to think about anything else because she will have so many suitors trying to pin her down that you will have to battle pretty stiff competition if you want to win her hand. Aquarius is the Sign of friendship, social life and aspirations. This woman does not make a show of jealousy herself, and will not forsake friends of long standing just because you wish to monopolize her time.

All in all, she could be an extremely difficult woman for you to live with. Undoubtedly, she has fine taste when it comes to furnishing and decorating a home, but on the debit side, you are going to find her reckless and extravagant to a frightening degree. You will constantly be lecturing her on the best ways to save—unfortunately, to little or no avail.

There are, of course, many good things about the coming together of the Ram and the Water-Bearer. On the credit side, she will force you to face up to your responsibilities and do all she can to ensure that you make the most of your considerable leadership abilities. She likes life to be full of surprises, so the best way you can ensure that she sticks by you is to keep her guessing. The trouble is a lifetime of games-playing does not really suit you.

It must be stated that this is not, on the evidence, an ideal masculine-feminine relationship. If you need a wife who will nag at you and constantly spur you into action, then all is well and good. However, you are perfectly capable of making your own decisions, so do you really want a nag?

If after a whirlwind romance with Ms. Aquarius you both decide it's not going to work out, you should have no difficulty in keeping her as a pal for life. She is perfectly capable of turning romance into friendship. And she will always be on hand should you need a shoulder to cry on. This is another reason for you never to get jealous if you see her on the arm of another guy when you are going steady with her—it could well be her kid brother or an old boyfriend. So don't go up and sock him without making a few inquiries first!

The qualities you will admire most in her are her sympathetic nature and the desire to help anyone who is in distress.

You will find you can take her anywhere. She will weigh the company that she finds herself in and will soon have a crowd around her. She doesn't have a jealous nature and won't be looking over her shoulder at you. Even when she's got a right to be jealous, she won't show it. If the man of her choice does go off the rails, she will try to ignore the fact and carry on as if nothing has happened. This is not to say that you should take her for granted—if your two-timing becomes a habit, like the rainbow, she'll be gone in a flash.

She makes a fine mother and will bring her children up in a sensible and adult way.

ARIES MAN—PISCES WOMAN

Dear, sweet Ms. Pisces. It looks as though this girl will always be paddling in circles, never sure where she is going, always confused—and getting nowhere fast. Many a man has thought he could be the one to give her direction, and you, Mr. Aries, are no exception.

She is certainly the dream-girl type. Nice to snuggle up to and very, very domesticated. She is able to keep a household running very smoothly with apparently little effort. She always manages to look cool and attractive. She likes a man who is masterful and will be happy to leave the big decisions to you. In many ways, this combination—you born under the first Sign and her under the last—can work out extremely well.

Ms. Pisces knows how to get her own way, usually by charm. Still waters run deep here, so you ought not be taken in by first appearances. There is quite a brain ticking away under that pretty and seductive exterior. Don't let this put you off, however, as it is not in her nature to wish to match wits against her lover—unless you rub her the wrong way.

She wants you to be the one who goes out and makes the money. She will have a hug and a kiss and a delicious meal waiting for you when you get home. There is not much chance of your hanging out with the boys after office hours are over; domestic attractions will lure you right back to adorable and feminine Pisces.

She will stand up for you at all times. Let no one breathe a word against you in her presence. A more loyal and devoted partner you could not possibly wish for. She likes to be totally honest about her relationships and would hate to do anything to hurt or upset you. Pisces women can be tremendous actresses, though. They can turn on buckets of tears at the drop of a hat. This does not mean they are not feeling the emotion; it's just that they know how to make the most of it. The Fish can play out whatever suits her mood. If you don't realize you are intended to be an audience, you may take the performance for total reality.

As we've said, she can do wonders in the home. She is very artistic and good at decorating, painting and arranging furniture. She loves natural beauty and will always try to have fresh flowers somewhere in the house.

On the debit side, this could be a very unsatifactory combination—you with your strong will and craving to be active all the time, and her floating around in a dream with her head in the clouds. Allow yourself to go along with what at first sight may appear to be her rather zany and way-out ideas—she could be doing her darndest to awaken spiritual understanding in you.

Sometimes she can be a little careless with money. But then, although you're a hard worker, you can play pretty hard yourself. As a partner, you will find your Pisces lady very astute at putting the pennies to one side, so you won't regret it if you put her in charge of the family resources.

Make sure you never forget her birthday or your anniversary because occasions are very important to her. She loves to feel wanted and you will never be able to spoil her with too much affection. So long as you are tender and patient with her, there is no reason why you two should not settle down into a very successful and lifelong partnership.

ARIES' HEALTH

Yours is one of the healthiest Signs of the Zodiac. You are bursting with reserves of energy and have great recuperative powers. But you can burn yourself to a temporary standstill more easily than is often suspected.

You endanger your health when you work strenuously for long periods at a time and ignore the "wilting" signs you should have learned to recognize by now. Your constitution is built for intense, short bursts of exertion. You are then capable of incredible achievements, both physical and mental. But when you try to spin out your vitality by keeping up a relentless effort, you go against your own spontaneous nature. Your metabolism is upset and psychological depression as well as physical strains appear.

Ill health makes you irritable, cramps your style. As sympathetic as you are, you don't even like staying for long periods with people who are sick. Your nature is to be constantly up and doing both physically and mentally. Any threat to this mobility is the worst possible news.

You seldom suffer from drawn-out chronic illnesses. And when you are temporarily immobilized, you become quite indignant about it. You're a terror to nurse or to have around the place. You so dislike being ill that you tend to ignore symptoms when they first appear, as though believing your can overcome them psychologically by refusing to acknowledge their existence. You have a point; sometimes this does work for you. However, there are obvious risks, and the Aries person has to temper self-treatment and willpower with common sense and not allow disturbing signs to continue without reporting them to a doctor.

You don't enjoy visiting the doctor, and will try as many home remedies as you can think of first. At the root of your dislike of doctors is your fear of death; or, more accurately, your lack of conviction of immortality. You don't want to be told the truth if the illness is serious. You would rather bear up and press on, hoping it will go away. For an Aries, this is not burying his head in the sand. Your lust for life refuses to contemplate an end to it. You are also a bad patient for any physician. You don't like following instructions and are likely to discontinue a prescribed treatment after the first day. If directed to remain in bed, you will probably be up and around before the doctor gets out the front door.

It is easy to tell when you are really sick. You lie there and won't move. At these times, you seem to be handing yourself over to unconscious Aries processes and, with your ego out of the way for a while, these are formidable. An Aries usually has tremendous powers of recovery once he can be induced to rest. You can come through fevers that would literally kill others. Convalescence, though is not an easy time for anyone around you.

Your Sign rules the head and face. There is also a reflex association with the kidneys, and it is possible you will suffer from nerves and stomach complaints. Particular care has to be taken against ulcers, especially among executives and high-powered business types. There is a tendency for severe headaches, such as migraine, sunstroke, inflammations and skin rashes. Toothache is also a common complaint among Aries who don't make a point of having regular dental checkups. A visit to the dentist can produce an extraordinary reaction in these people. Although they can face the scalpel and other physical trials with stoic control, the mere thought of the dentist's drill is often enough to bring on an extreme case of the jitters.

Hemorrhages through accidents are a danger. Because of their incessant haste, Aries often trip and collide with objects. They have a great love of sports, speed and the outdoor life, and the risk of injury here is considerable. Around the house, through not always looking where they are going, they bang into doors and regularly suffer from cuts and bruises. Not many Aries are without at least one scar on their bodies.

Despite usually robust health, the Aries individual is particularly vulnerable to drafts and dampness. He or she suffers quite often from head colds, which may develop into sinus infections, ear complaints and nagging headaches. Neuralgia is a common complaint. So is arthritis, which will sometimes affect the hands markedly.

Many Aries tend to abuse their tough constitutions in one way or another. There is a limit to the battering their bodies will stand. Three ways you can help are: slow down, don't overtax your stamina and pay close attention to diet.

ARIES AT WORK

The Job

You can excel in just about any field you choose. But don't kid yourself. You're not going to be happy or particularly successful in the civil service or any large organization that offers a humdrum existence in exchange for security. You won't be a cog in anyone else's machine. Security is not that important to you.

You must be where there is a challenge, where there is a doubt that the job can be pulled off successfully—and also where you can prove over and over again that you can do it better than anyone else around. To be happy and satisfied, you must have expression for your talents and enthusiasm. Money is secondary.

You prefer to batter things down, not in a destructive way, but in that sense that "There's the objective, here am I and here I come." You're all hustle and bustle and striding action. You think on your feet with the speed of a computer. You are at your brilliant best in the midst of the action, when the challenges are coming thick and fast. Ideas burst like fireworks in your mind. If one means fails, you are never stuck for an alternative. You can plug the holes in a scheme with almost intuitive grace as quickly as they appear. You are daring, combative—and quite often reckless.

One of your strongest points is originality. Many of the great inventors of our times have been Aries. So have the originators of the latest business techniques, methods and systems. You have a flair for coming up with the most outstanding idea.

As a salesperson, you are terrifyingly persuasive. This doesn't mean that you are good at knocking on doors and selling housewives goods they don't want. In fact, you won't find many Aries content with that sort of vocation. You're interested in the big time and you're always moving toward it or deeper into it. You like to be proud of what you are doing and it's extremely important that others have a good opinion of you. Your pride in yourself and your ability to perform can be monumental. You'd make an excellent "headhunter," convincing top professional and business leaders that they should take a new million-dollar job. As a promoter of pop stars and other talented temperamental people who know what they want but not how to go about getting it, you are peerless. You have a way of handling odd-bods. And you can sell practically anything. When selling, you are magnetic, convincing and diplomatically astute. But in normal relationships, you are just about as subtle as a fire engine.

Whatever vocation you follow, you gravitate toward a position of authority. Any boss who wants to make the most of your talents has to recognize this almost pathological need to take charge. Not that you want to take over his job ("But if it's going . . . I'm your man!"). You have more than enough know-how to be able to coexist with other ambitious types on the payroll. But you have to feel free, independent of the confines of the structure. You'll submit to the order of things and to a fair amount of cohesive discipline if you are allowed to make your own decisions. And you're not that keen on working regular hours, either. To you, nine to five sounds like a prison sentence. Some of you only reach your peak when others are thinking of retiring to bed. You'd much prefer to come and go at different times. If more bosses understood this and made allowances, they'd get twice the amount of work out of their Aries employees.

You won't remain in any job that does not sustain your interest. When the excitement goes, you go. If for some reason you can't quit, everyone in the place will soon get the message. When unhappy in a job, you become indifferent about it. You take no further active part and are likely to spend most of the day writing and sending off scores of applications for new jobs. The chances are most of these will be beyond your experience or qualifications. An Aries always believes in starting at the top—no bottom-of-the-ladder role.

A military life often provides just the right ingredients for a successful Aries career. The influence of Mars, your ruling planet, helps here. The Martian qualities of strength and the willpower to keep going in times of great stress and pressure also make an able surgeon or explorer. You should also succeed as an engineer, mechanic, dentist or even professional sportsman or sportswoman.

But it is as an executive that the Aries is usually found fulminating in the business world. Here you are in your element and display more capability than most other Signs. For one thing, the Aries approach to problems is quite simple. A situation is usually black or white; there are hardly ever any grays to consider. An expert has been defined as a person who makes quick decisions and is sometimes right. This is the Aries technique. While other wiser and more experienced men and women hesitate because they perceive the possible consequences, the Ram acts. You are an uncomplicated individual largely because you know your own mind. Your attitudes (until you suddenly discard them) are firmly set. You are also unbelievably sure of them. Other people might say life is not that simple—but to the Aries, it is. And you chalk up some impressive successes to prove it.

Surprisingly, you are largely a creature of routine reactions in routine situations. You make a very good authority because you have an unconscious rulebook in your head by which you lay down the law. This also allows you to impose a rigid and unbending discipline if required. When the unexpected happens, you are nonplused for an instant and likely to react impulsively. Then your agile mind gets working again and starts throwing out alternatives. You are similarly unable to cope well with people whose moral or intellectual approach is a bit abstract or out of the ordinary. You are somewhat narrow-minded and like things to be clear cut. When confronted with a viewpoint beyond your immediate comprehension, you are likely to reject it as unrealistic and never give it another thought.

You are not the type to work as a member of a team because you upset others by trying to take over. You do best working alone or at the head of a project. Basically, you are quite conservative—that is, you prefer to follow established precedents while trying to improve on them. Your style is to introduce a new version of an old idea in a new situation. This gives the appearance of originality—and in a way it is original, though essentially it is an act of pioneering, not invention.

Your ideas are often impressively audacious, clever and brilliant. At other times, the Aries technique lets you down and your ideas appear inept, inopportune and immature. You try things, give them new applications, and in this respect you are not as creative as some other Signs.

Aries people are often gifted with eloquence and make excellent orators. You can communicate your enthusiasm to others with a vital intensity and, if given the opportunity, are able to stir public feelings. You can make the best of politicians from a progressive point of view, but the chances of your remaining in a position dependent on the popular vote are not too good. The true Aries is too idealistic to compromise with the expediencies of politics. Democratic procedures are far too slow and laborious. And your supreme faith in your own ability to know what is best for others will eventually be resented and cause hard feelings. You are far from being an expert at wheeling and dealing because you can really only think of one thing at a time. Intrigue leaves you standing flat-footed and uncomprehending. You are too impatient and rebellious to serve the ponderous political machine or to mark time until the moment is right for this or that measure. You know what needs to be done and you want it done now. Goodbye, President Aries.

Writing is a talent that often distinguishes the Aries. It gives the scope to explain his or her ideas in a context where they can be more readily acceptable. Aries is an intellectual Sign. It produces extremely able journalists, especially reporters who must be constantly on the move, probing and confronting. Radio, television, advertising, lecturing and public relations also provide careers suitable for the Aries temperament and talents.

In choosing an occupation, the Aries person has to remember that he or she can't stand monotony. It's no good following Dad into the legal business unless you are sure you can put up with the long apprenticeship as a clerk. Accounting and similar professions requiring close concentration on detail are also apt to send the pure Aries racing for the bottle, or the door. When you get bored, you start trying shortcuts and make mistakes. Carelessness is always a danger with you people; once you lose interest, it is inevitable. Another hazard that has to be considered when selecting a vocation is misplaced enthusiasm. If the *idea* of a job catches your fancy, you are likely to surround it with highly imaginative expectations that have no relationship to the real job to be performed. Aries people are frequently disappointed because once they start a job, they find it's nothing like what they had imagined. This is one reason why they move on quite regularly.

The Aries nature is to start out full of beans, put a headlock on the task and throw it in three seconds flat! If the job drags on and becomes a repetitious exercise, it is a dead loss for you. To be happy, you must do work that provides continual opportunities to demonstrate your talents to the world (or to an appreciative superior).

You are a fine starter but a desultory finisher. Whatever you choose to do, someone will have to come along behind and clean up or fill in the details. You'll build the house on the edge of the mountain where no one else would dare. But when the time arrives for decorating, living in it or laying out the garden, you will have long since disappeared.

Money

To the Aries man or woman, money is not all that important. It certainly is not the main point of work. Money just doesn't have the same power to corrupt these people as it does others. Like love, money to an Aries is a thing apart from his reason for being. He uses it and seldom allows it to use him.

You like to spend money. You are extravagant in many ways. You'll squander your cash on others to create an impression, to give you a feeling of importance. Money fuels your impulsiveness, the dominant characteristic in your nature. It's the agency for working instant miracles. You haven't got something? Here, take this—now you have. You're poor? Now you're rich. You have well and truly noted that there are few vacuums in your society that money cannot fill.

You rarely save much during the first half of your life. It is usually around middle age that you begin to accumulate, when your life-style has become less erratic and urgent.

You are extremely honest with money, both personally and in business. You won't deliberately rob another individual. But you're not the world's best economist. Your ideas of accounting and balancing the budget, like your nature, are pretty elementary and straightforward. You take from here to pay there. There's no question of dishonesty or fraudulent intent. But you do get yourself in a financial mess at times.

Your impulsive actions in love and romance often cost you a packet. You can genuinely shrug off these expenses as being of little importance, but they still have to be paid. And it can be a long, hard haul at times.

You lend money with surprising alacrity. This doesn't mean you are a soft touch for everyone. To the contrary, you are quite discriminating about whom you give to or oblige. But though you frequently don't get all your money back, you're not the type to weep about it. You can't help it if you're often a rotten judge of character. Your faith in other people's integrity—or is it just your faith in life?—is as amazing as it is enviable. It's also a matter of pride with you not to complain if someone takes you for a ride. But it's not always easy to ignore the hollers of outraged dependants or partners!

It is the Aries way to throw a lot of bread on the water.

TAURUS' CHARACTER

Whatever in the world would we do without you, Taurus? Seasonally speaking, you come after Aries announces spring by poking his impulsive, fiery finger into the freezing earth. You grip the seed of life in a tight resourceful fist and give it its chance to live, to grow into tomorrow's crop. Taurus is the Sun's seasonal Sign of hope. Without Taurus and hope, nothing could survive. Good, solid, caring, patient and persistent Taurus gives every living thing the chance of a lifetime.

Taurus is the warmest and most humanistic of the three earth Signs. Its symbol is the Bull. Everything about this common-sense and practical Sign has an affinity with nature and the earth. Since nature is the greatest artist, it's not surprising that you are as likely to be found at a theater or an art gallery as on a farm or a game preserve. The ruler of Taurus is Venus, the planet of love, beauty and harmony, and this, of course, enhances your strong artistic tendencies.

You are not necessarily a Rembrandt or a Hemingway yourself. Your artistic tendencies are expressed basically in appreciation rather than creativity. And without practical application, art has less appeal for you. For instance, if you have paintings in your home, your enjoyment of them won't come from their beauty alone; you'll also get a lot of satisfaction from the knowledge that they are valuable—and becoming more so every day. You see, you're practical. You've got the down-to-earth touch that makes your taste elegant, but not arty, and therefore acceptable to most others. You are not like the Libra person, for example, who may get so carried away by the sheer idea of beauty that art becomes a rather precious and overspiritualized exercise. After all, though we all have a feeling for absolute beauty, we do live in a material world, and you manage to stroke a very nice balance between the two.

It follows, of course, that you love to go away to the country—or, if you can't manage that, to parks and other natural surroundings. There, with every deep breath of fresh air, you shed all the tension that may have built up in you. Nothing delights the Taurus man more than a fishing trip to some quiet out-of-the-way place where he can contemplate the trout (even if he doesn't catch any), slip and slide down the grassy banks and delight in the delicious earthiness of his surroundings. If he's not a camper, he'll love to go for a drive and park in the woods. He'll get there some way, because it's a therapeutic need.

The Taurus woman is a little more genteel and less likely to rough it. But she, too, must get out of the city and into a rural setting, even if it's only to visit people she's not particularly interested in. These women often become "lady farmers," that is, they employ others to do the work and delight in sharing their time between a town house and a country home. Most Taurus people do like to get back to the stimulus of people once their batteries are sufficiently recharged.

That kind of *gentle* change of scene is what you require, but you hate disruptive change. In fact, you don't really enjoy any change that means shifting your possessions from one place to another. Even when you're moving into a nicer home or a better job, you're all sixes and sevens inside. It takes time for you to settle down. But when you do settle, you settle as though it's forever. Of course, life being what it is, you're very disturbed when the time for a change comes around again.

This is easy to understand. Your whole nature is founded on the need for stability and security. You want to be left alone to build your own world and—it's got to be said—you're fairly materialistic in your urges. Security to you means possessions, objects you can touch, mortgage or sell if need be. You'll work hard for them, though. Your patience, endurance and determination are quite amazing. When others give up, you are still pressing on. If your life work was suddenly destroyed, you would be able to pick up the pieces and toil on. You don't complain. You are the essence of reliability. This makes you a wonderful employee. All the boss has to do is point you in a certain direction. He can be sure there'll be no shirking and that he'll get his money's worth. You are totally honest.

But you're not a great one for taking chances, nor for adapting to new circumstances, which is why you usually do better in an occupation where the guidelines are clearly laid down. You do get some inspired ideas occasionally, but often you're too cautious to act on them. Thus do you miss opportunities.

In an emergency, you certainly won't lose your head, but you are inclined to stand around flat-footed wondering what to do. It's a different matter if your own progress or welfare is involved; you have no trouble coming up with alternatives to protect yourself or what you own. This instinctive self-preservation is similar to your intuition, which is also very strong and protective. It often warns you about things that are going to happen and is a great help to you in summing up people you're meeting for the first time. You frequently amaze your friends with the acuity of your judgment.

Actually, you're more a feeling person than a thinking one. As a child, you probably found it difficult to learn certain subjects. You might even have gotten the reputation for being a bit slow at book learning, though no one ever questioned your basic intelligence. Unfortunately, both parents and teachers can show a remarkable lack of understanding of Taurus children. (This is discussed in some detail in the "Taurus Children" section.) In order to function happily and efficiently, it is essential for you to be emotionally involved. If your feelings or interests aren't aroused, you might as well forget about learning a subject. It's the same with the Taurus youngster, though naturally more distressing because he or she has not yet learned to accept this as a natural part of his or her character.

As a child, you also required a great deal of affection. Yet if it wasn't forthcoming, you wouldn't go looking for it. You might have felt starved, empty and unsure inside, but you'd never show it. In fact, you'd put on an air of self-confident indifference, though you weren't feeling half as brave as you pretended. If this kind of thing happened to you—and it does to most Taurus children—some emotional damage was done. Today it may manifest itself in great possessiveness toward the things you own and treasure—even more especially, the people you love.

You still require a great deal of affection. You are very attracted and attractive to the opposite sex. In the "Taurus in Love" section, there's quite a bit about you and your love habits. Briefly, you don't go looking for love. Oh, you're always on the lookout, all right, but that's not the same thing. You don't believe in overexerting yourself. You'd rather rely on your proven magnetic quality to draw lovers and admirers *to* you. If you're not already married, what you're patiently seeking is the man or woman of your dreams. You know exactly the type of person you want. It's a tall order, but you won't settle for less. And you're determined not to make any errors by rushing in when a prospect turns up. You'll take your time. You're cautious. You can wait. That's the Taurus style.

You are somewhat emotionally impulsive, which may sound odd after describing you as stable, methodical and conservative. You're not easy to shift in your habits, but emotionally you're often vulnerable unless you've learned to control this shortcoming. For a start, you can be too easily influenced by the feelings or opinions of others.

If you get on a certain person's wavelength, it's amazing how he or she can sway you in a different direction. You are likely to accept this person's prejudices and faulty reasoning as being true without subjecting them to any logical scrutiny of your own. It's as though you don't want to exert yourself mentally to form your own conclusions or are unwittingly prepared to be brainwashed for the sake of ease. It's a good idea for Taurus people to occasionally examine the opinions they've been putting forward and see just how many reflect their own true feelings.

Everyone knows that the Bull is a rather contented sort of animal that doesn't give much trouble as long as it's left alone. Handled properly, he'll work all day without complaint and even allow himself to be led by the nose. Harmony is what he seems to value most. You're much the same. But when it comes to temper, you are both capable of ferocious, irrational fury. Much has been written about this seemingly inappropriate flaw in the gentle, sympathetic and sensitive Taurus character. But is it really so inconsistent? No, not in psychological terms. The Taurus person's whole nature is to preserve what is, as it is. You don't object to anyone's progress through accumulation. This you understand. If people add more to what they've already got, it's okay with you, so long as they don't go round upsetting others. What you do object to is people making changes that others (yourself) don't want. You're conservative politically and socially. Taurus is the symbol of big business, finance and private enterprise, which abhors radical changes. What's been working well for decades, you firmly believe, should not be interfered with.

Taurus can be prodded and provoked a long, long time before he blows his top. No other Sign will turn the other cheek more often or deliver a firm resisting heave with such restraint. But finally, it happens: the Establishment explodes, the Bull charges, Taurus does his his block. The outcome is cataclysmic, positively dangerous to the life and limb of all in the vicinity. The blind fury of Taurus rage seems to give the person superhuman strength.

While we're on the subject of faults, we might as well mention your obstinacy. This has also been misunderstood to a large degree. Basically, it's your way of controlling your own temper! And the rest of us are grateful for it. But really, you should try a little harder to understand yourself. You're terribly fixed in your opinions. There's too much black and white, you and me—not enough us and the gray patches of compromise. You may be a loving and lovable creature, but we've all got to live in this meadow together. Now, hold off, no one's questioning your loyalty and devotion to those you love, or your ability to serve them and care for them through thick and thin without complaint. In fact, they don't come any more steadfast than you. But please . . . relent a bit from time to time.

And finally (we'll soon be into the good part), we come to your jealousy and possessiveness. It's as though everything you accumulate becomes a little part of yourself. You hold on to what you own with the same firm determination that the fist of Taurus holds on to the seed of life. Taurus conserves, holds the forces of sustenance around the spark of individuality and gives it its chance to shoot, to grow, to mature. Yours is the impulse of possession. And you are naturally extremely good at acquiring things.

First, there's your money instinct. You'll seldom find a Taurus person who's broke. No matter how lowly you start out, you invariably rise to a position far more comfortable than your early circumstances. Part of your success is due to your steady, methodical working habits and tremendous perseverance. Once you fix a goal for yourself, you stick to it, wearing down the obstacles with the persistence of the sea eroding the shoreline. You don't gamble and you don't take risks, so you won't rise quickly. But you most certainly *will* rise.

Then there's your Midas touch. You have the habit of turning money into more money. Quite often it's for other people, big companies and the like, but you share in the rewards and rise to considerable prominence. (Taurus people often finish as presidents of banks, stockbroking companies or insurance empires.) You generally do better under a corporate umbrella where speculation and risk-taking are minimized and where your conservative and traditional style can be fully exploited.

Taurus people just starting out will probably be drawn to jobs where they can put their artistic inclinations to practical use, such as in picture framing, hair styling, interior decorating, architecture and the like. Many make their first pile as actors and singers, and then go on to make even greater fortunes through canny investments. There are a lot of Taurus people among the millionaires of this world.

You're careful with your cash but no one could ever call you miserly. You're just determined that if that proverbial rainy day does arrive, you'll be able to afford a raincoat. And you *are* a bit pessimistic where money is concerned. Since it's the symbol of your psychological stability, you're careful with it and inclined to take frequent mental inventories (especially when you're feeling low) of what you own and how much you could probably raise *if*. . . . You also take a quick reassuring look at your bank book every now and again—it does make you feel better, doesn't it?

These, of course, are your very private secrets. Your friends probably wouldn't believe you do these things. To them, you are a very generous and kind person with an admirable common-sense way of handling your finances. You don't allow your silly personal fears to inhibit your natural sympathies. If any of your buddies is in need, he or she won't have to ask twice. It's just that you seldom get *yourself* into a mess with personal finances. If you're a man and married, your wife is likely to be the envy of the neighborhood because she has a husband who takes her on a winter vacation to the islands. If you are a woman and in control of the family finances, your budget somehow always stretches to cover a nice holiday in a pleasant place for the whole family. That Taurus golden touch certainly makes life pleasanter for the people you love.

Talking about travel, even though you're a bit of a stick-in-the-mud, you do enjoy getting away because it gives you a chance to get a new slant on things and you're sensible enough to know this is most desirable for you. It's meeting new faces that pleases you most, along with the touch of good living and extravagance that normally characterize travel. It's funny, but though at home you're a little reserved making new friends, on a trip, you're positively effusive. It's the atmosphere—change without disruption . . . change without risk—and the knowledge that you will find everything back home exactly as it was. What bliss! You swing along with the bouncing verve of the good-neighbor tourist (still very selective, though) and make some charming new contacts. If that element of refinement you so admire is absent in a would-be acquaintance, it's no deal. You're very firm about this. You can't stand pushy, loud-mouthed, boisterous people. You don't want opinions thrust down your throat. With a Taurus man, even the most glamorous woman doesn't rate recognition if she shows off her intellectual brilliance in company to impress him. When he fixes her with that dead-cold stare of absolute indifference, she'll know she's met a man and not just a male.

The Taurus woman likes to converse with an intelligent fellow as long as he doesn't get domineering. She's wonderful at giving advice and often attracts the quiet handsome guy in the corner with a lot of troubles on his mind and no one to tell them to. How this lady and her male counterpart can put her finger so deftly on the key to happiness for others is one of the mysteries of this Sign—but Taurus people frequently can do this for others. It could be because you're such good listeners (if the person appeals to you) and because you have such a logical-thinking brain.

A very definite quality in you Taurus individuals is your acceptance of a person's right to do or be what he or she wants—rat catcher, laborer, agitator or dropout. To you, they're all people first. Because of your genuine tolerance, you usually number a few odd-bods among your closest companions, and you're as much at home with them as you are with the governor. Remarkably, you can gather together very different types of people in a room and make it seem the most natural thing in the world. It's phonies who make you mad, people who put on airs and graces and haven't got the guts to be themselves. Basically, you are a terribly sincere person and believe that dishonesty begins when people pretend to be what they're not. You are conscious of a lot of your own faults and you're prepared to live with them—but you refuse to cover them up. When you meet a person you don't like, you just avoid him. It is not your style to make scenes.

Both the Taurus man and woman are very sexy. To begin with, they are extremely aware of their bodies. Sensuality is something they truly understand. Instinctively, they know how to move, stand and sit to attract—whether they are conscious of it or not, every one of their movements is designed to stir the physical interest of whoever happens to be around. This Sign does include a higher proportion than most others of homosexuals and transvestites. The sensual distinctions are not so clearly defined here.

Taurus is the Sign where the Moon, the planet intimately associated with the emotions and desires, is exalted or at its strongest. And the ruler of this Sign is the planet of love and beauty itself, Venus. Since both of these influences are expressed in earthy and practical ways rather than idealistically, the potential for sensual excitement and enjoyment is exceedingly strong in the Taurus person. The sense of touch-feeling is highly developed. Fortunately, you have a great deal of self-control (especially if you are a woman). Your willpower—if you choose to use it—is tremendous, a built-in protection against the allure of excess.

Taurus people usually have attractive bodies, but not necessarily because of any particular feature. They often appear slimmer than they are, more rounded in the right places and more pleasingly proportioned than is a measurable fact. In other words, as they used to say in the twenties, they've got It.

It's not unusual for the male to pamper himself with bath oils and salts, and a husky male scent or talcum powder. This guy is usually so masculine and down-to-earth that it's difficult to imagine him taking so much care with his toiletries, but make no mistake, they're very important to him. He loves fragrance. He also loves romantic imaginings. A girl would never guess what goes on in his mind from his placid, easygoing, low-key approach.

Unlike the Taurus woman, he probably hasn't got anywhere near the wardrobe you'd imagine. The secret is that whatever clothes he does own are of superb quality (beautiful to the touch) and impeccable in taste and style—and he knows all about coordination. The Taurus lady does all the above and much, much more, depending on her financial resources. If she's rich, she'll surround herself with every luxury and her bed and bathroom will resemble something out of the Arabian Nights.

Blessed with such seductive magnetism and intense sensual curiosity, the Taurus person's sexual tendencies are often determined in his or her early years. Promiscuity or control? Deviationist or heterosexual?

It has already been mentioned that youthful Taurus is more emotional than mental. The reasoning powers are slow to develop in this Sign and while they are maturing, Taurus requires a great amount of love and affection, including physical cuddling and petting. If this is not forthcoming from the parents, the child is apt to look for it elsewhere, to fall into precocious experimentation with other children or salacious adults.

Mature Taurus manages to balance his or her love of sensation with good common sense. In other words, if dependent on another person, you know where your bread is buttered or exactly what you want for yourself. You won't deny yourself physical pleasures, but you won't plunge into them ingenuously, either. You'll weigh everything against your big aim in life, which by early adulthood is usually quite clear—a nice home, a good income, the partner of your dreams and some solid assets. Sure, you want plenty of diversions while you're waiting and working, but you allow nothing to interfere with your splendid vision. That's willpower. And that's Taurus.

Now, about the "nice" home Taurus wants. "Superb," "beautiful," "sumptuous," "magnificent" would be the words to describe it if you manage to have your way because the home is the most cherished of all the Taurus possessions. In it, you crystallize the sum total of your worldly aspirations. Everything you do is essentially to realize the home of your dreams. You go to work for it, marry to help beautify it and have children to give it a social purpose. The home is not just your castle. It is your grip on the ever-loving earth. Naturally, then, your home is as beautiful and comfortable as you can afford to make it.

Your contentment comes through your possessions, and you have a great feeling for them. You luxuriate in what you own, but extravagant style doesn't appeal to you much unless it has a useful purpose. You enjoy blues and pinks and frequently different shades of green. Your penchant for green, in fact, often expresses itself in a love of gardening. Many of you have a green thumb, and if you have the space, you're certain to create a tidy and attractive garden where you will spend many unhurried hours. Even if you live in an apartment in the city, you will install window boxes filled with flowers or have a tasteful sprinkling of indoor plants. If the space is available, the Taurus male will have part of his garage or another room or shed adapted for his favorite hobby. This will usually be a pastime involving a fineness of touch such as painting, sculpturing, music, restoring, woodcarving and so on. The Taurus woman also likes these things, and in addition, embroidery.

Quite often you'll have a keen interest in *objets d'art* and greatly enjoy browsing through antique shops. The past, with its refinements, unhurried pace and more elegant style of living, appeals very much to the Taurus heart. Though you may be aware of historical social injustices, still, you would like to see a restoration of the better qualities of former eras, especially the leisurely enjoyment of simple pleasures.

The place where you were raised often enters your thoughts, especially if you were happy there. You seldom fail to notice the beauty of the architecture around you. There's a deep nostalgia to your nature you can't quite explain. Copper, that beautiful old-fashioned metal that covers itself with a greenish-blue patina (your favorite color), is your favorite metal.

It's not easy for you to express your feelings. You're not a particularly avid talker or gifted writer, though when your emotions are aroused, you become far more descriptive and communicative. But generally speaking, you are more an observer and listener than an expounder. Mind you, the Taurus male when he's in love can write some lovely little poems guaranteed to make the deserving heart beat faster, but that's *emotion*—whenever you feel it, you must express it in some meaningful way.

In later life, when you're successful and you've made a mint, are you happy? What does power mean to Taurus? Well . . . you enjoy giving orders as much as anyone—for a while. But once you realize you've got the resources that command power, you're inclined to lose interest in it. You're in this life to enjoy its aesthetic and sensuous pleasures, not for the ego trip of bossing others around. If you have to take stern measures to protect your position or capital, that's a different matter. Behind that cold impersonal stare of yours, you're quite capable of ordering punitive and sometimes ruthless action if the threat is urgent enough.

Taurus men and women are often first-class cooks. When they're entertaining, which is one of their special joys, they plan their meals with infinite care and patience. They like to put out a substantial meal with as many homemade foods as possible, including oven-fresh bread. They do not favor exotic kinds of dishes with elaborate sauces and taste-obscuring garnishes. As in everything, the Taurean individual prefers quality and substantiality: thick steaks, roasts, potatoes, turkey, duckling—all very nicely presented, all very basic. For salad, you like lots of chunky tomatoes and fresh greens—and a very light dressing that doesn't spoil the natural good taste. And for dessert, strawberries, apple pie, loads of fresh cream, Danish pastries, cakes—rich, delicious food that horrifies people perpetually on a diet.

Here we come to another fault, weakness, defect, failing—call it what you will. Taurus people often eat (and drink) too much. Sometimes they're downright gluttonous and stuff themselves at table as if it were their last meal—but always, mind you, with studied good manners.

Under the sturdiness of its own rude health, the Taurus body has a natural inclination to bulge. The slightest indulgence of the appetite shows up in all the wrong places. Those who have learned to control their love of good dining usually find that they have to miss at least one meal a day to stay at their normal weight! It's not easy, but considering that your capacity to enjoy the delights of the flesh is about twice that of most mortals, what would you expect—and still retain a sense of justice?

That's another point—a good one. You are an extremely fair person. Whether you're dealing with children, employees or a recalcitrant spouse, you don't expect miracles overnight. You always remember how long it took you to learn things (even though when you did, you seemed to remember them longer than others).

You put a lot of store in tried and true methods. You're inclined to distrust new methods and may even reject them altogether. Some would say you're not very progressive. Others (less kind) might venture the opinion that you're stodgy and unimaginative.

It's true that you're not a great one for taking the initiative. You're inclined to postpone decisions for as long as possible, so you can think about them carefully, deliberate. Sometimes in the end, someone has to light a fire under you. But when you finally *do* get going, Taurus, you're unstoppable.

TAURUS IN LOVE

YOUR TAURUS MAN

You like him? Love him? Just what sort of a guy is your Taurus? He's a wary one. He loves women. He feels with every emotion in his body. But he's not going to be caught by any gold-digger female who thinks she can twist him around her little finger. Not strong, silent Mr. Taurus. He knows what he wants in a woman. From the moment he meets you, he'll be summing you up. He doesn't have to think much about it because he's got a lot of intuition in these things. He wants a woman who'll pet him and love him. And he won't object at all if she's got a little money of her own or is socially well connected.

This man has many love affairs before he settles down. If you're one of those, he'll treat you right, give you a good time and walk away.

If he wants you for keeps, you'll be able to tell by his slow but sure technique. If you want to throw yourself on the bed, okay, he's a hot-blooded male and it's not by accident that his symbol is the Bull. But otherwise, he'll give you the full matador treatment, circling you gracefully while displaying his smooth and artistic manner—before going in for the kill.

As you no doubt know, this guy is ruled by the love planet Venus, which also happens to be the planet of beauty and harmony. He can really turn on the charm. And if he's a pure Taurus, it will be roses (literally) all the way—expensive gifts and stimulating conversations over pleasant meals in first-class restaurants. Once he's sure you're the girl for him, he won't spare any effort or expense.

But don't expect a whirlwind romance. He's looking for someone to put on a pedestal, and that kind of woman is not easy to find, he's discovered. He wants a someone who'll be true. He's prepared to overlook numerous minor faults (well, several anyway) in exchange for loyalty. This he treasures most. And if you're the kind of woman he's looking for, you can depend on him being true to you. Oh, he'll make goo-goo eyes at pretty girls and indulge in mild flirtations, but as long as he believes that you love him, he will never let you down.

He's a bit careful with the pennies—not so much when you're dating, but when the responsibilities come after marriage.

He is basically an insecure person inside, unsure of himself under all his brave talk about how well he's doing in business and what big deals are coming up. He'd love to have his own private gold mine, not to finance an extravagant existence, but for the sheer comfort of knowing it was there. He regards his home in the same way. It's his personal El Dorado. He loves to make it attractive, fill it with beautiful paintings, furniture—all the best that he (and you, if you marry him) can afford—so he can experience the delicious feeling of security that comes (he feels) with owning valuable possessions. He won't blow his cash at the racetrack or the gambling tables.

He's also a very good businessman, so your chances of having a comfortable life are good. He's not a spectacular wheeler-dealer, mind you, but he's so steady and reliable that he may end up heading a bank or another large financial institution. Taurus people have this knack of turning money into money, without taking any risks.

He's a passionate lover—and jealous. You mustn't tease him . . . about anything. He takes offense terribly easily. He's also unbelievably stubborn, though actually, this is a curb on his rather violent temper. He can take a heck of a lot of provocation, but if you push him too far, he'll erupt—in a fury that can be physically dangerous! You must be feminine at all times. He can't stand aggressive women. He wants soft lights, sexy music and a suggestion of feminine fragrance (try spraying a little perfume in the room). Comfort, warmth and love . . . he's turned on by his senses and is very susceptible to first impressions.

Talk to him about records, art, food, theater, but never, never try to pretend you're what you're not because he can't stand phonies.

YOUR TAURUS WOMAN

You like her? Love her? What sort of a woman is she?

She's sexy. In her youth, unless she controls her sensual desires, she's inclined to do a fair amount of bed hopping. But if she has managed to restrain herself, she's a choosy one. This miss is not going to make any mistakes that might endanger her idea of what love and marriage are all about.

You've got to understand Miss T's surprisingly simple outlook on life. She's not inclined to surrender fully to her passions (well, maybe once or twice) because she believes strongly in security. And the man she intends to end up with is the one she decides is most likely to give it.

Now don't get the idea that this woman is a heavy-witted fortune hunter. She's got a heck of a lot to give. It's just that she's a teeny-weeny bit mercenary. You could say practical. Or calculating. Or down to earth. But all these are euphemisms for the desire for a lovely, comfortable home, money in the bank, plenty of possessions, smart clothes, social position—and an adoring husband.

Now what does she offer in return? Loads. She's artistic, feminine, intuitive, easygoing, cheerful. Her aesthetic appreciation of beautiful objects will make you understand why Taurus is said to be ruled by Venus, the planet of love and beauty. She's no idealist. She knows that life can be difficult for people like her who have an innate love of luxury, unless the money is there. Naturally, she adores an extravagant lover.

Once she commits herself, she's yours. She'll never ever look (that might be a bit strong) to have an affair with another man. And that is why she's going to take her time making up her mind about you. Even if you're well-heeled (hurdle no. 2), can she depend on you to be true to her? This is terribly important because she can't stand the thought of her man cheating on her. She's one of the most possessive females in the Zodiac—and she's got a temper as violent and dangerous as the Bull's, which is her particular symbol.

Yet, if you do get hitched to this woman and you're not so well off to begin with (don't worry, she'll have assessed your potential), she's a wizard at making do. She will put up with great hardship side by side with her man and never fail to encourage and praise him, no matter how hard things become. Her strength of character in adversity is astounding.

Miss Taurus is one of the most loving and affectionate of people. She'll have your drink poured when you arrive home from the office and you slippers out warming by the fire. She's dependable in every way.

She may appear a bit headstrong at times (some people call it stubborn). Once she gets the idea she wants to do something, that's it. Nothing will induce her to change her mind. This might alarm you the first time you encounter her obstinacy, but it will help you to know it often means she's not getting enough love and attention. Without it, she gets irritable and life with her then can be a bit of a strain.

Miss Taurus, as you've probably guessed, slips into the domestic routine like a wall-to-wall carpet. She's absolutely great at setting up a home, and her love of luxury and beauty means you'll be surrounded by these things as fast as she can help you get them. She's a bit pushy in a quiet way, but she'll never go against her man. She wants the best for both of you. And although she's quite capable of soldiering on alone if need be, she makes a stunning job of appearing dependent.

This woman is determined to enjoy her life, and if you've got money and position, you'll enjoy yours better with her.

TAURUS WOMAN—ARIES MAN

Although you may be attracted to a man born under the Sign of the Ram, it's unlikely you will settle down comfortably together in married life. It's not impossible, mind you, just unlikely. The trouble is you have so many qualities in common—and in this world it's more often opposites that attract.

Do not think you can dominate your Aries partner. This will have to be a union where power-sharing is practiced. If you are one of those domineering types of female born under the Sign of the Bull, you will certainly have to change your ways to keep this man.

This guy will have a host of qualities you admire. He's industrious and hard-working. Like you, he's terribly ambitious and success is very important to him. He's the no-nonsense type. He won't take your side in an argument if he feels you are in the wrong (and how you hate being in the wrong).

Public shows of love and affection will embarrass Mr. Aries. For him, romance is something private to be shared between two people. It will take quite a lot for him to hold your hand or link arms with you when strolling down the street. He's a bit of an old stick-in-the-mud. You both like a comfortable home.

He has a very active and inventive mind. Sometimes you'll find it a little hard to keep up with his speed of thought. Although he's a hard worker, he does tend to switch jobs pretty quickly. You might find his ways a little extravagant. Mr. Aries could easily lay out a lot of cash on a new hobby, and after a short space of time completely lose interest.

He will make many demands on you. Aries men like to share as much of their life as they can with their chosen companion. He will expect you to be all things at all times—good housewife, perfect hostess at a dinner party and calm and dedicated mother to his children. As far as money goes, he doesn't have the sound business mind you possess. If possible, it would be in the best interests of you both to have a joint account. It isn't that you won't be able to trust him. It's just that he is easily tempted to spend extravagantly and on impulse.

It is obvious two such determined and strong-willed people will have their differences. With the tempers you both possess, it will be difficult to control your emotions. You will have to keep your jealousy under control. Don't always think the worst when he's late coming home from the office, and never give him the feeling he's being cross-examined when you inquire what sort of day he's had. Our Aries friend will become aggressive and soon blow his top if he gets the impression he's being fenced in.

One area of your life where you need have no doubts is child rearing. Aries men make wonderful fathers. He will never tire of seeing to the needs of his offspring. And you can go out for the evening to visit mother or a friend without worry—he is more responsible than any babysitter (though he may get a bit irritable if the children act up). He is such an indulgent father, in fact, that you will have to make sure he doesn't spoil the children. It may require the firm hand of Taurus to exert the discipline. When your youngsters hit their teens, it might be best for you to take a back seat. Girls in particular will probably need a good sized chunk of his sympathy and understanding.

Neither of you bears grudges for any length of time, and that's a good quality in any kind of partnership.

TAURUS WOMAN—TAURUS MAN

At first sight, this would appear to be an ideal pairing, and in many cases, it certainly can be. You should, however, give the matter of marriage to a fellow Taurus serious consideration. Don't forget that being born under the same Sign means you'll be quick to recognize each other's faults as well as each other's good points.

You are both ruled by Venus, the planet of love, and erotically you should have a perfect understanding of each other's needs and desires.

You will find his company gay and stimulating. He's lots of fun to go out with and you will very rarely be bored in his company. If you become convinced he's the only man you could possibly settle down with, you'll still have to proceed with extreme caution. You both like to get your own way, and if there are serious differences of opinion, the sparks will really fly.

It is essential that you both have the same ambitions in life. It would be a disaster if you were to marry a fellow Taurus who doesn't totally share your hopes and dreams.

Don't forget there's a lot more to him—as indeed there is to you—than is apparent on the surface. Although he likes to give the impression of being a good-time Charlie without a care in the world, this is very often only a facade. Mr. Taurus often has a bit of an inferiority complex, which compels him to pretend he's doing better than anyone else in his group. This, of course, can be helpful in business. But you must make him feel secure enough not to have to try to impress you with big talk and big ideas.

You both have a great love of home and family life. Security is very important in your lives. Many evenings will be spent together sharing domestic bliss. You'll never want for anything if you do decide to share the rest of your life with him. He's the sort of man who hates being in debt and always settles bills promptly. Not being an extravagant person himself, he'll expect you to make financial sacrifices when they are called for. He will deeply appreciate your ability to run the home smoothly.

You will know how to soothe him when he comes in hot and bothered after a hard day's work. In his warm and inviting house, with his favorite drink poured out and his slippers warming by the fire, he'll soon forget his troubles and give you his undivided attention.

He likes hard work and can become very irritable if life is too quiet. He'll need you to boost his confidence when times are difficult. Although he's a very masculine sort of guy, he likes the gentle treatment and is particularly attracted to soft and feminine women.

You both have a great love of art and will probably share many of the same tastes in entertainment. It is also true you'll be in agreement on matters of furnishings and decoration.

He will certainly be pleased he can bring important business associates home to dinner. Being a born hostess, you can't fail to make a good impression on his boss.

You will probably have the same tastes in friends—both of you are likely to choose the sort of people who don't inquire too deeply into personal matters. What you feel about each other is not something you like to be the subject of public discussion.

This is the sort of a marriage in which it would be disastrous for either partner to have an affair because once the bond of mutual trust is broken, you will feel there is very little point in staying together.

Woe betide you if you're caught two-timing him. You are a Taurus, too, remember, so you should know all about temper, jealousy and possessiveness.

Children will help to bring you even closer together. Your ideas about how to bring up youngsters are likely to tally.

TAURUS WOMAN—GEMINI MAN

If Mr. Gemini is really gone on you, it will be very hard for you to resist becoming involved because he's a great charmer. Being a down-to-earth person yourself, though, you might find his changes of mood very wearing. You like to see things through to their logical conclusion, whereas the man born under the Sign of the Twins can easily have half a dozen projects on the go at the same time.

He gets bored very easily and you may feel you never know where you really stand with him. If the circumstances of your first meeting are right, however, he may sweep you off your feet. You're not likely to experience a dull moment when he's about.

For this relationship to work, you will have to be prepared to reach certain compromises in order to have a quiet and tranquil life. As much as you resent change, you are going to experience quite a lot of it if you team up with him.

Give yourself plenty of time before saying "yes" to his marriage proposal because once you've grown accustomed to his charming way, you may discover he's a little too shallow for you. Don't forget you will have at least two people to cope with—it's not for nothing that Gemini is known as the Twins! One day your Gemini man will be all over you, declaring there's never been anyone quite like you in his life. The next, you'll be trying to get him on the phone only to discover he's taken off for Timbuctoo. He will often try to buy your love if he doesn't feel he's getting through to you. It would be wise not to accept his gifts unless you're really serious about him.

If you happen to meet him at a party—or for that matter, at any social occasion where a large group is gathered—you will definitely be attracted to him. He'll be the guy in the corner with a crowd around him. He's highly entertaining and has the ability to make people laugh at the strangest situations. You can't help be stimulated and impressed by his sheer presence. If you decide to keep your relationship purely platonic, you'll have a friend for life.

The trouble with Gemini is that if he's physically attracted to you, he'll want to make a conquest. If you go along and happen to fall in love with the guy, you will have a big problem because the Gemini man is the hardest person in the world to tie down to a one-to-one relationship. The Taurus woman needs a man who is there when she wants him. It could become very frustrating for you trying to keep tabs on this man.

If you're lucky enough to come across a well-adjusted and serious-minded Gemini, one who has come to terms with his desire to run away, you could prove to be an ideal team. The Gemini man is usually a reasonably intelligent being; it's just that he has a Peter Pan quality and doesn't really want to grow up or be tied down for any length of time.

If you are prepared to have a short-term affair with Mr. Gemini, you'll have a lot of fun—so long as you don't expect too much from him, that is. Be happy to enjoy the time you are together and ask no questions about what he does on the other nights of the week. If you pressure him, he'll skip away into the shadows. Don't try to discover what makes him tick. He can't bear people probing too deep.

He may talk like a great lover but he's not the most passionate of men because his active mind is always ticking away and is usually one jump ahead of his body. If you love him, make sure he's totally honest with you. It will be up to you to make him play it straight with you.

If you decide you can't live without him, it would be advisable for you to hold on to the purse strings because Gemini folk are pretty useless with money. If he has a walletful of bills, he's liable to blow the lot on having a good time.

You will have to be the disciplinarian with the children because the Gemini father tends to let his youngsters walk all over him.

TAURUS WOMAN—CANCER MAN

You'll find the Cancer man a bit hard to get to know. When you first meet him, you may feel there are one or two secrets he wishes to keep to himself. Actually, he's a rather shy person and needs to trust someone absolutely before he'll allow her to get really close.

If you decide he's interesting enough to spend time getting to know, you'll discover you have quite a lot in common. He's a steady and reliable sort of person. Like you, he's practical and has his feet firmly planted on the ground. You both need a secure home life. On the outside, our Crablike friend may appear to have a rather hard attitude to life, but nothing could be further from the truth. He cares greatly about his friends and will do anything for them when they're in trouble.

About money, you'll find you think very much along the same lines. Like you, he can't bear to be in debt, and you can rest assured he'll move heaven and earth to pay the rent on time.

If he does fall for you, you'll know all about it. Mr. Cancer is a charming and considerate lover. He will want to understand you and will go all out to please and make you feel happy and desired. You can't help but be flattered by the way he treats you. His Old World manners and charm will make many girls envious of your catch.

If you're thinking about marriage, you needn't look much further. Mr. Cancer has all the qualities that add up to a first-class husband for the Taurus woman. He will never be stingy with the housekeeping money, though he won't be pleased if he feels you've been unnecessarily extravagant or wasteful because he strongly believes in getting value for money. He will be perfectly prepared to take you out to the best restaurant in town as long as the service and food live up to his expectations. If, however, he feels he's being taken, he'll raise the roof, demand to see the owner and refuse to pay the bill. His attitude to the financial side of life should make you feel secure. Because he's interested in getting value rather than in making a big impression, he will go for a solid and dependable car rather than something flashy.

Where romance is concerned, you may find him rather shy. He does not like to display his feelings in front of a large audience. To him, love is a personal matter. He'll satisfy you in bed all right, but don't expect great shows of passion when he's courting and saying good night on the front porch. He'll be far too worried that Mom and Dad are peeking through the curtains.

If he's a typical Cancer, you'll find him a rather conservative dresser. He'll follow his personal tastes rather than the latest fashion—and won't buy anything that will go out of style before it wears out.

Let's hope you get on well with his family, especially his mother. Cancer men usually make model sons. If you don't see eye to eye with your mother-in-law, life could become rather unpleasant for everyone.

Much of your life together will center around the home. You will find you have a very domesticated guy who is quite happy to share the household chores. If you continue to work after marriage, he'll be just as capable as you at preparing the evening meal should he arrive home first. Although you both enjoy the company of others, your happiest periods will be when you spend an evening alone at home together.

You needn't worry too much about his straying because Cancer men make remarkably faithful husbands. You will also be delighted to discover he can be safely left in charge of the children. He is a very patient, loving and understanding father.

TAURUS WOMAN—LEO MAN

This teaming up will be something of a mutual admiration society. There will be many qualities you admire in each other. Your temperaments are such that you'll each ignore aspects of the other's personality that don't particularly appeal to you.

Since you are both no-nonsense types, you will not descend to the level of playing games with each other's emotions. But there could be a bit of a power struggle, as both of you like to get your own way. If you fall head over heels for the Lion, the secret of catching him is quite simple: be his audience. He is a flamboyant sort of a character who has very firm opinions on life. Fortunately, you will probably have little difficulty in going along with his notions.

He may seem a quiet sort of person on the surface. Certainly when you stroke his mane, you'll have no trouble making him purr. Woe betide you, though, if you rub him up the wrong way. Bear in mind that he is only *pretending* to be a meek soul. If you try to lay down the law with him, you'll soon discover why he is known as the

King of the Jungle. Though you are hardly a pushover for any man, once he has swept you off your feet, you will find it extremely difficult to regain your composure. And once under his spell, it'll be hard to put up much of a struggle. He will make you feel all woman.

Romance is very important to him because when love is missing from his life, he is not a happy creature. You'll be wined and dined and taken to the best places. He puts his partner on a pedestal. Basking in such wonderful treatment, you might think you've got the King of the Jungle exactly where you want him. Think again. You are not being pampered and sheltered for nothing—he wants you to belong to him, body and soul. And he's a very jealous person. Woe betide the lass who's caught flirting and woe betide the man who is giving her the come-on!

Being Taurus, however, you're the sort of woman who likes to play it straight with her man. You might find it a bit hard to accept his very definite opinions on how you should wear your hair and what kind of clothes you should buy. He does tend to get carried away with the idea that every action in your life is taken just for him.

You will have to be on hand when he's had a bad day at the office and needs soothing. Occasionally he has to blow his top and needs someone around to comfort him and show understanding and sympathy.

Once he's decided you're the one for him, he'll be very persistent. If you are not very careful, he could sweep you off your feet with a whirlwind courtship. Don't allow this to happen because it's important that you give yourself plenty of time to make up your mind.

You need have no worries as far as security is concerned. You will always be provided for. Like you, Mr. Leo is careful with money, though never mean. He probably likes home entertaining more than you and enjoys a good party. You'll have to be prepared to share him with others because he likes playing to an audience.

One thing you will like about your Leo husband is that he's a great handyman. He'll be very good at fixing things around the house, whether it's a stopped-up sink or a broken window.

Don't expect to have a life of your own. It would be unwise to plan on having a career if you get hitched to a Leo because he won't be happy at all to come home from work while you're still out attending to your own affairs.

It's unlikely you'll raise a large family if you marry him. His children will be brought up strictly but fairly. Just allow him his occasional ego trip without attacking him and you should have a happy and contented life together.

TAURUS WOMAN—VIRGO MAN

The Virgo man may be a bit too fussy and methodical for you. He certainly has a tidy mind and a logical approach to life. Usually a quiet and respectable type, he may lack the fire and aggression you look for in a man. He will admire you for being practical. He'll also be impressed by the fact that once you start a job, you do your damnedest to see it through to a successful conclusion.

Mr. Virgo tends to look for more than ravishing beauty when deciding on a lifelong partner. He's not the great romantic, so don't be disappointed if he doesn't bowl you off your feet while you are dating. It might take him quite a while to get around to that first good-night kiss—and then it's likely to be merely a peck on the cheek. You may end up taking the initiative yourself out of sheer frustration.

Social gatherings are unlikely to be the places where you first meet. He would be far too shy to try to make overtures at a party, especially if he were surrounded by friends. He could be the guy who asks to look at your program at a concert or remarks on the beauty of a painting while passing you in an art gallery. He's a very sensitive type and does not like to be thought of as pushy with members of the opposite sex.

The male of the Virgo species tends to marry late in life, and it is unlikely he will marry more than once. He won't try to rush you into marriage, partly because he wants to be 100 percent certain himself. His mind is a bit like an electric clock. He is not an intuitive person, as a rule, and he sets great store by conservative behavior. He'll not easily forgive you if you don't keep your word. One of his faults is that he does tend to bear grudges and judge other people. In fact, he is very quick to find fault. Another irritating trait is that he's one of those people who are usually right!

A love affair with Mr. Virgo will probably be the last thing on your mind when you meet up. He will be very formal in his approach. But chances are, he'll have been doing a lot of thinking about you since he first saw you. He will not make his intentions clear until he's positive, or as near to positive as he can be, that he isn't going to get his fingers burned.

Physically, the Virgo man is usually much stronger than he looks. He is no coward either and is capable of taking on men who look as though they could make mincemeat of him.

The Virgo man is sincere and reliable, and faithful in marriage. No matter how much temptation is put his way, he's unlikely to have an affair once he has promised himself to you.

He looks after his appearance. That nice smell in the room is likely to be the aftershave Mr. Virgo is wearing. He's also likely to take more baths than any other Sign of the Zodiac.

Virgo men tend to hit middle age rather early. It will be up to you to see that he keeps himself in good shape. Very often this type is not enthusiastic about exercise, and can develop a spread around the waist in his thirties. Keep him on his toes, get him out on the tennis court. Don't allow him to become too set in his ways. He'll certainly look after you. If you're feeling one degree under, he'll have you tucked into bed with a piping hot cup of milk. Some of the best doctors were born under this Sign.

He will make a gentle and loving father but will never spoil his children.

If you decide not to have a family, this won't worry your Virgo man. He'll be able to channel all his love into looking after you.

TAURUS WOMAN—LIBRA MAN

Both of you are strongly influenced by Venus, the planet of love and beauty, and should therefore have a great deal in common. Your love of art and all things beautiful could bring you together in the first place. You are both fairly realistic people. You will like the sense of humor of the Libra man. You will also like his practical way of going about things. You'll get plenty of advice from him. Although you're not a person who likes to be told what to do, you won't find it so difficult to accept a certain amount of bossing around from Mr. Libra—he does it so beautifully, and besides, his advice will make sense to you.

He is very charming, and once you've become involved with him, you'll find it very hard to break the spell. In the end, you'll find yourself giving in to his persuasive ways. He will notice all the little things you do to make him happy, from the way you arrange your hair to the flowers you've set on the table for dinner.

Where you may run into trouble is dealing with the fact that he's a bit of a wanderer. Since you are a homey sort of person, you may find it difficult to keep up with his wanderlust.

Sometimes you'll have to be very bossy yourself because he finds it hard to make up his mind. You'll have to give him a good nudge every now and again to stir him into action. Although naturally talented, he's inclined to be on the lazy side. If you really love him, you mustn't judge him too harshly. He's a very romantic person and finds it hard to settle down to a one-to-one relationship. You'll have to make allowances for his flirtations. It will be hard for him to stop making eyes at a pretty girl who takes his fancy at a party. But don't allow your jealous Taurus nature to come to the surface because there's probably nothing serious in his little games. He needs to be appreciated, and it's important to his ego to feel he's desired by members of the opposite sex. Rarely does it go any further than that.

You may disagree over financial matters. It's possible that he will accuse you of being hung up on money.

As a lover, you'll find he leaves little to be desired. He is a very sensual character and it will be extremely important to him that you are totally satisfied in bed.

You will probably do best with a Libra male who is fully mature. If you meet him when he's young and callow, you will find it hard to get him to lead a reasonably settled life. He'll want to experience everything that's going.

Mr. Libra will allow you your secrets. He's not a prying person. You'll also be allowed to follow your own career after marriage if you wish. He doesn't like trouble and will do anything he can to avoid a head-on collision. Sometimes he'll hide his own feelings to avoid having an argument.

The Libra man hates confusion. Basically he needs to lead a harmonious life. You'll be able to make the sort of home he really needs. He has to have a shelter from the trials and tribulations of the outside world.

As a father, he'll be extremely fair. Don't forget that the symbol of Libra is the Scales, and that means justice. Libra fathers exercise discipline with quiet authority. They always try to reason with difficult youngsters rather than resort to the heavy-handed approach. He may not always be as ambitious to get to the top as you'd like, but you should be able to give him that little extra push when he really needs it.

TAURUS WOMAN—SCORPIO MAN

It's true that Scorpio is one of the hardest Signs to understand. Scorpio people can be moody and at times downright nasty. Don't, however, be too quick to write a Scorpio man off without looking a little closer.

He is a very passionate and self-assured person. If you don't feel you can take a relationship that's built to a large extent on physical attraction and a deep involvement in politics, religion and schooling—in fact, everything that makes the world go round—then move on.

You, Miss Taurus, may be just the woman who can cope with his restless searching. Scorpio is, after all, the Sign opposite to your own, and you know how opposites attract.

But since you are pretty sure of where you are going in life, you could very well find Mr. Scorpio a bit to aggressive and determined to dominate.

You will always know where you stand with Scorpio. He can be blunt to the point of hurting others' feelings. This won't matter too much to him as long as he's being truthful to himself.

He can be very mean with money, although this is often because he's short of cash. He can be given to sudden extravagance without having anything of value to show for it.

On the first meeting, you may think he's in complete control of himself. You'll be impressed by his apparent ability to cope with awkward people and situations. Don't be fooled. If he's pushed too far, his passions can explode and you'll be amazed at how physically violent he can suddenly become.

He is very much a family man. His home is very important to him. He likes to feel he can get away from the trials and tribulations of work and relax with people he really cares about. You'll have much in common in the way you prefer spending leisure time. Never push him too far and don't attempt to dig too deep into what makes him tick. Like you, he must be allowed his private moments.

He will wish to put you on a pedestal. Although he can be on the tight side with money, he'll be sure you never go without new clothes—in fact, he'll want you to be dressed in the latest fashion. He likes his woman to be admired by the other guys at the golf club or the office. Woe betide the man who makes a pass at you if you are his girl. He's quite capable of taking on someone twice his size and giving him a good beating if his passions are aroused.

He is a hard-working man to whom success is very important. You'll seldom have to entertain his business associates, which is fortunate since you are not enthused about home entertaining. He will leave his working problems at the office.

He's not much of a dresser. You'll probably have to remind him when he needs a new suit.

Don't try two-timing him, because if after you marry, he discovers you've been playing around, he'll probably show you the door. He finds it almost impossible to continue a relationship once faith has been broken. He's not too concerned with what others think of him. He's very secure in his own opinions. Once he's made up his mind, it's unlikely anyone will talk him out of something. He has a strong sense of right and wrong.

Sexually, you're likely to hit it off in a big way. You will understand each other's physical needs perfectly. Both will react instinctively to changing moods and passions.

It's pointless to try to hide your feelings from Mr. Scorpio. If you have a problem, it would be better to come right out with it. He likes to know where he stands with others and can't tolerate being ridiculed or made a fool of.

As a father, he'll be strict but fair. Scorpio people often have quite large families.

Your friends may be amazed if you decide to get married. You could surprise them all by making a success of it.

TAURUS WOMAN— SAGITTARIUS MAN

You have many strong points, but putting a lot of effort into making a relationship work may not be one of them. With a Sagittarius man, you would have to give far more of yourself than you are usually prepared to do.

He is an easygoing sort of guy who's not particularly interested in settling down. You will discover if you get to know him well that he has something of the gypsy in his nature. Home-loving Miss Taurus may find it very hard to accept the wanderlust in his blood.

You will certainly get on extremely well as friends, especially since he's great fun to be with at parties and gatherings. But you may not find it quite so much fun sitting up in bed at four in the morning waiting for him to creep in. Don't get the idea he's out serenading some other lady—nothing is likely to be further from his mind. You'll probably discover he's been at the local bar or out with a gang of buddies, being the life and soul of the party.

Mr. S. needs a lot of looking after but will resent it if you try to tell him what's good for him. You, Miss Taurus, may not have the patience to cope with this guy, who can be a baby at heart.

He is likely to make many mistakes in his life and is also rather accident-prone because he enjoys taking chances. He rarely bothers to think about the risk involved—he is perfectly capable of attempting to ride a horse bareback or speed around the track in a car with no experience!

When you first take him home to meet Mom and Dad, they are likely to be shocked and appalled that you could even contemplate marriage with him. His good points are not always instantly recognizable. You see, basically he's a very insecure person. In order to hide his true, sensitive feelings, he feels he has to be the life of the party. He can't bear silence in the room if he's with strangers. He'll keep telling the most boring stories—and laughing louder at them than anybody else. When people get to know him a bit better, they discover there is far more to him than they originally thought.

If you are in any sort of trouble or need help, turn to the Sagittarius man. He's the person to sit with you all night while you cry on his shoulder. But don't expect him to be a great romantic. Even when you're romantically involved, he'll treat you like a very close friend. You may wonder if he is capable of deep and lasting love.

Home is very important to you so you may be rather upset when he doesn't even notice the new curtains you've made for the living room. He'll eat your food without complaint, but don't expect compliments when you lay out something really special. He is as happy with a hamburger as he is with that complicated recipe you dug out of a cookbook.

He likes to look his best and can be rather a stylish dresser, although his clothes may strike others as a little eccentric. Since handling money is not his forte you had better make sure you get the household money before he goes out with the boys.

He is a great lover of children. A family could help him to settle down.

Unlike some men, he won't try to change you. If you can accept his love of freedom, you could find happiness together. The Archer may not always be wise, but he will never set out to hurt or upset you. So long as you can forgive him for the silly mistakes he is bound to make and be prepared to go out with him at the drop of a hat, you could have a successful marriage.

TAURUS WOMAN—CAPRICORN MAN

The Capricorn male is the sort of guy who could really appeal to you. While others tend to write him off because of his slow and pedantic ways, you will see his potential. He is certainly a challenge to any woman.

He is shy, and this leads many people to conclude he has little to offer. You with your great patience and understanding could be just the woman to bring him out of his shell.

You may have to take the lead in this liaison because Mr. Capricorn is afraid of getting hurt. You might, in fact, have to ask him for a first date. Don't worry, he won't think you're foward. He likes to be organized and feel he is sought after. Once he has decided he can trust you with his love, you'll find you have a reliable person who won't let you down.

The hidden depths of this man, who to many appears superficial, will fascinate you. You'll enjoy finding out more and more about him. He is not the most romantic fellow in the world, so forget about words and fiery passion.

The Capricorn man is very interested in getting to the top in his occupation. He's a great respecter of authority and of people who have made a success of their lives by hard work.

He is not an impulsive person. Rarely will he make an important life-changing move without giving it serious consideration. Others label him overly cautious because of this, but it's probably jealousy on their part because they are unable to organize their lives as well as he can.

People born under this Sign of the Zodiac rarely rush into marriage or long-term relationships. Once you've both decided it's for keeps, however, he's unlikely to be unfaithful. If you're the type of Taurus woman who likes to take her time about making important decisions, you'll feel at ease with this man. He won't try to pressure you into making up your mind.

Mr. C. is very good at avoiding stupid mistakes. He will make the right decisions in business. Competitors may appear to be leaving him way behind, but like the tortoise this persistent old Goat is likely to be first past the finishing post.

He's careful with money and will make sure the future is provided for. He'll take out insurance policies on almost everything so that you are both covered where it counts. He'll also make provision for you should anything happen to him. He takes his responsibilities very seriously.

You will share the same sense of humor, and that is not all you will have in common. Home is important to this man. He will appreciate your efforts to make it a comfortable and beautiful place to live in.

Never embarrass him in public. He can't bear to argue in front of others. If you wish to criticize him in any way, wait until you are alone. He can be a bit of a pessimist and this is where you could be a help to him. Your positive attitude to life will lighten his darker moods and depressions. He is also a great respecter of tradition. You will have to be comfortable with his family—especially Mom and Dad, who in his eyes don't do a thing wrong.

You may have to be a little firm with him about having in-laws over for Sunday dinner every week. Gently point out that although you love his family dearly and always enjoy seeing them, you married him, not the entire brood.

He takes responsibilities of parenthood very seriously and will expect children to show him respect as head of the household. He's a stickler for routine and a great one for discipline. It was probably a Capricorn who invented the edict, "Little children should be seen and not heard."

There's no doubt that you and Mr. Capricorn have a lot in common, and this should make your partnership a lasting and happy one.

TAURUS WOMAN—AQUARIUS MAN

Many people think the partnership of Aquarius man and Taurus woman is one of the most impossible imaginable. But it is not necessarily so.

It's true you will have a very different way of viewing many things in life. You are a very practical person and he is the complete opposite. But when Cupid's arrow strikes, it's amazing how differences can be overcome. He is definitely a dreamer, always going on about the wrongs in the world and how things should be. You with your practical and down-to-earth approach could find this head-in-the-clouds attitude rather irritating. However, you have a great deal to learn from each other. You are the patient one, so it will be up to you to show him how important it is to have a practical outlook to life as well as visions of how things should be.

Money is not very important to him—at least, saving it isn't. You'll have to be quite firm in preventing him from supporting every charity that exists. What is likely to strike you about him most on first meeting is that dreamy faraway look in his eyes. This should be a clue as to what you can expect.

He needs looking after. He can be very forgetful. It will be your business to keep an engagement book and to note down all his business appointments because they easily slip his mind. This is also true of social engagements. You'd better call him at the office to remind him when you have a function on, as he's likely to forget all about it and arrive home halfway through dinner.

Don't write off all his hopes and ideas as idle dreaming. The Aquarius man is often ahead of his time, and this can be very frustrating for him. His ideas for today will often be put into practice by the planners of this world tomorrow. Life with Aquarius will not be all frustration. You can do a great deal to help him come to terms with himself. Being an open-minded sort of guy, he'll be willing to listen to what you have to say and give you free rein in expressing your opinions. He may not agree with them all the way, but he'll defend your right to think the way you do.

Sometimes you may get the feeling he's forgotten you're a woman. You might have to make the advances. He's a kind and considerate enough lover, but that old wandering mind of his needs to be jogged about romance.

He will admire many of your qualities. He likes the house to be tidy and clean as a new pin, though he's unlikely to lift a finger to tackle any of the housework himself. He'll keep himself impeccably clean—he's the kind of a man who likes to take a bath or shower at least once, and probably twice, a day. He can get a bit neurotic about germs and is something of a hypochondriac. He'll take to his bed at the first sign of a cough or cold and will expect you to be on hand to look after him. He won't be against your having a career. If you're very ambitious, though, he might have difficulty understanding why.

Let's be frank—Aquarius doesn't take easily to permanent relationships so this man will be hard to tie down. It is difficult for him not to become emotionally involved with other people. You'll have to control your jealousy, and that's not an easy task for a Taurus woman. But Mr. Aquarius will always come back to you after he's had one of his flings, though he will find it hard to understand why you carry on so about his casual affairs.

He may not be the greatest money-earner around, but he often surprises everybody by coming up with an invention that takes off.

If you can accept the fact that he won't be tied down to routine, that he is absentminded, rebellious and unpredictable, then you might decide Mr. Aquarius is the most exciting male you've ever met!

TAURUS WOMAN—PISCES MAN

The Pisces male is one of the easiest of all the

Signs of the Zodiac to misjudge and misunderstand. When you first run into him, you may feel you've come across a sweet and gentle soul who needs mothering and protecting. This may indeed be half the story, but it's certainly not all of it.

Don't forget that the symbol of Pisces is two Fishes. Still waters run deep, and way down in these Neptunian depths there are many contradictions. He will usually go along with your ideas of how to spend the evening. Whether you want to stay quietly at home or go to the movies, it will seem all the same to him. He's a very intuitive person and often you won't need to put your feelings and thoughts into words. He'll sense them.

Once your courting days are over and you settle down into marriage, the other side of the coin is likely to be revealed. It won't be that he has fundamentally changed—it's just that Pisces people have a habit of discarding today what they thought was a great idea yesterday. You with your set ways and need for roots may find this a little hard to take. You know exactly what you want out of life, and exactly where you stand. When you describe your practical plans, he'll listen intently and then come up with his own ideas, which may at first seem irrelevant or zany. Give a bit of thought to what he says, though—you may discover there's a method in his apparent madness.

He could be just the right mixture of dreamer and realist to excite you. One thing is for sure—you may get the feeling you'd like to throw things at him, but you will never find that life with him is a bore!

It is important to you what your closely knit circle of friends and working associates think of you. Pisces people, on the other hand, always speak their minds, though this is not to say they won't care what others think of them. It's just that they don't like pretending they are something they are not.

If you marry the weaker type of Pisces man, it would be advisable not to give up your job too quickly. You may discover after a few months of life together that you're going to need every cent you can lay your hands on.

It doesn't make too much difference to this man where he lives. He likes his home comforts, but being rather a restless creature he doesn't mind moving on. It is change, in fact, that keeps him young. You with your strong desires for security may find it a little upsetting to live this kind of life.

You could be the one who has to look after the broken windowpane or keep the grass cut. It's not that he's lazy, it's just that he's likely to tell you he has more important things on his mind and will get the mundane chores done tomorrow. His tomorrow rarely comes.

Mr. Pisces loves excitement and thrills. You are unlikely to find him in the sort of job where he's waiting to collect a pension. He can be a bit of a gambler, but very often his gambles pay off.

You'll rarely need to be suspicious about his getting involved with other women. If he does have an affair, it's likely he'll let you know all about it. As a lover, he will be romantic and giving. You may have to control your own jealousy. He can't help flirting with a pretty girl even if you are in the room. He doesn't really want to seduce her—he just admires beauty and can't help flattering and praising it.

It'll be your job to keep the youngsters under control. He's much too easygoing and will rarely tell them off. He enjoys his parental responsibilities and will never mind telling them a good-night story and tucking them into bed.

TAURUS MAN—ARIES WOMAN

There could be a personality clash here. The Aries woman likes to be in command. So do you. She is very ambitious and keen to ge to the top of her chosen career. Sometimes work is more important to her than romance. It will take quite a man to win her over.

You both like a comfortable home life and, like you, Aries people are perfectly capable of looking after themselves. Where you tend to differ is that you are rather a plodder, while people born under the first Sign of the Zodiac are always in a hurry to complete tasks. If your approach proves to be the right one, for goodness' sake don't be smug about it. An I-told-you-so attitude could mean the dishes start getting thrown in your direction.

You may wonder what attracts you to Miss Aries in the first place. Well, for one thing, she has a great sense of humor. It's likely you will find the same sort of jokes and situations extremely funny. You will never find it dull to be in her company. She'll always be full of interesting ideas and suggestions for fun things to do.

She's extravagant, and you'll have to be pretty well heeled if you're going to be able to satisfy her expensive tastes. A night out with an Aries woman is not likely to be a cheap affair, though if she realizes you're a bit short of cash, she'll usually offer to pay her own way.

Beneath all her bravado and fire is probably

lurking an insecure being. Although she wants to lead and be one of the winners, she dislikes arguments and scenes. Renowned as a great lover (though not perhaps a great romancer), you should have no trouble in your physical relationship. Basically, she likes a man to be her master in bed, although she may put up a bit of a fight. She'll make a lot of demands upon you. If she really fancies you, it's unlikely you'll get much sleep.

Miss Aries will cause you quite a lot of heartache if it's a one-sided relationship. It will be very hard on you if she's not certain you're her man because it's easy for the Aries person to be involved with two or three very different types at the same time. You will have to make your intentions clear from the start if you're not prepared to share her. You must never allow the relationship to get out of balance. If she gets the feeling you're going to submit and be her slave, she'll soon get tired of her conquest.

A long courtship is advisable. Many Aries girls get married on a sudden impulse. They do, after all, like to be first at everything—and when young, it might appeal to them to be the first of their set to get the little band of gold on the left hand. Aries women often marry more than once. It will need your steadying influence to make certain you aren't merely the first of many.

Life together will hardly be a bed of roses, but then, marriage rarely is. You'll have to be kind and understanding and help her in every way you can to shed her aggressive urges and impatience. She may say things she doesn't really mean on occasions and you mustn't take her remarks too much to heart.

Miss Aries is quite an outdoor girl and loves sports, especially those that are really competitive. She'll keep you constantly on the go. In business, she'll be good for you.

As your wife, you'll have no reason to grumble about her cooking or the way she entertains important people. As a mother, she's wonderful. She's strict with the children, but you'll find you're likely to agree with her ideas about the upbringing of children.

As long as you are prepared to settle for compromise solutions in areas of your life where there are real differences, there's no reason why you should not have many happy years together.

TAURUS MAN—TAURUS WOMAN

Since both of you are ruled by Venus, the love planet, sparks are bound to fly. In Miss Taurus you'll find a person who can love and feel for you deeply without neglecting her duties to friends and family.

You must never doubt her. Just as you demand freedom of thought and action, so will she. It will be a stormy liaison if you try to humble your proud lady and expect her to trot along behind you. This woman does not take kindly to having a ring slipped through her nose; on the second finger of the left hand is the only place for you to put it.

It will take a long time to woo this girl if you do have marriage in mind. She'll be looking for a secure and stable home life. Adventure appeals to her, no doubt about it, but behind all her energy and drive is a longing for something to fall back on in an emergency.

She has the same strong instinct for possessiveness that you have. You'll find she is very hung up on owning things. She will always be very fair in these matters, though.

Miss Taurus can be jealous, so woe betide you if you go off the rails after having vowed undying love. And you'll have to watch your own jealous streak. Men will be very eager to be in the company of this woman, and you won't be able to hold her if you try to protect and shield her from the outside world. Give her independence and the opportunity to make her own decisions.

There will have to be plenty of give and take in this alliance. Don't expect to settle down to stability and a life of pleasantries. If anyone knows about the Taurus ability to fly off the handle at the drop of a hat, it should be you. You'll never get your own way by adopting a heavy-handed approach. Unfortunately, the only way to keep the peace is to give ground, and that's a thing neither of you finds easy. Being loved, understood and appreciated is terribly important, also. You'll both have to rid yourselves of selfish tendencies.

Being artistic people, you should have a lot in common. Your love of beautiful objects could well have drawn you together in the first place. Your first meeting could occur at a theater or at an art gallery.

You need a woman who is not going to hold back when it comes to lovemaking. There'll be no problems here in bed because this woman is as passionate as you. She may take a lot of satisfying physically, but that should be no great problem for you.

Where you will really score is in getting a home together. You both adore spending a good deal of time in the place you call your own. A cozy winter's evening by the fire will never be a bore for either of you.

Taurus wives are very good at keeping the house in good running order. They also make excellent and inventive cooks. She will be very capable at keeping within her budget. Although a careful person yourself, you are not stingy. You'll make sure your beloved never wants for anything. Mrs. Taurus knows how to shop wisely and will be able to prepare a tasty and imaginative meal at a very reasonable price.

You are a very ambitious person. It's extremely important to you to get to the top and be well thought of. It might make for a stable relationship if your marriage partner is socially well connected. It isn't that you are snobbish, it's simply you need the person who shares you life to be able to hold her own in any company.

You'll both make devoted parents. Just keep an eye out for that Taurus trait of being rather too strict with youngsters who don't always toe the line.

TAURUS MAN—GEMINI WOMAN

On the face of it, this doesn't look like a very successful coupling. Can you, Mr. Taurus, with your feet so firmly planted on the ground, knowing exactly what you want out of life, put up with our charming Mercurial lady friend, who appears to be quite contented flitting from one impermanent relationship to another?

Her changes of mood will dazzle you. If you're the kind of guy who likes life to be full of surprises, then you've found the right person here. The lady born under the Sign of the Twins blows hot and cold. You like life to have a certain pattern and conformity; she doesn't like to keep two pieces in the jigsaw together for very long.

Many women of this Sign become involved rather seriously with the opposite sex when very young. A number of early love affairs—many of them ending disastrously—are possible. If you're really crazy about her, you'll have the patience to listen to her tales of how rough the world treated her in her youth.

She is very caught up on physical sensations and may sometimes appear to forget it takes two to tango. Not that sex usually plays a leading role in Miss Gemini's life. She'll keep experimenting physically in order to try to satisfy an emotional need. Perhaps with love and patience, you'll be able to help her overcome her hangups.

It will certainly help if you are an older and more experienced person. Being immature herself, she needs a big daddy to turn to and a strong shoulder to rest her pretty little head upon. You married men had better watch out. Gemini ladies sometimes want a semipermanent relationship without all the security trimmings. This is where the guy who is hitched could come into the picture. She'll tempt you and tease you and say she wishes to move in with you. But if you did leave your wife for her, she'd probably run a mile.

Let's not be unfair, though. It is possible for you two to form a lasting and successful partnership. If you catch her at the right point in her life—that is, when she has truly grown up emotionally and realizes that all her flitting around is getting her nowhere fast—then you could strike it lucky. If she thinks in her heart of hearts that you're going to be her man for keeps, you'll have nothing to worry about. She's great fun to be with, and a wonderful hostess to boot. Have no fears about bringing the boss home to dinner.

Miss Gemini is an honest critic. If she feels you're in the wrong, she'll tell you so even if it's against her best interests. She's not a hypocrite.

You'll have to keep active and alert because she's not too happy spending a great deal of time sitting by the fire warming her pretty little toes. To keep her, you'll have to stir yourself out of that rocking chair and take her out on the town once in a while.

Another important point: Give her your advice *only* when she asks for it. People born under the Sign of the Twins hate to feel someone is putting them under the microscope. There will be times when she'll appear to be a complete stranger. Don't dig too deep. Take what she's willing to give of her own free will and don't push for more.

This lady will do her best to keep the home clean and tidy but Gemini women don't make the greatest housewives in the world. You'll need to do a fair share of the chores yourself if those comforts you care so much about are going to be guaranteed.

Where money is concerned, you'll have to keep a hold on the purse strings. Give her a good allowance; a joint account could end in disaster.

TAURUS MAN—CANCER WOMAN

This little lady could be the perfect love match for Mr. Taurus. You certainly have a great deal in common. Both of you are keen home lovers. Also, she needs protection from the big outside world, and you are the kind of guy who likes to take on the masculine protective role.

Don't think you have to prove to her you're something you aren't—this would be a wrong tactic. Being a very intuitive person, she sees through amateur dramatic poses very quickly. Your steady ways and reliability are what will impress her. She'll like the fact you are a person who keeps his word. When she gets into one of her down moods—and these are something you'll have to learn to cope with—cultivate the happy knack of comforting her and stopping those tears running down her cheeks.

There's no question about it, the female born under the Sign of the Crab has her ups and downs. One minute she'll be riding on the crest of a wave, the next she'll be fighting off one of her depressions. But she should bring out enough of your true manly patience for you to calm this stormy sea.

It's a very rare occurrence for Miss Cancer to get hitched to the first guy she goes out with. Being a discerning lady, she prefers to have more experience of life before taking the big step. And she doesn't like to let go of her admirers, either. Until she finds the right man she'll keep a lot of poor males dangling like puppets on a string.

But if the day should come when you decide you were meant for each other, marriage to this woman should be about the best move you've ever made. She'll devote the rest of her life to giving you the sort of home you dreamed about and doing all she can to ensure you get right to the top in your career. Household chores are no real problem to her, so she'll never make heavy going of her domestic responsibilities. No matter what sort of a day she's had while you have been toiling away at the office, she'll always be looking feminine and attractive when you get home.

There are quite a few females born under different Signs of the Zodiac who can settle for men with certain weaknesses. Not so Miss Cancer. She'll want you to be commanding and dominating, not only with her, but with other people. Although outwardly she appears to be able to face the world on her own, her basic need is for someone to take control and give her the right sort of guidance.

She's a great cook and an inventive one, too. Another thing you'll notice (and might not be so pleased about) is that she's constantly changing around the household furniture. Although she's a great home lover, she likes to ring the changes.

You couldn't choose a better mother for your children. Of all the Signs, this woman is the most maternal. But don't assume that your offspring will be spoiled; she knows how to be strict when discipline is called for.

As your life together rolls on through the years, she will become even more gentle and tender. As long as you go on wanting and desiring her, you will be happy and satisfied bed partners for many years to come. Never take her for granted. Always woo her as if it were the first time you are making love together. She's a sensitive person with deep and passionate feelings under a sweet-tempered surface.

TAURUS MAN—LEO WOMAN

You'll need to be pretty well heeled to keep up with the expensive tastes of our catlike friend. Don't expect a cheap evening out with Miss Leo. A hamburger and two seats at the movies are hardly likely to keep her happy on a date. She certainly likes the best things in life—but then, so do you.

More than any other Sign in the Zodiac, the women of Leo can drive men to the point of insanity. Many lose both their heads and their hearts to such a woman. She finds it very difficult to settle down with one man and her tastes are not limited to one particular type. People may talk about her many and varied lovers, but she's immune to gossip.

Don't believe all you hear, though. Being feline by nature, she will often attract catty remarks. (Other women don't always appreciate her honesty.) When it comes to marriage, however, be careful for this is not likely to turn out to be a successful match. Taurus and Leo living together have a number of serious personality clashes to overcome. Of course, as the saying goes, love conquers all. If your feelings for each other are deep enough, then you do have a chance of making a harmonious life together.

She can be very unpredictable and even outrageous. Your friends may think you've gone off your rocker if you get serious about her (to say nothing of what your mother will say). If, on the other hand, you are going out to try to clinch an important business deal, take her along. Whether you are permanently hitched or just going steady, your Leo partner will certainly help that special business luncheon go with a swing. When she knows it's important, there is no one better at putting members of the opposite sex at their ease and in the right frame of mind.

When she is really in love, she is deeply passionate and yet extremely strong-willed. If she fancies you strongly enough, you could well find she's the one suggesting you head for the bedroom!

Be very careful about criticizing her. Keep your opinions to yourself. When she hits (or should we say, spits?) back, many men will run a mile from her because they feel their masculinity is threatened.

If you do decide on marriage, do not expect life to be a bed of roses. Once you've got over the first flush of romance you'll find it very difficult to keep your good lady tied down. She is *not* prepared to accept a secondary role. She certainly will not be content to be left home holding the baby while you go downtown to live it up with the boys. If you do leave her alone for nights on end, you may well come home one night to an empty house. And more likely than not she won't have gone home to mother but to the arms of another guy.

Many Leo girls are career women. This is an important factor you'd better face up to early on in the relationship. She doesn't consider marriage enough of a reason to give up her job.

As a mother, she'll be kind and considerate but not overly emotional. It's important to her that children be brought up to face the problems of the outside world in later life.

If you wish for a partner who is sweet and feminine, but also eager to wear the pants, all is well and good. So long as you're prepared to allow her to find her own fulfillment in life—a difficult thing for any man as well as being your partner, then you'll be able to rely on her loyalty and devotion. And these are two of the strongest characteristics in the Leo personality.

TAURUS MAN—VIRGO WOMAN

Virgo is the second of the earth Signs. You are the first. Does this mean you are very alike? Well, you certainly both have your feet firmly planted on the ground. Like you, Miss Virgo knows the value of things. She'll be very careful with money. She's also serious about life, and will expect you to be the same.

People born under this Sign where Mercury rules don't fall in love easily. They are very particular about whom they date. And you needn't expect to be put on a pedestal. It would be pointless to try to pretend you are something you're not. It's not an easy task for any man to woo Miss Virgo.

She'll admire in you the fact you can take care of yourself, but you won't win her by being overly protective because she, too, has an independent streak and doesn't like to feel anyone is taking over her life or stifling her individuality. You may find she's very shy about showing her feelings in public. Be careful you don't embarrass her by great shows of affection in front of people she doesn't know very well.

On your first couple of dates, you'll probably have to do all the courting; just be careful you don't try to take her along too fast. Virgo people like to make up their own minds. You won't get very far by being pushy.

If you are interested in really knowing this woman, you'll discover that she is striving for perfection. She also possesses a strong desire to serve, not just the people she loves, but also the entire community.

There's a strong sense of responsibility here, so if you marry, you couldn't possibly ask for a more faithful and loyal partner. You may even find she's prepared to take on obligations you don't consider necessary. There could be arguments about this. Like it or not, it's something you'll have to learn to live with.

Don't give up if you seem to be getting nowhere after taking her out a couple of times. You mustn't be disheartened if she turns her cheek to you when you go to give her a good-night kiss. If you love her enough to give her patience and understanding, you could be just the right guy.

You may discover she isn't as free and easy about sex as you are. It may take time to get her to overcome the feeling that making love is something you don't talk about. She's got a rather puritanical streak. Still, don't give up. You'll be amazed at the sudden transformation that can take place in this woman once she's decided she can trust you with the precious gifts she has to offer.

Virgo people are great observers. They find it very easy to put their finger on people's strengths and weaknesses. You will probably find this a little irritating at first—until, that is, you discover how right-on her value judgments usually are. If you're contemplating going into business with someone and are not too sure if your future partner is 100 percent trustworthy, have him meet your Virgo lady. She'll be able to tell you within five minutes whether or not it's a good idea.

You'll have to learn to be open and aboveboard in all things because Virgo people expect straightforwardness. If you two-time her, she'll probably never forgive you. She is constantly striving after perfection and looking for it in others. Even if she knows deep down that perfection is beyond all of us, she won't be deterred in her quest. She will do all she can to help you in your career. As a homemaker you couldn't ask for more. She'll nurse you through ill health with the dedication of a Florence Nightingale—and will always be striving to make a better man of you.

TAURUS MAN—LIBRA WOMAN

People born under the Sign of Libra are interested in everything and everyone. They can be very changeable in their moods. You may find it difficult to cope with this miss. In fact, she could drive you around the bend.

Miss Libra is perfectly capable of being all over you one moment, offering you her undying devotion and love, and cool as the proverbial cucumber the next. Don't try to put her in a pigeonhole because she defies all analysis. Most people born under the seventh Sign of the Zodiac are born diplomats-artistes in human relationships.

Being rather a possessive person, you will find it hard to come to terms with the fact that although she may love you deeply, she has many friends and many outside interests. A lasting relationship with Miss Libra would be difficult— impossible may not be too strong a word. A love affair would suit you better, perhaps. In fact, you are both likely to get a great deal—and learn a lot about life—from a short-term alliance.

Flirting is something of a sporting pastime to Miss L. You, being rather a jealous person, could find it very difficult to control your impulses when she flutters her eyes at the handsome guy in the corner. It may only be harmless fun, but you're unlikely to see it that way.

Let's take a look at the positive possibilities of this relationship. Libra women are very feminine—all woman, in fact. She will never knowingly set out to hurt you. One smile from her and you'll feel the warmth of her heart. If you can give her the self-confidence she needs and sweep her off her feet, you'll feel bigger than St. George after he took care of the dragon.

In marriage, you'll have to dominate and make most of the important decisions because if you leave it to her to control your life together, you'll never get anywhere. Libra sees so many possibilities that she often does nothing. If you do find the key to her heart, you'll discover a very passionate person.

You'll have to work hard to give her all the material things she likes to be surrounded with. She's a lover of beauty and usually has a very expensive taste in clothes. Money is no object to her where beauty is concerned.

Libra women often carry on with a job long after marriage because they find it difficult to give up all outside interests for domestic life. Usually they have the happy knack of being able to combine both.

You'll be proud to bring people home to dinner. She will make an excellent hostess at parties and gatherings. She is never lost for words and knows how to make people who are shy feel relaxed and completely at ease in her company. She can adapt herself to any role she's required to play. She's at home with people from all walks of life. And she is not a snob. A person's mind will be more important to her than his wealth or social status.

You'll find you have many artistic tastes in common, such as your love of music and theater. You'll have a great deal of fun going out together. Miss Libra may not be as content to stay in one place for as long as you are, though. You may also have differences of opinion when it comes to decoration. Just when you have accepted the way she's arranged the furniture in the living room, she will want to throw it all out and start afresh.

Think very carefully before you pop the all-important question. The biggest danger to marriage between Libra and Taurus is your jealousy and her laissez-faire attitude.

TAURUS MAN—SCORPIO WOMAN

Here is a woman you'll really have to mind yours p's and q's with, for when Scorpio loses her temper, there is only one thing to do—get out of range as quickly as possible.

In many ways this would appear to be a most unlikely match. Of all the Signs, Scorpio and Taurus are the ones who most like to get their own way—and usually do. Certainly you'd both have to learn far more about compromise if you are contemplating a permanent relationship.

People born subject to the rulership of Pluto and Mars find it extremely difficult to control their emotions. Passionate and loving at one moment, she could be throwing a vase at you the next if she feels you are getting out of line.

Scorpio people are deeply interested in the occult, reincarnation and the secret or mysterious. You'll find you have a woman who can match you for jealousy and possessiveness. You will have to decide from the start that you are going to play it straight with each other or life will not be worth living.

Usually, women ruled by this Sign (whose symbol is the Scorpio or Eagle) are very sexy and seductive. Physical satisfaction is very important to them. It takes quite a man to satisfy a Scorpio woman's desires and needs—it could even be too much for the hot-blooded Taurus.

This woman can be very secretive. You'll find it takes a long time to get to know her. As a rule, Scorpio people are wary of strangers. You'll have to do all the running in the early days. You'll also have to be a real man.

Scorpio is a great worker and usually gets to the top in any profession she chooses. She loves challenges and craves excitement in her life. You won't find her sticking at tasks that give her little scope to use her imagination if she can possibly help it.

You may find her bad temper a little too much for you at times. Her critical faculty is also extremely high and she has a habit of speaking her mind—which often scares away possible boyfriends and lovers. At times Miss Scorpio will appear to be fighting the whole world. She certainly has the knack of blaming others for her own errors. She's constantly striving toward perfection, though, whether in work or making herself more attractive.

When she falls in love, it's total. She finds it very hard to carry on two affairs at the same time. There's a strange conflict in her alliances with the opposite sex. Miss Scorpio can't bear to be dominated, and yet, conversely, she craves a masterful man.

Miss Scorpio can sum up character very quickly. You won't be able to give her that old love, moon, June line. This is a woman you will have to play straight with all the way along. If you think you can take the rough with the smooth, it might be possible to settle down to a happy and lasting married life. She will never embarrass you in company because she doesn't like to carry on arguments in public. In fact, if you are having an argument and a couple of friends suddenly walk in, it's unlikely they will ever know it.

As a housewife, she's not going to measure up to your dreams. Domestic chores are a big bore to her. She's not the greatest cook in the world, either.

You'll have to be prepared to include her in most of your outside interests. You've got the wrong girl if you're expecting someone who is happy to wait patiently at home every night until you come in. If you've decided you can't live without a Scorpio woman, you'll have to be prepared to change your ways.

TAURUS MAN—SAGITTARIUS WOMAN

A Sagittarius woman may be a little too fond of constant moving about for you. You'll find it hard to keep tabs on her. One day you'll ring up to make a date with her, and twenty-four hours later you'll discover she's packed her bags and gone off on a holiday. You'll never be sure what to expect.

You both have a highly competitive streak that makes it important to you to come out on top when faced with a new challenge. Known to be very sporting, people born under Sagittarius get on very well with animals, especially horses and dogs. They also have a strong gambling streak, which you may find very hard to accept.

You will admire many of her qualities. She never complains and is able to accept quite a degree of hardship. She is a very good-natured girl, always looking for the best in people.

Miss Sagittarius likes to keep on the go and can't stand to be kept waiting.

Just when you think you've won her she'll surprise you by a sudden change of attitude. You see, she's sometimes more interested in catching her man than in keeping him.

She's quite a career girl and likes to be a leader. She has a very inventive mind and often ends up in a job calling for creative talent of one sort or another. She's never dismayed by hard work and is capable of carrying on through the night if she finds the task an interesting one. No job will tie her down for long if it doesn't offer good opportunities for improvement in status, though. If you fall in love with each other, there'll be quite a few problems to overcome. The need to be free and be her own boss often interferes with this woman's romantic involvements. You will have to curb your strong desire to dominate and learn to share all the important decision making. She would find it extremely hard to give up her friends and outside interests to look after you every day. If you attempt to make a go of the matrimonial stakes, you'll probably have to accept the fact that you've married a career woman.

At first meeting, a Sagittarian woman is likely to be instantly attracted to you. You have many of the qualities she admires, such as self-assurance and the strong belief that your opinions are right. She needs someone who appears to know exactly what he wants from life and she'll often turn to him for advice.

As a marriage partner, she'll be a driving force. She'll have great faith in your abilities to get to the top, and be a wonderful confidence-booster as well. Your friends will be extremely fond of her. Perhaps you need to be a bit careful about inviting influential people to dinner, though, because Sagittarians do have a rather unfortunate knack of saying the wrong thing at the wrong time. Diplomacy is certainly not one their strongest points. She will not become a model housewife overnight—but you can bet your bottom dollar she'll keep trying.

If finally you do decide she's the girl for you, you're unlikely to regret your decision. One word of advice is that it would probably be in the best interests of you both for you to keep control of the pruse strings. Sagittarians are not too good at balancing the books and they do have an extravagant streak.

Women born under this Sign make wonderful mothers, though they are inclined to be a little too possessive. It will be easy for you to become jealous of your own children. You may feel she is overly protective—and at your expense. You might have to step in at times and make sure she doesn't keep her kids tied to her apron strings for too long.

TAURUS MAN—CAPRICORN WOMAN

You two should get on extremely well. When you are introduced to Miss Capricorn for the first time, you'll get the sensation of having met her before. It's not to be wondered at as you two have a great deal in common. Both of you are earthy types, and therefore realists. She has an inquiring mind and is very interested in other people and their jobs—what they do, how they do it and why. She is very faithful to her friends, a quality that can border on possessiveness where her lovers are concerned.

A nice home means a lot to her. Capricorn people find it very hard to function socially in uncomfortable conditions. She is not really interested in acquiring a great fortune, but she has a true understanding of the value of money and certainly likes the things it can buy. She has no trouble putting cash aside if she sees something in a shop window she really wants to save up for.

Capricorn women, as a rule, are hardy types. The outdoor life appeals to them. They can stand up to difficult conditions without complaint.

People born under this Sign hate making enemies. They are worried whenever they get bad vibrations from a person; their inquiring mind will want to know the reason.

Underneath what may appear to be a gay and fun-loving exterior, you probably have one of the most serious-minded Signs of the Zodiac, if not the most serious. A very practical person, she is also extremely ambitious, not only for herself but for her man as well. Her feelings run very deep. Once you've won this lady, she'll stick by you through thick and thin and be rooting in your corner all the way.

Success is very important to her. If you are lacking in ambition, she'll give you an extra push to get you to the top in your career. She'll be full of ideas and suggestions and she's absolutely wonderful at home entertaining. You need have no worries about bringing influential people home to dinner, and it's just possible your Capricorn lady will help you to clinch that all-important deal.

She's not the most romantic woman of the Zodiac, but let's face it, you're not exactly Rudolph Valentino. You'll find her earthiness refreshing. You will always feel you can speak your mind with her; in fact, she would not want you to do anything else.

Family life is very important to people born where Saturn rules. If you begin dating, she'll soon be wanting to take you home to meet Mom and Dad. Don't get cold feet, it's just that she likes to include her family in most compartments of her life. If you do decide to get married, it will certainly help for you to be on a good wavelength with your prospective mother-in-law. This is one area where you may have to be on guard. Don't be critical of her relatives; she'll take criticism of her family tree very personally.

Any challenge she undertakes she is likely to carry off successfully.

Not many men are able to give the Capricorn woman all the appreciation she demands. Remember, she won't give herself to you unless she's sure you care deeply. This is not a woman to play about with. It takes people born in Capricorn a long time to make up their minds about a permanent relationship. You must not attempt to rush her into a quick decision. She needs a man who will be a driving force, but she won't allow you to submerge her individuality.

As the years roll by, you're likely to become even closer. It is important for Mrs. Capricorn to have some outside interest, though, because if her life centers around the home, she's likely to become extremely jealous and possessive.

As a mother, she should leave little to be desired. Your children will be brought up with good manners and respect for the feelings of others.

TAURUS MAN—AQUARIUS WOMAN

This is one of the most difficult Signs for the Taurus man to figure out. Being a pretty practical and down-to-earth sort of guy, you'll find Miss Aquarius mysterious to say the least. You will probably never know where you stand with her. It's possible her eccentricity is what attracts you in the first place. As a permanent relationship, this would appear to be something of a nonstarter. You will constantly be trying to bring her down to earth and put the stars in her eyes back in the heavens.

Aquarians' heads are certainly full of wonderful ideas about making the world a better place. They are extremely interested in progress and change. They can also be very persuasive talkers. You might find it hard to hold your own verbally. In fact, Mr. Taurus, you'll have to be prepared to have your ego dented if you are going to get serious with Miss Aquarius.

She is a creator of fashion rather than a follower. You, being rather a conservative type, could find her manner of dress rather embarrassing. But don't let her see your blushes because then she'll enjoy teasing you more than ever. The frustrating thing for Aquarian people (and they usually know it) is that their ideas are way ahead of their time. You will have to learn to accept her for what she is and not try to mold her into what you think she should be. Never try to pin her down. Her active mind will always be one jump ahead of you.

Be very careful and sure before you marry Aquarius. Don't go from a whirlwind courtship straight to the ring on the third finger, left hand. It might be an idea to have a "trial marriage" first. Since they are artistic (more spiritually so than you), it's very difficult for Aquarius people to settle for an ordinary humdrum life. Home is a place this woman hangs her clothes at night (or perhaps leaves them on the floor). Tidiness is not important to her, and this cavalier attitude could be irritating to you. Possessions are not at all that important, either. People matter much more to her. Don't be surprised to come home from work and find the house full of strangers. If anyone needs help, Aquarius will feel duty bound to do all in her power to provide it.

She can lose interest in things overnight, though. It is extremely difficult for her to see any job through to the finish if she becomes bored with it.

On first meeting, you may feel she is the most unselfish person you've ever met. As you get to know her better, you'll discover this is not always the case. It's very difficult for the Water Bearer to form lasting relationships. It might be best to let her come and go as she pleases. A dazzling affair would probably do you both a lot of good, and after it's over, it should be possible for you to remain the best of friends. For her, the transition from an affair to a close friendship is not hard—it's the most natural thing in the world.

It's quite possible you will find yourself having an affair with an Aquarian woman and dating someone else at the same time. As a rule, she'd prefer to know all about it than to discover later that you were hiding the truth. She's not a jealous person and will seldom be angry.

If, in spite of all that could go wrong, you do decide she's the only woman for you, you won't have any trouble getting nights out on your own. It's possible she'll never even ask where you've been. Unfortunately for you, however, she'll expect the same sort of freedom and herein lies the danger. You will have to be very careful you don't end up leading separate lives under the same roof.

She makes a wonderful mother. All her hopes for the future of the world will be channeled into her children.

TAURUS MAN—PISCES WOMAN

Down-to-earth and methodically minded Taurus can make a good match for romantic Pisces. It will be up to you to bring this woman, whose Sign is the two Fishes, out of the deep waters of self-analysis. You won't find Miss Pisces at all easy to get to know; she may seem wrapped up in her own feelings and emotions. You will have to keep your temper under control during her emotional outbursts which could be a little too much for you to take at times.

The Pisces woman places a great deal of value on love and romance. She's a very kind person and feels very deeply about injustice. She also has very high standards, so only the man who sticks to his principles can win her.

There could be something of a problem about who wears the pants. Like you, this lady does not like to be bossed or told what to do.

Beneath that soft and cuddly feminine exterior is a very quick and intuitive brain. She will always speak her mind. If she feels you aren't doing as well as you could in your career, she'll let you know it. It's not that she is given to criticism. It's simply that because she loves you, she wants you to realize your potential and live a happy and fulfilled life.

There's a part of Pisces that is selfish and lazy. And there is another part that is somewhat scheming. She has a tendency to live in a make-believe world. It will be up to you to get her to face reality and understand her dreams and fantasies for exactly what they are.

She will admire you for your ambition and drive. She is terribly loyal; woe betide the person who says anything behind your back. Still, you may feel you never know where you stand with Pisces. If you marry her, you may always have a lurking fear that one day she will run off with someone else. Probably this fear is groundless—you just find it difficult to believe her passionate interest in other people is only that.

Basically, she needs a dominant male. She mustn't be allowed to get out of hand. As a homemaker, she is first class. Pisces people are naturally good at running a home. When you first set up housekeeping together, you'll discover she has a keen eye for bargains, and being rather artistic, will know exactly how to decorate. She's very fond of beautiful things and can at times be rather extravagant. She won't give much thought to the cost if something catches her eye.

You will have trouble getting her to mix with strangers. Being rather shy, she may be frightened by big crowds. But with your boldness and confidence, you should be able to bring her out of her shell.

It is a matter of pride to her that her man is well turned out. You are never likely to be wanting for a clean shirt or a carefully ironed pair of pants. Never try the heavy-handed approach with her because she abhors violence and you'll never win her through shows of brute strength. If you can control your jealousy and suspicions, this relationship could turn out to be a very happy and successful one.

You must never give her the feeling of being trapped. Be sure you get her out of the domestic environment as much as possible. Don't allow her to hide herself away. Since she has such a vivid imagination, it is unwise to leave her alone for long spells. In this union, it is important that life and its experiences be shared as much as possible. It might be an advantage if you are a more mature person than your Pisces mate. As a rule, these people, whose element is water, need an anchor to hold fast to.

Pisces mothers have very strong feelings for their children. She will want them to be independent and stand on their own two feet, but at the same time will give them things she might have been deprived of as a child.

But that's Pisces for you—two Fishes swimming in opposite directions!

TAURUS' HEALTH

You are a creature of habit and therein lies much of the secret of your continued good health—or otherwise. If your body is subjected to sudden changes in climate or diet, or if you switch from gentle to violent exercise, you are likely to become ill. Therefore you should make all changes slowly, working up to them so that your body has plenty of time to adjust and adapt. If you abide by this rule, you should remain quite healthy.

You have probably noticed that in most departments of your life it takes you some time to develop an aptitude. You have to practice more than most others and then go over the routine until it becomes a firmly fixed regimen. After you do do this, you're well on your way. Once you've learned something, you never lose it.

This is why Taurus people can attain high levels of physical competence and timing in acrobatics, trapeze work, gymnastics and the like. Other Signs are more naturally lithe and will *mentally* grasp a physical discipline more quickly, but they don't possess the staying power of a Taurus. You master technique through long and arduous training. (As one famous astrologer put it, the mind of Taurus people is in their muscles.)

Since yours is an earth Sign with great natural affinity for the body, as distinct from the mind, you usually possess above-average strength. Your constitution is remarkable for its stamina and endurance, and the burdens of work you can carry under a gradual buildup are extraordinary.

Because of this, you are reluctant to give in to illness—in fact, scorn to even acknowledge it. You feel you can shake it off. You go on and on—until you exceed your magnificent stamina and have to go to bed. You won't go quietly, and fortunately, because of your powers of endurance, you won't have to go often. But when you do get sick, it tends to take you longer than average to get back to par again.

The most vulnerable part of your body as a rule is your throat. There are very few Taurus people who don't find that any infection or breakdown in general health appears here first. The neck and shoulders are also weak spots. Taurus folk have a tendency to suffer from earache, mumps, tonsillitis and goiter. Through the influence of Scorpio, the Sign directly opposite yours, you may be troubled with genital problems. Otherwise you're as strong as a horse—or Bull. But there are certain precautions you should take. Even the beasts of burden have fundamental requirements for enjoying continued good health.

The first very definitely is, don't overeat. This temptation has been mentioned already, but it can't be overstressed. Apart from excessive intake, you should also avoid fats and rich food. Overweight puts a strain on your heart, which is likely suffer under any prolonged excess.

It's too easy for most men born under this Sign to take in a huge meal, wash it down with a full-bodied red wine, swallow some port as an aid to digestion—and then put up their feet and enjoy the full feeling. This sort of luxuriating (and the obesity that inevitably accompanies it) is likely to impose a severe strain on your kidneys and impair circulation. Taurus people who don't take care with their diet are also prone to gout, varicose veins and weak ankles.

Most Taurus individuals have an inordinate fondness for comfort and the good things in life. Remember, you were born with a splendid constitution, that if looked after should see you through to a ripe old age, but if you begin to overeat and follow your natural tendency to avoid all forms of exercise, your health problems will quickly multiply. You do love the country and the wide open spaces, but are inclined to do your deep-breathing exercises from behind the wheel of a car.

One thing you should try to remember is that obstinacy sometimes clouds your common sense. You are inclined to pooh-pooh the concern of close friends and loved ones if they happen to notice that you're looking a bit seedy. You're also a terror for disregarding doctors' orders.

Bend a little, huh?

TAURUS AT WORK

You are suited for a wide range of occupations, mainly because you actually enjoy working and would feel lost without a job. The jobs you're inclined to favor fall into four categories. Which of these you'll eventually end up in depends on other influences, including the part of the Taurus month in which you were born.

Generally speaking, Taurus people will be attracted to, first, work connected with the land and building; second, commercially artistic enterprises; third, executive positions of all kinds, especially those connected with financial management; and fourth, professions such as law, medicine and teaching.

These categories might seem to cover just about every vocation. But it's not as simple as that. You are *not* an adaptable person, and unless there are strong influences to the contrary in your horoscope, you will be most unhappy in any job that requires you to handle constantly changing scenes, such as a Gemini person would excel in. You need a job that has a certain pattern requiring repetition of your particular skills. Coping or adjusting to fluid situations is just not one of your strong points.

The Taurus person has no hangups about working for others. In fact, he or she is one of the ideal employees of the Zodiac. But as a rule, because of your sound common sense, determination and capacity for hard work, you tend to rise from the ranks. A Virgo person, for example, who also makes an excellent worker, may remain for years in the one position. But not Taurus. You'll rise at least to a trusted management or executive position—here you'll still be following instructions, but at a more responsible level. If you have entered the field of finance, you are apt to finish as one of the respected and influential heads of a banking or some other leanding or investment concern.

Taurus people work just as well for themselves as for others. Their nature urges them to be productive in just about any occupational situation. They can't sit back and simply do nothing. It doesn't occur to them to work harder just because they're in business for themselves than they would if they were making money for someone else. Once committed, they put aside such considerations and get on with doing the job to the very best of their ability.

The personal profit motive is high in the Taurus individual's calculations. But where you differ from others is that you're prepared to work and wait for long-term gains rather than risk short-haul rakeoffs. The fear of loss while waiting for the results of an overnight "killing" would give the usually phlegmatic Taurus person a crop of ulcers. You simply are not a gambler or a speculator. If you try to become one, you will invariably lose one way or another.

When starting out on a career, it may take Taurus people a little time to decide what they really want to do. Despite your dislike of change and uncertainty, you are apt to move out of your original line of work after a couple of years and try something else. Not that you will switch and change jobs every few weeks. No, you'll give whatever you began a chance and genuinely endeavor to get ahead through patient and dogged effort. But it is essential for you to *feel* happy in your work. And this is something you can never tell in advance—you have to *do* it to know if you will enjoy it. Unless you have a deep-down conviction that what you are doing is the job or career for you, you'll fret inwardly because you must feel at one with the nature of your work. Then, no matter how menial, uninspiring and uninteresting it may appear to others, you will be able to plod along quite contentedly forevermore.

This trait must not be confused with the Taurus person's admirable ability to continue to work under the most difficult and oppressive conditions. You can literally "slave" to maintain your position, particularly if it is for the sake of someone you love. But to be in such a position to begin with, you usually have to feel a strong affinity for the type of work. Your willpower is such that if it suits you, you can disregard the ugly conditions around you and sacrifice your immediate self-interest for the sake of the future.

Quite often a Taurus person will train for one profession, say the law, and on graduation move into an unrelated field. This may be public relations, designing or work connected with one of the beauty industries. You will usually finish learning a job, though, before quitting it for another—another small gesture of insurance.

Your love of nature and the outdoors often leads you to dabble in real estate, especially in properties outside the city. You are also likely to be a sales representative whose territory includes the suburbs and semirural areas. But for you, an itinerant occupation has to involve a regular routine and not demand much instant initiative. It is also terribly important to you to have a fixed income rather than one dependent on commission alone. You really need that reassurance because you can't be happy without some security you can put your finger on.

The Taurus caution and reluctance to jump to conclusions often earn him or her a reputation for being stolid and stodgy. This is an unfair, judgment really, and it's often leveled by people who are themselves superficial and lightweight. You are not a particularly imaginative or exciting operator and colleague, but you are solidly reliable and honest as a boss, employee or co-worker. And, best of all, you possess a fineness of feeling and responsiveness that go straight to the heart.

A true Taurus person never lets people down. You are the loyalist of associates, your common sense is truly remarkable and you have an instinct for giving good advice about business as well as personal problems. You would make an excellent consultant in any practical field. Your own natural fondness for security imparts a calculating shrewdness for assessing material effects and values. Anyone who wishes to make a move that's going to affect someone else's hip pocket, and wants to know how that person will react, should confide in a Taurus person in that field.

Basically, the Taurus person is a long-winded empire builder. Give you a start in any job, and you'll lay foundations on which to build a monolith. You work slowly, deliberately and persistently. It may seem to others that not a great deal is going on, but every day you will be stamping down the ground without letup and looking around for building materials. If you can't build, you're not interested. You'll quit, because as much as change goes against your grain, you must have the incentive of productive advancement. If you are given a target to reach, it must be a moving one.

In this way, with your quiet manner, unobtrusive style and extraordinary financial acumen, you are often by middle life in a position of considerable power and influence.

What do you expect from your employees? Loyalty and persistence. Since you are rather fixed in ideas, you will lay down procedures and methods and expect them to be adhered to. You admire anyone who works to a system. If his happens to be different from yours and you think it's good, you won't mind his doing it his way—sometimes. Other times, you can be stubbornly unprogressive. You are also suspicious of optimists and enthusiasts, and you can be painfully obdurate, unresponsive to reason and impossible to persuade once you get a bee in your bonnet (which is quite often). On the other hand, you frequently turn out to be infuriatingly right about business matters.

If you were born between April 21 and 30, you may do well in an entertainment field, especially as a singer or actor. Your voice is apt to have a distinctive quality, which may attract popular attention. Your Taurus gift for handling and making money should be quite pronounced. You should aim for high goals rather than settle for midway comfort. You have a greater business potential than your conservative nature may attempt to exploit. Banking would suit you well as a career. You should also shine in scientific work connected with crops and animal husbandry, as well as medicine. Occupations and businesses connected with the manufacture and sale of farm machinery may also be lucrative. Too much emphasis on materialistic aims may fail to win you many friends and sympathizers; try a little altruism. Old friends and habitual routines may land you in a rut. Travel should be good for you. Overwork is a health hazard.

If you were born between May 1 and 10, you are an intellectual type of Taurus and your creative capacities are above average. You should be a competent writer with impressive down-to-earth ideas, and may make a name for yourself as an advertising copy writer or a public relations executive. You may also have a flair for scientific reporting on actual experiments and new products. It would be a pity to miss opportunities through being overcautious, so be a little more adventurous! But don't act on your emotions alone; use cool logic. Plan deliberately and avoid allowing prejudices, especially old grudges, to influence your decisions.

Jealousy and possessiveness may interfere with your career. You can also guard your secrets too closely and hinder the progress of deserving subordinates. If you allow loved ones to live their own lives, you may find they make fewer demands on you.

For the sake of your career, it is important that you have a lovemate with an intellect at least equal to your own, but who does not share identical interests. You need as much change as you can get in any palatable form.

In partnership, do your best not to be stubborn over trivial matters.

If you were born between May 11 and 20, you have a particular talent for organizational work and running a large concern. Although you may start your career in an undistinguished way, you have what it takes to get to the top. Chances are you will outdistance those of your contemporaries who were regarded as whiz kids.

Your ability to work hard is outstanding, but you shouldn't overlook the importance of leisure activities; a less serious and intense approach to life should be beneficial for you and those around you. Materialistic ambitions are apt to absorb all your time and conversation without your realizing it. It may help to find a friend with some spiritual leanings that have practical application to everyday life.

Indiscretions may lead to damaging publicity. Business associates and friends should be selected with care; some may not be all they pretend. People born at this time need to be careful that their preoccupation with material success doesn't make home life a mockery or their loved ones feel unhappy and neglected.

Money

You have a way with money. You can make it and manage it, for yourself or for others.

The Taurus woman can look after financial affairs to the great benefit of her family. She is firm, yet kind; saving, yet generous. She has no trouble deciding what is needed and what's not. She can be extravagant in buying for the home and her loved ones, yet she is capable of making substantial economies that involve little hardship for all, whenever necessary.

Money naturally gravitates to Taurus people, usually by their middle years. You often marry wealth and sometimes begin a successful business career through your marriage partner.

The self-made Taurus person seldom fails to acquire a pleasant home of his or her own and all the creature comforts.

GEMINI'S CHARACTER

No Sign of the Zodiac is quite as smart, sharp or communicative as Gemini. Your mind functions with the instantaneousness of an electronic circuit. The ancients used to call you the Messenger of the Gods, and, seasonally speaking, you bring the good news of the start of summer. But then you apologize, you must be off . . . because everybody knows that good news and Gemini travel f-a-s-t!

If you are a true Gemini, the odds are against your reading this chapter through without taking a quick look at the last couple of pages. This isn't because you're uninterested (no one is more curious about himself than the person born under your Sign), but because your searing curiosity demands the message faster than the written word can convey it.

It's the same with everything you read. You skim a page like a photo scanner and your comprehension is as swift as your eye.

Yet, one subject continually eludes your powers of understanding—yourself. Others seem certain of who they are, where they are going and what they want. But you, despite your brave and confident show to the contrary, are quite frankly baffled by your own nature. Now, settle back for a few minutes and enjoy a quick run-through on your favorite topic.

Gemini is the third Sign of the Zodiac. On its own, it's as unstable as quicksilver, the metal of the Sign. Add to this the fact that its zodiacal element is air and its disposition mutable or changeable, and the result would be an impossibly zany character. But the Sun's presence in this Sign gives the remarkable Gemini intellect a stability that, if not too upset by other influences in the horoscope, produces a highly intelligent, inventive, quick-witted, versatile, lively, never-say-stop character.

It all began the day you first sat up in your crib. You've seldom laid down peacefully since. As a toddler, you must have driven your poor mother mad, for unless she was a student of Astrology, how was she to know that all you lived for was to learn about everything by experiencing it for yourself? It was no good trying to keep you quiet each day with the same old toys, your favorite teddy bear and all that routine kid stuff. You wanted variety, novelty, action—and you screamed and ranted until you got it. To put you in a playpen, where most other kids are content to while away a few hours with their blocks in the sun, was like ramming a pound of dynamite into a tin and lighting the fuse. If you did explode and your mother didn't understand, it must have been very painful. To develop ideally, a Gemini child must have as much supervised freedom as possible to satisfy his or her almost insatiable inquisitiveness.

Rearing a Gemini child is hard on the parents, but then again, it has its compensations. The Gemini youngster is a very easy little person to be proud of as well as to love. For instance, you probably started walking long before other youngsters your age, and likely as not you made some intelligible remarks when your contemporaries were still emitting cooing noises. The versatile Gemini child has a natural ear for music and frequently astounds the household by picking out tunes on the family musical instrument. You probably drew a recognizable outline of Donald Duck before you could write, and may even have gotten a big hug for doing some cute little dance steps off your own bat at two and a half. From the very beginning, you were quick to imitate and learn things.

That a Gemini birthday produces a mental creature rather than an emotional one is usually evident from the person's physical characteristics. Geminis are built for speed. Even though other factors in the horoscope may round them out and add weight, there's a lightness about their precise sharp movements and darting agility that suggests instantaneous response.

The true Gemini person usually speaks quickly (certainly fluently), and in extreme excitement, may stutter. Even when the verbal rate is controlled, there's an ease of articulation and a pronounced ability to turn a phrase. Gemini frequently illustrates his or her words with hand movements. So, if Gemini's fingers, hands or feet aren't moving or tapping, he's probably asleep.

Gemini men and women are likely to be found wherever there's a touch of risk, mystery or novelty. Speed attracts them, skill fascinates them. As competitors, deftness characterizes them. They love sports and enjoy participating, though not so much in heavy-endurance activities. Ideal pastimes for these intensely mobile people are skiing, scuba diving, waterskiing, horseback riding, ice skating, even sky diving—in other words, activities that demand swift, responsive physical involvement. Golf may be a bit slow but tennis is a game Gemini probably invented. The Mercurial man and woman like to drive fast cars and fly airplanes if they get the chance. They thrill to danger.

As spectators at sporting events, they have the habit of arriving on time to witness the beginning, but darting off midway through (lord knows where), only to return for the finale. Their rationale is that it's the beginning and the end that count, and what goes on in the middle—well, you could be out watching something else starting or finishing, couldn't you? It's agony for Mercurial people to sit through an evenly matched game. Even at the movies you'll find them eating, chewing, drinking—and making at least one visit to the washroom "just to stretch the legs."

The Gemini male often likes to watch boxing (the gorier the bout, the better). An evening's television at a Gemini house can be pretty wearing—the sound is likely to be turned down and everyone expected to engage in an animated conversation while following the story line. Gemini has no trouble performing two, even three actions at the same time—this is your life-style.

You're magnetic. Just as you love to meet new people, so others are drawn to you. Even if you could resist dialing the phone for one night, it would keep you busy ringing. No one manages to make more acquaintances and friends than people born in the merry month of May. After all, you've a lot to offer in a social sense. You are witty, bright and charming. You radiate a beguiling insouciance. Your enthusiasm refuses to be squelched by the usual accumulation of mundane worries that effectively inhibit most of us.

Your personality and life-style are an exercise in self-expression. You are positive (and uncharacteristically consistent) in this regard, and many of us secretly respect and admire you for it. It's not that you're always particularly sincere or honest in what you say or do, it's just that you're prepared to meet each situation afresh, to change your attitudes and moods outrageously. You refuse to be constrained like most of us by the irrational desire to be consistent. Why adult human beings should sacrifice self-expression for consistency is something you can't understand. To you, consistency is an indecent four-letter word spelled d-u-l-l.

Naturally, you're the life of the party and probably the most interesting person there. Intellectual types enjoy your company and you invariably choose them for your closest buddies. Rough and ready types amuse you—especially if you can send them up—but being a sensitive, sensible, sidestepping spirit, you make sure they don't get too close for comfort. You are usually well informed on current affairs and can discourse knowledgeably on any topic that crops up. People do get the feeling when you talk that you're something of an authority, although your modest manner does not suggest this. Talking off the top of one's head is a Gemini specialty. Your active mind is constantly devouring and analyzing all sorts of ideas and theories; in conversation, they emerge with an inventive little twist that frequently astounds your listeners. You do not initiate much, but you can certainly put the pieces together in an original way.

You can change your entire personality walking from one room to another. It's not by accident that your zodiacal symbol is the Twins. No one—including you—can be sure which Twin is going to appear next. You are a human chameleon. Skeptics who fail to understand your true nature may describe you as a quick-change artist; in more sinister circumstances, as a turncoat. Actually, you give an audience what it wants, but nothing of your real self. If people want to hear fables presented as fact, you'll have no compunction about obliging them. You take on the character of the company you are in and respond accordingly. Whether it's afternoon tea at a genteel club or a hard-headed business dinner, you're unbelievably convincing and effective.

But what about those fantasies of yours? They do cause problems, don't they? And you never seem to learn from them. Gemini, you see, for all his rationality, is an incurable romantic, an idealist, a dreamer. Your imagination soars to incredible heights of glorious speculation where all is rosy. Then you plunge with optimism into the real world, only to be disillusioned and shattered. You who possess such a great amount of common sense in so many things never seem to sober up where your dreams and ideals are concerned.

If controlled, your flights of fantasy can be directed into constructive pursuits and planning. Your gift for visualization can be developed and applied to practical projects. To be happy and to feel fulfilled, the Gemini person has to learn to be the master of his or her mind, not its lackey.

This nimble brain of yours must be put to work in *specific* directions. You can be powerfully creative in several artistic fields as well as in more practical occupations. But you tend to waste your time and talents by chopping and changing, and by continually starting new projects without finishing the old ones. If you are a mature and successful Gemini individual, you must already know how to curb this dispersiveness. But no one has to tell you that the tendency is always there.

Your mind should be trained along academic, professional or technical lines. However, this is easier said than done. The early educational years normally are the hardest for a Gemini individual. Youthful curiosity and impatience frequently impel him or her to drop one subject after another, to switch courses in midstream or to veer off in a different direction altogether. Although you possess a voracious appetite for knowledge, it can easily degenerate into an incurable addiction for any novelty and excitement.

Your powerful intellect must be harnessed by a real and abiding interest. You must genuinely be intrigued by a pursuit if you want to bring it to fruition. Be honest with yourself. Apply this test. You will then avoid scattering your energies and be equipped to accomplish that which you really desire.

A fault of Gemini people is that they find it difficult to accept advice. They are likely to retaliate against fair and helpful comment with a witheringly skillful and logical justification of their own actions that leaves nothing more to be said. By being clever enough to win an argument, they too often lose a chance.

Does this scintillating, Mercurial shaft of energy ever know the pangs of loneliness? Indeed you do. More so than others. You plunge into awful crevices of despair and mope around, hit the bottle, perhaps even take a pill—anything to try to lift yourself out of the black depression that crushes your spirit like a giant boot. But like all Gemini moods, this despair doesn't last long, and it lifts abruptly. Your misery often begins with frustration, impatience at your inability to cope with your own restlessness and to achieve some lasting satisfaction. The latter, of course, is a hopeless goal since the dual nature of the Gemini character can only be satisfied by ever-looking, never-finding curiosity. Contentment, like everything else you experience, is transient.

Another cause of despondency is being trapped among negative, introverted and doomy companions. Being adaptive to your environment, you relate to these people's moods and repressions as though they were your own. In other words, you con yourself into thinking that their emotions are yours. So whenever you are down, be sure you're not picking up secondhand vibrations. The best cure for this sort of depression is to get out into the mainstream of life as fast as you can. Meet a buddy, go to a party—or if it's really serious, make a major change you've been thinking about. You should learn to follow your intuitive hunches because they will often extricate you from sticky situations (as you've no doubt noticed). There's nothing quite so terrifying to a Gemini as the thought of being isolated, emotionally or intellectually, from his fellow man.

The way some astrologers speak about Gemini emotions you'd think these people had no heart at all. It's not true. You have as much love and sympathy within you as anyone else. The problem is it lies under a crackling mesh of intellectual brightness. And intelligence is a fundamentally cool and detached impersonal force. For instance, in a tragedy or emergency, one can usually be of more help by keeping one's head and not giving in to emotions. If others could imagine living just about every moment with a crisislike feeling of tension, they'd have a fair idea of what it's like to be a Gemini. You hum with nervous energy, the power source of your intellect. This energy twangs in your brain and body twenty-four hours a day. Often you can't sleep because of it. And if you do, you twitch, toss, turn and dream.

To reach a Gemini's heart, it is necessary to hit him hard. Love and compassion always do this, but never sentiment. And since a great deal of human emotion is based on sentiment, you can expect to be called everything from "heartless" and "cold" to "sterile" and "indifferent." And yet another point that is obvious about your affections—you recover very quickly from emotional disappointments, bitterly painful though they may be at the time. Not being the type who can moon around for long, you will be projected, even against your will, into new company and fresh diversions. With your unique talent for doing two or three things simultaneously, you can also be at an emotional low tide whenever you're bubbling over with mental interest in a new pursuit. You really are different.

It follows, of course, that you are a bit selfish. When preoccupied with the logic of a situation, you are likely to trample on the emotions of others, especially the ones who live with or love you. Your compulsive need for variety and change also makes you a creature of the moment who will disregard another's interests or anxiety to satisfy your own passing whim. This does not apply to the same degree to every Gemini person, but all of you need to cultivate more awareness of and respect for other people's feelings.

A calculating or cunning streak is very much a part of the Gemini personality. You do or say nothing without being conscious of the effect it will have on your own interests. Certainly, if you are the mature type, you can ignore your petty selfish urges and are capable of great generosity and sympathy. (You can't help it if the logistics of the situation are immediately apparent to your alert brain—this is a tribute to your integrity.) But it's decidedly different with the unevolved type, the Gemini who gives his brothers and sisters a bad reputation, the one who can't resist the opportunity to look after old number one. He is the fast-talking con man, petty swindler and small-time crook. Gemini, when he turns to crime, seldom goes in for the big-league conspiracy or the long-term caper. He's too impatient and impulsive. He wants what he wants *fast*, so his particular pattern is smash and grab, a deft dip into someone's pocket or till. Well, every Sign in the Zodiac has its negative type who's drawn to crime in one way or another. Fast-moving, plausible, unpredictable Gemini just happens, in this instance, to be fairly predictable.

Here again, you are the victim of your mental processes. In you, these are more mechanistic than in any other zodiacal type. The human mind, epitomized by Mercury, the planetary ruler of Gemini, is just as capable of plotting terrorism as devising ways to save lives. Essentially, it has no morality; it will busy itself with any objective. Therefore, it is extremely important for you to apply your mind to elevating and productive goals so that society may benefit from your talents. The artistic as well as the moral side of your nature—especially in youth—require encouragement and cultivation so that you can develop discrimination. Even the most brilliant intellectual discovery may be rejected by humanity on moral grounds.

As a lover, you are sensitive and affectionate, but inclined to blow hot and cold. The "Gemini in Love" section deals in detail with your inclinations in this regard. But briefly, your love moods depend on your mental outlook at the time and are as unpredictable as everything else about you. You are more flirtatious than deeply sensuous, and Miss Gemini particularly is apt to be a very elusive bedmate. Today she will, tomorrow she won't. Mr. Gemini is seldom difficult to coax into bed, but getting him to the altar, unless it's an impulsive decision, takes considerable maneuvering. Both sexes look for a companion who stimulates them mentally rather than physically. They both adore a conquest, but tire extremely quickly of people who want to tie them down or who become jealous. However, their curious natures often lead them into curious entanglements. They extricate themselves from these by the simple expedient of suddenly disappearing, oblivious to the problems and complications they leave behind. Lovemaking for both the male and female has to be imaginative and romantic to sustain their ardor.

You dislike scenes immensely and are particularly adroit at dodging them. Seldom does a Gemini person have to cope with violent confrontations, unless he's caught in an act of impulsiveness. You have a sixth sense for anticipating trouble and usually manage to skirt potentially disturbing situations. If you can't dance away, you tend to fall back on your gift of gab, which may vary from cutting verbal riposte to a beguiling display of eloquence. Your great capacity for producing "facts" out of thin air temporarily mollifies or disarms your antagonists.

Still, you are exceedingly able at debate. You can, in fact, deliver a convincing case for either side of an argument and will sometimes deliberately provoke your friends for the sheer excitement of sharpening your wits on another intellect. It doesn't bother you on these occasions to take an opposite point of view to your own. As a rule, the Gemini individual is extremely flexible in his opinions and seldom feels really strongly about anything—well, not strongly enough to become involved in prolonged and physically demanding campaigns. The exception may relate to your loathing of all forms of censorship and attempts to restrict freedom of thought and speech. You may publicly employ your oratorial skills to condemn these practices if you feel they are a threat. You may even make a quick sortie into politics or onto the platform to support women libbers and the like. But one day or night when the organizers or party stalwarts look for you in your usual seat, you won't be there. There are too many exciting causes in this world for you to devote your full-time allegiance to any one of them.

You don't enjoy domestic routine. Setting up house is great. So is moving. But once life settles down to an everyday affair dictated by the kitchen clock, you nearly go off your rocker. You quite enjoy having family members around as long as they do things your way and don't interfere with your personal activities. You think you're very easy to get along with in the house, but you are far from it. Those who live with you contend you're a bit fussy and far too quick to become irritable over little things. If you're prevented from getting out and making the fraternal rounds, everyone suffers. Gemini women with children to look after and no job to take their minds off the sameness of housework are likely to become highly neurotic—and may suddenly take off.

You tend to carry your independence too far, using it as an excuse to escape responsibility. Unconsciously, you may pick an argument with family members just so you can make a dramatic escape for a few hours. You don't possess a great deal of self-confidence and often hide your uncertainty behind a flurry of criticism, cynicism and superficial belligerence. Your ability to change attitudes with lightning aplomb and to copy other personalities makes you a convincing actor or actress. Your urbanity and charm are usually reserved more for acquaintances and friends than close family.

You make a great host or hostess. This is where you shine. All your friends will agree that a party at your place should never be missed. There's likely to be some very wacky goings-on—odd games in which anything can happen and usually does. The music will be fast, modern and loud—unless, of course, you've got your eye on some romantic who enjoys sentimental gush.

You are apt to do most of the entertainment cooking yourself because you enjoy fiddling around with attractive dishes—the more rare and exotic looking, the better. If your finances can encompass it, you'll make a point of having some really different items on the table—reindeer steaks, kangaroo-tail soup and amber caviar.

You enjoy visiting gourmet restaurants. Food is something you are very fastidious about. You don't like a lot of it, but you do relish variety. It must be clean, attractively served and of good quality. You'd rather go without than settle for hash. Alone in the house, you're a virtuoso at concocting a quick snack and usually fill your kitchen shelves with cans of interesting soups, salmon, imported ham, smoked oysters and the like; in the refrigerator, there'll be munchy celery, tomatoes, fresh milk (it's not hard for a Gemini to get on the health-food kick or to go vegetarian) and eggs that can be curried. Your penchant is for tasty, spicy foods, not for solid, full-course meals.

Gemini characters usually like to dress in extreme clothes and definitely abhor the very conventional. If a man, you have expensive tastes. If a woman, you do also, but are not quite as fussy on this point. Both sexes like their clothes to be clean and to fit well. Unless they're short of cash, neither will keep their garments long enough for them to wear out. You are not a great jewelry fan, mainly because you haven't got the time to fiddle with it. Besides, it catches on things and gets in the way as you slip in and out of doors and tight corners. You'll often wear a ring with a distinctive motif as a gesture of independence.

One of the most common faults of both the Gemini man and woman is gossiping. You mix with so many people and keep up such a torrent of conversation that you usually know all that's going on in your immediate circle as well as in half a dozen neighboring sets. If you are an advanced type, this minus quality becomes a sophisticated plus and you are well informed, poised and conversant. But if you are a Mercurial gossip, you scatter fact, fiction and innuendo around like banana skins for numerous others to trip on so they will confide secrets and confidences to you. It is why some astrologers have suggested the chattering chimpanzee would be a good substitute symbol for the Twins.

The Gemini individual changes friends quite often. You don't deliberately break with your old buddies, but keep on making new ones, to whom you give the bulk of your attention—for a time. Unless your emotions are very deeply penetrated, you are not capable of profound relationships.

It must be remembered that diversity is the key to the nature of the individual born under this Sign. Your role as a type is to communicate a continual stream of information and original ideas to as many people as possible through a plethora of activities. Admittedly, you sometimes spread yourself pretty thin and appear lightweight, superficial and immature. The youthful appearance that goes with Gemini's alert expression and quick, darting movements seldom deserts you, even if you live to a ripe old age.

The true Gemini person continues studying new subjects for most of his or her life. There's always something worth learning, you feel, and even in advanced years, you rarely lose the aptitude to absorb facts quickly.

Most of you manage to do a part-time job as well as follow a regular occupation. You are also likely to engage in one or two spare-time activities, probably associated with writing, speaking or handicrafts.

Some Gemini women, if it appeals to them, make ideal companions for sugar daddies who are not too demanding physically. The youthful Gemini male is also known to make a successful gigolo for wealthy aging ladies. Both Twins revel in the opportunities for social gadding about that money and position provide. They are also detached enough not to be troubled by their emotions and realistic enough to know that a kid, a car and a cottage in suburbia are not their scene.

Both the Gemini man and woman frequently marry more than once and are notorious for keeping two or three love affairs going at the same time—while they are searching for the companion of their dreams. But since their ideal lover is an abstract idea they couldn't describe even if they wanted to, they seldom find what they are looking for. Gemini's frantic search for the beloved is often as amusing as it is heartrending for the people involved.

A Gemini girl born in Australia and living in London telephoned her mother down under to say she'd found *him* at last—she and Alvin were getting married the following week.

Mom made a cake and took a quick flight over, arriving the day before the wedding.

"I brought your wedding cake, darling," she said proudly, plonking it down on the table with the happy couple's names beautifully iced on top.

"It's lovely, Mom," said Gemini, "but we couldn't wait—we got married yesterday."

"Oh."

"And there's something else. You would have had to change the name, in any event. I married Desmond."

GEMINI

IN LOVE

YOUR GEMINI MAN

You like him? Or love him? Just what sort of a guy is he?

Fascinating. In fact, he's two guys in one. But until you settle down together (assuming that's your intention), you'll probably spend most of your time with only one of the Twins, which is his zodiacal symbol. Mr. Gemini is probably the most flirtatious male in the Zodiac (and that's saying something), but whereas most of the others want to possess you body and soul, Mr. Gemini doesn't play that way. Oh, if you hook him, he'll settle down and probably make a darned good husband, but you'll have to be a special kind of understanding woman.

He's suave and dashing and terribly interesting. His mind is so quick and sharp that you'll feel at times he knows what you're thinking. He'll often answer questions you were just about to ask. He's got a way of getting on a girl's wavelength—which is delightful, especially if you're used to some of the more earthy types. This guy talks and moves like quicksilver, which is not surprising since his planetary ruler is the ever-restless and intellectual Mercury.

He's easily bored. He wants a woman first for her mental abilities. Sure, he's interested in sex, but if you're just a beautiful dummy, he'll take what you've got to offer and be out the door without taking his hat off. This is a guy you've got to keep guessing. Play his own game. Tease him. That's what he'll be doing to you.

He knows he's the life of any gathering and that people instantly take to him. They might not want to be around him for days on end, but how many parties last that long? This fellow gives the impression that he hasn't got a worry in the world, that he enjoys himself perpetually and that anyone who takes life too seriously is a fool! Oh, what a tonic these Gemini folk can be to all of us world-weary people.

It's an act, of course. He's got just as many hangups as any of us—which you'll soon find out if you live with him. But as a date, he's terrific. He's actually looking for deep and lasting love, but can seldom manage to stay in one place long enough to recognize it. He makes friends everywhere he goes. Women love his wit and charm. He'll eye two or three girls in the same room and manage to make each one feel she's the only female there.

If he starts to concentrate on you alone at a party (this is where you're sure to meet him), you'll feel you've never been wooed like this before. Even before he gets around to giving your hand a suggestive little squeeze, you'll believe you're terribly important to him. It's the little things he thinks to say and do that will convince you. He never misses a trick.

But is he sincere? Yes and no. He's always sincere at *that moment,* but he changes like a flash. It's those terrible Twins. One is always searching for novelty, variety and excitement in both people and situations. The other is a romantic who believes in fidelity and ideal love, but is doubtful about ever finding them.

When Mr. Gemini does fall for a woman, he's impossibly urgent. He'll pester her to distraction to marry him. If she doesn't reciprocate his passion, he may threaten to take his own life as a final dramatic gesture—which threat he'll mean but won't carry out.

If, on the other hand, she feels the same way, he'll have her in front of a justice of the peace ("We'll have a nice little church wedding later") in five seconds flat. If it's just a matter of hopping into bed, it'll take two and a half seconds. He just can't wait, this guy.

So where does that leave you, a woman in love with a Gemini man? If you get married, he'll be faithful as long as you don't try to cramp his style. He'll still flirt outrageously, but if you laugh it off, so will he—afterwards, in bed with *you* and not the other woman. He only wants the excitement of the chase. And as far as he's concerned, that's largely a mental exercise. He wants to know, to convince himself, he can make it with any woman he fancies—if he wanted to. It's his ego trip.

YOUR GEMINI WOMAN

You like her? Or do you love her? What sort of a girl is she?

She changes her partners the way she changes her clothes. She's looking for love, but not at the price of freedom. She believes that somewhere in this world there's a man who's her intellectual equal, capable of responding to her (bewildering) changes of mood and prepared to let her live her own life—within reason. Not surprisingly, she seldom locates him. Even if she does, she's likely to dismiss him with some superficial criticism in her rush to move on and keep looking.

This woman is frequently her own worst enemy. She craves an emotionally settled existence, but as soon as it materializes, she's bored stiff. Any man who wants to hold her will have to be enthused about going out a lot and meeting other people. And he can't afford to be the jealous type, either, for flirting is as natural to Ms. Gemini as breathing. Her man-for-keeps must also possess a very romantic imagination that indulges her constant flights of fantasy. This will have to include an aptitude for varying love-making scenes. One thing this girl can't stand and won't tolerate is sex that comes with the regularity and predictability of a three-course meal.

You'll spot your Gemini girl at any party surrounded by males. She's vivacious, witty, charming, tantalizing—and very, very seductive. She's basically a mental creature and the feminine allure she exudes is not unlike the elusive fragrance of an expensive French perfume. She has a will-o'-the-wisp quality—as you talk to her, you'll see it, feel you could touch it (if only you dare) . . . and then abruptly she's looking elsewhere, spellbinding another guy. This girl is terribly hard to pin down. She loves light and flirtatious situations.

Before she marries, Miss Gemini is likely to have numerous affairs. They won't mean a great deal to her because she won't give herself permanently to any lover. Declarations of fidelity just aren't in her book. Making love and being in the company of an exciting and stimulating man are vitally important to her—at that particular moment. She'll give herself over with gay abandon. But try to find the permanent part of this lady, because, if and when you do, she'll definitely be yours forever.

Miss Gemini will break off an affair at the drop of a hat—another man's hat if he happens to be more interesting. It's your job to see she stays interested in old number one. She'll tell you right from the start that that's how it is because she's a straightforward woman. If she's not yours, she won't think twice about having two or three affairs simultaneously. If she doesn't confide in you, it's because she doesn't think it's any of your business. If she does, it's because she feels she's a free agent. Nothing matters quite so much to the single Gemini lady as her precious freedom to do and think as she pleases.

Now marriage, that's different. If you fail to live up to courting-day promises and become a boring old stick-in-the-mud, she's likely to leave you. But otherwise, she's an intelligent woman and therefore realizes there's a great deal of give and take in living together. She wouldn't have married you unless she thought you were the kind of guy she'd be happy with. But if it doesn't work out, she won't meekly carry on.

She'll probably want to continue with her career, at least until the kids start coming along. This could be good for your relationship because the odds are against married life providing enough interest to keep a Gemini woman occupied with household chores.

She's a very efficient person when she wants to be and has no trouble keeping the house spick and span and the home fires burning as well as going out to work.

If you're a professional man, a doctor or a lawyer, for example, and can use her in the business, especially for social contacts, you'll really have it made. The same elusive charm that seduced you from bachelorhood will now be working *for* you.

GEMINI WOMAN—ARIES MAN

When you first become acquainted with Mr. Aries, you will be impressed by his apparent confidence and self-reliance. You will feel he's the sort of guy who could overcome almost any obstacle placed in his path. Like you, he has an inquiring mind and is very interested in other people. He can be a bit domineering, though. He feels he was born to rule, and if you decide to go steady with him, you'll have to battle to get him to tone down his bossy ways.

He may be too butch and masculine for you. In many ways, he's a man's man who prefers the company of his own sex. He thinks a woman is someone who should spend a lot of time in the home. This attitude to the fairer sex might not appeal to you with your freedom-loving ways.

Chances are you'll get a bit bored with his huntin', shootin' and fishin' chat. Aries males are known to be great sports lovers. You'd better cultivate an interest in his baseball team or tennis club if you wish to share in his outings.

Males born under the first Sign of the Zodiac can blow hot and cold. One minute, he'll be wooing you like a passionate Latin lover; the next, he could seem like an Eskimo lost in the far reaches of the North Pole.

You both have pretty quick tempers and that's something you're going to have to learn to control if this liaison is to last. He's the kind of guy who really needs a woman and his little-boy charm will bring out your maternal instinct.

Both of you can be very impulsive and a few words of warning here would be opportune. You might be smitten by love at first sight and feel you've met the only person you could share your life with—but give yourself more time, get to know each other really well, make sure you've got more in common than a transitory passion. As adaptable as you are, this man who feels he's the only person competent to make the big decisions could be too much of a trial.

Home life is very important to him. He loves to spend peaceful evenings in front of the fire. So long as you can keep on with your career after marriage, all should be well. You'll need an outside interest to give you a balanced life. Let's hope you have an exciting and interesting job to provide activity apart from running the home and warming your Ram's slippers.

He's a bit of a flirt but you should take his games playing with a pinch of salt. He enjoys having his ego boosted and likes to give his pals the impression he could make it with any woman if he really tried.

He'll never tire of you because you'll be something of a puzzle to him. He'll never quite work out what is going on in that pretty little head of yours.

As a rule, the Aries man is an excellent provider and homemaker.

You are not the greatest at handling money. You can also be a bit impulsive and self-indulgent when it comes to shopping. Mr. Aries will be fair and give you a generous allowance.

Don't try to make him jealous by flirting because he is not the sort of person you should play games with. He doesn't like people to torment him. He can be extremely possessive and jealous when aroused.

Aries men make wonderful fathers because they have a great sense of responsibility.

Very often the Aries man will take on more than one job. He doesn't like to feel he's trapped in routine forever. Encourage him to be independent but try very tactfully to put the brake on his impulsiveness at the same time.

GEMINI WOMAN—TAURUS MAN

You'll find the Taurus man easy to get along with so long as you don't try to tell him what to do. He hates being dictated to. If you have a talk with his mother, she'll no doubt tell you about the time he threw the baby food at her when he was in his high chair because she tried to force an extra spoonful down him.

In speed of thought, you'll feel he's a million light-years behind you. He is very solid and dependable, though, and—let's face it—you do need a bit of looking after.

You are both terrible flirts. It would seem wise not to marry a Taurus man before you've both had quite a lot of experience with the opposite sex. You both have very inquiring minds and it would be advisable to quench your thirst for knowledge before you walk down the aisle.

Both of you delight in meeting others, going to parties and being out with groups. But when Mr. Taurus gets hitched, he becomes a home lover. You may have trouble playing the housewife and entertaining all his friends. It's very difficult for any woman to keep up her own interests with this guy. He'll want you to become part of his life, but it's extremely unlikely he'll go overboard for your friends.

Can you play the role he casts you in? Well, if you love him enough, you can. But you'll have to be really crazy about him, hero-worship him, if you're going to change your ways enough for this union to work out satisfactorily. He's a very sexy guy. You may feel his appetite is almost insatiable. You'll have to be quite a lover yourself to keep him from going after other girls.

You both have a great sense of humor and this will help to overcome many of your differences. Neither of you likes a bad atmosphere in the home and you're both big enough to admit it when you're in the wrong.

You'll have to change your ways about the house. He's very particular about cleanliness and tidyness. You aren't all that keen on housekeeping, so let's hope you're rich enough to have these chores taken care of. You'd better enjoy cooking (a lot of Gemini women do) because

Taurus men are very fussy about food and he's unlikely to be happy with hamburgers and french fries for Sunday dinner.

Mr. Taurus is in many ways an old-fashioned type of person. He usually believes in the traditional standards and values. If you're unfaithful to him after marriage, he'll never completely believe in you again. On his side, if he does marry you, he'll try to change his wandering ways and settle down to being good and faithful.

He's a good businessman and as a rule has an excellent head for figures. He'll prove to be a great provider and will always expect you to look your best. Your appearance will be something of a reflection on him, he'll feel, so never let him down in front of his friends or colleagues.

He will plan for tomorrow very carefully. Everything in the house will be insured. He'll make sure you are taken care of if something happens to him.

Although he's not an extravagant person, Mr. T. does do some things on a lavish scale. Your vacation will usually be spent in luxurious surroundings and you'll get many second honeymoons with this man.

In a lot of ways, you'll be very good for him. He needs an honest critic, and you'll be quick to tell him when you feel he's on the wrong track. Your intuition about people and situations will be invaluable because he doesn't possess a great deal of that quality himself.

Stand up for your rights. Be sure he takes you out once in a while. Occasionally he'll need reminding you're not exactly like him and that change is important to you.

With children, you should make an excellent duo. Mr. Taurus will make sure they never step out of line and you'll give them all the love and devotion growing youngsters need.

GEMINI WOMAN—GEMINI MAN

On a platonic level, you and Mr. Gemini will hit it off like a house afire. Chances are you'll be in agreement on most matters, whether it's religion, sexual equality or solving the world's problems. Living together as man and wife needs a little more consideration. One Gemini in the house can be enough. Your restless ways are catching and may throw more settled people off balance. How, then, can you cope with someone who likes to ring the changes as much as you do? You two might end up buying a caravan and moving gypsylike from place to place.

You'll need to be the motherly type because a Gemini man needs a strong woman to give him a push. Like you, he has a quick mind and a talent for invention. But as you well know, these qualities have to be channeled in the right direction. Since you both hate arguments and will do all in your power not to rock the boat, you may grow apart without ever discussing your problems. Besides intensely disliking scenes, neither of you can stand to be told when you are wrong.

Going out with Gemini for the first time may seem an odd experience because he'll usually know what's going through your mind and vice versa. And when he calls you to cancel a date at the last minute, you won't be surprised because you were probably just about to call him to do the same thing. If you meet at a party, you'll probably spend the whole evening in his company. It's likely he'll be the most interesting and stimulating person present.

You should get along famously with each other's friends. You are both excellent mixers and enjoy meeting people from varied walks of life. One problem may be, who will look after the savings, because, let's face it, neither of you is the greatest at keeping pennies in the piggy bank. For a while, you can both be very careful, live on crusts of bread and scrimp and save; then the day comes when, bored with the frugal life, you blow your roll on some totally useless article.

You both like to be independent and it's possible you'll wish to keep on working after you marry. Beware of allowing your different interests to cause you to grow apart. You are both quite happy as loners and may discover you're not seeing as much of each other as perhaps a married couple should.

You are both outrageous flirts. This is another area where you'll have to be very strong-willed. Of course, you can't deny your natural instinct for playing games with the opposite sex. You'd both just better be determined it's not going to go any further than that.

You'll laugh in the face of adversity together. You can both take the knocks and get up and carry on fighting whatever the odds. Your home life will be very happy. Although your Gemini man likes going out as much as you do, he's very handy around the house and he'll be willing to take on his fair share of the chores.

The house will rarely be empty at nights. Your Gemini male is a bit of a night bird and it's odds on you sparkle after midnight, too.

You're both very artistic and enjoy going to the movies and the theater. Music is apt to play an important part in your relationship. When you've got the cash, you're more likely to buy a stereo than something practical like a washing machine—but there you are, that's Gemini.

You're likely to bring up the children with a sense of personal responsibility and freedom. Neither of you likes being dictated to so it's highly improbable that you will lay down the law with your offspring.

GEMINI WOMAN—CANCER MAN

Mr. Cancer could be a bit too sensitive for the likes of a Gemini gal. Go easy on the jokes, especially if they're at his expense. You may be a bit too fun-loving and outward-going for him. He can be very moody and subject to fits of depression. You'll just have to get used to his lunar moods if you're going to make a permanent relationship work.

As a rule, he's a pretty good businessman with a fine head for figures. He is very hard-working and success is important to him. He's a real tryer and rarely takes on a job he doesn't feel he can see through to its conclusion.

He is a home lover and likes his comforts. You, on the other hand, are a lass who enjoys going out to different places and meeting different people. You may not be too happy about the number of evenings you find yourself sitting on the other side of the fire gazing at your Cancer man sitting oh-so-happy in his rocking chair. You are intrigued by the new and modern—the latest fashions—while he prefers antiques and loves discussing the past. You'll often hear him say how much better life must have been a couple of centuries ago.

You'll have to live for Mr. Cancer. He won't be too happy about your pursuing your own interests; he's bound to take it personally and feel you don't really love him.

Just because he's careful with money, don't think he's a miser. Security is terribly important to this man and he likes to be sure he can always pay as he goes. For advice on how to invest money, ask a Cancer man. He'll know which shares to buy and which to avoid.

Though he is rather quiet and introverted, you mustn't make the mistake of imagining he doesn't know exactly what's going on. He's not the kind of guy who enjoys a flaming fight. If he feels insulted or slighted, he'll crawl into his shell and scuttle away to lick his wounds. He can be a bit of a loner and tends to work out his emotional problems in solitude instead of seeking the counsel of friends and family.

Mr. Cancer will make sure you never lack for the essentials and will always buy you beautiful birthday and Christmas presents. But you won't be able to get away with extravagant shopping sprees. He'll be quite disgruntled if you waste his hard-earned cash on what he considers unnecessary luxury items.

Being a water Sign, he is usually fascinated by the sea. His idea of a dream vacation is likely to be a slow cruise on a banana boat to the West Indies. In fact, he doesn't like to do *anything* in a hurry. Before he makes an important decision, he thinks about it from every possible angle. This could be a bit frustrating for an impetuous woman like you.

It will help if you get on well with his mother. Cancer people are usually very close to their family. He won't exactly compare you to Mom, but you'll have to accept the fact that her name will pop up in conversation quite a bit. This man often marries late in life—the maternal nest was so cozy he wasn't in a hurry to spread his wings.

You'll have a lot of fun together, though. He's artistic and you'll also find, much to your surprise, that he's a magnificent chef. When he casually asks you to drop over to his apartment for a snack, you'll be amazed at the spread he has put out and his fine culinary touch. This man does not believe in half-measures; when he does something, he does it well.

He will make a terrific father. The responsibilities of parenthood are very serious obligations to him. He'll spend his last buck giving his children the best education he can afford.

If you are tactful and patient, you'll find Mr. Cancer is happy to meet you halfway. If you really love him and are prepared to pamper him, it won't be too long before you find yourself taking the place of Mother.

GEMINI WOMAN—LEO MAN

Mr. Leo is a strong-willed character, a born leader, in fact. He's a very proud person, but then, he is the King of the Jungle. Your close friends will shake their heads when you tell them you're going steady with a Leo man. They'll tell you he's far too bossy and domineering for you.

Without love, he will pine away. He needs a lot of pampering. Although he is a very capable person, his ego must constantly be boosted. But he will have many qualities you admire, and being an intelligent person, you won't mind giving his confidence a shot in the arm whenever you deem it necessary.

You'll have to play second fiddle to him. He puts his woman on a pedestal, but he'll shout her down if she voices opinions in company that don't coincide with his own.

When you first go out together, you will notice how gallant he is. He will take you to the best restaurants and get good seats at the theater. His manners will be impeccable. You will feel like a real lady. He likes his women to be feminine. You'd better forget all about individual freedom and living your own life if you settle down with him for keeps. Don't tease him or make him jealous. He can't bear to lose face in front of others.

You will be a bit of a mystery to him. For all his intellect, you'll usually be one jump ahead of him in speed of thought. He is extremely possessive and will want you to belong to him body and soul. When you go out alone, he will want a blow-by-blow description of where you've been, whom you met and what you talked about.

Mr. Leo is very handy around the house. He won't want you to do any of the heavy work. And you'll have little cause to worry about the future because he's a good provider. He can be a bit of a worrier, though. You'll have to soothe him on occasions. He'll get very upset if his work is criticized by his boss because he always does his best and it hurts him if people are not satisfied with the results.

You won't have to worry too much about his fidelity after marriage because he's not a womanizer. This is not to say he won't be tempted to have an occasional affair—but usually only when the woman makes the advances. So keep your eye on your female friends.

You'll lead a fairly active social life with your Leo man. He'll want you at his side at office parties and when he is entertaining an important business associate. He'll take great pride in bringing colleagues home to meet you.

Leo men are not too happy about staying up late. They worry if they don't get their eight hours in bed. (But after all, you will be there, too, won't you?)

You are a romantic person and your Leo man will do all he can to keep the romance in your marriage. You'll find that for all his shouting and masculinity, he's a gentle and considerate lover. He's very amorous and will expect similar attention from you.

Occasionally he can get lethargic. Then you have to flatter him and tell him what a waste of a great talent it is for a genius like him to be slouching around doing nothing. This guy will certainly be a challenge and, as you well know, there's nothing a Mercurial woman likes more than that.

He is unlikely to want a large family and you should be in agreement there. He will love his children but you mustn't give him the feeling he has been relegated to second place when a baby comes along.

His secret fear is failing at anything; you'll be happy together as long as he doesn't feel he has failed to hold your love.

GEMINI WOMAN—VIRGO MAN

To be frank, it's hard to believe you could find long-term happiness with a Virgo male. He is too fussy for a romantically oriented woman like you. Mr. Virgo has his feet firmly planted on the ground. He lacks your imagination and quicksilver mind.

He'll find you a bit too easygoing, perhaps. He likes to have things laid straight on the line. He's a cool, calm and collected sort of person, and would find it very difficult to adapt to your style of living. When you first begin to go out together, you will be impressed by his calm and Old World manners. He'll usually be dressed impeccably and will smell terrific. Mother is likely to say, "Now, why didn't you bring a nice polite boy like this home before?"

After two or three dates, however, you may find yourself getting a bit restless. Heavy romancing is not for him. He may, in fact, find your passion too much to handle. He's a difficult man to stir emotionally. Perhaps he's afraid of being rebuffed. He couldn't stand to be turned down or to be made to feel he isn't desired.

There are many good qualities in the Virgo character and they shouldn't be ignored: he is as straight as an arrow, he will always treat you with respect and courtesy and his cool ways are strangely attractive.

He will make a faithful husband. Not for him the odd fling. Once he's walked down the aisle, he'll take his vows seriously. He'll want his marriage to be for keeps.

He does not like public displays and will be rather embarrassed if you take his hand or give him a big goodnight kiss under the lamp post. He's terribly sensitive and sometimes you may get the feeling he's acting in order to secure sympathy. He won't be prepared to go along with any of your crazy schemes. He likes to deal in facts. You may be disappointed at the way he shoots down some of your ideas for making extra money. He'll be difficult to impress. If you work in an artistic field, you had better earn a lot of money because he believes financial reward is the proof of talent.

Mr. Virgo will *try* to understand you but will probably not succeed. You'll find his analytical approach rather destructive. He'll be able to defeat you with words and more words, as any logical person usually can.

He remembers all those important dates like wedding anniversaries and birthdays, and he's quite a home lover. He won't mind your pursuing a career after marriage so long as he knows he comes before anything else in your book. He's very strong on self-discipline and does not easily forgive those who are not.

If your heart is set on catching a Virgo man, you'll need to tidy yourself up a bit and change some of your sloppy ways. He won't mind doing his fair share of the household chores, but he'll get pretty exasperated tidying up after you all the time. He's quite domesticated and will be just as capable of cooking Sunday dinner as you are.

As a rule, the Virgo man has no great desire to be a father. He doesn't get the emotional fulfillment most men derive from parenthood. He makes a terrific uncle or godfather and really loves kids—other people's.

You will be expected to fuss over him when he has a chill. A Virgo man likes to be waited on if he is feeling out of sorts.

Now that you have some idea of what you are in for, go ahead and tie the knot. So long as you can come to terms with his ways, you'll have a happy marriage.

Many women would find Mr. Virgo the man of their dreams—neat around the house, a good provider and happy to share the daily chores.

GEMINI WOMAN—LIBRA MAN

You should have much in common with Mr. Libra. From the first meeting, you are likely to get on extremely well with this man who shares your zodiacal element (air).

His charm and extraordinary powers of reason will impress you. On top of these qualities, he usually has a zany humor and will share your sense of fun in life. He's so sweet and gentle you'll be prepared to turn a blind eye to the inconsistencies in his character.

He has a way with impulsive and intelligent women and will readily accept your changes of mood as if they were perfectly normal. You'll love him for knowing exactly when to take you seriously. He'll understand you because he, too, is given to fits of impulsiveness. Making up his mind to a definite course of action is as difficult for him as it often is for you. He can always see the other point of view, and this often makes it hard for him to retain strong convictions.

Mr. Libra is the sort of man you will want to impress. You'll love looking your best for him because he will notice when you are wearing a new dress and will pay you the sort of compliment that gives you a warm glow—especially since you will know he does not indulge in idle flattery. You'll find you have the same tastes in art. He can be something of a dreamer. He is also romantic and will know how to woo you. He has a gift for words and will be forever whispering sweet nothings in your ear.

Mr. L. is not a promiscuous type. He is rather choosy about whom he gives himself to. You'll find that other women will be envious when he asks you for a date. Sometimes you may have to do some of the chasing. He can be rather vague and in the early days of courtship could suddenly disappear every now and again. He hates to hurt people's feelings and you may discover he still has one or two old girlfriends hanging around. Once involved with a Libra man, most women don't like to let him go.

He's a peace-loving person. The sight of blood makes him wince. Very often you'll find he earns his living by using his artistic talents. Libra people, although gentle and sensitive, are often leaders and teachers.

He won't try to solve your riddle; he would never dream of prying into that part of you you wish to keep secret. Occasionally, you may feel he doesn't care enough. He sometimes seems to be unaware of another's need to be understood. He will respect your desire for freedom and will not try to tie you down.

The problem in marrying this man is that you could easily slip into the habit of pursuing different interests and leading separate lives. Mr. Libra abhors jealousy. He hates to feel he is being hemmed in or smothered. Don't question him too closely if he's late coming home from work. He will tell you where he's been if he wants to. He hates shows of temper or big scenes, and will think you're being adolescent if you stamp your foot and demand to know where he's been.

He won't like it if you fill your home with lots of people. He wants the place where he lives to be quiet and peaceful, somewhere he can escape to from the trials and tribulations of the outside world. He dislikes confusion and must have order in his life. You'll be the one to answer the telephone—and very often you'll have to say he's out if business people call. He doesn't like crowds, either. If you still want to be a party girl after marriage, it's unlikely you'll be able to drag along your Libra husband as escort.

He will make an extremely fair and understanding father. If his children act out of line, he'll always try to talk reasonably to them before resorting to harsher means of discipline.

You are an extremely loyal person; he is wonderfully patient. Together, you should make a fine pair.

GEMINI WOMAN—SCORPIO MAN

Though you will be very drawn to each other, this could be a dangerous and destructive union because you are likely to bring out the negative side in each other's nature. Sexually, you'll be immediately attracted to a Scorpio man and he attracted to you.

When Scorpio stings, it can be fatal. You may find yourself swept away by the hypnotic effect he can have on women. It is very easy for a girl to lose control of herself when this man's around. He is terribly jealous and possessive. He may strike you as being a bit of a brute, but you'll find it difficult to say no to him. He won't have much use for your escapism or dreaming. He will always be bringing you down to earth with a bump. You'll be constantly arguing with yourself whether he is good or bad for you. He hates being tied down to home life, and so do you to a certain extent. He does like his comforts, though, and in marriage he may desire a woman who is prepared to stay in the background and look after him.

Mr. Scorpio is the sort of person who wishes to make his way in the world. He's got a very ambitious streak and can't stand for anyone getting the best of him in business. He can also be a bit mean with money—you'll have to struggle with him about spending. He's secretive about his cash; it's unlikely you'll know how much money he has in the bank.

This man is very virile. No matter what sort of a day he's had at work, he will usually have plenty of energy left over for lovemaking. He can be aggressive in bed, too; you'd better be the sort of woman who likes to be dominated.

He will make you face up to yourself. He won't allow you to stay up there on cloud nine. You may find his ego too much to take. He can become very depressed at times. When a Scorpio man is in this mood, keep out of the way; there is little you can do to shake him out of the doldrums. Don't ever laugh at him. He has no sense of humor about himself. He does love flattery, though. Most men born where Pluto rules have strong physiques. He will be able to take care of himself in a fight. If anyone tries to flirt with his woman, he'll most likely throw a left hook at him and ask questions after.

Scorpio people like to be leaders and very often surround themselves with camp followers. They don't have many close buddies because essentially they are loners.

Mr. S. is unlikely to share your views on politics. Whereas you are able to see the other person's point of view, he has very fixed ideas and always appears to know exactly where he is going. He does not entertain opinions that differ from his own. If you are really under his love spell, this liaison can work. You'll have to turn a deaf ear when he expounds views you don't happen to agree with.

He is very interested in religious matters and in questions concerning life and death—so preoccupied with this subject, in fact, that many people find him rather morbid. Prepare yourself for lots of ups and downs. Certainly you'll not live a quiet life with Scorpio.

He's not much of a dresser. You'll have to look after his wardrobe and make sure there's a clean shirt and pressed suit ready for important business meetings. It would be very unlikely to find a Scorpio man on the list of the world's best dressers.

Frequently Scorpio has a great affection for animals. Not always able to communicate with people, he may be very close to a dog or some other household pet. He is often quite interested in sports and usually one of his hobbies will keep him out of doors. You are likely to share the same taste in books and television programs, but it's doubtful whether you will find that you enjoy the same type of music.

He's a great family man and loves his children passionately. He can be rather too strict, though, and is a bit Victorian in the way he disciplines youngsters. You'll have to balance his approach with plenty of love and affection.

If you can take the rough with the smooth, you could survive together. One thing is certain, you won't have much time for your own interests. It's unlikely you'll be able to continue with your career if you marry this man.

GEMINI WOMAN— SAGITTARIUS MAN

Mr. Sagittarius is a difficult man to pin down. He likes company and you'll usually find him surrounded with buddies. He talks big and delights in being the life and soul of the party, but he's really a bit of a baby at heart. He's unsure about marriage. He prizes his freedom and is afraid of getting involved in a relationship that would curtail it.

You could be the right sort of woman for this man. You are unlikely to give him the feeling he is being pressured into anything. Whether you have a whirlwind affair with the Archer or decide it's got to be forevermore, you'll find the time you spend with him most enjoyable. He may appear to be rushing hither and thither to no real avail, but behind all his tomfoolery is a man who knows the score and one who can sum people up pretty rapidly.

You both like gadding about, but it's unlikely you'll enjoy the same sort of evenings out. He is a raucous type, while you prefer to get involved in long discussions with friends. The sort of company he chooses may be entirely too masculine for you.

If you get to know him well, you'll discover he's more practical than crazy. He is definitely an optimist and always tries to look on the positive side of life. This could be very important to you as you tend to get down in the dumps from time to time. He is always prepared to help someone he believes in.

He can be absolutely outrageous in company because he will speak the truths others may resent. He doesn't care what people think of him; he'll always come out with what's on his mind. This is the reason he doesn't last five seconds with a lot of women. You, however, will admire and respect his frankness.

For all his gypsylike ways, he needs a home where he can feel safe and secure. If he does go off the rails, it's likely to be on a night with the boys. He may give his body to another woman but his heart will remain faithful to you. Before you met him, he probably had numerous affairs. Sagittarius men rarely get hitched without tasting the fruits of life. Your marriage is unlikely to be a spur-of-the-moment idea.

Mr. S. is great fun to be with. You may get jealous at parties because lots of people will want to monopolize him. He's not too keen on staying in nights. He's very restless by nature and likes action. Although you're a late-night person yourself, you could be the one who's yawning when he's still holding the floor and dawn is breaking over the hills. It will be extremely difficult to drag him away when he's having a good time.

His fire could warm that rather cool breeze that often blows around a Gemini person. He will want your total love. His confidence needs a lot of boosting. In his private moments, you will see how insecure he feels. Don't nag or cross-examine him too closely. Personal freedom is a necessity of life where he's concerned.

He will spoil you like mad. He's a bit careless with money but will make certain there's enough put aside to meet next month's bills. You'll never want for new clothes. Anything you ask for, he'll try to provide. He loves to visit distant lands. You'll usually end up in a different place each year for your vacation.

Erotically you should click. Your lovemaking will be a mixture of physicality and fantasy. He'll make your vivid imagination sparkle.

It would be foolish to become involved with other men after marriage to this fellow. He is unlikely to become violent if you are unfaithful to him, but he will be terribly hurt.

He is not particularly good with babies. You won't find him showing a great deal of interest in his children until they are old enough to communicate with him.

GEMINI WOMAN— CAPRICORN MAN

Don't be fooled by his shyness and sensitive manner, for under the surface, your Capricorn man is a tough cookie. He is extremely gentle and his manners are usually perfect, but when the chips are down, he can be hard and ruthless.

He may be a little too introverted for you. You may get the feeling a part of him is always hidden away from other people. You are a free-thinking person who tends to show her emotions whenever strong feelings well up. This guy rarely loses his cool. When he does show his temper, it's likely to come in sudden bursts. Then he can make the most cutting and hurtful remarks.

Under all this front, the Capricorn man secretly yearns to be admired and desired. He is terrified of rejection and is an incurable romantic at heart. Any close involvement, he fears, will not live up to his dreams.

Work is terribly important to him. Capricorn people usually hold down responsible jobs. They are thorough and workmanlike and can be depended on in an emergency. Mr. Capricorn does tend to be a bit of a worrier. You'll be able to help him in his career by pointing out with love and tact that many of his anxieties are quite unconnected with reality.

He may be too slow moving for you. A long relationship with the old mountain Goat could be a drag for an all-action woman like you. His plodding ways, and his conviction that you should play second fiddle to his work, will get on your nerves after a while. As he grows older, though, he will mellow. A liaison between Gemini and Capricorn would probably work best when he has overcome his adolescent ways. This change often only takes place after he has reached his mid-thirties.

He is extremely tidy about the home. The motto "A place for everything and everything in its place" might well have been written by him.

Most men when they reach fifty appear to be on the dowhill path, but this man will just be coming into his own. He believes in the old values. Basically, he is a conservative who doesn't like change. He loves talking about the past and the good old days. Family life means a great deal to him. He will usually go home for Christmas if possible to see Mom and Dad, no matter how far the journey, and even if he's only got one day off.

At a gathering or party, you may not even notice him because he's far from flamboyant. You can bet your bottom dollar, however, that he's been chatting with someone influential who can do his career a bit of good.

You will have to be a pretty good cook and housekeeper. He'll also want you to keep up a public image that is flattering to him. He's unlikely to get along very well with your set of friends, although he'll always show kindness and friendship to your family. He'll be extremely possessive about you which you may find irritating.

He won't agree with your attitude about money because he's so hung up on security and responsibility. Everything in his home, from the grand piano to the fish bowl that stands on it, is probably covered by an insurance policy. You'll be given a reasonable allowance but he'll frown on any extravagance.

He budgets carefully. He'll work out your vacation money down to the last cheese straw.

Mr. Capricorn becomes nervous in the company of the opposite sex. Once married, he's likely to feel far too guilty to have an affair.

He's not the sexiest of guys. Lovemaking could well be reserved for weekends only.

He can be a bit cold with children. You'll probably have to provide most of the affection.

GEMINI WOMAN—AQUARIUS MAN

If you've decided marriage is far too dull for you and that you're going to spend the rest of your days *not* settling down to routine, wait until you've gotten involved with an Aquarius man. He could be everything you want. You will never be tied down. Life will be full of surprises. You are both pretty scatterbrained, but will muddle through, much to the amazement of your friends.

He is an extremely open guy and you can learn a great deal from him. It could be that you'll know him quite a while before getting involved romantically. Perhaps you'll be good friends for years before you discover there's more to it than friendship.

You'll feel very much on his wavelength. He'll never challenge your actions. He's a dreamer and a wanderer himself. He loves people and usually has lots of friends. He doesn't like to be alone for very long. He feels much happier in crowds. He desperately needs something or someone to believe in. You'll often find that the guy leading a protest march is Aquarius. People born under the Sign of the Water Bearer are very keen to put the world to rights.

He's a bit of an eccentric so you'll never know what to expect next. He doesn't harbor grudges and he can't stand being enemies for long. Romance comes first with him, long before he thinks about the physical side. He's a bit more analytical than you and has a great thirst for knowledge. He's prepared to ask questions other people would never dream of posing, so keen is he to get at the truth.

He lives in the future more than the present. He is not a realist. You'll have to be the sobering and steadying influence in the partnership—an unusual role for you to be cast in. He's not a traditionalist. He'll tell you democracy has failed, though when you question him further, you'll discover he hasn't quite worked out what to put in its place.

You probably won't be able to discover a great deal about his background. Old family ties are not all that important to him, and he doesn't like any involvement that holds him too strongly to the past. He is quite content mixing with people from all walks of life. He feels equally at ease drinking cocktails with the beautiful people and listening to the problems of those who live in the ghetto.

You'll delight in the way he chops and changes. He doesn't like to make precise appointments. Rather than say, "I'll be over tomorrow at three-thirty," he'll be much happier to part company with the words, "See you around."

His attitude to life is very much live and let live. He won't tell you how to think and he'll expect the same consideration from you. He's no coward but he doesn't like violence. He will do all he can to avoid angry scenes and confrontations.

Aquarius people feel the cold and it's easy for them to become ill in winter. Very often their circulation gives them problems.

He is rather useless around the house so you will have to take care of most of the chores. If you send him out to do the shopping, make sure you write everything down. He's very straightforward about money and he won't tolerate lying or cheating. He doesn't like to run up big accounts and won't be first in line to get a credit card. He much prefers to pay his way.

Mr. Aquarius won't mind your being a bit extravagant. In some ways, he will admire your attitude about money. He'll be quite pleased to see you furnishing the house beautifully, though he would never dream of spending money on that sort of thing himself.

You may have an odd difference of opinion but it's never likely to be serious. In fact, you'll find your arguments will stimulate the union.

GEMINI WOMAN—PISCES MAN

After one or two meetings with Mr. Pisces, you may think you've got his number—but the fact is, he's far more likely to have yours. There are hidden depths here and you should never underestimate him. He may appear to be a bit of a dreamer—and on one level he is—but he rarely misses the subtleties of what is going on.

He may seem a little sluggish and slow-thinking for you. It's true he's easygoing most of the time, but the speed with which he can swing into action when it's necessary will amaze you. When he decides to go into business, he is unlikely to fail. One of his problems, however, is that it may take him a long time to decide what he wants to do with his life. He needs a woman who is a bit pushy.

He's a kindly man and will always bend over backward to assist anyone who is in trouble. People will often pour out their troubles to him and bask in his understanding.

He's very romantic. You'll love it when you are alone together because he'll make you feel you are the only woman on earth. Still, remember you can't live on love alone. It would be well if you have an income of your own. Certainly, you will want to think very carefully before leaving your job to marry this man. He can't stand the idea of working for the sake of work. You'll rarely find him in a nine-to-five job where he has no power to make important decisions or use his imagination.

He doesn't possess a lot of aggression; but you do. He won't be able to take it if you try to order him about. You'll have to be careful how you suggest he needs a bit more drive.

You won't be expected to be the greatest cook and housewife in the world, but he does need a place that is comfortable and secure. He has to feel he can get away from all the trials and tribulations of the big bad world. Give him lots of affection. He needs looking after.

Mr. Pisces is not a critical person. He's very fair-minded. People born under this Sign are rarely prejudiced by the color of people's skins or the politics or religion they subscribe to. They prefer to take individuals as they find them. He can be secretive. His past may well be a closed book. He doesn't like discussing private old times. Often as not, he sees little of his family. Be careful of hurting his feelings. The Fish is high-strung and would be terribly wounded if you were unfaithful to him.

He's not much of a handyman. Let's hope you are good at fixing things yourself or can afford to get someone in when things go wrong. If not, you are likely to sit in a pool of water together and say, "Isn't it a shame the roof's leaking?"

But you'll make an interesting couple—or perhaps we should say foursome. You are both capable of projecting different personalities at different times.

He could easily get involved in all sorts of different religions. He may dabble in the occult or explore Oriental philosophies. You'd better take an interest in whatever he does because otherwise he'll bore you to death.

When he gets really down in the dumps, it will fall on you to lift him up. He loves treats and surprises. Do a quick change and whisk him off to the theater and dinner and he'll soon become his normal self again. He's not too good at handling money. It's not that he's as extravagant as you are, but he's capable of making bad investments. Let's hope you're the type of Mercury lady who has a good business head on her pretty shoulders.

Mr. Pisces is great with kids. Youngsters love him and he enjoys romping around the playroom and acting like a child himself.

Never shatter his dreams. Always tell him he's going to make it. Chances are he'll surprise a lot of people and do just that—in a most unconventional way, what's more.

GEMINI MAN—ARIES WOMAN

Miss Aries is quite a gal. You should hit it off very well together from the start because you have a lot in common. Both of you find it difficult to settle into a permanent relationship. Like you, she's perfectly capable of being deeply involved with two people at the same time—at least, you both talk yourselves into believing you are deeply involved if it fits in with your plans. You'll find it very easy to confide in this woman. It's often possible to have a relationship with her that neither of you wishes to be permanent.

A high-key involvement, on the other hand, could present problems. You may find yourself caught up in something of a power battle. She had a fiery temper and you like to avoid head-on collisions if at all possible.

You'll admire many qualities in the Ram that you don't possess yourself. She's a little fighter and will do her best to get to the top of her profession. Her attitude to her work could inspire you to push a bit harder to achieve success. You have a tendency to lose interest and to drop a new hobby as quickly as you picked it up. Your mind is inclined to wander and you abhor the idea of working for the sake of just earning money.

She's a woman who can stand on her own two feet. She will never put pressure on you. Miss Aries will stand alone rather than ask for help. But once she knows what she wants in life, she usually gets it. It may take a long time, but she refuses to take no for an answer. She likes a good time and will enjoy your company and your quick sense of humor.

Loving freedom so much yourself, you'd never dream of putting curbs on your Aries lover. You'd be foolish to try, anyway. Don't forget her ruling planet is Mars and her element is fire. If you decide to get married, it would be a good idea to support her desire to continue with her career. An Aries woman doesn't particularly enjoy living in the reflected glory of her man for very long, however much she loves and admires him. It will be very good for the relationship if she has some outside interest.

Although you are never backward in coming forward where the opposite sex is concerned, you might find Miss Aries has fixed up the first date and asked you around to supper or to meet some friends of hers for a drink. Being quite intuitive, you'll realize early on that she hates being pressured and you will probably enjoy letting her take the lead. Be sure she really wants it before you give her that first good-night kiss or nod in the direction of the bedroom, because she's perfectly capable of slapping your face or showing you the door if she feels you are taking liberties.

Miss A. is one of the few women who have the pep and drive to keep up with you. It's advisable for you to try to get the upper hand in this relationship. You can be insensitive to the feelings of those who care for you and trample all over them if they give you half a chance. But you won't dominate this woman and shouldn't try.

Chances are you'll turn out to be handier about the home than she is. You could be the one who does the cooking and the shopping.

As lovers, you should be very well suited. Your Aries woman has a lively sexual imagination. She'll realize early on that you are quickly bored with routine, whether it's in the office or in bed. She'll know how to ring the changes and you could find her aggressiveness in lovemaking very exciting.

If you decide to marry, you'll both have to give up a little bit of that freedom you treasure so much. The match won't last very long if you're selfish and keep to your old bachelor habits.

She'll make a good mother to your children. Where you have a tendency to give way to the demands of youngsters, she'll make sure they get the discipline young minds need.

GEMINI MAN—TAURUS WOMAN

The Taurus woman is quite a handful and may be a bit too much for you. She's a no-nonsense type. Her feet are firmly planted on the ground. Whereas you are a bit of a dreamer, Miss Taurus faces up to reality. But you've heard about opposites being attracted, and it's possible you two could hit it off. However, you'd both have to make certain sacrifices.

Undoubtedly there is a great deal you could learn from each other. She's a girl you will not win easily. People born under this Sign rarely do anything on the spur of the moment. Don't expect to sweep her off her feet. She may fall in love with you in five minutes flat, but she's unlikely to agree to any sort of permanent relationship until she gets to know you really well.

If you do manage to strike it lucky with this little lady, you'll not be disappointed. Taurus people hate to fail at anything they take on, whether it's work or marriage. Don't forget her ruling planet is Venus. This should be enough of an indication that she's all woman. She's very passionate and has no sexual hangups as a rule.

Miss T. can be a bit bossy and this is where your difficulties could start. Oh, how you hate being told what to do, even if it's for your own good. It's not that you shirk responsibility, it's simply that personal freedom is terribly important to you. You hate being tied down, and those itchy feet of yours might be too much for your Taurus companion, who needs a settled home life. You will certainly have to accept spending quite a few nights of the week at home.

Never try to force her to do something against her will. If you do, that missile whizzing past your head will probably be the fruit bowl mother gave you last Christmas. Once her temper is aroused, you'll know it. If she's really gone on you, however, she'll love looking after you and your home will be something to be proud of. It will be a pleasure to bring home friends and business associates. She's a terrific cook and her artistic touch will be recognizable in the dishes she serves.

It might be a good idea to let her help manage your financial affairs because she is extremely capable at sticking to a budget, whereas you can be a bit irresponsible about money. She will resolutely put enough cash aside to cover taxes and mortgage payments.

Miss Taurus will take your friends for what they are without quibbling. She finds it easy to accept people whose way of life is different from her own.

Woe betide you if you play around. Of all the Signs of the Zodiac, Taurus is the most jealous. Never give her cause to doubt your fidelity. She won't mind the odd flirtation and some games playing, but if you go beyond these bounds, she may well walk out on you.

You are both quite artistic. You'll find you have a love of nature and all things beautiful in common. She loves to surround herself with pretty objects. There will usually be a bowl of freshly picked flowers on the dining table. You are both pretty fond of animals, too, so it is probable you'll have a few pets around the house. She will readily accept the stray dog you bring home and make it one of the family.

Don't try to pry too deeply into what makes her tick and don't misunderstand her natural reserve. She likes her private moments and you'd be wise to accept this.

Miss Taurus won't push you to do things you don't want to do. So long as you're doing your best to get ahead, she'll be happy and willing to stand by you through thick and thin.

She makes a wonderful mother. You could be just the right combination to give children what they need most.

GEMINI MAN—GEMINI WOMAN

This relationship will put you in paradise—or be a total disaster. You'll get that strange feeling on being introduced for the first time that you've met before. Miss Gemini will certainly reflect a lot of what is going on in your head. She'll either show you a side of yourself you find flattering, or the shadow you've been trying to ignore. When you two are together, you'll never be at a loss for words. Someone sitting behind you on the bus will cheerfully observe that the art of conversation has not died when he hears you two rattling on.

In intellectual matters, you will have met your match. You'll find you share many of the same tastes, especially in politics and music. You both like to be contrary and enjoy a good debate; it could be a bit tiresome to have someone who agrees with your point of view so readily.

You both like to flit about and hate the idea of being hemmed in. So long as you enjoy wandering together, all will be well. If, however, you're determined to lead separate lives after you set up house together, you're soon going to grow apart. Romance with this woman born under the same Sign as you is likely to be passionate. You should have a pretty good idea of her sexual needs and desires. You are both imaginative so your bedroom scenes will never become a bore. She'll appreciate your aims and desires because she feels the same urges.

Very often the female of this species is a career woman. If you're looking for a girl who'll sit patiently at home knitting you a pair of socks while awaiting your return from the office, you're barking up the wrong tree.

Gemini men very often form platonic friendships with Gemini women. You have no difficulty getting along so long as there's no emotional element. People seeing you out with your Gemini girlfriend often believe you are brother and sister, if not twins, because of the mental affinity you appear to share.

You also share a great sense of humor. It's crucial if you plan to take up with your Mercurial friend to make sure the laughs keep coming. You can both get pretty depressed if you allow external pressures to get you down. It's important you try to lift each other out of the doldrums.

Money and financial planning could be something of a problem because neither of you is particularly adept at handling cash. Oh, you'll start out with the best intentions in the world and carefully put aside a portion of your salary to meet regular bills. Then your eye will light on a new gadget or something fashionable to dress up in and bang—there goes the rent!

You're both inclined to flirt and this could be dangerous. When one of you decides to play around, the other may also have an affair rather than try to heal the rift. You both find it easy to be irresponsible.

In domestic life, you'll have no difficulty sharing the chores. You may discover you are both happier doing the artistic jobs like cooking and picking the flowers as opposed to digging the garden or scrubbing the floors.

Your Gemini loves people as much as you so social life together should be great fun. When friends see you out, they may get the impression you never stop arguing and disagreeing. They may not understand you only do this in order to stir other people to join in the fun.

You'll both take a cab rather than a bus if your funds can cover it, and you'll spend your last few dollars on an expensive dinner rather then eke out a miserable existence on hamburgers and french fries. Let's hope you are both highly successful in your chosen careers so you can live the sort of life that most appeals to you. As parents, you'll probably allow junior plenty of freedom to develop his own personality.

GEMINI MAN—CANCER WOMAN

You like change and don't really feel happy if you know what's going to be around the corner. Well, dear Gemini buddy, Miss Cancer could drive even you round the bend. You'll never know where you stand with her. Water is her element—like the river, she is constantly flowing, like the sea, she has her highs and lows.

One minute, she'll be telling you you're the only man for her. The next, she'll be relating the story of the attractive guy who has just come to work in the office and how much she fancies him. Although by nature you're not a jealous person, if you get mixed up with this bundle of dynamite, you could be driven crazy.

Don't assume she's playing with your emotions. She's certainly not out to hurt your sensitive feelings, but in matters of love, people born under her Sign find it extremely difficult to make up their minds.

If you've been going steady and have to part company for a while, you'll have to be prepared for anything on your return. She is not the sort of woman who finds it easy to remain faithful when her man is not around.

You'll have to watch that sense of humor of yours, too, because your offbeat jokes may not go down very well. Cancer people are not good at laughing at themselves. Don't, whatever you do, ridicule her family or close friends because she'll take it personally. She can't stand being made fun of and she needs very gentle handling. But you must not get the idea that she likes a man to be putty in her hands. She is, in fact, a mass of contradictions.

Miss Cancer is yearning for someone to dominate her and yet fights every inch of the way if anyone tries to tell her what to do or how to run her life. If you're smitten with the love bug, you could find yourself acting totally out of character in thinking up ways to cope.

If you do manage to forge a worthwhile relationship, you'll never regret it. Once she's said those magic words, "I do," she's likely to be yours for life. She'll make a devoted wife and do everything she can to make your home comfortable. She's the sort of woman who would give up a promising career if it was affecting your success in any way. When it comes to the family funds, you may not be very compatible. She'll scold you for your extravagance because security is important to her. She is terrified of not being able to pay bills on time.

Although people born under the influence of the Moon are great home lovers, she'll be wise enough to realize it would be bad for your relationship if she tries to keep you home too much, so she will go out with you and keep in contact with mutual friends. It's this combination of the settled domestic life and the pleasant social one that could be just the balance needed to keep you contented.

You will have to cope with her moods. She needs a lot of help and understanding to get through those low patches. You are a sensitive man and ideally equipped to give her the comfort and understanding she requires.

July women prefer to save their deepest emotions for the people who are really important to them—mother, father, lover and children. She will not allow others to get very close in case they pierce the hard shell she's built up around her sensitive personality. It is important that you keep her from hiding in that shell, because once she buries herself inside, it will be extremely difficult to coax her out.

She's a wonderful mother. Some men would be jealous of the love and devotion she expends on her youngsters, but not you.

So long as you never stop trying to communicate and understand each other, your partnership will endure.

GEMINI MAN—LEO WOMAN

Leo women make wonderful marriage partners—once you've done battle to win them. Her number is one, her metal is gold, her element is fire and she's usually in big demand by members of the opposite sex. Leo people are no-nonsense types. Whatever they involve themselves in, whether it be career or love, they do wholeheartedly. You will always know where you stand with a Leo woman.

A born leader, Miss L. doesn't like to be told what to do. At school she was probably the leader of her gang and a bit of a tomboy to boot. If she joined the Brownies or Girl Scouts, she probably earned more badges than any girl in her group.

If you do marry, she will retain her independence. No matter how much she cares for you, she'll insist on keeping up with her own interests and friends.

Nature appears to have shown some favoritism here because Miss Leo is endowed with more than her fair share of fine qualities. Often she appears to have more drive, glamor and sex appeal than two or three other women put together. She has an inquiring mind and is very interested in other people.

Let us hope you are one of those positive types of the Gemini species because you won't be able to stand the pace if you have any sort of inferiority complex. If she does give herself to you, you'll feel on top of the world. Miss Leo never does anything without being pretty sure. If your intention is to win her, don't play hard to get. Lay your cards on the table and woo her full force.

Count yourself lucky if this Miss accepts your proposal of marriage. She'll be a wonderful confidence booster. Her attitude to life is so positive it will help you keep your feet on the ground. Your pals will love her and probably fancy her like mad. Don't get jealous if you see her holding hands with your best friend or putting her arm around his waist. Leo women are very affectionate and any friend of yours will probably become a friend of hers. You have no reason to get jealous at her outward physical displays.

You couldn't ask for a better wife from the business and career angle. Your boss will love her, and if you are entertaining influential people, she could help clinch the all-important deal for you.

Very often Leo wives carry on with some sort of work after marriage. It's highly unlikely this woman will be satisfied doing the menial household chores while you're out earning a living. Never try to suffocate her or deny her freedom of movement. She's unlikely to try to hold you down or stop you from going out when you wish. You will have to accept that she is to be treated as an equal.

She loves fur coats and pretty things and you'll have to earn good money to supply her with them. She's not extravagant but does like to keep up with fashion—which she often helps set. On the surface, she appears to be soft and gentle, but don't be fooled. If you step out of line, you'll be in the Lion's den.

Because of her inquiring mind, she's always keen to acquire knowledge. You may find it hard to keep up with a hobby for very long, but your feline partner doesn't. You'll still be walking around in a dream while she's on her way to her language class after taking her dancing lesson and before going on to study art!

Neither of you is particularly good at handling money. You won't find it easy to save.

She makes a good and practical mother. In fact, as a parent team, you are one of the best of all the possible permutations of the Zodiac.

Don't let her dominate you. And don't try to organize her life. Strike the right balance and you'll be very happy together.

GEMINI MAN—VIRGO WOMAN

Miss Virgo may be a little bit much for you to take. She's a very practical person and you could find it rather difficult getting a good vibration going between you. There is a strong wish for perfection here and a sound analytical way of thinking. You are a bit of a dreamer, and in this particular combination, there would be quite a few problems to overcome.

Your ways may appear very strange to her. She's dependable and sincere and may look upon your sudden changes of mind as a sign of weakness and superficiality. This is not to say you are absolutely incompatible. Don't forget you have one important thing in common: you are both ruled by Mercury. The trouble is her element is earth and yours is air. Very often you'll discover you are in complete agreement about life and how the world should be. It's just that you approach such questions from opposite directions.

If you wish to win this little lady (Virgo people are not giants as a rule), you'll have to learn to be a bit tidier around the home. You've heard the saying, "A place for everything and everything in its place"? Well, that could have been penned by Miss Virgo herself. She's very keen on hygiene, both personal and environmental. You can be a bit sloppy. One thing you'll have to cut out is eating in bed because she can't stand breadcrumbs on her sheets.

Whereas you tend to be ruled by your emotions, Virgos are ruled by their mind.

She likes a man to be a man. She doesn't want to be put on a pedestal and worshipped, so get up off your knees and prove yourself to her.

Don't get the idea that all Virgo people are heavy-handed and lacking in humor. There's a quick mind here, and a Mercurial wit to match your own. If you really love her and are prepared to meet her halfway, you could have a very happy life together.

She'll want you to look smart at all times. You tend to be the sort of guy who likes to wander around in jeans and can't understand why people want you to wear a tie on certain occasions. Your Virgo woman will soon take you to task. It's likely she'll refuse to go out with you unless you tidy yourself up. She'll take it as a reflection on her if you can't be bothered grooming yourself with care. You are an impulsive person. That little rule book your Virgo Miss brings out may be too much of a mind-blower.

After dating her a few times, you may decide the chemistry isn't working. However, after a few days of not seeing her, you could well be on the phone asking her to meet you because you'd like an opinion on the new suit you've bought. She's a mystery woman and you could be coming back for more without really knowing why.

Making love is very important to you. When you first go to bed with a woman born under this Sign, you may feel she's cold and lacks imagination. This is not true. Once aroused, she's very erotic; underneath that cool front, there's a passionate fire burning. When this girl really loves, she pulls out all the stops.

She's probably the most loyal type of all the Signs. If you do marry her, she'll take her vows seriously and will expect you to do the same. She will not abide hypocrisy. She's a perfectionist, but this doesn't mean she doesn't have her faults. Don't be too critical of her, though, because she hates being told when she's in the wrong. She's very good at telling others what to do, but not so good at sorting out her own hangups.

She is careful with money. Quite a few Gemini men like to gamble. If you fall into this category, you could be in hot water. You'll have to face quite a scene before your regular weekly poker game.

Mrs. Virgo will run your home efficiently. When you come in, that mouth-watering smell wafting through the house is likely to be homemade bread or some new and exciting recipe she has devised. If you love her enough to change your ways a little, it could work out very well. It's up to you, really.

GEMINI MAN—LIBRA WOMAN

It's a pretty safe bet that a woman born under Libra is going to get along better than most with a Gemini man. You are the first air Sign, she is the second.

This is the sort of woman you'll hit it off with on first meeting. When you walk into a room, that dainty and vivacious girl sitting in the corner who immediately catches your eye, sending a shiver down your spine, is likely to be a Libra lady.

She has a fabulous sense of humor and a lively and positive interest in life. She's one of the few people you would allow to wear the pants and make many of the important decisions, mainly because she'll do it in a charming way without being domineering. As a homemaker, it's hard to top her. She's often able to combine the many duties of mother and housewife with a successful career. If you do marry a Libra lady, you will probably discover she wants to remain in her job. Don't let this worry you. You'll never get the feeling you come second to her work. She'll always make sure your dinner is ready and that your house or apartment is spick and span.

She's all woman and it's unlikely you'll be able to resist her. If she accepts you as her man, you are indeed fortunate. Apart from finding yourself on an excellent physical wavelength, you'll also be extremely close buddies. You can be a bit secretive, but you'll wish to confide your innermost thoughts to your Libra partner. She will never judge you; her main concern is that you do right by yourself.

She'll want you to be successful in business and will do all in her power to help you achieve your ambitions. She instinctively makes the right decisions, so if you need advice, hers will be well worth following. Venus girls like to have plenty of money around. Success is important to them, mainly because they like the things it brings. Like you, she enjoys going out and meeting people. You'll have great times together at parties. Another thing you will have in common is your dislike of solitude. Neither of you can stand to be left on your own for very long. You both have to keep on the go all the time.

Typically, this is a woman who has quite a few boyfriends before settling down with one man. She wants to be sure she's found her dream guy before giving up her freedom.

Miss Libra will never pry into your affairs. You needn't worry about your letters being opened or your diary being read; this sort of behavior would not occur to a Libra woman. She'll never betray your confidences, either. Your secrets are safe with her.

You are both very sentimental, though family ties are probably more important to her than to you. You may be surprised to discover you get on very well with your mother-in-law; your Libra wife will have seen to that. You'll find her mom and dad popping over quite a lot, but this is unlikely to be a problem.

If you do get hitched, you'll lose a lot of your restlessness. There'll be many a winter's night when you enjoy snuggling in front of the fire, listening to your favorite music, with your Libra lover all dressed up in silk and resting her pretty little head on your shoulder.

Just because she's all woman, don't be fool enough to think she can't protect herself. She's a very strong character and when forced to act independently is perfectly capable of doing so. Never take her for granted and always treat her with respect. Next time there's a domestic crisis, keep your eyes on your partner. Watch how she swings into action and makes the right decisions immediately. You can't help but admire her.

The Libra lady will stand by you in sickness and in health. When you feel a bit down, she'll do everything in her power to help you get your confidence back. She makes a wonderful mother. You'll never come second to the children. She has enough love to share among her whole family.

GEMINI MAN—SCORPIO WOMAN

There's little doubt you'll be attracted to this woman. The question is, will she be a bit too hot for you to handle? You don't go in for big scenes and emotional outbursts as a rule, and these are very much a part of the life of a Scorpio woman.

What will immediately attract you to her is her sexiness and sensuality. It is highly improbable, though, that you will choose each other as marriage partners. You're more likely to have a great affair together and become lifelong buddies ever after, with no regrets on either side.

The Scorpio woman can certainly be a mass of contradictions. When her temper flies, you had better duck as she'll sling any missile handy in your direction. But when she's in a good mood, she is loving kindness itself. Living with a Scorpio woman will have plenty of ups and downs. She's likely to sink into black moods and you will find it very difficult to shake her out of them. Don't try to do it with that old Gemini sense of humor; you won't get many laughs. Her withering scornful look could send you straight to your neighborhood bar.

She doesn't like to display her emotions in front of others. Certainly, she doesn't like strangers knowing her innermost feelings. She is a very private person. Miss Scorpio is the secretive type. If you do decide to live together, or even to marry, there may be a few skeletons she will choose to keep in the closet.

You both love to travel. She's very much a party girl and, like you, will rarely refuse an invitation to go out. She's quite talkative, and on first meeting you'll have so much to discuss there won't be many pauses in the conversation.

She's the jealous type and revengeful, too. It would be unwise to cross her on the smallest thing. It may take her many years, but one day she'll even the score if you hurt her or let her down. She's one of those Old Testament eye-for-an-eye and tooth-for-a-tooth women.

You'll be magnetically drawn to her deep and mystical beauty, for like the water that is her element, she has hidden depths. She's often a vehement feminist and has little use for fluttering females. She's quite capable of looking after herself and sticking up for her rights. Many men find her a bit frightening. Very often Miss Scorpio has a husky voice. She looks most seductive in tight blue jeans or an old flat cap you might have discarded long ago.

If you can't live without her, you'd better make up your mind not to stray off the straight and narrow. Difficult as this is for the Gemini man, the liaison won't work if you slide into your old familiar way of life.

She may think you rather foolish and extravagant with money. She is not herself the type to throw cash around stupidly, but if she loves you, she'll give you her last cent. Once under her spell, you'll find her difficult to live without. Miss Scorpio is very often interested in the occult and all things supernatural, and you may feel she's used some of her special magic on you.

If this woman doesn't settle for one man fairly early in life, she's liable to go on searching for Mr. Right even though she's convinced deep down that he doesn't really exist.

If you think you can handle her, well and good. But be warned, you are taking on quite a handful. She will be deeply devoted to her children, though unlikely to be openly demonstrative.

GEMINI MAN— SAGITTARIUS WOMAN

This miss is terribly easy to get along with. Like you, she prizes freedom—individual freedom above all. She'll never try to tie you down. The Sagittarius woman gets along extremely well with men. She is usually the outdoor type and quite a sport. She doesn't like to be bettered in anything and will try to beat you at tennis or any other pastime you take her on at.

In some ways, you, Mr. Gemini, will find it hard to make a go of it with the female Sagittarian. She's outspoken and deals in fact, not fantasy. She likes travel but not wandering. You could be a bit too much of a drifter for her.

She's the hard-working type and tries to make a success of anything she takes on. She's not as mysterious as some people would try to make out. She may withhold the truth, but she's unlikely to lie to you.

There is a danger that if Gemini and Sagittarius do get hitched, they'll end up leading separate lives because so many of their interests will be different. As neither of you is forceful, you prefer to let the other go his/her own way, and your marriage could disintegrate.

You may wince at some of the dialogue your little fire lady comes out with. It's not that she's trying to be rude or to upset people, but she always speaks as she feels and never minces her words. She's certainly not malicious. It's just that she's a very patient person and expects things to happen almost to order.

Miss S. will never try to boss you around or tell you what to do. At times, you may feel she doesn't care enough. This is not the case. To her way of thinking, you should be able to make your own decisions and conduct your life as you see fit. Never point out her mistakes. This is a woman who doesn't accept personal criticism easily. She'll turn to ice if you try to tell her how she should behave in company.

There's something you must learn early on if you really want to make a go of it with a Jupiter woman. Never *tell* her what to do—*ask* her. She'll come around to your way of thinking so long as she doesn't feel she's being ordered about. Never show her up in company, either. You are quite likely to be the boss when you're alone together, but in front of others, she may enjoy giving you the odd command to show she is in control.

Never take her for granted. She'll be a devoted and loyal companion as long as she feels you are not taking her for a ride. Woe betide you if she discovers you've been two-timing her. Sagittarius people are not prudes by any means, but they do expect their marriage partner to play it straight with them. If you let her down, it's unlikely she'll give you a second bite of the apple. Once her mind is made up, there's little you can do with all your talk to change it.

She loves her home but you, having more artistic flair, might be the one who arranges the furniture and pictures. She dislikes arguments and will go along with your ideas as far as she can.

You may get fed up with her butterfingers. She tends to be on the clumsy side. After a few years of marriage, that beautiful dinner service Mom and Dad gave you on your wedding day is likely to be reduced to one chipped plate.

Miss Sagittarius always tries to look on the bright side of things, and this trait could be invaluable to a Gemini man. When you mope around, she'll try to shake you out of your depressions. If you find your salary has been reduced, your Sagittarius wife will tell you it could be worse—you could have lost your job! That sort of remark just about sums her up.

She's a terrific mother and knows instinctively how to bring up children.

GEMINI MAN— CAPRICORN WOMAN

It is extremely difficult to put the Capricorn woman into any sort of category. She is often a contradiction. She's intensely interested in success on the one hand, but it's possible she'll love you like crazy if you are down on your luck. She's unpredictable and there's no telling what she will be drawn to.

After a long involvement with a successful businessman, she could go to the other extreme and hitch up with a freedom-loving hippy. It is basically a man's mind she's first attracted to, especially if she gets the feeling he's into something exciting and new.

She's an inquisitive type who loves to know what motivates others and why. She'll try to push you as far as she can to see how you react.

Once Miss Capricorn knows you well, she may endeavor to change your ways. It's not merely that she wishes to dominate you; she will truly feel she knows what course of action you should take. And many times she will be right. She recognizes talent and hates to see it wasted.

If she loves you, she'll do anything for you. You may, however, find the sort of love she offers a little suffocating. She's an all-or-nothing girl. She'll expect you to break it off with your other lady friends as soon as she enters your life.

This woman is an excellent mixer and feels at home in any company, though she can be quite biting and catty when she wishes and some of her remarks will make you wince. She's great at entertaining and loves to bring together people from different walks of life. She will usually end up striking it rich, often in the most unlikely way. Capricorn people have their ups and downs, but they always learn from their mistakes and are unlikely to repeat them.

One thing you will have in common is a sense of humor. Both of you can see the funny side of life.

You may find she gets a little too heavy for you if you become deeply involved. An affair with a Capricorn woman can begin in a lighthearted way and then suddenly become terribly serious—on her side, at least. Don't say you love her unless you really mean it; she'll believe everything you say.

This miss won't wish to give up her freedom in marriage. Capricorn females make excellent businesswomen. It would be a waste of her talents to expect her to stay at home while you go out to earn the bread and butter.

She can get deeply depressed at times and it's difficult to shake her out of these moods. She can be extremely demanding and has a very suspicious nature. Don't tease her. The one thing she doesn't have is a sense of humor about herself.

Your sex scene should be a treat. Capricorn people can be very demanding physically, so don't plan on getting much sleep. She makes a great lover and you should find you are romantically in tune, as well.

Being an all-action, constantly on-the-move type of person, Miss Capricorn can be a great asset. She is excellent at entertaining. She'll know exactly how to treat your boss should you bring him home to dinner. If you are out to clinch an important deal, your Capricorn wife will help put the much sought-after contract in your pocket.

She is a family-loving type. It's likely she'll be asking her mother's advice throughout her life. Getting along with your in-laws will be quite important to your relationship with her. Let her look after the savings. She's much better at handling money than you are.

Underneath her cool exterior, this woman very often lacks confidence. It will be up to you to help her overcome her fears and secret doubts.

GEMINI MAN— AQUARIUS WOMAN

This could be quite a combination. If you find you're in love with a woman born under the Sign of the Water Bearer, then hold onto your hat, you're in for quite an experience. You'll discover she's like no other woman you've ever come across. She's full of wonderful ideas about how the world should be and she's a great lover of freedom. These women hate to tie themselves down to timetables and appointments. They are likely to turn up at a party a couple of hours late because they got deeply involved in a conversation elsewhere.

The Aquarius woman will always give her opinion honestly and frankly without trying to dictate how you should see the situation. She may disagree with you, but she'll respect your right to think as you do.

You like life to be constantly changing and find it hard to settle in one place for long. You'll have met more than your match in Aquarius. She is self-reliant and will never be a drag on you. She likes to look after herself and hates to be dependent on others.

If you have a date, you'd better give her a call a couple of hours beforehand—it's quite possible she'll have forgotten all about it. She finds it very hard to remember appointments. (Next time you buy her a present, make it an engagement book.) She's likely to come home from the supermarket with all the vegetables for the Sunday lunch but not the meat.

She despises cheats and swindlers. Remember, she wants the world to be a better place for everyone to live in. She might find it a bit difficult to come to terms with the duality of your nature. She likes to know where she stands with people and your sudden changes of mood could confuse her.

Aquarius women can be mixed-up characters who take their adolescence right through life with them. You'll find it hard to tie this woman down to a permanent relationship because she will be frightened about making long-term arrangements. She doesn't like to feel she belongs to anyone. It's very unlikely she is an old-fashioned type of girl who meekly accepts that her place is in the home.

The qualities she'll be looking for in a man are kindness and a deep feeling for humanity. She also wants a person who is true to himself and refuses to sell out on his principles.

She's not the most passionate of women, either. You'll have to do all the courting because though she feels the sexual side of a relationship is important, she won't want to place much emphasis on it. She's likely to be faithful because she has so many outside interests that she won't want to complicate her life with a love affair.

She's not a skinflint by any means but (perhaps surprisingly) she knows how to look after the bucks. You won't need to worry about her having an account at the big department stores; she's unlikely to run up big bills on lavish items.

Don't go jumping to conclusions if you see her walking along arms linked with another guy—it might well be an old boyfriend she's just bumped into. She is the type of woman who finds it perfectly reasonable to go on seeing her ex-lovers after the romantic side of the relationship has died away.

She's a very artistic person. You should share a love of art and theater. You both enjoy going out a lot. Although you'll delight in each other's company, both of you may find it difficult to turn down invitations to parties—solo.

She's a bit of a prophet. What she forecasts for tomorrow is likely to come true.

GEMINI MAN—PISCES WOMAN

Take a look sometime at the lists of famous people born under various Signs. As a rule, when you come to Pisces, you'll discover the men far outnumber the women. On the other hand, take a look at the number of successful men who have or have had a Pisces woman by their side; you'll find a heck of a lot of them.

Many men find Miss Pisces is the girl of their dreams—and Gemini is no exception. She is extremely feminine and has a wit and imagination that match your own. Life for you both will be something of an adventure. One thing is certain: you're unlikely to get bored with each other because there's one important thing you share—unpredictability.

You like to lead and your Pisces mate will allow you to do so with the greatest of pleasure so long as you're leading her in the right direction.

She'll be a wonderful confidence booster. She likes to think her man can take on the whole world if necessary and win. She'll be quick to recognize what talents you possess and make sure you exploit them to the best possible advantage. She mixes easily with people from all walks of life. Although adaptable, she's always herself. She's a sharp one, though, and will know exactly how to deal with your boss. She is also a good homemaker, though she refuses to be tied to the house. Like you, she enjoys ringing the changes, and being a water Sign, has a penchant for long cruises and holidays near the sea.

She won't allow you to sit back and take things easy. But with a Pisces woman, you won't want to. Of all the Signs, she is the one you will feel most protective toward. You'll enjoy earning loads of money so you can buy her all the things she loves and appreciates. She is extremely loyal. If anyone says a word behind your back, she'll not let the remark pass. She has quite a temper and is never afraid to speak her mind.

She doesn't have a great head for business matters. She'll leave that side of the partnership to you. Miss Pisces will enjoy spoiling you. She'll soon have you feeling relaxed and comfortable after a wearying day at the office.

You are both apt to change your minds very suddenly about social plans. Your symbol is the Twins and hers is those two little Fishes swimming in opposite directions. You of all the Signs are likely to understand her difficulty in making up her mind. She is very vague and dreamy. You might get the feeling she lives in a little world of her own—one that is totally divorced from reality. She doesn't like to live alone, but enjoys the company of small groups rather than large ones.

She is very ladylike and unlikely to be the Women's Lib type. She's quite happy to be feminine; in fact, she loves it.

The Pisces woman is wonderful at understanding shy people and helping them come out of their shells. If someone is sitting alone in a corner at a social event, the lady born under the twelfth Sign will go out of her way to make him or her feel wanted and interesting.

Treat her with tenderness and love and the relationship will be a successful one. She's such an understanding creature she may even forgive you if you go off the rails (but don't count on it).

Pisces women can be a bit extravagant, but so, for that matter, can Gemini men. You'll both have to restrain your extravagant impulses.

GEMINI'S HEALTH

Any form of suppression, physical or mental, is likely to make you ill. Nowhere in the Zodiac are body and mind so entwined as in people born under Gemini. The water Signs, such as Pisces and Cancer, are influenced by the emotions, and these, in turn, affect their bodies. But you are an intellectual Sign, and the mental processes are far swifter than the emotions. As a consequence, your body movements are rapid, darting, agile, continuous—like thought—while the water Sign people are generally languid and rounded in their movements.

An inactive mind is a dull mind. And generally speaking, an inactive Gemini individual is not likely to be in the best of health. However, it is important to remember that a still mind—one that is alert but not the tennis court of indiscriminate and undisciplined thoughts—is a healthy and receptive instrument. It is this kind of "stillness" in activity that Gemini has to aim for in order to enjoy the health he needs to keep happy and constantly on the go.

Endeavor to get as much rest as possible in your very busy life. This doesn't mean going to bed for ten hours at a stretch every night—an impossibility for most Gemini people, anyway. It does mean that when you do sit or lie down to rest, you should give yourself up to it completely. Don't permit random thoughts and nervous body movements. You of all people must learn to relax totally in mind and body, even if it's only for a few minutes at a time. As you practice falling into this "instant" relaxation, you will find it becomes easier and easier.

One way of clearing your mind and relieving body tension is to get out in the sunshine and fresh air. Go for a stroll, take the dog for a walk, jog around the park. Nothing is as mind-ventilating for the Gemini individual as an opportunity to commune with nature, even briefly.

Yours is the first air Sign of the Zodiac, so it's not surprising that it rules the lungs. Polluted air is very detrimental to your health. When you're feeling a bit frazzled, get out of town and take in some good deep lungsful of fresh air. We all know how a few deep breaths can relieve nervousness—and as a Gemini, you have much more than your share of this sort of energy.

Because your Sign is so closely linked with the respiratory system, you have to guard against colds, chills and influenza—which, if neglected, can develop into bronchitis, pleurisy or pneumonia. Asthma may also be a problem. Keep yourself well protected in bad weather and don't sit around in damp clothing.

Generally speaking, the typical Gemini person, because of slender build and nervous manner, appears delicate or physically weaker than is the case. Although you are seldom robust, you usually do not contract serious illnesses. However, when under strain for any length of time, you are prone to catch whatever happens to be going around (though you also tend to throw it off more quickly than others). Your recuperative powers are acutely dependent on the state of your nervous system (which is ruled by Gemini). The nervous system—and the diseases it is subject to—is the key to your extreme sensitivity. You are quickly upset by feelings or thoughts of confinement. Your bedroom, therefore, should be light and airy. You are vulnerable to insomnia, which may be aggravated by stuffy, dark or depressing sleeping quarters.

It is essential for you to maintain an optimistic and objective outlook. You should not allow your vivid imagination to take control. It can quickly raise you to intense peaks of excitement and anticipation, often culminating in nerve-fraying disillusionment and despondency. It can just as easily induce depression through brooding and worry. Your uncurbed imagination tends to cause violent mood fluctuations.

Bad posture can cause discomfort in your arms and shoulders.

Through Sagittarius, the Sign opposite yours, there may be a reflex association causing occasional sciatic pains in the hips and thighs. These problems can often be traced to poor circulation, underlining again the need for a reasonable amount of exercise to stimulate the system. Don't try to diagnose your own pains; leave this to a doctor.

GEMINI AT WORK

You will be successful in any job requiring an active and inventive mind—but it must provide plenty of scope and freedom for self-expression. You should be able to make a name for yourself in journalism, advertising, publicity, broadcasting, lecturing, teaching—in any job that utilizes your gifts for writing or speaking.

You are also, as a rule, an affable and congenial person with a high degree of personal magnetism. This, combined with your outgoing style, fits you extremely well for all kinds of public relations work. You would make an excellent social secretary or professional host or hostess, as well as a contact person or go-between for organizations dealing with government departments or political parties. You often make an ideal "fixer."

As a personal assistant, private secretary or just plain stenographer, you have few peers. But no matter how attractive and glamorous these jobs may appear to others, unless they offer considerable personal liberty and out-of-the-ordinary involvement, you won't stay in them. You're not going to be anyone's intellectual lackey; nor will splendid isolation in some luxurious ivory tower suit you. You must obtain satisfaction from your job, and that doesn't necessarily consist of top status, good salary and plenty of additional privileges.

Gemini people are so adaptive and mentally capable that they can be successful in practically any career they choose. But they do have a couple of weaknesses and blind spots that ensure it's not always plain sailing. For example, you tend to imagine a job is going to be better than the specifications. You look on the rosy side and ignore the often tedious realities. Thus you may eagerly accept a position in a travel firm after a night of delicious imaginings, only to discover that numerous telephone calls to distant places from a nine-to-five desk in a downtown office are not very exciting.

You become restless and nervous if you have to remain too long in one place. Your ideal job is a nonstatic one where you can blow in and out. You would make a wonderful salesperson. Even if you aren't traveling around, you will be quite happy dealing with the public all day, provided you can vary the routine. Because you are tirelessly curious and love to chat when your interest is aroused, because you genuinely enjoy hearing what's happening in the lives of others, you are memorable company. And the fact that you don't judge others also makes people warm to you.

You are not so capable in positions that impose constant pressure. You can handle emergencies with magnificent aplomb, but when the problems drag on and solutions are not clear, you're inclined to become irritable and depressed. If you are a boss, you are likely to disappear on urgent business for a few hours (or days), leaving the sticky bits for subordinates to sort out.

You are resourceful and inventive in business and have the knack of anticipating problems and sidestepping them with great skill. Many Gemini businessmen and women have built a successful company on the strength of their ideas, contacts and timing—while leaving the entire organizational side to others. Gemini insists on being where the creative action is—way, way out in front—and is always a swerving target. Your character is indeed difficult to pin down.

Your attitude to employees is likely to be a bit severe and standoffish. There's not much you can gain from these relationships, and you tend to show it. There's you in command, and them. What you say, you want done. You are straightforward and precise. You are prepared to listen to suggestions and will act on them if they're worthwhile, but you don't generally open your heart to the people who work for you with the same alacrity as you do to equals. In handling labor disputes, you're likely to antagonize the other side. You're inclined to look for reasonable solutions and to rely on argument rather than grapple with the fundamental causes. The human side of a grievance may escape you. Palliatives providing time and respite from disagreeable situations are likely to be the foundation for your attempts at conciliation.

You are a Twin, remember, so it's not unusual for you to have two jobs or two careers. Your dislike of regular working hours and your remarkable versatility often allow you to dovetail your activities so that you end up virtually working for yourself, or at least as a pretty free agent. The Gemini person's dual personality fits him extremely well for an acting career, and many of these people combine this with some kind of literary work. Their plays, books and articles are notable for their lucidity of expression and entertaining style. Since Geminis love to wander, they often write travel stories.

A Gemini person is likely to be a jack of all trades without ever really becoming proficient in one. You are quick to learn and cover any gaps in your knowledge with extemporization and verbal diversion. You have great difficulty sticking to one thing for long.

Your talent for constructive criticism may give you entree to the world of professional critics. The Gemini flair for journalism is quite extraordinary and frequently people born under this Sign rise to prominence with very little training. The fast-talking, quick-thinking, resourceful reporter typifies the Gemini character. Being an airy, intellectual Sign, Gemini has strong leanings toward art. You are often gifted musically, able to play instruments as well as compose. Dancing is another activity that may attract you. Your characteristic manual dexterity may make you an able sculptor, wood-carver, engraver, handicraft or needlepoint worker.

On the technical side, the Gemini man or woman is suited for a career in engineering, aviation, radio mechanics, mathematics—in fact, there's no limit to this list provided the subject stirs Gemini's imagination and the job or business allows him the freedom to put his ideas to work. Too often, Gemini is unfairly criticized for turning established procedures upside down when what he's actually doing is drawing attention to outdated and inefficient practices. People born under this Sign are exceptionally progressive. Although you are not as practical in your thinking as, for instance, a Virgo person, your concepts are far more original. And out of the abundance of bright ideas and bewildering abstractions is likely to emerge a real money-maker.

As an employee, you will take orders willingly and pursue with great gusto any line of mental work required. You'll make rapid-fire suggestions, point out where economies can be made, tighten a communications system—and keep the rest of the work force amused with a constant stream of high-spirited chatter. But Geminis don't have a great amount of staying power. You become bored very quickly, especially once you realize a job is well within your capabilities so that it no longer offers a challenge. Once this is obvious to you, you are apt to disappear for a while into another department.

Gemini employees won't cheat on their boss. You are very conscientious and an employer must understand you in order to make the most of your considerable talents. You'll work three times as fast as most others but you are incapable of concentrating on one task for long. You need to be made responsible for several projects so you can divide your time between them. If you are also allowed the freedom of a fairly loose schedule, you'll deliver all the goods—on time. Of course, you might turn up for work in time to give the others a wave on their way home because Gemini is a night owl and often is most productive when others are thinking of turning in.

You are easily discouraged in your work, especially when things are not going well. Then you're likely to throw down the tools and walk out. You are also upset by criticism and are very unlikely to remain in a job where you don't feel appreciated and liked. You prefer to do things your own way and people offering unsolicited advice feel the sting of your sharp tongue.

Before taking a job, be sure it doesn't involve too much routine. But remember, it will pay you to knuckle down as much as possible and to become proficient in at least one line of work.

Gemini people as a rule are not well suited for heavy physical labor and will seldom attempt it voluntarily except as a means of keeping fit. The skilled trades also are unlikely to attract you unless a fineness of touch or unusual ingenuity is required. Many of you are able to use both hands with equal dexterity. Since your hands and your mind are delicately coordinated, you can often form abstract designs in metal and other unusual materials. If you are this type, you may produce modern art shapes with arc-welding gear.

Whatever a Gemini's occupation, he or she likes to use the most up-to-date machines and equipment. Your mind automatically and continually analyzes the systems you are involved in with the object of improving them. Speed and efficiency are second nature to the Gemini worker.

If you were born between May 21 and May 30, you are capable of considerable intellectual accomplishment. But you should learn to master your restlessness and cultivate concentration. There is a likely future for you in one of the arts, in business or finance (as a stockbroker, for instance) or in invention. You have a particularly fine memory and probably by now have learned to resist cramming it with useless information as weaker types of Gemini people usually do. Your mental processes are first rate, your intuitive hunches frequently brilliant. A career as a linguist may give you the opportunity to travel as well as make a name for yourself.

If you were born between May 31 and June 10, you have a very pleasing manner that fits you for all occupations dependent on the cooperation of others. You quickly win the confidence of associates and usually can count on the help of influential persons, who seem to trust you. You should endeavor never to let others down by walking away from your responsibilities. Partnership should be lucky for you provided you can adhere to mutual goals. You are a born diplomat.

If you were born between June 11 and June 20, you have a most aware and alert intellect. You are something of a visionary whose ideas may be too advanced to be appreciated by mundane minds, which causes great career frustration. You possess high humanitarian ideals. At times your intuition is phenomenal and should help you obtain a leadership position. You would be wise not to be discouraged too early by conservative oppostion to your proposals; be patient, but be sure your ideas are practical. Travel and unexpected happenings are likely to lead to opportunities.

MONEY

You have a higher regard for money than your lighthearted and easygoing manner would suggest. Although pay is secondary to your need to enjoy your job, you won't work for nothing. You have a very good idea of what you are worth. And you are well aware—down to the last cent, in fact—just how much should be in your pay envelop each time.

You spend a lot—though where others are concerned, no more than is necessary. You aren't stingy, but few people would ever call a pure Gemini person overgenerous. You like to keep a little cash in reserve, which nobody knows about. This allows you to feel you can always "get out" if you need to.

Most of your extravagance is prompted by your sudden changes of interest; you spend money on new activities and pastimes and then abandon them for something else.

You are a good provider, particularly because you are capable of working at two or even three regular jobs. You may not be prepared to wash dishes, but you'll usually hustle up some lucrative spare-time work to provide a comfortable income. It is what you spend, not what you earn, that causes problems. You are a canny saver when it suits you. But you are also quite likely to blow the lot on a night out or on a wildly extravagant purchase.

In your home, you enjoy all the creature comforts but don't believe in buying lavish furnishings and the like. You do believe labor-saving devices are well worth investing in.

High times with friends—particularly the gambling kind—may keep Gemini people on a financial treadmill.

CANCER'S CHARACTER

You are a seriously misunderstood character, Cancer. You love to laugh, your sense of humor is delicious, you are a great listener, a loyal and openhearted friend and a gentle, sympathetic person all around. But those deep melancholic moods of yours . . . they've given you an awful reputation. Most people view you as an enigma, but anyone worth his astrological salt knows you are just a Moon child, born under that mysterious zodiacal Sign where the emotions ebb and flow between fantastic heights of exhilaration and deep lows of inexplicable dread.

Cancer is the Sign of man's beginnings and its unknown depths are said to contain the secrets of the womb and the grave—happiness and sorrow, one might say. With such weighty and intriguing matters to reflect on, it's no wonder that you sometimes leave us and hide inside yourself.

In no other Sign of the Zodiac are the virtues and the faults so distinctly different. Undeveloped Cancer individuals have very little will of their own, regard sentiment as love, seldom originate anything, accept what comes without discrimination, are unreliable and irresponsible and will live any kind of existence that offers the easiest way out. This type, thankfully, is in the minority. In this book, we are describing the typical Cancer person who sits comfortably between the two extremes.

Cancer is the fourth zodiacal Sign, the only one ruled by the Moon. Its element is water, which is understandable considering the lunar planet's influence on the oceans of the world. But this watery connection is more complicated, and from an astrological viewpoint tells us much about you. The Moon and Cancer represent all the life-giving and live-sustaining liquids, including amino acids, which support the embryonic cell structures in all living things. Cancer also rules the reproductive system, the stomach and the gastric juices. In other words, it is the mothering Sign of the Zodiac. It symbolizes mankind's desire to nourish and take care of.

So as a Cancer-born person, you are very protective toward everything you consider yours. And first on this list is your peace of mind. You do everything in your power to keep trouble at bay. Your technique in dealing with problems is not to venture forth to grapple with them before they arrive on your doorstep. No, indeed, for that would be to expose yourself unnecessarily, and the Cancer philosophy is to bide one's time in the hope that the difficulty seen in advance may never eventuate. If forced into action, you will generally circle the problem, very rarely going in for a frontal attack. Like the Crab, which is your symbol, you prefer to move sideways or backward, pausing with inscrutable detachment, then darting in for the kill (or the pickup) when the quarry is exhausted or momentarily distracted.

Security means a great deal to you. Being a Moon and a water creature, you have a very tenuous grip on the earth. But it is your intention to hold on at all costs—you cling to your old possessions with a tenacity equaled only by your resourcefulness and enterprise in adding new ones.

You are not mean, though your alacrity in giving depends considerably on your emotional involvement. For instance, as far as your family and loved ones are concerned, you are likely to be an all-year-round Santa Claus. Just about everything they ask for you'll provide, if you scrape up the cash. Sure, you'll look worried on occasions and make the usual observations about money not growing on trees, but deep down you love their demands for nothing gives you greater pleasure than delighting and serving those you love, especially when they show they love you. You want to be liked, and this moves you to the kind of openhanded generosity that gives you a reputation among your neighbors and others for being kind and helpful.

But your heart really beats with selfless concern when the suffering or privation of another arouses your compassion. Then you never hold back with time, money or effort. You simply cannot bear to see anyone or anything suffer unnecessarily, so you will share all you can without depriving those who are dependent on you.

None of this is to imply you're the type who spreads largesse among institutionalized "worthy causes." You're too individualistic for that—and far too canny with your shekels. When you give, you give directly to someone in need; this method is far more satisfying personally—and it cuts out the middleman. Your generosity is hardheaded to the extent that frequently you'll wait to see what others do to help a person in need before you make your move. The reasoning behind your delay is impeccable: perhaps the recipient will receive twice as much if you wait; or perhaps if someone else gives first, it will be sufficient and your money or time will be saved. One thing is certain, though: you'll come to the rescue at the last moment if needed. Your initial caution is tied up with your fixation about security.

In business, Cancer types are usually outstandingly successful. Although passive and reserved by nature, they are more ambitious than they appear. They desire money and position as a form of insurance for themselves and their loved ones, and this preoccupation with security drives them on with rather uncharacteristic zeal. Not that the Cancer businesswoman or man is a spectacular operator. They prefer to work in roundabout ways, manipulating from the sidelines, never attacking the task directly if possible. They are adept at playing the waiting game and often display the steel-nerved calm of the professional gambler by holding off till the very last moment.

Cancer has tremendous powers of perseverance once a commitment is made. It may be very difficult for you to get started in a direction, but once you're on your way, you seem psychologically impervious to setbacks. You never expect to achieve your goals overnight. If difficulties mean you've got to begin all over again, you are quite prepared to do so. Where others would grind their teeth down to the gums in frustration you just chew away at the opposition and the obstacles. There's something very akin to the inexorable action of the waves on the coastline in the Cancer person's business technique.

You Crabs, of course, are inveterate worriers. But in business affairs, you're usually so well organized and prepared that there is very little risk involved. If you can help it, you won't initiate a move while there is the slightest chance your plans will come unstuck. You're anything but impulsive. Like a true tidal creature, you realize the current will change eventually and you're prepared to cling to your rock until it does and then swim along with it.

In private and social life, though, the Cancer individual's stomach (also ruled by the Moon) is in a constant turmoil. It's because you've got so much to lose, and not necessarily just material items such as a house, money, possessions, job. There are intangible things like reputation, respect, esteem and privacy that you treasure and dread losing. The pessimistic possibilities that flash through the Cancer consciousness in one day would fill a book, and because many of these feelings are vague, unnamable fears and doubts, you easily become despondent. Which is only another way of saying you simply don't understand what's wrong with you.

Here, Astrology can help. It is amazing just how closely the comings and goings of your planetary ruler, the Moon, correspond to the character and behavior of a typical Cancer person. The Moon is unbearably hot on one side and abysmally cold on the other—something like your moods. We see it for a couple of weeks and then it disappears for the rest of the month. Again, this reflects your regular need to scuttle off to a quiet place where you can repair the damage done your psyche by strain and tension. Yet, even when we can't see it, the Moon is always out there, just like your basic character. In fact, the Moon, despite its reputation for inconstancy, is wonderfully dependable, a perfect clock whose regularity of movements allows us to prepare tide timetables years in advance.

So . . . it can be predicted that you will have your high and low moods with clockwork precision, but underneath you'll always be a lovable, sincere and gentle person to those who understand you. You are certainly changeable, and present a slightly different face to the world (like the Moon) just about every day. But you're *consistent* in your inconsistency—which is more than can be said for some of the other Signs who are likely to be your most voluble critics.

You have a great affinity with the past. This is not to say that you necessarily go around collecting antiques or digging for archeological treasures, as is often suggested in descriptions of the Cancer type. Although you may do these things, the implications are far more subtle and comprehensive than that. Again, we return to the Moon, which astrologically represents the senses. These are developed in the first years of childhood—the life period governed by the

Moon—when we respond instinctively to feelings of hunger, discomfort and the like. Instinct is an evolutionary hand-me-down that all living things need to preserve themselves. Human beings, of course, gradually build up a more personalized and intelligible substitute for instinct called discrimination. So, Cancer, your emotional origins are instinctive, straight out of the *dear,* distant past. Is it surprising, then, that you hanker for the "good old days"?

You Cancer people like to act on precedent, on what's been established by experience—either your own or some recognized authority's. You are not innovators and not the slightest bit adventurous when there's any risk to the things you hold dear. At times you can be quite daring and amaze others with your courage and fortitude—but the thing at risk will always be something you feel is expendable, even if it's your comfort or life. There are as many dashing heroes and heroines among the Cancer people of the world as any other Sign. It's just that Cancer values are often, well . . . different.

Some Cancer individuals possess an unconscious desire for martyrdom that makes them court their own destruction. If they take pleasure in their misfortunes, this is not some masochism. Cancer people, through the intensity of their introverted emotions, occasionally gain tremendous spiritual insights, which elevate them to the ranks of prophets and mystics. Death becomes significant against their vision or glimpse of a higher purpose in life. They are prepared to sacrifice all—for a greater, more permanent security (that word again!).

Genuinely inspired Cancer visionaries are few and far between. The danger for the less-developed person is self-delusion. If they believe they are prophets or savior material, they go looking for a cause or opportunity to exalt them. Usually, with this type, the vision-splendid is quixotic: that which needs to be "saved" exists only in their imagination. A contempt for others engaged in ordinary worldly pursuits is likely to lead to supreme egotism; given the right (or wrong) circumstances, such a misguided Cancer person may cause needless anxiety and problems for others. Here again is the Cancer fascination with the past: behavior is styled on the example of the saints and many of the great secular martyrs of tradition.

You are first and foremost an emotional creature, acutely responsive to the changes in your environment. You "feel" things, sense them, long before they happen. You can't stand bad vibrations and will often quit a place for no concrete reason because it feels too distressing or uncomfortable to stay. You are also extremely sensitive to the presence of others and usually sense a person's character before he utters a word. Although you hate to cause scenes, you'll dart off without a word of explanation if someone you can't stand enters the room.

Similarly, you are very quick to take offense; the most innocuous remark can send you into a black mood of brooding resentment. It doesn't take much to throw you off balance emotionally. Any form of criticism tends to trigger an exaggerated reaction, a scowling, sullen silence. On these occasions, you feel very sorry for yourself, and anyone who lives with you will know it. There's nothing so downright depressing as the damp atmosphere the Crab can exude while sunk in a low-water mood.

There are times when you will sink into depression for no apparent reason. This can be really maddening to those around you because you disappear into your shell and stay there without any spark of communication. Although you may go through the motions of eating, sleeping and working, your psychological isolation is as effective as if you were in deep space—and if a Cancer person were to describe what goes on inside him at these times, his profound alienation, it would seem another world.

You have an extremely vivid imagination. Your fantasies soar to almost ecstatic heights where sensation and ideas blend into some kind of otherworld euphoria. It's all exceedingly pleasant while it lasts, but your dreams have a nasty habit of backfiring. The higher the trip, the lower the slip, so to speak. It's as though you stir memories in the universal mind stuff, and in their clamor to get out, they pull you down into the pit of despondency.

You should aim to keep your imaginings either artistic or optimistic. This will help you keep at bay the vague feelings of sadness and sorrow you are prone to. Dwelling on the past, particularly on unhappy times, you corrode your health and well-being.

Cancer people are romantic sentimentalists. They are the knights and ladies of old, living on in a tolerable but far, far inferior world. There's something courtly and yet a little dusty about the Cancer man. He likes to wear old clothes and even his best gear has a touch of the traditional or stylized convention. Sometimes it's not hard to imagine him in the role of a polished courtier, particularly when he's demonstrating his charming gift for words and phrases. When talking about his favorite subject, he will get a faraway look in his eyes as though he's got a private peephole to the splendor of the past. He knows those eras were cruel and impoverished, but he'll never admit that the quality of life has improved—because for him it hasn't. He lives mostly in his imagination.

The Cancer woman shares the male Crab's respect for bygone days and has considerable affection for her ancestry. She likes to wear old things, too, mainly because she admires lavish gowns and the graceful sophistication that went with them. Both these Old World romantics manage to recreate their dreams of the past in their homes. Whichever period of history appeals to them will be represented here, in the furniture, furnishings, paintings or knickknacks. It might be a Georgian fireplace, a coat of arms, the family tree in heraldic form, some flintlock pistols on the wall or genuine buccaneer swords (which Cancer knows were made in Taiwan, but he or she is not going to allow that sordid fact to spoil a good story). The Cancer home will be well stacked with an interesting assortment of objects, musty souvenirs, memorabilia and sometimes plain junk. If Cancer is married to a sparse, no-nonsense type of mate like Virgo, the redolence of antiquity may be less pronounced. But if you look under the bed, in the stored suitcases or on the back shelf of the wardrobe, you'll find bundles of faded photographs, blue-bowed parcels of ancient love letters and yellowing books with presentation inscriptions on the flyleaves.

Rock of ages cleft for me . . . it is in the crevices of the past that the Cancer Crab finds his most comforting seclusion. And where on earth is there a more vital manifestation of yesterday than in the family? Cancer people adore the family idea and serve their loved ones with almost smothering affection and attention. Their children are brought up to respect all the traditional values, including good manners and respect for elders. It's usually a major crisis when a teenager comes home to a Cancer mother or father spouting ideas about liberation. This Age of Aquarius is understandably a hard era for the typical Cancer parent.

Though devoted and self-sacrificing with her offspring, the female Crab has a jolting habit of suddenly losing her temper and dishing out punishment far more severe than is deserved. This is likely to occur just after she's petted and spoiled the child, who may feel he can get away with some extra naughtiness.

Both sexes often get cranky, which is another manifestation of the famous Cancer moodiness. Some small irritation sets them off and for the next few hours they're crabby and crotchety, snapping off people's heads at the slightest contact. They don't mean it, and no real harm's ever done, but an emotional alarm clock sometimes goes off to remind these otherwise placid and easygoing people that the world's not such a good place to live in after all and that they'd better quit dreaming and get to work to improve it.

Basically, Cancer people would rather do nothing hurriedly. You like to get around to things in your good time. Psychologically, you can be a little flabby. Some might even call you fundamentally lazy, self-indulgent and luxury loving, but that would be a description of the negative Cancer type who has not yet developed the timbre of his own nature. What keeps you evolved types in trim is your persistent concern for the future, your need for self-preservation. You are prepared to work diligently rather than run the risk of . . . well, you never know what might happen tomorrow, do you? For a Cancer-born person to become wealthy early in life before discovering what he or she can really do is often disastrous to character development.

Cancer people of both sexes are usually fabulous cooks. Cooking is an artistic delight for you. You love to prepare an impromptu meal for half a dozen or so select friends, one of whom is a bona fide gourmet (the kitchen is one place where the Crab is supremely confident). You are usually an imaginative and creative chef and even the common roast can become a masterpiece in your hands. Ms. Cancer is usually particularly active in the kitchen and likes to prepare as many homemade dishes as time will permit.

As much as Mr. Cancer enjoys eating at home, he occasionally surprises his family with an invitation to eat out. This can be a very satisfying and instructive experience. He always chooses a first-class restaurant—quality and atmosphere are essential. And he eshews places that feature noisy music—with Mr. Cancer it's more likely to be a nostalgic violin or a soft solo piano. All will be very traditional and pleasant, even down to the carefully calculated 15 percent tip. As much as he loathes a scene, this man will not tolerate bad service or poor food. When he feels imposed upon, something gnaws at his insides until he's just got to act or comment. He'll shoot an offending meal back to the chef with a peremptory wave, or carve up a sloppy waiter with three curt words. He believes things should be done properly when he's paying for them.

Cancer people enjoy their food tremendously. It doesn't require much of an adverse influence in the horoscope for them to take up overeating as a hobby, especially if they've established a bit of a reputation as a gourmet. Cancer being the Sign of nourishment, growth and liquid refreshment, it's not surprising that a good proportion of the round and jellifying characters you run into are self-indulgent Moon children. Ms. Cancer has more of a problem with her weight than her male counterpart. Yet, irrespective of their hearty appetites, these men and women usually have impeccable table manners. There's a conspicuous sense of refinement about them, a genuine appreciation of the social graces that shines through no matter what their circumstances in life. They are wonderful hosts and hostesses at parties and are also always in demand as guests.

Being ruled by the lunar Queen of the Senses, your taste is highly developed. You enjoy variety rather than quantity in a meal, but the first of these too often leads to the other. One Cancer male, part of a small party at an expensive Chinese restaurant, after surveying the extensive list of dishes on the menu, told his host, "I'm not that hungry—I'll just have a little of everything." And he wasn't joking. Another Cancer gentleman, having Sunday dinner with his wife in a cozy out-of-town restaurant, was asked by the proprietor what he thought of the roast. "Excellent," said Mr. Cancer. "But I suggest a tureen on the table for the gravy rather than assuming in the kitchen that we all like the same amount." This fastidiousness is the trait of a person who regards eating as an art and not just an intake.

As a typical Cancer person, your sense of humor frequently puts you at the center of a gathering. When you're amused by others, you're vastly amusing and entertaining yourself. You're a very good audience. Your wit is dry and memorable. You see the funny side of life at the oddest times and an appreciative world often laughs with you. When you're in the mood, you're also a fine raconteur, especially if you're a male. You can spellbind an audience with atmosphere; your words may be few, but the images they create are vivid and alive.

Here, you are aided by an exceedingly facile memory. The Cancer power to recall is frequently phenomenal. And there's a good reason for it. Whereas most people file away intellectual impressions, which when not frequently revived fade and lose their potency, you store your memories as emotions. You are a feeling creature, and every emotion you ever felt lives on in you along with the memory associated with it. Memories may die but emotions never do. It is they, as Cancer knows, that are the spice of life, its meaning and reality.

You are fond of the limelight and popularity but you won't push or contrive to acquire them. Things must come naturally for you to really enjoy them. When you start jostling and pushing, you often upset the applecart.

Among the most important things in your life are respect and admiration, and you are therefore rather difficult to live with at times. Your family and loved ones are probably well aware that to stay in your good graces they must continually demonstrate their love and appreciation—which can become very tiresome (ask someone who's close to you). And what happens when the acknowledgment and recognition you crave are not forthcoming? You feel neglected, discontented and restless; you slope off into your room without saying a word; you start picking on other people around the house. You should try to remember it's not always as easy for others to show their feelings as it is for you. Besides, you sometimes upset others with your fussiness and your insistence that people (especially your children) conform to standards or rules they consider outmoded. This applies mostly to Mr. Cancer, who can be incredibly obstinate when his authority is questioned. Mrs. Cancer is likely to be overly possessive and try to run her children's lives long after they are able to make decisions for themselves. This woman may dissolve in tears when she feels pressured or opposed. Despite her intensely devoted nature, she is apt to make unreasonable demands on the time and effort of her family members.

As a lover, you are emotional and tender; once aroused, extremely sensuous and pleasing. Refer to the "Cancer in Love" section; it deals in detail with your inclinations in this regard. But briefly, you learn from life's experience, and with each new romantic possibility, you like to take your time. You're inclined to beat around the bush, to range over the whole conversational gambit, while you assess the other person, get the "feel" of him or her. In every partner, you are looking for your ideal mate; once you locate that person, you won't let him or her go.

It is this searching that sometimes earns the Cancer individual the reputation of being fickle. Your standards are high and usually result in a fair turnover of rejects. But fickle you are not. Your possessiveness and tendency to take over the other person will probably cause many arguments and heartaches. But you are such a loving and responsive individual that making up could be among the happiest moments of your life . . . each time.

You're always on the lookout for a good cause to identify with. Your business acumen makes you just the person to head a large charitable organization. Despite your natural timidity, you are skillful in public and can make a fine crusading speech guaranteed to bring an audience to its feet or to its senses. You possess a talent for spotting which social ills are ripe for attention and for making them popular issues.

You will work for very little reward if a cause means enough to you. And you're not beyond badgering others to contribute to your charity appeals. There's always a danger, though, that enthusiasm for a cause will upset your sense of proportion—like the Cancer lady who knocked on all the neighborhood doors collecting for a worthy down-and-out family, overlooking the fact that some of the people she approached were retired and just as hard up as the people she was trying to help.

When it comes to hobbies, you have a natural instinct for collecting. It might be stamps, antiques or even national flags (Cancer is very patriotic as a rule). Whatever you do in your spare time is apt to have commercial possibilities after a while. Old discontinued collections may be worth quite a bit of money. Remember, anything that's rare or is no longer made is salable. Have you checked lately?

If this natural urge to collect does not follow a definite line, the Cancer person is apt to hang on to junk instead of throwing it away. Bedrooms may be cluttered with outdated clothes, shoes, hats, and kitchen cabinets stuffed with empty jars, plastic containers, paper bags, silver paper "that might come in handy sometime."

One thing rarely lacking in a Cancer-born person is an innate affinity for the artistic side of life. You may not be engaged in the arts yourself, but your intuitive understanding and and appreciation allows you to move easily in artistic circles if you are so inclined. Most Cancer people at some time or another write a little poetry; free verse suits their wanderings and vivid imagination. Their insights into human nature are often remarkable. Sometimes their artistic urge expresses itself in a profound love of nature, particularly rivers and the ocean.

Finally, dear Cancer, you should know that we know you're not half as tough or detached as you sometimes pretend to be. All that swagger and bravado are a shell you've built up to ensure that the sensitive creature inside—the real you—doesn't get hurt too often.

CANCER IN LOVE

YOUR CANCER MAN

You like him? Love him? Just what sort of a man is he?

He's one of the most romantic velvet-tongued men in the Zodiac—if you get the positive type and not the negative, that is. He will make you feel one thousand percent woman. If he desires you, he'll lavish you with attention, affection and delectable words. His highly emotive and sensitive presence is often enough to turn a girl on without a word being said. He communicates sensually.

But before he does any of these things, he'll have to be convinced you're not playing around with him. He is terribly serious when it comes to love—you could even go so far as to say that he lives for love, to give and to receive it. He feels his way very carefully in any romantic affair. He's not going to make any rash mistakes. Even if its only a brief affair, he will treat you as the only woman in the world. Respond appropriately, and this coolly sensuous romantic is all yours.

You can't be the aggressive type of woman because this guy likes to pussyfoot around the women he fancies, picking up their vibes with his supercharged senses. He's looking for the ultimate in femininity. Any raucous female will send him scuttling off in horror. You know, of course, that his Sign is the Crab, he's remarkably like this fierce-looking armor-plated little creature. The Crab and Mr. Cancer pretend to be tough and invulnerable, but inside they're so soft it hurts. Your Cancer guy desperately wants to be loved and fussed over—though he would deny it. When he asks you out, let him take over completely.

He's got so much love to give, he can't bear the thought of giving it to a girl who shares hers with other boyfriends. If you go with him, he's yours and you're his. All or nothing at all, that's him. He's possessive and jealous, and this may be a problem. He's jealous because he's got such a massive inferiority complex he can't believe a woman like you could possibly love only him. He needs to reassure himself of this wonderful fact constantly; so he's likely to start questioning you: where've you been? who with? what did you talk about? All the self-torturing questions that can drive a loving and sincere woman like you nearly mad. Still, that's Cancer when he loves you; he can't believe his luck. It's a bittersweet affair for him.

He'll make you the queen of his castle. His woman and his home are the most important things in his life.

If you love him, tell him and tell him often. Show him, as well, not only with physical love but with an occasional small gift such as a fine old book, an antique, especially a souvenir of your own happy first meeting or that special evening out. He's sentimental and he'll treasure whatever you give him. He'll be loyal as long as you both love each other. He has no desire to move on once he finds the girl of his dreams. But if he feels you don't understand him—which usually means you've failed to give him sufficient attention—you'll have problems.

He's a pretty busy guy, with a great head for business, but if you call him at the office and want to drop in, he'll always make time for you (and slyly enjoy the opportunity to show you off to the other guys).

The negative type of Cancer man? You wouldn't like him at all. He's lazy, self-indulgent, wearyingly passive and indecisive. He's a good actor, though, and with his charming manner can pose as a winning guy—if it's worth his while. This type wallows in all forms of luxury and extravagance and often marries—fast—for money so he can settle back and do nothing.

YOUR CANCER WOMAN

You like her? Love her? What sort is she?

She's a moody, tempestuous, soft, lovable and changeable lady. She knows exactly the sort of guy she's looking for, and *if* she can find him, she'll never let him go. The trouble is she frequently goes through a lot of men in her search for Mr. Right. She surrenders completely to her emotions. She goes through the whole syndrome of lovesickness, from an inability to eat and sleep to desolation when she's parted from him. If it is Mr. Right, then Miss Cancer will take to marriage for the rest of her life (like a Crab to water so to speak), without ever looking over her shoulder at another man. If she can't marry him or live with him, she's likely to carry a torch for him for the rest of her days. That's the tenacity of pure love, Cancer style.

But . . . if you're not her ideal mate, Miss Cancer's supersensitive machinery will start sending disturbing messages to her brain. Without being disrespectful to the lady, this is the last part of her anatomy she consciously makes use of. She is so instinctive about the rightness and wrongness of situations and people that she seldom bothers to develop intellectual judgment—in normal circumstances. But in the situation just described, she finally gets the message. She starts to pick at her erstwhile lover, seeing him in a new light, spotting the areas in which he doesn't measure up to her idyllic image. She's likely to nag him to death if he sticks around. Not being a great one for initiating action, she'd rather he walk out than have to make the move herself.

This girl loves her family and home. If she fancies you, she'll want to take you to meet Mom and Dad at the first opportunity. You'll feel very comfortable and at ease in her apartment; it will be cosily furnished with lots of little knickknacks that remind her of sentimental events and interludes in her life. She'll be a very attentive hostess, genuinely concerned with your comfort and pleasure. And as a cook, she's a honey. If you really want to please her, suggest that sometime soon she might like to prepare you both a meal either at your place or hers.

Miss Cancer is very temperamental. She'll plunge into a mood of shattering despondency in the time it takes you to turn on the light switch. She'll be bubbling like champagne one minute, and as emotionally inert as an empty glass the next. She goes so deep inside herself that you'll wonder if you're with the same person and what you could possibly have said or done to bring about such a violent change of personality. You've probably done nothing. These Cancer people are ultravulnerable to psychic changes within themselves and in their environment.

When a Cancer woman is depressed, you'll have to be understanding or you'll lose her. She can throw a weird emotional tantrum that will make you feel you're the one who's lost touch with reality. Trying to reason with her will have no effect at all. Only love and patience will work. If you haven't got enough of these qualities, go home—next time you see her she'll be her old happy self and will never mention the incident.

To win this woman, you must constantly show her that you love and care for her. She, in return, will treat you as though you were the only man in the world—literally. The danger is she may smother you with affection and attention until what once was delightful becomes stifling. The more she loves, the more possessive and jealous she is.

Once a mother, Mrs. Cancer is likely to transfer all her love and attention to the infants, leaving poor you out in the cold.

CANCER WOMAN—ARIES MAN

A man born under the first Sign of the Zodiac may be too demanding for a girl like you. He'll always be questioning you, and in your frequent quiet moments, you don't like people constantly asking what's on your mind. He'll find your sudden mood changes hard to understand. A Mars-ruled person will look you straight in the eye and expect honest answers. The problem is you won't know what you really think at times, and even if you do, you're likely to send him into confusion by changing your mind the next day.

It is difficult for you to conceal your emotions. He finds it hard to show his. He doesn't go in for open displays. He'll save the tears for when he's alone. He likes to present a strong and robust image to the world.

You will have to coax him into taking more of an interest in home life because he's not the most domesticated of animals. In general, he prefers the company of his own sex. He's a man's man and quite a sporting type.

His lovemaking is rather physical. You may have to teach him to be a little more gentle and subtle in bed. But he's not a little-boy type, and you do like a man who can dominate you.

At some period in his life, this man will indulge in rash behavior. He may get involved in some stupid incident that he'll regret for a long time. He's not devious or deceptive, but he doesn't always think about the consequences of his actions. If he's had too much to drink, for example, he wouldn't dream of leaving his car where it is and getting home by other means; he'll imagine he is perfectly capable of driving, whatever his condition.

This is the sort of romantic combination that could amaze your friends. In so many ways, Cancer and Aries are opposites. You have hidden depths. Like your element, which is water, people find you hard to fathom. Our friend the Ram is an honest, open being. He finds it difficult to lie—to lie convincingly, that is. He is what you see before you.

You have great tenacity. Once you start a project, you will see it through come hell or high water. Mr. Aries, on the other hand, is constantly searching for something new. As a little boy, he probably hardly looked at his Christmas presents as he opened them, so keen was he to get to the next brightly wrapped parcel.

He's a great fighter for what he wants. If an Aries man has his sights set on you he'll battle to win your love. He's an aggressive type so your other boyfriends had better watch out. He doesn't mind a fight to get what he wants. He'll act first and ask questions later.

He's quite a dreamer. He will come up with the craziest ideas, which he'll be convinced can earn him a fortune. You, for all your dreaminess, know what is likely to work and what is not. As far as some of his business projects are concerned, you'll have to be the steadying influence.

He's not a subtle guy. In romance, you should be able to read him like a book. You will realize early on in the relationship that you have entirely different ideas about life. It's how you bridge this gap that will decide whether or not you have a contented marriage.

With an Aries man as your mate, you'll be mixing more than usual with other people. He loves a party and enjoys meeting characters from all walks of life. He will do what he can to get you out of your shell. Of course, there will be disputes and clashes of personality from time to time, but neither of you is the type to bear grudges for very long.

He makes a wonderful father. After all, he's something of an overgrown schoolboy himself.

CANCER WOMAN—TAURUS MAN

There is every possibility you two will get on together like a house afire. Mr. Taurus is a real man. He's got a big shoulder for you to rest your pretty head upon. He likes his comforts and he's interested in anything that will make life more comfortable. You are a home-loving person. He will love looking after you and will provide everything you want.

He likes to be the dominant one in his relationships with women. He's down to earth, practical and sensible. He will have all the qualities you desire in a man. You want someone to look up to and respect. This man, whose element is earth, should fit the bill.

You will probably fall head over heels in love with him at first meeting but he will take his time about you. He's not going to make any promises of undying love until he's pretty sure you're the kind of woman he's looking for.

You will always know where you stand with this man because he's incapable of handing you a line. If he is only interested in a fling, he'll tell you so straight out. There could be one problem for a dreamy girl like you: this guy is not so good when it comes to romance. Oh, he'll know how to wine and dine you and will give you the cash to buy the pretty things you want. But if you expect him to hold your hand and whisper romantic words on a moonlight night, you could be disappointed.

He is not a mean man with money but he does know its value. If you decide to marry, you and he should soon accumulate enough cash to put down a deposit on your first house.

Mr. Taurus will be good for you in many ways. You'll wonder why you ever wanted to escape reality when this man has shown you what a joy life can be with your feet firmly placed on the ground. You find it difficult to put your trust in other people, so afraid are you of being hurt. He will help you face the world and stop burying yourself away where nobody can reach you.

Some women find him a bit too much to take physically. It's unlikely you will share this point of view. He is not oversexed; he's just normal and uncomplicated. You should make an extremely good match. He will never try to take over your domain, the home. He will leave you to arrange the furniture and to cook the evening meal. In turn, you'll allow him to get on with his work and enjoy playing the housewife and entertaining his business associates.

Mr. Taurus is a very jealous man so don't let him catch you playing games with others. He has no sense of humor about infidelity. If he asks you to marry him, he expects it to be for keeps. He likes flattery. You'll have to keep telling him how clever he is—which is okay because you'll probably mean it.

He plans tomorrow very carefully. He doesn't like to be short of ready cash. Your house is likely to be fully insured, as is everything else you own that is of value. He's quite keen on possessions and can also be a bit of a snob. Here is where you could differ. You are not impressed by public images but success is very important to him and he likes to rub shoulders with people who have made the grade.

You will have to watch those moods of yours. He is likely to be rather intolerant if you brood. That faraway look in your eyes and the sudden stabs of pain you feel will be extremely difficult for him to understand. Your moments of sorrow, which even you are unable to explain, will have to remain secret.

As parents, you should make a wonderful couple: he will be a strong and masculine father and you a loving and giving mother.

CANCER WOMAN—GEMINI MAN

Something is sure to spark between you and a Gemini man. Chances are you will break his heart or he'll break yours. Whichever way it happens, this will be a relationship you are unlikely to forget.

He could overwhelm you with his speed of thought and lightning wit. If you fall for him, you could find yourself disappearing into that shell of yours, frightened to say anything he does not agree with. You will have to be extremely careful he doesn't take your personality over completely. It's very difficult to keep track of Mr. Gemini because he has a hundred different interests. If he is really enthralled by you, he'll make you feel terribly important. Most people find him either exceedingly attractive or shallow.

If he does hurt you, you're bound to suffer deeply. It's very hard to get away from a Gemini man because he likes to take people over and control them. You will probably try everything in your power to make him settle down. From your vantage point, it will be only too evident that he is getting nowhere fast.

Don't misjudge him, though. He'd never set out to upset anyone. He tends to live in the moment. If surrounded by an interesting group at a party, he will forget all about little you sitting in the corner waiting patiently for him to show you some attention.

He's a terrible flirt. He'll promise you undying love, and mean it—and then be unable to resist trying to seduce the next pretty girl he meets when he's out of your company.

He's terribly generous when it suits him. On a date, he'll never let you pay for anything. He likes eating in the best restaurants and sitting in the best seats at the theater. He won't take a bus if there's an empty taxi passing. With your attitude to money, you'll think he's crazy.

Let's face it, he *is* a bit crazy. He's certainly unpredictable, and this is part of his magnetism. You may get the uneasy feeling that a liaison with this man who's ruled by Mercury is not doing you any good; but you'll want to hang on to him to catch the next exciting installment in his unusual life.

He wants to experience everything at least once. It is advisable to play somewhat hard to get because once he takes you for granted, his interest will quickly wane. This is not to say that marriage or a long-term affair with Gemini would be disastrous. There's a lot you could teach this man, and once he gains some insight into what makes you tick, he could become very dependent on you. Basically he needs security, but can only accept it if he feels confident his freedom is not being taken away.

He loves long deep talks and so do you. Romance is an important part of his life. For all the silly mistakes he makes, you will have to treat him with gentleness and understanding. He needs a companion who is on his mental wavelength. Unless you talk the same language, the union won't last very long because he can't be held on a purely physical plane. The problem is, he may not always be around when you need him most. He has a way of vanishing into thin air when there's any hint of emotional upheavel. He likes comfortable surroundings but is not a great home lover. He gets restless if he has to spend more than a couple of evenings a week at home.

He won't take your moods too seriously, which is probably a good thing. If you want to grow more independent and self-reliant, then Mr. Gemini will be a big help to you.

Being a bit of a baby himself, he's very good with children, though he can't stand to be constantly pestered by them.

CANCER WOMAN—CANCER MAN

You and your Cancer man will understand each other well. You'll certainly sympathize when he goes into one of his moods. And when it comes to dreaming about the perfect life, you two will be a compatible duo. Your problem might be getting back to reality and doing something practical to realize your ideals.

You could do a lot worse than marry this guy. He will be gentle with you and show great sensitivity and compassion when you're down in the dumps. He's a hard worker and wishes to get to the top of the ladder. He's also dependable and will always live up to his responsibilities. Cancer men can suffer for years from what appears to be the most dreadful luck. People often write them off and think they'll never make it. Then suddenly they will hit the jackpot—and usually in a most unlikely way.

If you are one of those lady Crabs who wants her man to be masterful and dominant, you should not get too deeply involved with Mr. Cancer. He's not the sort to offer a shoulder for you to cry on. Actually, he often needs looking after himself.

Even when you hit hard times, he'll always see to it that the rent is paid on time. He's very security conscious and you will both be keen to build up your savings.

He's fussy when it comes to romance. He's looking for his ideal woman and is unlikely to have many casual affairs.

Mr. Cancer takes the responsibilities of marriage seriously. Like you, he would not walk down the aisle before giving the matter a great deal of consideration. Thus it is likely your courtship will be quite a long one.

This man is very often connected with the arts; many famous writers and musicians were born under his Sign. They possess the kind of creative talent that allows them to give the public what it wants.

You will both wish to spend a good deal of time at home. When first married, you'll love getting the house organized. You'll have no difficulty, agreeing on furnishings and decoration. He won't want to waste money on extravagant entertainment. He would much prefer to have a few close friends in for dinner and an interesting discussion.

You may be tempted to take each other too seriously, weighing every little gesture and word and reading more into them than you should. You are both very easily offended and often feel shattered by the most innocent remarks. However, neither of you is very good at sustaining a feud. It's important to try to avoid sinking into those isolating Cancer moods at the same time.

Don't make the mistake of looking for compliments and gratitude from each other, which is another Cancer failing. Both of you give generously to friends and loved ones, and you should not expect thanks when you give to each other.

Mr. Cancer will be a marvelous dad. He'll show all the feeling and understanding for offspring that you do. After all, you are both the mothering Sign of the Zodiac. You will have similar ideas about how children should be brought up, particularly from the discipline angle. Despite your loving natures, you can both be quite strict. You believe that children need to be shown how to conduct themselves by their elders and have no use for a child-rearing philosophy that says youngsters should be allowed to do as they please. However, this stiff attitude will be tempered with warmth and understanding of the problems of growing up.

If you love your Cancer man and are prepared to give as much as you take, yours will be a happy and lasting relationship.

CANCER WOMAN—LEO MAN

Will you be too wrapped up in yourself to give this man the constant ego boosting that he requires so desperately?

In many ways, he will be your dream come true. But there are certain drawbacks for a Cancer girl in this liaison and they should be examined closely before you take an irrevocable step.

You have an uncanny knack of seeing beneath the surface of people and, unlike many women will not be taken in by his strutting and roaring (he really does believe he's King of the Jungle). What you may find disconcerting is his lack of humility. You do like people to be aware of their faults and to own up to them. Mr. Leo has great difficulty admitting he is ever in the wrong. If necessary, he will twist the facts around to suit his case.

He's determined. If he decides you are the girl for him, it will be hard to escape him. When the Lion is in love, you can't ignore him. He's overpowering rather than masterful. You could find yourself under his spell and acting completely out of character. Leo males have a peculiar knack for making people think as they want them to. He's a persuasive talker and very difficult to influence or dissuade.

He needs loads of affection. When you are waiting for him to take you in his big strong arms, you could discover that he's lying back with his paws in the air expecting you to tickle him under the chin.

You will have to balance his great enthusiasm for life with calm and reason. He's an extremely hard worker and will do everything in his power to provide for you. He'll love to see you looking your best and will always try to buy you what you want because he considers your appearance a reflection on himself. He will enjoy showing you off to his friends and making you feel like the most beautiful woman in the world.

In many ways, he will work wonders for you. He'll draw you out of your shell and refuse to let you creep back into it. He'll make you face up to yourself. He's terribly possessive. When you slip out without him, he'll ask for a blow-by-blow account of your day. You'll have to explain what you did, whom you met and what took you so long getting home.

He likes to be the center of attention, surrounded by admirers. When things are going really well for him at work, he's apt to become a bit full of himself.

It's important for Mr. Leo to be number one. He hates taking orders from anybody. Very often he will work more hours than his associates, not so much for the money, but for a promotion.

You'll have to provide the sort of home he needs. He'll love coming in from the office, finding dinner prepared and you standing by the front door in your pretty little apron, waiting to throw your arms around him. He adores the romantic scene.

Although he loves his home, he also enjoys a good party. He's a bit of a showoff. By the way, don't get too jealous if you see him dancing with lots of different girls. He can't help flirting. There's unlikely to be anything serious in it. He simply likes to feel he's attractive and desirable.

Don't be too disappointed if you only have a small family. Leos like their home to be a peaceful place and can't stand too much disruption to their orderly way of life.

CANCER WOMAN—VIRGO MAN

With this man you'll have to accept one thing from the start: you are both likely to judge people and situations from opposite ends of the scale. You are emotional and make many of your judgments intuitively. He is reason itself. He believes that any and every problem can be worked out logically.

You'll have to be absolutely crazy about each other to overcome these very important differences. You could be greatly attracted to him on first meeting. He's charming, gentlemanly, well-groomed, often a real dandy. It's only when you get to know him much better, perhaps after a couple of months, that you'll begin to discover he might be too much of a fusspot for you.

He is old-fashioned and a great upholder of law and tradition. You need a level-headed person, certainly, but he may have his feet sunk too firmly in terra firma.

You are the type of dreamer who probably went on convincing yourself Santa Claus really did exist even after the kids at school broke that particular bubble for you. He will continually make you look at the facts. It will be difficult for an intuitive person like you to show this man that two and two do not *always* add up to four.

His love is very unselfish. He's devoted to his parents as a rule and will show great respect for his father in particular and for his older relatives in general.

You could get disillusioned with each other pretty soon after the affair begins. In most cases, the differences are just too extreme to overcome.

You may find him far too touchy. Sometimes you may even believe he's putting on an act just to get his own way. When you point this out to him, he's likely to lose his temper. Why, you may ask yourself. Because, Miss Cancer, you have pierced his Achilles' heel.

If you are able to form a workable relationship, you'll discover you have a faithful and devoted husband. Virgo people usually have plenty of opportunities for illicit affairs but rarely take advantage of them. He would not risk his security with you for anybody.

He likes his home and his comforts and will be very appreciative of all you do for him. His love is the steady kind that lasts a lifetime. You will have to do what you can to fire his imagination in bed. It is through your lovemaking that you will probably discover the best opportunity to get through to him.

He will want you to be a smart dresser but not a flashy one. He'll want you to appear a beautiful lady rather than a seductive woman who draws wolf whistles from men on the street.

His privacy is sacrosanct. He will always be courteous to your friends and family, but when you're alone, he'll ask if it is really necessary to have Mother over for dinner *every* Sunday. Like you, he's careful with money. He's definitely not mean but he rarely goes on a spending spree. This should not bother you because what he saves he's likely to put into the house and invest for your old age.

Virgo men as a rule are not that enthused about becoming fathers. He may even go so far as to try to talk you out of having children. He doesn't like interference with his settled and orderly way of life.

If you do have children, he will expect them to be clean and dressed neatly always. He can't stand dirty hands and faces and toys strewn around the living room.

CANCER WOMAN—LIBRA MAN

Mr. Libra won't be prepared to take over and make all your decisions for you. He's the sort of person who feels it is up to you to stand up for your own rights. You are a dreamer, but you're practically a realist compared to him. Lots of women find him far too wrapped up in his own make-believe world.

He's sociable, enjoys the company of good friends, loves to talk politics and discuss the world's problems.

You are looking for a permanent mate and he may be something of a puzzle. One moment, he will be all over you; the next, he'll seem like a stranger—distant and aloof. At times you will get extremely cold vibrations from him without a word being uttered in anger.

Don't try to work out where you went wrong because it's unlikely that you did. It's just that Mr. Libra has strange ways. He's extremely charming and it's terribly easy for a woman like you to fall under his spell. But he finds it difficult to make up his mind. He has an amazing ability to see a situation from all angles. He knows how to treat a woman—when it comes to picking restaurants and giving his lady loves a good time, he's fantastic.

You'll find his mind fascinating. He will have a fund of knowledge and stories that will keep a room enthralled. He knows how to pay a compliment, too. It will rarely pass his notice when you're dolled up in something new.

He likes to cry alone. He does not allow friends to see him in his down moods—even close friends. He feels that the world situation is bad enough without adding to its problems with his personal gloom.

He's ambitious without being pushy. If bad luck strikes him down, he's capable of picking himself up off the ground and fighting his way to the top. This is because of his positive attitude and his refusal to blame others when things go wrong.

Mr. Libra could be very good for you in many ways. He will teach you a great deal if you're prepared to listen. To him, marriage is an art and well worth working at. He's a wonderful and considerate lover. It will be a matter of personal pride with him to keep you happy and satisfied in every way.

Libras are always shouting about peace. Perhaps in their idealistic way they think the human race is better than it really is. They frequently support a more just government and a welfare state, but they are rarely found working in prisons or other squalid places. They will do anything to avoid an argument—and they can't stand physical violence.

Neither of you is very decisive and this could be a disadvantage. You both prefer to muddle along rather than make hard and fast decisions. Perhaps after a few years of marriage to you, he'll realize that one of you has to take responsibility.

Your best bet will be to catch this man well after he's reached maturity because he could be much too difficult to cope with in youth. He tends to trifle in his teens and early twenties, and get involved with more than one woman time after time.

He may not know how to satisfy your innermost needs. It might be impossible for him to understand your emotional outbursts. Still, taking everything into consideration, you should be able to rely on him and know he will be on your side at all times in this ever-changing world.

CANCER WOMAN—SCORPIO MAN

He will be one of the most fascinating men you come across in your life. If you get involved with Mr. Scorpio, it will be difficult to break the spell. He may not be all that good for you, but you will learn a great deal about yourself from an affair with him.

He refuses to be beaten in anything. He's jealous, possessive and a real fighter. Although there are many things you will disagree about, there is a considerable amount you'll have in common. Remember, you are both water Signs, which means you're both far deeper than most people suspect.

You are pretty passionate and so is he, so your sex scene will be exciting and stimulating, though it could become a little too intense for you at times. He's not a great romantic but he is fascinated by sex. He likes to try out anything different in his lovemaking. Unless there are other aspects to your relationship, it will most likely not last very long.

He won't stand for your moodiness. If you sulk a lot, he may ask why you don't pack your things and go home to Mother. He's blunt and doesn't believe in either mincing his words or hiding his emotions.

If he feels he is not being treated fairly, he's quite capable of quitting a perfectly good job. He won't allow himself to be dominated for very long by authority. Sometimes you may feel he is merely out to make trouble; especially since the scenes he creates usually have an unfortunate way of backfiring on him.

Love without jealousy does not exist for this man. He will always be suspicious, even when there is nothing to be suspicious about. He can't help it; it's second nature to him.

He may easily misunderstand your patience with him and take it as a sign of indifference. He wants your constant attention. He likes to be told how much you love and desire him.

Mr. Scorpio enjoys his home comforts but you shouldn't expect him to stay home every night. He likes to have his time out with the boys. He's something of a man's man, though essentially he is a loner. Apart from his own woman, he doesn't enjoy the company of the opposite sex that much. He needs respect. He likes to be thought of as a good guy. Very often he is unable to admit the truth about himself.

He will adore your femininity. He likes his woman to be all woman. When you are going about your domestic chores, you may catch him watching you with an adoring look in his eyes. If you are his, he will want you and admire you right to the end.

Of course, there is no long-standing partnership that does not go through difficult times. You will have your arguments and fights—you may even think he's a monster on occasions.

People rarely get the better of him in business. He knows how to spot a con man when he sees one, and he can usually see through the most convincing lie if he is being two-timed. He has a knack of getting to the bottom of things.

Mr. Scorpio is terribly ambitious for his children. He may wish his youngsters to be carbon copies of himself. If there is a family business, he will want junior to take his place in it. Of course, children don't always fall into line with his careful plans. Perhaps you will have to bridge the gap between father and son.

The biggest problems that will face you both is in parenthood. You have a strong mothering instinct, and he could become exceedingly jealous and bitter if he feels he's being superseded by his own children.

CANCER WOMAN— SAGITTARIUS MAN

He's difficult to catch, and some people would say difficult to live with. Certainly, there would be quite a few obstacles to overcome for a Cancer girl.

Mr. Sagittarius hates to feel trapped. He loves freedom and dislikes planning too far into the future. A settled life terrifies him. He's a roaming sort of man who loves company and enjoys telling a yarn in the neighborhood bar.

He's lots of fun. You will be overwhelmed by his strong personality, but underneath that brash exterior, you will find a bit of a baby. He really needs looking after, although if you told him so, he'd be terribly offended. You must ask yourself seriously if you want to get deeply involved with a man who very often does not know when to stop.

Of course, you are not altogether staid. You sometimes revel in excitement and parties. If you don't give too much thought to the morrow and are prepared to drift through life taking whatever fate casts your way, all will be well with you and Mr. Sagittarius. But there are very few ladies born under the Sign of the Crab who feel this way years on end.

He attracts people like bees to the honey pot. He's always joking and fooling, and when you're out, a crowd will often gather around him. He seems so bright and full of energy that few people remain depressed in his company. You may get a bit bored traipsing around with him because you have heard his yarns two or three times before.

Just when you've despaired of Mr. Sagittarius and written him off as a fool, he'll allow you a glimpse of the real man—a deeply intelligent being. Basically, he's extremely sensitive and terrified of being hurt or let down. Perhaps that is why he's wary about permanent relationships. He puts on an act so others can't get too close to him. Once he feels absolutely sure about you, he'll open up and you will begin to see the man he really is.

Whatever arguments you two have—and there will be many—life will certainly not be dull. Although you may feel like throwing something at him on occasions, he'll never bore you. He is as honest as the day is long and delivers straight from the shoulder. A Sagittarius man has great insight. You may feel he doesn't notice what's going on around him, but he does. He's a very good judge of character.

You will undoubtedly do wonderful things for him and he for you. If you're prepared to dedicate a good part of your life to looking after this man, he'll help you come out of your shell. He may flirt with other women, but only to boost his ego. It is highly unlikely that he'll ever get involved in a serious affair once he's given his name to you. He's not the greatest romancer but you will not have many complaints about his lovemaking. He is passionate and aggressive. If you don't try to hold him down or limit his freedom, he will always come back to you.

Mr. Sagittarius enjoys the company of his own sex so let him have his night out with the boys. He needs to let off steam occasionally. He'll come home to you, seeking shelter from the storm, and will give you every opportunity to indulge your maternal instinct.

This man will love the home you make, but don't expect him to spend a lot of time in it. There won't be many evenings when he can unwind enough to snooze in front of the fire.

He's generous with money and he'll do his darndest to ensure you never want for anything. If you work at this union, it will improve with time. He won't get tired of you when the gray hairs begin to show. And he'll love the way you look after the kids.

CANCER WOMAN—CAPRICORN MAN

When you're first introduced to a Capricorn man, you may feel he's exactly like you in temperament and character. But don't believe it. He is a past master of the coverup.

Being very shy and retiring, he finds it necessary to put on a front when meeting people. He's wary of letting others get too close to him. He may seem independent, debonair and cheerful, but there is much more to him than that. And the longer you are in his company, the more complex you'll discover he is.

The Capricorn man often lives alone. He rarely gets married early in life. He's terribly fussy and perhaps a bit afraid of sharing his life with another. He needs to be loved and admired. Very often he will throw himself into his work. He has so much energy he usually gets to the top of whatever career he pursues.

He's something of a romantic and lives in a dream world. He has some difficulty in facing the harshness of reality.

He admires hard work and success. He doesn't get along too well with people who are flippant. He loves intelligent discussion. With him, words often speak louder than actions. You are a fairly thorough person and quick to recognize the good qualities in others. He won't get involved in romance lightly; you can be sure he means it if he does whisper that he loves you.

Mr. Capricorn will be quite happy for you to continue with your career after you get married. Your having outside interests won't worry him and he'll probably encourage you in your job. The reason he does not expect you to give up everything for life at the kitchen sink is that he is not the sort of guy who expects others to make sacrifices he is not prepared to make himself.

Your Cancer attitude to work is likely to make him think you're a little lazy. He'll tell you you should plan ahead more.

He can be quite passionate but is unlikely to make a pass at you until he's convinced he won't be rejected. Criticism can be excruciatingly painful for him. You will have to give him confidence in himself as a lover if you desire him.

Although not a mean man, he is careful. You will find you agree pretty well on how to handle joint finances. He will do what he can to ensure a secure future for you both.

If you do decide to be a career wife, Mr. Capricorn will be prepared to take on a fair share of the household chores. Mother has probably had a strong influence on this guy, so you'll find he comes to you already house-trained. Talking of families, you are both likely to want to remain close to your relatives after marriage so it is essential that you get on with his parents and he with yours.

He may want to check up on how much you are spending at the supermarket each week. It isn't that he doesn't trust you; he simply wants to make sure you are getting the best value for your money.

He will make a very good father and take his parental responsibilities seriously. More than likely he'll model himself on his own dad, whom he is likely to have admired tremendously. Even if they didn't get along too well, you'll find his father made a big impression on him in his youth. Mr. C. is old-fashioned enough to expect respect from his youngsters. He's a stickler for routine and discipline. You should make a pretty good combination for any child to grow up with.

Don't let him get too set in his ways. Coax him into casting off that grave exterior occasionally and having a good laugh.

CANCER WOMAN—AQUARIUS MAN

If you want to wear the pants at home, you've got the right man in Mr. Aquarius because he will completely accede to you in domestic responsibilities. As a matter of fact, he's seldom interested in mundane things at all.

You like to have positive views on things. It

is important to you to form definite opinions. Mr. Aquarius could therefore confuse you. He's likely to be the most broad-minded chap you've ever met. He's very impractical. He swings into action without considering the consequences—a startling mode of living to a person like you.

Of course, love can change a man. If he feels you need protection and can't look after yourself, he might make it his life's work to take care of you and see to all your needs.

Mr. Aquarius needs a cause. He doesn't want to reveal his true feelings but he'll enjoy dissecting others and trying to discover what makes them tick. An Aquarius man is adept at telling you what is wrong with the world. He tends to look outside rather than within.

If he finally gets around to proposing marriage and you say "yes," prepare yourself: he'll expect you to feel as passionate as he does about his causes. You may get fed up having a houseful of people all the time.

A Cancer girl is likely to intrigue the Water Bearer because he can't fathom you. When you have one of your moods, he'll never tire of discussing it with you. Since you quite enjoy talking about yourself, you'll probably feel flattered by his interest. He's no bully or brute. In fact, he'll be terribly gentle with you. The trouble is he might want to change you (gently). Aquarius men do try to mold people into what they think they should be.

He's so proud of being reasonable and logical that others find him a bit of a bore at times.

Strangely, Aquarius men often get to the top of their profession despite their apparent efforts to the contrary. People are surprised when they do make it because they always seem so wrapped up in their other interests.

These men need a stable influence in their lives. And you may be just the woman to give Mr. Aquarius the kind of settled background he can best function out of.

He won't infringe on your freedom. Since he is something of a revolutionary, "freedom" is very important to him. He wouldn't dream of telling you whom you should see and whom you shouldn't.

Aquarius men find it rather difficult to express themselves in lovemaking. You will have to use your womanly wiles in bed to get him to relax and give himself to you.

It might be a considerable time before he summons up the courage to say that first "I love you." When he does get it together, it will have been well worth waiting for.

He may get tired of your closeness with your family. It's quite likely he stopped seeing very much of his parents a long time ago. He's not very good at keeping friends. Always on the lookout for something new, he is constantly finding new acquaintances to stimulate his alert and active mind. He's quite an intellectual type, you know, and you should have some very interesting discussions over the dinner table.

Mr. Aquarius is never likely to be short of money, though he's not really good at amassing it. Still, he'll often come up with a new idea that will help to keep his head above water.

He makes a fine father and usually has a pretty good understanding of children.

CANCER WOMAN—PISCES MAN

Do you believe in love at first sight? If you doubt there's such a thing, a Pisces man is likely to convince you otherwise. This person, who was born under the twelfth and last Sign of the Zodiac, will probably have a special appeal for you. Just when you had given up hope of ever finding true love, a Pisces man could enter your life and make you believe it's spring again.

He's artistic and easily moved by beautiful poetry and music. Although a dreamer (like you), he's no slouch when it comes to work.

He's sensitive and romantic. He will do his best to look after you. A Pisces man will try to give you everything your heart desires. He is a very kind person and will seriously try to get you to face up to yourself. He will never be cruel but he will be honest. He certainly won't allow you to go hiding away from reality for too long.

Mr. Pisces is not petty, and that is something you will appreciate.

Very often people born under the Sign of the two Fishes are involved in creative work in one form or another. He may be an artist or be connected with theater or television. Whatever his occupation, he is likely to bring an individualistic touch to his work, for though he is a dreamer, the modern Pisces man does all he can to ensure that his dreams come true. His head may be in the clouds but his feet are firmly on the ground. He's always on the lookout for something new. He's inventive and will take a chance on any project he believes in.

When he is courting you, he will ply you with gifts—something all women, but especially Cancer women, love. His love letters are missives you'll wish to keep forever. He won't forget your birthday and will appreciate your love of nature's delights and be forever sending you beautiful flowers. A relationship with a Pisces man could be the experience of a lifetime.

He's quite intuitive. He will understand your moods and know how to cope with them. He'll always have the time and patience to hear you talk yourself out of your depressions. This man doesn't harbor any deep prejudices. He won't judge a fellow human being by class or creed. He believes in giving everybody a fair shake. He's also prepared to forgive mistakes.

You are both water Signs so you should have a keen understanding of each other's personality. He will share your love of the home and will never try to tell you how to run it.

You should be very much on the same mental wavelength. Your opinions on world situations are likely to coincide. You will also find you both get on very well with the same people. Many of your friends will be mutual friends.

You both need security. He will be willing to work hard to maintain a good living standard. If you wish to pursue a career, this will not worry Pisces—so long as it doesn't detrimentally affect your life together. To him, this is paramount.

Any drawbacks? Well, yes. He can be very easily hurt so you mustn't be too blunt with him. If he loves you, he'll want your respect. Never tease him because he won't know how to take it. He needs lots of encouragement. When he gets down in the dumps, you may have to push him back into the fray.

If he gets really depressed, be positive. Get him out of the house. Have an evening on the town together. You are just the sort of woman to inspire him to get to the top of his profession.

Mr. Pisces is a permissive parent. You will have to be the one who exercises the discipline.

CANCER MAN—ARIES WOMAN

This woman could drive you out of your mind. Let's be honest, she likes to wear the pants. She could be much too forceful and dominating for a dreamer like you.

She's an all-action girl who does not indulge in wishful thinking. Very often women born under this fire Sign are terribly ambitious. Although they have a fairly strong maternal instinct, you'll generally find their career comes first. Often an Aries girl won't get married until late in life. Nor will she want to contemplate starting a family until she has fulfilled some of her other cherished hopes and dreams.

This woman is a fast worker. If she really fancies you, she could well sweep you off your feet. Whereas you like a peaceful life, she is full of drive and finds it hard to stay put for one minute. The nervous energy she burns up may be quite frightening to you.

You prefer to proceed cautiously in personal relationships as well as in matters connected with your career. A Cancer-Aries union is a bit like the tortoise and the hare. You could well be first past the finishing post, though, because you will avoid the obvious mistakes. You will look right and left before crossing the street; an Aries person won't.

Don't underestimate her. For all her forcefulness, she's very sensitive. She doesn't like to show her emotions, though, because she can't stand to appear weak in front of others.

She's a bit complicated. For a start, she's extremely jealous. Woe betide you if you deceive her with another woman. She's not incapable of violence. Miss Aries is quite prepared to confront the woman who's taken her man from her. She's impulsive; she'll act first and face the music later.

Underneath all that vivaciousness and cheery courage lurks an inferiority complex. Deep down, she doubts herself. Success and acceptance are terribly important to her. She can't stand criticism, mainly because she feels there may be something to it.

What she is basically yearning for is someone who can take command. She would really love to be the dominated little housewife, but the trouble is there are so few men she feels are worth sacrificing her independence for.

She is quite capable of deep involvements with various men before settling down. This is because she's searching for Mr. Right. Very often she'll go for the wrong type and get badly hurt.

In her lovemaking, she is warm and passionate, and she is quite capable of becoming the dominant partner.

If you are her man, she'll want to go everywhere with you. She is a great confidence booster and will do all she can to ensure that you make a success of your chosen career.

She prefers male company to that of her own sex. You'll find she is likely to have only two or three close girlfriends. She's the sporty type and quite an outdoor girl. Don't try to take her over when you first start courting. And don't read more into her relationships with other men than is really there. You will have to trust her and not cross-examine her.

When she does settle down, she usually

makes an ideal wife and a fantastic mother. She can get a little possessive with her children, especially when the time comes for them to leave the family nest.

CANCER MAN—TAURUS WOMAN

This liaison will certainly have its good points because you will have so many things in common with a Taurus woman. You both have a deep-rooted need for a secure home life. It is difficult for a man born under the Sign of Cancer to function properly unless he feels right in his surroundings.

A Taurus woman is a wonderful homemaker. Although when you first meet her she may appear to be totally absorbed in her career, she's capable of giving it up and settling down when she meets the right man.

She's not inclined to take the initiative but she's ambitious enough to give you a kick in the backside to get you going on occasions. Although you are ambitious yourself, your plans frequently stop at the "if only" stage. She will get you thinking and acting in terms of "I can" rather than "I should."

She's very passionate and alive. She's materialistic and will expect you to provide her with comforts. If you really love her, she's the sort of woman who could make you want to get on, not so much for yourself, but because you would love to prove you could make it for her sake.

Miss Taurus takes people for what they are without asking too many questions. In other words, she accepts reality. Apart from her interest in her home, she is also likely to have a great love of nature. She will enjoy puttering in the garden and growing beautiful flowers.

She dislikes change. You are a man who, although home-loving, enjoys moving from time to time and perhaps even living abroad. You'll find it extremely difficult to get your Taurus woman to go along with such plans.

It will be impossible to talk this lady into going steady with you if she's unsure of her emotions. It's perfectly simple really; either she fancies you or she doesn't. There's little you can do or say that will change her mind. She is faithful and loyal. She doesn't like to get involved with more than one person at a time.

She's not a flirt herself and won't be able to accept your showing an interest in other women. She finds it difficult to forgive her man if he gets involved in an affair. She expects him to be stronger-willed than that. She's extremely jealous and possessive. She's not an easy woman to fool, so don't try to pull the wool over her eyes.

Miss Taurus is quite artistic. People born under this Sign are often good at drawing and painting. She usually loves the theater.

Food is very important to your Taurus lady. She's finicky. Everything must taste just right. She usually goes in for plain cuisine and won't be very impressed by exotic dishes. You will love her cooking. She takes a great pride in her culinary expertise.

She has a very sensitive sense of touch. She loves things to be soft and feminine. She won't like it if you have a beard. You'll have to shave it off before any petting can commence.

Surprisingly, this little lady can be quite a tomboy. Despite her love of pretty things, she won't complain about petty irritations. She can look after herself when she has to. If things are a bit difficult financially, she'll be prepared to take a part-time job to help out. She likes to feel she's pulling her weight.

She won't argue with you for the sake of arguing. If you are in the wrong, though, you'd better duck. Wow! What a temper.

You'll be the one the youngsters try to win over. They'll come to you and ask if they can stay up a bit longer to watch a favorite TV program. They'll know darned well that once Taurus mommy has said "no," she means it.

CANCER MAN—GEMINI WOMAN

Gemini is the Sign of the Twins. You may sometimes wonder which twin you are dating when you go out with this Mercurial girl. You will certainly have some difficulty keeping up with her moods and changes of thought. She likes to keep on the go and finds it extremely hard to stay put in any one place for very long. She's full of new ideas and is no slouch when it comes to the art of conversation.

She's a bit of a flirt and you might find this side of her nature hard to come to terms with. You must learn not to take her playing up to other guys too seriously. At times she might not even know she's doing it. Her changes of mood will dazzle you. You like a certain amount of stability in your love relationships, and it's possible Miss Gemini will cause you too much pain. So be sure you know what you're doing before you make it permanent.

Her mind is always traveling. She's not too good at living in the present. She's always curious about tomorrow and what it will bring. If you're looking for a woman who will settle happily into the routine of domestic life, then move along, friend. Marriage makes little difference to the Gemini woman's basic attitude. She loves parties and meeting people.

You like to get eight hours' sleep, more if you can manage it; she's a night person. If there's any action going, she's likely to be out till cockcrow.

Mind you, she's not really heartless. She certainly doesn't go out of her way to hurt people. She's a sensitive woman herself and does not relish the idea of causing another human being pain. Very often she'll be well aware of her faults and desirous of changing her ways. For the right guy, she probably could.

It's the same with work. One day your Gemini woman will be telling you she's going to be a photographer. But after taking a reel of film, she'll decide she'd rather be a mountaineer. Halfway up her first climb, she'll change her mind and hurry back home to take singing lessons. One thing is certain: you'll never be bored when you're in her company.

Miss Gemini fascinates people. When you go to a party and see a crowd around someone, it's likely to be pretty Miss G.—capturing the hearts of a fair proportion of the males in the room. Her attraction is magnetic.

Don't get angry with her. She needs help, not admonishment. Cancer-Gemini unions can work; but they do require lots of patience and kindness on the part of Cancer. You will not get her to change her ways by bullying. If you try to lay down the law, you'll find that her ruler Mercury has whisked her away.

She loves speed. She gets a great kick from being driven fast in a sports car. All sorts of travel appeal to her—especially jetting to other countries. You might prefer a cruise on a luxury liner, but this mode of travel of yesterday will be far too slow for her.

A Gemini woman is in love with the idea of love. If you want to be her man, you'll have to help her direct that love into one channel. In her youth, she may get involved in quite a few affairs, some with married men. Basically she is looking for security. She is often able to settle down better with an older and more mature person. But she needs to be able to respect her man.

Don't try to dig too deep with her. It's a pointless exercise to attempt to work out what makes her tick. The time will come in her life when she realizes she can't be the life and soul of the party for eternity and will want to settle down. If you catch her then, you'll never regret marrying her.

CANCER MAN—CANCER WOMAN

This liaison will have its good points and its bad. There is no doubt you will understand each other well, but you may find it hard to come to terms with your fellow Cancer's moods.

When you are both down in the dumps, it will be really heavy going because both of you tend to withdraw into your own little worlds and become so wrapped up in yourselves that you forget all about the feelings of others. Of course, you'll have a great deal in common: love of your home, pleasure in traveling, the desire to hang on to old friends. You are both deeply involved in the past and have difficulty facing up to tomorrow. Family life is terribly important to you. She will always be on the phone to her mother and both of you will maintain very close ties with relatives.

Miss Cancer's a woman of many moods. That quiet reserved lady you see going about her business in the day could easily become a giggling Moon loon at night. You will share the same sort of humor and are likely to be attracted to the same types of friends.

Your attitude to cash should be identical because you have a common interest in making sure of the future. She will be as keen as you to save money wherever she can. Like you, she is terrified of not being able to keep up the mortgage payments or any other regular bills.

Clothes are her big weakness, the one area where she can't help being extravagant. Her closet is likely to be packed with beautiful robes, suits and dozens of pairs of shoes. She finds it hard to walk past a fashionable department store without going in to try something on.

Remember what you don't like yourself when dating a girl born under the Sign of the Crab. She hates criticism and can't stand to be ridiculed or laughed at. Take her seriously when you know she is being sincere.

She loves to be spoiled with presents. She will be truly happy if you buy her boxes of chocolates and dozens of roses. She'll never take you for granted. She needs to be constantly shown how deep your love goes.

A Cancer woman is not aggressive. While you are capable of suddenly blowing up and even becoming physically violent when driven to it, she is not.

In your love relationship, you'll have to make the first move. She needs to be dominated and likes a man who can master her. The little-boy type who needs mothering will definitely not last the distance with a Cancer woman. If she should marry one, she'll love him and protect him in a way—but walk right over him.

If you do decide to become husband and wife, you'll have married a woman who is capable of making your home exactly what you want. She'll look after you well. She'll have your evening meal ready, darn your socks and do anything else she can to make you feel happy and contented.

Play it straight with your Cancer woman and she'll put you on a pedestal. She'll be terribly hurt if you have an affair after marriage. Deep down, she will blame herself and wonder where she went wrong. It is really not fair to play with the emotions of someone so trusting and loving.

Never lead her to believe you care more for her than you do; when she's really gone on a guy, she wants to believe everything she's told.

Naturally, she makes an excellent mother, although she does find it difficult to cut the apron strings—especially with her sons.

CANCER MAN—LEO WOMAN

You'll have to shake yourself out of your introverted ways if you want to catch a Leo girl. She simply won't have time to cope with your moods. A Leo woman is a positive woman. She's very quick to sum up people. If she feels a man is going to be too much trouble, she just won't allow herself to become involved with him.

This Lioness has great willpower and self-control. She doesn't like to be bossed around. She is extremely logical in her approach to life. This doesn't mean there isn't a sentimental side to her nature; of course, there is. But it will always be tempered by the practical.

She's likely to be a leader in her group. With her girlfriends, she'll be the one who makes the suggestions about where to go and what to do. She's not a sit-at-home. She can't stand mooning around talking about what is wrong with this world of ours. Miss Leo gets up and does something about it.

If you do decide to marry, don't expect a meek wife. She has an inquiring mind and will wish to go on learning new things all her life. A Leo woman could be terribly good for a Cancer man. But if you want to keep her, you'll have to change that negative side of your nature.

She may appear to be soft and gentle, but when aroused, she can be quite stormy. Don't try to get away with anything with her. She'll know what is going on and would rather you come clean than take her for a fool.

Miss Leo has expensive tastes. Don't expect her to be happy with a hamburger and a movie on your first date. She likes the good things in life, although she's not really extravagant. And though she's quite capable of looking after herself, she does like to be treated as a lady.

Be original. She can't stand people who are carbon copies or who try to be fashionable for the sake of making an impression. She's not seduced by flashy manners and flashy dress. She'll see right through any man who's trying to put on an act for her.

She's quite athletic, while Cancer people rarely are. She loves to keep fit and it's quite possible she'll be interested in yoga or some similar form of discipline. A Leo woman will often be a health-food addict. She reasons everything through and tries to do what is good for her.

In bed, you will find her very physical, very attuned to sensation. She likes to be taken. She doesn't like her lovemaking to become routine. She desires her man to be an imaginative lover.

If you decide to go as far as marriage with a Leo woman, you'd better get busy and cash in on that Cancer business flair of yours. Although she's for equality of the sexes, she does expect her husband to be the provider.

You'll probably find yourself going out more than you did before you met this girl. She's fond of her home, but having an inquiring mind, she can't bear the idea of being buried away.

A Leo woman is superb at entertaining. You need never fear to bring the boss home to dinner; everything will be just right.

She is also excellent at getting along with members of her own sex. If you have any business dealings with women, far from being jealous, your wife will get on very well with them.

Leo women rarely go in for large families. They love children but don't want to devote their entire lives to motherhood.

CANCER MAN—VIRGO WOMAN

You are just the sort of man to bring out the woman in a girl born under the Sign of Virgo. People are very unfair to those whose symbol is the Maiden (the only female figure in the Zodiac, remember), insisting they are cold and indifferent and lack imagination. So many are quick to write Virgo off on first impression. You, Mr. Cancer, are just the man to see beyond the veil.

She happens to be very particular about her men. Romance is not something she's prepared to become involved in lightly. So many people these days expect to go to bed with someone almost before they have been formally introduced. Not so Miss Virgo. People call her old-fashioned. Well, she has standards and she tries to adhere to them.

She is basically terribly shy, so it's not easy for her to show her emotions. Perhaps she has a deep-down fear of being rejected or hurt. She finds public display distasteful so don't embarrass her in front of others. (You yourself don't like a girl to hold your hand walking down the street or give you a good-night kiss in front of her friends.) And don't try to force that first "I love you" out of her, either. She likes to make up her own mind and can't tolerate pressure.

Miss Virgo is basically pure-minded and interested in real love. She goes overboard for all those weepy movies of the late thirties and early forties. Not for her the casual pickup. To go to bed with a man, she has to feel more than physical attraction.

You'll have to improve your sense of time if you date a Virgo woman. When you say you'll pick her up at 8:00, be sure to be there on the dot. She's a very punctual person herself and doesn't think there is any excuse for you being late.

A Virgo woman's obsessiveness with neatness could drive you a bit crazy. Although a great home lover, you do tend to be a bit messy. You like your home to be comfortable. Her orderly ways and efficient manner may make you feel you're being institutionalized.

At first, she'll be very shy about going out with you alone so your best ploy might be to arrange with a mutual friend for a foursome. Earth is her element and actions always speak louder than words with her. She lays great stress on good manners. She also clings to the past. She would far prefer to shop in an old-fashioned grocery than in a brash new supermarket.

Don't give up, though, because love can conquer all. It will take all your patience and understanding to get her to relax and forget what other people might think of her, but you could find it well worth the effort.

It will be terribly important to her to succeed as a wife. She'll want to make you happy. She can't stand failure, especially in something as important as marriage.

Like you, this girl can't bear to admit she's in the wrong or to have her faults pointed out to her. What will be rather annoying to you is that most of the time she'll be in the right.

You couldn't find a more loyal woman. It is a very rare thing for a Virgo type to be unfaithful. Oh, she'll have her opportunities, but thinks about the long term and won't be prepared to risk her future for fleeting physical pleasure.

She'll bring up children quite strictly and try to equip them to cope with the realities of the outside world.

CANCER MAN—LIBRA WOMAN

Women are well known for changing their minds and Libra women probably change theirs more often than any other Sign in the Zodiac. It's not that they lack steadfastness; it's just that they have difficulty making definite decisions. They can always see an argument from all points of view, which doesn't leave much room for personal maneuver. They will bend over backward to be fair to everybody.

This chopping and changing could drive you absolutely mad. You do, after all, like to know where you stand with a person, especially someone you're romantically involved with. Miss Libra will keep you guessing. She's capable of promising you undying love and devotion one minute and disappearing into thin air the next. When you take her to task over this, she'll probably wonder what you're carrying on about.

She is tremendously interested in life and people. She's a great observer and possesses an inquiring mind.

She may be a bit too logical for you. She thinks that any problem can be worked out scientifically. You may get very irritated at times because Libra people have the habit of being right.

She is quite a woman. Lots of guys fall head over heels for Libra girls. They have a vivacious quality that is very attractive. Miss Libra is soft, exceedingly feminine, knows how to wear clothes and gives off extremely warm vibrations. When you get to know her a bit better, you'll discover she has lots of close friends.

She doesn't go in for obvious feminine wiles to catch a man. She likes to be herself. If she fancies you, she'll let you know. She's the party type. You will find it difficult to get her away from large gatherings. She is in her element flitting from group to group, joining mildly in an argument here, a conversation there.

She is not a loner. It is extremely rare to find a Libra girl living on her own. On leaving home, she will prefer to take an apartment with a friend than to live in isolation.

Women born under this Sign are pretty astute at business. They have a nose for what will make a profit. They don't wish to be too dependent on a man so after marriage they like to work. It's quite important for a Libra woman's self-respect that she contribute something to the family's financial well-being.

Being a person who likes his home comforts, you'll be pleased to discover that a girl born under the second air Sign is capable of flitting between work and home without allowing either to suffer. She would not take a job if she didn't feel she could cope with domestic life as well.

You'll love the way she fits in with your old friends. New relationships pose no problems for her. She's adaptable and feels at home with people from all levels of society.

She won't try to dominate you, but she will expect you to work hard and try to be successful. She's no slouch herself and will have little patience with your moods and bouts of depression. Don't get the impression she doesn't need your love. It will be terribly important to her in marriage to be desired.

This could, in fact, be a very successful union. You need someone positive and bright, and Miss Libra may be just the sort of woman you want to work for and prove yourself to.

Whatever job you have, your Libra wife will do her best to adapt to your way of life.

Be grateful you've got an independent woman. Never doubt her; she'll be rooting for you all the way.

CANCER MAN—SCORPIO WOMAN

Can you take the honest truth about yourself? If not, it might be a good idea to skip the next couple of pages.

Miss Scorpio is a no-nonsense type. She doesn't put on a front. She will make you face up to yourself and what you really are. Many people think she is cruel and sadistic, but this is not true. However, people who live in a dream world are shocked by this girl's frankness.

Certainly, she'll praise you when you are worthy of it because she really wants to look up to her man, but she won't pay you a false compliment. Her honesty is not for your sake as much as for her own—she doesn't wish to delude herself. When she does say something complimentary, you should feel great because you'll know her remarks come from the heart.

You are both water Signs, remember, and as such are susceptible to bouts of fearful depression. Whereas you like to be surrounded by lots of admirers and talk out your problems, Miss Scorpio is quite the reverse. She doesn't like people to see her weaknesses and thus prefers to brood alone. Watch out for that temper of hers. She can be a wild mountain cat when aroused. Being an extremely physical person, she's quite capable of getting violent if you two-time her. Scorpio people are exceedingly jealous and possessive.

You may find her fascination with matters related to birth and death very morbid. People under the influence of the Scorpion are usually deeply interested in the occult and all things mysterious.

She sets great store by her friends, although she's unlikely to be close to many people. Still, she'll stand by someone she has affection for through thick and thin. She identifies herself with the loser because she understands only too well that it is the sensitive and gentle people of this world who suffer most.

She likes to dominate. You'll have to be quite a man to keep the relationship balanced.

Scorpio people very often go off the deep end. Their great curiosity often leads them to excess in sex, drugs and drink. The trouble is they don't know when to stop. They occasionally blame the outside world for their own faults. Although very astute at summing up others, they tend to overlook their own glaring weaknesses.

When you meet her eyes sometimes, you will get shivers down your spine. Scorpio women have a way of looking at you as if they can read your mind.

Don't make an exhibition of yourself in public. If you are out with this girl, she'll want you to keep up a good appearance. Although a whirlwind of passion and emotion, she doesn't like to put on displays when her friends are around.

It's quite something to get really close to a person born under this Sign. If you only have an affair with her, you can be sure it will be something you'll remember for the rest of your life.

She's the sort of female you'll be attracted to on first sight. You may feel you have found Eve sitting in the Garden of Eden. One of her great attractions is that she often seems, for some mysterious reason, like forbidden fruit.

Scorpio women love their homes. She will like her surroundings to be comfortable and attractive. You both enjoy feeling secure and there will be many nights when you'll be perfectly content to sit snuggled up cozily in front of the fire together.

This woman will be terribly ambitious for her children. She'll sacrifice anything to help them fulfill their potential.

CANCER MAN—SAGITTARIUS WOMAN

While you tend to float across the waters of

life, occasionally encountering stormy seas and tidal waves, the Sagittarius woman is like a sleeping volcano. She may be calm for eons. Then suddenly, when you least expect it, she'll erupt, showering considerable devastation. Life together would need much mutual adjustment because you two have a very different approach to the ways of the world.

She's a no-nonsense type. She likes to deal in facts. She wants to keep on the move. A Sagittarius woman is not prepared to tie herself to the kitchen sink. She's difficult to get to know. There are hidden depths here. She has to be deeply involved with a man before she'll open up to him.

You may be a bit too much of a dreamer for her. She's very outspoken, sometimes to the point of rudeness. Many a time you will squirm with embarrassment when you are out with this woman. She doesn't mean to offend or hurt people's feelings; it's simply that she doesn't have a stockpile of tact.

Miss Sagittarius has a way of making one remark that puts a stop to all arguments. You could be sitting around with your friends for hours, debating a fascinating subject, when suddenly this girl will throw her few cents' worth in and bring the room to silence.

She's terribly impatient and sometimes appears to be rushing from one thing to another for no real purpose.

She's a bit bossy, and not in a way you'll readily take to. She always feels she knows what is best for everyone else.

Being an independent type, she's very good at looking after herself. It does not worry her to be alone from time to time. Though she loves her family, she won't wish to live under Mom and Dad's roof once she reaches her late teens.

Never try to boss her. If you want this girl to do something for you, *ask,* don't command. She can't stand people who try to dominate her. One of the reasons she left home was because she couldn't bear being cross-examined when she crept in late from a party.

Occasionally, she can get out of control. When the mood is upon her, a Sagittarius woman will drop the most terrible remarks; she just can't help saying what comes into her mind.

She's a bit marriage-shy because she doesn't want to get involved in any long-term union that could stifle her individuality. Chances are you'll have to do quite a lot of chasing before you track her down.

Many men are capable of having great buddy relationships with Sagittarius girls. You'll never find her company boring. Even if you aren't physically attracted to her, you'll love going to parties and out on the town together.

A Sagittarius woman will work hard to make the home a wonderful place to live in, but she's not always the greatest cook so you might find you're the one who spends more time in the connubial kitchen.

Being in such a rush all the time, she can be a bit clumsy. You may be forever having to replace the teacups and dinner plates that slip through her pretty little fingers while she's trying to break the world record for cleaning up.

She can be overly dependent on her children. She will sacrifice anything for them. Although a wonderful mother, she'll often have a guilty conscience and feel she's not doing enough.

You may have to work harder than you would with another woman to maintain your role as head of the family. If you're not careful, she'll take over the responsibilities of the home completely.

CANCER MAN—CAPRICORN WOMAN

The Capricorn woman is fascinated by people. Although in many ways a conservative type, she is intrigued by character. She's quite a complex person, although you might not think so on first meeting. One might almost say the longer you know her, the less you know about her.

Prestige and recognition mean a lot to the Goat tribe. These people are very often found in the public eye, and if not, they are almost certain to be manipulating power from behind the scenes. They like to be well thought of themselves and they admire those who have made a success of life.

Very often this woman is ultrafeminine and will quite happily play the little girl who needs looking after in the big, wide world. Her pouting and posing get on a lot of people's nerves. If you take the trouble to dig beneath the surface, you'll find there's a great deal more to her than she is prepared to project.

But how will you get on as a duo? Well, she's not the most romantic woman in the Zodiac. Don't try to throw her a line. She'll see right through you if you don't play it open and aboveaboard. She is looking for true love and is unlikely to be interested if all you have to offer is a casual affair.

She likes company and can get very depressed if left alone and neglected. She can also be rather overpowering. If she's really gone on you, she won't try to hide it. Although basically careful and responsible with money, she will give you her last cent if you are her man.

If you're looking for a one-night stand, then move along and don't waste this girl's time. Like you, she's quite concerned about security. When Capricorn and Cancer set up home together, the bank balance will be very healthy. Don't try to tie her to the home. You needn't worry about her meeting other men at work. She's the faithful type and wouldn't dream of an office romance that could put her private life in jeopardy.

She's terribly efficient and makes an excellent secretary. Her earthy qualities calm excitable bosses. Your friends and co-workers will see her as a real lady no matter what her background. This woman has a natural ladylike quality that shines through. She has a way of gliding into the room that makes heads turn.

She's wonderful at parties and at entertaining influential people. She knows exactly how to break down an icy atmosphere and make people relax with one of her warm and charming smiles. People would never believe it, but underneath all this grace, she is likely to be the most nervous person in the room. She'll never show it, though, because she doesn't want to let you down.

She can't bear to waste time. She'll soon put you straight about those projects you thought up in a moment of insane inspiration.

You had better get along well with her mother and father because if you do get married, you'll be seeing an awful lot of them. In lovemaking, she has an insatiable appetite. It takes a lot to satisfy her, so you'd better keep yourself in pretty good shape.

She won't be extravagant with your money. She'll never go on wild shopping sprees unless you've given approval. You may be quite happy to hand her your paycheck and let her take care of the budgeting.

Marriage improves this girl and brings her to maturity. She'll have no trouble with children. She'll be able to give them all the love they need without excluding you.

CANCER MAN—AQUARIUS WOMAN

Stranger things have happened than a Cancer guy getting it together with an Aquarius girl. It would appear on first sight, though, that this girl's progressive ideas and inability to live in the moment could drive you stark raving mad.

There could be just too much mystery about her for you to cope with. You are by no means a slow-thinking man, but her speed of thought and sudden changes of mood will dazzle or confound you.

She's out to change the world and make it a better place to live in for all. You tend to be an introspective kind of guy; she's just the reverse.

Aquarius people often get caught up in revolutionary movements. They make up the slogans and carry the banners. Freedom for all is the motto of the Water Bearers. They are not very concrete about *how* they're going to achieve their purposes, but they usually uphold the idea of equalitarianism.

She is unconventional and envisions home as a place to put her sleeping bag. She's not too interested in the comforts of family life. If you find yourself drawn to a woman born under this Sign, you'd better get ready for life on a roller coaster because it's unlikely she'll settle down to a stable life until she's older. Aquarius people who do marry young very often find themselves in Vegas for a quick divorce before the first twelve months are out.

She's the kind of woman who could really embarrass you among your more conservative friends. In fact, you'd better give her clothes the once-over before you take her home to meet your mother. She's liable to turn up in a Che Guevara T shirt, open-toed sandals and a duffle coat with a stick of incense burning behind her ear for good measure.

Don't underestimate Miss Aquarius, though, because what she preaches today, the world often adopts tomorrow. Frequently she is ahead of her time. Aquarius people have been responsible for many of the improvements in living and working conditions throughout the world over the last centuries. More mundane types take them for a joke until the realization suddenly dawns that there is a grain of truth in what Aquarius is preaching.

The Aquarius woman is likely to fall in love only once. If it doesn't work out, well, she'll be cautious about getting deeply involved with anyone again. Not that this will be a great tragedy to her; she'll always be able to find many other interesting things in life to absorb her energy and interest. She's usually got lots of friends, too.

For all her zany ways, she knows how to look after a buck. She's not extravagant with herself. The latest fashions are not terribly important in her life.

She's not a jealous person. Just because you date her once or twice, she won't think she owns you. She's also unpredictable, and just when you think you know her really well, she'll behave in a manner that leaves you stunned. You enjoy quiet moments when you can forget all about the turmoils of life, but she'll never stop arguing the toss. You'll find this tiring—and in the end, perhaps boring.

Miss Aquarius is very analytical. She doesn't like to talk about feelings. She'll put your famous Cancer emotions under a microscope. You won't get very far wooing her with soppy romanticism. Songs about love, moon and June strike Miss Aquarius as being rather silly.

She's quite a forgiving person. If you have an affair or two, she won't worry too much.

She can be a bit of a contradiction, so when your children are of school age, you may find, to your surprise, that she's dead set on sending them to the most conventional school going.

CANCER MAN—PISCES WOMAN

When Miss Pisces comes into your life, you may wonder why you have wasted so many years messing around with other women. You are likely to feel an immediate affinity with this woman, who shares your element, water. There is so much you will have in common. You are both dreamers and, like you, Miss Pisces places great emphasis on love and romance. She needs to feel more than a physical vibration before she'll give herself to anyone.

When you first meet, you may get the strange feeling you already know each other. She has a vivid imagination and can easily get carried away with her dreams and fantasies. She will never try to boss or dominate you, but she'll expect your love and devotion. She's a trusting girl and will believe anything you tell her. If she does find you've been deceiving her, though, it will be a long time before she puts her total faith in you once again.

She's a sucker for anyone with a hard-luck story, including animals. Your house would be a refuge for every stray dog and cat in the neighborhood if she had her way. A girl born under this Sign has a way with small and helpless creatures.

She's all woman. Men love her company. She talks to them, not to flirt, but because she has a deep and sincere interest in them as people. She will do all in her power to help you make a success of your career. Not because she necessarily wants money and power, but because she knows that a man who is happy in his work is easier to live with.

She's a very dainty dresser. In the winter, she'll look cute in a woolly hat; in the summer, she'll look graceful in a long flowing skirt. There's something of the "other world" about her that will always keep you guessing. You will never get bored in her company because she is so changeable (her symbol is two Fishes swimming in opposite directions).

If you want to play big daddy and protect your woman from the outside world, she will happily let you assume that role. She can make a man feel like Superman and Robin Hood rolled into one. She's no women's libber. She's intelligent enough to realize she's equal to you already.

You'll discover there's something very precious about married life together. Even when you are out with close friends, you'll feel there's a secret world that only you two inhabit and no one else can enter.

She'll never blame you when things go wrong. She's not a nagger. If you don't get a promotion when you think you should, she's likely to tell you to move on and find a boss who appreciates your talents.

She's not too clever at handling finances. She doesn't know a thing about economics and doesn't want to. She'll leave those things to you.

Don't get the impression that life will be a bed of roses, though, because Pisces ladies can be terribly moody and act like bad-tempered little children sometimes. In this mood, she may have you running all over the place seeing to her every whim and fancy.

Miss Pisces will never try to usurp your position as head of the household. She'll be very proud of you when you do pull off a successful deal. She's a great cook and enjoys preparing dainty and imaginative dishes. She's fond of decorating an apartment or house.

She loves her children dearly but can be a bit unpredictable in the way she treats them, depending on her mood.

Although she may cause you to lose your temper at times, you're likely to feel that marrying her was the best move you ever made.

CANCER'S HEALTH

Most of your health problems are connected with the stomach. And they are not always easy to diagnose. You often feel unwell when there's nothing evidently wrong with you.

Cancer rules the solar plexus, that highly sensitive nervous center in the abdomen commonly called the pit of the stomach. There, if you are a typical Cancer person, you feel a constant play of emotions, and these make your stomach churn. It is here—not in the brain—that you first register what goes on around you. As a result, your digestion is frequently upset.

This weakness is exacerbated by the fact that many people born under your Sign tend to overeat and to select foods that are palpably bad for them. Spices, curries and condiments may titillate the taste buds, but the discomfort they cause after a meal is hardly worth it in the long run. You also have a penchant for sweets, pastries and other rich foods, which can play havoc with your waistline.

What makes this a greater health hazard is that you're not the type to go in for much exercise. Most Cancer people would prefer to sit around than take off on a good brisk walk or to play a regular game of tennis. As far as sports are concerned, you're probably more at home on the leisurely fairways of the golf course. But ideally, most of you would probably choose an afternoon of sunbathing on the warm sand beside the sea or at the edge of a lake.

You do love the fresh air and outdoors and it's always a tonic for you to get out into natural surroundings. That's why you enjoy puttering around the garden and doing small jobs on the house. The Cancer lady may be inclined to spend too much time indoors looking after her family's needs. If she feels dispirited at any time, she should desert her housework, go for a walk in the park—and let the wind blow the cobwebs from her mind.

Cancer people are not usually robust in youth and seem to catch more than their share of childhood illnesses. Their recuperative powers are also weak and they tend to remain on the sick list longer than other children. Chronic ailments are also prevalent. Once adulthood is reached, these rather delicate individuals gather physical strength and can go on to live to a fine old age. But they must use some common sense in their middle years, when the results of earlier excesses, brought on by their fondness for sensation, are likely to demand attention.

No other Sign in the Zodiac (except perhaps Pisces) is as susceptible to psychosomatic illnesses. Worry and tension have a most deleterious physical effect on Cancer people. It can either put them off food and make them irritable and complaining, or it can create an inordinate appetite. You should avoid eating whenever you are emotionally upset because of the effect this has on your digestion. You should also avoid eating in places or surroundings you find unpleasant or disturbing. The more you can remain calm and contented in your daily life, the healthier you will be. Try to cultivate a sanguine outlook. Don't give in to feelings of gloom, bitterness or doubt, which invariably lower your resistance to disease. Retain your sense of humor; it's a natural tonic.

Just as you can literally make yourself sick, so can you "think" your way to recovery and good health. You are one patient who should not be pampered with too much sympathy; it's too easy for you to lapse into self-pity.

Cancer also rules the female reproductive system and the breasts, as well as the gastric juices. It has a close connection with the kidneys, which makes a sensible diet very important, particularly in the middle years. Other vulnerable areas are the skin and knees.

Sometimes Cancer people are accident-prone because their reflexes are a little slow.

You are subject to complaints involving excess fluids and mucous congestion. Asthma, bronchitis and chronic coughs may cause discomfort. Sunshine is extremely therapeutic.

It will help your general health if you face the fact that as a typical Cancer individual, your vitality is naturally low. But remember, vitality is *not* enhanced by lounging around and consuming calories, any more than it is stimulated by overexertion. The happy medium of normal physical activity and moderate regular exercise, along with a diet of low-starch foods, is what you should aim for. Don't drive if you can walk. And try eating only fruit between meals.

CANCER AT WORK

Most of you Cancer people have the happy knack of ending up in a comfortable position by middle life. And some of you—through your peculiar talent for gauging public taste--go on to make fortunes. Millionaires who forged empires selling goods and services to the masses are conspicuous among the successful people born under your Sign.

But often the rewards come after a very shaky start or a period of hard times. Cancer people generally are very slow to get moving. Although ambitious, they think too much about what they should be doing instead of actually doing it. They tend to dream of what they would accomplish "if only. . . ." Sometimes after being written off by most people, they're suddenly on top, surprising everyone with the brilliance of their success. You Cancer people also have a habit of making a name for yourselves in unsuspected and unusual ways. Cancer is a dark horse, and anyone who underrates him or her is likely to be proved a fool.

You possess a very strong creative streak, which may fit you for a career in one of the arts. Your deep yearning for self-expression may find an outlet in painting, writing, poetry or music. Even if these activities are only part-time to begin with, chances are you'll develop a style or technique that can be turned to commercial use in the future. There's nothing esoteric about your artistic productions—you always aim to create something that has practical appeal. You are artistically inventive and may be skilled at presenting unusual materials in old and traditional forms. Swift-changing conditions, which may unsettle or inhibit other artists, are apt to inspire you along original lines.

Whatever job you do is likely to have some connection with the home and its requirements. You may be in the furniture or furnishings business. Interior decorating could have a strong appeal. And, of course, there's no one quite so well suited as a Cancer individual for dealing in antiques or pursuits related to the past such as archeology, historical research or anthropology. Your rather scholarly nature may also induce you to take up a career in education that culminates in some kind of professorial appointment. You prefer to work in a relaxed and unhurried atmosphere. Many Cancer people are librarians. Those who write for a living often specialize in biographies, historical novels and travel accounts.

Your flair for business is well known. You are guided instinctively in commercial matters and are helped by a shrewd and taciturn manner. If you choose a career in the rough and tumble of the commercial world, you are likely to do best in an industry or profession dealing directly with the masses. Your planetary ruler, the Moon, governs public moods and modes through the senses, and it is that connection that enables you to tune in to popular tastes and to know what people will want in the near future.

You are tremendously sensitive to your surroundings and will often respond to a group situation without knowing why and delight everyone concerned with your action. It is this faculty, along with your keenly sympathetic and sentimental nature, that frequently makes you a successful doctor. Cancer doctors are inspired diagnosticians and their bedside manner is incredibly comforting and reassuring. Their extreme sensitivity makes them so aware of their patient's feelings that they actually suffer with them. Your carefulness and responsible patience also fit you for pharmacy and chemical analysis.

Obviously, a tender and gentle character such as yours is eminently suited to nursing and social work. Your innate gift for easing the anxieties of the sick through sympathetic conversation and empathy sometimes earns you the reputation of a healer.

As an actor or actress, you possess very special talents. Your emotional repertoire is almost inexhaustible. When you immerse yourself in a role, you throw off your natural timidity and are able to communicate a fine emotional attunement with the audience. This can be truly captivating. You know instinctively what people want and you give it to them through the character you are playing. Cancer people also make first-class mimics.

You are a conscientious person and will do your best in whatever you undertake. You don't like to fail and this fear is sometimes responsible for your tardiness in getting started. But once you're on the road to success, you seldom have any more problems. In the beginning, though, you must be sure the occupation or career you select genuinely interests you and is not just a passing fad. Since you're not much of a self-starter, when you do make a move, it shouldn't be one that's going to fizzle out. Strange and unfamiliar surroundings and people put you off. You're always much more efficient and self-confident once you settle in. You seldom allow co-workers or others to glimpse your uncertainties. You can put on a most convincing—even aggressive—front when you want to.

In working for yourself, you have to be on your guard against becoming discouraged during the establishment period. Few businesses get off the ground without setbacks and problems. Although you are capable of great perseverance, you may be inclined in the early days, when expenses are heavy, to lose heart and give up. It would be a good idea to prepare yourself psychologically for these periods of uncertainty; then when they come, you can put your head down and keep going.

Because of their rather nervous disposition, some Cancer folk are far happier working for an employer. For them, the security of a regular imcome outweighs the ambitious urge to make a fortune. Another point is that Cancer finds it extremely difficult to stand up to any pressure outside of a business situation for too long. To cope with family worries on top of running a business may be damaging to health. Your individual preference will be indicated by other influences in the horoscope. For example, if Mercury and Venus are both in Leo, you will have a greater desire for self-assertion and independence.

As an employee, you should be very successful. If your boss understands your Cancer nature, he'll have a loyal and industrious staffer, maybe for life. But there's no one in the Zodiac with a better idea of what he's worth than the Crab. You're not the type who rushes in for a job demanding a fabulous salary and all the perks. You want to be sure, first, you can do what you're being paid for. Once you've determined that, and your efficiency and know-how improve, you will flex your muscles by demanding the salary you're worth. If it's not forthcoming, you'll quit—even though the change goes against your conservative grain.

The plain fact is that a typical Cancer man or woman will never take a job without intending to get to the top. There's not enough room for everyone up there—you know that and are prepared to wait your turn. You won't initiate a palace revolution or crudely undermine your rivals—not so that anyone would ever notice, anyway. You leave those knock-down and drag-out tactics to Leo and Aries. You're prepared to wait, to take orders to do your job diligently—while the wheels you've set in motion slowly but surely carry you to the corridors of power.

As a boss, you expect everyone to do his job without excuses. You're kind and fair, and very aware of the special problems of those who work for you. You won't ride a man or expect him to accomplish anything beyond his capacity; you wouldn't have hired him in the first place if you didn't believe he could do the job. You don't have much trouble with your workers; you're too good at summing them up at the first interview.

Your methods as an employer are pretty conventional except when it comes to the wheeling and dealing side of business. Here you are superb—flexible, responsive, able to anticipate reactions five moves ahead and to quietly place your money bags in just the right position for a refill. It's not so much what you do at a given time but what you've already done in advance that pays off in the long run.

But back in the office, you're a bit of a stickler for formality. You want the rules you've laid down to be followed; these are usually taken from something you've read or learned. Procedures that have been proved over the years are best, you believe; experimentation leads to errors. You like your employees to be neatly dressed in the traditional way and to show you the courtesies and respect due someone in authority. Any excessive hilarity during office hours is likely to evoke a wry comment from you. You don't exactly lose your sense of humor at work, but it does get drier and drier. The fact is, you're in business for the money. What else is there?

If you were born between June 21 and June 30, you are extremely well suited for welfare and other work requiring a humane and sympathetic approach. A career in medicine, nursing or teaching is likely to prove satisfying. You may enjoy working with money, but should be careful not to allot it too large a place in your life, or it will undermine your sensibilities. A choice may have to be made between selflessness and selfishness in connection with your career. Some sort of public recognition for your work is likely. You are splendidly diplomatic and have a gift for expressing yourself aptly and persuasively. Don't allow doubts and apprehension to unsettle you in your career. A partnership may well suffice.

If you were born between July 1 and July 10, you have a good chance of attaining your objectives. You will be more inclined to fight for what you want, to come out into the open and take your chances. You won't give up easily, and stress and strain won't have the same deflating effects on you as it does on other Cancer types. You could make your mark in literature, or you may be tempted to try politics if a social issue fires you sufficiently. Your emotions may be volatile; if so, you will learn to control them if you are to avoid creating a bad impression on those in authority. With your birthday in this part of the month, you won't be quite so docile or eager to obey orders. You are patriotic and should enjoy working for the government, especially in foreign affairs. International trade and travel may also offer opportunities.

If you were born between July 11 and July 20, you will probably do best in one of the professions like writing, teaching or medicine, or in a definite artistic field. Your main problem in getting ahead is likely to be your own changeable and unpredictable nature. You may wonder at times if all the effort is worthwhile—of course, it is, so you must endeavor to remain optimistic. You work well with money and should be able to make your mark in community affairs where the handling or control of public finances is involved. You are inventive and enterprising. But be careful not to chase the shadow instead of the substance when you're deciding on a job.

MONEY

Money is the stuff with which you buy protection from worry. You're not the type to be concerned about keeping up with the Joneses, or using your cash to assert your ego in some megalomaniacal power struggle. Money makes you feel secure, and you do your best to hold onto it for that reason.

You usually do well investing in real estate, government securities and the stocks and bonds of large blue-chip corporations. You're not as a rule a lucky gambler or speculator, and these activities, even if they are profitable in the beginning, may cost you in the end.

As much as you like to fill your home with reassuring possessions, your tastes are not extravagant. You seek only to establish around you the permanence that money can buy. You will never buy a luxury yacht, for instance, unless there's a justifiable (business) reason for the outlay. You might be chauffeur-driven around the city all week in a splendid limousine, but spend your weekend fooling around the countryside in your Volkswagen. When you spend money, it's got to be justified. If you pour it into your home, you feel like that's money in the bank. If you buy antiques, you consider it an investment. If you spend on things for your family, it is to repay them for the love and affection they show you.

Your artistic inclinations ensure that when you do spend, you will buy quality. If you're down to your last dollar, you'd rather purchase one lovely red rose—and starve.

LEO'S CHARACTER

At your best, Leo, you are without doubt the most complete, balanced, commanding and unforgettable personality in the Zodiac. You are Leo the Lion, King of the Jungle, the symbol of royalty, regality and rulership. You were born under the patronage of the Sun itself, the undisputed center of the planetary forces and the source of all life. Like the Sun, you pour out your influence and beneficence without restraint. Unlike the Sun, you are human and your lack of restraint is often your undoing.

A lot of your trouble is that you're too well-meaning. You want everyone to share in what you feel you've got to give. The crunch comes when others resent being told by you what's good for them. They think you're being arrogant, presumptuous and downright interfering.

Still, you're probably one of the easiest people in the world to forgive—especially when you flash that wonderful, ingenuous smile of yours. It's pure sunshine, guaranteed to warm all but the bitterest heart. When a person who matters to you responds, whether it's to excuse your impulsive ways or out of sheer admiration, you're as happy as a lark. When such a person doesn't respond, you are disconsolate, discouraged, shattered.

But only for a brief time. Leo is a champagne Sign; it sparkles with an irrepressible faith in life. As a Leo person, you possess a strong self-sacrificing quality. Your life is virtually a search for a cause to devote your existence to. You have a sense of destiny. Somehow, you're convinced that the world needs you, that your life just won't be allowed to pass unnoticed.

You take command easily in any situation because you are a born leader. Power falls on your shoulders like a royal mantle. And you can be counted on to give a royal performance in any crisis you happen to be coping with. Your self-confidence is immeasurable. So is your self-awareness, or, as some might describe it, your self-centeredness. You seldom do anything without endeavoring to draw attention to yourself.

Have you ever watched a fellow Leo going about an important task? One that he or she is really on top of? Heard the sighing, heaving and snorting? It's all a part of that rather youthful desire to attract notice, in this case to show how hard Leo is working, how deserving he or she is of everyone's recognition and gratitude. An amusing thing to do to friend Leo is to offer to help. Help? Leo? Watch him parry the offer, pooh-pooh the task as a piece of cake *for him*—yet at the same time make a lot of huffing and puffing noises.

The simple fact is that you Leos are usually extraordinarily capable at your job. What you lack in expertise or knowledge you make up for in energy, determination and tenacity—not to mention organizational flair. You have an almost pathological fear of failing to live up to what is expected of you or what you have promised. You will toil day and night to deliver the goods. It is even possible for a Leo to work himself or herself to death, if identification with the task is strong enough.

What else would one expect from a noble and kingly type? Leo's so-called arrogance has deep and worthy origins. Like Caesar, he gets carried away sometimes with his own divinity.

Leo men and women very seldom ask for help. If they do, the request is usually framed in such a way that some sort of exchange is implied. Your unsubtle attempts at subtlety are a rich source of amusement to trained Lion watchers. (If you don't believe this, consult the guy or gal in the next room.)

Proud and self-sufficient Leo is not too convincing, either, when it comes to expressing gratitude. You can be enthusiastic, even fulsome, with your thanks; you can weep if the occasion warrants it. But the astute observer will see that you are merely going through the motions, that you *really* believe when someone does you a good turn, it is only what you deserved. You will repay a favor at the very first opportunity, perhaps in such an extravagant way that it's out of proportion to the original deed and more like a reward. It's the Leo way to be magnanimous, and to make large gestures at unexpected times. You like to receive out of homage, to bestow out of beneficence. You are like a monarch dispensing favors to worthy and devoted subjects.

No matter from which angle they are studied, there is something about Leonine individuals that makes them stand out in a crowd. They have presence, sometimes charisma. What they say or how they say it is usually arresting.

There are, of course, immature Leos whose only claim to recognition is their ability to make a great amount of noise in drawing attention to themselves. These types are boisterous, conceited, critical, boasting, snobbish, swaggering, domineering and—if they get the chance—tyrannical. But because of the Sun's sole rulership of this Sign, even the negative types have a noticeable urge over the years to improve themselves. The spiritual awareness of this Sign, through the Sun's influence, is very strong and in the more evolved types usually takes the form of an intense yearning for self-knowledge. In extreme cases, self-centered awareness can suddenly explode into a self-realization.

Leos generally move quickly and gracefully. They are among the doers of the world. Yet they are sometimes said to have a lazy or indolent streak. This criticism arises from the fact that they don't like wasting their time. They won't build a bridge where there's no river. They've got to be convinced that whatever they put their energies into is worthwhile. Some other Signs, such as Aries or Sagittarius, are so intent on participation and action that they'll go off half-cocked with impatience. Not Leo. What he starts, he finishes. He's inclined to take total responsibility. There'll only be one person to be thanked when the task is finished (the way he looks at it), and he can't afford any white elephants. So when others rush in fired by enthusiasm, Leo often sits back disinterested, languidly sunning himself (and noting every mistake that's being made). He'd love them to ask him to get them out of trouble. Then he'd spring into action. But otherwise—no deal.

Leo is a fixed Sign. This means you're set in your ideas. It doesn't mean you're rigid and inflexible. You will change your opinions. You won't cling to a notion just out of stubborn pride. You'll listen to reason. Perhaps you'll bristle and stamp a bit, but in the face of evidence, you'll concede. First, you may stride off and think about it, but you'll come around.) You are strongly impelled by the desire to be just even when it erodes your own position and standing. It is this quality that wins you the trust and respect of others.

You are acutely observant of all that is happening around you. You hear everything within earshot and are instantly aware of any changes. You have an almost sixth sense about where even the most unimportant objects have been left. Your ideas come mostly from your own experience. You don't rely very much on what others report; you have to find out for yourself. This is the clue to your rather fixed ways. You establish as you go along what works in practice and you remember it. Others are more imaginative, speculative and fanciful, prepared to assume things will be different next time. Not you. You stick to what you know until the facts prove otherwise. Meantime, you tend to disdain or reject the efforts of others. You think you know it all.

Your energy is fantastic. And by a curious quirk of nature, you often seem to be able to transmit it to others, both physically and mentally. Partners born under Pisces and Cancer are apt to draw emotional and vital strength from you. Others are simply inspired by your example or encouragement and go on to realize potentialities that may have lain dormant within them for years. You go out of your way to help others to make the most of their talents. In this regard, you are not the least bit selfish; you don't hold back information others would consider their "trade secrets." It is this helpful tutorial urge that makes you prominent in the teaching professions. Whatever occupation you follow, you will make a point of seeing that others, especially younger people, receive the benefit of your experience and knowledge.

You are very fond of fun and pleasure. All kinds of entertainment appeal to you. You love parties, first nights, all gala occasions where you can dress up and engage in your particular style of theatrics. But however much you clown about in public, you never lose sight of your essential dignity. And woe betide anyone who takes you for the fool you sometimes go to so much trouble to pretend you are. Your gamesmanship has one object only: to draw admiration and applause. You *know* you're the life of any party, but you feel compelled to demonstrate it to others every time. And you are a lot of fun. You've got a sunny, happy personality that inevitably breaks the ice of formality. Your vivacity and magnetism can't help but communicate itself. Quite often you are able to sing, dance or play a musical instrument. This, along with your innate talent for acting and showmanship, makes you a very popular party guest.

There are, of course, quiet Leos, controlled, dignified, very much together. But under that restrained, complaisant exterior beats a boyish or girlish heart waiting for the right circumstances or person to reveal itself. There's no true Leo on earth who won't let his or her hair down . . . sometime. And not one can hide the proud dignity or arrogant vanity that will flare if anyone dares to try to rule him or her.

Astrologically speaking, Leo is the Sign of pleasure and happiness secured through self-expression. So there's little wonder that you're such a natural at entertaining. As a host or hostess, you're fabulous. If you've got the money, you love to live in style. A life of luxury—but not without ambitious effort—is your idea of material paradise. Your home may well reflect your exotic tastes, which can tend toward ostentation if you're not careful. But everything in your home will work, including the color scheme, which is likely to have a strong bias toward gold, scarlet and yellow. You enjoy glamor and like to mix with famous, influential and wealthy people. You're quite prepared to cut down on vacations and other things to ensure that your home is everything that you want it to be.

Both the Leo man and woman are generally fashionable dressers. They're anything but inconspicuous in their choice of clothes, and yet the colors and styles they choose, which might seem outré on others, on them blend into pleasing harmony. The Leo male, unless he's influenced by one of the more subdued ladies of the Zodiac, is likely to be quite a dazzler. He'll splurge on the very latest styles and manage to combine startling reds and golds that no one else could get away with (or want to). Unusual accessories like hats, ties and jewelry give him the chance to express his fondness for sensational contrasts. Being a courtly type of peacock, he can wear frilly cuffs and ruffles without detracting from his vibrant masculinity. Mr. Leo, when he can afford it, loves velvet and rich colors. He's a vest man, more for elegant effect than sobriety. He relaxes at home in satin bathrobes and brocade smoking jackets. In snow country, he looks fantastic in a rugged sheepskin jacket or a sleek fur-collared topcoat—with jaunty fur hat to match, of course.

Ms. Leo is also an expensive dresser when she can afford it. She usually manages to look great in original styles and offbeat color schemes. There's elegance and distinction to her taste, though. As a rule, she loves expensive jewelry and adores furs. Everything about this girl's wardrobe has a touch of class. She'd rather go without than settle for cheap, poor-quality stuff. She spends a fair amount of time in front of the mirror making sure she looks attractive.

Leos are tremendously ambitious. You *have* to get to the top. Although you enjoy the rewards of power and success, it is the position that counts most—the being there. Whatever your scene or group, you have to be top dog, the undisputed focus point of all that is happening. Imperious at work (which is discussed in another chapter), you are just as autocratic where your home and family are concerned. You insist on things being done your way and get irascible when they're not. Your attitude is that if a thing was black yesterday, it's black now. You forget that although the color might not have changed, the people affected by it have. You don't make enough allowance for the preferences and moods of others, which generally waver more than your own. (We'll come to emotions, later.) You know where you are going and what you want. This is the strongest single factor behind the incredible Leo drive. But others don't have the same patient fixity; nor do they always see the necessity for or wisdom of it.

You usually get along well with your family, but not because you're easy to live with. Despite your bold and liberal ideas abroad, you frequently make an issue of trivial matters at home. You can be a Captain Bligh and psychologically keel-haul everyone for hours over an inconsequential point. Once your family has learned how to handle you (they've got to or it will be hell), your quite tractable and domesticated. As long as you feel the whole household revolves around your presence, all is well. Court must be constantly paid you, your efforts on behalf of everyone acknowledged and appreciated. This can become a bore to others—and even if you haven't woken up to it yet, all your loved ones know exactly how to calm you down, how much flattery and praise is required to get you to go along with their plans. It's certainly easier to indulge you than to fight you. You're an absolute terror when opposed. You'll hit the roof with a lightning flash of temper and round on the offending party with cutting acerbity.

Your indignation when you are doubted or disbelieved is monumental. What hurts is the implication that you could possibly hold fallacious opinions or beliefs. Of course, you know you're wrong at times; you are no fool. But a challenge of this kind always seems to catch you off guard, and you instinctively react to defend your infallibility. Fortunately, your anger is short-lived and you are often intelligent and fair enough to realize your own blindness or stupidity. On these occasions, you are apt to apologize and admit your error. This is the humility of the Lion, which because it is so surprising and apparently out of character frequently makes him or her an irresistible partner or buddy.

Sometimes you will take out your worldly frustrations on your family. If you don't build up some sort of empire through work, you may attempt to run your home like a feudal fiefdom, demanding your rights as head of the household while everybody waits on you.

But Leo can't endure an unhappy or discordant situation for long. It is your nature to bring differences and grievances out into the open where you can deal with them. For this reason, you find it difficult to sustain a grudge; you must either forget it or confront the other party and clear the air once and for all. The Lion will choose a fight to the death, any time, rather than have something hanging over his head. It's this attitude that often discourages antagonists and saves you a battle to begin with. But in a cat-and-mouse game, you, the mighty battler, are frequently at a loss.

You like to imagine that you're cunning when it suits you and that you can outsmart the schemers and intriguers of this world on their own ground. You don't stand a chance because you're an open book. All your wily stratagems are usually hopelessly naive. Leo is a noble character and basically uncomplicated. There is no room in your nature for ill-will, for petty squabbles and sinister conspiracies. Only your misplaced pride allows you to think you could outwit those who deal in deception and the double cross. Your duels are fought in the sun. You believe in giving an opponent an even chance. You're fussy about the weapons you use, too. You'd rather perish honorably than prevail dishonorably. Villains who skulk in the shadows taking potshots from behind or who poison with innuendo are out of your league. If a guy won't come out and fight, you'll tear the place down to get to him (perhaps Samson was a Leo).

You're not a very tactful person. You make some horrible gaffes, though never unconsciously; it's your style and you're very much aware of what you're doing. Like all the fire Signs, you're terribly wrapped up in yourself. You have very little time for the frailties of others or the minor subterfuges people use to hide their uncertainties. You can be blunt to the point of insult. One wonders how you do it; you get away with murder. Sometimes you expose courtesy as a front for cant. You want the truth out. You mean well. But damnit, it does hurt.

It's a pity you're not so adamant in exposing your own hangups, or tolerant of others' criticism of you. Few can dish it out better than Leo, and none is more outraged when he or she is on the receiving end. Fortunately, others appear to sense the absence of malice in your statements. You never seem to see any reason for withholding a frank opinion, whether harsh or favorable. To be fair, though, you are just as likely to hand out an extravagant compliment to an archrival as you are to criticize him.

You have a great deal of heart. In fact, your emotions are both your strongest and your weakest point. You are acutely sympathetic and can't bear to see a person unjustly treated. You have immense respect for the dignity of man and the right of all to find their way (with a little help from you) to a fuller and richer existence. As competent as you are at describing abstractions, you're not sure what they mean; still, you are supremely confident that your advice and wisdom will move others in the right direction. When your compassion or sense of purpose is stirred, you throw yourself into the cause with courage and complete disregard for your own interests. You never give up. You keep pushing and pushing until there's no room left for anyone to maneuver, yourself or the opposition. It's then showdown time, black-and-white time, when you're either victorious or vanquished.

As far as Leo is concerned, the time for compromise is *after* the battle has been won. And remarkably, the loser often receives all or more than he would have had he been victorious. Leo in victory is the spirit of magnanimity. You will never humble a defeated enemy; you will respect a person's pride. The only thing that matters is to prove you were right. As has been said, the only battles you can be bothered waging are those you identify with your own unshakable principles. After victory, you show superb generosity of spirit and mind.

But what an easy person you are to mislead. You're one of the world's worst judges of character. Anyone who makes the effort to praise you can usually win you over. It takes only a few words of flattery to change your countenance and attitude. It doesn't matter what you're doing at the time—you beam. You have a habit of responding to the most outrageously phony compliments. It's not that you're fool enough to believe all of them, but you are unwise enough to feel there is no harm done in benignly excusing an attempt to humor you. After all, it is human nature to try to please the king, isn't it?

When your weakness for flattery is combined with your simple and laudable faith in human nature, there are all the ingredients for a first-class deception. Being a pretty simple and straightforward character yourself, you think others are the same. Perhaps you should read the other books in this series. Until you've learned the errors of Leo's prideful and conceited ways, you're likely to be an easy person for crooks and confidence men to deceive. You may also be a soft touch for the not-so-crook as well, as you've probably discovered by now.

Leo is the Sign of love, romantic love. It represents the passion of the fiery, masterful ideal lover. With this supremely powerful motive force behind you, there's no wonder your emotions are often your Achilles' heel. It seems that as strong, stalwart and steadfast as you are in just about every other department of your life, where love is concerned, you are incredibly vulnerable and quite frequently make an awful mess of things.

Love makes the Lion (both man and woman) throw caution to the wind; his usual discretion seems to desert him (or he it). He is impulsive, erratic, impelled hither and thither by every random wind that promises to head him in the vague direction of his or her beloved.

The Lion doesn't fall this hard every time. But when he or she does, there are no half-measures. In your more temperate romantic affairs, you are still compelled by irresistible ardor. But in the face of unrequited love, you are able to sadly switch your affections elsewhere—happily resuming the chase of another beloved.

Leo is not an easy Sign for women to be born under. The temptation to go wild is very, very great. Perhaps that's what is meant by women's liberation (this is obviously written by a man!). Seriously, though, there is no doubt about the radiant femininity of these Leo girls, their grace, beauty and dignity; no Sign is more female or just plain sexy. But the basic love drive is initiatory, thrusting; the impulses radical rather than conservative. The instinct is that of the huntress—who waits. The mature Leo woman develops a fine balance, giving her a remarkably attractive poise and reserve, despite her vivacious outgoing manner. Ms. Leo can resist any man, except *the* man, if he comes along. The Lioness enjoys her affairs, padding sleekly and untamed among her men. But when she goes overboard, like Mr. Leo, there's no predicting what her emotions will compel her to do.

It seems that both the Lion and the Lioness are fated to learn to control their emotions, eventually. Very few men or women born under this Sign escape at least one torrid love affair that ends disastrously. But Leo's recuperative powers are great. Once restraint in love is learned—and it may take several painful lessons—these people often go on to make happy and enduring marriages. The chances of this happening are discussed in more detail in the "Leo in Love" section.

Leo is also the Sign of children, as well as ideas, which are, of course, the offspring of the mind. Although not fruitful in itself, the Sign inspires productivity and creativity and encourages self-expression in others. Leo people don't possess the same passionate maternal love of children as Cancer-born individuals, for instance. They usually don't have large families. The Leo instinct, rather, is to prepare children—all children—through teaching to carry the flame of creative understanding to the next generation. So you see, Leo's tendency to preach and teach, as maddening as it is, is basically an altruistic urge.

Leo's love is not purely sexual. That's Scorpio's department. It's not discriminating mental love, which is the realm of Libra. Nor is it the love of Taurus, which is feminine, earthy, enveloping. Leo's love is a bit of each—the romantic, unrestrained and compelling starting point of it all.

Your ambitious nature frequently induces you to accept responsibilities beyond your capacity. Out of excessive generosity, you bind yourself to those you love. You're the type to attempt the impossible. Sometimes you go so far out on a limb that you leave yourself without any resources to fall back on. If you don't make it, you don't complain. Often, only your strength of mind and robust constitution get you through. Even so, you are always in danger of undermining your health through taking on too much.

You are fond of sports and the outdoor life. It is imperative that you release your energy in some creative way and not allow it to stagnate or be wasted in gossiping and accumulating useless information. You are more an intellectual being than a physical one, so unless there's a good proportion of creative thinking involved in your activities, you won't feel fulfilled. Your capacity for intense short bursts of concentration should help you to be successful as a professional sportsman or sportswoman.

Artistically, you possess great potential. Your intuition is a rich source of original ideas that can be applied to a wide range of pursuits and interests. Most Leos are naturally skilled at writing and speaking. If they can overcome the tendency to dramatize their statements, they can communicate quickly and expressively. Your love of the dramatic often induces people born under your Sign to join amateur acting groups or to try their hand at other types of entertaining. You have a deep appreciation of nature and a rather poetic turn of mind. Even if you don't write, you use apt, lyrical phrases to describe events. You are quite sentimental and are likely to keep mementos, especially love letters and photographs, long after the people concerned have disappeared from your life.

All typical Leos possess a hidden talent that is not always developed: they can perceive changes that are necessary for society, and sometimes individuals, long before they are generally evident. It is this talent that will cause you to work toward reform often without knowing why. You are frequently at the center or head of a movement. When in charge, you have a knack for distributing jobs to the right people; you can "feel" a person's potential achievements. Unfortunately, your emotional nature often distorts your prophetic gifts. You succeed most when working for others and along idealistic lines. A selfish life makes a Leo-born person shallow and discontented.

You are exceedingly loyal to your buddies and many of your friendships last a lifetime. Although popular, you don't have many really intimate associates. You prefer to keep a degree of aloofness in most relationships.

Probably the most remarkable characteristic of all true Leos is their optimism and almost mystical faith in life. A Leo wrote the following:

My friend Life is death and birth
My friend Life is the whole wide earth
My friend Life is sorrow and a tear
But my friend Life does not know fear.
All the people would drag me down
But not while my friend Life's around
My friend Life is change and pain
But that's all part of my friend's game.
Play the game and it can be fun
Fight to win and the fun's all done
My friend Life is an outstretched hand—
It's your friend, too, if you grab it Man.

LEO

IN LOVE

YOUR LEO MAN

You like him? Love him? What sort of guy is the Leo man?

He wants everything his woman has to give—and more. Sometimes it seems he wants her very soul. And what does he offer in return? The same—all of him. No half-measures are possible on either side.

He puts his woman so high up on a pedestal that sometimes she can't do anything but stand there and be worshipped by him. This can be a bit of a strain on the lady unless she's very, very much in love. In that case, she'll have every single thing her heart desires because Mr. Leo will lay it all at her feet. And while he loves her, she will be the only woman in his life. She will be unable to do any wrong (except one) in his eyes. He will adore her, serve her, idolize her, and with his urgent and passionate lovemaking, make her feel like a goddess.

But if you are disloyal to him, things will never be quite the same. He is big enough not to bear a grudge or want to get even, but his nature is such that he can't ever forgive a woman who destroys his dreams. Disillusionment has an emotional finality for him. If he decides to stay with you (he is feafully noble and proud), he'll continue to demonstrate his affection as though nothing had happened—but the fire will be gone. In these circumstances, unless the woman is able to prove to him that she truly loves him, he will gradually pine away and eat his heart out. A Leo man without love is a dying man.

Of course, in a less than absolute love affair, our Leonine friend won't hang around once a woman's betrayed him. For a time, he'll be dazed because his self-esteem is so towering he just can't believe a woman who said she loved him could possibly change her mind. He'll shake his mane and lick his wounds as he sadly saunters off into the jungle. But don't worry, he'll spot another she-mate shortly (or she him) and it will be the same thing all over again.

Not surprisingly, Mr. Leo is very often unlucky in love. It's one area in which he doesn't seem to have much discretion or judgment.

He's great fun and is usually to be found right in the center of a crowd, roaring about how well he can do something—and then probably doing it even if it kills him. The lengths this guy will go to prove he's the greatest are almost unbelievable. He lives for love and applause. He's a born showman and showoff. If there are any ladies around, he'll be playing up to every one of them, waiting to pounce on the one whose eyes show the greatest admiration and interest.

He's a masterly type who likes to *win* his women. If you fancy him, sit back and be lionized. If you want him to come on a little stronger, just a couple of compliments will do the trick. Even downright flattery is not lost on this guy. He's so sure that every girl he meets is knocked out by him that it never occurs to him to take praise, no matter how extravagant, with a grain of salt.

Despite his domineering and lordly way, he's a bit of a boy at heart, sometimes even naive where love is concerned. It's not difficult for a woman to mislead him. He's terribly trusting in a way, probably because of his simple faith in his own magnetism. There's no doubt he has a compelling presence, and he uses it to great effect in business, where he is generally a top executive or leader.

If you land this man, you may find him difficult to live with at times. He can be exacting and infuriatingly self-centered. He is always looking for approbation and appreciation from his mate and is absurdly wounded if they're not forthcoming. Tickle him under the chin with a little praise, and he'll bounce back to his happy, charming self. Neglect him, and he'll moon around the place as though he's carrying the weight of the world.

When it comes to parties and entertaining, he's a wow. He loves to flirt but will never neglect you. He'll also enjoy showing you off to his buddies. If a Leo male takes to you, it's a safe bet you're an attractive personality with some very special feminine qualities.

YOUR LEO WOMAN

You like her ? Love her? What sort of woman is she?

She's a golden girl, a child of the Sun, a real dazzler. A Leo woman can take her place in any company and make her man feel ten feet tall. She's sexy and very attractive to men. You'll have to love her sincerely and give her all the adoring affection she craves to hold her.

Once this woman says she's yours, there'll be no doubt about her loyalty. She'll give you all her attention. She'll wear the type of clothes you admire most and do everything in her power to please you. If you've decided to save up to get married, she'll work just as hard as you and make sure most of her paycheck goes into the joint account. Once she commits herself to a course of action, she seldom swerves.

So what are the disadvantages? Well, you've got to win her first. And with all the competition, that's not going to be easy. Even when you're sure she's yours, your heart will sink with doubts whenever guys crowd around her (which is often). She's terribly confident and sometimes says the most outrageous things that everyone else but you (biting your nails near the door) will think is hilarious. Her quick-thinking mind is a match for just about any male's repartee, and her open sense of humor is infectiously winning.

When you show her off to your buddies, they'll probably all fancy her, much to your chagrin. She's got physical magnetism, charisma, this girl, so she's going to make you jealous even when she's not trying.

She's also likely to infuriate you at times with her bossy manner. Oh sure, she can be one of the most pleasing and agreeable types you've ever met, but when you tread on her ego, or even give it an accidental nudge, watch out! She can turn arrogant and overbearing in a second. Her temper will flare in a thunderous roar of indignation—but as fast as it came, it will be gone, and your Leo girl will be genuinely smiling like the Sun coming out from behind a cloud. She doesn't cherish ill-will. There's no malice in her.

She loves to dress up in the latest fashions and go to parties. She's great at making an impression. Whereas others may be embarrassed at being made a cynosure, she laps up every minute of it. A Leo woman just can't get too much attention. Perhaps because Leo is a royal Sign, the symbol of kings and queens, she loves to hold court. And as the "royal consort," you'll be pretty important to her. She usually makes a point of only getting involved with men she'll be proud to have by her side.

As a lover, she's fiery and passionate and aggressive in the bedroom. She'll be prepared to leave the lovemaking initiative to you provided you're able to keep her charmed and interested. She doesn't want any caveman haste, though. She wants a *lover* in every sense of the word. Only real men need apply.

Your Leo girl will shower you with presents. She wants to show you in every way she can that she is yours. She is extremely romantic and your flowers, perfume and chocolates will delight her. No one will dare say a detracting word about you in the presence of this proud and dynamic woman. Once she regards you as her man, everything about you will be as dear to her as if it were her own.

Unfortunately, unless her husband is a virile and fairly dominant type of person, this woman will gradually take him over. She won't want to, but her powerful personality and natural talent for making decisions and taking responsibility will make her preeminence almost inevitable.

Always remember that underneath is a kind-hearted, generous and intelligent female. With a strong and masculine husband who loves her, this lady will be content to be his queen and they should live a good and happy life together.

LEO WOMAN—ARIES MAN

He's a feet-first kind of guy. When he falls in love, it's impossible for him to hide his emotions. His passion will overwhelm you. You'll be able to read him like a book, and what you read could put him on your list of bestsellers. He's the sort of man who will fit your ideal pretty well.

He's positive, hard-working and fairly straight in his relationships with the fairer sex. It is not necessarily true that in marriage one person has to lead—doubters will point out that Aries and Leo are born rulers and the fight for power would make this union a nonstarter. This, of course, is rubbish. If two people are in love, a liaison in which all decisions are reached by mutual agreement is the perfect one.

You do both have a very special talent for ruling and it will be in finding out which partner takes the lead and when that will keep your affair alive.

It would be wise to have a fairly long courtship with the Ram. In, the beginning, his passion could sweep you off your feet and make you feel you've met your true love. Do get to know him a little better. He's more fickle than you are and it's not easy for him to settle down to a one-to-one relationship. Certainly, he's the most passionate of all the Signs. His lusty sexual appetite is virtually insatiable.

You may think when you first meet him that because he's so quite, he'll be afraid to make romantic overtures. Don't be fooled. He is ruled by Mars, and you'll find that for him, actions speak louder than words.

There are so many nice things you'll enjoy sharing together. Like you, he will have a fairly acute interest in what's going on in the outside world. You may not have exactly the same attitude to how society's current crop of problems should be solved, but you'll enjoy discussing different approaches.

You are both quite artistic. He will enjoy going to the theater with you and to music concerts as well; one of the special things you have in common is a love of music.

Mr. Aries likes a feminine woman, but he will also admire your guts—your ability to make important decisions and to stand on your own two feet when the going gets rough. He won't mind your having your own career after marriage so long as it doesn't interfere with the smooth running of domestic life. Knowing you, you will be able to cope easily with both.

He is prone to sudden plunges into a new hobby or career, and you'll have to be ready for this. His enthusiasms are boundless but short-lived. He could be absolutely crazy about a pastime for a couple of weeks and then suddenly forget all about it.

Of course, you'll have your arguments, but then, what couple doesn't? You must be sure never to dent his ego. Mr. Aries can't stand being nagged or criticized too harshly. He's really a bit of an overgrown boy in many ways and will need to be constantly reassured of your love.

Don't do too much flirting with other guys when your Aries man's around. He won't be able to take it, even though you think of it as merely harmless fun.

If after you settle down together you have an affair, with another man, it's extremely unlikely that your partnership will ever be the same again. If you love him, your marriage will be far too important to you to play with fire.

You will be a tower of strength to your Aries mate. You are the sort of woman who is clever at bringing out the very best qualities in this man.

LEO WOMAN—TAURUS MAN

Let's hope you're the sort of woman who likes to take her time over courtship because Mr. Taurus refuses to be rushed into any kind of permanent relationship. He's difficult to pin down because he has a fear of being trapped. He doesn't usually fall for a woman who does the chasing. Where romance is concerned, he likes to feel he's got the initiative. It may take him quite a while to finally decide that you are the woman for him.

It is true that people born under this Sign never reach a decision quickly. Usually they are pretty shrewd businessmen; it is rare for anyone to get away with a sharp practice when dealing with the Bull.

He's a home-loving creature. He likes his comforts and is not too keen on change. He's very true to his friends. If he believes in someone, he'll stick by that person through thick and thin. You may get somewhat bored with his desire to spend so many evenings at home. You're an active kind of person so it will be up to you to put a firecracker under his rocking chair from time to time.

He's very bright and can talk pretty well on any subject. You are both good conversationalists so it's unlikely you'll get bored in each other's company. You could have some fearsome disagreements—but that's another matter.

He has quite a roving eye. You may be surprised to discover how many girls he has lured to the bedroom. It's unlikely, though, that he's found real love with any of them. If he does fall in love with you, his promiscuous ways will soon become a thing of the past.

You both have a penchant for beautiful things and you'll be happy to discover you've met a person who is also a great lover of art. Possessions are important to him. He will want to furnish his home carefully and won't worry how much he spends on decorations and comforts so long as they please him. He's quite handy, too. He can do repair jobs around the house. If you leave him to visit your folks, you'll find he's quite capable of keeping your love nest tidy and of looking after himself.

He's also adept in the kitchen. If you continue your career after marriage—and it's quite likely you'll want to—he will be able to prepare a tasty dinner for you both if he gets home from work before you.

He's a hard worker and will appreciate the drive that keeps you going. You both have inquiring minds and would make a pretty interesting business partnership if you decide to work.

He's a lot of laughs. You'll like his rather aggressive attitude to life. He's a bit of a storyteller. Because he has a vivid imagination, he can't help making out that he's really tougher and shrewder than he is. You will be good for him because you'll help him face up to himself and his failings without being unnecessarily cruel.

This man will be able to offer you security. He's very skillful at looking after the shekels so life will be okay with him from the material point of view. He likes to keep on the right side of the law and will do all he can to stay out of debt.

You will have to be his friend as well as his lover because it's important to him to have a good relationship with his lover outside of bed. He goes in for crazy gadgets and always likes to have the latest in anything.

If you both agree about what you want out of life, there is no reason why you should not be very happy together.

LEO WOMAN—GEMINI MAN

You've heard about the little boy who never grew up? Peter something? Well, it's a dollar to a cent he was a Gemini. A man born under the Sign of the Twins usually maintains his youthfulness throughout his life. What appeals to women most about this character is his naughty schoolboy quality.

The question is, how strong is your maternal instinct? It is extremely unlikely that Mr. Gemini is going to turn out to be the hero type who sweeps you off your feet.

He's very cuddlesome and lovable and you'll always find his company stimulating and entertaining. He has a sharp mind and is quite intuitive about people and situations. His sense of humor will appeal to you, although you may find it a little sick at times because he doesn't know when to stop—which is one of his major problems in life. If he has a drink, he usually has to finish the whole bottle. He finds it almost impossible to cry, "Enough!"

He will admire many of your fine qualities. In fact, you could be the woman of his dreams. He likes a woman with a strong personality. Although he adores freedom and can't beat being dominated, it's important to him to have someone by his side who can pull him up from time to time. But—it's sad to say—that if a woman allows him to, he will trample all over her after a while.

You will certainly have to drive him on at times. He needs plenty of incentive and can easily become bored if he feels tied to his job. He likes change and has the idea that the grass is greener on the other side of the fence. He won't mind your having outside interests so long as they don't interfere with your life together. In fact, he'll encourage you to continue working after marriage because he doesn't want to feel that his partner is going to be a millstone around his neck. He will not expect you to do all the domestic drudgery, either, because he's quite fair and won't demand sacrifices he's not prepared to make himself.

Mr. Gemini loves to move around. Travel excites him. He rates friendship very high and is likely to have numerous close buddies. Let's hope you get on well with them; he'll want to bring them home quite often.

Although he likes a strong lady love, don't ever try to boss him or tell him what to do. He'll run a mile if he feels he's being ordered around. The way to get through to him is by discussion and suggestion.

When it comes to kids, he's great at buying toys and handing out sweets, but not so good at disciplining them. It looks as if that will have to be your department.

He can't help flirting, but then, neither can you. He's not the jealous type unless you go out of your way to tease him.

If you are really hung up on this man, you should be able to cope with him. Remember though, he's not the kind of fellow you should try to change. Don't go into marriage with the idea that he will alter his ways and settle down. He never will.

So long as you can keep up with the all-action life he likes to lead, all will be well. As far as entertaining goes, you'll have a lot in common. When you get into one of your flamboyant moods at a party, he'll sit there genuinely amused. He's quite prepared to let you make a fool of yourself; that's his idea of freedom.

When the children do come along, you must be sure you don't divert your love from him to them. If he feels left out in the cold, it won't be very long before he goes elsewhere in search of love.

LEO WOMAN—CANCER MAN

You'll find it difficult to understand a man born under the Sign of the Crab. When you're first introduced, you'll think he's an easygoing, fun-loving sort of guy without a care in the world. As you get to know him better, you're likely to discover you have gotten involved with a rather complex character. He'll storm into a roomful of strangers and fairly take over. You'll feel you've never come across a man with more confidence. But underneath this bravado, he's basically insecure and is only putting on a big front to cover up his self-doubt.

It may take a long time to discover what he's all about. He won't expose his true feelings until he's sure he can trust you because he is terrified of getting hurt. He will hold out for an inordinate time before he says those three little words.

You'll probably feel that in Mr. Cancer you've met a man who knows exactly what he wants and where he is going. As it turns out, he is very easy to influence and capable of amazingly abrupt changes of mind.

He is quite interested in power and wealth and is usually careful with money.

If you really fall for him, you will have to help him find himself. His tough outer shell hides an exceedingly lovable and gentle soul. Don't think he's a weak man; he's not. He is quite capable of looking after himself and will want to protect you as well.

Both of you will have to be ready to give up rather a lot if you're thinking in terms of marriage. Neither of you really likes to be advised or told what to do. He may talk intimately about his problems to you, but when you give your opinion, he's quite likely to go out and do the reverse. For a straightforward person like you, this can be terribly frustrating.

If he does pop the question, it means he intends to stick by you. Marriage is not something anyone born under the Sign of Cancer enters into lightly. He usually makes a faithful husband. He will want to make your union just what the good book says it should be—for keeps.

He's not mean with money but he can't stand the thought of insecurity. He will make sure you never go without, although he's not one to indulge extravagant tastes. You should not have a problem in this area because you're pretty capable at living within a reasonable budget.

Occasionally, you will have to be his psychiatrist. He needs to talk out his hangups. He knows this will not solve anything, but he can't keep emotions bottled up in an intimate relationship—a thing he feels he has to attempt when dealing with comparative strangers.

You will have to be quite hard on him at times to get him to make the most of his talents. The best way of doing this is to constantly remind him of what he is capable of achieving. Although he's not lazy, this guy's not exactly a self-starter, except when clinching a business deal.

Mr. Cancer will love the way you run the home. He delights in efficiency. His domestic life is very important to him. He likes to know he has a secure refuge to retreat to when outside pressures build up.

In your lovemaking together, there are not likely to be any major problems. He's intuitive about sex and will know what to do to bring you satisfaction.

His family is immensely important to him. His mother will probably be a frequent visitor. You'll just have to make it clear from the start that you rule the roost, not her.

LEO WOMAN—LEO MAN

This might seem an ideal team on the surface: the King and Queen of the Jungle brought together in a right royal linkup. Don't fool yourself—there could be quite a few problems to contend with here.

This is the union of two active and proud personalities. It might be too explosive to be contained under one roof.

You are generous and loyal, and will have to make the most of these qualities if the marriage is to succeed. You both like to lead and this could be a major stumbling block.

You and Mr. Leo will find it easy to become friends because you have a great deal in common. It is essential that you don't mistake friendship for love. Your way of making a marriage partner happy is not likely to be this guy's idea of how his woman should behave.

On first sight, you may feel he matches up to the man of your teenage dreams—strong, courageous, bold and capable of making difficult decisions. Well, he does possess all these qualities, but when your youthful fantasy is offered in the flesh, you may well find out you don't really want what you thought you did. You will find he insists on making certain big decisions on his own, which will not please you because you like to have a say in anything affecting your future well-being and security.

Mr. Leo also craves a great deal of attention. Sometimes you won't be in the mood when he wants petting. Every time he comes into the house, he'll expect you to drop whatever you're doing and give him priority. He can't stand other people finding fault with him, either. You are the sort of woman who says exactly what is on her mind, and this may be a bit too much for him to swallow at times.

He won't be prepared to make many concessions. Once he's laid down the law, he will expect his decisions to be carried out. This all-or-nothing attitude is difficult to live with, especially for a woman as proud as you.

Both of you are capable of extreme jealousy

and possessiveness; this is another area where the relationship could founder. Though both of you like to flirt, neither of you can stand flirtatiousness in your lover. But it's not all bad news. It is possible that you could work out your problems, and this process of accommodation could be rather exciting in itself. In bed, you are both rather aggressive types and neither of you is prepared to play a totally passive role when making love.

He will expect a great deal from you in many other ways—as a housewife and hostess to his business associates, for instance. This could be quite a challenge.

You will need to be many things rolled into one. Sometimes he will treat you like his teenage daughter—yes, he does incline to paternalism—and will like to feel he's looking after you and protecting you from the dangers of the outside world. So long as you can live up to his demands, there will be no problem.

You're the kind of woman who tries very hard to make a go of marriage. You're independent, but you're always on the lookout for Mr. Right should he come along. Like Mr. Leo, you've got fairly high standards, befitting one of the royal Sign. If you can surmount all the difficulties together (which largely means facing up to them to begin with), this could just turn out to be a happy and fruitful union.

LEO WOMAN—VIRGO MAN

Mr. Virgo is too good to be true for a realistic woman like you. He could be just too much of a fussbudget. He's certainly finicky and particular.

Everything has to be spotless, especially his home. You are no slouch when it comes to housework, but there are things you rate as more important in life. He'll notice immediately if the rug hasn't been vacuumed when he comes home from work. He won't overtly criticize you; his method is to get the vacuum cleaner out and go to work himself. He can't help being this way.

He's quite a cool character when it comes to dealing with the fairer sex. His approach is subtle. Though sex is often on his mind, he can do without it for a surprisingly long time.

All this is not to say that your Virgo man does not have a great deal to offer. He does. If you decide to change your name to his, you couldn't ask for a more devoted or loyal husband. He will put you on a pedestal and try to give you everything your heart desires.

The real point is, can you accept someone who is this straightforward and down to earth? He's a man of habit. When his favorite TV program is on, it will be very hard to get him to go out, no matter how exciting the invitation. He's a thinking man who is ruled by logic. If something can't be worked out systematically, he will have little time for it.

If you're going to make a success of life together, it's important that you share many mutual interests. When dating him, note just how much you have in common. It is awfully important to him that his woman have the same taste in music and art and the same opinions on politics and religion. He won't mind converting you, but what a bore that could be if you're already pretty sure of what you enjoy.

You are both fond of going abroad for vacations, and this penchant for travel is one thing you're likely to share together—once Mr. Virgo gets a taste of it, that is.

You could be the right woman to make old stay-at-home Virgo change his ways. You have many qualities he admires, and you'll be able to give him that extra push he so often needs. Although extremely talented, he does not tend to knock himself out getting to the top.

Try to induce him to take more of an interest in sports. Virgo men can often go to seed earlier than they should because they hate physical exercise. You will have to shake him out of his complacency.

He will also have quite a lot to teach and show you. He's pretty sharp about money. He's also exceedingly adept at summing up the strengths and weaknesses of people he meets. He has a computer memory and usually knows a surprising amount about a lot of topics.

You've probably heard wicked rumors that Mr. Virgo is frigid when it comes to lovemaking. He's not. He just has to be turned on, which is the sort of challenge a girl like you might enjoy. You're not forward, but with the right guy, you're not averse to making the overtures. Being a Leo woman, you could find it quite exciting to see what you could do. You'll be able to show him that sex is something to be enjoyed. He sometimes does have a bit of a problem expressing his true feelings.

Mr. Virgo will take his time about proposing. He will want to be really sure before he decides you're the woman for him.

This man usually wants only one or two kids, which will probably suit you. But you can be sure he'll make a fine father.

LEO WOMAN—LIBRA MAN

Your relationship should look pretty good right from the word go. You will admire his mind and speed of thought. The only trouble is the foundations of this affair may not go deep enough to make a permanent liaison possible.

He's super to be with, a charming and amusing companion. He'll know the best places to go and you will soon realize what a compassionate and caring man he is. He feels very deeply for other people and will go out of his way to avoid hurting or upsetting another human being.

Where you may come unstuck is when it comes to setting up home together. There are likely to be a lot of basic differences in your attitude to life and how it should be lived. You look for some sort of consistency and permanence in a man. Mr. Libra will be something of a puzzle to you. In romance, he blows hot and cold. It is extremely difficult for him to settle down with one woman. It isn't that he's madly promiscuous but rather that he's in love with love. He is a great romantic.

Never put pressure on him because he can't stand feeling he has to live by a rule book. Don't tell him dinner will be on the table at a certain hour every night. He's not a person of habit. You will have to be prepared to go along with his moods and lightning changes of mind.

He doesn't like violent confrontations—in fact, he will do everything in his power to avoid them. He doesn't understand why people can't settle their disputes through discussion. He is a real gentleman. He knows how to pay a compliment and will mean what he says. It will not escape his notice when you are wearing a new outfit or have changed your perfume. He's also very tactful; he won't pass comment on matters that aren't his concern.

You, on the other hand, speak your mind. You prefer to bring differences out into the open than to keep your feelings bottled up inside you.

In your courtship with a Libra man, you may wonder if he is really serious in his intentions. He doesn't like to commit himself in a hurry. Like all air Signs, he is terrified of being trapped.

You will enjoy listening to him talk on the subjects in which he specializes. Libra people are often very good teachers because they are capable of making the most dreary and trivial matter sound interesting.

He will love taking you out and showing you the things that really interest him. Art in some form usually strongly appeals to this man. He should be able to open up new worlds for you.

He can be rather cynical at times, and this could get you down. He can also be very tough. If someone tries to double-cross him, he can be absolutely ruthless. Once his mind is made up on a certain course of action, he's very difficult to budge.

Mr. Libra is a survivor because he is able to take the rough with the smooth. He is a good provider, though amassing great wealth and numerous personal possessions is unlikely to appeal to him.

He enjoys traveling. He usually ends up in the sort of job that gives him plenty of scope for being inventive.

Home is important to this man, though he does tend to think of it as a place to recuperate and restore his lost energy. He has lots of acquaintances, but only one or two close friends. He's very tolerant of other people and will always try to see their point of view.

He's a kind father and finds it very difficult to exert discipline with children.

LEO WOMAN—SCORPIO MAN

Oh lady, you'll wonder what you've discovered the first time you get involved with a Scorpio man. He's very passionate and you will have to summon all your strength to keep up with him.

There's no way you can dominate this guy. There isn't a woman going that can lay down the law to him. He likes his women to be feminine and cuddly.

When you have a disagreement, it's unlikely that either of you will be prepared to give ground. If you want a marriage partner who is going to keep you constantly on your toes, then don't look further. You will bring out the man in him and he'll make you realize what being a woman is all about.

When it comes to lovemaking, you should have a ball together. He's lusty and has an insatiable appetite.

You may not hit it off so well when you first meet. This is the kind of union that develops with time. But you won't be able to ignore him when he walks into the room because there's something magnetic about this man.

Mr. Scorpio is not the most romantic man in the world. To him, actions speak louder than words. He won't be standing under your bedroom window trying to woo you with a guitar; he'll be doing his darndest to climb up the ivy and get through the lace curtains. Being a passionate woman, it's unlikely you'll be able to reject his advances for very long.

You will have to curb your flirtatious ways if you do move in with Mr. Scorpio. Of all the Signs, he's the most jealous and possessive. Woe betide you if you're caught having a secret liaison. And woe betide the guy you're caught with. Scorpio's quite capable of resorting to physical violence if aroused.

He probably won't share your tastes in music or art. He likes fairly straightforward reading and theater.

He will regard the house as your domain. He is one of those old-fashioned types who thinks a woman's place is in the home. He will expect your main interest in life to be looking after him. He'll enjoy an odd night out with the boys, and won't mind your having an evening out with your girlfriends, so long as his supper is left ready for him. He can be a bit of a brute. But you may be one of those Leo girls who can take his rough treatment.

This guy is an exceptionally hard worker and, as a rule, pretty astute with money. He is careful about how he invests his cash and his methods are fairly conservative. He will do his best to make sure you have everything you want, but he will frown on unnecessary extravagance. He'll try to get to the top in his career and you'll be very good for him in this respect.

He's not a great night bird. He likes to unwind and relax after a day at the office.

Your Scorpio man keeps his home life and his work in strictly separate compartments. When work is over for the day and he's settled down in his favorite chair, he won't wish to get too involved in discussions with business associates who happen to drop in. If he's got any shop talk to get done—or to listen in on—he prefers to dispose of it over a drink on the way home.

You must try to do what you can to avoid serious confrontations. You are a bright enough girl to know when to draw the line with this man. He needs to be loved and wanted. However, he can be a bit of a loner at times. He requires solitude when he's got problems to work out.

He's extremely fond of children. He will want to rear them in what he considers to be the correct way.

LEO WOMAN—SAGITTARIUS MAN

The Sagittarius man, whose symbol, you'll recall, is a centaur with a bow and arrow, certainly shoots to kill where romance is concerned. Known simply as the Archer, he is often shown galloping along and still trying to speed his effect on the world ahead of his physical presence by means of a well-aimed arrow.

Although he was known to ancient astrologers as the Sign of wisdom and the seeker after truth, we must be a little more critical. His so-called love of adventure is no more than adolescent irresponsibility.

He is a difficult man to trap. He is a bit wary about accepting routine life. You could say he is marriage-shy. He's the kind of guy girls like to have a wild fling with. He's good fun and makes a great companion and escort at parties. You won't forget time spent in his company.

He would not enjoy being trapped in a nine-to-five job. Give him the chance to break through new frontiers, even if it means taking great risks, and he'll jump at the opportunity. He loves the dangerous and unusual and is willing to take a gamble.

He is not exactly what he appears to be on the surface, though. There are hidden depths here. He is basically a sensitive and gentle person. He will always go out of his way to make shy people feel relaxed and at home. Underneath all that bravado and shouting is a man who suffers from an inferiority complex. He has to put on an act for his own sake as much as for the world around him.

He is a faithful person in marriage. Surprisingly enough, there is a strong religious streak in this man. He will take his vows very seriously.

Miss Leo and Mr. Sagittarius should hit it off quite well. You can be a bit wild at times, and you do like a man who speaks his mind and has a touch of the swashbuckler. You are both fire Signs, remember, and you'll discover that you share a great many opinions and beliefs.

You are both fairly sporting types. You could find he is the ideal partner for you at any competitive pastime.

He's something of a Romany, so you might think it's impossible for him to settle down. As a matter of fact, Mr. Sagittarius can quickly adapt to the home life once he has found what he's searching for. He will still like his night out with the boys—some nights he won't be in till the milkman is arriving—but don't get suspicious because it's more than likely that he's been up all night playing poker with his buddies.

This man is generous with money. In fact, he can be rather extravagant. He will spoil you with beautiful clothes and presents. Probably you should have some say in the handling of finances as he doesn't give much thought to tomorrow.

Mr. Sagittarius thinks of money as something to have a good time with. You'll have to remind him from time to time that there are rent bills and income tax payments to be met, and that if you ignore them, landlords and tax agents will get very, very uptight!

He's not the greatest with kids. Oh, he loves them all right, and he's good at telling bedtime stories, but he's not thrilled about changing a diaper or drumming responsibility into a rebellious teenager who got that way from observing his zany example over the years.

Still, if you can accept an occasional screaming match, you could both live happily ever after.

LEO WOMAN—CAPRICORN MAN

He may be shy, but don't be fooled because basically he's as tough as they come. He builds his defenses high around him, so it's not easy to get to know Mr. Capricorn.

He wants a lot of attention and loves to be the center of interest. He may appear self-sufficient but he decidedly is not. Underneath he is an incurable romantic. His trouble is he has great difficulty transforming his dreams into reality. He is a terribly disciplined person and a great conformer. You like helping people and all you expect as a reward is a word of thanks. The trouble with Capricorn is that he finds it very hard to admit he needs help.

If you want to get through to him, you'll have to work your way into his life in exceedingly subtle ways, and subtlety isn't your strongest point.

His humor is of the tongue-in-cheek variety. He can be a bit of a gossip and occasionally he lives his life through other people.

Capricorns like to pretend—especially to themselves—that they can live without compliments, but in fact, they absolutely thrive on them. Just try saying something really nice to a man born under the last earth Sign and watch his face light up.

You adore the good life, he's a bit frugal. He can't bear to waste money. He will travel second class on a train and stand all the way even if he can afford to go luxury.

One wonders if he offers enough to keep you contented for a lifetime. He's not a great mixer, and is likely to have only a handful of close friends. He doesn't feel comfortable at large gatherings. He has a private world that is difficult to break into. It would certainly be easier for you to make him happy than vice versa. The problem is to do this, you would probably have to give up many of your outside interests.

Perhaps the best chance of a successful liaison is with a Capricorn who has weathered the problems of his youth. By the time he hits his late thirties, he's likely to be a far better adjusted person.

If is very difficult to get him enthused about matters outside his sphere of interest. He will find it hard to become involved in something just because it's important to you.

He's unlikely to stray because it's against his nature to have secret love affairs. Of course, you will have to contend with his family. If you marry this man, you'll be taking on another mom and dad and a host of uncles and aunts into the bargain. Be sure you get on well with your mother-in-law because he's likely to have an extremely close relationship with her.

In bed, he'll try to take you by storm. It will be up to you to teach him better and show that you like the slow and gentle approach in lovemaking.

You will have to look after him when he's ill. He likes mollycoddling. He will often retire to his bed at the first sign of a cough or cold.

You'd better give him the idea right from the start that you expect your life with him to have plenty of passion. If not, your relationship will soon develop into something that's mainly platonic with thrill-night coming around every other Saturday.

He will love showing you off to his friends. He will be very proud of the capable way you run the home. He'll always adore you. To him, you'll never look a day older than the day you got married.

LEO WOMAN—AQUARIUS MAN

Mr. Aquarius has certainly struck it rich if he can get hitched to a woman like you. You are exactly the sort of person to bring out the very best in him. This man has many fine qualities; unfortunately, they seldom see the light of day. He needs a woman who can recognize his great potential and coax it out of him.

You will discover he's quite a thinker. If he falls madly in love with you, he will go to the ends of the earth to win you. He's extremely forceful when communicating his own ideas. Don't forget, his is the Sign of friendship, social life, hopes and fears; Aquarius is also known as the house of brotherhood. You will have to bring him down to earth a little bit. If you can stop him from thinking so abstractly all the time, you'll make a more lovable human being of him.

He has many varied interests and it will be better for both of you if you share a few of them. He's very enthusiastic and addicted to causes. Being inquisitive, you'll want to discover what makes him tick. It will be terribly important to him that you care.

The domestic chores will be left to you because he won't even know whether the house is tidy or not. He is out to change the *world* and make it a better place to live in, not the house. What is frustrating to Mr. Aquarius is that he's so often ahead of his time. The innovations he is trying to bring about now could well be generally accepted in fifty years. The Age of Aquarius (we hope) is going to bring us peace and brotherly love—something very dear to this man's heart.

So, how will you fare as a twosome? Well, he doesn't function on quite the same level as you do sexually. With him, love starts in the mind, and from that, all else follows. It is not easy for an Aquarius man to give himself on a casual basis.

He won't share your respect for tradition. As far as he's concerned, the world is in the state it is today because we have hung onto the ways of our ancestors.

Family is important to you; not so with this man. Of course, he loves his parents and his brothers and sisters, but what he believes in usually comes first.

At times you may feel he has lost interest in you completely. This is unlikely to be the case. He just gets so preoccupied with a cause that he becomes vague about everything else.

He will realize what a strong person you are and will expect you to be able to fend for yourself when he's not there.

He's unlikely to be jealous, and this could have its drawbacks. In sheer desperation, you could turn to another man just to see if he cares enough to come and get you back. Unfortunately, you won't get the reaction you hoped for, for he is likely to be philosophical about such matters.

You'll never know what time he's going to arrive home or whom he'll be bringing with him. Often as not, you'll come down in the morning to find some stranger sleeping on your couch; the poor guy probably didn't have anywhere else to go for the night.

Mr. Aquarius is quite likely to change jobs a number of times during the course of his life. Routine doesn't appeal to the Water Bearer.

Don't get too pessimistic, though, because in many ways you will hit it off together. You will learn a lot from each other. Your differences could unite you, if you resist the Leo urge to try to prove you're in the right all the time.

You should be able to show him that what is felt between a man and a woman is just as important as putting the world to rights.

LEO WOMAN—PISCES MAN

Well, one thing is for sure—your life together will be full of surprises. Fortunately, most of them will be pleasant.

When you first meet this man, you may think he's far too dreamy ever to be able to get anything together. True, he is a bit of a dreamer, and he does tend to wander around with his head in the clouds, but when it comes to action, watch him move. He's an expert at clinching business deals in record time. He's also capable of working in sudden spurts that leave even his close friends and family gasping.

Don't forget what his symbol is—two little Fishes swimming in opposite directions. He is a living contradiction. He can be everything you want—and, at times, everything you could well live without. He will keep you guessing.

He is not a weak man but he finds it hard to work up the energy for a project unless he can see a point to it. Work for the sake of work never appeals to him.

Mr. Pisces can be extremely naive. He will take people on face value. When you first go out with him, he'll think you must be the most even-tempered and placid girl he has ever come across. (This is an impression you often give to people.) He'll be very surprised when he finds after a few dates that you're pretty near running the whole damn show.

Let's be honest about Mr. Pisces. If he hasn't got the ball rolling by the time he's 30, he's unlikely to go terribly far in his career. If you don't mind that, all will be well. Being a Leo, though, you'll probably have ambitions for your man.

He can be a loner. This type of man has been known to live without other people for a lifetime. He doesn't hanker after riches or power. Give him enough to fill his belly and a jug of wine and he'll be quite content. If you've got a lot of money, okay. But you must face up to the fact that life with Mr. Pisces is not going to be plain sailing.

That's one Fish. Now, let's have a look at the other Fish, the go-getter. He is a real catch for any girl. His mind will amaze you. He will combine the qualities of many other Signs: the speed of thought of Gemini, the strength of Taurus, the leadership qualities of Leo. He has a live-and-let-live attitude toward life. He won't judge another human by his religion or the color of his skin.

He will do his level best to get on with your family, even if he disagrees with them on many subjects.

Mr. Pisces is not exactly a secretive person but he does believe in letting others know only what is good for them. He may occasionally conceal the truth from you because he doesn't want to hurt your feelings. He's a good talker and is usually capable of holding his own on most subjects. He appreciates a comfortable and settled home life.

He loves company as a rule but the time will come when he wants to be alone with you. You will have many a happy evening together snuggled up in front of the fire. He might take the phone off the hook to make sure you're not disturbed.

If you want to get your own way with him, appeal to his imagination and his feelings. If you try to lay down the law, he will balk.

He's great fun with kids, more like a big brother than a father figure.

LEO MAN—ARIES WOMAN

You'll find her very sexy and a real charmer. She's as bright as a button and her wit is razor sharp. She may be a little too forceful for a man like you, who prefers his relationships with women to be masculine-feminine in the old-fashioned way, because Miss Aries likes to dominate. She won't take orders from anyone. She's positive. And once her mind is made up, she rarely budges.

You do like to be spoiled and made a fuss of and her no-nonsense attitude could be a bit deflating to your male ego.

A woman born under the Sign of the Ram is always on the move. Adventure fascinates her and she is prepared to accept almost anything in the way of a challenge. She knows what she wants, and what is more, she knows how to go about getting it.

Like you, she doesn't play around with passion. If she returns your "I love you," you can bet she means it. You will admire her practicality. But at times you'll wish she relied on you a little more. You can't help wanting to play the protector. Her independent streak may be a little too much for you to take.

Of course, if you both know exactly what you want from life and it happens to be the same thing, then this union could work extremely well.

In a business partnership, you would be unbeatable. A Leo-Aries liaison would be just the right chemistry for getting to the top.

Don't try the masterful approach. She doesn't take kindly to being banged over the head with a club and dragged off to a jungle clearing. She dreams of a more romantic approach, and this should not be difficult for a Leo guy. You know all about soft lights and sweet music.

If this woman is attracted to a man, he soon knows it. It's not uncommon for her to take the lead in a love affair. In fact, she quite likes to do this. Being a bit proper in these things, you may think her rather forward when she asks you out to dinner.

There is no affectation or pretension in this woman's nature. She'll always lay it straight on the line. As a man who likes to know exactly where he stands, you will appreciate her honesty.

It would be wise to keep her guessing. She doesn't really like to get the upper hand in a relationship, although her manner may suggest this is what she's striving to do. Actually, she's only testing you. Play a little hard to get; this sort of behavior always intrigues a Mars-ruled woman.

Miss Aries can be an extremely jealous female. If you start having a bit of fun on the side, be sure she doesn't hear about it because she has a terrible temper and she won't think twice about going to the other woman's place and throwing things at her.

She'll be a great help in your career and will do all in her power to help you get on. A man with an Aries woman behind him will have an advantage over many of his competitors. In marriage, she'll put your interests before her own. She feels you should be the breadwinner.

You'll have no complaint about the way the home is run. She can look after the domestic side of your life together with apparent ease. Her cooking will be different without being exotic. She has the ability to rustle up a tasty snack in five seconds flat. This girl loves licking a house into shape. She's also adept with a pail of paint and a brush.

Basically, she prefers the company of men to women. You must not get jealous if she continues to keep in touch with old boyfriends after marriage. She'll think you're being silly and old-fashioned if you try to lay down the law on this score.

You will admire her fighting qualities, and if you believe in power sharing, all will be well.

LEO MAN—TAURUS WOMAN

This could be an interesting combination. Like you, she's extremely romantic, though people might not guess it on first meeting. Miss Taurus is a bit introverted. She will not easily show what she feels. She's very strong-willed and resilient. She doesn't like to take orders and occasionally seems to be totally without humor. You may find her a little too down to earth. You like a woman to be really feminine. Miss Taurus doesn't always give this impression.

She has great self-control. It is difficult to bait her into losing her temper, but when she does lose it . . . watch out! Try to boss her around, and you'll soon regret it.

This woman doesn't judge other people and expects them to extend her the same courtesy. She has no difficulty mixing with characters from all walks of life. You will find her equally at ease chatting with the postman or the President.

She's not interested in a casual affair. A Taurus woman only subscribes to the real thing. If you are hoping for a weekend with this girl and nothing more, save your breath and imagination. Still, she's very passionate. If you are really gone on each other, there will be no complaints coming from the bedroom. Your type of lovemaking will definitely appeal to her and vice versa.

Miss Taurus is a very reliable person. She would never let a friend down. If you get married, you can be sure your Venus-ruled woman will stand by you come hell or high water.

Her mind may not work as quickly as yours. She reaches the important decisions in life with deliberation. She refuses to be rushed by anybody. She loves feminine things. Angora sweaters and fur coats that she can nestle into will send her into ecstasy. Her sense of touch is highly developed.

She's very good with money and a guy like you may find that with Miss Taurus two can live as cheaply as one. She's quite a saver. She knows a bargain when she sees one and will be able to save dollars on the weekly food bill.

This lady is very set in her opinions, but then, so are you. As long as you are both on the same mental wavelength, all should be well. But it would be a good idea to have a fairly long courtship. Don't trust too much that the first explosion will last a lifetime.

She won't mind you if you wink at a pretty girl or even dance too closely with another woman when you've had a couple too many at a party. Don't go too far, though, because she doesn't miss a trick. She's very jealous so don't take her for a fool and cheat behind her back.

Miss Taurus is quite fashion-conscious. She knows what she looks best in. You will find she's extremely elegant, favoring nicely cut suits.

You are unlikely to be sorry if you do decide to marry a Taurus woman. Once you sort out your differences and come to an understanding, your relationship will be fruitful.

She will be prepared to give up her career if necessary to look after you. She takes great pleasure in doing things for her guy. She's an artist in the kitchen and delights in creating her own dishes to tickle her husband's fancy.

She's great with children in the toddler stage but can be a little too domineering when they hit their teens.

You'll find you haven't married a woman who runs home to mother. And though she won't be after you for your worldly possessions, she will help you to add to them.

LEO MAN—GEMINI WOMAN

A Leo man does like to feel he is following some sort of pattern in his life. You like order and can be quite methodical, so you may run into problems if you get too deeply involved with a girl born under the Sign of the Twins. She can be very confusing. She's apt to change her mind in the blink of an eye. You may feel she's just out to tease you, but this is unlikely.

You see, people born under this Sign have extreme difficulty in working out exactly what they want from life. With patience and understanding, you could help her a great deal. You will soon discover that in linking up with a Gemini, you have taken on more than one woman. After a few dates, you'll be wondering which girl you're going out with next. She just can't hide her moods or her feelings.

Age is quite important. If you meet a Mercury-ruled woman after she's had a chance to mature and experience life, it will be much easier for you to make a go of it. It takes her a long time to grow up and to come to terms with herself. Don't get angry with her or try to lay down the law, as you are in the habit of doing. You won't win her by wielding the big stick. She needs your sympathy and understanding. She'll run a mile if you try to dominate her.

You are a practical man and she certainly needs that. Show her by example and she will learn quickly. She has a sparkling personality and great presence. Just watch the heads turn when you walk into a room together.

Your Gemini woman loves travel and changes of scenery. She can't stand to feel trapped. She always wants to be experiencing something different and new. Jet planes and fast cars are likely to be terribly exciting to her. She's not the type who likes to go to bed early, either. Very often she comes alive at night. She'll get very restless if you expect her to stay home more than a couple of evenings in a row.

It is highly unlikely that this Mercurial woman will allow herself to be cast in the role of the little housewife waiting patiently for the breadwinner to return home demanding dinner. You'll have to allow her to carry on with her own interests or she'll go crazy with boredom. She's not great shakes in the kitchen, as a rule. She doesn't have the patience to prepare lavish banquets.

Miss Gemini needs a lot of loving—but she's capable of giving a lot of love. She can't bear to go on living with someone once the romance has gone out of the relationship, so don't forget to tell her continually how much she means to you. Buy her little presents and remember to take her in your arms occasionally. Even after years of marriage, she'll love it if you flirt with her and hold her hand under the table at a restaurant.

She has a good sense of humor. She'll try to make the best of it if you hit hard times. Miss Gemini can get down in the dumps, but on the whole she's a positive person and a great believer in tomorrow.

Life will never be dull with a Gemini woman. It's unlikely she'll lapse into silence for long. She loves stimulating conversations and discussions.

She makes a great hostess. When you bring your boss home, he's likely to be captivated by her charm and vivacity. She's not too particular about the background of her various friends and may arrive home with some pretty strange characters on occasions. All she requires of people is that they be interesting. When you have a party, leave it to her to do the organizing. She knows how to make an occasion go with a swing.

Her kids may not be the smartest in the playground, but they will be loved and well cared for.

LEO MAN—CANCER WOMAN

Hold on to your hat, Mr. Leo. If you get involved deeply with a Cancer woman, you won't know what's hit you. And the only way you can get involved with this woman is deeply.

You'll find her a constant puzzle. You won't be able to make up your mind whether she's the sweetest, most intelligent woman you've ever met, or if she is totally governed by her ruler, the Moon. Yes, you'll soon discover what an influence the Moon and her element, water, have on her. She turns like the tide itself and is as fathomless as the very deepest portion of any ocean.

Miss Cancer is a rather uncertain lady. She rarely appears to know in what direction she's heading. One minute she'll be vowing undying love, and the next she may be telling you she never really cared for you anyway. The strange thing is she will always appear to be telling the truth—and she probably is. She has great difficulty in recalling what she felt yesterday.

When this girl hits a low, she really gets down. It's almost impossible to shake her out of her mood. Perhaps a powerful personality like you can do it. But you'd better form a good idea of what you're getting involved in.

On first meeting, you'll find she has a way of concerning others in her life and her problems. She likes to be the center of attention and doesn't enjoy competition at all. Her symbol is the Crab, and a pretty apt one it is. When she withdraws into her shell, it will be very difficult to get through to her. Your phone bill could be fairly high because she loves to have long conversations with Mother, which could drive you absolutely insane.

You will have the task of getting her to face up to herself and to accept life for what it really is. She always fears the unknown. Although she is often on the run, she hates to be on her own. She'll worry if she's too fat, likewise if she's too thin. It will be the same with age.

She can be pretty tight with money. Desperate to secure her future, she'll hang on to the last buck. Mind you, she can suddenly go on a spending spree and come home with parcels of expensive new clothes. Her one great weakness is her wardrobe.

If she does fall in love with you, there won't be any doubts about it. She's all woman and will give herself totally. This won't happen, though, until she's absolutely certain of you because she's terrified of being hurt.

You will need to boost her ego constantly. She really does need compliments about her looks and dress. She will never take you for granted and will always be bowled over when you bring her a dozen red roses.

She hangs on to her friends from the past, probably for reasons of security.

Your Cancer wife will make a wonderful home for you. There's nothing she won't do for her man. She'll want you to be a success in your career and will do all she can to help you get to the top. Although she's not a stay-at-home, she does love domestic life because she feels most relaxed in familiar surroundings.

In marriage, she'll become more gentle. Once she feels settled and secure, she will stop hedging and walking sideways. She is devoted to her loved ones. As a mother, no sacrifice is too great for her to make for her children. But you'll have to watch your step when the babies come along. Being a man who needs constant admiration and flattery, you may feel a bit left out when she's fussing over her offspring.

There could also be trouble when the time comes for her kids to find their own way in the world because she does have a tendency to keep them tied to the apron strings.

LEO MAN—LEO WOMAN

This linkup will not be the plain sailing you might imagine. Although on the surface you'll have a great deal in common, there are fundamental differences that will have to be sorted out. When someone is very similar to you in so many ways, there are bound to be aspects of your own personality in them that you find difficult to come to terms with.

Miss Leo is proud, a born leader and unwilling to take orders from anyone. Her freedom is terribly important to her. She hates to feel hemmed in or suffocated. You, on the other hand, like to be cast in the role of protector and provider. It might be hard for you to swallow when this girl proves she is quite capable of taking care of her own affairs.

It will only be because she loves you that she'll allow you to make important decisions. She's not a golddigger. She seeks something higher than money or security in her marriage. She won't be prepared to sit quietly in the background while you hold the floor. She is much admired herself and has plenty to offer other people.

Miss Leo is all woman. Your male friends won't be able to help admiring her, and perhaps even desiring her. She is well aware of the effect she has on men. You will have to hide your jealousy and let her cuddle and hold hands with whom she pleases. You'll soon realize it's all quite harmless and that she'd never dream of doing anything to hurt or upset you. There is definitely something special about a Leo woman. Your friends will be forever reminding you what a lucky guy you are.

Never take her for granted or expect her to sit quietly at home while you live it up. You had better get it straight right from the start that she likes the exciting things in life as much as you do.

She's not the greatest cook or housekeeper. She'd much prefer to eat out if she's not entertaining. She's capable of rustling up a quick meal or experimenting in the kitchen, but to cook a roast every Sunday is one big yawn for her.

Other women will be pretty jealous of her, or perhaps we should say envious. They'll probably wish they had the strength of character to stand up for their own rights that she has.

Don't expect a lot of flattery, you who like to be tickled under the chin and told how clever you are. Your feline mate will make sure those feet of yours are planted firmly on the ground. You won't be able to pull the wool over her eyes and she certainly won't allow you to fool yourself.

She will be terribly good for you in business. You will never be ashamed to bring home important people. In fact, she could help you to clinch that contract you've been angling for. It won't be what she does or says that tips the scales; it will be her very presence.

She loves to dress up in pretty clothes and you'll enjoy buying them for her. She's very partial to chunky jewelry, expensive perfumes and fur coats she can snuggle into.

Your Leonine partner is a competitive pussycat. She'll give you a run for your money at any card game and will never admit defeat on the tennis court.

Her lovemaking is passionate. She has a vivid imagination and will enjoy experimenting and playing games in the bedroom.

Always remember her birthday. She loves pretty things. Your home is likely to be distinctly feminine. Neither of you is likely to want a large family.

LEO MAN—VIRGO WOMAN

You have a tendency to rush in feet first with your women announcing, "Well, here I am, girl, come and get me." You'd better change your style if you've got your sights set on a Virgo lady. She's quiet, reserved and hates big emotional displays in public. She will never respect you if you embarrass her. If you are interested in more than a casual affair and are prepared to woo her as romantically as only a Leo can when he tries, you'll find her more fascinating every hour you're in her company.

Miss Virgo is not prepared to show her true feelings until she can trust a man. She will expect you to prove yourself before she opens up to you.

Basically, she's shy. People would be amazed if they knew the thoughts that were running through her mind on occasions. It is very often the Mercury-ruled woman who ups and leaves her husband and two kids because she suddenly discovers true love. Her friends will pass such remarks as, "Well, who would have thought that she. . . ." Still waters run deep here. Little Miss Virgo cannot be put in a pigeonhole or stamped with a serial number.

She simply cannot or will not admit she's in the wrong, so don't think you can win her by criticizing her. She won't like it at all if you nag and try to change her. The aggravating thing is she's likely to be right most of the time. She's extremely good at summing up people. She may not have joined in the conversation, but when you get home you'll be amazed at how cannily she can pinpoint the strengths and weaknesses of the people you were out with.

If you are at all unsure about which decision to take in connection with your career or an important business deal, you could do a lot worse than discuss the matter with your Virgo woman. Nine times out of ten her advice will be worth following.

Marriage will be about the most important thing in her life so she will certainly try very hard to make a success of it. If, however, something goes wrong, she won't hang on. One thing she won't be able to accept is infidelity. She'll find it extremely hard to trust you again if you betray her.

A Virgo woman will want to share in your life as much as possible. She'll do her best to make your friends her friends.

Keep yourself looking smart. This lady can't bear a man who looks a mess. Keep that beard under control and be sure to splash on plenty of her favorite after-shave lotion.

When it comes to lovemaking, don't rush her. She needs to be treated gently. Whisper sweet nothings in her ear and keep the candles and the incense burning. You have to provide more than physical stimulation to satisfy her. Never say you love her unless you mean it. A woman born under this Sign takes those three little words very seriously. Don't make any promises unless you can deliver the goods.

She's quite capable of keeping on with her career after marriage. She's so well organized that she can run a house and hold down an important job at the same time.

She loves evenings at home but not too many of them. Her happiest times will probably be when you are alone together. Her idea of heaven will be to snuggle up with you in front of a fire on a chill winter's evening. She will keep the home tidy. In fact, you may find it hard to get used to her fetish for cleanliness. Every time you stub out a cigarette, she'll empty the ashtray, and she'll do the washing up while she's still chewing the last mouthful of her dinner.

The Virgo woman makes a good mother but you needn't worry about being displaced by the kids. You'll always come first with her.

LEO MAN—LIBRA WOMAN

You'll hit it off with a Libra woman from the word go. Out of all the Signs of the Zodiac, she is perhaps the most compatible for a man whose symbol is the Lion.

Miss Libra will depend on you without losing her individuality. She will make you feel all man without playing little-girl-lost. You will never feel suffocated or held down by her. Her interests are many and varied. She's an extremely good mixer. She is deeply interested in people and has a very inquiring mind. She is capable of continuing her career and running the home. She's very adaptable, equally poised when having a cheery joke with the mailman and when dazzling your boss with her charm and vivacity.

Harmony and balance are very important to her. She needs more than one interest in life to feel fulfilled. Don't worry, you'll always come first, but you must allow her her independence. Let her carry on with her career after marriage if she wants to.

The Libra woman is usually on the petite side and feminine to their fingertips. Although capable of looking after herself, she will bring out your protective instincts. She will never try to wear the pants. She'll be perfectly happy for you to be head of the house. She likes a man to be a man.

She's very logical and will be able to hold her own in any discussion. There's a mind as sharp as a razor's edge ticking behind that doll-like expression.

Don't forget that Libra is the Sign of partnership and human relationships. You can imagine how important it will be to a woman born under the symbol of the Scales to make a success of her marriage.

You'll have to accept the fact that she likes to flirt. She knows she's attractive to men and can't help playing up to them. You, too, like to play games with the opposite sex, so you will have to be prepared to allow her the same freedom. Don't get hot under the collar. It's unlikely she would ever do anything to put your marriage in jeopardy.

Your Libra woman will be a great ego

booster. She'll put you on a high pedestal. She will tell you you're capable of achieving anything if you really put your mind to it. With this woman behind you, there is no reason why you should not fulfill all your ambitions. For her part, she'll do all she can to get you into the executive seat.

She's just as romantic as you are. She'll adore bouquets of flowers and candlelight dinners. She'll throw her arms around you and shower you with kisses. She does not play games with men so you'll soon know if she is really attracted to you.

This woman needs other people. You aren't likely to find her in a job where she's shut away in some cubbyhole with only a typewriter for company. She'll want to join in as much of your life as she can. In many cases, it will be an advantage to have her along on business dinners.

She will never allow her emotions to get in the way when making an important decision. If she feels a relationship is going wrong, no matter how much it hurts her, she'll break it off. Her analytical powers are quite astonishing.

You'll love the way she organizes things at home. The kitchen is likely to be streamlined. She'll have all the latest gadgets to make life's daily chores easy to handle. The den will be comfortable and in perfect taste.

She's tops with kids—those of others as well as her own. You'll be as proud of her as a mother as you are of her as a wife.

LEO MAN—SCORPIO WOMAN

Brother, if you want to take on a real challenge, if you like to stick your chin out, if you want to dedicate your life to a woman, then pick Miss Scorpio. She'll fit the bill on every count.

She'll be a constant puzzle to you. She's not an easy woman to live with or to understand. Being a very passionate person, her feelings run deep. If she loves you, she'll do anything for you. But if you let her down and make her feel like a fool, watch out.

She's got quite a temper. She will not be dominated unless she wants to be. If you try to lay down the law in your usual way, she'll tell you where to get off in no uncertain manner. Basically, she likes to be in charge. Although she's all woman, she wants to have the upper hand in her close relationships.

Don't try the old-fashioned caveman approach. You won't win her over by dragging her off to the bedroom. She likes to make her own decisions and freedom is very important to her—not just freedom of action but freedom of spirit.

Life with a Scorpio woman will not be smooth sailing because she actually requires a certain amount of conflict in her life in order to function successfully. Her feelings are intense. It is rare for her to be indifferent about anybody. Her opinions are important to her.

She has no use for simpering little girls who play Miss Innocent with men. She's direct to a frightening degree.

She can be pretty ambitious. Scorpio women are usually leaders in their group. She will always retain her individuality and likes to make up her own mind. She is not a camp follower. Her work is pretty important to her and she likes to get to the top in her career. She can't stand to play second fiddle to anybody.

Never make a fool of your Scorpio woman in public. She'll let your remarks pass while others are around, but watch out when you get home. She's extremely truthful. She'll want you to be a success in your job. A hard worker herself, she can't abide laziness in others.

Scorpio people never know when to draw the line. They can go to excess with alcohol and drugs; when their senses are aroused, they lose their self-control.

Sex is one of the dominating factors in their lives. The physical relationship will have to be good for the union to survive. Her appetite in bed is insatiable. Strangely enough, though, she can go for months without sex if she has had a bad experience or doesn't meet the right person. She is quite choosy about whom she gets involved with, and usually goes for a very definite, distinctive type of individual.

You can trust your Scorpio mate to keep a secret. Her friends are terribly important to her. She tries never to let down anybody she respects and loves. She's not as romantic as you are. She'll always put the practicalities of life before her dreams.

Being the type of man you are, you could find life with a Scorpio woman a little draining. It would be advisable to get to know her really well before you marry. Make sure you have a lot more going for you than a purely physical attraction.

You'll find she mixes extremely well with your friends. She'll be just like one of the boys when you go out in a group. Miss Scorpio doesn't mind being the only girl in the party. In fact, she revels in it.

She makes a possessive mother. But then, she is possessive about everything she considers rightfully hers.

LEO MAN—SAGITTARIUS WOMAN

You will have to go easy on a Sagittarius woman. For one thing, she will not tolerate being told what to do. In your Leonine way, you often feel you know what's best for everyone. You appear to be bossy because people sometimes misunderstand your motives. A lady born under the third fire Sign will allow you to make the big decisions as long as you don't try to interfere with what she regards as her domain.

At times she will make you cringe. Sagittarius people have a habit of putting their opinions in a very strong way. She won't mince her words. People will know exactly where they stand with her.

You do like to have your ego boosted regularly. She is not prepared to do this. This woman will bring you to a greater understanding of yourself.

You can't help but appreciate her honesty and good intentions. She will do everything in her power to fulfill her duties as a wife and mother. She will make sure you are always well turned out. It will be important to her to run the home smoothly. She's no slouch when it comes to doing housework and all other duties connected with domestic life.

You'll find her great company. She's very good at parties and is interested in meeting new people. Although a home-loving person, she won't be prepared to stay in the background all the time and play the role of the little woman. You are a bit of a man's man; too many nights out with the boys could land you in hot water with your Sagittarius lady.

She's very ambitious, not only for herself but also for her man. She will stand up for you with other people. You have a bit of a career girl here. Most Sagittarius women go on working after marriage. The home is unlikely to be enough to occupy her mind.

She's quite the outdoors type. Very good at sports, she'll be a willing partner at tennis or squash. She'll enjoy it when you bring your friends home. Even if you give her only a couple hours' notice, she will be able to lay out a nice spread for your poker-playing and beer-drinking pals that will satisfy all.

This woman is exceedingly trusting. Tell her something and she'll believe you. Woe betide the man who lets her down, though, because it is not easy for her to forgive and forget. She'll tolerate the odd flirtation, but if you get involved seriously with another woman, she'll never have quite the same respect for you again.

Miss Sagittarius is a little shy of romance. She's not too keen about displaying her emotions in public. For her, love is something to be shared between two people only.

You haven't got the greatest cook in the world here. Sagittarius women simply don't have the patience to spend hours in the kitchen being creative with a casserole.

A Sagittarius lady will not pry into your business affairs—or into your personal life outside the home, for that matter. She'll feel that as the man of the house, you'll know the best decisions to make as far as your job is concerned.

One motto to remember with your Sagittarius lady is: "If you want a job done, do it yourself." Ask her to mail an important letter and she's quite capable of forgetting to put a stamp on it. Be careful you don't scold her, though. Even if she makes a mess of things on occasions, she'll always do her best to keep you happy.

With kids, she's an absolute wonder, although she does have a tendency to live her life through them as they grow older.

LEO MAN—CAPRICORN WOMAN

All will be well if you are one of those Leo men who are born leaders (that is the category most of you fall into) because Miss Capricorn is an ideal partner for a man who is out to make his mark in the world. Success is very important to her. She will always be there at your side, boosting your confidence and telling you you're the greatest.

Remember, we are dealing with the third of the earth Signs here. This woman is very hung up on possessions and getting to the top. She'll want you to be ambitious and will do all in her power to make you realize your full potential.

A woman born where Saturn rules and Mars is exalted is interested in wealth and security. She wants to feel secure about the future. She's wonderful at getting a home together.

Don't get the wrong idea about her—she doesn't worship money; but she is well aware of its value. She will help you to save and is expert at balancing the family budget. She's also capable of whipping up an interesting and exciting meal for next to nothing.

If you fall for little Miss Capricorn, you will have made a very good choice. If the feeling's mutual, you can count yourself a lucky man for she's a very choosy lady. And you can bet your bottom dollar she's spotted your leadership qualities. It may take some time to get to know her well because she's quite complex. Her head does not always rule her heart. Her emotions are very deeply felt, but she will usually pull back if she thinks she is going to get hurt or is wasting her love on someone who doesn't really deserve it.

Miss Capricorn will take the rough with the smooth and make the necessary sacrifices for the sake of the future. But she is emphatically not the kind of person to put up with second best for the rest of her days.

She has great patience, and if she is really attracted to you, she'll be prepared to play the waiting game. You'll find her wonderful as a partner when it comes to entertaining influential business associates. Miss Capricorn could well help you clinch that all-important deal. She knows how to flirt with men and make them feel very important without allowing the relationship to become heavy.

You won't have any complaints about her lovemaking. Her sexual appetite is pretty near insatiable. She will make you feel all man. As a woman, she likes to be taken. Variety is the spice of life for her. In bed, she has a vivid imagination.

Her family is very important to her, so once you get married, be prepared to see a great deal of her mother.

She will help you build up your bank account. She's shrewd about bargains. You'll never cease to be amazed at how economical she is when shopping for the family groceries. And she's adept, as well as artistic and inventive, at making her own clothes. Occasionally, she might go on a spending spree, but then, can you name a woman who doesn't?

A Capricorn lady can't help being a bit of a flirt. If you catch her fluttering her eyes at another guy, try not to let that jealous streak of yours take over because it's likely to be harmless.

She will make a good mother to your children. As a parent combination, you should agree on how youngsters ought to be brought up. You'll both be firm but just. And she'll give them all the maternal love they need.

LEO MAN—AQUARIUS WOMAN

So you want to marry an Aquarius girl? Well, friend Leo, you'd better decide on a long courtship. Get to know this woman really well before you decide she is the one you want to spend the rest of your natural life with.

There would appear to be quite a lot against this liaison. But then, as they say, love can always find a way. It's possible you two will view life in very opposite ways. She's an extremely difficult girl to pin down. Just when you think you've got her number, she'll do or say something that appears to be totally out of character. You like to know where you stand with a lover, and this is something that's almost impossible to ascertain with Aquarius.

She has a very independent streak and won't allow anyone to lay down the law to her. No sir. She'll always shout "freedom," though when you ask her what exactly that is, she'll find it difficult to articulate.

Plenty of other guys find her desirable so you'll have to contend with a lot of competition if you're out to become the only man in her life.

Aquarius is the Sign of friendship, social life and aspirations—and unexpected happenings. There is not, as a rule, a great deal of interest in domestic matters here (don't forget how much you like your home comforts). An Aquarius woman is likely to be on the go all the time. She's a woman of ideas and can get deeply involved in causes.

As a Leo male, you can be pretty possessive if you feel your woman's life doesn't center around you. A woman born under the Sign of Aquarius could drive you insane. When coming in from a hard day at the office, it's possible you'll find the house empty. You'll have to get used to preparing your own supper quite a lot.

When it comes to getting a home together, this lady has excellent taste. But she's not too good at economizing—in fact, she rather enjoys spending money. Your little chats about how to cut down on unnecessary expenditures will have little effect on her.

This relationship need not be all gloom and despair. She'll ensure that you make the best use of your powers of leadership. She is extremely attracted to people with powerful personalities.

If you can accept change and the fact that Miss Aquarius likes life to be full of surprises, all should be well and good. You do like a certain amount of order, though, and a lifetime of games playing could be a little too much for you.

It could be that a whirlwind romance that ignites great passion for a short period would suit you both best. It is quite likely you'll go on being great chums once your affair is over. She's that sort of woman.

You can't help but admire this girl's pluck. She's always willing to put herself out to help a person in distress.

You'll enjoy taking her out to parties. She doesn't have a jealous nature. If you have an affair with another woman, she'll be very understanding. There is a danger that relationships outside of marriage could become a problem for you both. You will have to work pretty hard at mutual fidelity.

Contrary to expectations, she makes a very responsible mother, who strives to bring up her children in an adult way.

LEO MAN—PISCES WOMAN

The Pisces woman is all woman. She will impress most men with her feminine charms, and you, Mr. Leo, are no exception. She is the zany type who often goes around in circles, occasionally getting confused and frequently changing her mind. She'll have you in a dither, but when you get to know her well, you wouldn't have her any other way.

She's dreamy. Not only is her head in the clouds, but her feet are off the ground: She'll come up with the craziest ideas for travel and for making money—and the surprising thing is that her plans so often pay off.

She likes a man who can take the lead. Masterful Leo is likely to be very much her type. It will be up to you to make the big decisions. She knows who should wear the trousers around the house, and she'll expect a great deal from you. Any lack of confidence you have about your prospects will soon be dispelled by her.

You two make an excellent combination in so many ways because your various strengths and weaknesses balance each other out perfectly.

Don't be taken in by her rather blank and wide-eyed expression. A Pisces woman knows exactly what is going on. There's not a man around who could pull the wool over her eyes for very long. You'll find yourself waiting on her quite often, bringing her a cup of coffee in bed and making sure she's got most of the clothes she desires. But then, what man who loves his woman doesn't enjoy bringing pleasures into her life?

She won't try to match her wits against yours and will enjoy hearing you speak out on your favorite subject.

You are pretty careful with money, although you do enjoy an occasional spending spree. She likes to be extravagant at times, too, but Pisces knows the value of a greenback. You'll have no trouble saving cash for a luxurious vacation or the proverbial rainy day. By the way, Pisces women are reputed to be very astute about property. She knows a bargain in real estate when she sees one.

You will be keen to get home to her most nights after a hard day's work. If occasionally you stop for a couple of beers with the guys, she won't object. Just be sure to let her know if you're going to be late as she may have prepared some special surprise for your supper.

She's an absolute wow at decorating. Her taste is impeccable. One of her pleasures in life is buying new things for the home. One or two of her purchases may turn out to be shrewd investments.

There are, of course, certain drawbacks to this duo. Where you like to be positive and stick to your decisions, this lady born under the last watery Sign of the Zodiac is likely to change her mind as quickly and as many times as the tide ebbs and flows in a day.

The Pisces woman places a lot of importance on anniversaries and birthdays. She'll like you to remember all special occasions. It's one of her ways of reassuring herself of your love. It would be a good idea to keep a record of them.

Physically, you'll discover you are well attuned to each other. She is an uninhibited lover and will like your very masculine attitude. Don't play with her affections. If you let her down, she can be ferocious.

To keep her self-doubts at bay, it will help if you tell her, without being patronizing, whenever she's done a good job. This girl is very artistic and poetic, but in her vain search for perfection, she's likely to destroy her creative efforts in disgust—and the world could miss out on something unusual. She will make an excellent mother for your children—and she'll never relegate you to second place.

LEO'S HEALTH

Since you are one of the hardest workers in the Zodiac, it's not surprising that nature has provided you with an extremely robust constitution. You are probably the healthiest Sign of all. Your nerves, muscles and vital organs are arranged in a fine functional balance, and your fiery, outgoing temperament gives you the will to survive in the most difficult situations.

Leo rules the heart, the central source of the organism's power. Any serious health problems are likely to appear here. Heart disease, epilepsy and rheumatic fever are possible disorders. But generally speaking, the heart is especially strong and healthy in Leo people. They are capable of tremendous exertion (while in good shape) without any ill effects.

You throw off illnesses very rapidly. Your powers of recuperation are quite extraordinary. You can stage a recovery that in other less vibrant types would be impossible. In any kind of sickness, your immense vitality seems to radiate from the heart into every cell, quickly revivifying your entire body.

However, you should never disregard the important effect your emotions can have on your well-being. There may be nothing physically wrong with you, but sorrow, sadness and especially pining disorganize your system. Then you feel unwell and you look unwell. You become lethargic and depressed. You are likely in these circumstances to imagine yourself ill and even talk yourself into going to bed.

Fortunately, the Leo temperament is extraordinarily sanguine. You are usually able to snap out of depression. You can be assisted in this by a person with the right bedside manner, one who admires your strength and capacity to fight back, or by an appeal from a loved one who is dependent on you. The need to take some sort of authoritative action will eventually force a dejected Leo to throw back the sheets and start giving orders.

When you do go succumb to an illness, if it is not heart disease, it is usually connected with the spine, the circulation or the throat. You may suffer from pains in the back, side or shoulders, weakness in the ankles or problems of the reproductive organs. Hoarseness and sore throats are also common. There is also a danger of pleurisy, fevers and convulsions, especially in childhood.

You seldom suffer from chronic or lingering diseases, although periodic eye trouble can be a complaint. When sickness strikes, it is usually sudden. As a patient, you are inclined to require a lot of attention and frequently convince yourself you are in worse shape than you are. You will first think it wonderful to have an opportunity to rest (at last), but soon you will get bored with the inactivity and want to get up.

You are prone to accidents. You are not the most patient driver on the road. Although normally very safety conscious and aware of your responsibilities behind the wheel, you tend to be easily irritated by other motorists and to take silly risks out of churlishness.

A distinct danger period for Leo-born people occurs in middle age. This is when you are likely to become absorbed in a wide range of mental pursuits and take insufficient exercise. Or, being inclined to extremes and recklessly confident of your own strength, you may suddenly throw yourself into intense physical exertion, which puts a great strain on your heart.

You are usually a great sports lover, the kind who likes to participate. When plunging into superactive games, remember to treat your back with extra consideration.

It is important for Leos as they get older to develop the art of relaxation. You should endeavor to create a philosophical outlook and not react automatically to every emotional situation. In the space of one hour, you can go up and down like a yo-yo, getting all heated up over the most trivial provocations. In middle age, the superb nervous system that served you so well in your youth is easily upset.

Leo's great fondness for pleasure can also be a health hazard. You may burn the candle at both ends just once too often. There is also a danger of drinking and eating to excess because you love good food and are an inveterate party-goer.

Leo individuals are psychologically fearless in the face of danger but not so well equipped to cope with physical pain. You are a sensitive person who can literally fight a duel to the death if necessary to defend a person or a cause, but you may protest at a pinprick and perhaps even faint while giving blood.

LEO AT WORK

You yearn to be a celebrity. This is a basic Leo urge, so don't be ashamed of it (especially if you're young) and wonder why the limelight seems so much more important to you than to your friends. Leo is the Sign of personal projection. You're going to get to the top in whatever you undertake. If you bury yourself in a dead-end job just because it's safe, you'll always be discontented.

You are a colorful and dominant personality. There's a great deal of the showman in you. You should choose a job or career where you can make the most of these qualities. The entertainment and amusement fields are naturals for you. Many of the most successful actors and actresses were born under your Sign. You possess a wonderful physical magnetism; in the theater or on the screen, this is what is called "star quality." You also possess a fine sense of the dramatic; in fact, you probably have to guard against overdramatizing your actions and words in whatever occupation you follow. The desire to create a sensational effect is not always appreciated by others and may even hinder your advancement.

Leo-born people make fine entrepreneurs, promoters and managers in show biz. They are attuned to public taste and can usually spot talent at a glance. Their promotion methods are usually spectacular. Glamor and gimmickry are props Leo loves to use. Motion picture production, with its almost unlimited opportunities for spectacle, is an excellent medium for your vivid and flamboyant imagination.

But no matter what work you're engaged in, you'll do best when you occupy a position of sole authority because your strongest characteristic is the power to rule. It is as a leader that you make your greatest contribution and impact on the world, and at the same time satisfy your deepest instincts. You'll never be happy in the role of an understudy.

Naturally, everyone has to make a start and learn the business. It is good if you have to knuckle down in your early days and learn to follow orders. There's nothing to stop you from dreaming of the day when you'll be on top while you're working diligently toward it. Fortunately, people born under your Sign have good minds. They can work with great determination and against tremendous odds as long as they know they're progressing. But they need the encouragement of loved ones at home, and appreciation and recognition of their talents by their superiors.

As a Leo, you are well suited for work in one of the professions. Medicine or the law frequently offers the chance of individual expression leading eventually to public acknowledgment. Your vigorous sense of purpose and desire to serve mankind in a dramatic fashion often allow you to change the established order and pioneer new developments and techniques. As an authority, you will have a powerful influence.

Politics is an extremely fertile field for the Leo man or woman. Here you can lead in your inimitable, individualistic style and at the same time satisfy your altruistic urges. Although you may never cease to complain about the weaknesses of the system and the shortsightedness of your colleagues, you have the patience and perseverance to work incessantly toward your goals. Your tactlessness and brash criticism of others is only equaled by your ability to get away with it.

Many Leos end up in executive positions where they can command, organize and distribute duties. Although infuriatingly critical and demanding, they are also extremely fair. They are trusted by their workers.

As a boss, you like to hog all the important jobs for yourself—that is, the ones most likely to impress your clients or the board of directors. But if you get overloaded—which means you can't take a two-hour lunch, meet a client for a game of golf and do the innumerable other things you pack into a single working day—you'll hand the jobs around. Even so, everything has to have your imprimatur on it before it goes out. The fact that someone else worked all night on a job doesn't change this. You'll see that he is rewarded more than amply for his efforts; but when it comes to accolades, you make sure you're the only one in line. Still, your employees usually respect you and will do anything for you, which means working for you can't be all that bad.

In fact, if a worker is having a hard time because of illness or unexpected expenses, you're likely to be on his doorstep as soon as you hear about it with a good-size check in your hand or airline tickets for a holiday in the sun. And no one's ever likely to hear from you what you've done. You might like to blow your trumpet about your achievements, but helping others is one thing you're in no rush to take the credit for. A significant proportion of famous anonymous philanthropists have later been revealed as people born under the Sign of Leo.

As an executive, you expect your staff to be creative and extremely active. You enjoy conferences and think tanks. You like to take the floor and outline your plans with great flourish. You certainly know what you want—and you expect your subordinates to get going on it. You're not a great one for detail yourself (you're strictly an idea person), but you do like everything done precisely, accurately and efficiently. You'll listen to other people's suggestions and encourage them to contribute, but you'll always retain personal control. Everyone must report to you finally. Lone wolves are outlawed in Lion territory.

Although at times you like to appear informal and one of the boys, you want your due respect. Then you are generous in your compliments for a job well done.

You are honest and frank, and therefore sometimes lacerating in your criticism of employees. Insubordination or lack of faith in your pronouncements or leadership is likely to be met with howling rage and derision. There are no palace revolts in Leo's domain. Mutineers get the boot with the first insolent look. The Lion makes terrible enemies while on the warpath putting down a revolt or dealing with a cannonade from the top. He or she shows no mercy and looks for none. You usually win, or die in the attempt. If you do neither, you will simply walk out. Leo, though, only quits as a last resort. You prefer to stand and fight.

As an employee, you've always got your eye on another guy's job—up the ladder. It won't be your boss's job, as a rule, because if he treats you right, you're absolutely loyal. You'll be his number two in no time, and then you'll move sideways, around him, through some other department, so there'll be no collision of loyalties.

If you've got to wait around to obtain a big promotion you know is coming, you're supremely patient and philosophical. As long as you can see the light at the end of the corridor (burning over that other guy's desk), you can wait in good grace. And in an emergency, you're ever ready to take over, no matter how big the job may be. Can you handle it, Leo? "Yes, just tell me his name and I'll get all I need from him."

You prefer to have a job with a fancy title than an extra few dollars in your paycheck. You'll never really forget a boss who overlooks you. If he does, he's also likely to be a Leo. You're too fond of telling everybody how good you are and too critical of those in command to ever hit it off with a Leo boss, who thinks you're supposed to be telling *him* how great he is. Between the two of you, each jockeying to impress those a little higher up (not to mention all the other employees on the floor), it will be a genuine two-ring circus.

You're a quick thinker, a daring and adventurous operator. Anyone can bounce a decision off you; in a crisis, they come in sure-fire volleys. You'll never pass the buck once you've accepted responsibility. But if anyone's foolish enough to overule you, you'll let him stew in his own juice and watch the ship go down without batting an eyelid. There's nothing quite so immovable as the imperious disdain of Leo scorned.

You'll be happiest working for an organization where there is contact with the public. You'd prefer a receptionist's job in a high-class or glamorous establishment to working as a secretary-typist. As a personal assistant to a company chief or executive, you are sure to shine, provided you are allowed to achieve the required results your way. You are exceptionally good at implementing orders as long as you are left alone. You also need a job where you can make full use of your vivacious and winning personality.

If you were born between July 21 and July 30, you will do best by pouring your considerable energies into worthwhile projects. There is a danger you'll be distracted by glittering propositions that have no real substance. Glamor and fame may attract you more than solid achievement. You have a talent for writing and for expressing original ideas. You may make a name for yourself in advertising, journalism or public relations. You should be able to rise through the ranks to a high executive post.

The teaching profession, religion and public

welfare work may also serve as an outlet for your talents. You are intense, spontaneous and dynamic. An excessive love of pleasure could affect your health. Emotions may be difficult to control at times, especially where romance is concerned. Work and love affairs may conflict.

If you were born between July 31 and August 10, you will probably do well in some travel-connected occupation. You may write or lecture about your travels. Your judgment in finance and business is first class; your organizational and executive skills excellent. You are quite capable of heading an international operation or company. Artistic decoration and design may offer good commercial prospects. Your personality is forceful, commanding and attractive; you should make friends easily wherever you go. You need to stimulate your thinking by mixing with intellectual types.

You should be able to succeed in a high-level government career where you have responsibility for the interests of large numbers of people. Your vision is broad and independent. Whatever you write or say will have a wider influence than you suspect. In times of stress, you may have to strive to keep your emotions under rational control.

If you were born between August 10 and August 21, you have a good legal mind that is able to perceive the motives of others. Your sharp and alert intellect may be a little daunting and frightening at times. You probably have a strong interest in occult subjects that, given the opportunity, could be turned into a career. Publishing and writing should appeal to you. You may also do particularly well in the entertainment industry or another field that demands close contact with public opinion.

You are likely to gradually build up your estate and by midlife have considerable assets. Much of your success will depend on your ability to control impulsive and speculative actions.

Money

You like to spend money but seldom squander it, except perhaps in your youth. You have expensive tastes but are prepared to work hard and put money aside to buy the best. You are a methodical saver.

People born under your Sign have to learn to make money work for them. Once you mature emotionally, you usually manage to accumulate investment capital. You are a shrewd investor and are often helped by information from people in high places. The real estate and property business can be a bonanza for August-born people.

Your home is often your first worthwhile investment. You enjoy a change and by moving residence can usually manage to improve the value and size of your assets. You should never underestimate your intuition when buying or selling. Leo people often "feel" the right thing to do with money but can be swayed off course by the opinions of loved ones.

You are a good and generous provider. You often find it difficult to say "no" to those who depend on you. You may run yourself into debt for them. Extravagance by family members can cause you considerable anxiety.

There is the danger of loss through gambling. Once started, it's very hard for Leo to stop. Romantic involvements may also be costly.

VIRGO'S CHARACTER

Virgo the Virgin, of course, is no more the Sign of virginity than any other. But it does represent the primitive human drive for purity and perfection. If you are a typical Virgo individual, this is the key to your character. You want to see those rare and fleeting virtues established for keeps here on Earth. It is a magnificent and impossible ideal at this stage of human evolution—but that does not deter you. You seek perfection where you perceive it is most conspicuously absent—in your work and in people. Which explains why you are so determined to introduce method and efficiency into the office and to tidy up the place wherever you happen to be. It also explains why you are so critical of the rest of us—and why your verbal incisions are so uncannily accurate.

Virgo is the sixth Sign of the Zodiac and one of the most misrepresented. You are adaptable and busy, yet practical and cautious. You are reserved, modest and possess sound mental qualities. You are also extremely trustworthy, impeccably honest and straightforward, sincere, loyal, courteous, diplomatic and exceedingly reliable.

The Sun passes through Virgo at a time of the year when the grain is ready for harvesting—when prudence dictates that all that is worth keeping should be put in its correct and proper place. Put another way, Virgo represents the conservation principle.

Virgo is the Sign of discrimination through intellect, not rejection through habit or instinct. It bestows the ability to tell the difference between this and that by logic. It is also the Sign of healing, which explains your avid interest in good health and food. It has a special affinity with nature; not every Virgo-born person has a green thumb, but all possess a psychic understanding of Mother Nature's first law of cause and effect. And finally, it is the Sign of true celibacy (not to be confused with sexual fears and disgust). Here is the paradox of celibacy with pure fruitfulness—symbolized by a maiden holding two ears of corn in her hand, and the Virgin and child. There is far more to this wonderful Sign of yours than is usually guessed.

It is difficult to determine a person's Sun Sign from physical characteristics because, as a rule, there are too many diverse influences in the horoscope. But in the fairly typical Virgo, several distinctive qualities are quite easy to spot once you know what to look for.

First, they retain an extraordinarily youthful appearance into late middle age. Gemini does the same, but Virgo is less restless and urgently communicative, and this serenity shows in the calm and confident set of the face as well as in body movements. These are measured, though fluid, and somewhat dignified; they certainly lack the sharp, darting mannerisms that distinguish your fellow Mercury-ruled Gemini.

In a crowd or at a party, the Virgo man or woman can often be found standing in a central situation with a questioning gaze, observing others and listening to their conversations while deciding who would be the best person to talk to. You are concerned with improving your knowledge and mind and can't be bothered wasting time talking to frivolous lightweights. You have a studious and intent expression, which can flash into a smile or a look of animation when your interest is stirred.

Both male and female Virgos have a cool, pleasing I've-got-it-all-together demeanor. You don't stand out in a crowd, but one never fails to remember meeting you. You are like that definition of the well-dressed person: people can't remember what he was wearing, only that he looked good! Some people have twisted this "anonymous" quality of Virgos and described them as being the face in the crowd no one ever remembers. But your unobtrusiveness stems from your sense of what is appropriate, your innate desire to fit properly and inconspicuously into the scenery. You're not out to draw attention to yourself. You are, essentially, an observer.

Your instinct is to analyze, to sift the minutest details of what's going on in an effort to discover the significance. So you listen, evaluate, and remain quiet until you are sure of your audience. You have no wish to make waves.

The typical Virgo is appearance-conscious and very aware of good grooming. Even the most unsophisticated Virgo is neat and tidy. You can't stand sloppy habits and carelessness in dress. You can be extremely snooty about mixing with dirty or unkempt characters. Cleanliness is terribly important to you, sometimes to the point of obsession.

The Virgo man is a spick-and-span figure and quite often a natty dresser in his own quiet way. He favors simple and subdued colors, like gray, brown, black and navy. For accessories, he may wear touches of blue; he may also favor small patterns on ties and scarves. This man makes sure that his hair, even if worn long, is trimmed and clean. If he sports a beard, it is shaped and presentable. His nails, irrespective of his job, are always clean.

The Virgo woman is usually a chic dresser in the traditional sense. She favors different tones of blue and gray, but will often wear white to accentuate her cool, meticulous, well-groomed image. She likes to be comfortable in what she wears, but must also feel she looks good—which to her means looking right rather than dazzling. The Virgo woman can on occasions let her appearance go and become quite sloppy. But this usually occurs only when she is lonely or depressed. Depression, as a rule, is short-lived with her; loneliness is something of a chronic complaint. She bears up with determination and courage, but these are seldom enough.

The problem of loneliness is an extremely difficult one for all Virgos to come to terms with. At heart, you are shy and retiring. You are inclined to take a back seat. Fortunately, you are particularly efficient when it comes to doing a job. The world needs you, and it keeps you busy during your working day. But when that is over, typical Virgos often go home to an empty house or apartment. They tend either to take work home with them or to immerse themselves in cultural interests, which usually include reading and listening to music. As important as books and records may be to their fulfillment, these things can't be considered a substitute for human contact: its warmth, intellectual stimulus and earthy togetherness. Despite your aloofness and cast-iron emotional control, your soul yearns for release with other human beings.

You want to belong as much as anyone. But your intellect too often rules your heart. You analyze and mentally skirt your deeper longings. Too frequently you feel that to reach out to others will complicate your life, when in fact it would do nothing more than release your tensions and nervous inhibitions and contribute to your overall good health.

If you look closely at your life, you will probably notice that although you declare you want meaningful relationships, you deliberately avoid them. This is a conflict between nature and character. Remember, it is your nature to insulate yourself against the emotional imperfections of the world—but if you do so, you will be unable to make the world the perfect place your basic character desires. Your nature doesn't relish involvement with people because of the possibility of personal hurt. You don't wish to take any unnecessary risks. And yet, your character wants you to give yourself, to strive after happiness, to experiment with life and its emotions—to step out in faith. Loneliness is only the absence of reaching out to others.

One of your most admirable traits is your modesty and lack of egotistical posturing. Those fiery and self-centered Signs that are so often disdainful of your devotion to work and detail could certainly learn a thing or two from your example. You don't cloud issues with your own egocentric intolerance and prejudices. You can see a fact clearly and are able to discard all that's not essential to a proposition. Because of this, you learn much faster than others. You are able to assess a situation correctly while they are still struggling to overcome their preconceptions.

Basically you are a thinker who endeavors to apply your ideas in practical ways. Though you have an active imagination, it's only likely to get out of hand in romance. Otherwise you employ it to try to improve the conditions and circumstances around you. A shrewd and discerning observer, you are very much aware of what is missing or needs attention. You don't project yourself outside your immediate environment; but you certainly do your best to redress any failing or imperfection you encounter within it.

This brings us to your penchant for finding fault. It's not a quality that endears you to people, yet it does gain you considerable respect. As a critic, you are without equal. You can always be counted on to give a fearlessly honest opinion. But too often you are searingly personal. And the fact that your criticisms are amazingly accurate doesn't help. Your intuition invariably picks up the weaknesses in others, and being a sincere individual, you see no necessity to hide what you see. The result is puncturing outspokenness. Your intention is to help, but instead you often wound and offend. Frequently it is only your obvious lack of aggression and malice that saves you from being slapped in the face or punched on the nose.

You do not, however, like having your own faults pointed out. Let someone try to tell you you're fussy, pedantic, hypercritical and interfering, and you respond with a perfectly reasoned argument to show your critic is mistaken. The fact is you are well aware of your weaknesses and faults, but you believe you're the only one competent to deal with them. True enough—but shouldn't that apply to us all?

Still, you honestly do try to make a better person of yourself. Self-improvement is very high on Virgo's list of priorities. Sometimes you can even make a fetish of it. But at this stage of human evolution, Virgos seem more intent on improving themselves physically than on rectifying their character defects. Most of you are preoccupied in one way or another with health, hygiene and diet.

Your interest here is in bringing about purity and perfection in the body. But too often it degenerates into faddism. There are more hypochondriacs among people born under this Sign than any other. Their bathroom cabinets are usually stocked with all kinds of fast cures. Actually, the Virgo philosophy is "prevention is better than cure." You tend to stuff yourself with vitamins and take all kinds of other precautions, such as mouth-washing and gargling, to ward off the *possibility* of infection. Consistent with this is your great attention to personal cleanliness and hygiene. It is not uncommon for a Virgo-born person to wash his hands ten or even twenty times a day. As soon as you touch something that is not your own, you have a compulsive desire to get to a washbasin. Some of you shower or bathe two or three times a day. Your clothes actually get worn out from overwashing.

Virgos don't as a rule like people touching them or strangers preparing their meals. They often try to avoid crowds, not for claustrophobic reasons, but because they fear "germs" in the air and infection from the close proximity of bodies.

Strangely, the Virgo individual is not so conscious of the benefits of physical exercise, apart from a few desultory jerks. In your early years, you are likely to be active in light sports, but seldom anything boisterous or rough. In middle age, however, you get so wrapped up in your intellectual pursuits that you go to seed. You need plenty of fresh air and sunshine to keep your nervous system functioning properly. Without some outdoor activities, you will become addicted to the medicine chest.

Virgo's keen interest in diet and hygiene is not so odd because physiologically the Sign rules the digestive organs (the intestines) and the bowels. You invariably possess fine discriminatory powers as to the choice of foods best adapted to your particular organic requirements. Many of you are vegetarian or semivegetarian. Few of you chronically overindulge in food or drink. Your idea of pleasure is to enjoy most things in moderation. You are much more likely to starve yourself than to be gluttonous.

If you are a typical Virgo, you develop habits very easily, though this is not the unconscious process it is with some others. Just about everything you do you examine carefully first. Once you've decided that a certain procedure is desirable, you quickly make it a rule. It could be the most convenient drawer for your underwear or the best day of the week to go shopping. God help anyone who tries to interfere with your routine.

One of the first habits you acquire is punctuality. Few Virgos could be late for an appointment even if they tried. This is part and parcel of your great penchant for order, method and efficiency. The simple explanation is that the typical Virgo person has proved to himself through practical experience that being on time is the easiest way of avoiding inconvenience and aggravation for all concerned (please spread this around!). You know that this kind of precise attention to detail actually makes work easier. And it is in work that Virgo strives to attain the highest perfection he or she can.

It's a pity you don't see with the same clarity that there's another side to life, a more intimate, more personal, more meaningful side, that also deserves perfect development. This is the emotional side, the side that has to do with the love between a man and a woman. At this point in human evolution, this world of our affections is sweet and torturing, unpredictable but splendorous. The trouble is that the typical Virgo usually knows exactly what he or she is doing in this department. You seldom succumb to an emotional impulse. Certainly you will experiment with love, but it's usually just that—the inquisitive urge to find out what you're missing rather than the surrender to an insane, head-over-heels, irresistible attraction. Virgos can resist just about every emotional temptation if they want to because their sharp intellects are always dominant, holding back feeling, pushing aside impetuosity, calculating the consequences. You are fastidiously discriminating, and frequently you miss out on love through too much analysis.

The "Virgo in Love" section deals in detail with your romantic inclinations. Briefly, you can certainly be stirred in this way, but only if the other party measures up to your idea of a lover and a person. You don't participate in sordid affairs if you can help it. If you do get caught up in one, you'll extricate yourself as quickly as possible. You demand a decent relationship based on trust and honesty.

The Virgo man is likely to be more curious about sex than the Virgo woman. He'll have his first affair with a convincing show of casualness and pretense of experience. Inside he'll be literally trembling, not with lusty passion so much as with trepidation. This man does not have a great physical need for sex, but he does suffer grave doubts about himself. He often wonders whether his masculinity is of the same order as the rest of the boys, who never seem to have the problems he has. Once he's proved himself (don't worry, you're as virile as they come), he can wait a remarkably long time for the right girl to come along without doing any more casual bed-hopping.

The Virgo woman is not inquisitive about sex. She wants one thing only, and that's pure love. And she won't compromise if ever she finds it. As much as she loves order and doing the right thing, she won't put up with a disastrous marriage. She's lily-white but not lily-livered. She'll leave everything for true love. The problem is the Virgo woman seldom finds her sublime idea. This is a mental image that only one man in a million could possibly measure up to. In ordinary marriage, she usually spends most of her time trying to create this ideal out of mere mortal material.

Both the Virgo man and woman often have trouble with their relatives. They are happier and more contented living apart from their family. Sometimes they marry distant relatives but these partnerships seldom work out satisfactorily.

As a typical Virgo, you have very high ideals about home life. You believe in sharing responsibility with your mate. Because of your reasoned approach to problems, you are a tower of strength when the going gets tough. You are prepared to pull in your belt when economies have to be made and to work hard toward mutual aims without complaining. You are ready to make the best of things. Although basically idealistic, you have few illusions. You aim for the best but accept necessity. You are a very sensible, down-to-earth character.

You run your home with natural expertise. There's a place for everything and everything is in its place. You are not the type to put up with slovenliness. You can make life pretty tiresome at times for those who believe a home was meant to relax in. You're likely to be too exacting, fussy, house-proud. It's not uncommon for a Virgo to follow household members around, straightening cushions, emptying ashtrays and generally succeeding (with the best intentions) in making them feel thoroughly uncomfortable.

Though disorderliness is foreign to your nature, excessive neatness and the effort to maintain are apt to affect your sensitive nervous system. Your passion for perfection can literally drive you mad. This applies particularly to the Virgo housewife and mother, who has to depend on the uncertain cooperation of a husband and children. When faced with the impossibility of imposing their exacting standards, it is not unknown for these women to suddenly let the place fall into total disorder. This is your built-in safety mechanism, which helps prevent a nervous breakdown.

Although an exceptionally methodical person, you are easily upset by monotony. You don't like the idea of changing residence, but when the time arrives, you enjoy the activity immensely. You are great at making arrangements and organizing masses of detail. Things get done when you're in charge. You can pack and unpack with the dexterity of a professional. With a paintbrush or wallpaper, you are marvelous. In no time at all, you can transform three bare rooms into a cozy and comfortable apartment. You are very particular about the appearance of your home and will spend a lot of time choosing furniture and furnishings.

Despite your intense interest in your home, you do need to get out of it into other surroundings. Vacations and long weekends are especially important for the Virgo housewife, who is apt to get home-locked and wonder why she's feeling irritable and depressed. Again, your nerves need to be considered. Astrologically, you represent a somewhat incompatible combination of two elements—earth and mutability. Earth makes you practical, material-minded and in-drawn; mutability makes you crave variety. This basic incongruence is experienced as nervous pressure—in your own way, you want to go but you also want to stay. The solution is to have both a regular job and a permanent home that allow frequent changes. In your job—even if this is running a house—you must have ample opportunity to get out, frequent communication with others, short trips, visits—that is, numerous small, detailed but different tasks.

A Virgo who is forced to stay in enclosed surroundings will soon become tense, irritable, demanding and hypercritical. (Husbands and wives of these sensitive people, please note.)

There is another interesting astrological theory about the Sign of Virgo that may have significance for future generations. It concerns the so-far "undiscovered" planet Vulcan, which is said to be the true ruler of Virgo.

At present, Mercury, that quicksilver, intellectually brilliant but somewhat irresponsible planet, is the co-ruler of Virgo and Gemini. Mercury signifies the airy qualities of Gemini far more than the practical, earthy and meticulous attributes of Virgo.

What sort of a ruler is Vulcan? What difference would the sighting of this planet (said to be imminent) make?

In Astrology, only when a planet is discovered do its properties begin to appear in the people born under the Sign it rules. As Vulcan hasn't yet been seen, Virgo people to date are stuck with the Mercury influence, which is not really compatible with them and which creates the conflicts we've referred to. Vulcan's attributes, on the other hand, complement the Virgo character splendidly. Vulcan was the ancient god of the blacksmith's forge, the deity of silversmiths who fashioned small and finely worked objects. He was a cheerful, obedient and extremely intelligent entity who had a reputation for being conscientious and industrious (definitely not Mercury traits). He was also said to be the crippled servant of the other gods. Many astrologers have remarked on the peculiar gait of Virgos, which often suggests some irregularity if not "lameness."

Vulcan will eliminate much of the nervousness that now characterizes Virgo. You will be more sure of yourself, less inhibited, and you will reflect that amiable strength and inner courage that is personified by the hard-working smithy once your true ruling planet is discovered. Interestingly, the mental brilliance of Mercury will always remain with you because this planet is exalted in Virgo alone.

At present, it certainly seems that Virgos do have an unfair disadvantage. Their emotional world seems to be locked inside of them. They feel so much and yet just can't manage to communicate or express it. There is a fire burning within, as every Virgo knows only too well. Perhaps Vulcan the smithy will release it.

It's time to touch on some Virgo faults. Surprisingly, there are not a great number of them. In fact, all that can really be said is that you make vices out of your virtues by carrying them too far. Take your crystal-clear mind, for instance. This is a wonderful help to us all. If we can't sort out ourselves or our problems, you are a most reliable person to turn to. You can see a saving fact in the middle of imaginative chaos. When everyone else is running around in a panic screaming something like "We're trapped, we'll never get out of here," you're likely to be the only one who coolly tries the "locked" door and finds it wasn't locked after all. Yes, you're a realist. It's not that you necessarily disbelieve others, but you prefer to ascertain the truth for yourself. This is a very admirable trait when action is required, but you often go too far and start splitting hairs. You get hold of some inconsequential fact, and to make your point, hammer it home relentlessly until everyone else is ready to climb the wall. Factual trivia might be important to you, but lots of others don't give a damn. They don't want to know *how* a thing's done; just that it's done, thank you.

Your main weakness we've already touched on—you tend to find fault in all and sundry. Your inspired criticism we all appreciate . . . in moderation. It helps us to know ourselves better. But do try not to make a pernicious habit of it. Not all of us want to be as perfect as you would like us.

You're also something of an actor or actress. In fact, the typical Virgo has a tremendous flair for drama. A number of thespians were born under your Sign. Nonprofessional Virgos have a habit of dramatizing their illnesses because they want sympathy. Frequently there's nothing wrong except that you are feeling a bit lonely or neglected. You enjoy sympathy, and you are very good at extending it to those in trouble. It's a sentiment that doesn't require great attachment or emotional commitment; hence it doesn't frighten you and make you want to retreat.

One of your favorite ploys, when you want to get out of a tricky or an unpleasant situation is to pretend to be ill. One Virgo lady going for an interview arranged by her employers at another branch decided in the crowded waiting room that it very definitely was not the sort of job she wanted—and fainted. At precisely the same moment, a Virgo guy opposite her clutched his chest and slumped to the floor groaning. It was a terribly good piece of mistiming. Later, when the two became firm friends as a result of the incident, they confided the truth to each other.

Lastly (still discussing faults—but this is only number three) Virgos are a little too practical-minded to ever be classified as overgenerous. You are not selfish, as is sometimes reputed. The explanation is far more profound. You are self-centered in the sense that you seldom make a move unless there's a good reason for it. You like to be liked, respected, appreciated—and generosity is often a means of ensuring you will be. Others may be impelled by the same motives—*unconsciously*. That's precisely the point. With Virgos, it is almost impossible to act unless the move has been thoroughly analyzed. You analyze automatically. Every impulse is referred to your intellectual center. And naturally, where intellect dominates, spontaneity is inhibited.

But can you be blamed for being continually aware of your own reactions and mental processes? After all, this is only another way of saying you are alert and fully conscious. You are highly intelligent and your gift is for conservation and prudence—for having what you need and for being able to share it with others because you haven't wasted it.

Virgo people will give for a good reason but seldom out of sentiment. What you give is usually needed and deserved. Because of your fine discrimination, you often succeed in helping your fellow man whereas others who give out of sentiment and attachment fail.

So another Virgo fault turns out to be an extension of a virtue—your gift for logical analysis, which you apply to every department of your life. Logical analysis must be as impersonal as space, which—like Virgo—gives factual existence to everything.

All you Virgos need to be happy is a place where your critical attention to detail can be used in practical ways and your reliability appreciated.

VIRGO

IN LOVE

YOUR VIRGO MAN

You like him? Love him? What sort of person is Mr. Virgo?

He'll either fascinate you or bore you to death. It depends very definitely on what kind of woman you are. If you're fiery, passionate and want to be swept off your feet into the bedroom or down the aisle—forget it. This guy takes his time. He pussyfoots around the subject of romance as though he were dancing around the maypole. It takes him ages to get to the point. He'll often date a girl for weeks before getting around to a good-night kiss.

But once he's broken the ice with you and feels sure of his ground, you're likely to be pretty busy satisfying his rampant curiosity. This man loves mostly with his mind. He reaches for love through his body, but he's never one with it. Passion as an exquisite pain of sensuous longing is something he very seldom experiences. He doesn't know the agony and hopelessness of surrender to unrequited love or the insane abandonment of the lover who gives up all just to get to his woman.

No, Mr. Virgo is a cool customer. And that's what can be so fascinating about him. He can resist the most seductive advances—look vaguely interested or glance right through you if he thinks that's likely to do the trick. He's shrewd, analytical. His blood doesn't race and his heart doesn't pound.

The Virgo man is frightfully unsure of himself with the opposite sex. He just doesn't know how to deal with passion. He's a guy who's basically self-centered. He can't take and he can't give—he's emotionally straitjacketed. He's too selfish to offer himself and too cautious to demand the surrender of another. Frankly, he wouldn't know what to do with a woman who gave him her soul as well as her body.

All this makes him very different from the usual hot-blooded male. To many women, he's a refreshing change. And he does play the flirting game delightfully. This he understands. He's a glib talker when he gets going, yet honest as the day is long. A woman can't help but be struck by his lack of male egotism. He doesn't want to dominate her, to conquer her, and yet . . . what is it about this fellow that gets to so many women?

Well, for one thing, he's pretty safe to have an affair with if you are looking for the thrill of conquest and can manage to bed him. He won't make trouble. He won't make demands on you and he won't accuse you of playing him along. He hates all kinds of public demonstrations, especially emotional ones. He is acutely embarrassed if a girl kisses or hugs him in front of his friends. He'll never speak to her again if she persists in such demonstrations. He reckons romance is something only two people share—and that they should express it in privacy.

This guy's ideas about lovemaking and romance come mainly from what he's read and heard. He's a great stickler for form and tradition. If he starts courting you, you can expect all the traditional overtures—red roses, boxes of chocolates, Valentine cards and a very important meeting with Mom and Dad. He's a perfect gentleman, as a rule, and he'll want your father's consent before he marries you. He's such a straightforward, clean-looking, reliable, upright sort of chap that most fathers will think him excellent son-in-law material.

He hates vulgarity and can't stand a woman who's sloppy or careless in her dress or habits. He is very punctual and expects everyone else to be on time. He mightn't say much if you've offended him, but you'll certainly feel the temperature rapidly dropping to zero minus five.

He's one of the most critical people you'll ever meet. He can make the most damning personal observations in about three words. And the trouble is he's so often right that an honest girl just can't answer back.

If you marry him and come up to scratch, he'll never be disloyal. If you let him down, he probably won't divorce you because of the fuss, but since he's had a taste of the love game, he will now be capable of illicit romances.

YOUR VIRGO WOMAN

You like her? Love her? Just what sort of woman is she?

She's going to be very, very hard to get. She knows exactly the type of guy she wants—or let's say she knows precisely the type she doesn't want the very moment she meets him. She's fussy, choosy, very hard to please. She analyzes every male she meets. If you fancy her at all and start turning on the charm, you'll feel that cool scrutiny of hers. Her detached assessment of your character can be so infuriating, so frustrating—so sexy. Here's a girl that's just waiting to be won—daring you to show her it would be well worth it!

Everything about Miss Virgo symbolizes the Virgin, the untouchable, the unstained. She can go to bed with a different man every night (most unlikely)—but that delicate reserve will still be there. Yet when she gives herself finally (most unlikely), it's a total surrender.

This woman's problem is that she has great difficulty finding a male she can trust with her emotions. She keeps them locked up, deep inside, because she sees so many flaws in people wherever she looks—especially in men who can hurt her. She's a perfectionist. What guy can ever be *that* right? Only Mr. Right himself, of course.

She's extremely outspoken. It's a sort of compensation for her constant judgmental attitude, especially toward would-be lovers. Being a very honest person, she feels that if she judges someone, she should at least be frank and come out with it. This can be very irritating—or more to the point, ego shattering.

Still, Miss Virgo is no fool. She's acutely intellectual, and if you're dating her and want to make an impression, you'll have to be a good conversationalist who is able to discuss both people and current affairs. She's very interested in what others think—more so, in fact, than in what they feel.

She's witty, articulate, and if she does flirt, she does it in a very intangible way. She definitely won't dart behind the curtains with you for a quick kiss and a cuddle. This female, in fact, doesn't like to be touched much at all. A man has to get the chemistry working just right to enjoy the fountain of passion the Virgo woman keeps so rigidly capped. There's great pressure there if you can only find the formula to release it.

The Virgo woman hates vulgarity and coarseness. She doesn't want to listen to smutty jokes. Bad language appalls her. You won't get anywhere with the he-man approach. She sees no reason why a man can't be a perfect gentleman. The casual, slangy guy will probably draw a withering acerbic retort from her if he tries to get fresh. She's the type who likes doors to be opened for her. The right guy will get the message quickly; she'll stand there expectantly with a touch of regality that seldom leaves any male in doubt about the treatment she is waiting to receive.

Miss Virgo is quite capable of going through life without sex, even though she is terribly curious about it. The type—but not the individual—is the personification of spinsterhood, as it is quaintly called. She has to be convinced mentally that a romantic involvement would not do her harm. She weighs it all carefully. The physical part is secondary. She does not have much vital spontaneity.

First, she must be sure that she's not burning any bridges. This woman lives a well-ordered, methodical life. The future is terribly important to her, and she does not intend to live now and pay later. She owes no one anything and is very independent. You'll find this out if you fall for a Virgo lady.

She'll expect you to be true to her once you've agreed to make it permanent. It's not that she's jealous or possessive. She just believes everyone should live up to his word. She demands fidelity because it is the correct thing; to her it gives meaning to a union. She doesn't, as a rule, believe in one-night stands.

She'll never let you down. But if you are disloyal, things will never again be the same between you. Not because she can't forgive, but because she can't forget the imperfection of cheating.

VIRGO WOMAN—ARIES MAN

It is often a mistake to go on first impressions and you might find it advisable to remember this when you meet an Aries man. There are many qualities that will attract you to him. The question is, will you be compatible over any length of time? He's an impetuous kind of guy. Like his symbol, the Ram, he has a tendency to rush into situations head down and ask questions later. You are a very different kind of person. You take your time. You weigh the pros and cons before deciding on a course of action.

Opposites do attract, and this could well be so in your case.

He's aggressive—a born fighter, in fact. So are you. But you tend to be a bit shrewder and to use strategy to defeat the opposition.

Don't get the idea that you can control your Aries partner by soft-soaping him. If you decide to get together, you would have to come to an understanding about who makes what decisions. Perhaps a power-sharing arrangement would work out; its lines would have to be clearly drawn, however.

He loves changes and brings about quite a few of them himself. You are more the steady, reliable type.

This man born under the first Sign of the Zodiac is quite a womanizer. It is important to his male ego to be found attractive by the opposite sex. Could be you will get a little bored with his game-playing even if you know it's all harmless fun.

On the plus side, there will be many fine qualities to admire in an Aries man. He's hardworking and willing to accept almost any challenge if it gives him the opportunity to better himself. He's certainly no shirker. Always willing to learn, he's quite capable of changing jobs fairly late in life. He's very ambitious, perhaps a little more than you. He wants to get to the top.

Your friends won't think you two have much chance of lasting the course together. But the staying power of true love has surprised a lot of people down through the ages. He will certainly have a lot of admiration for you. He'll be absolutely knocked out by the way you run the home and will be happy to leave that department to you. He is handy around the garden and never shirks work that calls for manpower. You won't have to call in your local builder to put up new shelves.

Mr. Aries is very straightforward. He won't side with you in an argument if he feels you are in the wrong.

Like you, he is not too keen on public displays of affection. They embarrass him, especially in front of his male friends.

You may find his ways a little extravagant. It might be a good idea for you to have some control over the family finances because he can get carried away by his enthusiasms. For instance, he's likely to spend a lot of cash on a new hobby and then suddenly lose interest in it.

The sexual urge is strong in this man. Women find him attractive and he knows it. He finds it difficult to say no when they issue an invitation. This is where the relationship could fall down. You may not be able to accept the fact that he is likely to have an affair from time to time.

You might get the feeling he's not all that interested in what you feel and think. He can't help this. He's not a great one for analyzing people, even people he loves.

Never give him the feeling he's being fenced in. An Aries man can't stand not being able to come and go as he pleases.

VIRGO WOMAN—TAURUS MAN

This could be a marvelous combination. Taurus will make a wonderful friend for a Virgo girl. Since you are careful and methodical, it might take you a few dates to discover he is the man of your dreams. You are both earth Signs, which means you're a pretty sensible and straightforward pair.

You will admire his patience and frankness. He will feel he can trust you, and this is terribly important to the Bull. He hates to be abused and won't allow anyone to play with his emotions. You'll find his company stimulating. He'll bring you out of yourself. He is wonderful at taking a girl out. He's all man and he'll make you feel all woman.

He's solid, steady and dependable. Once he offers someone his friendship, he'll be a friend for life. He's not the sort who changes his mind every five minutes. If he talks to you about settling down together, you can be sure he's serious.

Like you, he's a traditionalist. He doesn't like change. He tends to hold fast to the old values. He'll always employ methods that have proved themselves down through the ages.

You love music and so does he. You both have an artistic streak. It's important that you have the same sort of tastes in art and books.

Occasionally he likes to give the impression to his friends that he's a big man. Actually this is a front. He can't help wanting to impress people. He has to make his associates feel he's doing a bit better than they are. Make sure he doesn't feel he has to give you the same impression. You must make him feel secure enough in your company to be himself.

One thing you have in common is a great love of family life. The home and its comforts are terribly important to both of you. You will be quite happy to spend many evenings at home together. You are not likely to get bored in each other's company.

Mr. Taurus is a great provider. He would never let you go without anything. Although an extremely good businessman who knows all about making money, he won't be stingy with you. He will love buying you all the pretty things you want. He'll do all in his power to make you feel happy and contented.

You will have to accept the fact that he's a bit of an adventurer in the field where he has proved himself. He will always be involving himself in new projects there. Don't try to interfere in matters connected with his work. He hates to be told what to do in that area of his life.

He can be a bit bossy and this is where you could clash. He will expect you to run the home and leave it to him to do the providing. He won't be too happy with a wife who keeps up her personal interests after marriage. He's quite a lover but needs to be aroused physically. You will have to work at being more of a siren. Don't rebuff his compliments; if you don't respond to his overtures, he will sulk.

He likes to work hard and can get very irritable if life becomes *too* dull and routine, even though that's what he seems to like. You'll have to put up with his moods.

It would be disastrous were either of you to get deeply involved in an affair. Like you, he finds it hard to forgive infidelity. He would be hard pushed to trust you completely again.

Be sure you have plenty of mutual friends. You could end up spending too much time together and that would make him a bit stodgy and grumpy. He does need some outside stimuli.

VIRGO WOMAN—GEMINI MAN

You will not respond tepidly to this man. Either you'll go overboard for him or find him a scheming, artful, worthless character. Love and hate, though opposite emotions, sometimes overlap. You have a great deal in common with clever, witty Mr. Gemini. You are both ruled by Mercury, which gives you speed of thought. On the other side, he is an air Sign while your element is earth. He wants variety and you cherish the status quo.

He's a charmer but you might find his sudden changes of mood a bit too much to take.

The man born under the Sign of the Twins can easily have half a dozen projects going at the same time.

He gets bored very easily. You may often feel he is wasting his talents. You will never know where you stand with him. He will appeal to your intelligence; he's an excellent talker and very good at convincing people to adopt his point of view.

He may not appear to need much protection, but he really does require a secure home life to retire to when he's gone too far (which is quite often).

If the circumstances of your first meeting are right, he could sweep you off your feet. If you meet Mr. Gemini at a party (he'll be the guy with the crowd around him), you're liable to find him fascinating. You are never apt to experience a dull moment when he's on the scene.

Don't let him rush you into making a quick decision. You are usually the sort of woman who takes her time, but he can be very forceful and he could easily confuse you.

Once you've seen him go through his routine a few times, you may discover he's too shallow for you. Don't forget you'll be coping with two of him—his Sign is the Twins.

Bright as a Gemini man is, he can also be stupid and superficial. He may feel a little inhibited by your efficiency and your steady pace.

As a good friend, you will never tire of seeing his face. Very often this man gets on better with the opposite sex than with very masculine company. He's a bit of a gossip and feels flattered by being surrounded by a lot of women.

He enjoys sex, but more for the feeling of power it gives him than out of sensuality. Life without making love would be a dull affair. He's not too good at making love relationships last.

Mr. Gemini know how to get a woman to fall for him but he might not be around when she needs him most. He has trouble facing up to responsibilities. It could be frustrating for you to try to keep tabs on this man. If you are lucky enough to come across a well-adjusted Gemini, one who has stopped running, that is, then you could prove to be an ideal team.

You are not the promiscuous type but you would learn a lot from an affair with a Gemini man. It is likely to be an experience you would never forget.

He is not interested in getting involved in a project where he will not see the end result. He's excellent at organizing but he won't stick around once a job becomes routine.

If you decide to try to make a go of it, then it is advisable for you to hang on to the purse strings. Money definitely burns a hole in this man's pocket—after all, there are two of him to spend it.

VIRGO WOMAN—CANCER MAN

On first meeting, you will feel you have met a charming and straightforward man, one who has come to terms with himself and has very positive views on life. He has excellent manners and a great sense of fun.

If you get deeply involved with him, though, you will soon discover he is a complex character, one of the most complex in the Zodiac. You will begin to feel there are one or two secrets he is keeping to himself.

If he feels he can really trust you, he'll confide in you—and you'll discover you are mixed up with an extremely shy person, a man who basically lives by his emotions. Can a logical person like you take this sort of thing for very long? It's doubtful.

He is a romantic; you are very much a realist. His chopping and changing will infuriate you. He is an inward-looking individual; you tend to take your values from the outside world. You will rarely hear a Cancer person ask someone else how he or she is doing. But if you ask the Crab the same question, you could get an answer longer than Hamlet's soliloquy.

Of course, there are many things you will agree on. Finances, for one. Like you, he can't bear to be in debt. You can rest assured he will move heaven and earth to pay the rent when it's due. You will be extremely good for him in so many ways. He needs someone who is ruled by her head and not by her heart.

He can be charming and very romantic. If you do decide to take him on, he'll always be kind and considerate. It would appear, though, that you need a slightly stronger character around you. He's a homey type and he needs some pushing to get him to the top of his career because he has a tendency to settle for second best. If he's earning enough to get by, he won't be all that ambitious.

He needs to be treated gently at all times. When he arrives home from the office, he'll expect you to drop everything and pour him a drink. You could find him a bit of a moaner.

If he is a typical Cancer type, he will be a conservative dresser. He will follow his personal tastes rather than the latest fashion. He refuses to buy anything that will be out of style before he wears it out.

When things go wrong for him, he retreats into his shell and it takes a lot to coax him out. When he's having a tough time, he'll become a recluse, refusing to see even his friends. He can't bear to have other people aware of when he's doing badly.

Let's hope you get on with his family. A Cancer man is usually very close to his mother. In fact, this fellow is often found living with his folks long after he should have be out fending for himself. He just hates to forsake a secure nest. If you don't see eye to eye with your mother-in-law, life could be pretty miserable.

He's very good at coping with domestic chores. He won't leave you to deal with all the household problems yourself. With kids, too, he's prepared to take his fair share of responsibility. If you decide to continue with your career after marriage, you'll find him perfectly capable of preparing the evening meal.

You need not worry too much about infidelity because Cancer men make remarkably faithful husbands. Since your inclinations are similar, this mutual trust could hold you tightly together into a happy and companionable old age.

VIRGO WOMAN—LEO MAN

Let's hope you are one of those Virgo women who like to be dominated because Mr. Leo is a man who has to be boss. He will pamper you and put you on a pedestal. In return, he will expect you to provide him with a good home and be 100 percent woman.

Don't play games with this man. And don't attempt to wrest power from him.

If you fall head over heels for the King of the Jungle, the way to snare him is quite simple—be his audience. He is a flamboyant character who has very firm opinions about life; you will find you have little difficulty in going along with him because he's very good at proving himself right.

He is confident, even overconfident. He would never let it enter his head that he might be wrong about anything.

He's extremely passionate. Any woman finds it difficult to refuse him. He enjoys sex. He is the sort of man to free you of any inhibitions you may harbor in that department.

The Lion will be generous with you, perhaps overgenerous. He is careful with money but can't bear people to think him mean. If he decides you are the girl for him, he'll move heaven and earth to supply you with your heart's desire.

Once he has swept you off your feet, you'll find it exceedingly difficult to regain your composure. He will certainly make you feel all woman. He's a romantic. If love is missing from his life, he's not a happy creature.

You will have to be prepared to change a little and this you find difficult. Mr. Leo does need to be flattered. You'll have to go along with his view that he's almost perfect—perhaps even absolutely perfect. You will also have to learn to keep quiet when he loses his temper. The King of the Jungle must be allowed to stand on the top of the mountain and roar his head off from time to time—without his mate hollering back.

He will want you to belong to him body and soul. He's a very jealous man. Don't flirt with other guys when he's around. He won't stand for any nonsense. Being a Virgo lady, however, you are the one-man type so you should not find it hard to stay faithful.

He will also have very definite opinions on how you should wear your hair and the way you should dress. He will prefer you in pretty clothes to jeans and a sweater.

He thinks most of your life should center around him. He won't be too happy about your having a job that keeps you away from home. Likewise, he won't be too keen on your having too many of your own friends. (Well, he is the King of the Jungle, isn't he?)

You will have to be on hand when he's had a bad day at the office. He'll need your comfort, understanding and sympathy. Don't make any career plans. A part-time job may be okay, but he'll want you at home when he needs you.

He is very persistent. Once he has decided you are the woman for him, he'll never let you out of his sight. He could well sweep you off your feet in a whirlwind courtship.

You need have no worries about the future. You will always be well provided for.

You are both careful about money. You will agree on priorities. He likes staying in quite a lot, but like you, enjoys a good party, especially if it gives him the chance to take the floor and spout his views. He's super around the home, quite a handyman. And he truly enjoys fixing things.

VIRGO WOMAN—VIRGO MAN

A union between a man and a woman born under the Sign of Virgo could be paradise—or the most boring liaison you could possibly imagine. You have a lot in common, of course, and this in itself could be the biggest stumbling block to happiness.

You might find him a bit too fussy and methodical. It could be that he wants to take over all the aspects of the relationship that you consider your domain. He is quiet and respectable, but you may want a guy with more fire.

He's not a great romantic. A Virgo male will not move you with his passion. He is pretty shy and you may get the feeling after a few dates that perhaps he doesn't care for you at all, so long does it take him to get around to that first goodnight kiss.

You both love the home and are searching for peace and harmony. You're the sort of person, though, who will understand that in life, and especially in human relationships, a certain amount of conflict is needed. How long can two people last together who tend to agree about everything under the sun?

It is unlikely that you'll meet at a party or some similar social gathering. He would be far too shy to come up and ask you for a dance. Very likely you'll meet through a mutual friend.

Your love life will be more tender than passionate. He's no cave man in the bedroom. This will probably work out well, though, as you usually prefer to be treated gently.

He is a very sensitive person and would never be pushy or take liberties with the opposite sex. Male Virgos rarely rush into an early marriage. They are also very much one-woman men. It is extremely rare for them to give up on a marriage.

He won't try to rush you into saying "yes" because he won't want the decision to get married to be his alone. He will want you to be absolutely sure that he is the man you wish to spend the rest of your life with. Neither of you has a great deal of intuition.

He's pretty conservative in his ways. He is a man of his word. He doesn't find it easy to forgive a person who is not able to keep hers. As you are well aware, one fault of the Virgo character is the tendency to bear grudges and judge other people. Both of you are quick to find fault; this could lead to a lot of niggling arguments.

Physically the Virgo male is neatly built, as a rule. He's tidy in manner and dress, something of a dandy, in fact.

Sincere and reliable, he will always be on hand to help you to weather a crisis. Nothing's too much trouble in the way of effort. He is also terrifically loyal to his close friends.

You will have to get your Virgo man to watch his weight. He's not all that keen on physical exercise and tends to go to seed rather early. Keep him on his toes. Get him out in the open air. Tell him a long walk would do him more good than forty winks after Sunday lunch.

Like you, he's very clean and particular about his food. You'll really have some fun thinking up recipes for health dishes.

He's great with kids. But if you decide not to have a family, it won't worry him all that much.

The desire to be a father is not particularly pronounced here.

VIRGO WOMAN—LIBRA MAN

You should find you have a great deal in common with a Libra man. He is charming and terribly attractive to most women. He will know how to keep romance alive in marriage, too.

Your love of art and music could draw you together in the first place. You will certainly like his sense of humor. Occasionally you take life a little too seriously. He will teach you to see the comic side as well. He is also very practical.

You will also have to get used to his advising you. You shouldn't mind because his suggestions are usually well worth following. Although you are not a person who likes to be told what to do, you won't find it too difficult to take a certain amount of bossing from him.

He is very charming and has a strongly developed sense of justice and fairness, as well. The idea of cruelty is repellent to him. He really does feel it deeply when he hears of other people's misfortunes. Intellectually, you will have quite a lot in common. Although he is an emotional person, he usually allows his head to rule when it comes to making the really important decisions.

Once you have become involved in his life, you'll find it hard to extricate yourself.

He will notice all the little things you do to make him happy.

He is a bit of a wanderer and this might be difficult for you to accept. You are a home-loving girl and the fact that he doesn't have regular habits might be hard for you to adapt to.

Sometimes he needs a push to stir him into action. Although he is naturally talented, he can be somewhat lazy if given half an excuse.

Partnership is essential to people born under this Sign. He needs a partner in business or in one of his artistic schemes. Having someone to talk his ideas out with helps him to bring his projects to fulfillment.

Mr. Libra is a flirt, but don't take this too seriously. It is practically impossible for him to resist chatting with a pretty girl. You must not become jealous or possessive or he will get the feeling he is being trapped and run a mile. He needs to feel appreciated. So long as he knows you desire him, that is usually enough for him.

Friends may tell you that you've fallen for his charm and that he's really a superficial sort. They may say that as a twosome you are really not suited to each other. This is not necessarily true. However, you might be well advised to marry a Libra male only if he is mature because if you marry him when he's very young, there could be problems. He needs to experience everything that's going before he settles down.

This man will not try to probe too deeply into your psyche. He will accept that there are certain things you wish to keep secret.

He hates troubles and confrontations, but he will stand up for his rights. Still, he would never consciously do anything to upset another human being. Sometimes he will even hide his own feelings if by doing so he can avoid an argument.

He likes his life to be orderly. The Libra man hates confusion.

Children find him an extremely fair father. He can be a bit of an old softy and is a real pushover for a daughter.

VIRGO WOMAN—SCORPIO MAN

If you fall for a Scorpio man, it's likely to be against your better judgment. You may realize deep down that danger lurks here but simply be unable to resist getting involved. Certainly there is something mysterious and exciting about him.

You will find his sheer physical presence stimulating. He can send a shiver down a girl's spine just by walking into a room. And when he fixes you with those eyes . . . wow! This could be one of those love-at-first-sight scenes. Both of you will wonder just how long such an explosive romance can last.

Scorpio is probably one of the hardest Signs to understand. He can be moody and on occasions downright nasty. You are going to have to accept that a fair portion of this relationship will be built on physical passion.

If there was ever a union of opposites, with all the excitement and drama this implies, it is the liaison of a Virgo woman and a Scorpio man.

He wants power. Power is everything to him: in his business life, in friendship and—most of all—in his love life.

You will always know where you stand with a Scorpio. He can be very blunt even to the point of hurting people's feelings. This will not bother him unduly so long as he is being truthful.

He can be mean with money, even miserly, though occasionally he will be very extravagant for no good reason. Certainly you will never go without your comforts. It is a fact, though, that security is important to him. He is terrified of being broke.

When you first come across Mr. Scorpio,

you will be impressed by his ability to cope with difficult people and awkward situations without batting an eyelid. Don't be fooled into thinking he's easygoing. If he is pushed too far, he can be extraordinarily violent and rather frightening.

He loves his family and is devoted to home life. He likes to feel he can get away from the hurly-burly of business and relax with people he really cares about. He doesn't want too many others around. You will be quite compatible in the way you like to spend leisure time.

Never push him too far and don't ask too many questions. He doesn't like to feel he is being cross-examined. He's something of a natural psychologist, so you'll probably get the feeling (quite rightly) now and again that he knows exactly what you're thinking.

Sex is of vital interest to Scorpio. The sex act is for him a way of showing strength, virility and personal power.

He will put you on a pedestal. He likes his woman to be admired by the guys at the golf club and at the office.

He is not a natty dresser himself but will love seeing you all dolled up in your glad rags. He will want you to keep up with the latest fashions. For him, you will never cease to be the most attractive woman in the room.

You are not a flirt, which is a good thing. Woe betide the man who makes a pass at you. Even if the guy is twice his size, Mr. Scorpio is capable of flattening him if his temper is aroused.

He's not that concerned about what other people think of him. His own opinion is quite enough. Once he has made up his mind on a certain course of action, it is unlikely that anyone will get him to change it.

People will be amazed if you two do get married. You could surprise them even more by actually making a go of it.

VIRGO WOMAN—SAGITTARIUS MAN

You are not a jealous woman by nature, but even your well-balanced personality is likely to be put to the test by outward-looking, easygoing Mr. Sagittarius.

No matter how much he loves you, he prizes his freedom above all else. He has more than his fair share of Romany blood.

You would have to give far more of yourself to look after him than you normally are prepared to give to a man.

He's a freewheeling sort of chap who is not too keen on settling down. The idea of marriage frightens him.

You will certainly get on extremely well as friends. You'll find him great fun to be with. He's very entertaining and you'll enjoy his company at parties. He's kind and considerate, too. You might not find him quite such fun or quite so considerate, though, when you are sitting up in bed at five in the morning waiting for him to arrive home. Don't be too suspicious. He's probably been out with his buddies. He's really a man's man, you see.

If you can respect his desire for freedom and give him the feeling he can go out just as much as he likes, he might settle down a bit. But don't count on it. He needs a lot of looking after. It's no good trying to tell him what's good for him. As you're a bit inclined to do this, there could be stormy weather ahead. If you do have a fight, he'll walk right out, slamming the door hard behind him. But chances are, he'll be back the next day; despite his wanderlust, he does love to have a home and a woman to come back to.

This man is likely to make a lot of mistakes in his life. He does have a tendency to go into situations feet first. He's also accident-prone. He takes so many chances because to him, life is really a game. He's not interested in a job with the same firm for 40 years and a gold watch and pension at the end of it. He rarely thinks about the risks involved when he gets carried away with one of his hairbrained schemes.

When you take Mr. Sagittarius home to meet Mom and Dad, they may be taken aback that you are actually contemplating marriage to this guy. Well, his good points are not always instantly recognizable. They may get the idea that he has an extremely high opinion of himself. It's true. He has. But this is only a coverup for his nervousness and insecurity. When your folks get to know him better, they'll discover there is far more to this man than they originally thought.

If you're in a jam, the first person you would think of turning to is likely to be a Sagittarius friend. He will be deeply sympathetic and prepared to put himself out quite a lot if he can be of service in some way.

A highly developed Sagittarius man will treat you as his equal in sex. He will want to be sure he gives you satisfaction. He is not a selfish lover. Neither is he a great romantic. But you should be able to adapt to the way he shows his love. Home means a lot to you. It may be rather upsetting that he tends to treat it as a place to hang his hat. He'll never notice things like a fresh vase of flowers or new curtains. Neither is he hung up on food. He's as happy with a hamburger as he is with a Sunday roast with all the trimmings.

He's very good with children. A couple of kids would probably give him more interest in the home.

Never stop saying "I love you." He wants to be told he's needed.

VIRGO WOMAN—CAPRICORN MAN

If you were to feed all the facts about yourself into a computer and program it to come out with the best Sign for you to hitch up with, nine times out of ten the answer would be Capricorn. Rationally and logically, there is no other choice. Love is strange, however, and it does not admit of certainty.

Mr. Capricorn could really appeal to you. Many people would write him off because of his rather slow and pedantic ways. You will not. You will soon discover that he can be witty, social and cordial. He is also extremely ambitious, dedicated and determined to get to the top.

You may have to be a little more forward than you like to be. A Capricorn man is very shy when it comes to love and is terrified of getting hurt. It might be up to you to suggest dinner or a drink some evening.

He likes to be organized. He probably keeps an engagement book. He loves to feel that his company is in demand—and very witty company it is, too.

You'd better look elsewhere if you are seeking a man to sweep you off your feet. He can get very depressed, and he finds it exceedingly difficult to hide his true feelings when the black clouds roll overhead.

He is a great respecter of authority and of people who have gotten to the top by sheer hard work and industry.

He is not an impulsive person. Rarely will he make a life-changing move without giving it serious consideration. Career ups and downs have a great effect on him. He will not be happy in any other area of his life if he is not contented with his work.

You will have to comfort him and cheer him up when things go wrong. You will have to constantly bolster his sagging spirits when he feels he has been rejected. He can suffer from persecution feelings. Occasionally the rat race gets to him. He's a perfectionist, something like you.

People born under this Sign rarely rush into marriage, or into any sort of a long-term relationship, for that matter.

He's very good at avoiding stupid mistakes. He can usually see the pitfalls that lie ahead and he thinks before he acts. He neither overrates nor underrates the importance of sex—like everything else it has a place in his life. That is to say, it is meaningful to him, but in no way rules his life.

Mr. Capricorn is a careful person and will make sure the future is provided for. He will take out insurance policies on almost everything. He will make provision for your future security were anything to happen to him.

He can be a bit of a pessimist; your positive attitude to life will make you a tower of strength to him. Never embarrass him in public. He can't bear to be shown up in front of others, especially strangers.

Another thing you have in common is your respect for the tried and trusted traditions. Let's hope you get on well with his family, for his ties to Mom and Dad are usually close long after he has left home.

He will take the responsibilities of parenthood very seriously and will expect his youngsters to show him respect. He's a stickler for routine. He believes that a bit of discipline never did anybody any harm.

A partnership with this man should be a lasting and happy one.

VIRGO WOMAN—AQUARIUS MAN

At first glance, this linkup doesn't look too promising. Be very careful before you allow yourself to fall in love with Mr. Aquarius. It takes a heck of a lot to keep him happy and occupied. He is the perennial seeker. He's always interested in what is new, what is different—in fact, in anything that arouses his curiosity.

You have a different way of viewing life. You are fairly practical; he most certainly is not.

He won't be particularly interested in the home. The beautiful things you collect will not intrigue him. He will only feel you are making life more complicated by acquiring a lot of possessions. He likes to be free.

Chances are the reason he'll fall for you is that you're so different from the people he's used to. It is quite possible he's never come across a woman like you before. The fascination for you will be in the challenge of whether you can hold him or not.

There are quite a few difficulties here. You, with your practical down-to-earth approach, could find his excessive idealism irritating. You will have to be patient with him.

Certainly he needs looking after. He can be forgetful (you may have to remind him when he has important appointments). He's not too good with money, either, so you will have to watch the family finances. He finds it very hard to refuse to support what he considers to be a worthy cause.

Aquarius-born people often have a dreamy faraway look in their eyes. This should give you some clue as to the character of the Water Bearer.

It would be unwise to write off this man as an impractical dreamer because frequently he is merely ahead of his time, which can be most frustrating to him. To know you are right and to find people will not accept your ideas does make life rather hard. What this man is thinking today will probably be picked up in a few years' time by the people who make the big decisions.

He is unpunctual and unpredictable. You will never know whether you are coming or going with him. He doesn't like to be confined to regular habits, and he may have a point. To him, the most natural thing in the world is to eat when one is hungry and sleep when one is tired. He hates to be governed by the clock.

You may be sitting patiently by the stove with a casserole cooking to a frazzle only to get a phone call telling you he's run into an old crony and doesn't know when he'll be back. Yes, dear girl, that's what life with an Aquarius man will almost certainly be like.

Undoubtedly he will admire many of your qualities. He likes his home to be tidy and clean. He's a bit of a freak about personal hygiene, too. It's quite likely he'll take one or even two showers a day. His lovemaking is more of an exploration, an adventure, than a madly passionate delight. He doesn't take his own emotions all that seriously.

What will surprise you is what a loving and devoted father this man makes. He takes parenthood very seriously and will do his best for his children because in them he sees the future of the world.

Aquarius people don't take easily to permanent relationships. It is always hard for them to get involved with people on an emotional level.

To keep him, you may have to make out that you're less capable than you really are. This will help to convince him you do in fact need looking after. This kind of appeal he understands.

VIRGO WOMAN—PISCES MAN

Very often this man lives in a world far removed from reality. This does not mean that Mr. Pisces is not perfectly capable of looking after himself. He is. He's just a very different type of person.

When you first meet him, you'll think you have come across a sweet and gentle soul who needs protection. This is only half the story.

The symbol of Pisces is two Fishes. Still waters run deep, and in the Neptunian depths of his character, you will find many contradictions.

He is terribly easygoing. He'll usually go along with your ideas as to how an evening should be spent. If you are looking for a man who knows his own mind and is decisive, then look elsewhere. He can take things in his stride. It takes a lot to rattle him and throw him off course.

He is afraid of being hurt or rejected, though. He's frequently overly sensitive. He sometimes feels people are taking advantage of him when this simply isn't true.

Since you are a rather stable person, you may find his habitual reliance on intuition highly irritating. When you describe your practical plans, he will listen intently and then come up with his own ideas, which may sound highly impractical. Give some thought to what he says, though. There is quite likely to be some method in his apparent madness.

He could be the right mixture of dreamer and realist to excite you. He is a charming lover. He's rather sexual. You will be excited by his imaginative physical approach.

A Pisces man will speak his mind. This doesn't mean he doesn't care what others think of him. He does. It's just that he doesn't like to pretend to be something he's not.

One thing you can't help but admire about this man is his concern for people less fortunate than he is. He will always be on hand to offer sympathy and aid when others really need him.

His advice is usually well worth following. He has a way of pinpointing people's problems and coming up with a simple solution.

It doesn't make much difference to him where he lives. He likes his home comforts, it is true, but he is restless and finds it difficult to settle in any one place for very long.

He's not too handy around the house. You could find it is your responsibility to do jobs that are often considered the man's domain. He can't get enthusiastic about mundane routine chores.

He loves excitement. He thrives in the sort of

job that throws new challenges at him all the time. He can be a bit of a gambler, but more often than not his gambles pay off.

Mr. Pisces is likely to be the faithful type so you will rarely need to be suspicious about his getting involved in affairs. He does, however, have difficulty in restraining himself from flirting with pretty girls. Don't get too worried about this; it is, as a rule, just harmless fun to Mr. Fish.

You will probably have to take more than your fair share of responsibility for the kids because he will be far too lenient with them. He finds it difficult to mete out discipline to youngsters.

If you can face the fact that you're not going to get everything spelled out by this man, that he likes to play things by ear, you could make a quite happy and successful combination.

VIRGO MAN—ARIES WOMAN

There could be certain basic problems to overcome if Virgo and Aries are going to become a team. You could say the personalities will clash. The woman born under the Sign of Aries is a bit on the bossy side. You are an easygoing chap in many ways, but you hate to be told what to do.

It is also wise to remember that you have a career girl here. Success is very important to her. She is unlikely to be contented playing the role of the little woman in the background for very long.

Miss Aries is perfectly capable of looking after herself. Perfect gentleman that you are, you're perhaps more suited to a woman who prefers the old-fashioned charms and graces.

Although you have an agile mind, you're a methodical person. You feel if a job's worth doing, it's worth doing well. This little fireball is always in a hurry to complete her tasks.

There are a number of things you will have in common, and it is these you'll have to cultivate if you wish to make something of your relationship with this woman. For one thing, you both have a good sense of humor; this should stand you in good stead when serious differences of opinion arise. Her company can never be called dull. She lives life to the full.

An Aries woman has quite expensive tastes. But if you are short of bread, she won't mind eating at the local hamburger house.

Actually, underneath all her outward aggressiveness there lurks a shy and rather neurotic person. She often takes people's remarks the wrong way because she's terrified of being criticized. She can't bear to be proved wrong.

You are a bit of a romantic. She is much more basic in her attitude to sex. You may be rather taken aback at how forward she can be if she really fancies you. She's all for cutting out the frills and this attitude could shock you.

If the relationship is unbalanced, she will cause you quite a lot of heartache. She can be very tough on men she doesn't really care for. It is quite easy for an Aries person to be involved in two—perhaps even three—relationships at one and the same time.

You will have to be strong with her. Tell her from the start that she is your girl and don't allow her to play games with you.

It would be advisable to get to know her really well before you think of setting up home together. You never rush important decisions, so it is unlikely you would rush into a union as important as marriage.

Aries girls often get married more than once. Certainly 90 percent of them have more than one very close relationship in their lives.

You are a kind and understanding person and will be a great help to her in coping with her insecurity and aggression.

She loves sports and will do what she can to get you out on the tennis courts and on long country walks. Since you are the indoor type, this will be good for you. She'll make sure you keep yourself in pretty good shape.

An Aries woman will be a great help to you in your career. She'll know just how to treat your boss. She's also a pretty fair cook and enjoys experimenting in the kitchen.

She will be quite strict with the kids, an attitude with which you'll wholeheartedly agree.

VIRGO MAN—TAURUS WOMAN

You should hit it off with a woman born under the first earth Sign (yours is the second). You both have your feet firmly planted on the ground. She will understand you better than most women—and let's face it, you are not the easiest of people to understand.

A Taurus girl loves the home. It is extremely important to her to have a base from which she can function properly. You are a good provider and should be able to supply her with most of the things that make her happy.

Critics sometimes say Taurus people are exceedingly bossy. This is actually not so. They don't like to be told what to do and can't abide people taking liberties with them. You are a kind and considerate person and these qualities will be much appreciated by Miss Taurus.

She's serious about love and marriage. Her ruler is Venus, remember. She will like the respect you show her. She will also appreciate your excellent manners.

She's very artistic and is likely to share your tastes in art, literature and music.

It will take quite a while to woo this woman. She does not make important decisions in a hurry. She will be looking for a secure and stable home life.

Don't get the idea that Miss Taurus is an old stick-in-the-mud and nothing more; far from it. She has a great love of travel and adventure. But she does like to know there is a secure place she can come back to.

She loves pretty things. She can get very hung up on possessions. Clothes are important to her; they are often her one big extravagance.

You are not a womanizer, and thank goodness for that because woe betide the man who two-times a Taurus woman. If you never see her lose her temper, then you're lucky. If you do, you'll probably have to duck to miss a saucepan that comes flying somewhere near your left ear.

You will have to let her pursue her own interests. If she wants a career after marriage, it would be foolish to stand in her way. Give her plenty of freedom and you will always have her love and respect. You're a pretty intelligent guy so you know these things make sense, even if you haven't run into a woman like her before.

Of course, it will not always be pleasant and easy. Occasionally you will have to give ground even when you feel you are in the right. You will both have to rid yourselves of selfish tendencies to make a go of it. Miss Taurus will do her best to be reasonable.

In bed, Miss Taurus is quite something. She's all woman and will help rid you of any inhibitions you may have. She's extremely passionate and it takes quite a man to satisfy her. Evenings at home together will be wonderful. You will like nothing better than drawing the curtains and cuddling with her, listening to your favorite music and burning your toes in front of a fire.

She's wonderful at keeping a home tidy and that is something you'll be pleased about. Her cooking is usually quite plain but wholesome. Virgo men often like taking charge in the kitchen and she will be quite happy for you to do so.

She's economical. You will have no difficulty in working out a budget together and sticking to it.

She will make a fine mother to your kids. She is inclined to fly off the handle with junior when the going gets heavy, though, so you have to take the child to one side and tell him that "Mom didn't really mean it."

VIRGO MAN—GEMINI WOMAN

To be honest, this does not look like a very workable relationship. You are a man who knows pretty well what he wants out of life. You know your own mind. Once you have worked out a plan of action, you usually stick to it.

This charming little lady (who, incidentally, is also ruled by Mercury) hardly knows whether she's coming or going. She appears to be quite happy flitting from one relationship to another. Her sudden changes of mood could be a bit too much for you to cope with. After all, you do like to know where you stand with a woman.

One minute she'll be all over you. When you call her for a date a few days later, she'll tell you she's fully booked for the next couple of weeks. If you like lots of surprises, then go right ahead.

You are basically a conformist. You believe in the Establishment and old-fashioned values and graces. She is constantly looking for novelty. Once she feels she understands something thoroughly, she discards it and continues her search elsewhere.

She can be promiscuous. Many females born under the third Sign of the Zodiac get involved in heavy romances when in their early teens. They find it very hard to take their mother's advice to "wait awhile." But don't get the idea that she is a nymphomaniac because, like you, she is ruled by her mind first and foremost. It's simply that she will keep on experimenting as part of her search for knowledge.

With your great patience and understanding, you may be able to help her to know herself a little better and stop constantly looking outside for all the answers.

It will be to the advantage of you both if you're a few years older. Gemini women need a man they can rely on. The little-boy-lost type would be a total disaster for her. She needs someone to run to when the going gets rough.

Beware if you are already spoken for. A Gemini woman often takes a strong fancy to guys who are hitched. A married man gives her the opportunity to form a strong relationship without getting trapped. She values her freedom above all else and is basically apprehensive about marriage.

Of course, this doesn't mean you can't find true happiness together. If she has come to terms with herself emotionally and realizes that all her rushing hither and thither.is getting her nowhere fast, then you could make a striking partnership. She's great fun to be with. You'll discover she's pretty sharp. You are both likely to find the same sort of things funny.

She may be a little too critical for you. You sometimes find it rather hard to take outspoken criticism. She won't pull her punches if she feels you are in the wrong. She has a hard streak and you may find her brutally frank at times.

Miss Gemini won't feel strongly inclined to spend her evenings at home. She loves people and parties. It is meeting new faces all the time that really sparks her off.

Don't try to change her. Give her advice when she asks for it. If you tell her to take a certain course of action in a heavy-handed authoritative way, she will probably go out and do the opposite just to declare her freedom.

She'll do her level best to keep the home tidy but you could find yourself doing more than your fair share of the chores.

It's advisable that you take care of the family finances. She's not too good at handling money.

VIRGO MAN—CANCER WOMAN

It's difficult to say exactly how this one would work out. Certainly you have many likes and dislikes in common. But though you will agree in *principle* on what is right and wrong, you are likely to approach matters from a totally different angle.

You are ruled by intellect, she very much by instinct and emotions. And that, friend Virgo, always poses a problem in a close relationship.

You are both great home lovers. She needs protection from the ill winds that can blow her little boat off course so easily. You certainly like to play the role of provider and protector. It isn't quite so simple, though. Don't think you have to prove yourself to her in any way. Being such an intuitive person, she will see right through any posturing on your part. You are a sincere man but you do give the impression of putting on an act at times.

Miss Cancer will like the fact that you are a person whose word is his bond. You will also be just the sort of man to comfort her when she's down—and she is often despondent.

It is extremely rare for a woman born under the Sign of the Crab to marry the first man she gets seriously involved with. She takes her time and wants to experience quite a lot in life before she settles down.

This girl loves to have a male entourage and hates to lose an admirer. She will play some poor unsuspecting guys along in order to keep them in tow while she's looking for Mr. Right.

If you and she decide that you were really meant for each other, the walk down the aisle with Miss Cancer is a move you'll never regret. When she finally gives herself to a man, it is a total commitment. She will work very hard to make a go of life with you.

You are not the type of man to cheat on his wife, which is a good thing with this woman. Never give her reason to doubt you. If you have won her over, she will trust you absolutely.

She loves keeping her home running smoothly. She makes a wonderful housewife. She will make sure you are provided for. When you come home after a hard day at the office, she will make sure that everything is just as you like it. She will also do her best to look attractive for you at all times. No matter what sort of a day she's had while you've been slogging away on the job, she'll always be there to soothe your fevered brow and comfort you.

Your Cancer woman will make a marvelous hostess at gatherings and dinner parties. Your friends and business associates will probably take to her instantly.

She likes a man to dominate her. Power sharing doesn't work too well in this union. You will have to be careful here. She doesn't want to be nagged; she wants her man to be masterful. She needs someone to give her the right sort of control and guidance.

The Cancer female is very inventive with food. She'll prepare dishes you have never heard of. You need not look further to find the perfect mother for your children. The only trouble is your nose may be put out of joint a bit when the first child comes along.

Never take her for granted. Always treat her as you did when first courting. Don't forget that under that sweet surface, she's a sensitive and deeply passionate person.

VIRGO MAN—LEO WOMAN

Let's hope you're pretty well heeled because you'll need to have quite a bit of loot to splash about if you're going to keep Miss Leo in the manner she feels befits her. You cannot have a cheap evening out if you date this little kitten. She won't be happy with a hot dog and a trip to the local movie house.

Miss Leo wants the best things in life. She can't bear to do anything on the cheap. She'd rather stay home than stand in a queue for hours, even if her favorite pop group is appearing. Since you are a pretty selective person, you should be able to understand how she feels.

She can drive a man absolutely wild. If you lose your head and your heart to her, she will turn you off your work, your food and all your other passionate interests.

She finds it difficult to settle down with any one man. Her tastes are not in any way limited. People may gossip about her but she takes no notice of bitchy remarks. She's very much a woman who makes up her own mind on what particular life-style she is going to adopt.

She's unlikely to have a lot of girlfriends. Other women find it rather difficult to take her particular brand of honesty. She gets on much better with the boys and is likely to have a number of platonic male friends.

There are quite a few drawbacks to Virgo and Leo living together. Your personalities are likely to clash in a number of ways. She will not be fond of your slightly quaint and old-fashioned habits. You may be disappointed that she is so capable of looking after herself. Certainly she has an independent streak that can make things difficult for a man.

She will be extremely good for you in many ways. From a business point of view, this is a terrific woman to have on your side. She will know exactly how to put influential people at their ease. Your Leo partner will make that important dinner party go with a bang. Your boss will love her.

If she desires you, you'll know it. Once she sets her sights on a man, she can be very determined. She's very passionate and you could find that she is the one who whispers in your ear that it's time to climb the stairs, turn out the lights and head for the bedroom.

You will have to be prepared to let her do her own thing. She won't be content to stay in the background once you are married. She has an active and inquiring mind and will want to go on learning as long as she has breath in her body.

Don't leave Miss Leo on her own too many nights. Never take it for granted that she will always be there when you come tripping in at odd hours. If she feels you've lost interest in her, she'll look for attention and affection elsewhere.

Yes, this girl certainly likes to retain her individuality. One way of doing this is to keep up with her career after marriage. You'll have to face the fact that whatever job she holds down, she'll probably pull more rank than you do in yours.

She's unlikely to want to have a family right away, and probably won't want more than a couple of kids anyway.

If you can accept a partner who is a combination of so many things—sweet and feminine on the one hand and bossy and a bit domineering on the other—fine. Just remember, she will never be willing to live her life through your success.

VIRGO MAN—VIRGO WOMAN

This union will not be as straightforward as you might think. You are both earth Signs and should be quite alike. Well, maybe you will discover you are a bit too much alike for comfort. Like you, Miss Virgo knows the value of things. She's careful with money and she's serious about life.

You may think you know her really well and she may feel the same about you. Don't believe it, though. Still waters run deep and you might discover after a few dates that you've been playing a role with her and she with you.

She's capable of keeping things hidden. She's finicky about almost everything. The two of you together could be forever dusting the house and cleaning the ashtrays.

She's very particular about whom she goes out with. It is unlikely that she will have a great many men in her life.

You won't win this woman by playing the strong man. Like you, she has an independent streak. Don't pretend you're something you're not; she easily recognizes game-playing.

She will like your well-groomed appearance. She's a neatness fanatic herself.

Don't try to sweep her off her feet. She takes a lot of wooing. A grope in the corner at a party is likely to lead to a swift kick to your shins—but then, groping isn't really your style anyway.

She's pretty shy about showing her feelings in public. It will be quite a while before she allows you to kiss her good night at the front door.

Miss Virgo has a strong desire for perfection. If she takes on a challenge, she will do her best to see it through. She takes responsibilities very seriously and will never let you down.

It will be important to her to remain a good daughter to her parents. She will even be prepared to change her ways if possible in order to win the approval of Mom and Dad. It must be hoped that you get on well with her family, as this will make life much easier all around.

If you do decide it's a good idea to marry, you'll find she's determined to stay faithful and loyal. It would be one of the worst things that could happen in the life of a Virgo female for her marriage to fall apart.

If lovemaking means a great deal to you, you

could be in for a bit of a letdown because she's not the most passionate female in the Zodiac. She will not rate sex as the most important thing in any permanent relationship. But if you are patient and romantic, you could get through to the Virgo female and stir her into a state of frenzied excitement.

You will enjoy going out together, especially to parties. You will find you get on with the same sort of people.

You will have to be open and aboveboard in all things. If you two-time her, it is unlikely she will forgive you. She's honest to her heart and will be true to you so long as you never try to betray her.

She is just the sort of mother you would like your kids to have. Junior is likely to be the best turned out child in the school. You'll never see him with dirt on his face or a runny nose. She may not be able to supply all the emotional needs that a growing human being requires, but she will always strive to do her very best.

You should be able to thrash out many of your problems in a rational way.

VIRGO MAN—LIBRA WOMAN

Your Libra woman has a very inquiring mind. She's interested in pretty damned near everyone and everything. She can be changeful and moody. You may find her sudden switches a little difficult to keep pace with. You tend to prefer a more straightforward woman. One moment she will be offering undying love and devotion; the next she'll be as limp as yesterday's lettuce.

You have an analytical mind. It would be foolish to attempt to put her in one of your safe little mental compartments. Just when you think you've got her number, she will act in a way you find totally out of character.

She's wonderful at coping with people from all walks of life. She'll be just as relaxed chatting to the milkman as she will be having dinner with an important executive.

You tend to want a woman to be with you all the time. She's the type who has to maintain outside interests and contacts. She will make a loving and caring wife, but she has a lot more on her mind than just that and will refuse to allow herself to be chained to the kitchen sink.

You can be rather possessive. A lasting relationship with Miss Libra would mean you would have to change a number of your preconceived ideas about marriage.

Perhaps a short-term liaison would suit you both best. There is certainly a great deal you can learn from each other. Miss Libra can't help flirting. To her, it is more of a sport than anything else. You will not understand this. Probably you will take her little games far too seriously. You will have to curb your jealousy and realize that her flirtations are only in fun.

Don't get too despondent, though, because this combination has several things going for it. She's very feminine, and you certainly favor that type of woman. You will be able to give her confidence in herself, although it might come as something of a surprise to learn that she lacks it. Miss Libra has an easygoing manner that suggests she hasn't got a care in the world. In marriage, it is essential that you make the big decisions. She will want you to be the leader. You'll get nowhere fast if you rely on her to plan your future together. Although she's bright, she's overly imaginative at times.

You are quite a hard worker and she will admire you for this. You'll have to keep your nose to the grindstone to give her all she desires.

You will enjoy showing her off to your friends. Her ability to get on with almost anyone will stand you in good stead when you are doing business entertaining at home.

This girl is no snob. It is of no interest to her what a person's pedigree is. She won't care, either, what sort of a background you have. She will be more interested in the qualities you possess as a human being.

Artistically speaking, you will have much in common. People born under this Sign often have strong links with the entertainment or literary world. She's fun to go out with. It's quite likely you'll be dining out as much as in.

The Libra woman makes one of the best mothers in the Zodiac. Her rapport with children of all ages is sometimes quite amazing.

Take your time before you ask for her hand in marriage. You may think she's the girl of your dreams, but her love of freedom and your rather possessive nature could mean you're both heading for trouble.

VIRGO MAN—SCORPIO WOMAN

Your stable and steady nature will undoubtedly have a calming effect upon Miss Scorpio, but one wonders if either of you has the powers of adaptation to make a lasting union possible. You do possess a number of qualities that would obviously appeal to her. She needs a man she can trust and rely on. If she is crossed on even the smallest thing, she never forgets it.

In many ways, this would appear to be a most unlikely match. Of all the Signs of the Zodiac, Scorpio is the most passionate. She likes to get her own way more than almost any other woman.

These people born with Pluto and Mars ruling find it exceedingly difficult to control their emotions. Miss Scorpio is likely to have a deep-rooted interest in the occult and life and death. You might find this rather morbid.

She is extremely jealous and possessive. She won't be willing to stay at home if you are out. She also has an insatiable sexual appetite. You may be a bit too romantic for her. She's very basic in her urges.

You like to share your secrets with the person you have chosen to be your partner. A Scorpio woman can't help being fairly secretive. It takes a long time to get to know her. And there are certain aspects of her personality she will feel you should never see.

She's quite difficult to track down. It will be up to you to make the running in the early days of the relationship. She's suspicious of strangers and it will be some time before she's willing to go out with you unless you hit it off physically.

A Scorpio woman is a great survivor. She may take plenty of knocks, but she'll go down fighting. She loves a challenge and can get to the top of her career if she really sets her mind to it.

This girl loves excitement, and although she enjoys her home, she won't be prepared to stay put in it for very long. She can be pretty bad tempered. She doesn't believe in keeping her feelings bottled up. You may find her tantrums a bit too much. After all, you do like a peaceful life. She speaks her mind and this trait often scares away potential boyfriends.

Moody and morose on occasions, she does have a habit of blaming the world for the mess she often finds herself in. She is always striving for perfection and will not settle for second best.

This woman is often in conflict in her relationships with members of the opposite sex. Though she is looking for a guy who can dominate her, she'll put up stiff resistance if she feels she is losing her individuality.

She likes to keep her family battles confined to the home. She is embarrassed by public scenes or spectacles.

If Miss Scorpio believes in you, you couldn't hope for a better second in your corner. She'll stand by you through thick and thin. She will be prepared to put her own career interests aside for a man she really loves. And for a woman born under this ambitious Sign, that is really a great sacrifice.

As a housewife, she is unlikely to measure up to your high standards. Let's hope you are in a position to afford help.

She will love her children dearly but may not be able to give them a great deal of affection. You would both have to work hard on this angle.

VIRGO MAN—SAGITTARIUS WOMAN

You should get along famously with a Sagittarius woman. She's good-natured and always tries to look on the positive side of things. Sure, she likes to keep on the move, but she could be just the person to put a little fire into you. Sometimes you don't take all the opportunities that are available. With a Sagittarius woman behind you, your career should shoot forward rapidly.

She's outspoken but not malicious. You will like her straightforward manner. She loves a challenge and is always prepared to take on a task that promises excitement.

You appreciate a woman who has good intentions. This girl is always striving to do the right thing. She won't keep any secrets from you. She does not complain. She will be willing to go through the rough times as well as the good with her man.

Occasionally she may embarrass you by speaking out of turn. She can't help being blunt with people sometimes. By tactfully pointing out to her exactly what reaction she invoked in the company you were with, you might be able to cure her of this.

Many people—but not all—born under this Sign are the outdoor type. It is likely she excelled at swimming or tennis in school. She probably likes long walks and keeps herself in pretty good shape. Being a bit of a slouch, you will benefit from accompanying her on a long walk every now and again. You like fresh air and that's a better way of getting it than standing at the window.

She's a busy person who sets great store on mobility. She can't stand to be kept waiting, although ironically she is often late for appointments herself.

Hard work will never worry her. If she takes on a job, she will do it to the best of her ability. No one can accuse her of being a shirker. She can't bear to be tied down to any one job for too long, however. No matter what the financial rewards, she'll move on when her interest wanes.

Your Sagittarius lady will be ambitious for herself as well as for you. You will never come second to her career. She's one of those capable people who can hold down a good job without allowing it to affect her married life.

Don't try to tie her down. She needs friends and outside stimulation.

You possess many qualities she will admire. She is more attracted to a man's mind than to his physical attributes. She will like your fairness and logical way of arriving at decisions. She likes someone who has strongly held opinions, too.

She's great company and won't mind your asking your buddies over for a drink. She won't become a model housewife overnight but she'll work at it. You may find you do more in the kitchen than she does. She doesn't have all that much patience with routine affairs.

If she feels she is in the wrong, she'll be the first to admit it. Even when she knows she's in the right, she won't crow.

If after careful deliberation—and you always do take your time when reaching important decisions—you decide that Miss Sagittarius is the woman for you, it's unlikely you'll ever regret the choice. You are both fairly competent at handling financial affairs. You are likely to find yourselves in agreement on what the priorities are when it comes to setting up home together. She's not the suspicious type.

As a mother, she'll always make sure her children get the very best.

VIRGO MAN— CAPRICORN WOMAN

Miss Capricorn is not the most romantic woman in the world, though you couldn't call her cold. People often misunderstand this girl, which is a pity because she has so much to offer.

Like you, she believes in true love. In fact, that is what life is all about with her. When you meet her for the first time, you might get the strange sensation that you've come across each other before. Certainly you will have a great deal in common. She is not interested in a casual romance. She wants a man who is serious.

Don't waste her time and put her in promiseland if you are not serious. She will believe everything you say and will feel deeply hurt if she discovers you were only after a one-night stand.

When she really goes overboard for a man, she becomes the most faithful and dependable woman you could wish for. She can't help being possessive and even a little jealous. Usually she is aware of this and does her best to curb it.

A nice home means a lot to Miss Capricorn. She finds it very difficult to function if she doesn't feel relaxed in her surroundings. Money is important to her only for what it can buy. Amassing a great fortune does not interest her.

People born under this Sign hate making enemies. They get rather worried if they feel people don't like them. Though she may appear not to have a care in the world, this is a front. You are dealing with a very serious-minded woman indeed.

The Capricorn female is terribly ambitious, not only for herself but also for her man. She will boost your confidence no end and will do everything in her power to help you get on. She will never settle for second best. She will stick by you through the rough times as well as the good. Her love is not the sort that blows hot and cold depending on the state of a man's bank balance.

She is always coming up with new ideas and suggestions. Listen to what she has to say; one or two of her original projects might turn out to be a winner.

She's a super hostess. You will be amazed at the way she entertains. She has a wonderful knack of mixing people from various walks of life. Her parties are events to remember. She can be very influential when your business acquaintances come to dinner.

You will find her earthy quality most refreshing. You will feel you can always speak your mind with her. She would rather you gave it to her straight from the shoulder than beat around the bush.

Family life is very important to people born where Saturn rules. Never say a word against her mother or father. Being the diplomatic type, you should have no trouble getting along with your in-laws.

Whether she comes from a working-class background or a high-class family, she has natural refinement. She's a lady through and through.

She likes to be flattered. Never stop telling her how beautiful she is and how much you desire her.

She won't give herself to you unless she's sure you care deeply. It will take her a long time to make up her mind about marriage. She is not the type to rush a decision as important as this.

You could be just the right mixture for her. You are precise and methodical and will never trample on her precious individuality.

The Capricorn mother is usually able to exercise discipline without losing the love of her brood.

VIRGO MAN—AQUARIUS WOMAN

If you have fallen for the Water Bearer, then fasten your seat belt, you're in for quite a ride. This is one of the most difficult Signs of all for a steady, down-to-earth type like you to figure out. She's a mystery. She's unlike any other woman you have ever come across. You will never know where you stand with her.

She is very eccentric, which is what will probably attract you to her. She can be a bit of a hippy and her way-out clothes and odd manners may fascinate you.

Whether or not you would contemplate marriage with this woman is another story. Her head is full of crazy notions about how to put the world to rights (well, to you, they are likely to seem pretty odd). Don't kid yourself that she will mellow as she gets older. Very often she becomes even more cranky.

Miss Aquarius is very caught up with the idea of progress and change. She's looking for utopia. She's out to make a heaven on earth. She's an extremely persuasive talker and can often get other people to go along with her ideas. She is exceedingly tolerant and open-minded.

Even though you are pretty good at expressing your opinions and ideas, you could be overwhelmed when an Aquarius girl gets going. If you do get serious about her, be prepared for your ego to take something of a battering.

You will have to accept her for what she is because no amount of persuasion on your part will change her attitudes toward life and people.

Never try to pin her down. Her active mind is always likely to be one jump ahead of yours.

Be very careful you don't marry too quickly. You may feel after a couple of dates that you could not live without this woman, but get to know her well before you pop the question because there are a number of drawbacks to building a little nest together. It might be a good idea to have an affair and live with each other for a while; at least this would afford you the opportunity to get to know all aspects of each other's personality. If you are too old-fashioned for a trial marriage (which, since you are a Virgo, is quite likely), then make sure you see her at work and at play and meet her friends and family as well.

Possessions are not important to her. They are to you. She cares more for people than for things. Don't be surprised to find your house full of strangers when you come home—an odd assortment of characters she picked up on her travels. Aquarius people feel they are duty bound to aid others not as fortunate as themselves.

You may think you have come across the most unselfish woman in the world when you first begin to date. This is not always so. It is very difficult for this girl whose element is air to form lasting relationships with members of the opposite sex. She is not a jealous woman and will seldom show suspicion. This in itself may be a problem because you might feel that she doesn't care if you get involved with someone else. Of course, she would care. It's simply that she shows her love in unconventional ways.

If, in spite of all that could go wrong, you do decide to make a go of it, you will become better individuals as a result of the experience. Children could do a lot to cement the relationship.

VIRGO MAN—PISCES WOMAN

Down-to-earth and precise Mr. Virgo could find his soul mate in romantically minded Miss Pisces. She has qualities that make her the dream girl of many a man. It will rest with her lover to bring this woman out of the deep waters of self-analysis. She's an introverted type and it doesn't do her too much good to be constantly thinking about herself.

She's quite a mixture. But then, she is a split Sign—two Fishes swimming in opposite directions.

She needs a man who can look after her and whom she can run to when things go wrong. At first, you won't find it at all easy to get to know her well because she's extremely shy and retiring. You may be attracted to the rather mystical aura that surrounds her. Mind you, this is only one side of the coin. She has quite a temper when she feels she's been wronged and her outbursts can be quite frightening.

She places great value on love and romance. You are a bit of a romantic, too. She will make sure that the love between you doesn't fade away after a few years of marriage. Miss Pisces knows how to keep a man interested. You will want to be of service to her and do all in your power to keep her happy and contented.

Your friends and colleagues at work will all adore her and keep telling you you're the luckiest guy in the world. Not that you will need any reminding.

Miss Pisces may not be all that career-minded herself but she will be very ambitious for you. She will want you to fulfill your potential and will make sure that you do your best to make a success of your life.

There is a side to her character that could be described as selfish and lazy. She likes to pamper herself and can take hours in the bath and putting her face on. She also has a tendency to live a Walter Mitty existence. It is easy for her to lose touch with reality. You will have to do what you can to help her understand her dreams and fantasies for what they really are.

She will be terribly loyal to you. She will never sit quietly in the corner if she hears someone knocking her man.

She's terribly interested in other people, usually of the opposite sex. There's no need to get jealous, though; her interest in life simply makes her curious about what makes men tick.

She needs to be kept in order as well as being placed on a pedestal. It would be unwise to allow her to become the dominant figure in your relationship. You could end up being little more than a slave.

She's a wonderful homemaker. She knows all about decorating and color schemes. She also has a keen eye for bargains and is likely to spot something really valuable when browsing through antique shops.

You will have to help her with strangers. She won't be too good at entertaining large groups of people until she feels confident of success.

Treat her with tenderness and the relationship will be an enjoyable one. Don't forget those special dates like birthdays and wedding anniversaries. And never, never take her for granted. Don't try the big he-man approach. You will never get your way with her by being heavy-handed and laying down the law.

Be sure she gets out of the house quite often. She's a bit of a stay-at-home and it doesn't do her any good to sit around brooding.

She'll be good with kids. She'll help them to become independent and to stand on their own two feet—even while she spoils them.

VIRGO'S HEALTH

The typical Virgo-born person lives to a ripe old age. An yet, for most of your life, you are inclined to worry about your health and to take all kinds of protective measures against illness. You might reply by pointing out that it is this concern and practical prevention that gives the Sign its long life expectancy. No one could argue with that. The question, is, do you overdo it and knot your high-strung nervous system with unnecessary anxiety?

Undoubtedly you have good reason for being health-conscious. Your Sign represents the meeting place of the nervous system and the digestive process. You're always on edge a bit in the intestinal region even when there's nothing wrong. If it's not your nerves affecting your digestion, it's the other way around. So you're very aware of the necessity for a correct diet.

Many Virgo people are food faddists. Other Signs don't understand just how important it is for you to ingest only those foods that agree with you. By the same token, many of you don't appreciate that a lot of your diet problems are peculiar to you; you are inclined to try to convert everyone to your particular regimen.

You are probably a semivegetarian or at least have a high regard for fresh, natural foods. Many Virgo individuals buy only organically grown vegetables. They are frequently among the best customers at the local health-food store. They often enjoy salads of chopped raw vegetables, all kinds of lettuce, dates, nuts, natural cheeses (definitely not pasteurized or manufactured), yoghurt—everything that's wholesome and healthy.

But there can be a problem because Virgo people have to make sure that the foods they choose intellectually do in fact agree with them. Sometimes you will persist with a diet because it conforms to your *idea* of pure and nutritious food, when actually it is unsuited to your digestive system. Raw food, for instance, is not always easily digested. You should be guided by how you feel after a meal and not solely by what health magazines and other faddists say is good for you.

To enjoy the best of health, a Virgo person needs loads of fresh air, adequate exercise and as much sunshine as possible. There's always a danger you'll get caught up in your work, even if it's just housework, and put off taking a break in the garden or going for a walk in the park. You're also inclined to work through your lunch hour or to spend it in the office. And when you arrive home, you may become absorbed in cooking or preparing a meal (usually a favorite Virgo pastime) and not bother to go out.

You're the type to keep fit through light exercise at home and perhaps some yoga. You may also be a regular visitor to the local sauna bath. But it is light, active exercise in the open air that you need to keep your nervous system and physical constitution in proper balance.

People born under your Sign are quite prominent among the hypochondriacs of this world. They are inclined to take far too many pills, and use vitamins and tonics to supplement a very selective menu. One thing, though—they are very fussy about checking that any preparation they use is the real thing; all ingredients must be pure and products true to label. They are quite prepared to have a test analysis made if they feel it is necessary.

The most difficult time for health is usually during infancy. This is when the nervous and physical components, so pronounced in the Sign, are learning to live together. There is a danger of convulsions and infantile diarrhea. But once this stage is passed, the threat of serious illness is fairly remote.

However, worry and inner anxieties can have a most harmful effect, causing obscure and persistent disorders. These may not be serious enough to confine you to a sick bed (Virgo people hate to be immobilized), but can make you miserable. Imagined illness is always a likelihood where there's any faddism.

The Virgo person frequently has regular medical checkups; he or she doesn't allow any symptom to go on too long without reporting it. Because of this, an illness seldom develops to the stage where it is difficult or impossible to treat.

Sometimes you may suffer from foot trouble, possibly a limp. Appendicitis, peritonitis and nervous disorders are common. You are prone to ulcers because you worry or eat poorly. Highly seasoned foods should be avoided.

VIRGO AT WORK

To the typical Virgo, work is a pleasure. You are one of those people who does not mind how much is required of you. The only condition is that you must be happy in your work—and feel appreciated. A Virgo who is discontented in his or her job can be pretty sure it's not the right one; a change may well be worth thinking about. Virgos are the natural routine toilers of the Zodiac; dissatisfaction affects not only their performance, but also their health. So many occupations are open to them that they should never settle for a compromise position.

To begin with, though, you must face one basic fact. That is that you do not want to exercise a great degree of personal power. You work for satisfaction, not for some ego kick. Sure, you want to get to the top, but unlike so many others, you don't aspire to the dizzy heights where one is inclined to lose touch with the production line. You are practical, a realist, a producer. Management level is usually enough for you—or your own business, where you survive or go down on the strength of your performance. You will serve a wise boss as his assistant without angling to get his job. You're not interested in ivory-tower abstractions and game-playing. You must be able to see the results of your efforts at first hand.

You are better suited for intellectual work than physical labor. You need a certain amount of variety. You won't be happy digging a trench all day or working a jackhammer—although you are capable of these and other menial tasks as part of a particular job. An occupation has to be a challenge to your active imagination. Your analytical mind is extremely well suited to accounting, bookkeeping and statistical work. You would be very good in charge of a department in a large organization. You have a particular flair for devising new methods for handling detail.

Currency exchange and the careful management of money on behalf of others could also offer opportunities. You are not, as a rule, the tycoon who rises to riches and prominence on the strength of his willingness to speculate and take chances. You are conservative. You can make money work efficienctly for those types of people by setting up systems for them, devising economy campaigns and generally handling the finer details of financial control. You would excel as a bank clerk or cashier.

Whatever your occupation, you are superbly reliable. You can be counted on to do six days' work for five days' pay. In fact, when you are happy in your job, you have to be careful not to work too hard and undermine your health. Virgos are scrupulously honest with other people's money and time. They normally manage to save both for anyone who employs them.

You are well adapted for professional life but usually prefer a business career. The commercial side gives you an opportunity to employ your flair for balancing budgets. You enjoy working for yourself or for a large organization where you can concentrate wholly on the job and let someone else worry about where the week's wages are coming from.

Medicine and science often attract you. Your particular gift for painstaking analysis and careful judgment frequently makes you an ideal researcher or laboratory worker. Many Virgos have a healing gift, and they are often found working in hospitals, clinics and institutions. They may also be employed in health clubs or on health farms. Generally speaking, Virgo individuals are apt to specialize in the technical side of medicine. You would make a good physiotherapist, work therapist, dental mechanic and the like. Your practical turn of mind and ability to communicate lucidly makes you exceedingly successful in training and educating handicapped people.

As researchers, many Virgo people are leaders in their field. Their innate humility, studious approach and willingness to serve creates a receptive atmosphere for learning. Although you are not the type to greatly inspire others, you are certainly gifted at putting abstract matters in practical terms. You also make an excellent lecturer. You never lose your enthusiasm for routine work that interests you (but would tend to bore others to death). Your capacity and patience for processing details is indeed rare. You get genuine delight out of being able to enlarge other people's knowledge and understanding. You are among the born educators of the world.

Virgos are often found in religious and quasi-religious movements where they have an opportunity to preach. Here your views tend to be orthodox and rather narrow. You are probably a fundamentalist, animated less by the passion of belief than by the fervor of erudition and form. The peculiar perceptive powers that make you so adept at spotting faults in others enable you to play upon the weaknesses of an audience and whip up emotion and enthusiasm without being affected yourself.

As a typical Virgo, even if you don't know it, you possess a talent for writing. Some of the most famous authors of modern times have been Virgos. They have an amazing eye for detail and describe their characters and the periods in which they live with remarkable accuracy. Virgos are also very good at writing reports, putting complex subjects into easily assimilated language. They are sometimes employed by newspapers and magazines to interpret medical and scientific discoveries in layman's language. With your unusual discriminative powers, you have to be careful in your writings or lectures not to become dull and tedious in your striving for accuracy. The really famous Virgo authors have all learned to restrain their love of detail so that the reader's interest doesn't flag.

You will never do a sloppy job. You would rather refuse work than leave it half-finished. You always aim at perfection.

Your analytical ability well fits you for a career as a lawyer. You don't give in to your emotions and can handle others with tact or firmness, as required. Your practical nature makes you seem understanding, but only extreme cases arouse your sympathy.

As a boss, you are inclined to be strict and unforgiving—at least until everyone understands that you won't put up with slovenly work. You want the job done as quickly, quietly and efficiently as possible. After the first hour on the job, no employee will doubt that you are a practicing perfectionist. You don't make (many) mistakes yourself, and you don't see why others should. And anyone with the temerity to draw attention to where you might have gone wrong had better watch out.

To be fair, you certainly do try to give your staff the benefit of your experience. Anyone who really wants to learn will never find you too busy to answer questions or to explain procedures. The office or factory will abound with methods and systems you have worked out or approved. No one can plead ignorance. You make sure that all employees know precisely what they have to do and how to go about doing it.

You are not so confident or talented at organizing the social and public relations side of the business. You're a little too reserved and aloof to become fast friends with a client over a martini lunch, or to get high and fraternal at the office party. Your style is to play it correct, cool and strictly traditional.

You're the sort of boss who likes to employ people with talents you yourself don't possess. And you're modest enough to listen and learn. In fact, you never cease gathering knowledge whatever occupation you follow. It's a Virgo trait to try to be as much of a human encyclopedia as possible. You give credit to others where it is due. You have no desire to hog the glory. Although you prefer to work alone, you are excellent at heading a small team. No one will ever be jealous of you.

You are very quick to criticize your subordinates. Punctuality is your first rule. As an employee, you are a boss's dream. He can put you on just about any job and needn't look in again until it's finished. You attack every task entrusted to you with diligence and efficiency. Your sense of responsibility is total. You are more concerned with getting the job done properly than with impressing anybody. Certainly, you like to be appreciated, but since you are so capable, you undoubtedly will be.

You may be too outspoken and critical for some people in authority to put up with. Your criticism is usually well founded, but not everyone appreciates this, especially superiors. You don't spare them the benefit of your observations any more than you do your co-workers. But you dislike being reprimanded or criticized yourself, and too much of this either from your boss or your fellow employees will prompt you to quit a job that otherwise pleases you.

If you were born between August 22 and August 31, you are an extremely adaptable and inventive person. You may make a name for yourself in a mechanical or technical field. You possess acute mental powers, including highly developed intuition. You'll often know what others are thinking, and this could help you forge a career in big business or finance. You can argue clearly and forcefully without being undiplomatic. You should be successful as a power behind the throne, advising and influencing someone in authority.

If you were born between September 1 and September 11, you possess an impressive talent for organization, particularly where masses of people are concerned. You should make an excellent personnel officer in charge of computerized systems for a large company. Your business sense is highly developed. You won't make a move unless you've given it a great deal of thought. Sometimes you may miss opportunities through too much rationalizing. But when you do act, you move swiftly and make few tactical errors. You are likely to work from the bottom up to a position of authority and respect. Well-tried conservative methods should be used. Solid, blue-chip financial transactions are more likely to succeed than speculative attempts.

If you were born between September 12 and September 22, you are artistically inclined and able to make a living through one of the arts. Your creative endeavors will be more successful if you give people what they want rather than try to break new ground. Keep to what you know, and if you must experiment, do so practically. You have a keen and well-balanced mind; you should not inhibit it with too much musing on the past or future. Your inspiration lies in the present. You should aim to be with people who need you. Friendship and partners are likely to be lucky for you. But be careful you are not imposed upon by relatives. Try not to be too aloof and independent when others offer help.

Whatever date you are born within the Virgo month, you should never try to take shortcuts in your work. It is your nature to endeavor to evolve easier and more productive ways of doing work, and this requires considerable application and inventiveness, strong Virgo characteristics.

You have the distinct advantage of being able to do manual as well as mental work and to combine them in a wide variety of ways. You are as much a builder as a draftsman. You are as much at home in a trade as in a profession. Just be sure you enjoy whatever you take up.

Money

You are extremely good at making pennies grow into sizable sums. By middle age, most Virgos are in a comfortable financial position. But frequently their well-laid plans for security are upset by loved ones and other relatives whose needs and spending habits may be extravagant.

You try to spend your cash wisely and are very seldom extravagant. You like most of the creature comforts but would rather live in a convenient style than a luxurious one. You worry about money but do your best to hide this from others. You want to appear open-handed, but with your rationalizing nature, it's not easy to be generous except in obviously deserving cases.

It is usually disastrous for Virgos to gamble or speculate. The safest way to acquire money is through persistent effort and careful saving, which is natural to you, anyway. Your sound business sense allows you to make money in straightforward deals where success depends on acumen rather than risk taking.

LIBRA'S CHARACTER

Let's get it right. You Libras are lovely people. No other Sign in the Zodiac is endowed with such an abundance of pleasing attributes. You are charming, artistic, gracious, intelligent, amiable, generous, sympathetic—a wonderful companion. So why do you spoil it by suddenly turning your own character inside out and becoming argumentative, critical, moody, fiery, sullen, jealous and unyielding?

Astrologically, the answer is simple: Libra is the Sign of peaceful coexistence . . . and of *war.* This is a point frequently ignored or understressed when this reputedly "balanced" Sign is discussed. Libra is *not* a *balanced* Sign; it's a *balancing* Sign, which is something quite different. Still, there is more peace than war in the world, so peace (or the craving for it) is the dominant theme in the typical Libra character.

According to ancient tradition, each zodiacal Sign has a special contribution to make to mankind's development. Libra's esoteric assignment is to reconcile the two opposing forces of harmony and disharmony wherever they are encountered (especially in relationships) and to eventually bring "peace on earth and good will to all men."

Obviously, there's a long, long way to go yet, but at least we know Libra is winning because (if you are typical) you are an example to us of charming and unruffled good-naturedness.

Yet there is a peppery side to your nature. For someone who yearns for congenial and happy relationships, you manage to stir or get mixed up in an amazing amount of strife and discord.

The key to this is the symbol of your Sign, a pair of Scales—held aloft by the blindfolded goddess of Justice herself! Justice aims to balance the scales and restore peace. Hence, your sense of fair play is exceedingly well developed. And it is in trying to right the scales wherever you sense imbalance, disharmony or injustice that you exhibit most of your so-called negative traits.

Let us remember that appearances are not always what they seem. Otherwise the goddess of justice would not be blindfolded. Her judgment depends on her ability to compare or weigh facts, plus her intuition. This is a pretty reasonable description of how your nature works. Though your judgment is not yet perfected, you're moving in the right direction.

None of this is an attempt to whitewash or excuse your weaknesses. But the fact remains that for the typical Libra—as for nations concerned with justice—war is sometimes the means to peace.

For instance, you will often deliberately start an argument by taking an opposite view because generalizations and dogmatic statements irritate you. They imply that other opinions are wrong. To you, this is unjust and infuriating. You mightn't give a damn about the subject but you can't resist defending the "other side," trying to restore equilibrium, trying to "end the war" of differences.

When aroused, you tend to favor the underdog, the person accused, the long-suffering silent majority or minority. You make a wonderful lawyer or judge.

For this we can thank your remarkable intellect. You have a gift for comparative analysis and logical deduction. You don't bore with detail; usually you employ just enough to build a crushingly effective argument. You try to deal in facts. You genuinely want the truth. You know there are always two sides to an argument, and in this perception lies both your strength and your Achilles' heel.

In your personal life, you find it extremely difficult to make decisions. You are, in fact, one of the most indecisive people in the Zodiac. You may be dazzling at demolishing another person's certitude or swinging him or her around to another point of view, but when you try to make up your mind, you consider and reconsider so many possibilities that in the end everything seems to balance out. Result: equilibrium and too often procrastination. This vacillation can be infuriating to your family and friends.

Yet those who are close to you know better than to try to rush you. One jarring word of impatience or exasperation and you're likely to dig in your heels with astonishing stubbornness and very definitely refuse to be definite if you don't want to! This uncharacteristic taking of a precise stand is really plain cussedness. As said before, you're moving in the right direction, but you're only human.

You can't stand impulsive or pushy people. You never try to pressure others (not so they would notice, anyway). You find it disturbing to be badgered yourself, so, like the civilized person you undoubtedly are, you give everyone ample time to make up his own mind.

This ability to put yourself in another person's place is one of the most admirable facets of your character. It makes you outstandingly sympathetic, kind and considerate. Unless a high principle is involved, you find it extremely distasteful to be drawn into an argument. Apart from the fact that any interpersonal conflict upsets your nervous system, you genuinely do appreciate the point the other person is making. This makes it difficult for you to pursue an argument with determination. You are much more inclined to offer a compromise solution or to placate. It is this sort of compliance that gives you a reputation for seeking peace at any price. On some occasions, it's true. But most of the time you merely want to give the other person as fair a shake as you hope he would give you. When your attempts at personal peacemaking are rebuffed, you can slide into a pretty sullen mood.

There is much of the escapist in your makeup. You spend a great deal of time in a fantasy world. This is your protection against the harsh realities of life that won't be appeased or pacified or won over by your conciliatory tactics. If you are forced to live in sordid or depressing conditions, you retreat more and more into this dream world. At these times you are very much aware of what is going on but you refuse to acknowledge it. If you have to perform, you go through the motions but you drift into a sort of mobile oblivion. Eventually, though, under the pressure of a long-term problem, the tempestuous and fiery side of your nature will suddenly erupt—you explode in indignant rebellion and break your chains. This subconscious process can astound even you with its vehemence.

This high-powered energy comes and goes in Libra individuals. It makes you difficult to understand; some of your closest associates become a little wary of you. People born under this Sign can drift indolently for weeks, seeming to get nothing done and having no desire whatever to exert themselves. Then suddenly, as though the scales of inaction had dipped far enough, they break into a flurry of productive activity that may continue for two or three months. You Libras don't have great reserves of energy; but there's always just enough for what you want to do. You have distinct highs and lows. It is essential for employers and the people you live with to understand this characteristic. As much as you love to keep your home tidy and presentable, you are likely to become quite slack and neglectful at times. Then you spend much of your time lying around, not even bothering to get dressed, allowing the dishes to pile up and leaving your clothing where you took it off.

During these enforced "rest" periods, you are apt to speak very little and to withdraw as much as possible from contact with the outside world. When your psychic and physical reserves are restored, you become your old cheerful communicative self. Your home is spick and span, once again a showpiece; at the office, you are an example of nonstop effort and conscientious efficiency. Over the year, "Lazy Libra"—as those who don't understand the Sign sometimes dub you—probably manages to get more done with less fuss than most of the critics.

If you are a typical Libra, your nature contains much that is contradictory and confusing. Astrologically, this is attributable to the position of your Sign in the Zodiac. Libra is the seventh Sign, and according to tradition, it is the last Sign added, specifically to represent the evolution of humankind as two separate sexes. Before that, time-shrouded tradition has it that there was only the human spirit—a sort of a unisex being composed of both masculine and female principles. Your Libra longing for harmony and unity (this is the Sign of marriage) arises from the primal desire to embody the man-woman principle through an ideal partnership. You are always seeking this in your relationships with people. It makes you (theoretically) the perfect mate. It explains why you can always put yourself in the other person's position, why you are so diplomatic, tactful, courteous, attractive—in other words, combining.

According to ancient esoteric teaching, we

human spirits for the past few billion years have been living out our incarnations not as whole beings but as our masculine or feminine half—and we will continue to do so until the Libra evolutionary force succeeds in reuniting us in spirit.

It is said that before the appearance of Libra, Virgo and Scorpio—the Virgin and the pure sex drive—were one Sign. Libra now stands between them and the only eternal link they have is love.

A lively social existence is terribly important to you. But strangely, you are not the type of person who makes profound, soul-knitting friendships. (Romantic attachments are somewhat different, and we will touch on that aspect shortly.) Friendship to you is like a delightful dance in which you move harmoniously from one new partner to the next—never pausing long enough to link arms and form a deep attachment. You never give all of yourself in friendship. You are pleasing and companionable, but in your charm and unruffled courtesy there is a reserve, an inviolability that is very seldom disturbed by anyone. You may sometimes feel a deep attachment—especially when you are in love—but generally speaking, your nature is to enjoy and let go, to circulate gaily and freely.

You are also happy bringing people together. You delight in seeing them share each other's pleasures, emotions and talents. This is the pure Libra social role epitomized by the gracious host or hostess who wants the company to enjoy themselves, refusing to show any personal favoritism.

Looking at the astrological explanation for this rather impersonal approach to relationships, we see that Libra is the first of the "impersonal" Signs of the Zodiac. The first half-dozen Signs, from Aries to Virgo, are concerned mainly with personal activities and with building up the individual ego. The last six, beginning with Libra and ending with Pisces, are more concerned with activities entered into with other people, the broader scene of humanity as a whole. Personal attachment is not so pronounced.

There are, of course, many social butterflies among Libras. The temptation to be frivolous and superficial, to gossip and become preoccupied with inconsequential social affairs, is almost irresistible to the less mature type. Here are the pouters, the affected, the poseurs. Many of these less evolved types—even though they have no money or position—are compulsive social climbers. They adore keeping up with the comings and goings of wealthy and prominent people and are always angling for invitations and meetings that will admit them to "elite circles." A distortion of the innate Libra craving to be accepted is clearly at work here.

Every true Libra, through work or a pastime, expresses his or her intrinsic affinity with the artistic and beautiful. This is the part of your nature that is governed by Venus, the planet of lovely things (and the means to acquire them). The world being what it is, wealth and position usually signify some appreciation or patronage of the arts, even if only a pseudo-interest. Into this world all Libras, given the proper circumstances, will tend to gravitate. If this is impossible, you will still exhibit distinct leanings toward the aesthetic. Though you might live in the poorest of homes, you will exhibit a refined taste. Whatever your environment, coarseness and vulgarity are alien to your nature.

Still, you are rather materialistic. You may not cling to your possessions with the same stranglehold as, say, Taurus does, but you do delight in them and aspire toward having rich and lavish things. A pleasant or comfortably furnished home is not quite enough for you. The more luxurious the appointments, the happier you are. Though seldom ostentatious, your taste does incline toward the extravagant if you can afford it. It is difficult for you to accept an austere or spartan existence for long. Life loses its luster if you have to put up with purely functional accommodations. Utility is something of a dirty word to you. You adore things like oriental rugs, velvet-piled wall-to-wall carpet, fine mosaic floors, polished pine floorboards, richly colored and fine-textured drapes, downy cushions and pillows, soft, luxuriant Chesterfield sofas or button-backed leather Davenports, Old Masters, as well as Picassos and very stylish modern furniture. You possess a gift for blending the antique with the contemporary. Your tastes are elegant and fashionable. You are essentially a mental creature, highly intuitive. You sense and think rather than feel. You know invariably what goes with what; you can visualize, compare, distinguish, re-create—all in your mind's eye.

Clothes are very important to the Libra man and woman. This is one department where both can be lavishly extravagant. Addicted to entertaining and mixing with sophisticated and well-to-do company, you like to have a wide selection of elegant up-to-date gear. You choose your accessories with great care; coordination of materials, color and line are paramount. Whether a man or a woman, you wear clothes with distinction. You avoid extreme fads. If a woman, you know instinctively that you've got what it takes without having to resort to see-through blouses and that sort of gimmickry to attract attention.

Libras have natural grace. You move with fluid ease. There is seldom hurriedness in your actions. If you are a woman, your body is probably rounded and well-proportioned. If you are a man, you are probably smoothly masculine. Yours is a Sign to which beauty of line is intrinsic, and there is often less here than in the other zodiacal types to distinguish between the two sexes. There is a type of Libra man who is so good-looking he is almost effeminate. In all Libras, the regularity of features is usually extremely pleasing, the speaking voice often softly modulated and a little drawling. The typical Libra person has a remarkable smile that shines from the eyes; it is an eye-stopper in a crowd.

Both the Libra man and woman love to laugh (they seldom guffaw). You have an inner gaiety that responds immediately to company. You love to converse with all types of people. You accept others for what they are and never expect them to act contrary to their natural disposition. Yet you are quite prepared to accept affectation if that's how the other person wants to behave. You are both a fluent and an intelligent talker and a wonderful listener. You can hear a story right through to the end, managing to convey the feeling that it's the best thing you've ever heard. You never show a flicker of impatience or disinterest—and if someone recites a problem to you, you are likely to come up with a brilliant suggestion or even a solution. A typical Libra never gives the impression of trying to pry into people's affairs. You are extremely respectful of the individual's right to privacy. Even in your most intimate relationships, you recognize that there are areas in everyone's life best left undisclosed.

You Libra people often don't know what you want—that old indecision again. If you were given a twenty-four-hour magic wand, you'd probably exceed the deadline because you wouldn't be able to make up your mind what to wish for. If you are a typical Libra person, you want as much, if not more, than the next person. But you can't help but hesitate because you perceive all the complications and difficulties that might arise. By the time these considerations are weighed against other alternatives, you're back to square one—still wondering and waiting hopefully for someone or something that will render a decision unnecessary. Libras have a dreadful habit of leaving the initiative to others because they are afraid of making a mistake. Your theory is that if you never initiate an action, then you can't be blamed for the consequences. You are at your best when responding to a suggestion or a request, or in pursuing mutual aims with a partner. Then you know the direction in which you are heading and can employ your many particular talents to that end. This is why you are so successful in partnership: you have no desire whatever to set, or upset, the pace. Although undeniably artistic, you are not originally creative. You produce by combining refinements of what has gone before. You aid a partner by advising and guiding so that both of you benefit. You Libras are the luckiest partners to have because psychologically you are built for double harness. On your own, you are unsure and lack self-confidence. You need someone to relate to at all times.

Sometimes you are so malleable that people tend to take you over. Immature Libras can become almost slavish in their obedience to stronger personalities. Fortunately, you have a superior sense of independence that (in the typical Libra) exerts itself at the first sign of constraint. You may be very happy with a romantic or business partner, but as soon as either tries to tie you down or limit your freedom to do as you please within due bounds, you'll rebel.

Despite your easygoing and unhurried manner, you are basically a restless individual. You must have variety of scenery and people. Your attachment to freedom is often misunderstood by other Signs, particularly in romance. You can be married and loyal to one person but you'll never be bound to him or her. You won't be instructed about whom you can see and whom you can't. You'll meet whom you please when you please—so there! That's your feeling, but it will seldom have to be said if you find the right kind of mate.

You have an inordinate desire to be liked. You can even be deceitful if you feel your popularity is endangered. You are inclined to overlook old friends to gather new ones. You blow hot and cold according to the excitement you feel around people. You want to be where the action is, and if an appointment made yesterday doesn't look as promising as something new today, you'll cancel it—but tactfully because you want everyone to have a good opinion of you, even those you let down! You usually manage to charm your way out of tricky situations without offending a soul.

You are capable of deep philosophic reasoning even if you don't make a practice of it. You like to be at the center of groups of learning, and this desire often expresses itself in some kind of teacher-student relationship. There are many Libra gurus around. When these individuals are highly developed, they give off such a splendid aura of peace and spirituality that others want to bask in their presence. It is not difficult for disciples to see them in a saintly context. The Libra with his or her impersonal idea of love can be a devotional mystic.

You are, however, seldom an eccentric. You shy away from ostentation, exhibitionism and humbug. You practice and preach moderation, and don't exaggerate. Since you believe in treating others as you hope to be treated yourself, you are a great and respected peacemaker. You can make decisions worthy of Solomon, sending both parties away completely satisfied that justice has been done, even though one of them has lost.

You are particularly skillful at diverting attention from your own weaknesses. When these are brought up, you defend yourself by introducing red herrings. Though you don't necessarily tell lies, you are adept at putting others off the scent. If anyone accuses you of being indecisive, quarrelsome, moody or opportunistic, you'll confuse the issue completely with a splendid display of logic and self-delusion. Those who don't immediately accept your logic you'll probably contact and try to convince later. The oil can is your favorite weapon.

Your main trouble lies in your emotions. Whenever they are aroused, you lose your wonderful talent for impartiality and straight thinking. You become quite silly in a way and often irresponsible. At such times, you will accept the most incredible suppositions and fantasies, which normally you would scorn. Of course, it is in the emotional quicksands of love where you suffer most and often go under. The chapter "Libra in Love" deals in detail with your inclinations in this regard. Briefly, as a lover, you are terribly impressionable. You bend over backward to see your ideal man or woman in any individual who takes your fancy and who happens to measure up to a few basic specifications. You are inclined to make allowances for distasteful qualities, in a sort of compromise deal. After the first phase of euphoric mateship is over, you come thudding down to earth. Sometimes by then you are married.

Libras often marry young or several times. And they usually manage to get involved in at least one very peculiar love affair in their lives, which causes tremendous personal upheaval or disillusionment. They are sometimes parted from their true love forever and live the rest of their days in a romantic dreamworld of hopeful expectation—frequently safer for them than searching amid harsh reality for a mate they can love and live with.

Libras fall more in love with the *idea* of love than the person. You make such a smashing marriage partner that if you can team up with a compatible guy or girl, your imagination will do the rest. You can then settle down to a highly workable and successful relationship. You sometimes become depressed in marriage because of your habit of constantly comparing the faults and virtues of your mate. Thus you exhaust yourself and become moody, when really you are quite capable of accepting the discrepancies in human nature.

One problem Libra men and women have in romantic affairs is that they don't like to say no. You are so anxious to please and to avoid unpleasantness that you often take the line of least resistance and suddenly find yourself in an intolerable situation. Many of you have such an idealized vision of everlasting love that you are easy prey for sweet talkers. You also believe that madly romantic situations will last forever.

When it comes to breaking off an affair, you are sometimes shockingly lax. Rather than say you want out directly, you may just disappear without a word. Though you believe you are saving the other person the trauma of a scene, it is really yourself you are protecting. Otherwise considerate and kind, in this type of situation you can be selfish and thoughtless enough to ignore the pain that can be inflicted by uncertainty. You know it's over, and you feel that's enough.

By trying to please everyone at the same time, you Libras frequently give the impression of being shallow and insincere. People do talk, you know, and you can't expect to get away with agreeing with two opposing factions. It's that emotional thing again, you see. If two strangers want someone to make a fair adjudication between them, no type in the Zodiac can be relied upon to hand down a more just decision than Libra. But if your popularity is at stake, you'll endeavor to sit on the fence or trot out your bag of red herrings and no one will be happy. To avoid dissension, you may purposely falsify facts.

There is a great deal of nobility and high

purpose in the Libra character, and in order to be happy, you have to continually accentuate these qualities. Unfortunately, you have a strong tendency to give up when the going gets rough, to seek any haven in a storm. Resolution will be found in sticking to the Libra principles of justice and honesty irrespective of any unpleasantness they may cause.

As expert as you are at delivering judgments, you are probably frequently accused by those close to you of failing to understand their deeper feelings. This is true; but in a way, it's your essence, so you certainly can't be condemned for it. Your incisive mind is often able to carve very edible slices of wisdom off a loaf of abstractions, and your intuition can be impeccable. Why, then, do you find it so hard to understand the small irrational fears of others, the little torments that make us all so vulnerable and incomplete inside? Is it because your emotional mechanism, when stirred, is too self-centered? For all your sunny companionship, you Libras usually extract more from your close relationships than you put into them. Perhaps this is the price of peace.

You are a great admirer of books, and not just their substance. You love the feel and look of them; the smell of an old leather tome delights you. Although you are capable of understanding quite weighty subjects, you frequently choose lighter kinds of literature. You enjoy reading magazines and keeping informed of world affairs through the newspapers.

Spare-time activities are very important to your health and happiness. Whatever you do all day every day, even if it's looking after your own home, you need to get away to a different environment at least once a year. You must know there's something to look forward to, a change of pace in your daily routine. Painting, writing and dancing are apt to appeal to you, although you'll enjoy them more if you're not put under any pressure to practice and can resort to them at will. You must feel relaxed to benefit from your hobbies. In the summer, you should enjoy sunbathing and lazing around reading. When you're feeling productive, you Libra ladies should try your hand at making some stylish clothes. The results may astound you.

Finally, you should always remember the unconscious effect that your surroundings have on you. Your feelings of irritation or gloom are sometimes caused by very minor events or changes in the office or home, or in the people you live or work with. Clashing color schemes, shrill voices, dirty clothes, offensive smells, even a curt greeting can put you off balance.

You are not a temperamental person, just sensitive. Combine your sensitivity with a strong sense of social duty and you will have much to contribute to the community.

LIBRA IN LOVE

YOUR LIBRA MAN

You like him? Love him? What sort of man is your Libra?

Charming. Absolutely charming. He's a man most women have no difficulty falling for. The trouble comes after you've got him, and especially after marriage. Mr. Libra requires a great deal to obtain fulfillment. If you can give him what he wants and delight in so doing, you'll have a wonderful time. If you can't, you'd better just sit back and enjoy a brief and glorious affair. Libra is the Sign of marriage, so there's a lot going for a permanent liaison with this man. The Sign is ruled by Venus, the planet of love and beauty.

The typical Libra man is one of the most cultured in the Zodiac. (As you know, there's the undeveloped type, but we're not discussing him here.) He is urbane, suave, well mannered, diplomatic and highly intelligent. He loves women. He views them as the natural complement of man. To have a gracious and beautiful girl on his arm is his idea of the supreme luxury of the good life, which he enjoys very much.

Not surprisingly, this man commences his love life very early. By the time you meet him, he's sure to have had numerous affairs and to be very experienced in the ways of women. He knows exactly how to treat them. He's deliciously romantic. He will never take you to a second-rate restaurant. Even if you're his partner at the local dance, he'll introduce a touch of elegance and style to the evening. He'll charm you, make you feel you're the only woman in the room.

This man says it with flowers and gifts and in a million other little ways. He believes in creating an atmosphere. His apartment will be delightfully furnished. His taste in color and fabrics is usually superb. He loves to luxuriate in comfort and ease. Despite his sex appeal, he has a smoothly indolent air. He regards food and dining as creative and is often a first-class cook. He'll serve you aperitifs and a sumptuous meal with a single, memorable bottle of vintage wine. He's likely to save the cork to remind you both of your "first night" alone. The right effect is paramount for his enjoyment of all occasions. He's the original smoothie.

Mr. Libra is not an easy man to please. He thinks he knows what he wants, but it's impossible to satisfy his desire for refinement in all things in the sort of world we live in. This man doesn't want to know about ordinariness, clumsiness, uncouthness—all necessary components of everyone's life. He's a bit of a dreamer who has trouble facing up to reality. He's always trying to gild the scene with his own charming style, diplomacy and fastidious taste.

He doesn't like women who tell dirty jokes. He can't stand coarse or strident female laughter. He appreciates fine grooming and will never fail to notice a new hairstyle or dress and to give an appropriate compliment. If he doesn't like what he sees, he will never make an embarrassing comment. But his ladies get the idea because the inappropriate speaks for itself in his presence.

This man needs to be loved. He wants a woman who can give him peace and protect him from the shabbiness and discord of the outside world. But at the same time, he's a guy who can't help racing around "out there," stirring up dust that inevitably causes his biggest problems. He loves being with people. If you set up home with him, you'll have to do a great deal of entertaining. He'll want to show you off—along with his home.

The Libra man's home is terribly important to him. It is here where he actually succeeds in recreating the ideal world he finds so elusive in reality. He is probably the most superb homemaker of the Zodiac.

This man is no fool. His judgment is impeccable and his reasoning powers of a high order. He possesses a keen appreciation of art and likes to share these interests with others.

He is a consummate lover. He knows how to please a woman. Lovemaking is an art with him. He is more sensual than sexual. He uses his body with passion and refinement, an exquisite experience for the woman who does not resent the fact that he usually takes more from a relationship than he gives.

YOUR LIBRA WOMAN

You like her? Love her? Just what sort of woman is she?

Delicious. She can be the plainest woman in the world (which is most unlikely), and still an indefinable, almost spiritual quality of beauty will shine through. They've all got it, these Libra women, that quality that attracted you to her—and a hundred other guys before you. This girl is made for love, physically and emotionally, so you're going to have a hell of a lot of male competition.

She has many, many friends. She's one of the most social-minded creatures in the Zodiac. With her friendly, delicate and charming manner, she makes the perfect hostess. She can't help bringing people together. If you think of yourself as her new, most important love, you may find this a bit off-putting. Whenever you want to be alone with her, someone's likely to turn up. And more than likely it will be a man. If you're the jealous type, you've got some terribly tortured times ahead.

The jealous man doesn't understand this woman. Although she possesses a finely voluptuous passion, she's not promiscuous. She won't hop into bed with any guy who asks her. (If she did, with her super-sex appeal, she'd have time for nothing else.) This girl is a romantic. She believes strongly in a man-woman relationship. She's gently wending her way through all these men looking for the ideal lover. She won't experiment much physically because she doesn't take lovers who don't measure up to her notion of a lover. Are you Prince Charming? Because that's who she's looking for—someone who is gay, humorous, amusing, loving, chivalrous, well-mannered, polished, decisive, intelligent, determined, adoring, masculine, caring. Well?

You can sweep her off her dreamy feet (several men will do this in her lifetime), but can you hold her? Usually she makes a bit of a mess of her love life while sorting the boys out from *the* man. Once she's found him, she settles into marriage with an ease and naturalness that makes Mr. Right never stop thanking his lucky stars.

She is not the jealous type unless you give her occasion. It wouldn't enter her mind to doubt you. She will give you all the freedom a reasonable man would want and won't cross-examine you. She, too, will want a fair amount of opportunity to pursue her outside interests and to keep up with her friends. But you'll never have any reason to think she's having an affair unless you've failed her somehow. This woman will stick to the man she loves and be true to him. But she will never be tied down to any man's will.

Miss Libra is flirtatious and prone to imagine that every man is in love with her. She revels in the role of *femme fatale*. The more attention and admiration she receives, the more she radiates her personality. But it's usually not serious. If she ever finds herself emotionally involved with another man, she will own up to it and try to work something out. There is nothing underhanded about this woman. She is a strongly ethical creature.

You'll need a fairly good income because she can be extravagant and a bit cent-wise and dollar-foolish. She loves to surround herself with beautiful things, especially clothes. Being avidly social, she requires a large fashionable wardrobe.

If you do marry a Libra girl, you'll find she's a great sharer. She won't shirk her share of the responsibilities. If times get hard, she'll be prepared to economize and improvise. If you lose your job, she'll willingly act as breadwinner without feeling in the least put upon. She is quite capable of maintaining a career and running a home without neglecting either. She is wonderfully adaptable.

This woman is so intent on preserving harmony in a relationship that she may tell a white lie to protect you from worry. She doesn't want anything to disturb your happiness with her. She really aims to make her man contented. This tendency to ignore bad news is deep and sometimes results in her glossing over reality. In this way, she often fools herself, refusing to acknowledge the necessity for action or resolution.

No woman in the Zodiac is more satisfying as a wife to the man she loves than a Libra.

LIBRA WOMAN—ARIES MAN

You are the sort of woman who finds it fairly easy to get along with most people. You're the adaptable type. Being positive in outlook, you tend to seek out the good in others. In Mr. Aries, you have a man with the exact opposite temperament. Still, we all know that opposites attract, which should make this a very interesting combination, to say the least.

You will hold a strange kind of fascination for each other. He's a strong-willed up-and-at-'em type of character. He will be absolutely stunned by your elegance and womanly charm.

When you first become acquainted with an Aries man, you'll be impressed by his apparent confidence and self-reliance. He will not take no for an answer; he simply doesn't know the meaning of the word. Your calming and restraining influence can do him nothing but good. He tends to rush in head first.

He will probably get the idea that you are much more passionate than is the case. But then, much of the Ram's life revolves around the sexual urge.

He is in many ways a man's man. He likes to stand at the bar and knock down a few beers with the guys. He carries a lot of old-fashioned notions in his head, one of which is a woman's place is in the home. This sort of attitude toward the female of the species might be a bit much for you to swallow.

Aries men are known to be great sports lovers. You're usually more comfortable as a spectator than a competitor.

He gets overtaken by his own whims and fancies. Under the spell of one of his sudden enthusiasms, he will expect you to get as carried away as he is.

People born under his Sign of the Zodiac can blow hot and cold. One minute, he'll be all over you; the next, he'll have disappeared with his male friends for an afternoon at a baseball game.

You love to share things; the idea of partnership definitely appeals to a Libra woman. Though he will adore you, he will wish to dominate the union. It will offend his male ego if he's not the one who makes all the important decisions.

Don't get carried away by the first wave of passion. He's capable of overwhelming you and rushing you into a liaison you may later regret. Give yourself time to get to know each other really well.

He loves his home. He will think the way you run the domestic side of things is absolutely great; that is one area in which he would never dream of interfering. It would be wise for you to keep up with your outside interests if you do marry this man. You're far too active to be content twiddling your thumbs waiting for him to come home. He can't help flirting with other women, but it's usually quite harmless.

You are pretty good with money, although a bit on the extravagant side at times. Mr. Aries will always be fair and make sure you never want for anything.

Don't ever play games with this man because he is far too vulnerable emotionally. He can be extremely jealous, so don't push him beyond the limit. And remember, he is something of an overgrown boy so you should constantly praise him.

It's more than likely that he will earn money in his spare time. His regular job will not be enough to hold his interest.

He'll make a smashing father and will spoil his kids like mad.

LIBRA WOMAN—TAURUS MAN

You are just the kind of woman to bring love and happiness into the life of the Bull. There are a great many things you have in common. He's kindhearted, home-loving and pretty well sorted out in his head. You like to know where you stand with a man, and Mr. Taurus is unlikely to try to keep any secrets from you.

This guy can't stand to be bossed, but then, you are not the domineering type. He has to operate at his own pace. He's never fast at making important decisions and he refuses to be rushed. People might get to the top in their career quicker than he does, but this man is likely to last longer than most once he does make the grade.

He will want to protect you. You do like having a fuss made of you, and he will certainly make you feel all woman.

You will have a lot to teach each other. Being an air Sign, you will probably be light-years ahead of him in speed of thought. But occasionally you need slowing down. When you feel outraged by something you read in the paper and perhaps wish to do something about it, he will remind you to keep your nose out of other people's affairs. Many times you'll look back with relief at his restraining influence.

He won't be too keen on your having outside interests. He won't like it if he has to come home to an empty house. He expects his woman to be on hand to see to all his needs.

You are both artistic types. You will enjoy evenings at the theater or ballet. Although he's usually a bit macho, you'll find him extremely gentle underneath his aggressive facade.

He's a sexy man. He has quite an appetite for lovemaking.

Where the red light will flash in this union is

when he becomes possessive and jealous. He will want you in his sights all the time. Mutual trust in a relationship is important to you. You may get the feeling that he is overly suspicious whenever you go out without him. Will you manage to control your desire to form strong (nonphysical) relationships with other men? Remember, you are the outward-looking type, and being interested in people usually leads to making lots of friends.

He's a good businessman and as a rule has an excellent head for figures. He will love spoiling you. He's unlikely to refuse to buy you new clothes when you want them. He'll feel your appearance reflects on him, so be sure you always look your best when he takes you out.

Your tastes in home decor will be very different. He will dislike the changes you constantly wish to make. He won't be able to understand why you want to buy a new living room set when the old one looks perfectly fine to him.

Always make a fuss over him when he comes home because he needs to feel wanted. Warm his slippers and fix him his favorite drink.

You may occasionally have to remind him that you would like to go out because he can be content to stay home night after night.

He's very good with children. As parents, you should be a fine combination. He can be strict when he has to, but most of the time you'll feel he has the situation well under control because he understands kids.

LIBRA WOMAN—GEMINI MAN

If a Gemini man comes into your life, it's unlikely you'll ever forget the impact he makes. One quality that will appeal to you is his sense of humor. You will never know a dull moment while he's on the scene—but do understand that he likes to keep the scene *moving*. He's ruled by the restless planet Mercury, and you are both freedom-loving air Signs.

He's witty, he's intelligent and he's capable of taking care of himself. He won't mind your having outside interests. If your work is important to you, he would never dream of asking you to forego it for the sake of the marriage. He'll be quite happy to do the cooking and the shopping if you are held up late at your job. He's not one of those dominant males who expects you to sacrifice your freedom to a man.

He likes a girl with a sensible head on her shoulders. He will expect you to be responsible for your own actions.

You will have to keep him looking his best. If left to his own devices, he'll slip into the quickest and easiest gear.

A Gemini man needs a fairly strong woman behind him to give him that extra push. This doesn't mean he'll stand for being bossed around. Always *suggest* to the Twins, never command.

You will find him pretty even-tempered. He hates big scenes and will do all he can to avoid a head-on collision.

Don't get the idea that life with a Gemini man will be full of wonderful, intelligent conversation and exciting happenings. You will have quite a lot to put up with. He loses interest in things and people very quickly. To hold his interest, you must keep him guessing about you. He is constantly searching for something new. He is also a bit of a wanderer. He craves excitement and travel and adventure.

He will do his best to provide for you, but don't rely on it. He often takes a while to find the right niche in life. He may change jobs a number of times before settling down.

You will probably have the same tastes in friends. You are both excellent mixers and enjoy a good party. It's rather difficult for this man to be hitched to a woman who likes to stay home most of the time. Never refuse his invitations to go out because he'll go alone rather than stay in. He's a night owl.

Mr. Gemini has a vile temper but it doesn't last. He can fly off the handle over minor incidents. He's also capable of becoming moody and morose when things don't go well for him. It will be up to you to shake him out of his negative attitudes.

If you really dig him enough, you'll be able to do a lot for Mr. Gemini. Slowly but surely you'll help him grow up. He's a bit of a child at heart. You will have to show him that it's better to face his problems than to keep running away from them. You will have many interests in common. Your love of art and music will help bind you together.

It would be a good idea to wait a bit before you have kids. Make sure your man is responsible enough to accept the role of father. After all, you don't want to be stuck home alone with the children so be sure he has grown up enough to take on his fair share of parental duties.

LIBRA WOMAN—CANCER MAN

Your mother will probably be enchanted by him because the Cancer man has a great way with older women. He always appears so gentle and well mannered. You may find him a little hard to understand as a lover. He is certainly a man of many moods.

Don't rush into marriage with the Crab. This is unlikely anyway, since he's not the type to do things on the spur of the moment. You must give yourself quite a long period of courtship. He sometimes talks himself into believing things when he wants to. He craves security and may mistake his emotions because he dislikes being on his own.

He can be extremely gloomy and subject to fits of depression. You will have to get used to his lunar moods if you're going to spend the rest of your life with him.

You are something of an extrovert. Although you like your evenings at home, you also like to get out once in a while. This is where Mr. Cancer can be less than your ideal mate. Once married, he may expect you to be the one to keep the home fires burning while he goes out with his buddies. When you want to go out, he'll want to stay at home and watch an old movie. He's a funny character, this one.

He is certainly a great home lover, and he thoroughly enjoys his creature comforts. You like new furniture and modern decor. He prefers antiques. He is always harking back to the past, saying how great life was in the good old days.

He's a bit of a pessimist who loves a good moan. You are an optimist who always looks for the pot of gold at the rainbow's end. Perhaps you'll be good for each other. If you can manage to strike the proper balance—which is your style—then all should be well.

He is a creature of feeling and emotions. Your head tends to rule your heart, even though you are capable of getting very caught up with your emotions at times.

You will have to curb your desire for independence because he will be unhappy if you leave him alone to pursue your own interests. He will take it personally and tell you you don't really care for him.

Mr. Cancer is careful with money but only to a point. That is, he's capable of saving wisely for months at a time, then blowing a large amount on something quite ridiculous.

He will do his best to see you are well provided for. Being a man who likes his home, he's bound to make sure that your domestic life is as pleasant as possible. He's quite sentimental and will always try to buy you something special for your birthday and anniversary.

Water fascinates him. It is his element, and he often has a great yearning for the sea. A cruise in the tropics is probably his ideal holiday.

You will never get him to do what you want by bullying him. The way to coax him out of his shell is to praise him constantly and at the same time boost his ego.

He's one of the handiest men around the home. He's also terrific in the kitchen and is also prepared to do his fair share of the housework if you have too much to cope with.

He will make a terrific father, one who takes the responsibilities of parenthood very seriously. Probably he's better with girls than boys. He may get a bit jealous of a son; he could see him as something of a threat.

LIBRA WOMAN—LEO MAN

This guy could be quite a catch for a Libra girl. He's generous, positive in his outlook on life and has a powerful personality. You like a man you can admire, and there is certainly a hell of a lot you will dig about the Lion. You will find his very physical presence exciting. Your heart will flutter whenever he walks into a room.

He's a leader. It is not for nothing he is known as King of the Jungle. Your friends may feel you are biting off more than you can chew if you go steady with this fellow. However, being Libra, you are just the woman to tame him.

He will make you feel all woman. He will compliment you on your beauty, not just physical beauty—he will look right into your soul. He will love showing you off to his friends. A charming companion for a night out, he usually knows the right places to go.

Without love in his life, he would pine away. In spite of his apparent aggressiveness, he's an incurable romantic at heart, a big softie. Tell him this and he would think you were talking about another guy, but it's true nonetheless.

He knows how to express his love—in words and in actions. He doesn't think that a couple's sex life begins and ends in the bedroom. He will take you whenever and wherever it is possible. This is another exciting thing about Mr. Leo. You will always be stimulated by him. Lovemaking will never become stale.

Don't neglect him. He needs to be constantly reassured he is the only man in your life. He won't mind your having friends, but he won't be able to take it if he feels you would rather be in their company than his. If you would, why stay with him? That's his attitude, anyway.

One little hangup may be the fact that he wants to rule and you can't abide being told what to do. Unfortunately, he will always be trying to tell you what is best for you.

Obviously there will be a certain amount of conflict in this union. If you can just remember that when he does offer you his advice it is only because he loves you and wants to protect you, you might be able to cope with this aspect of his personality.

He will put you on a pedestal but will shout you down if you voice opinions contrary to his when you're out with friends.

He's quite the handyman about the home. He likes a challenge and is always interested in acquiring new skills. He's also a good provider. You will have no need to worry about the future.

He can't stand people bossing him around. His superior had better be a man who gives him plenty of leeway or he'll be off in search of pastures new.

When you feel confused and unsure of the future, he will be great to have around. He will find simple solutions to your problems. His advice is likely to be sound and well worth following. He will be proud of you. He will like to feel that his friends secretly fancy you.

Keep your eye on members of your own sex. Leo is not likely to wander unless someone deliberately tempts him.

He can put on a bit. You will find he's capable of doing a Hamlet routine if he feels he's not getting your attention. You will know him much better than he realizes, and this will be part of the fun of living with a Leo man.

He is unlikely to want a large family. So keen will he be to fulfill the duties of parenthood that he's unlikely to want to take on more than two cubs.

LIBRA WOMAN—VIRGO MAN

Mr. Virgo is unlikely to sweep you off your feet. You will probably find any romantic link that grows between you will develop slowly. He takes his time. When he does say "I love you," you can be pretty certain he's sincere. He's very analytical. You may wonder if you could find permanent happiness with this man.

He likes to have things straight. He's cool, calm and collected—you may even discover he's a little smug. You may get bored waiting around for him to make up his mind.

You will be quite impressed with many of his qualities, though. His charm and rather old-fashioned manners will intrigue you. He's a smart dresser, though a pretty conservative one.

Your mother will probably be quite taken with him, although, on reflection, she may feel his charm is a bit superficial. You, too, may get the idea that he is constantly putting on an act. He's really a worrier beneath the facade. He will worry about his job and whether he can earn enough to support you both. No matter how much he has in the bank, lurking thoughts of insolvency will haunt him.

The Virgo man is difficult to stir emotionally. This is because he's terrified of getting hurt. He can't stand the thought of being rejected.

Mr. Virgo is very fussy and you may well find this his most irritating habit. He's extremely house-proud and hygiene-conscious. His rectitude could become a bit of a bore to a fun-loving Libra female like you.

Let's not ignore this man's good points. He is as straight as a die. He's a lover of truth. If you do get it together, he is likely to be faithful to you. If a woman makes a pass at him, he'll weigh up what he would be putting in jeopardy were he to have a fling. He will always treat you as a woman. He will try to ensure that you have everything your heart desires. He will want his marriage to be for keeps.

You will have to help him unwind. Show him that sex can be fun. You will be able to get him to overcome his inhibitions.

Your Virgo man will definitely try to understand you, though he will never quite succeed. He'll be a restraining influence, and this may be to your benefit.

He's quite romantic deep down. He'll never forget your birthday or your wedding anniversary. Who knows—he may even make you a better housewife!

Though he loves his home, he won't mind your pursuing a career because he wouldn't like to feel he has imposed unfair limitations on you.

He's quite big on self-discipline. He doesn't easily forgive people who don't take their responsibilities as seriously as he does. Because he's so fond of his opinions, he can't understand why others don't always follow his advice.

He's domesticated and usually takes pleasure in exercising his culinary expertise. He also won't mind doing his fair share of the household chores but he'll get exasperated if he has to go around tidying up after you all the time.

Parenthood is not always important to this man. You might find his instinct to father a son or daughter is not all that strong. He loves kids, but would rather play the role of kindly godfather or uncle.

He will expect you to make a big fuss over him when he's not feeling well. He tends to take to his bed at the first sign of a chill.

If you learn to appreciate his kindly ways, you'll come to love him more and more as the years roll by.

LIBRA WOMAN—LIBRA MAN

You will, of course, have a great deal in common with a man born under the same Sign. But usually same-Sign unions don't work out so well. A Libra-Libra combination should be the exception to the rule.

You'll have fun beling alone with him at home. You'll also enjoy his company at parties or out with a group of friends. And you'll have a ball in the bedroom.

Mr. Libra is likely to have the type of looks you find irresistible. You will also go for his charm and his powers of reason. He has many fine qualities, but above all, he will share your sense of fun and zest for living. He's not fond of simple country life. He's more likely to be a city man. People interest him so much he can't stand to live on his own for very long. He has a winning way with women. Like you, he can be impulsive.

He will love you because you are so feminine. You will enjoy putting on your prettiest dress when you have a date. He'll always notice how you look and will never be slow to pay the right sort of compliment.

You are bound to share the same interests in art. You will have no difficulty, either, in agreeing on how your home should be decorated and furnished. You will appreciate his feeling for beauty and harmony.

He will go to great lengths to maintain peace. Like you, he can't stand violence or a heavy domestic argument.

You are inclined to be flirtatious, and this is something you will have to watch. Both being Libra, you will probably be able to accept the other's odd game with a member of the opposite sex. You should be adult enough to realize it's only harmless fun.

He's diplomatic enough not to try to uncover your deepest thoughts and innermost feelings. He will even tell a white lie if he thinks it will keep you from being hurt or upset.

This man often earns his living through his artistic talents. Although extremely sensitive, he can be quite ruthless when he needs to be. He knows how to get the very best out of people, which makes him an excellent teacher or leader.

Occasionally you may feel he doesn't care about you—especially when he gets that vague, faraway look in his eyes. You will have to learn to fend for yourself quite a lot of the time. He loves his freedom and will expect you to be able to stand on your own.

Don't try to tie this man down. You will keep him by allowing him to make his own decisions. Neither of you is the jealous type, and that will work to the advantage of the union. You won't get your way by losing your temper or making a big scene.

He can take ages to make important decisions; he will always weigh both sides carefully before committing himself to a positive course of action. Sometimes this guy waits a little too long and misses opportunities. You suffer from the same indecision, so you should be able to help each other out here.

He prefers to go out for his pleasure and entertainment. The quiet dinner party with a few chosen friends may appeal to him occasionally, but as a rule he likes his home to be a place where he can escape from the rigors and trials of the outside world.

He will make an exceedingly fair and tolerant father. He will be firm but patient with the children.

LIBRA WOMAN—SCORPIO MAN

This will be an all-or-nothing relationship. On first meeting a Scorpio man, you will either be completely taken with him or feel he is the most opinionated, aggressive character you have ever had the misfortune to set eyes on. Even if the latter is your response, he may still arouse your curiosity. Many are the women who have damned this man only to come back for more of the same medicine.

He's tough. His approach to life is hard. He will want to dominate you. If you have had a number of experiences with weak men, you might find his attitude to love and sex quite refreshing.

You may well be swept away by the hypnotic effect he can have on a woman. It is very easy for a woman—even a well-balanced Libra —to lose control of herself when he's around.

He will certainly want to protect you. Many

women find in this man something of a father figure. He will be knocked out by your femininity and charm. He won't want any other guy to share it.

He needs his freedom, but he won't be too enthused if you entertain ideas about living a separate life from his. He won't want you to continue with a career after marriage. He is looking for a woman who will make a comfortable home for him. She will have to be there—or else.

Mr. Scorpio is determined to make a success of his life. He's a very hard worker and will take on almost any challenge.

He can be a bit measly with money. You will probably have a battle every time you ask for more money to keep up with rising prices. He likes to provide his mate with material things, but doesn't enjoy handing her cash.

His jealousy may be just too much for you to cope with. He's a frightfully suspicious character and he can be a bit of a brute. No flirting when he's around, for heaven's sake.

He hates to be tied down. Basically, he's a man's man, probably the sporty type. He tends to like the masculine atmosphere of the golf club. He doesn't have many close friends. He's not at all easy to get to know. He usually ends up dictating to other people. He likes power and he likes to be in control. It's not going to be easy, is it?

You are always striving to see both sides of an argument. You do your best to be impartial and fair. Here is a man with very fixed ideas. He never has any trouble making up his mind between right and wrong.

He may find you a little cool in bed, but then there are few women who can keep pace with his passion and fire.

You will find it a problem working out whether he is good or bad for you. He will expect you to stay in the background and to make looking after him your number-one priority in life.

He's ambitious. Woe betide the person who tries to pull a fast one on him in business. He never forgets a double-crosser; it may take him years, but he'll get his own back in the end.

It wouldn't be a safe bet that you will last the course together. One thing is sure: if you part company, you will be more mature human beings.

The Scorpio man can be an old softie with animals. Having a problem connecting with other people, he often directs a great deal of his love and affection toward a favorite pet.

He makes a good father but expects a great deal from his children.

LIBRA WOMAN—SAGITTARIUS MAN

Life will certainly have its vivid moments when a Libra woman and a Sagittarius man get it together. He's a difficult guy to pin down and you can be an extremely elusive female. This romance may start out as a battle of wits. He likes lots of company. He's the party-going type so you will hardly ever know a dull moment when you're out with him.

Since both of you are adept at summing up others, this will have to be a very honest relationship. Neither of you can abide it when people try to deceive you.

Many a woman has tried to pin down this happy-go-lucky gaucho. Being a bit of a strategist, you could be the one to win him.

He hates to be pressured. He likes to feel he is in the driver's seat. He refuses to be told when he's had enough. He's a night owl who comes to life when the sun sets.

Whether you have an exciting affair with him or find that your love is the real thing, he's not a man you will be able to forget.

He may appear to be rushing around to no good purpose, but don't get the false impression that he's just a wild dreamer. Behind all that tomfoolery you will usually discover he knows exactly what is going on around him.

He is positive. Sagittarius people always try to look on the bright side of life. He is full of drive and wonderful ideas. His enthusiasm is unquenchable.

He is a just man and a moral one. You both set great store by fair play. You won't be able to help falling for him when he flashes that infectious grin in your direction. You will also find that naughty schoolboy laugh rather attractive.

He can be outrageous. He will say things that make others squirm. He is not afraid to speak his mind. He'll always come out with what he thinks.

If you do end up married, it's important you become friends as well as lovers. Mr. Sagittarius needs a partner whom he can pal around with, someone who shares his interests.

If he is unfaithful, it probably is not serious. He is only likely to get involved with another woman on a casual basis. He has no wish to make his life any more complicated than it is already.

He's very broad-minded. Like you, he tries to see things from the other person's point of view. He tries to take a live-and-let-live attitude.

This man likes to be the center of attraction. He always has a story to top everybody else's. He can't stand to be second best in anything.

He'll try not to show it, but he will be upset if you come on to other men. It is important to him that he be the only person who really matters in your life. Basically, he is rather insecure.

He is often fond of sports. He's got loads of courage and is prepared to try anything once.

Mr. Sagittarius will make a great fuss over you. He will want to buy you everything you desire. It might be a good idea if you have a joint account; this way, you can make sure he puts some cash aside every week to pay regular bills.

He loves entertaining. It's likely friends will be dropping by your house most evenings.

Occasionally he will try your patience, but you'll find it in your heart to forgive him.

LIBRA WOMAN—CAPRICORN MAN

A lively girl like you might find life with Mr. Capricorn a bit of a drag. That is, unless you get the hard-working, hard-playing, burn-the-candle-at-both-ends type of earth creature.

Most men born under the Sign of the Goat are extremely difficult to get to know. Mr. Capricorn will probably be touchy, arrogant, sensitive and shy. He will also have perfect manners and hold to tried and trusted values.

In romance, he's a little backward in coming forward. So scared is he of being rebuffed that you may have to close your eyes and pucker your lips before he realizes he's got a chance with you.

A Capricorn man secretly yearns to be wanted. He is capable of concealing his true emotions by being extremely witty and making cutting remarks.

If you meet that odd Capricorn guy who does not fit into this category—the higher type—you will indeed be lucky. He will push you hard, but will be tremendously good for you. He will ensure that you make the most of your natural talents. This man can be a wonderful teacher. He is terribly ambitious himself and intends to go far in life, which suits you because you like a man who knows what he wants. He likes to invite people to his home; especially business contacts. He will be very proud of the superb way you organize a dinner party.

Work is terribly important to him. You will usually find he holds down a job that entails quite a bit of responsibility.

You could find the average Capricorn man's plodding manner a little irritating. He's afraid to take chances. He can be very shy in the company of people he doesn't know well. By nature, he's conservative. You may get the feeling he's always keeping something hidden, not just from you but also from himself.

He tends to be a worrier. He will make problems out of situations that have not even arisen.

He also tends to gloat. He can't help taking an I-told-you-so attitude when you go wrong.

There will be many fundamental differences between you. He works by logic; you tend to improvise and go by your intuition. Perhaps this will make you a good combination—if you accept that your talents are different and respect each other's point of view.

He will think you are terribly extravagant, especially in buying clothes. He's a bit of a hoarder himself.

He will be faithful. You are unlikely to catch him looking at another woman.

He's neat around the house. You may even find his habit of constantly cleaning the ashtrays and emptying the coffeepot before you've had your last cup somewhat exasperating.

If you marry him, you'd better like his family. He's very proud of Mom and Dad, and you can expect to be seeing quite a lot of them.

He will expect you to be a good cook and housekeeper. He does most things by the clock. He likes to keep to routine.

As a young man, Capricorn can be a bit wild, but he settles down eventually to the serious business of living.

You will have to be patient with him. Though he probably has a greater store of knowledge than you, he'll be nowhere near as quick or bright.

When kids come along, you'll have to keep them under control. He won't like to have his life pattern altered by the patter of tiny feet around the house.

LIBRA WOMAN—AQUARIUS MAN

You Libra women are supposed to be good at coping with people from all walks of life. You'll certainly be tested if you ever get involved with Aquarius. You'll find this man has an extraordinary range of friends—from genius to downright insane.

You could say that the Water Bearer is a collector of characters. It is likely you will be attracted to his mind before you get around to discovering you actually desire him physically.

He is a good talker and is capable of communicating his ideas to others. The more you are in his company, the more you'll find yourself falling under his spell.

Chances are you will know him for quite a while before you have your first serious date. This man seems to attract crowds of camp followers. If you get serious, you could become irritated that you have so little time alone with him.

He's friendly and as easy to read as a nursery rhyme. He's terribly enthusiastic and easily becomes involved with causes. He is dedicated to doing away with out-of-date rules and traditions and bringing in a new era. Well, you're not against progress yourself so this could be something firm to start with.

Very often you will find him at the head of a protest march. Though this may not be exactly your scene, you'll enjoy cheering him and some of his mad friends on from the sidelines.

He will certainly be a challenge to you. You will learn a great deal from him. You are both seekers of truth. You might wish to do your exploring together.

He will never try to impose rules on you. He's a wanderer and a freedom lover. You might want a more settled home life than he is capable of providing.

Mr. Aquarius doesn't like to be alone too much. Other people spark him off.

He can be a bit of an eccentric. You will never know what to expect next. He's not romantic. In fact, he has an ironic streak. He does not care whether or not he is popular. He stands by his principles and his ideals come hell or high water.

It matters not one jot to him if he doesn't win popular support. He'll keep on plugging away, convinced that one day people will see his point of view. People born under this third air Sign are determined to put the world to rights.

Success frequently comes to this man without his striving for it. He is often exceptionally talented. You both have inner reserves. You will each respect the private area in the other that remains taboo.

He will want to be your friend before he becomes your lover. He's not the type of man to get involved in a hit-and-run affair. Family ties are not terribly important to him. He won't be interested in talking about his life as a child. It is unlikely he is particularly close to his parents.

Even you may find the challenge of trying to keep pace with him too much. When he's away from you, it will be difficult to keep tabs on him. You will have to accept the fact that he will come home when he feels like it. Don't worry—he's unlikely to be with another woman; he's the faithful type of guy.

He won't mind your odd extravagance; if the money is coming in, he'll be quite happy to see you buy the things you want.

He's a sucker for kids. Once he has children, you could well be seeing a great deal more of him.

LIBRA WOMAN—PISCES MAN

You will have your time fully occupied running a home and looking after a Pisces man. He's adorable, but quite a dreamer. You'll have to be the one who does most of the organizing. His mental processes don't work as fast as yours; still, it would be unwise to underestimate him. You may find him difficult to get through to.

It might also come as something of a surprise that he can be an extremely astute businessman. He may not be much use around the house, but rarely does anyone put one over on him where money is concerned.

He has the wonderful habit of getting other people to do things for him. It is only when they have finished that they come around to asking themselves why.

He is extremely sensitive. You may sometimes get the feeling he can read your mind. He will change with your moods. He's kind and sympathetic. He will always try to do his best for you.

He has a vivid imagination, which strongly influences his actions. He's a kindly man and will bend over backward to assist anyone who is genuinely in trouble.

He's a romantic. He knows how to treat a woman. You will love an evening out with Mr. Pisces.

He does not possess a lot of aggression. He can be overly sensitive about his own feelings. This is because he is terrified of being hurt. Don't be brusque with him. This will only send him into a fit of depression.

It might be hard for you to forget all about your own career—which you would find difficult to continue if you become involved with a Pisces man. He would be extremely jealous of your outside interests. He might get even worse if you were to become more successful than he.

He won't expect you to be the greatest cook in the world. He accepts people for what they are.

He can be a little secretive. Attempts to probe into his past life are likely to be met by stony silence—unless he wants to recite some ancient personal history (which he frequently does). Be careful about hurting his feelings. He would be terribly upset if you had an affair with another person.

You will be amazed at his patience with people. He doesn't mind what time of the day or night they contact him if they need to pour out their innermost feelings.

The positive Pisces type very often gets to the top of his profession. He is a successful businessman who is quick to recognize a good opportunity when one presents itself.

He's not too handy about the home. When it comes to putting up shelves and fixing a broken windowpane, he's all thumbs.

It is true you will both have to work hard at the union. Whereas he needs mothering, you like a man who can make the decisions and show the way ahead.

When he gets the blues, you will have to try to lift his spirits. Don't let him sit around moping. When you can see him getting despondent, suggest an evening out. He loves treats. He's like a little boy when he goes somewhere special.

He's not too strong on disciplining children, but he makes a fabulous father. He will enjoy playing with the train set his son gets for Christmas just as much as junior.

LIBRA MAN—ARIES WOMAN

You should get along very well from the start with Miss Aries. You will like her aggressiveness and positive up-and-at-'em attitude. She's a great fighter.

There are quite a few things you have in common. Foremost is the difficulty you both experience in trying to settle down in any sort of permanent relationship. She's terribly ambitious and so are you. But you may find she lacks subtlety. She does have a tendency to say the wrong thing at the wrong time, and this could be a source of embarrassment to an intuitive and diplomatic man like you.

The Aries woman is proud. She can't take criticism. An I-told-you-so approach will send her into a raging fury. And, oh boy, has she got a temper.

A deep involvement may present certain problems. You like to avoid head-on collisions if possible, and an attacking Aries lady could make you something of a neurotic.

You will admire many qualities in the lady Ram. She will do her best to get to the top in her chosen profession. Her attitude to her work could inspire you to push a little harder yourself—which wouldn't do you any harm. You don't like the idea of working simply for the sake of earning your daily crust.

An Aries woman likes to be treated tenderly and with respect. You will have no problem here. She will love your quiet ways and charming manners. Handle her gently and she'll be yours.

Miss Aries knows what she wants out of life, and what is more, she usually has a pretty shrewd idea about the best way to go about getting it. She likes a good time and you'll enjoy going out on the town with her. She'll love the way you arrange things. She'll be crazy about the bistros you frequent and the movies, art galleries and other entertainments you take her to.

Being a great freedom lover yourself, you would not dream of trying to mold this girl into something she is not. Which is just as well, since she can't stand people who are unable to accept her for exactly what she is.

In lovemaking, she is giving if she feels her partner is worthy of her affection. Once she is crazy about a man, there's nothing she would not do for him. She wants a guy she can be proud of. As lovers, you will be well suited. The lady Ram has a lively imagination where sex is concerned.

If you decide you can't live without each other, it might be a good idea to encourage her to continue with her career for quite a while after marriage. This woman would get very frustrated if left to stew at home while you are out and about all day. An Aries female does not particularly enjoy living in the reflected glory of her man for very long however much she digs him. It will be very good for the relationship if she has an outside interest.

She has plenty of pep and drive and should be able to keep up with the pretty fast pace you set yourself. She's good at entertaining and enjoys laying out a spread for her friends.

If you have picked the cultivated Aries woman, you will find she has marvelous taste in decorating. You will love the way she organizes your home life together.

She makes a good mother. Although not an individual to be tied down by responsibility, she is extremely fond of children and will give them plenty of attention and training so she can be proud of them.

LIBRA MAN—TAURUS WOMAN

You do like a woman who sparkles and bubbles. You also are attracted to a girl with a sense of humor. Miss Taurus may be a little bit too down-to-earth and steady for your liking. She's quite a handful and can be very moody.

You are something of a dreamer. At times, you live in a fantasy world. This woman is very realistic. Of course, if you can overcome your differences, you could be very good for each other. Undoubtedly you would both learn a great deal from this liaison.

But one warning: you won't win Miss Taurus with your famous Libra charm alone. People born under this Sign rarely allow themselves to get carried away by false notions or emotions.

If you do strike it lucky with her, you won't be disappointed. Taurus people can't stand the idea of failure, so she'll work extremely hard to make the marriage a success.

She's an absolutely sensational lover. Like you, her ruling planet is Venus. She is very passionate and rarely has any hangups about sex.

As a Libra, you find it difficult not to flirt and this could land you in hot water because the lady Bull is fiercely possessive. She has a smoldering, jealous nature and will show her indignation in no uncertain manner if she catches you playing footsie with another.

Miss Taurus will stick by her man through thick and thin. She'll be quite prepared to go through hard times.

This woman can be a bit bossy, which could make difficulties for you both. You hate to be told what to do even if it is for your own good. You can't stand to feel hemmed in. You are also something of a loner. You will just have to accept the fact that several nights of the week will have to be spent at home.

Never try to force her to do anything against her will. Let her plod along as she likes. It's no good your trying to coax her. She has to do things at her own pace and in her own time, even if she does seem rather too methodical to you.

Your home will be something to be proud of. It will be a pleasure to invite your friends over. She is also good in the kitchen and the dishes she serves will reflect her artistic touch.

It might be a good idea for her to have some control over the family finances. She's not mean but she may have a better idea of the value of money than you. You'll find her extremely capable at sticking to a budget. She'll have no difficulty in putting cash aside to pay regular bills.

Don't give her reason to doubt your sincerity. This woman will never forgive you if you hurt her or let her down, especially if she has put a lot of trust in you.

You are both fairly artistic types and your likes and dislikes in art and literature will be pretty much the same. She loves to be surrounded by pretty things. Her taste in decor is likely to be very feminine.

The Taurus woman delights in looking after her man. She will spoil you like mad. When you get home from work, everything will be just right for you. She'll pour you a drink and run your bath. You'll feel relaxed and comfortable. She may not understand what makes you tick, but she'll always try to please you.

This lady knows all about children. She'll be strict with her kids but will always give them a cuddle when they need it and instill in them an appreciation of family life.

LIBRA MAN—GEMINI WOMAN

In Gemini, you might well find the intellectual compatibility you are looking for in a woman. This relationship will either be paradise or a total disaster.

You two are alike in many ways. The girl born under the Sign of the Twins should know what you are striving for. She will share many of your aims. The trouble is you could be *too* much alike.

Together, you will never be at a loss for something to say. You'll find you have the same sense of humor. You both tend to see the funny side of rather tragic situations. Neither of you is short on irony.

You will also share many of the same political beliefs. You are both great freedom lovers and hate to be tied down. The crucial question here is will you both want to do your own thing and go off in different directions?

The Mercurial female has a sparkling personality. You are likely to hit it off from the word go. You will also be attracted by her grace, not to mention her subtle seductivity.

Like you, a Gemini woman can't resist flirting now and again. You both find it enjoyable to play games with the opposite sex, but this may cause problems if either one of you is left out in the cold. So long as you don't take each other's little fun too seriously, all will be well.

Romance with this woman could be very passionate. You are both imaginative about sex. Making love is unlikely to lose its thrill.

Allow your Gemini woman her outside interests because without them, she will get very low. It is no good for the Twins to live through a man. She will soon get bored if she's cast in the role of the little housewife.

You will make an attractive couple. You are

likely to be drawn to the same sort of friends. You both like a party—especially the music and the dancing. Much of your time is apt to be spent away from the domestic environment.

Miss Gemini is a great talker. You may occasionally adopt a point of view you don't really believe in just to have a good discussion. She has a very agile mind, so as smart as you are, you're likely to discover she's your match.

You'll have no trouble getting on with this woman even if you're not emotionally involved with each other. On a platonic basis, this liaison would work extremely well.

You are both pretty hard to live with when you get down in the dumps. It is important to do your best to lift your partner's spirits when she hits a low. And if you can control those moody Libra silences, it will be a great help.

You are probably better at handling money than she is—though not all that much better. She's *very* extravagant. If she has a few extra bucks, she'll try to think of ways to blow them. Putting them into a savings account would never enter her pretty little head.

Miss Gemini is not the greatest cook in the world, but you'll probably both want to eat out a lot anyway. She's okay at knocking together a tasty light meal, but doesn't have the patience to spend hours preparing exotic dishes.

She loves people. She needs contact with others to keep her going. She has no difficulty in getting on with characters from all walks of life. Rich or poor makes no difference to her.

She's very fond of children but can be short-tempered if they don't do as she says at once.

LIBRA MAN—CANCER WOMAN

You had better be prepared for anything if you fall in love with a Cancer woman. You are pretty good at accepting change, but even you will have difficulty keeping up with the Crab's different moods.

Miss Cancer could easily drive you crazy. Water is her element, and like the faucets in the bathroom sink, she's either hot or cold.

At one moment, this lady will be telling you you're the only man she could ever be happy with. The next evening, when you phone to confirm a dinner date, she could well inform you she's mad about a guy she's just met at work.

Don't let us be unfair to this wonderful warm-natured girl. She is not out to hurt you. It's just that in matters of love, people born under her Sign find it very hard to control their emotions.

You will have to spend a good deal of time encouraging her and coaxing her to come out of her shell. Keep the compliments flowing thick and fast. She needs to be told what a living doll she is at least a dozen times a day.

And watch that sense of humor of yours. Miss Cancer can't take jokes about her, even if they are meant in a lighthearted way. She takes herself terribly seriously. Don't ridicule her family or her close friends, either. She's the type who needs to be handled with kid gloves. She's never far from tears during an emotional conflict.

In financial matters, you may not see eye to eye because this woman is probably more responsible than you are when it comes to saving and thinking of the future. When she observes your spending habits, she'll feel you are much too extravagant. Security means a great deal to her. She is terrified of the idea of running into debt.

This woman yearns for a dominating man—which is not a role that comes easily to you. You believe people should be allowed to make up their own minds. If you fall for her, you could find yourself becoming more aggressive and at times acting totally out of character.

If you do manage to get it together with this Moon child, you'll never regret it. If she returns your "I love you," you'll know she means it. She will make a devoted wife. She'll do all she can to help you get to the top in your career and she will love your success.

When this woman meets Mr. Right, she is prepared to give up everything for him. Even a successful career of her own won't count against the delight of being with her man. She will make your home comfortable. And she's a wonderfully inventive cook.

You must be sure to get her out of the house occasionally. Renowned as a great lover of domestic bliss, a Cancer woman can stay in too much for her own good. Be certain she meets your friends and takes an interest in your work; otherwise your interests will grow apart.

You will have to learn to cope with her moods. You are an understanding man and will be sympathetic if she needs a shoulder to cry on.

She is very caught up with family life, and not just the one she shares with you. Her mom and dad are terribly important to her. Let's hope you get on with your mother-in-law because you're likely to be seeing quite a lot of her after marriage. And you must accept the fact that she'll be ringing up Mother for advice even when she's a middle-aged woman herself.

Don't let this woman bury her emotions away in that tough shell she uses for protection. Make sure she shares her secret hopes and fears with you. The worst thing that could happen would be for you to become strangers living under the same roof.

LIBRA MAN—LEO WOMAN

A Leo woman won't be dominated. She is perfectly capable of taking care of herself. She can't stand a man who puts pressure on her. Since this is something you are unlikely to attempt, you could well hit it off splendidly.

Leo women make wonderful partners. You'll have to fight hard to win her, though, because she's no pushover. And she's sure to have quite a number of other admirers. The Lioness is a no-nonsense type. She wants her man to be straightforward. She won't be taken in by charming manners. She can see through anyone who is putting on an act in order to impress her.

A born leader, she doesn't like to be told what to do. If you do get spliced, you can be sure she'll retain her independence. No matter how much she cares for you, she'll insist on keeping up with her own interests and friends.

The Leo girl often has more than her fair share of good looks and glamor. Very often the tomboy type, she's apt to look as attractive in jeans and T-shirt as she is all dolled up to go out on the town.

Many women are envious of her. They admire her originality and willingness to stand up for her rights. Often she has more drive and sheer sex appeal than two or three women put together.

If she does agree to become your woman, you will feel really proud. Don't beat around the bush if you're serious. Lay your cards on the table and woo her full force.

Count yourself lucky if she accepts you. It will be a wonderful confidence booster for a man like you, who really does appreciate an attractive woman.

She is pretty talented, so it would be stupid to try to tie her to the home; she has too much to offer for that alone. She never stops learning. Her zest for life is absolutely fantastic. She will never have any trouble keeping herself occupied. More likely than not, her big problem will be finding enough hours in the day in which to cram all that she wants to do.

From your career point of view, she'll fit the bill perfectly. Your boss will be bowled over by this woman. If you are entertaining influential people, she could be the one who helps to clinch that lucrative contract you've been angling for.

She loves furs, jewelry and all pretty things. She's not extravagant, but does like to have a closetful of clothes. She likes to look her best at all times. It is extremely rare to find a Leo woman who has not made an effort to look smart.

Don't, whatever you do, step out of line. She may seem ultrafeminine, but she has one hell of a temper if she finds her man's been taking her for a ride. She is capable of anything then. You'll be surprised at the sudden change in her if she finds you've been cheating. What you can do, this girl can do a lot better—and it will hurt like hell into the bargain!

Neither of you is all that interested in acquiring great wealth. So long as you are earning enough to keep you both living in the manner to which you are accustomed, all will be well.

She makes a fine mother. She will always be practical with her kids. You're rather easygoing and have a way with children that will make them want to bring their friends home. You'll both enjoy this. Together, you make a pretty good parent combination. Although a pal to her children, she'll know exactly when they need strict handling and she won't hesitate.

LIBRA MAN—VIRGO WOMAN

It can take a little time to get through to a Virgo woman. She's not going to be an easy one for you to conquer. However, the more you try to understand her, the more fascinating she will become. Even when you think you've got her number, she'll suddenly act in a way that takes you completely by surprise.

She is a perfectionist. She's always striving for improvement. She'll be looking for special qualities in her man, too. This woman will want you to be the dominant force in the relationship. She can't respect a man she doesn't look up to.

Your ways may appear rather strange to her. She's very dependable and sincere. Your sudden mood changes could throw her off balance.

She's capable of being secretive. Virgo people keep their emotions under control. She will only confide in you when she feels she can trust you completely. She has a fear of being hurt or let down.

You may have to spruce yourself up a bit. This woman likes a man who is tidy in appearance and around the home. She's keen on hygiene. She's also very efficient and will probably want to acquire the latest household gadgets to streamline her work.

Miss Virgo can be a bit of a prude. She does not enjoy blue humor. Keep your near-to-the-knuckle gags for the boys at the office. But don't get the impression she is lacking in humor. There is a quick mind here.

If you really love her and are prepared to meet her halfway, you could have a very happy life together. But sometimes when you get home after a date with her, you may wonder if she is worth all the trouble. You may feel her standards are just too demanding. However, after a few days, you'll probably be running back for more. It's likely that the mysterious side of her nature will intrigue you.

She will be very good for you in so many ways. She will give you that kick you occasionally need to get into action.

Miss Virgo is not that passionate. Her lovemaking isn't fiery. It takes a while to arouse her. Being a patient and considerate lover, you could help this woman overcome her inhibitions in bed. It will be up to you to show her that sex is something to be enjoyed.

She's extremely loyal. She will take her marriage vows very seriously. She won't be able to accept your flirting ways. Don't make eyes at another girl when you are out on a date with your Virgo lass or she's likely to walk out on you.

She's straightforward and honest. She will throw herself body and soul into your marriage. She will be prepared to work hard to bring in extra cash if it's needed.

Don't try to fool her because she can't stand hypocrisy. She'd rather hear the truth, even if it hurts, than discover later that you have made a fool of her.

Miss Virgo can't take criticism so be very careful how you take her to task if you feel she is in the wrong.

She is very good with money. She knows how to budget and will save on the grocery bill. If you're the sort of Libra man who has difficulty saving, hand over the family finances to your Virgo wife. You'll be amazed at how quickly your reserves build up.

Your home will be run smoothly. She'll make sure you're well clothed, well fed and provided for in every way. If you are prepared to become more of a creature of habit and to meet this woman halfway, the future looks very bright for both of you.

LIBRA MAN—LIBRA WOMAN

There will be great understanding between the two of you. In many cases, when a Sign pairs up with its opposite-sex counterpart, disaster is in the offing. This is not true in the case of a Libra linkup.

This is the type of woman you will hit it off with on first meeting. You'll get on like a house afire. The rapport between you will be such that you'll probably have an uncanny feeling you have met somewhere before.

Miss Libra has a fabulous sense of humor and so do you. Humor is, of course, terribly important in any close relationship. You both have a lively and positive interest in life. Here is a girl with an inquiring mind just like yours.

With her, you will always come first. Be sure you return the compliment. It's immensely important to a Libra woman to be needed and loved by her husband.

She'll be wonderul when you have problems. Ask this woman for advice and she is likely to come up with a very balanced opinion.

You will be happy to leave all the decisions concerning the smooth running of the home to her. She's marvelously domesticated. She is also capable of combining the many duties of housewife with a career without allowing either to suffer. She will probably want to continue with her job after marriage. She has a lot to offer and it would be stupid to tie her down permanently to household drudgeries.

Miss Libra is all woman and it's unlikely you will be able to resist her. She will sweep you off your feet with her open, charming smile. She's diplomatic, too. She will be invaluable when you have to entertain important people at home. She knows how to create a relaxed atmosphere.

If she accepts you as her man, you are indeed fortunate. The physical side of marriage should be highly successful. You will be highly passionate lovers.

It is improbable that you will have any secrets from each other. She's the sort of woman you'll wish to share your deepest thoughts with. She would never set herself up as judge. Her main concern will be that you make the right decisions for yourself.

She will want you to be successful in your work and will do everything in her power to ensure that you get to the top. Venus girls like to have plenty of money around. Success is important to this woman.

Like you, she enjoys going out and meeting

people. She has a vivid imagination and needs mental stimulation.

You will have great times together at parties. You both like to keep on the go most of the time. She will never pry into your affairs, and she'll never betray a confidence. Your secrets will always be safe with her.

You will enjoy your evenings alone together. Romance is terribly important to both of you. Many an evening will be spent cuddled up in front of the fire together. It's quite likely she'll have had many boyfriends before you came along, but then, being a Libra yourself, you probably haven't led a monastic existence.

Like you, she's pretty sentimental. Friendship and family life mean a great deal to her. She's very loyal to those she loves and will stand by them through thick and thin. She is a strong person, perfectly capable of protecting herself and standing on her own two feet if she has to. Don't take her for granted and always treat her with respect.

You will never come second to the kids. She knows how to combine the dual role of wife and mother to perfection.

LIBRA MAN—SCORPIO WOMAN

The Scorpio woman is very passionate. Actually, that's an understatement. She *is* passion. She could be a bit too much for easygoing old you, who are appalled by big scenes, emotional outbursts and a constant atmosphere of tension.

You are likely to be physically drawn to her from the start because she's both sensual and sexual. Still, you probably won't choose to spend the rest of your life with her.

She is a mass of contradictions. She blows hot and cold. She tries to be honest to herself and will never do anything against her will or contrary to her principles. When her temper flares, you'd better duck. She's capable of resorting to physical violence if aroused. But when she's in a good mood, you could not find a more sweet-tempered or wiser woman.

Living with a Scorpio woman won't be smooth sailing. You'll never know what to expect next. When she's down in the dumps, it's almost impossible to communicate with her. Her black moods are very hard for any man to take and make yours look like a party atmosphere. It's hopeless trying to reason with her when she's in this frame of mind.

Miss Scorpio hates to be embarrassed in front of other people. She won't want to wash her dirty linen in public. To her, home is the place to bring out your differences. Scorpios like to keep their private lives very private.

She's the secretive type. There is a private area that she just won't allow anyone to be party to. Even if you do decide to live together or marry, there are likely to be a few skeletons in her closet you will never hear about.

This woman is a home-loving type. Oh yes, she'll love to go abroad for her vacations or in connection with her work, but she does need the security of knowing there's a comfortable base to come back to. She enjoys a party, too; you'll adore going out together. She's good at talking (in fact, she likes to gossip). You will find her very understanding. A Scorpio woman is sensitive and will make you feel like confiding in her.

She's the jealous type. And how! She's also capable of bearing a grudge. If you hurt her, she won't forget it. She'll bide her time and will be prepared to wait years to avenge herself. She's has an Old Testament eye-for-an-eye-and-tooth-for-a-tooth attitude.

It's unlikely she's an ultrafeminine type. She's all woman, but she doesn't go in for coyness. She's capable of looking after herself and sticking up for her rights. Many men find her too powerful and frightening a personality to take on.

If in spite of all the pitfalls you do decide to make a go of it with a Scorpio woman, you'd better remain faithful. She's capable of almost any action if you two-time her.

She's likely to think your attitude to money is rather silly. She's capable of being extravagant, but in a different way than you are. Most of her cash is apt to go on clothes. She'll spend a fortune on an expensive and impractical blouse when the only shoes she possesses have a hole in them.

If she doesn't settle down with a guy early in her life, this woman will find it increasingly hard to accept a permanent relationship.

She can be a little overpowering for youngsters. She's terribly protective of them.

LIBRA MAN—SAGITTARIUS WOMAN

A more even-tempered and sweet-natured girl you are unlikely to find. Like you, Miss Sagittarius is a great freedom lover and can't stand feeling hemmed in or tied down. You should get on terribly well together.

There aren't many people who don't hit it off with this woman. She's the sporty type. She's a fierce competitor who doesn't like to be bettered in anything she undertakes. She's a great fighter and will always stand up for people's rights.

One wonders if there would be enough drama in your life together to sustain you both over a long period. In many ways, you may find it hard to make a go of it. You could be a bit too much for her to take. She's not exactly domestic, but your wandering ways are unlikely to appeal to her.

She's hard-working and tries to make a success of anything she takes on. If she gives her word, you can bet your bottom dollar she'll do everything in her power to fulfill the obligation. She's not as mysterious as some people believe. She may withhold the truth, but she's unlikely to lie to you.

You will appreciate her good intentions, although at times you'll become exasperated at the way she puts her foot in things. You will have to be very patient with her. She has a habit of phrasing her observations in an awkward way. She's capable of making people feel very uncomfortable when she wants to.

She speaks her mind. She takes as she finds. It's not that she wishes to hurt other people's feelings. It's simply that she doesn't have a clue to the art of diplomacy. She's very impatient and expects things to happen almost to order.

Miss Sagittarius is lots of fun. You will never get bored in her company. She's very easygoing and will fall in with most of the plans you make for pleasure and entertainment.

She won't try to boss you around. She'll take the attitude that you're old enough to make up your own mind. You may even get the feeling that she's indifferent to you on occasions. This is not the case.

Don't try to change her. This woman hates to be criticized or told how she should conduct herself. The secret is never *tell* a Jupiter woman what to do—*ask* her. Don't show her up in front of others, either. She can't bear to be made to look foolish in company.

Don't ever take her for granted. She will not easily forgive you if you betray her. Give her any reason to doubt you and she'll never have quite the same respect for you again.

On the whole, you will find her kind and sympathetic. She's prepared to admit it when she's in the wrong—in fact, she sometimes blames herself for things that are not her fault.

She loves her home, but since you are likely to be more artistic than she is, it could turn out that you will be responsible for most of the decorating and furniture arranging.

She will leave it to you to handle your career as you see fit. She wouldn't dream of prying into your business affairs.

She dislikes confrontations. A Sagittarius woman will do all she can to avoid ugly scenes.

She's positive and will always try to look on the bright side of things. She won't be extravagant with your money, although she's not the greatest at sticking to a budget.

As a mother, she is devoted and will make almost any sacrifice for her children.

LIBRA MAN— CAPRICORN WOMAN

You'd better be dead set on getting to the top in your chosen career if you're out to catch Miss Capricorn because this woman is attracted to people who wield power. She likes to be involved with a man she can look up to and admire.

She's rather difficult to define in many ways. You could never call her cruel or heartless because although she is a bit of a social climber, she will do all she can to help a friend who is down on his or her luck. The simple fact is that she likes security and is terrified of becoming deeply involved with a man who does not guarantee to provide it for her.

She's terribly inquisitive. She wants to know what drives other people on.

Although she's interested in getting to the top, she would never resort to dirty tricks to get what she wants. She's extremely fair-minded and has a strong sense of justice.

She may try to change your ways once she has come to know you well. It isn't that she wants to exert power over you; it's simply that she will feel she knows what's best for her man. And it's quite possible that in your case she does. You're a bit slow to move. Very often you will find a Capricorn woman behind a successful man.

If she is smitten by the love bug, this girl will do anything for you. She comes on very strong, possibly too strong for a Libra man. The attention she lavishes on you may be suffocating.

She's an all-or-nothing woman. She will not abide your having other women if she's your steady. You don't like being cross-examined, but you'll have to get used to that sort of treatment from Miss Capricorn. She'll want a complete rundown on your activities whenever you're away from her.

She's able to get along with people from all walks of life. She's also great at entertaining, the kind of hostess who knows how to mix guests to make an interesting dinner or cocktail party.

She'll probably be able to give you some useful advice when it comes to business. There is a shrewd commercial mind here. She will make sure you don't miss any surefire opportunities.

This is not the right woman if you're looking for a lighthearted affair because she refuses to get involved with a man unless the commitment is total. Don't say you love her unless you really mean it. She will believe anything you say and it would hurt her deeply if you were to play with her emotions.

She will probably want to maintain some sort of career after marriage, at least until she settles into domestic routine. She loves her home but would hate to feel she's lost contact with the mainstream of life.

She can get really low at times. It is very difficult to shake a Capricorn woman out of the doldrums.

She's pretty abandoned in bed. As with everything else in life, she's curious about sex. Your lovemaking will be like an adventure. It will be important to her to satisfy you.

She's very involved with family life. You will find she's devoted to her parents. Family ties run deep with her. No mother-in-law jokes, please.

She will lavish attention on her children. It is important to a Capricorn woman to do all the right things as a mother.

LIBRA MAN—AQUARIUS WOMAN

You're through with dullness if this woman is your choice. Of all of the types of the Zodiac, you could be one of the few able to keep up with the pace she sets.

This could be quite a combination, a genuinely pleasant surprise for both of you. The Water Bearer and the Scales have much in common, although she's probably more determined than you once her mind is made up.

Anyway, she's likely to be the most open-minded and tolerant woman you have ever had the good fortune to meet. She can't stand injustice or prejudice. You'll always find her on the side of the underdog (a stand you like to take yourself).

She doesn't like to tie herself down to a set schedule. Routine work appalls her. You will rarely find this woman sticking very long to a job where she doesn't have the freedom to make use of her vivid and unusual imagination.

Miss Aquarius will always give her opinion honestly and frankly without trying to dictate to people. She may not always agree with you, but she'll respect your right to express your ideas. You're sure to have some very interesting and lively discussions.

This woman is extremely independent by nature. If you do get spliced, you will have to allow her more freedom than most other women.

Marriage is a very big step for her. She may fight shy of it for a long time. She'll want to be darned sure of what she's getting into. She likes to look after herself. She's self-reliant and will never be a drag on you.

The line between friendship and true love is not something this woman finds it easy to distinguish. She's the sort of woman you can remain the best of friends with even after the romance is over. She's adult enough to believe that two people can remain close once the sexual attraction has faded.

She may have problems accepting you as you are. She likes to know where she stands with people, and you're not always the best at conveying this sort of information convincingly.

Very often the Aquarius woman can be rather confused about her personal relationships. She can't stand being tied down and doesn't like to feel she belongs to anyone. She will not accept the notion that a woman's place is in the home.

She will be prepared to put her children into boarding school if she feels they are holding her back from fulfilling other aspects of her life.

The qualities she will be looking for in a man are kindness and a deep feeling for humanity. He must also be a guy who is true to himself and refuses to sell out on his principles.

She's not a jealous person, but then, neither are you. You will never understand her completely. Just when you think you've got her number, she'll do something that will take you back.

Miss Aquarius will always be on hand to help others. No matter what the time, day or night, she'll put herself at the disposal of a friend in distress.

She is not the most passionate of women so you should be prepared to do most of the chasing.

She's likely to be faithful. There will be plenty of outside interests for her to get involved in without complicating her life with an adulterous love affair.

She knows the value of a greenback and is more careful with money than you might imagine. You will both enjoy going out together. You make a witty twosome and should be very much in demand.

LIBRA MAN—PISCES WOMAN

Miss Pisces is the pinup of many men. More nights' sleep have probably been lost by men thinking about this girl than any other.

She's certainly a mystery—but what a delightful one. She will fascinate you and drive you a little crazy with her sudden changes of mood.

She's all woman, soft and cuddlesome, and will bring out your protective urge. She's the sort of girl you will really want to work hard for so you can provide her with the very best in life.

You are never likely to be bored in her company. Your business associates and friends are apt to be envious and will constantly remind you what a lucky guy you are.

Your Pisces woman will allow you to set the pace and be the dominant one in the relationship so long as you are bringing home the bacon. Should she feel you are not trying as hard as you could to get on, she'll let you know in no uncertain terms.

You will find her a wonderful confidence booster who will make you feel you can take on almost any challenge. She'll be quick to recognize your talents and will make sure you exploit them to the best possible advantage.

Let no one say anything rude about you behind your back in her presence. She's terribly loyal and will stand up for you against anyone. She's a very sensitive creature and finds it hard to take criticism herself.

Your Pisces woman is apt to change her mind in a flash. Some men find this difficult to live with, but you, a Libra, should have no trouble coping. You will learn to accept her as she is at that moment and not try to put labels on her.

She will delight in looking after you. She'll know how to help you forget about work problems when you arrive home weary after a hard day's grind.

She loves entertaining. As a rule, she takes great pride in her home. It gives her much pleasure to cook and do things for other people, and she does it all so effortlessly and delightfully. Although you have excellent taste, you can safely leave the decorating to her. She's very artistic and you'll love the way she gets your home together.

She doesn't have a great head for business matters, although one or two of her ideas may be worth listening to.

A Pisces woman needs to be treated gently. She is a lady and you would be wise never to forget this.

Always remember "special" days like birthdays and anniversaries; they are likely to mean a great deal to her. She loves to be spoiled and a box of chocolates or a dozen red roses will show how much you love and admire her.

She is understanding and helpful to people who are not doing very well. She knows all about loneliness and shyness and will do her best to make others feel more comfortable and relaxed in her presence.

Of course, she has her faults. She's very touchy, and you will have to watch what you say to her all the time. A word of criticism and she's likely to burst into tears—or strike back with a surprisingly barbed retort.

She can be a bit extravagant with money, especially in buying clothes and fancy baubles.

The Pisces woman makes a good mother. She will bring up her children well without spoiling them too much. She will want them to be able to fend for themselves. She relies on love and wisdom. But you'll have to do most of the disciplining—not something you enjoy.

LIBRA'S HEALTH

Libra men and women usually enjoy fairly good health, though you are not as robust as you seem. Therefore, you know you must conserve your vitality by not unduly exerting yourself. It is this self-knowledge that has given you the rather unfair nickname "Lazy Libra." Your attractive physical features, cheerfulness and generally pleasant manner give you a sleekly well-kept look. Many of you have an olive complexion, which contributes to the smoothness of your appearance. Actually, your constitution is very delicately balanced and easily upset by minor ailments and psychological conflict.

As a typical Libra, you should never allow even a slight complaint to go unattended. It is unwise for you to expose yourself unnecessarily to contagious illnesses. This includes the usual children's complaints such as chicken pox. You are more susceptible than most to whatever is "going around." But, on the other hand, you respond very quickly to treatment. An illness that might keep another person in bed for a week may only incapacitate you for a couple of days.

The most vulnerable parts of your body are the kidneys and the spinal column. There are very few Libras (especially mothers) who have not suffered some disability in these regions. Kidney complaints, "slipped discs," lumbago and the like should never be ignored.

When you do feel ill, everyone in the household knows about it. It's not that you're a crybaby, but you do enjoy being looked after and waited on. When you have to take to your bed, you won't moan about your illness as long as you're receiving plenty of attention. You require lots of visitors, news of what your friends are doing and loads of get-well cards, flowers and presents (especially Miss Libra). The trimmings of convalescence actually appeal to you, whereas other more physically active types, such as your opposite, Aries, pound the bed in a fury to be allowed to get up.

You are also prone to headaches, migraine and perhaps eye trouble. It is not uncommon for Libras to bump, bruise and cut themselves in mishaps around the house. You may also suffer from rheumatic pains in the knees and stomach ailments. These latter may be vaguely persistent and not so easy to diagnose.

The health rule for Libras is *moderation* in all things. Fortunately, although often excellent cooks and gourmets, they seldom overeat or drink too much; if they do they usually can't keep it down.

You are especially prone to colds, chills and influenza. With an attack of flu, the aftereffects may linger for weeks. Coughs can last through the winter, especially in children. Recurring attacks should be referred to a doctor; immunization may provide the chance to build up greater resistance.

Proper physical relaxation is extremely important to people born under your Sign. You should always aim at cultivating a balance, between the aesthetic side of your nature and the sensuous. A way to do this is to take up an activity that gives expression to your sense of rhythm. It will also satisfy your love of harmonious and graceful movement. Yoga and swimming might appeal to you; so might ice skating. But strenuous physical exercise and vigorous competitive sports are likely to induce tension and irritation in all but the very young Libra.

Whatever way you choose to relax, see that you get some of your like-minded buddies to join in because you need company and laughter.

Rest is the greatest cure of all for you (assuming the medical problem has been referred to the experts). Your recuperative powers, once you allow your body to flop onto a bed, are amazing. It is here that you can be at peace with the world for a while and at the same time quickly and quietly regain your health.

Never forget that despite your gregarious nature and love of companionship, you need periods of seclusion to sort yourself out.

Libra people can't stand too much psychological conflict. You have a natural revulsion for excessive noise, disharmonious surroundings, vulgarity, coarseness—just about every antisocial vibration. Your instinct is to run away from these things, and if that is impossible, to go off into an idealistic dream world while physically coming to a stop. An unhappy Libra can achieve very little.

Libra is also acutely self-critical at the subconscious level. At times, you will plunge into deep depressions which, on occasions, drain you so completely that you have to go to bed.

LIBRA AT WORK

The prospect of becoming well off is not sufficient incentive for the typical Libra to stick to an occupation. You have to delight in what you do. Young Libras are sometimes misguided by well-meaning elders who push them into safe or well-paying jobs that their peculiarly refined temperament is completely unsuited to.

There is a tremendous range of jobs in which you may excel. There are just as many that you should never contemplate. If you are unhappy in your present employment, chances are you are in one of the latter.

First, you should understand that you are the sensitive, artistic type. This doesn't mean you are a born painter, the instinct is more generalized than that. You can work happily in the business world so long as the goods or services you handle or provide are aesthetically desirable. Nevertheless, you will seldom be content in a commercial jungle where progress depends on cutthroat competition. Nor is it likely you'd enjoy working on the floor of an abattoir. But you could very easily excel as an importer or exporter of fine arts and crafts. Here your flair for friendly low-key salesmanship could be employed. The point is you must have faith in what you are selling and not just in your own ability to sell. Whatever you do, you like to take pride in; you aim to give all concerned satisfaction and a fair deal. The last thing you want to endure are complaints and bickering. If you are a typical Libra, you couldn't stand a job as a debt collector, for example. High pressure and ugly scenes are totally alien to your character.

Since yours is the Sign governing partnership, you do, of course, make a splendid partner. You are marvelous at working with others and help bring out the best in them. You are not so suited for the solo role. Oh, you can make a success of it, but you will never quite attain the same sense of fulfillment. Your life will also be more worrisome; your work, then, even if lucrative and important, could get you down. Ideally, you need someone to share your burdens with. You are a little too lacking in self-confidence and drive to work on your own. When things get rough, you have a tendency to walk away and think about something else; you don't like to battle with life's problems.

A successful partnership is likely in any field requiring a feeling for beauty. (It is, of course, important to select a compatible associate; you'd be wise to check the person's character in the appropriate book in this series.) Partnerships or work connected with interior decoration, furs, jewelry, hairdressing, clothing design, display, color coordination, millinery or high fashion should appeal. Many Libras have an affinity for flowers and plants and sometimes turn related hobbies into a full-time livelihood.

People born under your Sign also make competent teachers, especially of the arts. They are naturals as sculptors, painters and writers. You have a highly developed intellect and a lofty frame of mine. You are very concerned with humanistic problems and are frequently drawn to social work. You possess talent for bringing people together in peace and harmony. Libras are especially effective as marriage or guidance counselors. Even though your own marital affairs may be far from placid, you are gifted at putting your finger on the differences between others and helping to eliminate them. You are not inclined to tell anyone what to do; you operate by suggestion and persuasion. It is rare for the people you advise to take offense.

You are particularly well suited for a career in the diplomatic service, or even in the armed forces in a post where cooperation and coordination are as important as fighting. You are not so much a combatant as a negotiator, a mediator and a combining force. Certainly you are capable of making a point with fire and aggression, but violent emotions in you are very short-lived. Your style is to be courteous, polished and charming. You may be attracted to the clergy. You can also make a name for yourself in politics, but usually require the stimulus of dedication to a specific cause. Sordid, hypocritical party politics, with all the attendant in-fighting and bitterness, appalls you. In this field, either you are a leader or you avoid it like the plague.

Law is a natural profession for you. You would excel as a judge or a lawyer. Your analytical mind, with its strong sense of justice and objectivity, also fits you for a responsible position in law enforcement. You may enjoy work as a stenographer or assistant to someone in authority in these fields.

You have an excellent ear for music and a superb sense of rhythm. Given the right opportunities, you could be a dancer or a musician.

You also possess the ability to deal with figures. If this is pronounced, you may be able to make a career in accounting. It is also possible your mind has a scientific bias, in which case you may be drawn to physics or mathematics.

Whatever career you choose, you must guard against becoming disheartened or discouraged in the early stages. Persistence in the face of hardship and recurring obstacles is not your strongest point. Whenever you are in doubt, you would be wise to discuss your problem with someone you respect and trust. Remember, you need to feel you *belong*. Never try to go it alone and then wonder why you are unhappy. You must keep in the mainstream of life. It is also essential that you respond to your urge to move out of any rut you may have fallen into. Be firm when people try to cling to you after you know it's time to move on. Associates and co-workers must understand that you need to circulate to stay mentally alive. Don't allow shyness to prevent you from stepping boldly forward when you know this is what you must do.

As a boss, you have a most flattering habit of consulting your workers. You listen to their opinions with interest and attention. They adore you for it and do all they can to see you get the right information. This suits you fine because it is extremely important to you to marshal all the facts when making a decision. You dislike acting on impressions alone (your own included) because you know how notoriously unreliable they very often are.

You become extremely restless where there's a big decision to be made. Although you do not cause a commotion, everyone in the office will know something is happening. You are likely to disappear from behind your desk without a word and take a walk in the park, or wander through the building chatting amiably with the heads of other departments, who don't suspect you're sounding them out on what they'd do in a similar situation. You're smooth, you're cautious, you dislike foulups. You want to cover every angle.

When you do reach a decision, it's usually a gem of wisdom and straight thinking. Nothing is overlooked, every objection is answered. Still, sometimes by hesitating so long to find the perfect solution, you miss the boat. Other times, when you perceive the possibility of a snafu, you cover yourself right down the line so that if anything does go wrong, you can't be blamed.

You are often an inspired thinker. Whether or not you are a boss, you can't help but stand out at an office conference. You have a brilliant way of solving problems off the top of your head. But you are not so good in disharmonious company or surroundings. Your temperament is remarkably sensitive to your immediate environment. If something or someone is grating on you, you become snappy, difficult or moody. You may not even know the cause consciously. You owe it to yourself to let someone else handle clients who behave crudely or tell dirty stories in front of women because they will put you off every time.

As an employee, you are all that superiors could ask for—so long as they understand that every now and again you're going to have one of your lazy-hazy turns. When this happens, you won't get much done at all; you'll wander around in a sort of daze and the work you produce will be pretty sloppy (if you're a typical Libra). These "down days" are caused either by two things: one, uncongenial co-workers and sordid or depressing conditions; two, periodic exhaustion of your vital energy.

You must not work too hard. Don't allow yourself to get carried away with enthusiasm when you don't possess the matching physical stamina. Moderation is the golden rule for you. Your mind is likely to drive you beyond your physical capacities.

If you keep your thinking positive, work moderately and don't settle for the wrong job, you will be one of the most valued employees on the payroll. And your boss will love the way you help keep the peace in the office when rival personalities start clashing.

If you were born between September 23 and September 30, you are particularly artistic and possess a fine sense of proportion. You should not settle for a routine job; this would be a waste of genuine talent. Try to find satisfaction through self-expression. You have a well-balanced mind capable of grasping the larger issues of law, such as constitutional matters. You can see both sides of an argument very clearly. The public should figure in your most successful endeavors. Your career is likely to benefit through marriage. A decision to enter a business partnership may be the turning point in your fortunes. Try to avoid overconfidence. Your popularity may tempt you to try to succeed by wit and charm alone rather than by solid performance. You may experience a difficult period until you learn, through coping with necessity, where your real strength lies.

Be prepared to take orders if you eventually want to give them.

If you were born between October 1 and October 11, your occupation is likely to be concerned with teaching, medicine or art. You are interested in occult or philosophical subjects. Older people are apt to influence your choice of career. You may make a successful marriage late in life, or with an older person, that leads to a commercial venture. Don't make important moves on appearances. The job you succeed best in will probably involve difficulties and delays to begin with; persistence will tip the scales your way.

If you were born between October 12 and 22, you are a farsighted Libra who will probably do best in an occupation where originality is rewarded. You should be successful in any job requiring you to travel, especially to other countries. Aviation in all its aspects may offer opportunities. You need intellectual challenge in your work; mundane routine would drive you mad. You could be involved in the design and invention of machines. Too much display of your independence may ruin your chances. Be prepared to walk before you try to run. Train your mind along definite lines.

There is a mystical side to your nature that allows you to see the deeper significance of things. You may embrace some esoteric teaching that will give you greater understanding of yourself. Keep meeting new people; don't get stuck with the same old circle of friends.

Money

You are one of the big spenders of the Zodiac. Still, you are not money hungry. You are, in fact, a very generous person and will share whatever you buy with your friends. You love to entertain and to spend on your home and wardrobe. You are an extravagant present giver. When in love, you shower your mate with gifts; cash is no object. Whenever you have it, you spend it.

You are lucky with money. It comes to you sometimes without your having to earn it. You often marry into wealth or inherit it.

Although you can stick to a family budget admirably when money is scarce, you are pretty hopeless at saving or making economies in good times. If you do put a little aside, you're likely to spend it all on the impulsive purchase of one luxury item. You never bemoan what you've spent. Your attitude toward money is wonderfully philosophic, though it can be exasperating to those you live with.

You are both conservative and adventurous by nature, and are often tempted to back long shots that don't come off. You are too shrewd for others to impose on you if you don't wish them to.

SCORPIO'S CHARACTER

There's no point in beating around the bush—Scorpio is the Sign of *sex* in its pure, elemental form. Not *sexual appetite;* it is far more potent and meaningful than that. Scorpio men and women are human volcanoes of intense primal energy. The burning question for them throughout their lives is which way to release it—creatively or destructively?

The temptation to go to extremes is enormous here. No other Sign gives the individual such an awesome capability for good or evil. Perhaps that's why Scorpio is the only one of the twelve Signs with *three* astrological symbols—the Eagle, the Serpent and the Scorpion. Like the Eagle, Scorpios can soar to exalted heights of service to mankind; they can be as wise as the Serpent (and extremely successful) in worldly affairs; or they can be as devilish in their methods and motives as the poisoned-tailed Scorpion.

It is usually the scorpionic and sexual side of this mysterious and fascinating Sign that achieves notoriety. This is naturally irritating to the very intelligent and reflective October-November-born people who—perhaps like yourself—represent the typical Scorpio character.

To ascertain just how pure a type you are, it is essential to take into account all the planetary aspects and positions given for your birthday in this book. Particularly note the beneficial and uplifting influences. (These are clearly set out in the colored tables and described in the adjacent text.) Because the natural Scorpio urge is to go to one extreme or the other (more so than any other Sign), these other modifications are terribly important in making a correct AstroAnalysis.

The key to the Scorpio character is an insatiable desire to get at the truth. This urge can become distorted and badly corrupted, but it is present in every true Scorpio. In the underdeveloped type, the impulse becomes a search for self-satisfaction. Then there are no limits to the depths that may be plumbed. At any level of development, Scorpio is single-minded in whatever he or she undertakes. If it's sensual gratification, there will be no letup in the pursuit.

In the typical Scorpio person, the desire for the truth is recognizable in the way he or she is always endeavoring to get to the bottom of things. You Scorpios are the instinctive detectives of this world. You don't talk much (unless it is about a pet subject). You listen—at least until you have summed up the situation or the people you are with.

You can ask the most direct and embarrassing questions without blinking an eye. Your skill at handling and dealing with difficult and downright offensive people is incredible. You know just what to do, just what to say. You despise hypocrisy and affectation. Anyone with something to hide should avoid a confrontation with a Scorpio. Your intuition and understanding of human nature is phenomenal. You have a way of asking the right question at the worst possible time.

Although, you Scorpios are experts at unraveling the secrets in other people's lives, you manage to keep your own affairs very much to yourself. You relish secrecy. You revel in the cat-and-mouse game—you enjoy deliberately sparking the curiosity of others and then blocking their attempts to find out more. If anyone dares to try to pry into your affairs or take any liberties with your psyche, you get very haughty.

You are proud of your subtlety and skill at conducting intrigue. Nothing pleases you more than to prove your intellectual superiority in a contest of wits. You are not dependent on the acclaim of an audience, either; if your performance satisfies *you,* that is enough. In an extroverted world where ego satisfaction often depends on applause and admiration, you are a very difficult character to understand. You are proud but not egotistical, dramatic but not ostentatious. You are a little bit too self-sufficient and durable for mere mortals to empathize with. No one ever really gets to know you.

You rarely volunteer information of any kind. But when asked a question, you will give a straightforward answer. When you do share a confidence with another individual (it will be a minor matter as far as you are concerned), it will be because you want to encourage that person to talk. To you, life is a pretty serious business. You are always working toward some aim or patiently waiting for the next move. You may appear relaxed and amiable in company, but you are always the center of your own existence. This attitude has given Scorpio the reputation of being selfish, self-centered and more than usually calculating. That this is an accurate characterization no one knows better than you, but you are not necessarily immoral, as your critics try to make out. Rather, you are supremely self-aware. You are never little-boy or little-girl lost. You know exactly where you are. Other people may like to lose themselves, to forget the real world for a while and be comforted in silly and sentimental ways. Not you. You are no romantic when it comes to essentials. You can't bear to kid yourself. You want the truth, no matter how it hurts.

At first meeting, it is obvious that a typical Scorpio man or woman has something instinctively serious on his or her mind. It shows first in the eyes. The gaze is penetrating and compelling, uncommitted but very, very personal. There is a calmness to the face, a quiet intensity. In an instant, Scorpio seems to see all that matters in a person; something indefinable is communicated. The recipient of a Scorpio gaze usually feels immediate attraction or repulsion. Scorpios are such powerful personalities that their presence can often be felt in a room. They are certainly not the type that can ever be ignored.

If you are a typical Scorpio, you are intensely critical and skeptical. You can't help seeing faults and failings in others. Unfortunately, you are not so talented at perceiving your own. You have a stinging tongue when you want to use it; no other Sign is a match for your biting sarcasm. You are very fixed in your ideas and absolutely convinced they are correct. It's true, you are often right. Your golden rule is not to accept anything unless you've proved it to your own satisfaction. You listen to what others have to say but you don't readily believe them. In you, there's always a degree of reserve and doubt, which sometimes comes across as suspicion or distrust. Frequently you are just plain disdainful and contemptuous when others try to convince or impress you. In your search for what counts, you have learned to accept facts only. You are wary of opinions and impressions. Experience has taught you that others are easily conned, that they are far too willing to accept without question. You know better. You check everything out. You're pretty sure of yourself. And it shows in your bluntness, which can be quite brutal on occasions. You can't stand fools.

One drawback to your pragmatic self-certainty is that you may fail to move with the times—that is, you are inclined to stick to your views permanently. You won't listen to the advice of others, no matter how overwhelming their experience. Over the years, you become inflexible; with power or authority, a law to yourself—this year's H-bomb in last year's container. Too often you make the same mistakes over and over again. You don't mind a bit of pain and suffering to gain your ends, but what you're likely to overlook is that things don't have to be done the same way all the time!

As long as you are not opposed and don't have an axe to grind, you are a very likable person. You are helpful and courteous. You have good taste, a civilized outlook and an innate appreciation of the artistic and cultural side of life. People can overlook your rather caustic remarks because what you say usually contains the truth. The fact that people don't always like to hear the truth about themselves doesn't prevent them from admiring your straight-from-the-shoulder style. Of course, you make enemies, more than most. You are so darned independent and outspoken. When you've got the bit in your teeth, you don't give a damn about what others think. You won't compromise or pull your punches. You stand by what you say because if it weren't true, you wouldn't have said it. You'll never back down on a matter of principle. No authority can hope to compel you against your will more than temporarily. Eventually you will win out because you will continue to scheme and undermine long after everyone else has got tired of the fight and wants to call it a day. In some ways, you are as invincible as you are implacable. Victory sometimes comes to you by default. No one else cares enough. Times change. You don't.

There was a Scorpio woman with an adult son and two younger daughters. She was an excellent mother and a widow. It was common knowledge that if anything ever happened to her, the bulk of her sizable estate would go to her son. She took ill. Her son made the mistake of mentioning in passing that he'd lost two thousand dollars in business over the weeks through visiting his mother. She died a couple of years later.

In the will, she left the son two thousand dollars only, with no explanation. She'd changed her will in favor of her daughters the day after he made his remark.

You are the sort of person whose unconquerable nature can inspire others. Weaker characters gain strength from your example. Some who unwisely try to match your physical endurance collapse with exhaustion. When your mind is made up, you seem to be able to go on forever. Nothing daunts you, no added burden is too great; you personify indomitability. Yet, paradoxically, you can be quite lazy; you can sit back and seem to take it easy for very long periods. You won't exert yourself for anything or anyone that doesn't interest you. You'll only go through the necessary motions and spend your time in introspection. Too much self-study can have odd effects on a Scorpio. One is you may lose all interest in life and will your own death. The volcano must express itself or explode.

Sometimes you will take someone who has a problem under your wing. You are generous and patient when your sympathy is aroused, a steadfast and staunch friend. You *never* go back on your word. You seldom make promises of your own volition, but when you do, you keep them. You help bring out the best in others.

Your most outstanding quality is your persistence and determination to reach your goals. It is characteristic of you Scorpio people to fix your objectives years ahead and to tenaciously work toward them irrespective of the difficulties. You have a one-track mind. You don't go around obstacles or try to remove them; you confront them and destroy them. Anything in your path gets flattened, no matter how long it takes.

This is not such an easy Sign for a woman to be born under. It is too dominant, masterful and unyielding for the female element to cope with comfortably. The Scorpio woman has to learn to pull her punches in her close relationships. She can seldom be herself with a man and get away with it for very long, even in these liberated days. She is very good for any male she links up with, though. Even if the association doesn't last, he will be a far wiser man when it's over. She will teach him much about himself.

If you look at a diagram of the Zodiac, you'll notice that Scorpio, the eighth Sign, is exactly opposite Taurus, the second Sign. This has a particular significance for you. You and Taurus have one thing in common—you are both intensely possessive. But there is this difference: Taurus loves to possess objects and money (this is because the first six Signs are concerned mainly with personal activities and in building up the individual ego), while you love to possess people (yours is among the last six Signs, which are more concerned with activities entered into with others). You direct your feelings toward people. You are jealous and react violently to the feelings they cause in you and which you share. Although you enjoy creature comforts, you are not a materialistic person. What you gather are feelings, and you hold to them with even more emotional zeal than Taurus clings to his gold and belongings. Scorpio is a water Sign, which means it is unfathomable and charged with high-pitched unstable emotionality. Taurus is a solid, phlegmatic earth Sign. Your energy is like an arresting shriek, Taurus' a bear hug. It's the same primal urge expressed by opposite temperaments.

You are bold, self-willed and love adventure. Your courage in the face of danger is magnificent. You are an excellent leader, a born strategist, an astute tactician. In an emergency, you are cool, calm, decisive. You think and act simultaneously. Your powers of observation are acute. You are practical and shrewd. Your mind works more constructively under moment-to-moment pressure than when you are making decisions based on your strong likes and dislikes. Here, your capacity to hate and detest can take over and become a cold fury of absurd prejudice. In this mood, Scorpio may sink the ship and go down with it just to destroy the engineer.

Your self-control is tremendous. If ever you go off the rails in any way, it's because you wish to, not because you've lost your restraint. The exception is when your emotions are suddenly inflamed and you lash out or act on impulse. In these brief moments, you can do a terrible lot of damage to your own life and to other people's. Once you lose your cool, your judgment is either hopelessly impaired or completely subjugated by your passion. Fortunately, this happens rarely. Most of the time you maintain a facade of well-regulated control. Though inside you are usually in turmoil (not because of any doubts or uncertainty, but because of the sheer intensity of your feelings), no one would guess.

In weaker Scorpio types, this self-repression, instead of galvanizing the individual into productive effort, creates a smoldering resentment. Normal healthy expression becomes impossible. Vehement passions are generated, helped by a brooding imagination. An emotional venom reminiscent of the Scorpion's paralyzing poison builds up. No Sign is as relentlessly vindictive, cruel or sadistic as Scorpio raw and unregenerate. These characters never forget an injury, even an imagined one. Whereas others may be content to forget a wrong once the person who committed it is out of their life, unregenerate Scorpios will wait years for the moment of retaliation. These individuals are quite capable of engineering complex conspiracies to bring about another's downfall. Their power to harm is concealed in subtlety. They can be friendly and helpful while plotting mercilessly. Here, emotion contorts the Scorpio search for truth into the craving for retribution—the vendetta is a truly Scorpio iniquity if ever there was one.

There is much nobility in your character if only it can be released. No other Sign can love with the grandeur of the Scorpio individual who has managed to open the floodgates of his or her heart. You have the capacity for total devotion to a cause or a person. Scorpio men and women make the most inspired mystics. Their spiritual fervor and insights into higher truths can raise the consciousness and faith of others. If they can overcome the peculiar possessiveness of their affections, learn to forgive and release those who have hurt them, they can fervently love all of humanity. If not, their repressive nature makes them unconsciously despise mankind.

At heart, you are altruistic. You wish to heal your fellow man, to remove his doubts and uncertainties, to give him wings to fly like the eagle above the earth's limitations. For this reason, your type is often among the world's finest psychiatrists and surgeons. You are naturally adapted to probe or cut to remove the mental hangups and physical causes that prevent men and women from being what they are or ought to be. But before Scorpio can overcome the ills of the world, it must first conquer itself. This is indeed the Sign of the phoenix that rises transformed from its own ashes.

You have a fineness of taste that is evident in your home. You are rather traditional. As a rule, you prefer older and more elegant furniture to modern contemporary styles. You like your home to be a place apart from the world and its problems. You enjoy entertaining, but very selectively. You do not appreciate people who casually drop in uninvited. You rather enjoy formality. You are a sophisticated host or hostess, but enjoy letting your hair down in the right company as the evening progresses. You are likely to drink or smoke too much.

The Scorpio man is not likely to be numbered among the ten best-dressed males. In fact, he's rather lax in his sartorial habits. Unless he's got a girlfriend or wife who cares, he's apt to forget to have his trousers pressed. He's the type who gives his shoes a quick rub on the back of his socks. He's convinced that people are more concerned with what's inside the package than with the wrapping.

Lady Scorpio is inclined to be a bit old-fashioned in her choice of clothes. That is, she'll wear the latest gear in her youth, but when that's over, she'll tend to stick to the same styles. What she wears may suit her perfectly, but how can a woman look really smart in picture hats and corsages? Modern Ms. Scorpio is likely to wear the most masculine jeans and other old gear and still manage to look sexier than any female at the party. She knows instinctively that she doesn't have to try to look good to attract men. She knows about the bees and the honeypot. Some Scorpio women have a funny habit of buying their clothes piecemeal. They don't have the knack for coordinating a look. In a moment of impulse, they may invest in a smashing outfit, and then wear last season's scruffy old shoes with it. They are very good with colors but a bit square on image.

For pastimes, you Scorpio people like activities where you can use your body or put your intuition to practical use. Your tremendous energy and stamina, plus your natural ability to think and act at the same time, makes you extremely proficient at active, competitive sports. Given a choice, you usually prefer water sports. Both men and women like to keep in good shape. Remarkably enough, you often look older than your years in youth and younger in middle age.

The powerful libidinal energies of the Scorpio person are often very successfully released in artistic pursuits. You are very progressive in these fields. It is likely that you are quite ingenious in adapting existing art forms to your own ideas. You are inclined to pull down the established order and replace it with a different version of itself. You introduce depth and greater meaning; whether it's in art, poetry or literature, your work suggests a new dimension. When you get involved in art, it is not just a pleasing aesthetic experience; it's a labor of love into which you pour your energies with passionate intensity. To many of you, it is a therapeutic necessity. There is no such thing as a half-hearted Scorpio in any of the arts.

If you are a typical Scorpio person, you have a deep-seated interest in the occult. You may try to deny it, especially in your brasher younger years, but eventually it will intrigue you because all that is mysterious and unsolved fascinates you. You dream of discovering the secrets of life beyond the rational; you look for the keys to life contained in the esoteric disciplines and pseudosciences. You may not be a psychic investigator or clairvoyant, but you sense the reality of the spiritual and psi worlds. You are intrigued by discussions on magic, witchcraft and primitive cults. Astrology means more to you than you would probably ever admit. You know and feel things that make you realize your perception reaches beyond the senses. It won't surprise you to learn that Scorpio is the Sign associated with flying saucers, a mystery yet to be solved.

Sometimes Scorpio men and women are considered a bit morbid. Others can't understand your interest in questions concerning life and death, which often amounts to preoccupation. This is not surprising. Scorpio, as well as being the Sign of sex, is the Sign of death and regeneration. You Scorpios are not the least afraid of death as a physical ending. You are concerned with it as a *psychological* mystery that constantly taunts you to find the solution within yourself. The reason you don't fear death is that instinctively you know it is only a concept. You seek to demolish it, to release its hold on your psyche, with the same intensity with which you attack everything else. Similarly, your strong sexual feelings are nothing more than the primal urge to penetrate to the roots, to be at one with something, to identify with your source (whatever that may be) in a final ecstatic forgetfulness. If this sounds a bit flaky to you, you are not a true Scorpio. Only a true Scorpio can understand the weird profundity of his or her feelings.

As lovers, Scorpio men and women are superb. Your responses to the various Signs are discussed in detail in the chapter "Scorpio in Love." Briefly, Scorpio people are built to probe the mystery of sex. At this stage of human evolution, this irrepressible energy is expressed mainly in physical ways; as a result, Scorpio individuals are highly sensual. You are sexually magnetic, you give deep satisfaction, but your chances of forming a happy permanent relationship are not too good. Sexual fulfillment with your partner may be wonderful, but the psychological side of a relationship may prove difficult.

Scorpios are demanding, domineering and fiercely jealous mates. You often find it hard to resist a secret love affair. Despite your better judgment, you often yield to the impulse of passion and mystery, even if you are happily married. You may not, but it's always a lusty possibility, more so than with any other Sign. Few Scorpios seem to escape tragedy or disaster in their love life. Those who can sublimate their intense erotic desires in artistic or productive ways and free their imagination of constant erotic images have a chance at making a reasonably happy marriage. It depends substantially on compatibility, so it would be advisable for you to check out your mate in the appropriate book of this series.

An interesting astrological tradition exists concerning the Sign of Scorpio, which some authorities maintain is the most important of the twelve. Way back in the forgotten past, before the Age of Atlantis, there were only ten Signs in the Zodiac. Virgo and Scorpio were one; Libra didn't exist.

At this time, apparently, there was only the human spirit—a kind of unisex entity—comprising both the masculine and the feminine principles. The immortals in their wisdom split the then sixth Sign (Virgo-Scorpio) in two by inserting Libra (the balancing Sign) in between. Virgo, of course, is the Sign of the Virgin and represents Eve. Scorpio, of course, is Adam and represents the pure sex drive. It's clearly no accident that Libra, which now stands between them, is the Sign of partnership and marriage.

According to the ancient esoteric teaching, we human spirits for a few billion years have been living out our incarnations not as whole beings (Adamandeve!) but as our male and female halves. We must learn how to be reunited in spirit. By seeking union only through the physical body, we're apparently getting nowhere fast and binding ourselves to the earth. Love alone (through the true partnership principle epitomized by Libra) is the link and the way.

Now back to you, Scorpio. You have a highly developed intellect and a sharp, resourceful mind. Subjects you are interested in you learn very quickly. Your unquenchable desire to dominate often induces you to take on a job or duty that others would avoid. You want power, sometimes at any price. Your memory is excellent. You make a point of being well informed on the topics you discuss and the projects you undertake. You absorb facts easily and pay close attention to the details of a proposition.

You are a thorough and systematic thinker though sometimes narrow in your approach. Your preconceived ideas are both your strength and your weakness. You never go off half-cocked, but are sometimes inclined to delay matters. Your gift for visualization reveals defects in plans and possible problems long before they are evident to others. Your imagination sometimes gets out of control and you daydream about your love life. But as a rule, you keep your thinking straight and very down to earth.

One overriding fault is that you separate your life into various compartments, meaning you don't think in an integrated way. You can have two opposing feelings about one subject because you concentrate on *aspects* and not the total picture. This is one reason why you are so dogmatic. You don't admit grays to your vision, just blacks and whites, likes and dislikes. You can't weigh one fact *against* another; instead you sift and isolate facts and consider them individually, in succession. You are very quick, though, to discern what is relevant. What you want, you pursue; what you don't want, you shun; what opposes you, you demolish. Consideration is a compartment called the self: you are self-made and self-existing. This is a simple code for living at either the highest or the lowest level of human aspiration.

Sometimes you appear to be a very stubborn person, like your opposite Sign Taurus, which is renowned for obstinacy. But your obstinacy has a different root: you are just very hard to influence. Anyone who thinks he can win you over to an idea by the hard sell, or even the soft sell, will be sorely disappointed. You fortify yourself against outside influence by learning everything about a subject you are interested in. In your opinion, there's only one way to do something you're involved in, and that's your way!

Despite your calm and composed manner, you have difficulty keeping still for long. Your nervous energy often makes you an inveterate doodler, leg swinger or finger tapper.

You are one of these admirable people who don't think that life owes them a living. In fact, you don't expect much from other people, especially in the way of favors and handouts. You don't resent life's adversities because you're determined to make the best of things even in the worst of circumstances. This trait is particularly evident in the Scorpio woman. When hard times hit, she is quite prepared to share economic and other responsibilities with her mate. And she won't complain if she's got to go without things in order to bring up her children properly.

Is there such a creature as a lonely Scorpio person? Indeed there is. Loneliness usually arises from early rejection by a mother or father (or both), or later parental figures. The rejection grows into resentment of *all* others. A love-hate complex can develop regarding the opposite sex. Even amid intense physical intimacy, Scorpio can be joyless, loveless and lonely. However, true Scorpio courage can enable such people to face up to their deeper resentments and fears. Then they can rid themselves of their constricting and repelling emotionalism and discover the joy and fulfillment of loving from the heart.

SCORPIO IN LOVE

YOUR SCORPIO MAN

You like him? Love him? What sort of person is Mr. Scorpio?

Deep. Dominant. Passionate. Demanding. All male. But not always an easy man to get along with in a permanent relationship, unless *he* feels contented. He'll never be mastered or changed, so if you're a persistently dominated type of woman, or if you have hopes of reforming him after marriage, forget it. Your life together could be hell.

This guy has a subtle yet distinctive magnetism. When you meet him for the first time, he'll either turn you on or make you want to run a mile. The trouble is, even when you're running from him, you may want to look back. He's interesting. Arresting. When he makes an approach, you're either for him or against him. You can't ignore him. The vibes this man sends out are heavily sexual. You *have* to respond.

You'd better understand right from the start that there are two Scorpio men. In no other Sign are the differences between the evolved and the immature type so important to the woman who is thinking of marriage or a long-term affair. The undeveloped type can be a bully and a brute. He will use his suave Scorpio manner and sharp intellect to impress a woman, but his ulterior motives are sex or domination. This guy wants power over people. Men are quick to shun him, but his powerful physical appeal and disarming surface charm gull many women. He's not an easy man to get away from. He can be unscrupulous, violent, jealous, vindictive, cruel and revengeful. At the first sign that he's a baddie, you had better start running.

The good Scorpio guy, although a powerful personality, manages to direct his energies into productive channels. Sex is extremely important to him but it doesn't occupy his entire life. Given the right woman, he will settle down. In fact, this man can make a good husband. He loves his home and will do everything in his power to give the right woman all she desires. Mind you, he will always remain a law unto himself—that is, he will cooperate, but only so far. He insists on making all the major decisions. Once he sets his mind on an objective, he will never give up; *no one* will dissuade him. But he is sincere and honest. He can't stand duplicity. You must be open with him.

If you marry a Scorpio man, you may be lonely at times. He doesn't make many friends, and those he has have to be intelligent and able to discourse on the subjects that interest him.

He's a wonderful businessman. You should have some opportunities to play hostess when he invites clients home to help him swing a deal, but unless there's a good practical reason, he likes to keep his business and private life as separate as possible. His home is his haven. He expects his woman to be there always. He doesn't like surprise parties and similar lighthearted instrusions. He's very possessive, suspicious and jealous. He won't tolerate infidelity. He will never forgive the woman who betrays him. Once she puts her foot out the door to meet another man, she'd better keep going.

If you love this man, he'll give you the feeling you need never fear anything again. So self-sufficient is he that he seems capable of standing alone against any odds. His determination makes him almost invincible. *Almost.* His emotions are his weakness. He is impulsive where they are concerned. He has a fearful temper. When aroused, he is likely to do anything. When in love, he will throw caution to the wind and consider nothing more important than reaching his love mate.

He often makes the same mistakes in romance over and over again. His passionate nature seems to drive him on regardless of the consequences. When he finds himself in romantic competition, he can endure tremendous aggravation for long periods while working patiently at undermining the opposition.

Mr. Scorpio is not a flirt. He has two things on his mind: sex and finding the right mate. He won't confuse you. If you are all he's looking for in a woman, there's no reason why life together with this strange and often brilliant man should not work out—if he is the evolved type. Just be sure you AstroAnalyze the other influences working in his horoscope because you can't afford to make a mistake here.

YOUR SCORPIO WOMAN

You like her? Love her? What sort of woman is this person?

If Miss Scorpio wants to have an affair with you, she'll let you know. She'll sum you up as a male the instant she meets you; she'll know your weaknesses and your strengths. This woman is deeper, sexier and more realistic than any other woman you'll ever meet. And she has a voracious sexual and emotional appetite; boys had better not apply.

The Scorpio lady is a very puzzling combination of contradictions and extremes. She is highly intelligent and intensely physical. She loves to be complimented and appreciated, but resents flattery. She doesn't like to be criticized, but can dish it out bluntly to others. She has the cultured type of mind that appreciates the civilized and educated side of things. She's not arty, yet she understands art. She loves mysteries, especially the occult.

Miss Scorpio will attract you as soon as she enters the room. She has a reserved, aloof poise. Her look of interest is a deep penetrating gaze that reaches down into the depths of your being. You'll sense she's seeing things that even you don't know are there. She is. One of her unique armaments is her ability to divine a man's soul.

No male will ever put one over on her unless she is bemused by her emotions. Then she's a hopeless case of surrender to her own self-indulgent desires. Otherwise she keeps control of any romantic situation. She is quite capable of having affair after affair without her feelings being the least bit involved. Her body and its desires are one thing. Her emotional self is another. She keeps them in two separate compartments. If they ever get mixed up, it's dynamite.

A Scorpio woman is very direct. If she's married and needs an affair because her husband can't satisfy her passions, she'll tell you it's only your body she wants. Take it or leave it. She won't want her home life disturbed in any way. And she won't want you falling in love with her and making trouble. It's quite an experience to meet such an extraordinary woman.

If you marry her and are true, your Scorpio lady will also be loyal. But you will have to be intensely virile to satisfy her sexual needs. She will go to no end of trouble to make the home comfortable and attractive; she is very talented at selecting furnishings. She will adore her children, but she won't put them before you. She's rather old-fashioned in her domestic ideas and will endeavor to do everything correctly and in the best of taste.

She's jealous. And she's dangerous. Don't try to kid her along. If you cross her, she'll be on your doorstep at midnight letting all the neighbors know just what a so-and-so you are. Or she'll call the office and tell your boss a couple of secrets you've confided to her. Or she might just flatten you with a saucepan. Anything to hurt, anything to get even. This is a volcano of a woman you're thinking about.

She doesn't give a hoot what other people think when she's made up her mind to do something. She's courageous. Her ideas are fixed. She either loves, hates or is indifferent to something, and that's that. She's not the type to have many girlfriends. She spends a lot of her time just assessing people.

She won't put you on a pedestal. She'll see you exactly as you are. She won't kid herself and she certainly won't allow you the luxury of self-delusion. In three words, this woman can deflate any pretentious male or female. She's not a gossip. She doesn't confide in others. She's a bit distrustful of everyone. She's learned that most people are fools because all fools are people. She doesn't give anyone the benefit of the doubt.

Miss Scorpio needs friction in her love relationships to keep them sufficiently alive and satisfying. This gives meaning she can feel. She adores an argument with her man, the stimulus of bared, ferocious passion.

For her lover, the making up afterward—because she is so sexually proficient and desirable in her uncharacteristic surrender—is not infrequently ecstatic. Great. But can you stand the emotional workup to it? That's a question you're going to have to answer.

SCORPIO WOMAN—ARIES MAN

If you are the type of Scorpio woman who needs friction to keep your close relationships alive, then link up with an Aries man. He likes to dominate and you can't stand to be told what to do—which is pretty good for openers, don't you agree?

You both know how to dish it out. On first meeting, the sparks are likely to fly. When it comes to verbal battles, you're both as hot as horseradish.

There are many things that will attract you to him, although you may not like to admit it even to yourself. He has an air of stability. You'll get the impression he would know what to do in a crisis. He seems very sure of himself without being aggressive.

People find you hard to fathom. You seem mysterious even to your close friends. The Ram will find you rather magnetic. You are the type of woman who appeals to him, even though he will instinctively know you are going to be quite a handful.

It is difficult to work out just how long you would last together. There would always be an underlying tension in the union.

Even though you may be deeply in love, you will want to test each other all the time. You will bring out the fighter in him and vice versa.

If an Aries man has set his sights on you, he will certainly battle to win your love. This is a quality you admire in a man because, deep down, you're a bit of a romantic and the idea of a dream prince willing to try to overcome all the obstacles between you is very appealing.

You have ambition, although it can be misdirected at times. It is possible for Scorpio people to channel their talents and energies into pointless and nonproductive projects. This is where the Ram could help you. If you would take good advice for once in your life, this man could put you on the right track.

You are both spontaneous and abandoned lovers. Physically you will have no problems. However hurtful your verbal battles may be on occasions, you should always be able to make it up in the bedroom—and how sweet it will be.

You could not call an Aries man subtle. You will realize after two or three dates with him that your basic attitudes toward life are very different. If you can learn to respect each other's opinions, you will have overcome the major stumbling block to permanent happiness.

You may get worried at his chopping and changing. You will think him crazy when he gives up a steady job to earn less money elsewhere. The fact is he feels he has to rise to new challenges to keep alive. He can't stand being trapped in a routine for very long.

He doesn't go for the out-of-date or antique. He loves the latest in everything. He's very gadget-conscious and is fascinated by labor-saving devices.

You may find a man born under the first Sign of the Zodiac too demanding. He will always be questioning you, and you can't stand constant cross-examinations. On his part, he will be confused by your occasional sullenness and changes of mood. He always tries to do the right thing, though, and this will endear him to you.

Even if he doesn't always manage it, he will try to understand you. Remember this, and you will find it much easier to forgive this likable boyish character for some of his tactlessness.

SCORPIO WOMAN—TAURUS MAN

Look at any picture of the Zodiac and you'll notice that your Sun Sign is opposite Taurus. You know all about the attraction of opposites, and this could well be what draws you two together. He is a real man. He's the sort of guy you can turn to when you've got a problem. You will always feel secure in his company.

One of the difficulties for a water baby like you in this Taurus-Scorpio linkup is that you can't stand to admit you need anyone's help. No matter what sort of situation you get yourself into, you like to sort it out unaided. This fighting attitude is all well and good, but it's not what love is all about. Occasionally we must put trust in people. We have to be willing to take a chance of getting hurt if we are going to become deeply involved in a relationship.

You should not be too doubtful about the Bull. If he gives his word, he will usually stick to it. He is not the games-playing type of man you are likely to meet elsewhere in the Zodiac.

You will infuriate each other, of course. His stubbornness will drive you mad. Your black moods will seem to him like adolescent tantrums.

You will always know where you stand with this man. He doesn't use a line in order to attract or impress a woman.

If he meets you at a party, or even approaches you while you're walking down the street (yes, he's aggressive enough to do that), he will come straight out with what is on his mind: sex. He might ask you around to his place for dinner or suggest you have a crazy weekend in Vegas. You might feel like slapping his face. But you will have to admire his honesty.

He will know how to wine and dine you. Although a very astute businessman, he is never tight with money where the opposite sex is concerned. He will take you to the best restaurants and make sure you have a wonderful time.

Girlfriends will warn you about him. They'll

say he's a womanizer and will break your heart if you give your love to him. Find out for yourself. It's true he has an eye for pretty girls, but basically that's because he's searching for someone to give him the roots and security that every Taurus man deeply needs.

It is amazing how quickly this man settles down when he finds what he wants. You will love the home he provides. He will not interfere with the way you manage domestic matters, either. He will be proud to bring people home to dinner.

Mr. Taurus is noted for his jealousy—a quality you also possess in abundance. If either of you were to fool around after settling down together, it's likely you'd split up pretty quickly.

Being an honest sort of woman, you might find it difficult to give this man the flattery that makes him purr. Perhaps if you love him enough, you'll find it in you to praise him, realizing that by boosting his confidence you will make it possible for him to achieve greater things.

You both love kids. As parents, you will find you basically agree on how children should be brought up. As a pair, you must beware of being too strict with your children.

SCORPIO WOMAN—GEMINI MAN

As friends, you would be a great pair. As business associates, you would be a fantastic combination. As lovers, you will have problems.

It's possible that when you first meet him you'll decide he's a guy you couldn't trust as far as you could throw him. But then you'll discover you are drawn to him against your better judgment. If he falls for you, you'll have great difficulty shaking him off your trail. Once Mr. Gemini really wants something, he usually gets it.

He can be very childlike. He's like the little boy tugging at Mommy's arm to get the bicycle he sees in the shop window. Even though Daddy can't afford it, he usually gets his way.

If you do eventually fall under his spell, beware because Mr. Gemini is a great user of people. He takes everything he can from them. He sucks them dry and then moves on to pastures new. Don't misunderstand. He doesn't do this purposely. He just doesn't understand what motivates him.

It is very difficult for this man to form a permanent relationship. When he goes cold on something, you won't see him for dust. He doesn't like to face up to responsibilities. He hates feeling trapped.

If he does something to hurt you, your suffering will be great. You might try every ploy in the book to get him to settle down. You might even end up feeling rather sorry for him because you will realize he is getting nowhere fast.

He tends to live for the moment. He doesn't relish the idea of making definitive decisions—decisions that would bind him to a positive course of action.

If he is in a group at a party, you can bet he will be the one doing all the talking. He will forget all about you, sitting in the corner waiting for some attention and affection.

He's one hell of a flirt. He will promise you undying love and mean it. This is what is so difficult about the Twins. You can't call him a liar, because you'll be able to see by the look in his eyes that he means the words he is saying, *when* he is saying them.

In sheer frustration, you may decide to give him up, not because you don't love him anymore, but because you'll realize he's not ever going to do you any good.

Is there any chance of your getting it together in marriage? Well, perhaps, if you meet this man when he has had a great deal of experience of life and realized he can't go on chasing rainbows forever. Then there is a possibility you'll find true happiness. There will still be differences, of course, because basically you are very different types.

He's generous. On a date, he will insist on paying for everything even if he can't afford it. His generosity can become downright foolish. You are much better at money management than he, and you're no Paul Getty!

Mr. Gemini loves going deeply into subjects, and so do you. Romance is necessary for him. For all his blunders and irresponsibility, you will have to treat him with gentleness and affection.

He won't take your moodiness all that seriously, which is probably a good thing. His sense of humor will help you to laugh at yourself.

He gets on terribly well with people younger than himself—probably because he has such a youthful attitude toward life.

SCORPIO WOMAN—CANCER MAN

You will have much in common with this man. Both of you were born under water Signs and you will have the same sort of rhythms and composure. You will understand his moods and will certainly have a good deal of sympathy for him when he gets down in the dumps.

One of your problems might be that you will have a negative effect on each other. Unless you surround yourself with positive constructive people, you tend to sink terribly low. It is exactly the same for Mr. Cancer.

You both tend to be dreamers. You could spend many evenings talking about what might have been . . . and if only. . . . All very interesting, but is it going to get you anywhere?

He tries to be steady. He desires security. Cancer always appears to end up making the most dreadful mistakes, though. The way he tells the story of his life you will get the impression that the whole world has ganged up against him to plan his downfall.

He needs affection and he needs looking after. He also needs a strong woman to give him a kick occasionally and tell him to get out and on with it.

You do need a masterful man. It is not an easy task to control a Scorpio lady. It would appear to be beyond the capabilities of most Cancer men.

He's a fussy Crab, especially when it comes to romance. He has to desire a woman strongly before he makes a play for her. He is unlikely to get involved in many casual affairs.

It is in the home that you will both function best. You will love having quiet evenings together. Mr. Cancer is highly domesticated. He will enjoy doing the cooking on occasions. You will be amazed at how capable he is in the kitchen. He won't mind your continuing with a career after marriage if that is what you desire. He will be quite capable of looking after the kids if he is left to cope alone.

You both enjoy entertaining, though you prefer to have a few well-chosen friends over than large gatherings.

This man often has a great deal of artistic talent within him. Many people born under this Sign have turned out to be famous writers or musicians.

You must try not to take each other too seriously. Always look on the bright side of things.

Be sure he invests his money wisely. He is careful with loot, perhaps too careful. He's likely to put his cash in extra-safe government bonds that pay low interest.

If you love him and are prepared to give as much as you take, this could be a happy and lasting relationship. He will rarely step out of line because he would hate to jeopardize his marriage for a passing fancy.

Mr. Cancer will see to it that you are always provided for. He will pay the bills on time even if he has to work all hours to do so.

He makes a wonderful and loving father. Perhaps he is better with girls than boys. But then, very often the Scorpio mother is better with boys than girls, so you should balance each other out as parents.

At times, you'll think he is overindulging the children—and he probably is. But he does have a fine way of nurturing youngsters through kindness and understanding so that they grow up with an appreciation of basic values. For instance, he's a great believer in courtesy and moral rectitude. He thinks these are the qualities that hold the family and society together.

SCORPIO WOMAN—LEO MAN

Much will depend on the picture you have built up of your dream man. With Mr. Leo it is important that you are searching for a leader—a man who will look after you, protect you, enlighten you and occasionally dominate you.

You must ask yourself a number of serious questions before you get deeply involved. If you are too wrapped up in yourself and your own opinions to change—even when you know deep down it is for the best—it would be wise to forget any further involvement.

He is a no-nonsense type and will not meekly submit to your moods or tantrums. One thing you can be sure of is that whatever admonishment he metes out will be with your best interests at heart. He will not be trying to satisfy his own ego.

He can be a bit of an actor. He loves to make a dramatic effect. Basically, he needs lots of loving and fussing. The King of the Jungle likes to have his mane ruffled and to be tickled under the chin. You will soon see through his posing and strutting and realize that he is basically a wonderfully soft and sensitive man.

He can be aggressive. His temper is just as frightening as yours when it is aroused. He's tenacious, too. If he decides you are his woman, he'll stalk you until you submit. When the Lion is in love, it is impossible to ignore him or pretend he isn't there.

Let us hope your ideal man is not the sort who will meekly submit to your will. This is doubtful since you don't admire weakness, even if you do put up a struggle before you submit to a stronger power.

Mr. Leo is a hard worker. He does not like to

remain idle for long. He's always coming up with new ideas. Let us hope your Leo man gets to the top in his career. People born under this Sign hate to take orders. They always feel their ideas are best. Very often they are proved right.

He can be a bit of a showoff. He is inclined to become egotistical when things are going his way. This is where you will come in. One or two tasty remarks from you will remind him that he is only human after all.

He's great to go out on the town with. When you are courting, he'll really give you the treatment. Leos have the knack of appearing to have money when they are actually low on funds. It's wonderful the way they can put on a show when they haven't got two cents to rub together.

Leo is very possessive. He will not like to let you out of his sight. He won't be too keen on your having an independent career once you are married if it's going to interfere with your domestic life.

It's terribly important to him to be the number-one interest in your life. He will want you to be waiting to throw your loving arms around him when he comes home from the office. He will enjoy telling you what a successful day he had.

The physical side of your relationship should be quite something. He's a passionate lover and you will know just how to excite and satisfy him.

Don't get too annoyed at his flirtations because they are unlikely to be serious. It's part of Mr. Leo's character to play up to the prettiest woman in the room.

He's very good with kids. He doesn't usually desire a large family, only the number he feels he can handle properly and teach. He's a great one for giving kids instruction in practical matters. He's both strict and indulgent, depending on how he feels at the time.

SCORPIO WOMAN—VIRGO MAN

You won't find it easy to get it together with a Virgo guy, though he will have many qualities you can't help but admire. He is serious, dedicated, a man of his word. He would never welsh on a promise. He is certainly honorable. It would appear, however, that he's a little too tame for a woman like you. You like some drama and excitement in your life.

He's terribly fussy and pedantic. He's also a stickler for hygiene. He can't stand dust on the windowsill or dirty dishes in the kitchen sink.

Having rather a mischievous streak, you will find it difficult not to tease poor old earth-bound Mr. Virgo. Don't ever underestimate him, though. Remember he is ruled by Mercury and therefore has a very quick mind.

He is a logical man. He believes that you *acquire* talent by hard work rather than being born with it. He admires people who strive to get to the top in their careers. He tends to write off people like pop stars as useless members of society.

He is devoted to the old-fashioned ways, the tried-and-true traditions. If you are looking for a level-headed man, a fellow with his feet planted firmly on the ground, then look no further.

He doesn't do anything on the spur of the moment. If you decide to get married, he won't go for your idea of rushing into it. Everything will have to be planned down to the last detail. The invitations must be printed, the wedding cake ordered. Everything must be just right.

He's a bit slow where love is concerned. When you start to date him, you may feel that first good-night kiss is never coming. He doesn't believe in rushing *anything*. He feels that love should grow slowly. He will want to get to know you really well before he commits himself. But his love is unselfish. He will want to do everything possible for you. He tends to put his woman on a pedestal.

You are the no-nonsense type so you may find his overly sedate ways rather irritating. He is quite mannered because he often finds it necessary to put on an act to conceal his basic insecurity. He will not allow many people to get close to him.

He will always face up to his responsibilities, even if he occasionally finds them distasteful. He is neither a shirker nor a quitter.

He is a good son to his parents. He is likely to have great respect for his father in particular and his elders in general.

His lovemaking may be a bit too tepid for you. You are much more physical than he is so you will have to have great patience with him in bed and teach him to let himself go. He can be a bit of a prude where sex is concerned.

If you are able to overcome your various problems together, you'll find you have a devoted and loving husband. Although you may feel many men are more exciting, you will find him more dependable than most. This is sort of relationship that will gain in strength over the years.

He loves his home comforts. He will be happy to do his fair share of the domestic chores. He will want you to pursue your own interests and have your own friends. He's neat in appearance and quite capable of looking after himself. Virgos are never sloppy dressers.

He will make a fine father, though he might not want kids until you've had a few years of married life together.

SCORPIO WOMAN—LIBRA MAN

You will enjoy his company. He certainly knows how to treat a woman. He is a good talker. But whether he is a strong enough type of man for you is a question you will have to ask yourself. It is true you don't like to be bossed, but you do like your man to put you before anything else. Mr. Libra has many interests. He is also a bit of a dreamer.

You will be a mystery to him. He may not be able to cope with your moods. He can't stand arguments.

This man is interested in people, people from all walks of life. He blows hot and cold. One moment, he will be all over you; the next, he'll seem strangely distant and aloof. He becomes bored terribly quickly. If you want to keep this man, you'll have to keep him guessing.

You are a fairly possessive woman. If you throw scenes because he has arrived home late, he won't be able to take it.

He is a true romantic. It is possible for you to have a sexual relationship without becoming emotionally involved. Not so a Libra. If he is not in love, or at least convinced himself he's in love, he simply can't work up any interest.

You will find his mind fascinating. He knows how to tell a story. He is fickle. Being a girl who likes to know where you stand with a man, you could easily get your heart broken if you go overboard here. He hides his depressions, doesn't like others to see him when he is down in the dumps. The reason he tries to put on a brave front is that he feels the world situation is bad enough without adding his personal gloom.

You could be driven to physical violence by his flirting ways. He simply can't help playing up to a pretty woman. You will have to learn to turn a blind eye when you are out on a date together.

He can be vague. He will hardly notice all the effort you put into keeping the home tidy. He takes such things for granted. But when you wear a new dress, he'll always notice.

It's amazing how cold and ruthless he can be when he has to.

It doesn't take this man long to get over an affair that goes wrong. He bounces back pretty quickly after having suffered a rough time.

Your physical relationship should be good. He will love your uninhibited way of making love. He likes a woman who comes on strong, so he won't mind your taking the lead in the bedroom.

There is a lot you can learn from Mr. Libra. He is a good talker and you'll discover he can interest you in subjects that previously had no appeal. He's ambitious without being pushy. He is capable of fighting his way to the top. Once he has made up his mind on a positive course of action, he sticks to it.

Life with your Libra man will not be roses all the way. There is bound to be a certain amount of conflict. This bit of strife could help to keep your union alive. You will need to be interested in his work because his job is likely to be very important to him.

He will not try to pry into your secrets. He will understand that there are certain things about your past you want to remain buried.

It could be that you will have to make most of the important decisions in this liaison. You will have to be prepared to take on quite a lot of the responsibility for the children and the running of the household.

Financially, there will be a few ups and downs; neither of you is that good at budgeting.

He will be very fair with the children. He will make sure they are very well provided for.

SCORPIO WOMAN—SCORPIO MAN

It seems natural that people born under the same Sign be instantly attracted to each other—after all, they share numerous personality traits—but very often this is not the case. Either we recognize and abhor in the other person our own weaknesses, or the union has no mystery.

In the case of Scorpio-Scorpio, you need have no such worries. You are likely to be instantly attracted to this man. Chances are you'll fall for each other on first meeting. It is quite likely this will begin mainly as a physical attraction. As you get to know each other better, you'll find you both have much more to offer. Your love will be passionate on both a mental and a physical plane.

You will recognize each other's weaknesses, all right. But in understanding your partner, you will also come to terms with your own hangups.

Like you, he is jealous and possessive. He is a real fighter for what he believes in. You like a man who lays his cards on the table.

His lovemaking can be bawdy and aggressive or gentle and caressing.

You must both watch your tempers. You will have to treat your man with the same respect you expect from him.

He is, of course, a very direct person. He will fight to the end for what he believes in. He is perfectly capable of quitting a good job if he feels he is not being treated fairly. You should understand him well enough to be able to channel his fire and determination into worthwhile endeavors. Let's face it, if you are not working for each other's good, you will destroy each other and probably yourselves into the bargain.

He is not a great romantic, but then, you're usually not enamored of the soft-talking sweet-music kind of Romeo. Your sex scene is unlikely to become dull. It will be a matter of pride to both of you to bring satisfaction to your partner.

Love without jealousy doesn't exist for either of you. You both like to feel your partner is desired by others. But in order to keep this relationship alive, it is essential that neither of you become seriously involved with another.

Home is an important place for you both. There will be many nights when you will be content to stay in, cuddle up in front of the fire and take the phone off the hook.

As a woman, you can be very hard on yourself. Your understanding Scorpio man will help you to overcome this self-criticism. You find it hard to allow any man to make the important decisions, but you'll feel you can trust Mr. Scorpio more than most.

He will adore your femininity. He likes his woman to be all woman, not little-girl-lost.

People rarely get the better of him in business. He is very shrewd at psyching out others.

He will be terribly ambitious for his children and will do all he can to make sure his kids get to the top in whatever career they enter. Scorpio men are sometimes heavy-handed with the discipline. If he has a son, he may try to turn him into a carbon copy of himself.

If you can stick together through the difficult times, you will help each other to become better and wiser human beings.

SCORPIO WOMAN— SAGITTARIUS MAN

When you first meet him, he'll seem to have many of the qualities you demand in a man. He has a powerful personality, a certain magnetism and a good sense of humor—which will never be directed against his woman. But if you contemplate settling into any kind of personal relationship, certain major obstacles must first be overcome.

He is rather frightened of losing his freedom. He is hard to catch and harder to live with. He has to be constantly on the go. You do like to have your quiet moments. Mr. Sagittarius finds it very difficult to stay in on a cold winter's evening. You may begin to doubt the depth of his love when he constantly suggests you ask friends over.

This is a man who can't bear to be trapped. He refuses to make plans for the future. He is a bit of a gypsy at heart and he can never get his fill of adventure.

He needs a strong woman behind him, and you are certainly that. But you will have to ask yourself the serious question of whether you are prepared to play mother as well as wife to the guy you choose as a partner.

He needs lots of looking after. You will have to be prepared to go to bed alone some nights because he will want to have his evenings out with the boys. You are not the sort of woman who likes to stay home every night of the week, but the sort of outside stimuli he appears to want might not appeal to you.

You are possessive and you are jealous. It might be difficult for you to accept the fact that he needs so many other people. You needn't worry too much about his having an affair, though. Once you are living together, this is unlikely because he is surprisingly a one-woman man. Also, he will probably come to depend on you far too much to put your relationship in jeopardy. He will flirt with women, but this will be to boost his ego more than anything else.

He is lots of fun. You will never have a dull moment when out at parties with him. He is a great storyteller and his company is very much in demand. A crowd will often gather round him. He seems so bright and full of energy.

He is, as a rule, a good earner. There is a serious side to him. As long as his energy is channeled in purposeful ways, he can live a fairly settled life.

You don't like to play a background role. You are very much an individual, one might almost say a loner. You will have to decide whether you can make any man the main reason for your existence. You are likely to get bored following him around. He isn't the sort of man who takes to being dominated.

As you get to know him well, you will discover much of his antics are just a front. He is actually desperately shy. He puts on an act for others so they won't discover the real him.

There are bound to be quite a few arguments. But life will most certainly not be dull.

It might be a good idea for you to keep your own career going if you do get married to the Archer. He won't mind your having outside interests; it will probably do him good to have to get his own supper on occasions and not always take you for granted.

With this man, you'll find your marriage becomes better as you get older.

With kids, he's pretty hopeless and can rarely manage to give them the time they need. He tries hard, but he's never quite able to get close to them. You won't think his fun-loving party-guy image is a very good example for them.

SCORPIO WOMAN—CAPRICORN MAN

Mr. Capricorn is an extremely complex individual. He has great difficulty coming to terms with himself, let alone others. He wants love desperately, but he's afraid of it. To a certain extent, he is insecure. He finds it hard to trust anyone with his heart.

He is an emotional and passionate creature, and if you take the trouble to get to know him well, you will discover he is as sincere and straightforward as they come. He can't help covering up what he truly feels. He finds it necessary to put on a front when meeting people for the first time.

He does tend to be rather conservative in his outlook on life. In many ways, he could seem too prim and proper for you. You are the kind of woman who will fascinate him, though. Your very sexuality will make him want to get to know you really well.

He will also be rather envious of your habit of speaking your mind without worrying what others may think of you. One of Mr. Capricorn's basic personality problems is that he so desperately wants to be liked.

A Capricorn man often marries rather late in life. He can be very fussy and terribly set in his ways. He needs to be loved and admired. Basically, he is a logical person rather than an intuitive one. The longer you are in his company, the more complex you will discover he is.

He is an extremely hard-working person. His career is usually important to him. Whatever he takes on, he wants to do well.

He is probably the most loyal type of all the Signs of the Zodiac. If he tells you he loves you you can bet your last dollar he's serious. He is a romantic who fervently believes in true love. At times, he has difficulty facing up to the world as it really is. He feels let down if friends don't live up to his expectations.

In his youth, he can be a bit wild; it's as though he's having his last fling first. In maturity, he doesn't get on too well with people who don't take life seriously. He loves a deep discussion. You will find his mind is quick. He is usually a good conversationalist when he has something to say.

Your Capricorn man will be proud of you as a homemaker. He will adore the way you make the house attractive and comfortable to live in. He is careful with money. As a pair, you should have no trouble providing for the future.

He will not expect you to tie yourself to the kitchen sink. If you wish to continue working after marriage, that will be okay with him. He couldn't expect you to make a sacrifice he's not prepared to make himself.

There is a passionate side to his nature, but it needs bringing out. You will have to help him lose his inhibitions in bed. If you desire him enough, this should be no problem. Keep telling him he is the greatest lover in the world, and it will not be long before that is exactly what he is.

He will want to defend you against the outside world. Surprisingly enough, you will like the protective attitude coming from this man. So many people feel you are capable of looking after yourself and fighting your own battles.

He will make a fine father for your children. He will try to bring up his kids with the right values. He believes in discipline and good manners. Living with this man will not always be easy, but you will never doubt the depth of his feelings.

SCORPIO WOMAN—AQUARIUS MAN

Mr. Aquarius is a very outward-looking person. He is interested in the world around him to such an extent that his family life often suffers a great deal.

He loves discussion. He is usually highly intelligent and capable of putting his point of view across most forcefully. But when it comes to making any important changes, it is often another story.

He is more interested in tomorrow than today. He knows how the world *should* be. He looks for the best in people. He thinks it is possible to change human nàture.

You may find him a fascinating guy. His views will certainly interest you. When it comes to a permanent relationship, though, it is difficult to tell how long you would last together.

You like someone with a positive views on things, but you also hold to definite opinions. This is the sort of man who would confuse you. He is very broad-minded. He always tries to see things from everybody's point of view. He is neither jealous nor possessive. You may sometimes wonder if he is at all concerned where you have been when you come in late. The simple fact is he will feel you are perfectly capable of looking after yourself. He'll think you're old enough to decide how you should run your own life. That's a very adult way of looking at it, but will you agree?

It is true, of course, that love changes a man. If he feels you really do need protection, he might make it his life's work to provide you with all your needs and shelter you from the big bad outside world. He's a bit of an extremist, you see, sometimes even a downright fanatic.

Can your basic differences in attitude be overcome? Well, just because he doesn't agree with your philosophy doesn't mean to say he will stop loving you. But let's face it, it doesn't make it any easier when two people hold opposing views on everything except the love they share.

Mr. Aquarius needs a cause. He finds it difficult to reveal his true feelings at the personal level. He often hides behind a placard or a slogan. Often it is hard to find the real man. You are much more straightforward. You tend to tell people what you think about things. If they don't like your candor, that's tough.

He's the sort of man who has loads of acquaintances but very few close friends. You may get rather fed up with the constant comings and goings in the household. He may not even notice when you are ready for bed if he is in the middle of a heated debate.

He won't be very good at coping with your moods, either. When you get down in the dumps, he's likely to tell you to snap out of it and think about all the people in the world who are worse off than you are. He's not a bully or a brute, though. He is, in fact, a very gentle man.

He won't be able to understand your deep interest in the home. He is unlikely to notice the care you have taken with decorations and furnishings. He needs a stable influence in his life; if you provide it, he might take you for granted.

If you care deeply enough for your Aquarius male, you might be able to work up some enthusiasm for his various projects. However, think very carefully before you marry him. Be sure that you have a lot more going than a purely physical attraction. Have a wild affair with him, enjoy his zany company and particularly his crazy friends. But give yourself time to find out whether it's an impossible dream.

SCORPIO WOMAN—PISCES MAN

Your friends who take an interest in zodiacal relationships between men and women may pooh-pooh the idea that a Scorpio woman could ever get deeply involved with a Pisces man. Actually, you have much more in common than appears at first sight. To begin with, you are both water Signs, which creates an emotional understanding if not an affinity. Also, you both have a profound interest in the occult and life and death. Then, you are both moved by your impulses rather than by any logical thought processes. Finally, you both have a vivid imagination and you both love change.

This man is likely to have a special sort of appeal. He is artistic and can get carried away by beautiful poetry and music. The reason you would tend to be such a good combination is that you are so much more realistic than he is and he needs someone to bring him down to earth with a bump on occasions.

He is romantic, but not in a mushy way. He is sincere, and that is terribly important to you.

He will do his best to look after you. But you had better face up to the fact early on that you are likely to go through a few rough stretches with Mr. Pisces.

He is not petty. He will always consider your feelings before he makes any decision that would affect you.

At times, he will be amazed at your energy. He is a bit of a dreamer and may find it difficult to understand why you rush around so much.

Whatever work he does, he is likely to bring to it a distinctly individualistic approach. Very often you will find that a man born under the Sign of the Fishes has a creative kind of job. He isn't very good at knuckling down to routine. He needs more than mere financial reward to spur him on.

Don't question his motives too much. He doesn't like to be cross-examined. If you love him, he will expect you to accept him as he is.

People born under this Sign are the idea

type. He will always be on the lookout for something new. He will take a chance on a project or an invention even if it may be rejected.

In your courting days, he will make you feel like a million dollars. He knows how to wine and dine a woman. This man also has the happy knack of being able to choose the sort of surroundings that will appeal to the woman he is taking out. He will not try to foist his tastes or opinions on you.

He will understand your moods and do his best to cope with them. He will always have the time and patience to allow you to talk yourself out of your depressions.

He can be changeable and you may find this side of his nature rather difficult to live with. He may seem determined to get to the top one day, and the next suddenly become lethargic and lose all interest in his career. You also are subject to sudden ups and downs. Let's hope you manage to have these in turn rather than simultaneously. You'll find, though, that when your Pisces man knows he's the anchor in a relationship and things start going wrong, he'll rise to the occasion magnificently. He's got a lot more strength and nous than his manner suggests.

He needs security as much as you. He won't object if you wish to keep up with your career so long as it doesn't interefer with your being a good and loving wife.

Most of all, he will need you as a woman, and that is the most important thing in the world to a Scorpio girl.

SCORPIO MAN—ARIES WOMAN

Quite a few differences will have to be overcome if a union with an Aries woman is going to last for very long. To be honest, after you've been with her a while, she could drive you absolutely crazy. She's not as feminine as you like your women to be. She, like you, prefers the role of the dominant partner. Still, love can find a way.

She is terribly ambitious. You like to be the breadwinner. You will have to ask yourself seriously if you would be happy with a woman who follows her own interests as much as Miss Aries is going to want to do. Though motherhood appeals to her, she will probably want to continue with her work for quite a long time after marriage and postpone having a family.

You like to take the aggressive role with a woman. An Aries lady may be too forward for your liking. If she's attracted to you, she may well suggest the first date. This sort of tactic tends to scare off the Scorpion.

This girl goes into things feet first. She's no diplomat. She comes out with exactly what is on her mind. You do like to be pampered and made a fuss of. Underneath your tough exterior, you're a bit of a softie—especially where women are concerned.

She finds it hard to stay put. The nervous energy she burns up in a day is quite amazing.

The lady Ram hates to be told "I told you so." She can't take criticism, even if it is well meant. You like to protect your woman and advise her when she goes wrong. This attitude toward the female sex would not be acceptable here.

Don't get the wrong idea, though. For all her ambition and drive, she is extremely nervous and sensitive. She does her best to hide her emotions and her vulnerability.

Your sex scene is apt to be pretty hot. You will definitely click in bed. She is almost as passionate as you are. As a swinging affair, you could have a ball together. Whether your love would go any deeper is open to question.

She is quite complex. She's terribly jealous, but then, so are you. She's quite capable of resorting to violence if pushed far enough. An argument between you two could turn into a flaming battle.

Basically, she would love to be dominated by a man. She'd be quite happy to play the role of the little housewife. The trouble is there are so few men she feels it is worth sacrificing her independence for.

Miss Aries can be promiscuous. It's not easy for a woman born under the first Sign of the Zodiac to settle for one guy. She may, in fact, live with two or three men before she makes her choice. This might play on your mind, too.

Her lovemaking is warm and aching. She will want to be on your arm all the time if you are her man. She will desire to share in your success. She'll want to share your problems, too, and is capable of going through the hard times as well as the good. She's a survivor.

Miss Aries loves a party. She is great at entertaining. She is also extremely generous. She would do anything for a friend in need of help. Her spontaneous way of giving will impress you.

Your house would be well furnished. She's got imagination when it comes to decorating. And she's a good cook.

If you have the patience to accept her moods and tantrums, you could be happy together.

SCORPIO MAN—TAURUS WOMAN

It is possible you would hit it off with Venus-ruled Miss Taurus. She loves the domestic scene and is a great homemaker. Like you, she is not too keen on change. She will be prepared to settle down to being a housewife and mother without many qualms.

She possesses a very strong personality. You may find her a little hard to handle. She digs her heels in when anyone tries to tell her what to do. Still, she's as straight as a die. A very down-to-earth girl, she always lays her cards on the table.

You may get the wrong idea about Miss Taurus on first meeting. Chances are she will appear to be totally absorbed in her career. You will be amazed at how quickly she is prepared to give all that up when she meets the man who can give her a secure and stable home.

She may try to interfere in your business activities, which is not likely to go over too well with you. You like to keep home and work in distinctly separate compartments. When she asks if you've had a good day at the office, she'll want you to inform her of the minutes of your important meetings.

If you do score with a Taurus woman, you won't be disappointed with her lovemaking. She's all woman. She'll make you feel all man.

Possessions are quite important to her. She also likes a comfortable home life. You're fond of your creature comforts, too, and shouldn't have any trouble providing her with all she needs.

This woman takes people for what they are without asking too many questions. You tend to be rather critical of others and to make snap judgments.

She is likely to have a great affinity with nature. As a rule, Miss Taurus is extremely fond of animals, especially dogs, and is bound to want to have one or two pets. If you haven't got a garden, she'll want a window box or some indoor plants.

You'd better watch that roving eye, brother. The lady Bull won't tolerate your getting involved with another woman even if it's only on a casual basis. This is one area where she will not be quick to forgive. And she is not an easy woman to fool. She'll sense it if you are trying to put a fast one over on her.

If she loves you, she'll stand by you come hell or high water. She's not the type to run for the lifeboat at the sign of a storm.

She likes her food. As a rule, you will find a Taurus girl cuts out the frills when she's in the kitchen. She's likely to make an apple pie just like her mother used to.

Your Taurus woman likes her surroundings to be soft and feminine. You may have to get used to a pink bedroom. You'll also have to be prepared to live with the teddy bear she's had since she was two years old. She's a great hoarder and extremely sentimental.

Miss Taurus is a bit of a plodder. She refuses to be rushed into making important decisions. Her restraining influence could be good for you. You do have an impulsive streak, and she may make you think twice about important matters.

She will adore doing things for you. So long as she feels she is the only woman in your life, she'll remain faithful.

She can take care of herself if she has to. She's fantastic at facing up to reality. She likes straightforwardness even if it hurts.

She'll fight to get the best for her kids. You'll make a first-class parent combination. With Scorpio and Taurus in charge, your children are likely to be well balanced.

SCORPIO MAN—GEMINI WOMAN

It's hard to see how you would last very long together because you would appear to be completely opposite types. Fortunately, there are other influences working in both horoscopes that may help. Don't forget that Gemini is the Sign of the Twins. Two of her! You may find this dual personality just too much to cope with.

This woman finds it difficult to stick at things. She is always on the move. You will find it tough going keeping up with her moods. She's full of new ideas. It's difficult to get a word in edgeways because she's such a chatterbox.

She also blows hot and cold. One moment, she'll be the most passionate woman you've ever met; the next, she might be engrossed in a magazine and pulling on her bed socks. You like to know where you stand with women. Sorry, you're in for some surprises this time. Her sudden fluctuations will drive you right up the wall.

Miss Gemini is even more of a flirt than you are. Whereas you make your intentions clear from the start when you desire someone, she can be a bit of a tease. She'll play footsie under the table, flutter her pretty little eyes and let you drive her all the way home—then she'll open the door, let herself in and shut you out before you can say "Are you free tomorrow?"

She likes to be constantly active. She tends to live in the future. She loves people and enjoys meeting folks from all walks of life. She adores being surrounded by admirers. The center of attraction is what she's always aiming to be.

Though you can't help but be attracted to this shooting star, give yourself plenty of time to think about it before you ask her to be your wife. She would not be prepared to sit at home all day while you are at work. Do you think you could live with a woman who'll want to keep up her outside interests and old friends?

Miss Gemini is likely to be artistic. If she could stick to one subject for any reasonable length of time, she'd most likely have a very successful career. But routine terrifies her. She doesn't want to be tied down. Being a creative woman, she runs from the thought of a nine-to-five office job.

Other people find her fascinating. She usually has lots of chums. You must not get jealous at the number of telephone calls she gets from male friends. She will tell you these relationships are purely platonic; more often than not, she'll be telling the truth.

Don't try to work out what makes her tick. If you are really gone on this Mercurial woman, you'll have to accept her for what she is and leave it at that.

Don't get angry with her. And don't try to change her. Watch that temper of yours. She needs kindness and understanding, not the heavy-handed approach. You will not win this girl's heart by being aggressive.

Don't keep asking her if she loves you, either. She prefers her man to play a bit hard to get. If you're all over her, it will be too easy for her; she treats love as a game. It's not that she can't fall like a ton of bricks, it's just that she seldom finds the right man.

Miss Gemini is a romantic at heart. She loves to float on air.

Basically, she is yearning for peace of mind and security. Have patience with her and in time she will settle down.

With children, she will mature. The responsibilities of motherhood will make her realize that she can't be a party girl all her life.

SCORPIO MAN—CANCER WOMAN

Of all the twelve Signs of the Zodiac, the Cancer woman is perhaps the most likely to be the dream girl of a Scorpio male. She will have almost everthing you desire. She needs protection, she loves her home, her mission in life is to look after the man she loves and she makes a fantastic mother.

You like to dominate and she likes a masterful guy. There are few men who can control her, but you appear to fit the bill.

You will need to have quite a lot of patience with her. She's a woman of many moods. She can be terribly extravagant, too. Although's she's quite astute at managing a budget, she can go off the rails from time to time with a massive spending spree. Clothes are her great weakness, especially if she's a city woman. She'd buy a new outfit every day of the week if she could. Her closet is likely to be packed with many different fashions.

She needs security. This girl can get very down in the dumps. She does not like to live alone. She will turn to you for protection and understanding when things get too much for her. You will have that special talent for calming her down and, more important, for cheering her up.

You will share the same sort of interests. You love your home as somewhere to escape to after a hard day's work. She will like nothing better than preparing your favorite dishes and spending the evening alone with you.

Don't ever let your Cancer lady down. She is likely to believe everything you say, not because she follows blindly, but because she wants to have faith in you. She will put you on a pedestal. She will stand up for you at all times. No one will dare to say a word against you in her presence.

Don't ever nag her or be overly critical. She can't stand to be bullied. She gets upset very easily. The pain she feels when her emotions are aroused is very deep. Don't ridicule her. Take her seriously when you know she's being sincere.

She would be terribly upset if you were to get involved with another woman after you had pledged yourself to her. If she has built her world around you, she will be absolutely shattered and things will never be quite the same again no matter how much you change your ways.

When it comes to clothes, you are a bit sloppy. You tend to be absentminded about putting on a clean shirt and polishing your shoes. A Cancer woman will make sure you are always looking your best. And she'll do it unobtrusively. She'll darn your socks and do everything she can to turn you into a well-dressed man. If you really love her, you'll go along with it and probably enjoy your new image.

She loves to be spoiled with presents. Buy her the odd box of chocolates or bunch of roses to show how much you appreciate all the things she does for you. She will never take you for granted.

Don't play little-boy-lost. She's got no time for a man who is searching for his mother. More than likely, *she's* looking for her daddy.

People born under Cancer usually have great

respect for their parents, so no mother-in-law jokes, please. Even if you don't get on well with her side of the family, it would be in your best interests to keep your mouth shut and make the best of it.

It's quite likely you'll have a large family. She makes a devoted mother. In caring for and bringing up children, there is none better.

SCORPIO MAN—LEO WOMAN

If you can take a woman who has an independent streak as wide as a freeway, you should hit it off with a Leo girl. She is a positive, no-nonsense type. She is quick to sum up people. You will have to be straight with her or you won't keep her. There will be no room here for your usual jealousy and possessiveness. She simply won't put up with that sort of behavior. If you persist, she'll consider you extremely adolescent and not her type.

Your Leo lady won't be dominated. If you try it, she'll show you the door. She is logical and matter-of-fact in her approach to life. Oh sure, there is a sentimental side to her nature, but it's always tempered with the practical.

Other woman are often extremely jealous of the Lioness. They wish they had the nerve and strength of character to conduct their lives the way she does. She is not bothered by catty remarks. After all, she is the Queen of the Jungle. What comes first with her is to be true to herself. You'll admire this quality because you believe in sticking to one's principles.

Miss Leo is likely to be a leader among her friends. She's often full of bright suggestions about how to spend an evening. She's glamorous and feline. She likes bright lights, spotlights and lots of yellow and gold. She shines like a diamond when she's the center of attraction.

In bed, you'll find her a fireball. She is a physical creature. To her, lovemaking must never become routine. She needs an imaginative lover.

As a Scorpio male, you are probably on the lookout for a homemaker. Check your priorities and you'll find this is high on the list. Well, don't expect an old-fashioned homemaker if you link up with a Leo. She mightn't stray, but she certainly likes to roam around. She has a very inquiring mind and will want to go on developing it and acquiring more knowledge all her life.

Although this woman may appear soft and cuddly on the surface, don't be taken in. When she is aroused, she can be quite stormy. She won't be prepared to stand by and watch you playing up to other women. Don't try to get away with anything. She has an uncanny knack of being able to read her lover's mind. This could be a bit discomforting for a guy like you, who has such a vividly erotic imagination.

Her tastes are expensive, though not extravagant. She's artistic. It's quite likely she will be able to save you money on housekeeping and groceries. She's very good at making things herself. She will certainly make domestic life very comfortable. Where she could cause you to dig deep into your pocket is in entertainment. She loves dining at good restaurants and will expect to be taken to the movies or the theater at least twice a week.

Miss Leo can be pretty sporty, and she's quite a fighter. You might have some problem getting the upper hand in any games you play.

If you have an important business deal to clinch, be sure to take your Leo woman along. She's capable of charming the pants off any man when she puts her mind to it. Share the decision-making, don't be quite so demanding and overpowering, and this woman could do a lot for you.

She may not be too keen to have children early in the marriage. It is highly unlikely that you'll ever have a large family.

If you are well-heeled, you will probably be able to overcome your differences. But if you're never going to make a pile of money, it might be best to cross Miss Leo out of your little black book.

SCORPIO MAN—VIRGO WOMAN

You are likely to be confused by a Virgo woman. In many ways, you are a straightforward no-nonsense type. This woman takes a lot of getting to know. She can be terribly shy and reserved.

She is particular about her man. Romance is not something she enters into lightly. She's unlikely to have a lot of boyfriends in her life. She finds some difficulty in showing her feelings.

Of course, if you are really crazy about her and have the patience to bring her along slowly, this could be a successful liaison. People are often unfair to this damsel. So many in this day and age expect to make it to the bedroom before they even know a person's name.

You will discover you have come across one of the Old World types who believes in courtship and good manners. She has standards and she lives by them.

Don't rush the romance. Get to know her first. Be her buddy. You will have to take your time wooing this lady. Bascially, she is shy. She has to be sure of her man before she will give herself to him. The question is, can you stand the long preamble?

You'd better smarten yourself up a bit, too. Nothing offends a Virgo woman more than slovenly dress. She won't go out with you if you turn up looking like someone on his way to the poorhouse. She'll feel you don't care very much about her if you don't make a special effort to look presentable.

Don't ask her back to see your etchings. She won't find those corny old ploys amusing. You'll just have to keep your passionate nature under control for a little longer than usual. Try not to criticize her or dominate her. If you can't accept the way she is, it would be best to forget all about it. She's not one to change her ways to suit a man.

Miss Virgo does not like to show her feelings in public. She's likely to blush bright red if you hold her hand at the bus stop or get romantic when her friends are around. She is interested in true love. To her way of thinking, second best just isn't worth bothering about.

You are not the tidiest of men around the house and that could cause problems because she can't stand things to be in disarray. You tend to be a bit messy. You like to spread. Her efficiency could drive you up the wall.

If you are a true Scorpio type, lovemaking is one of the major forces in your life. A Virgo woman could be too cool for you. You will have to make Casanova look like Donald Duck to get her in the mood on occasions.

She'll be very shy about going out with you. When you first date her, it might be a good idea to make it a foursome.

She puts great emphasis on good manners. She clings to the past and sticks to her childhood friends.

You'd better keep to the straight and narrow if she does become your woman because Virgos can't tolerate hypocrisy.

Love can conquer all, of course. If you are wild about Miss Virgo, you can both overcome your differences. You could be just the man to bring her out.

She will do her best to be a good wife. You will always be able to bring friends back in the sure knowledge that your home will sparkle. She's fond of preparing food and is most certainly not an extravagant woman.

Like you, she believes in bringing up children strictly. Just be careful that between the two of you they get enough cuddling and affection.

SCORPIO MAN—LIBRA WOMAN

Your patience will be sorely tried with Miss Libra because she is forever changing her mind. Her main problem is she always sees two sides to every argument. On the other hand, you could be absolutely marvelous for each other. If you are prepared to give a little and not be so sure of your opinions, she will certainly make you wiser.

She is charming and she is extremely feminine. It is possible she'll be one of the few women who could actually have you eating out of her hand. You will find her sexy and irresistible.

You will need to be a man with nerves of steel. She will confuse you. Just when you think you have won her, she's quite likely to tell you she doesn't want to get too serious with any man as there is still so much she wants to do in life.

It's quite possible you will discover your Libra sweetheart is a career woman. She can be domesticated, but she won't be prepared to make her whole life revolve around you.

Being possessive, you may not take too well to the idea of her having outside interests and friends. She is interested in life and people. She's very quick to sum up other folks' strengths and weaknesses.

You two might find you are better equipped to handle a passionate affair than to spend the rest of your natural life together.

She's a woman through and through. Lots of guys fall for her and she often has the field to choose from. You enjoy a bit of competition. It flatters your ego to think other men would like to be in your shoes. You are a determined guy and what you want you usually get.

This woman does not put on airs. She is a seeker of truth and likes to be honest with herself. This causes problems, though; what she believes today she might not tomorrow. When she's emotional, she can kid herself. She gets carried away with enthusiasm and imagines things are better than they are.

You may find it frustrating that she is always surrounded by crowds of people. You could have some difficulty in getting time on your own with her.

There's quite an astute head on those pretty little shoulders. This Sign is often extremely good at business. If you can stand her going out to work, it's possible she'll bring a fair amount of cash into the family coffers.

She might keep you waiting for hours when you're going out together. She takes ages to make up her mind about what to wear. If you've got an important appointment, it might be an idea to set the clocks back an hour when she's not looking.

You like your home comforts and will have no complaints about her as a housewife or cook.

She won't try to boss you around, and she will expect to be given the same sort of personal freedom by you. She is fond of beautiful clothes and furnishings. Her surroundings are important to her.

You will have to earn her love. The way to do that is by trusting her. She will not be able to give herself to you completely if she feels you are a possessive person. You will have to want her happiness first and foremost.

She is a particularly generous person and will shower you with expensive gifts when you are courting her. Even when you are married, she will save out of the housekeeping budget if necessary to buy you quality presents for your birthday and special occasions. She genuinely delights in giving to her mate.

She loves kids and will be more than eager to have a family.

When you get to know your Libra lady really well, you'll consider yourself extremely lucky to be her man.

SCORPIO MAN—SCORPIO WOMAN

Can you put up with someone who is as powerful, aggressive and downright jealous as you are? The thought of a Scorpio-Scorpio linkup is quite a mind blower.

Since sex is the force that drives you both, from the physical point of view, you are likely to get on fantastically. When this woman's temper gets the better of her, you'd better run, though. She can't stand to be criticized or told what to do. To be honest, there could be violence if you both lose your cool at the same time.

Miss Scorpio is a no-nonsense type. She does not fall for that love-moon-June talk. She usually has an interest in the occult and things mysterious. Some people find her fascination with matters connected with life and death rather morbid.

She is very honest with other people. When she thinks you have done something worthwhile, she will praise you to the skies. She wants her man to be successful. But she won't be prepared to kid herself or you if you don't make it. She won't pay false compliments, either. You may find her brand of honesty rather brutal. Scorpio males like to be flattered sometimes.

This woman has a tremendous amount of tenacity. When she makes up her mind to do something, she does it. No one gets in her way.

You know all about the Scorpion's jealousy, so don't two-time her. One must feel sorry for the man who is foolish enough to get involved with another woman when he is going steady with Miss Scorpio. She'll get even with him no matter how long she has to wait.

Of course, life with this woman will be pretty bumpy. If you can make that first passion last, marriage might work. She is a very independent woman, though, and hates to have to rely on other people—especially a man—for anything.

Don't embarrass her in public. She can't stand to have ugly scenes in front of her friends. If you have any criticism to make of her, then wait until you both get home and give it to her straight. If there is a grain of truth in what you say, there's a very good chance she will admit it.

You will have to come to some arrangement as to who wears the trousers. She can be quite dominant if she senses weakness in a man.

She is capable of excesses, and this is where you could be bad for each other. When one partner does not know when to stop, it is a good thing if his or her opposite number can be a restraining influence. You both have a great curiosity about life; if you were to get involved in heavy drinking bouts or drug taking together, the results could be disastrous.

You are unlikely to tire of her in the bedroom. She knows how to win a man and how to keep him. She has a vivid imagination and enjoys playing sex games.

Never cross her because she has as much capacity for revenge in her nature as you have. You know how you seethe when another person plays a dirty trick on you. She feels exactly the same.

It could be you will find life with someone born under the same Sign as you a little too draining. You prefer your domestic scene to be peaceful. Probably you require a woman who is a little more obviously feminine. You should have a closer look at the other influences in her horoscope in this book.

When children come along, you could find yourself relegated to second place. The Scorpio woman makes a good mother, but she can be overprotective of her offspring.

SCORPIO MAN—SAGITTARIUS WOMAN

Although she's a girl who's hard to track

down, it seems likely that Miss Sagittarius will be attracted to a man like you. She needs someone who is self-assured and confident. She wants a man she can believe in. She is very cheery and always tries to look on the positive side of life.

You will have to watch that temper of yours, for when this woman is provoked, she can be quite a volcano.

She is straightforward. It would be extremely good for you to marry someone like this. She will make sure you face up to yourself.

She likes to keep on the move. She is also a bit of a mystery. It is not easy to get to know her.

She's very outspoken and capable of standing up for her rights. You will find the way she deals with difficult people most refreshing. You're expert at handling disagreeable types so you can't help but admire this girl's style.

Although you are a pretty astute businessman, you're not too good at dealing with everyday problems. This is where your fire lady will come in. She's excellent at shopping and budgeting. No tradesman will be able to cheat her.

It is in her dealings with friends that she may turn to you for help. She does have an unfortunate way of saying the wrong thing at the wrong time to people she loves. You might be able to advise her on how to be a little more diplomatic. She has a habit of making a remark that can bring an interesting discussion to an abrupt end. You could be sitting around for hours debating a fascinating subject with your cronies, when suddenly your Sagittarius woman will toss in a couple of her special observations, and *bingo!*—the room will come to a painful silence. Don't get the wrong idea—there is nothing malicious about her. It's just that when tact was rationed out, she must have been away on vacation.

She can be impatient. Even when she hasn't got anywhere in particular to go, she has a tendency to rush.

With a weak man, she can get a bit bossy. It's unlikely she will try this with you, though.

If you have to go away on business, you can feel confident she'll be able to run the house and look after herself and the kids.

Miss Sagittarius is the faithful type, definitely a one-man woman.

Don't try to get your way by shouting. She's very reasonable and will try to go along with your ideas as much as she can.

People born under this Sign are often somewhat marriage-shy. They think twice before they give up their independence.

It would be wise for you to allow her to keep on with her career after marriage. She will become rather insular if you leave her at home all day with little to occupy her mind.

Your love life should not give you any reason to complain. She needs a man who can take the lead. She's not a voluptuous type of female, but if a guy can stir her, she'll respond.

With children, she is terrific. A Sagittarius mother will make darned sure that any talents a child has are developed.

Even if you don't wind up marrying this woman, you'll probably go on being buddies long after the affair is over.

SCORPIO MAN—CAPRICORN WOMAN

Many people have called Miss Capricorn frigid. This is simply not true. Perhaps the reason so few men fail to arouse her is that they don't know how to treat her. It is true that she can be colder than Sunday's roast in the deep freeze if she meets a guy who does not know how to excite her. But she can be an absolute whirlwind of passion. Even a randy guy like you may be taken aback by her insatiable appetite for sex.

She will like the fact that you are ambitious and a hard worker because success is quite important to her. She is attracted to talent, not because she wants reflected glory, but because she she can't abide people who have little to offer.

If you win her, she will be faithful. She will do everything she can to ensure the marriage is a success. If, however, you let her down, there is no telling what she'll do. She might go straight out and have an affair herself—partly to get back at you and partly to experience what you have experienced.

She's hung up on security, just like you. As a pair, you won't have too many problems putting the shekels in the bank.

A Capricorn woman is clever enough to play little-girl-lost if she sees it makes you happy.

Don't try handing her a line. She is interested in true love, not a casual affair. Don't neglect her. She will pout and make big scenes if you have too many late nights out with the boys.

Basically, she is responsible about money. But if you happen to be broke, she'll give you her last cent and pawn her jewelry for you. For this woman, love is a total commitment, and she expects it to be the same for her man.

The Capricorn woman is a wonderful hostess. She is just the sort of woman you will want around if you have to do a lot of business entertaining. She knows how to make people laugh and can bring a twinkle to the eye of most men. She likes to be well thought of.

She is efficient. She makes a first-class secretary. Whether she comes from a high-class family or is a policeman's daughter, her innate elegance will shine through.

She loves parties and you might get a bit bored with the number of people she wants to invite over. Mind you, when she knows you are tired and want to be alone with her, she'll make sure you are not disturbed.

She doesn't like to waste time. She will make sure she keeps busy all day. She is generally very thorough in what she does.

Let's hope you get along well with her family because she is likely to be very close to Mom and Dad and have lots of favorite uncles and aunts, too. Relatives are important to her, and she will be particularly proud of them if they have achieved any sort of fame or recognition.

Marriage always improves a Capricorn person. For one thing, it stops any introverted tendencies from getting out of control.

Sometimes Capricorn women marry relatively late because they get stuck on some guy who is not free and out of loyalty won't leave him. They often have some sad or unhappy love experiences behind them.

Kids will love their Capricorn mother but she won't stand any nonsense from them.

SCORPIO MAN—AQUARIUS WOMAN

Chances are you'll find an Aquarius girl almost impossible to understand. Unless there are other favorable influences working in your individual horoscopes, this woman's progressive ideas and attitude toward life would be difficult for you to live with for very long. You would be well advised to check the Aquarius book in this series.

It may take you some time to discover what she's really like. She'll probably always remain something of a mystery to you.

Her mood changes are difficult to keep up with. You do like to know where you stand with a woman, and perhaps more important, you want someone who will provide you with a secure and stable home life.

She is independent by nature. She likes to stand up for herself and can't bear to admit that even she at times might need a dependable man to fall back on.

You see, she's a bit of a revolutionary and quite a woman's libber in her way. The Water Bearer is out to put the world to rights. She's a brave one and will battle hard for what she believes in.

Certainly there will never be a dull moment in your life if you do get involved romantically with this woman.

There is something magical about her. She believes in freedom, but if you ask her to define that word, she might have some difficulty.

When you come home after putting in a full day's work, it could be that your supper will be waiting for you on the table but your dear lady will be nowhere to be seen. You will be left to tuck into the lettuce and ham alone.

When she does turn up, you'll probably discover she's been out helping someone less fortunate than herself or enlisting aid for one of her causes. One doesn't wish to paint a gloomy picture, but your married life could be like this.

She is unconventional. Home to her is where she unrolls her sleeping bag. She is not that interested in comfort. She certainly would not be content to sit at home all day attending to the routine affairs that make up the average housewife's life.

She is likely to get many proposals of marriage. An Aquarius lady has a great personality and people are magnetically drawn to her. Perhaps if you meet her when she is past her banner-waving days, she will be ready to settle down.

Don't introduce her to your boss if you work for a large corporation because she will probably cross-examine him on how he makes his profits and what he pays his workers. *Bingo!* There goes your bonus for another year.

She isn't as crazy as she seems. Often many of her ideas are accepted by the more conservative members of our society in twenty years. She is ahead of her time.

Marriage is a big step for this woman. You'd better sort out your differences before you contemplate slipping the ring on her finger.

Unlike you, she's not a jealous person. Your possessiveness will be difficult for her to understand. She won't question you if you don't get home on time. She doesn't have a suspicious mind.

She's capable of going for long spells without making love. She can channel her energy into other things.

SCORPIO MAN—PISCES WOMAN

Never tell this woman she won't be able to succeed in what she's attempting. She needs to have her confidence built up, not shattered.

When a Pisces girl enters your life, you may wonder why you have spent so long searching for the right woman. In so many ways, you will be good for each other. There is much you have in common—remember, you are both water Signs, which gives you emotional similarity.

She has a fantastic imagination and is full of ideas. Her intuition is astonishing at times. She would never dream of trying to boss or dominate you, but if you ever ask her advice, even if it's about matters that are not of special interest to her, it is likely she'll come up with some interesting thoughts.

It is when she is trying to come to terms with herself that she experiences problems. So often in life she feels she has reached a crossroads. She can always see the possibilities offered in taking the other path. She is a seeker after truth, ever striving for honesty.

Miss Pisces is very much a woman. You will fancy her like mad. She will boost your ego and give you all the confidence you need to go out and wrestle with your work problems.

You will have to get her to accept more responsibility for herself. This will be for her own good. Although you are a protective sort of guy, you must insist that she make certain decisions on her own.

She can't help going out of her way to give a hand to others when they are down on their luck. She has a deep feeling for the sufferings of mankind. Not that she is stupid about it. She will quickly realize if someone is not doing enough to get himself out of the hole he is in.

Her clothes sense is wonderful. She knows what suits her. You must boost her in this area, too, and get her to buy clothes she admires.

In love, she is devoted. Once she has decided that you are her man, that will be it. A career is not all that important to her. She will find interests outside the home to occupy herself while you are at work. But she will always be around when you need her. You will definitely come before all else.

You will never be bored in her company. Although she changes moods very quickly, you are not likely to find this inconstancy more than you can bear.

She believes deeply in goodness. Just being with her will make you a better person. She will be a driving force. Any success you achieve in your career will be done for her just as much as for yourself.

She's not the sort to blame others when things go wrong. She'll stand by you through the bad times as well as the good.

Mind you, it will not be *la vie en rose.* She can act up like a spoiled brat on occasions. You will sometimes have to reprimand her for behaving like a kid. She can be extremely selfish, too, especially when she doesn't get her own way.

Never let her get the feeling she is trapped or confined; she can become too introverted then. It is important to take her out at least once a week and insure she meets interesting people.

As your wife, she'll look up to you as head of the family. She would never dream of disagreeing with your decisions about the children, although she may tell you when you are alone together that you were perhaps a little harsh.

If you land these two little Fishes, you'll think you're a lucky guy.

SCORPIO'S HEALTH

If you are a typical Scorpio-born person, your attitude to life is the chief factor determining the state of your health. So Strong is your willpower that you can actually will yourself to recovery. So pernicious is your power to resent and hate that you can poison yourself with your own emotions.

Generally speaking, your constitution is robust, rugged and healthy. No other Sign in the Zodiac has at its disposal as great a reserve of sheer tenacious energy. Your health is largely a question of what you do with it.

There is always a danger that people born under your Sign will push themselves beyond physical endurance once they've resolved to accomplish something. Scorpios are such demons for devoted effort that they can ignore the normal limitations and end up with a breakdown of some sort. You should always remain conscious of the fact that your will is far stronger than your body.

You are also a person who is prone to illnesses brought about by self-indulgence. Few Scorpios are ever able to satisfy their lust for total experience by sticking to norms. Moderation and normal living leave them with energy to burn. They work hard, they play hard, and still they can usually physically outdistance any of their associates.

Excessive drinking is often a problem. You can hold your liquor better than most. It takes a heck of a lot to break down your tremendous self-control. Sometimes you make a habit of eating too much. You know you shouldn't, but it is your nature to dismiss the protests of your body and to make it serve you as you please.

There is a strong self-destructive urge in the Scorpio character. You don't deliberately set out to damage yourself; you just refuse to acknowledge any limits. You want to experience all there is in life. Often this search for sensation and knowledge leads to dangerous experimentation with drugs. Occult phenomena, with their self-charging emotional energies and weird rites of invocation, are likely to interest you. The changes in perception that emotional stimulus and narcotics induce can be fascinating for the Scorpion. Sexual excess is another area you find difficult to resist.

If you are a typical Scorpio, you don't have any patience at all where illness is concerned. You are more inclined to ignore a complaint than go to the doctor. This can be dangerous because you tend to dismiss the serious symptoms as well as the trivial. Since you are a realist, if incapacitated by illness, you will take quick remedial action. The trouble is, you may wait too long.

Your most vulnerable part is the stomach. Various disturbances are likely in the digestive system, especially as a result of the excesses mentioned. It is difficult for you to overcome internal toxic effects. Once a poison is in your body, it is hard to eradicate it. A buildup of any kind, even constipation, is to be avoided. This is why it's so important that you prevent the buildup of emotional corrosives that weaken the organs and attack the stomach, causing ulcers and the like. Brooding, worry and depression should be watched.

The reproductive organs are also governed by your Sign. So is the bladder, urethra and rectum. You are also susceptible to minor ailments affecting the head and throat. Nasal congestion, adenoids and sinus trouble are not uncommon. Children born under this Sign frequently suffer from recurring bouts of throat trouble until well into their teens.

It is advisable not to expose yourself to cold or dampness without taking sensible precautions. Dress warmly in winter. Liberties you take now with your health will have to be paid for later. Being a fixed Sign, you tend to suffer from rheumatism with age. Colds and influenza can drag on and make life miserable and you irritable.

Normally, Scorpio people live to a ripe old age. They have the constitution to survive most conditions. But too much of too many good thingsin earlier years often wreck your chances of longevity.

You are accident-prone. Some of you may die suddenly and violently. Be extra careful when handling explosives, and inflammable materials.

Scorpio individuals are the stuff that heros and heroines are made of. They are disdainful of personal danger when principles are involved. They will suffer without complaint for what they believe in and will die for a cause.

SCORPIO AT WORK

You, Scorpio, have just about all that it takes to succeed in any profession or job you set your mind to. But it's amazing how often people born under your Sign mess up their careers through tactlessness. You can't help putting your foot in it, blurting out a truth nobody wants to hear, upsetting just about everyone who counts. Unless there are strong mitigating factors elsewhere in your horoscope, you'd be better off choosing a career where your advancement depends on the fewest number of people.

In your own business or as a professional consultant, you should certainly be successful. Your straightforward and often blunt manner is less likely to offend those who are paying for your opinion than a superior. Still, you've got to start somewhere before you set up on your own. The sooner you can find a boss or powerful figure who likes or admires you, one whose good books you can concentrate on staying in, the better. The more people you've got to please, the riskier are your chances.

You do possess immense personal magnetism, apart from your other considerable talents. As a rule, you should have no trouble *getting* a job; the problem of *holding* it will rest purely on personal relations. Those who take to you will tend to overlook your tactlessness provided you don't go too far. They can't help but admire your conscientiousness, drive and tireless energy, or the speed with which you are able to learn and assimilate.

You are extremely well suited for scientific research, medicine, journalism, investigation, industrial or political espionage, psychiatry and archeology. These fields will allow you to employ your natural talent for unearthing hidden information and finding out what others are doing behind the scenes. There are many other careers in this category that will offer you a fine opportunity for success.

Being natural investigators interested in benefiting all mankind, you Scorpios are often found in the forefront of laboratory programs intended to solve major problems such as a new source of energy, the global food shortage and biological scourges like cancer and heart disease. Because of your avid interest in the occult and the mysteries of life and death, you are often leaders in parapsychology and similar investigative fields. You write and publish books about their findings. Usually you are specialists. Scoprios will work indefatigably to find a cure or an answer. When dedicated, you are oblivious to failure, time or money. You will persevere long after others have given up or despaired. Frequently you are publicly honored for your discoveries.

You have a distinct flair for investment. You should be able to make a career as a broker, financial consultant or accountant. The foreign exchange or investment department of a bank may offer you the scope you need. Scorpios are also proficient auctioneers. You can spot a bargain anywhere.

You are the natural builder of the Zodiac. But your vision in this respect is vast. You are not interested in building a house or two; you want to transform the environment, turn deserts into farmland, build whole towns, community centers, shopping and office complexes. If you enter the construction industry, you are apt to rise to a position of considerable power and influence. If you don't see the opportunity for this, you'll probably quit and try something else. As a builder, you always favor the boldest, the biggest and the most dramatic improvements.

Your imagination is excited by travel to other countries and strange places. You also have a strong affinity for water and the sea. Many Scorpio individuals earn their living working with boats. A naval career is not an uncommon choice.

Other factors in your horoscope may make you adaptable for work connected with the mining, engineering or chemical industries. You are skillful with machines and instruments. Any inventive flair in this direction should be cultivated.

Your cool nerve, manual dexterity and innate desire to heal often make you a top-flight surgeon. Many people born under your Sign are also found in the butchering trade.

You don't like doing heavy manual work for a living. You prefer to use machines. You'll dig a trench in the back garden just for the wonderful stimulus of getting your muscles working, but you're too intellectual to be content with a purely physical role.

The same talents that make you such an admirable and clever worker make the Scorpio character most "successful" at villainry. October-November-born people are among the most notorious crooks in the country. To the criminally minded, the thrill of outsmarting the other guy, especially matching wits with the defenders of the law and all their resources, is an irresistible challenge. Scorpio hoods often rise to gang leadership where power is measured in life and death and bloody vengeance. Others operate in the vague area between the legal and the illegal, the thrill being to remain "respectable" and accepted by the solid citizenry.

As a boss, you are a smoothie—and something of a tyrant. You know exactly how to handle everyone on your staff. You can be tough, damn tough. You can tear a man or woman to shreds with the edge of your tongue. You can make them wish you were dead. And yet no one you reprimand will crack because you are a great judge of character and know precisely how much each individual can take and still learn. You possess an extraordinary ability for making people you like stronger while you are tearing at their weaknesses.

Of course, it's a different matter when you're dealing with an antagonist. But with your chosen subordinates, you take a deep-seated interest. You are not just concerned with them as working units but as people. They often love you even though they mightn't like you. They admire your quiet, cool efficiency. They respect candor and detestation of humbug and duplicity. They are intensely loyal. You make sure they realize they are your team. Mind you, they also know you'd make a terrible enemy. They are happy to be on your side when a fight looms.

The secret, of course, is that you never hire anyone unless he or she is a certain type. You have to like the person, and discern that his psychic chemistry fits with your own. All this is revealed to you in your first look at him. One deep gaze into his eyes and you know everything. If you take over a department, it's not long before you've weeded out the unacceptables. You may kick them upstairs (or down the stairs on those rare occasions when you lose your temper), but however you get rid of them, they'll be banished to the outer regions and never enter your orbit again. You are instantaneous and implacable in your likes and dislikes.

As an employee, you don't necessarily want to be the boss. Well, not yet. You're a realist. Apart from being the most consistently energetic and resourceful person around the place, you never want to make a move until you're absolutely ready. And that means knowing the business, whatever it is.

You will take orders. You will do a job over and over to satisfy a fastidious boss without feeling any impatience or ill will. You may think he's got hold of the wrong end of the stick, but this opinion will make no difference to your work. The boss is the boss, and you accept his right to have things done his way. That is, as long as you can see clearly that under him you are going places. You are a person who fixes goals well in advance. You are more concerned with the inevitability of the end than with the irritations in between.

You don't expect any special favors as an employee, only what is due you. You have a good opinion of yourself, but it is based on an honest assessment of your worth and capabilities. You're not a boaster, a showoff or a clown. Compliments don't impress you much. You see instantly through flattery. Your whole attitude is purposeful and workmanlike. You are forever learning and moving ahead on the strength of that knowledge. You are extremely loyal to your employer. You are a company man or woman—not a maverick. However, when the time comes (as it must) for you to make your push for power, you will discard all previous alliances. You will change sides without compunction and work just as earnestly and conscientiously for the opposition. You are committed only to your own goals. While these happen to coincide with those of an employer, you can be counted on never to let him down.

If you were born between October 23 and October 31, you are inclined to be dictatorial and domineering. No obstacle will delay your career for long. You should try to be more patient, understanding and tolerant of others. Your impulsive and headstrong methods are likely to create more opposition than is necessary. You have great self-control once you learn to use it.

You should be able to accumulate a fair amount of property during your working life. Involvement with large construction projects should provide a suitable outlet for your abundance of energy. You need to think big and operate on a grand scale. You should try to associate with people who have higher than average IQs. Business partnerships can be profitable provided you curb your urge to take over completely. You usually think in terms of large groups of people and have a way of handling them. Sales work, where you have a large area or network to supervise, is likely to be rewarding.

If you were born between November 1 and November 11, you should make a competent and forceful teacher in any field that interests you. You are likely to prefer employment with a very large organization and to gradually make your way to the top.

You are tenacious, and once you've chosen a course, your life should become much more settled. The early years may be notable for their lack of direction. You may have to try numerous jobs before finding what you want. You possess a dynamic personality and should cultivate the friendship and support of people in authority who like you.

Your executive skills and judgment are excellent. You will probably gravitate to a financial or organizational career. You have a marked ability for laying down guidelines that others can follow. Your associates should be people who are interesting, dramatic and able to discuss most subjects. You have a powerful desire to keep learning and broadening your knowledge.

If you were born between November 12 and November 21, you have a good mind for legal technicalities. You can judge people and affairs with great accuracy. You intuition in business matters is quite remarkable. You are inclined to be highly emotional with strong romantic leanings. Sometimes you are aggressively ambitious; other times, philosophically placid. There is much that is contradictory in your nature, particularly when your emotions are involved. You have to avoid impulsive moves. You may be successful in an artistic or dramatic field and you should be able to write with great power and imagination.

You are likely to be attracted to work that allows you to influence the public. Your personality is magnetic and sympathetic. You may be able to carve a career in publishing or politics. Given the chance, you are likely to rise to a position of considerable popularity or authority.

Money

Money seems to come to you pretty easily, mostly because your hard-working nature ensures an above-average income. Scorpio people often receive inheritances, but the sums are sometimes smaller than anticipated. You are a shrewd financial manipulator. You understand budgeting, fiscal policies and complex appropriations better than most. Running a household is child's play to you.

You spend freely on your home and personal comfort, but you are not especially generous. However, many of the world's most famous philanthropists who set up anonymous foundations for the public benefit turn out to be Scorpios.

By a strange quirk, the more Scorpios spend on themselves and their families, the more money comes their way.

SAGITTARIUS' CHARACTER

No one loves life more than you, Sagittarius. And no one is in quite the same hurry to make his mark on it. Your approach is different, daring, perhaps even a little crazy by orthodox standards. For a start, most people would describe you as keenly ambitious, yet it's not so much success that you're after; failure isn't all that important to you, either. What you live for is the thrill of trying, of having a go.

Most other types usually look for an end result. Sagittarius deep down disdainfully rejects this as a design for living. It's the *quality* of life you crave, not the measurable, miserable quantity. To others, you may seem impulsive, restless, extravagant, extreme, but recklessness is often the price of freedom. You go on exploring, taking your chances both physically and mentally, to find out what is at the end of the rainbow.

Sagittarius is one of the finest and most altruistic Signs in the Zodiac. Your innate love of adventure and change is not based on selfish whim. According to ancient astrological tradition, each Sign has a special job to do for mankind. Yours is to dare to go beyond conventional thinking, to discover what's new in the world of ideas and to hand on your information or wisdom to others so that they may go beyond themselves.

Every Sagittarius expresses this urge according to his or her unique personality. The important point is it is clearly recognizable in the Sagittarius person.

To begin with, you are optimistic, cheerful and staunchly independent and self-reliant. (If you're going to go charging off in exciting new directions and not worry unduly about what calamities might befall you, you'll certainly need these qualities.) And you love change, new vistas, broad horizons and the blood-thumping stimulus of physical movement. You are also sincere and open, very truthful and intolerant of those who are not. You possess a keen sense of justice, the quality of mercy, and are guided by a lofty personal ethic. You are highly intelligent and honorable and a kind and open-hearted friend. (What else could we expect from a character whose role—to help others—depends on being accepted, believed and trusted?)

It can come as no surprise, then, to learn that Sagittarius individuals are always found among the most respected leaders in any society or group, whether it be a commune or a corporation. They are natural teachers, philosophers and comrades, lawyers, churchmen, businessmen, politicians—and ordinary decent citizens. No matter how modest or undistinguished their circumstances, people gravitate to them for guidance and advice.

You also like to be noticed. This can be a fault if you go to extremes to secure attention. Your character is so buoyant and expansive that it's very easy for you to go too far. Your virtues can become weaknesses through excess.

The astrological symbol for Sagittarius is the Centaur, or the Archer with a drawn bow and arrow. This mythical figure embodies all the main features of the Sagittarius character.

The Centaur is an ancient symbol of authority and wisdom. It has the body and four legs of a horse and the upper part of a man. It implies the fleet-footed power of a horse and the brain and potential wisdom of man. It is the meeting point, the nervous nexus, of intellect and flesh. Nowadays, instead of a horse's feet, the symbol could be an automobile wheel. (Some modern astrological works do use the wheel.) No one enjoys the free-ranging travel represented by a car more than Sagittarius. With you, travel is not just a fascinating or exciting experience; it's a psychological necessity. To keep mental powers at their peak and emotional equilibrium, you must continually move outside your immediate and known environment. If you don't have the opportunity to travel physically, you enjoy making excursions through the pages of books and in your vivid imagination.

Looking again at your character as represented by the symbol of the Centaur, you are extremely vital and body-conscious, with all the instinctual precision of an animal in action. Even if you are middle-aged and inclined to be portly (always a possibility for a Sagittarius), there's a determined gracefulness to the way you move. Action becomes you. You look better on the go than sitting around, and you always feel happier moving. When enclosed or isolated for any length of time, you tend to pine.

You do have one odd problem when you're on the move: you're clumsy. In your haste, you trip over things, slip or bump into objects. You're so busy projecting your mind ahead of yourself that you forget what you're doing. The typical Sagittarius goes through a fair number of china sets over the years.

You love sports and all outdoor activites. But you are not so interested in combative types of games. Tennis and water sports are right up your alley. Like the swift horse (some might say the wise half-man of the Centaur), you prefer to avoid physical combat. Your style is to depend on your intellect and speed to outwit and outdistance your opponents.

Sexually, there is rarely any coarseness to your highly developed body consciousness. Again, you show the fineness of the thoroughbred, the lusty sexual straightforwardness of pure animal delight. The typical Sagittarius man or woman doesn't dwell on sex, is not preoccupied or obsessed by it. Sexuality has its place, and you express it with swift, ardent vigor and freedom. You don't like heavy love scenes filled with tears and pleas. Physical love is a splendid game played each time with refreshing newness and constant action. Sex to you can never be fulfilling when it is a habit or a duty.

Your Sign rules the hips, thighs and locomotor muscles of the body. These together (again, as represented by the Centaur) are the source of man's physical power and the stable foundations supporting his upper intelligent half.

No other Sign needs more rational restraint than Sagittarius. Often you require a dear friend or loved one to call *whoah!* The old drawings of the free-ranging Centaur show him not only in full gallop but also about to shoot an arrow ahead, as though his own speed were not enough for the urgency of his mission.

And what precisely is Sagittarius aiming for? What is the target? You don't know yourself. You pursue each passing interest with the same gusto as if it were the bull's-eye itself. You have no reserve of arrows because you fire them off as fast as they come into your hands. Seldom do you pause to see if you have hit the mark—or even to collect the prize. Your reward is the sheer delight of the chase.

This unstoppable, ever-hopeful Sign stands directly opposite, and therefore is closely associated with, Gemini, the quick-thinking, brilliant, intellectual third Sign of the Zodiac. But whereas Gemini lives largely in his head, his body dancing up and down like a puppet and often appearing to be going nowhere, Sagittarius matured conveys a sense of direction, a feeling of distant goals. Here, intelligence achieves control and guides the body purposely in a unity of flesh and spirit that pushes both the individual and mankind ahead boldly and fearlessly.

Your nervous system is high-strung, like Gemini's. This shows in your constant eagerness to be elsewhere, your fondness for the great outdoors and complete freedom. But unlike Gemini, you are practical. You apply your razor-sharp mind in down-to-earth ways. You may be impetuous, but this is often because you foresee in a flash the outcome of a proposition or transaction. You don't waste time in needless abstract reasoning. You get to the bottom of things quickly and act. You make mistakes, but seldom because of procrastination. Your swiftness is the secret of your commercial success.

Your judgment is excellent in everything connected with your work, but where your emotions and private life are concerned, you frequently make errors. One of your chief problems is that you get involved in too many projects at one time. Your love of novelty and variety inclines you to commit yourself to any interesting new proposition that comes along. Because you usually move at such a swift pace, you're constantly hearing about something that sounds promising. Frequently you underestimate the problems because you're not that afraid of failure. You have supreme faith in your own ability to get by playing it by ear. You tend to spread yourself too thin. You have very little patience for details and prefer to leave them for others to sort out. You draw your plans with sweeping flourishes. You see the ocean and not the waves.

It's not unusual for you to have to backtrack to avoid unpleasant situations you've brought on yourself through enthusiasm. You are a quick thinker in a tight spot. You get a lot of practice talking your way out of trouble.

You Sagittarius people are definitely idealists. You sincerely want to see the world put to rights. And what's more, you're usually prepared to do something about it. You're not just a talker; you're a doer. Frequently you are associated with projects for social reform. You are on the side of the little guy, even though you often run with the big fellows. You're usually too level-headed to be a radical. You know what can be achieved and what can't. You are one of the great visionaries of the Zodiac, yet not a dreamer. You use your vivid imagination in progressive and socially desirable ways. You are a wonderful organizer, a born overlord. You have a genius for reducing questions to their simplest terms. People can follow your ideas easily. You don't like to quarrel. Unless a real principle is involved, you'd rather give ground and make your point another day, another way.

You are a positive thinker. You look on the bright side and dispel others' doubts with the clearsightedness and simplicity of your statements. You are no fool, though, and won't attempt the impossible. You always believe in what you recommend. You can communicate your zeal and gather others quickly to your side. Because you have faith in people, you are good at delegating responsibility and utilizing the talents of others while you surge ahead like a shock wave.

You are a gifted conversationalist, as a rule, who enjoys the thrust and parry of an argument with a good opponent. You express yourself clearly in writing and speaking. Sometimes, however, you talk too much, carrying on about one subject after another without pause. Still, you're an exceptionally entertaining talker because of your wit and humor. You tell a good story, though sometimes you flub it by leaving out an important chunk here or there in your haste to get to the punch line. But your manner is so pleasing or funny or both that you get away with it. Often you can mesmerize an audience into a euphoria of goodwill. (That's why Sagittarius people make such wonderful actors and actresses.) Your sense of humor is finely developed. You're often a comic, but there is a distinct sophistication to your humor, a refinement that's evident even when you are playing the fool or acting a bit adolescent.

There's an interesting astrological tradition about Sagittarius and talking. Sagittarius is one of the Signs of articulation (Gemini, Virgo and Pisces are the others). People born under these Signs either talk a lot or very little. Sometimes they suffer from speech impediments. Apparently Sagittarius—the "preacher" of the Zodiac—has to learn the happy medium: to be neither garrulous nor taciturn, but to say it just right. It can take a lot of working on. Both the knowledgeable pundit and the happy-go-lucky chatterbox must learn (so it is said) that the potency of speech lies in the economy of its use.

A subconscious urge to get straight to the point is a characteristic that shows through in every typical Sagittarius. You are among the bluntest people in the world. In a sentence of five words, you can reduce a happy party to silence or send the hostess running up the stairs in tears. You have the unfortunate knack of making innocent remarks that are so loaded with the hurtful truth they can't be ignored or laughed off. No one could ever accuse you of being malicious. You are so warm, broad-minded and understanding that to deliberately set out to hurt a companion is beyond your ken. Neither are you addicted to petty jealousies. You don't hold grudges.

But you do possess this extraordinary truthfulness—you say exactly what comes into your head. In this candor, you are assisted by a powerful intuition that goes straight to the heart of the matter. Often you are genuinely bewildered by the consternation your tactlessness causes among others. Your problem is that you tend to speak from your subconscious mind, which just can't or won't recognize the restraints of social niceties.

You Sagittarius people possess a great desire to be liked. If you're the mature type, you won't toady or sacrifice a principle to gain popularity or acceptance, but you are inclined to make promises you forget to keep. Sagittarius men and women are splendid crowd pleasers, magnetic as well as effusive. Carried away by the excitement and fervor of the moment, you are likely to promise others the world—and then spend a great deal of time and effort either dodging people or trying to make excuses. You are as morally courageous as they come, but you leave yourself open to criticism when intoxicated with optimism and enthusiasm. Despite your sometimes upsetting candor, you have no trouble being diplomatic when you are trying to get your own way.

If you are a typical November—December-born individual, you instinctively love animals. You feel a sympathetic bond with them (remember symbolism of the half-human Centaur?). Even if you can't keep a pet yourself, you are unable to see one go hungry and homeless without doing something practical to help. Some people can actually ignore the suffering and needs of animals; this is a fact you probably find incomprehensible. You have a particular affinity for dogs and horses. Cats may also have a home with you, but as a rule, they are a little too aloof and ungregarious for a close association. You like to treat your pets like buddies and to share with them as much as possible.

Your home is extremely important to you. It's your base, the place you always look forward to returning to. Others live *for* their home, but that's not quite your style. You like a place that's as spacious and comfortable as you can afford. You hate being cooped up. If you could have a farm as well as a town house and split your time between the two, you'd be in your element. Because you delight in sharing your things with others, you have as many people to your home as you can. You love entertaining and giving paries—sometimes hearty fun affairs, other times intimate and relaxed soirees. You don't like having to consider expense when you play host or hostess. You want to provide the best in food, drink—everything—and you're quite capable of spending more than you should to put on a good show. Restriction in any form irritates you. You'd rather blow your bankroll on one memorable night than try to survive by eking out the pennies. You prefer to live for the present and take your chances on tomorrow.

You're not a devoted family person in the usual sense. Certainly you are generous, kind and sympathetic to those you live with or who are dependent on you, but your outside interests and warmhearted regard for humanity as a whole gives you a certain detachment.

Sagittarius people probably keep most of the world's gambling casinos in business. This doesn't mean that you're all betting men and women, but it is your nature to often push your luck to the point of recklessness. As a rule, you respect money for the experiences it permits you to have; saving or hoarding just doesn't provide any satisfaction. The spending habits of Sagittarius people often appal the more security-conscious types of the Zodiac. They brand you as irresponsible, extravagant, profligate. But there's a deeper astrological explanation. Though it might sound like an attempt to whitewash the flamboyant, fun-loving side of the Sagittarius character, it's amazing how often the astro-theory proves itself. Sagittarius is ruled by Jupiter, the planet of wealth and good fortune. It stands for the forces of growth, expansion and abundance. The pure Sagittarius person is invariably lucky. You have a way of landing on your feet. You have just as many problems as the next person, but somehow there's usually a happy ending, or at least a saving one, for you. Money seems to come your way: you may be rich and keep accumulating, poor and receive windfalls that save the day, or a big spender or gambler and live in luxury that depends on the knife edge of chance.

The true-to-type Sagittarius knows instinctively that he or she must not worry too much about the future. It is this trait that is at the bottom of your irrepressible optimism and general good humor. Mr. Macawber, the Dickens character who always insisted something would turn up to solve his chronic money problems, was a typical Sagittarius. There's another curious thing about you and your celebrated luck: you seem to know instinctively you must not to try to hold on to money, that the only way to keep it coming is to keep it circulating. The "unlucky" Sagittarius is usually someone who has upset the system by being greedy, excessively security conscious or overcautious. (This will show as an unfavorable influence elsewhere in the horoscope.) The "Jupiter theory" makes the generous, easygoing, cheerful Sagittarius character much easier to understand and appreciate. Even the word "jovial"—a distinct Sagittarius characteristic—is from Jove, the ancient name for Jupiter.

In romance, you have a distinct problem. It is absolutely essential that you choose a compatible mate. Avoid at all costs getting tied to a partner on the basis of superficial attraction. The prospects for a lasting partnership with the various Signs are given in detail in the chapter "Sagittarius in Love." Briefly, you frequently marry more than once, and it's difficult for you to avoid disappointments and disillusionment in romantic matters. Your emotions, which seem so stable one moment, are likely to go completely haywire the next. Your judgment here is poor. It is imperative that you select a mate who understands your need for freedom and independence. Any of the jealous or possessive types could make your life hell. The person you live with must be your comrade as well as your lover. A Libra mate would be ideal; a Scorpio intolerable. You are the type of person who is happier married than single, provided you choose wisely. Look for patience, understanding, affection, a sense of adventure and a good intellect in your mate.

You can be mule-stubborn, and you've got a

hot temper. You don't like personal criticism, especially when it concerns your appearance. And you can't stand being unjustly accused of saying or doing something. You'll really hit the roof if anyone tries this on you, and after your first burst of temper, you're likely to go ice cool. Your tongue can cut like steel wire. You don't stick around to pick up the pieces.

You are often diet-conscious and susceptible to fads. You enjoy trying out new dishes and new ideas. You are likely to go on a health-food kick for two or three weeks and give everyone an inferiority complex with the strength of your resolve. Then you'll forget it—and start working your way through the latest exotic cookbook. You're often quite a chef and love to prepare an occasional lavish meal. Even the most complicated dishes don't daunt you if you're in the mood. But if you *have* to cook, the whole thing loses its fascination and appeal. Cooking for a family every day is not your idea of the good life. Domestic chores and the routine that accompanies them bore you stiff. Little wonder few Sagittarius people have large families.

You are basically an artistic type with a natural aptitude for art, music or dancing. If you don't engage in these activities, still you understand and appreciate them. Your love of the social life often brings you into contact with people who are accomplished in the creative fields. Even though you may not be an expert, your opinions and insights are well worth listening to. You can talk on practically any subject. You have wide general knowledge. You prefer intellectual friends, but can mix well in any company. You enjoy reading and often possess a marked literary ability if you wish to develop it.

Impatience and hastiness frequently lead you to make unnecessary trouble for yourself. Sometimes you reverse your own good chances of success by acting prematurely. Once you decide on a positive course of action, you seem unable to wait for the opportune moment to begin it. You want to board the ferry before it docks. It can be a drenching business.

You're not the greatest dresser in the world. You value comfort too much to make the best-dressed lists. (You do like your gear to be spotlessly clean, but there are no awards for that.) The Sagittarius male is a very independent dresser. Being disdainful of convention, he's likely to dress for an occasion in just the opposite way to what everyone is expecting. He knows when clothes are important and when they are not; he knows that most of the time they are not as important as everyone makes out. A Sagittarius father once rolled up to an exclusive boarding school on the first day of the term with his two immaculately dressed sons, wearing a pair of shorts, a T-shirt and no shoes. He just had to make his point.

A Sagittarius head of a public relations firm when visiting a client's fashionable Fifth Avenue store strode through the building in a tatty old anorak, followed by an entourage of impeccably suited account executives. He'd actually just driven down from his farm, but couldn't miss the opportunity to draw attention to himself and his contempt for convention.

The Sagittarius guy seldom misses a trick when he has a chance to be dramatic (and comfortably) at the center of things. If you asked him why he didn't go without his trousers to make his point, he'd think you were some kind of nut. You see, he's pretty conventional in his idea of being unconventional. Sometimes the male Archer really does have no idea of how to dress and looks a bit like a schoolboy in his first suit, with turned-up collar points and a ghastly tie. But, he has an invariable youthfulness—not so much naiveté as good-humored boyishness. When the average Sagittarius man really wants to make an impression, he knows all the right things to wear. He just won't be told, that's all.

Miss Sagittarius likes to combine comfort with style, but her individuality always comes through. She follows fashion but refuses to be a slave to it and will often produce her own striking thing. She likes gear that gives freedom of movement. Her mood largely dictates the type of clothes she wears on each occasion.

Despite your impulsiveness and certain impatience, you have an admirable capacity for enduring bad times. Deep down, you possess strong philosophic leanings that amount to a kind of stoicism when the occasion demands it. Never underestimate your power to persevere. Though you may dash around a lot, under the surface you have a strength of character to be reckoned with. The mature Sagittarius man or woman lives life as it comes, and if it happens to come hard for a while he or she won't complain.

Despite the ardor and zeal of your Sign, your temperament is fairly stable. There is the sense of direction mentioned earlier, which confers a basic calm and equilibrium even though surface fluctuations may at times seem frenetic. There are two sides to your nature, which combine to produce your varying moods: on the one hand, you are venturesome, restless and bold; and on the other, retiring, receptive and sensitive. You intuitively pick up atmospheres of people and places very quickly. Your likes and dislikes are usually instantaneous.

Your ideal recreation is one that provides a balance of physical and mental activity. You are well suited to deep and serious study of any current interest. Going to lectures and attending meaningful discussions can supply the intellectual stimulation you require. But the call of the outdoors should never be neglected. You need to break up your mental pursuits with games, sports and hobbies like hiking, riding, walking and bicycling. Fresh air is a must; without this, your nervous system will start to play up. One of the most pleasurable and rejuvenating pastimes for the Jupiter-born individual is travel. Travel satisfies your need to meet new people and gives you the chance to absorb different cultures by mixing with other peoples.

Despite all the cheerfulness and good nature that make you so popular, you sometimes suffer the pangs of bitter and miserable loneliness. Depression is not so common with you as with most other Signs, but it does happen.

Sometimes you go out on a limb for a friend. You undertake to do something that rebounds and lands you in a complicated mess. Other times your impulsive, emotional nature gets you into romantic scrapes from which there appears to be no escape. Your deeply ingrained sense of loyalty can prevent you from taking the obvious measures to extricate yourself. You get mixed up with loved ones and friends who are all wrong for you. In such cases, you become sad and lonely.

Astrologically, the solution for you naturally lighthearted people is to face up to the causes of your unhappiness. They lie in the deeper recesses of your own mind. Despite your love of honesty and truth, you are not always so honest with yourself. You often refuse to adventure deep into your own psyche because it frightens you. What you see there may make you feel insecure and want to run. You are inclined to choose the superficial way, to stick to conventional values and suffer in hopelessness, when facing reality instead would liberate you.

Sagittarius people often shy away from bad news. You'd rather ignore it and keep up the pretense of business as usual. In undeveloped types, this fault degenerates into exaggeration and lying. The immature Sagittarius person's idea of freedom is a jaunty casualness that allows him to swagger through life borrowing, boasting and using anyone who happens to be silly enough to believe in him.

But that's the negative side. Traditionally, Sagittarius signifies the rainbow—the promise of clear skies, sunshine and clean fresh air after the storm. That bow again—without the arrow.

SAGITTARIUS IN LOVE

YOUR SAGITTARIUS MAN

You like him? Love him? What sort of a man is Mr. Sagittarius?

Impulsive. Lusty. Daring. And a very difficult man to get to the altar. You'd better face it right from the start, he's not good domestic material. But if you're looking for a lover whom you can treat like a buddy, a guy who'll give you plenty of laughs and a wonderful time, this is your boy. Mr. Sagittarius is a bachelor at heart, a jovial, high-spirited gypsy who is often well into middle age before he reaches emotional maturity.

Some Sagittarius males do make happy marriages, but this is largely up to the woman. You've got to understand this guy. He's not really the freewheeling clown he often pretends to be. He has a deep side, which only those close to him are allowed to see. You can't treat him like most other men. He's special and he needs a special kind of woman.

First, he's basically a good man. He'll never hurt another human being if he can help it. He's also high-minded. He wants everyone to get a better deal—including the women in his life. As a single man, he'll make it clear that he's not ready for marriage, that he wouldn't dream of inflicting a wanderer like himself on a girl for good. That's honesty for you. He's no romantic. He couldn't be with his technique. He gets a lot of refusals, but he also gets a heck of a lot of playmates.

To land Mr. Sagittarius, you've got to show him he's as free as a bird as far as you're concerned. He'll usually shy away like a frightened Centaur from any female who thinks she's got a claim on him. He wants a girl to be his pal, to have plenty of laughs with him. He won't want to see you every night because he'll often be out with the boys playing poker, getting drunk or just horsing around.

He'll have a way of dropping in on you at the last minute for a night out on the town. (If you say you've made other arrangements, that will be okay with him—he'll swagger down your front path, whistling happily as he thumbs through his little black address book.) If you can manage to convey that you just happen to be free and find it exciting to be picked up without notice to go out for dinner, he'll be as happy as a lark to take you.

Remember, though . . . no sign of reproof, jealousy, possessiveness; no prying questions like where's he been for five days or why the hell couldn't he just phone to say he was coming over? No . . . not if you want to hook him. This is good-time Charlie himself, the life and soul of the party, the roistering prince of fun. If you take him in stride (that is, if you're the woman for him), one day it will suddenly dawn on him that you're great, you're everything he ever wanted in a woman. Apart from your wonderful physical charms, he will perceive you as a buddy, almost as another guy . . . he loves you . . . will you marry him . . . now!

Every Sagittarius male has something of this caricature in him.

He's a very loyal person. This man will take his marriage vows to heart, but perhaps in a different way from what you'd expect. He may have affairs on the spur of the moment, but he'll never allow them to interfere with his marriage. They won't mean enough to him to force him to choose. He's very physical, and he's such a perambulator that he can't help running into a man-hungry woman every now and again. And he does like to be friendly. That's all. Honest.

This man will never fit into a pattern. He'll seldom be home on time for meals. Something will always crop up to delay him or change his plans. If he's in business, he'll frequently be required to go away for a couple of days. He'll be genuinely busy earning his crust, perhaps working far longer hours than many men. His stamina and vitality will stagger you. His ability to keep going for days on end, sustained only by a couple of hours' sleep each night and the stimulation of other people, has to be seen to be believed. The trouble is, he has such a flair for mixing pleasure with business that you may feel you're being left out in the cold. He'll be thoughtful. He'll buy you presents, lots of clothes, send you away on a vacation on your own. And he'll always be pleased to see you. The question is, can you take being a combination wife and hatcheck girl?

YOUR SAGITTARIUS WOMAN

You like her? Love her? What sort of a woman is she?

Trusting. Trustworthy. Breezy. Easygoing. Basically a bachelor girl, although not without her moments of swift passion.

Romance is not the biggest thing on this woman's mind. She can pretty well take it or leave it. She's more interested in congenial company. She prefers men to women, as a rule, because they make more straightforward pals. It's comradeship that counts with her, and all the laughs, conversation, gaiety, shared interests and especially freedom that go with it.

What about love? That's something this very discerning woman knows will happen in its own time. She's very philosophic about it. She believes in it, but she's patient. Since she's always on the move and meeting people, she feels one day she will see love in some man's eyes (perhaps yours). Meanwhile she's going to have a good time. She enjoys living and feels no need to search for love. It will come.

Miss Sagittarius is a wonderful girl to have on your arm. She's as bright as a button, witty, talkative and terribly honest. She'll never get involved in an underhanded affair if she can help it. No one must get hurt through any action of hers. But sometimes she's impulsive, especially in romance. She jumps in, carried away by the enthusiasm of the moment. She takes chances. She makes mistakes. Because she is so trusting, she is often misled. She's honest and she thinks everyone else is.

This woman wants to see the world. She's a great traveler and just can't get enough of people and places. She is enormously interested in sharing experiences. To feel fulfilled and happy, she must lead an active life.

It is absolutely essential for her to feel free in her relationships. Any man who tries to tie her down or tell her what to do hasn't got a chance. She's not the jealous type. She'd never think of trying to control someone else's life. She's very adult and liberal in her views. She believes everyone should be allowed to reach his or her own decisions. She expects her man to share her respect for individuality.

This doesn't mean that if you marry a Sagittarius woman, she'll want to go her own way. Far from it. You'll be mates, a real team held together by love and understanding rather than mutual restrictions. This woman takes her marriage very seriously. She wants it to be a success. She's not devoted to housework, but she's quietly efficient. She gets a bit bored by domestic routine. She will rush through her chores as speedily as possible and then do the things that appeal to her most. She'll make sure she's there when you need her. She only needs to know she's free. She won't take advantage of her man's understanding or kindness. She'll never be unfaithful while he loves and cares for her.

The Sagittarius lady has many friends and enjoys entertaining them in her home. Her enthusiasm and vitality are boundless. She is a splendid hostess.

This woman is a great sport, the outdoors type. She'll love to ramble through the woods with you or go on a day's hike into the mountains. Fishing, hunting and riding are all likely to appeal to her. She's a happy, good-natured companion to have along on a camping trip. She's unlikely to be a pushover on the tennis court. You'll find she has loads of nerve and is willing to try just about anything.

Your Sagittarius girl is a passionate lover when she finds the right man. If she's not passionate, there's something wrong with your technique. She doesn't make a big thing of sex, but won't put up with a man for long who can't stimulate her interest and keep the excitement going. Rather than settle for habitual lovemaking, this woman would rather forget about it altogether. Although vigorously responsive in the bedroom, she is highly refined. Coarse caveman tactics just don't turn her on.

If you marry a Sagittarius woman, you'll find she takes a great interest in your career. Her judgment is mature. You'll be amazed at the soundness of her advice when you ask for it. She's not the type of woman to pry. Neither will she nag. But she can be embarrassingly blunt.

SAGITTARIUS WOMAN—ARIES MAN

This man is something of a human dynamo, always on the go. You need someone you can believe in. Sagittarius women don't go for the moody type of male; they need a guy who's straightforward. Mr. Aries could be just the type for you. He will be by your side through thick and thin and never let you down once he's committed himself to you.

It's difficult for this man to hide his emotions. He's pretty passionate, too. When he tells you he loves you, it's for real.

Of course, there are other considerations apart from love. It would be dangerous to allow yourself to be swept along by the fire of his passion without taking into account such mundane things as his future prospects and his ability to provide for you. Being an Aries, he is likely to be the hard-working type, though inclined to change jobs. He is also something of a leader. There could be a minor power struggle between you over who makes which big decisions.

It would be advisable to have a fairly long courtship with this man. Get to know him really well before you decide to join him for life.

You have some difficulty explaining your feelings and he may find this a little hard to take. He also has trouble settling down to a one-to-one relationship. He can't help it; the Ram is a born flirt. You don't go in for games playing and will find it hard to conceal your jealousy when he starts giving the eye to every pretty girl who passes by.

He is a passionate lover, although perhaps lacking in subtlety. This is because he is a physical type of man. It will be up to you to teach him to be gentle in bed and show him the art of lovemaking.

You may think when you first meet him that he's far too shy to ask you for a date. Don't be taken in by this first impression. He is ruled by Mars and you'll soon discover that with him, actions speak louder than words.

He is more of an outward-looking type than you are. You may get a bit bored with his political chatter. The typical Aries man thinks he knows how to put the world to rights. It will take him quite a while to recognize that you are his equal in many ways. He is a man's man. Thus it will come as a surprise to him that you can actually offer him good advice regarding his career.

He likes his women to be extremely feminine. He has no use for the women's libber type.

He won't object to your having a career after marriage so long as it doesn't interfere with the way you run the home. He is one of those old-fashioned guys who feels that a woman's prime functions in life are to look after her man and bring up the kids.

He gets carried away by new hobbies and interests. His enthusiasm is boundless, but he tires of things very quickly.

He won't share your interest in religious or philosophical matters. The Ram lives very much in the moment. You will probably find he is the sporty type. This could be a common ground. You are both likely to enjoy a game of tennis or long hikes in the country together.

As parents, you should make a fine pair. You are just the sort of combination to bring up happy and well-adjusted children.

He's a proud man, and when you see he's about to make an obvious error, you're going to have a heck of a job getting him to listen.

SAGITTARIUS WOMAN— TAURUS MAN

You are a proud sort of woman and Mr. Taurus is an extremely proud guy. You may each be a bit too much for the other to take. Neither of you is prepared to budge an inch once you have decided on a positive line of action. Of course, if you do agree about most things in life, this doggedness could make you an extremely formidable twosome.

Taurus is actually very good husband material. If you can judge him objectively—and that's something a Sagittarius woman is pretty good at—you will soon recognize what an excellent catch he is.

He is practical and realistic, but by no means a bore. He has a good sense of humor, and that is something you will appreciate.

This is not the kind of man who can be rushed into a close relationship. He'll take his time before showing more than a passing interest in you. However, when he tells you he loves you, you can be pretty sure he means it. He is rather afraid of being trapped. Fortunately, you are not the type of woman who gives the impression of being out to catch a husband.

He is a pretty shrewd businessman. It takes a lot to pull the wool over his eyes. If he is let down by a person, he will never trust him or her again.

He loves his home comforts. You may get a little bored with the number of evenings he wishes to spend quietly in front of the fire. It will be up to you to get him out more.

He won't be too keen on your keeping up with outside interests after marriage.

You will have to get used to his roving eye. Don't take his flirtations too seriously. They are meant chiefly to boost his ego. If he does go overboard for you, you can be pretty sure he'll be faithful.

He's as bright as a button and can talk on almost any subject.

You both love beautiful things. He will admire the feminine touch you bring to the home.

He will be happy to leave the decorating and furnishing to you, although he'll have some excellent suggestions to make if you ask him because he's quite artistic. Possessions are important to him. He is careful with money but won't mind spending on items for the home that are a good investment.

He's quite a handyman. You won't need to get someone in to fix a broken window or stop a dripping faucet.

It may be difficult for you to make one man so completely your life, which is what the Bull demands. You will have to ask yourself the very serious question, can you take his possessiveness for a lifetime?

He is a hard worker. You need never be afraid the bills won't be met. He will make sure you have enough cash for groceries and the like, but you may have a bit of trouble getting a new dress out of him.

He has an aggressive attitude toward life. This man does not have too many close friends. He can be extremely self-reliant when he has to be. And if you ever double-cross him and see that icy obliviating look in his eyes, you'll understand what it's like to cease to exist in one man's calculations.

Mr. Taurus will want you to be a friend as well as a lover. It is important to him to be on a good mental wavelength with the woman he loves. So long as you both basically agree about what you want out of life, there is no reason why you should not be very happy together.

He is a man who will always be there when you need him. He will make sure the children are brought up to be obedient and orderly.

SAGITTARIUS WOMAN—GEMINI MAN

Life with Mr. Gemini will be go, go, go. If you are the sort of Sagittarius woman who enjoys living on the knife edge of drama and excitement, then this is the man for you.

He can't stay in one place for very long. He is quick-witted and you are unlikely to ever experience a dull moment in his company.

He is not the greatest at making important decisions. He hates to be definite about anything, really. He needs looking after, but can't stand to be told what to do.

He is an air Sign, and you are fire, so you should spark off something in each other. You'll be a constant puzzle to him—which is good. This man has a very inquiring mind. He wants to know what makes people tick. Once he feels he understands them, he can be rather ruthless in dismissing them. Because you don't like to put words to your feelings, he will find it difficult to fathom you. You could be just the kind of woman to keep Mr. Mercury coming back.

The question is, how strong is your motherly instinct? Are you prepared to be mother as well as wife, friend and lover to a man?

His restlessness can be rather catching. As a pair, you could be rushing from one interest to another without making any real progress. It would be good if you could become a stabilizing influence on this man without giving him the feeling he is being trapped. He needs a strong woman, and you are certainly that.

He can be a terrible flirt. You will have to constantly think up new bedroom games to keep him interested in the physical side of your relationship. This type of man can very easily go off the rails.

He will admire many of your fine qualities. It is important for him to have by his side a woman who tells him the truth about himself from time to time. Mr. Gemini can easily go to excess. He never knows when to stop, and can do himself serious damage if he gets heavily involved in drink or drugs.

You will find you're very much on the same wavelength. It will appear uncanny to you how often he puts into words exactly what you were thinking.

You will enjoy going out together. It's likely you will share identical tastes in the arts.

He will leave the housework to you. He can be a bit of a shirker when it comes to tasks that require physical exertion. He is pretty artistic and often makes an extremely good cook or gardener (so long as someone else washes the dishes and pulls the weeds).

You will have to drive Mr. Mercury on at times. He needs plenty of incentive. He finds it very hard to do any work that doesn't totally grip him. He likes change. He has this idea that the grass is greener on the other side of the fence.

He won't mind your having outside interests. In fact, he'll probably wish you to keep up with a career if you do marry.

He's pretty unreliable with money. And he might keep a separate little bank account so he can always dart off for a few days. If he's short, he'll borrow from the housekeeping funds. But he can be very generous when he's flush.

If you become involved with a Gemini man

who has come to terms with his wanderlust and matured emotionally, all should be well. If not, you will find you have to wander from party to party or bar to bar looking for the excitement that exists only in this man's mind.

SAGITTARIUS WOMAN—CANCER MAN

Sometimes even a woman like you wants to settle down and live a peaceful and quiet life. If you happen to make this sort of decision, Mr. Cancer could be just the guy for you.

It will take you quite a long time to discover what makes this man tick. On first meeting, you might see him as an easygoing, fun-loving kind of fellow who doesn't have a care in the world. As you get to know him better, you'll discover you're involved with a fairly complex character.

He is terrified of getting hurt. Therefore he won't expose his true feelings to you until he is absolutely positive you're dependable.

He will admire your confidence and ability to get along with people from all walks of life. But instinctively he will know you'd like to settle down, just as he would.

If you really fall for him, you'll have to take on the job of helping him to find himself. He does tend to make rather a lot of his problems. He can also get a bit of a persecution complex. He tends to think the whole world is ganging up on him when things don't go his way.

He is interested in acquiring wealth. He is very worried about security and will usually be rather careful with his cash.

If you do take him as a lover, you'll be surprised how passionate this quiet man can be. You will adore the way he makes love. He's got plenty of sexual drive. On the physical as well as the intellectual level, you should really get on well.

You will have to be prepared to give up quite a lot if you're contemplating marriage to the Crab. He doesn't like taking advice and neither do you. He will want to talk his problems over with you, but when you come up with what you consider to be the logical answer, he'll probably go out and do the opposite. For a straightforward person like you, this kind of behavior can be extremely irritating.

Once he's decided you're the girl of his dreams, he will stick by you through thick and thin. Marriage is not something that a person born under the Sign of Cancer enters into lightly.

He won't like your having any important outside interests. He will want you to stay at home and have everything prepared for a cozy evening when he comes in after a hard day.

People say that Cancer is miserly but it's not true. He's careful—and only because he wants to be sure he can provide for his loved ones in the years ahead.

You'll have to be hard with him at times, insist he make the most of his talents. Otherwise he'll sit around, talking about things that never eventuate. He needs to have his confidence boosted. He can become very despondent when things go wrong. With the right sort of encouragement, however, he is capable of remarkable achievement.

It is true that many Sagittarius people marry more than once. If you don't want to be numbered among these, choose a Cancer for your husband. He will do everything in his power to sustain a close relationship. What is more, he'll make sure the romance never goes out of your marriage.

Around the house and in helping to look after the kids, you'll find he's a gem.

SAGITTARIUS WOMAN—LEO MAN

All the indications point to this union working out extremely well. You are likely to share many interests and points of view. One thing you have to remember with Mr. Leo is that he can't stand having people disagree with him. It would be impossible for him to take on a partner who has different views on the most important things in life.

Emotionally and sexually, you are likely to have the same basic attitudes and expectations. This should be the right chemistry.

This teaming up will in many ways be something of a mutual admiration society. Your temperaments are such that you'll do your best to ignore those aspects of each other's personality that you don't really like. You both possess a great zest for life and you are both capable of being unselfish lovers. Marriage is sharing, and this is something you both can do well.

He is a flamboyant kind of character—in fact, a bit of a showoff. You do tend to go for a man who is prepared to push himself forward. You like to be involved with a person you can look up to and put on a pedestal.

You both want to live big. Petty issues and narrow-mindedness turn you off.

You'll have to keep the bossy side of your nature under wraps. The King of the Jungle is a soft and cuddly kitten so long as you don't rub him the wrong way and try to run the show.

You are both very powerful personalities. If you love each other, you'll both have to be very careful not to use that power unwisely. There will be occasions when one or the other will have to give way on important issues. Let's hope you realize that there is great strength in *not* fighting on occasions. Being no-nonsense types, you will both be aware how dangerous it could be for your relationship to play games with each other's emotions. You must make sure you don't turn your marriage into a power struggle.

You can be rather blunt, and this is something you will have to watch. You also have a satirical vein, which Leo would find extremely hurtful. He can't bear to be made fun of.

He is a pretty jealous guy. He won't take too kindly to any flirting on your part. But since this is not really in your nature, there should be no major problems on that score. The Sagittarius woman likes to play it strictly on the level with her partner. You want everything in the open where you can see it.

He will have very fixed ideas on how you should be. This rather masculine attitude to the individuality of the fairer sex could irritate you on occasions.

Mr. Leo is a very persistent man. Once he has decided you are the woman for him, you'll find it very difficult not to fall under his spell. He'll chase you night and day and never let up until you say "yes."

Your friends will think you are a marvelous couple. You will certainly be very popular as a twosome. The Lion likes a good party and you're no slouch yourself when it comes to whooping it up in the right company. You will find yourselves always in demand.

You need have no worries about security. Mr. Leo is careful with money but could never be called mean.

One word of warning: don't expect to maintain too many outside interests. The Lion will expect you to be at his side when he needs you.

SAGITTARIUS WOMAN—VIRGO MAN

You might find it difficult to adapt to this man's ways because your attitudes toward life are so different. He could be a little too fussy for your liking.

You are a very straightforward person. He is also sincere, but he does give the impression of being a little superficial on occasions.

To you, housework is not the most important thing in the world. You are looking for quality in life. He may expect rather too much of you in the home: everything has to be spotless. He can be a bit fanatical about hygiene.

You and he have very different temperaments. Your outlook is poles apart in many ways. You're fire, he's earth. You demand a faster pace of life. He tends to be very methodical. He will never make a decision in a hurry. You are also likely to have varying interests. Whereas you are the outdoor type, he is rarely keen on any sort of sport or exercise—as a participant, that is.

This man is practicality itself. He could drive you crazy because he will always be able to find something wrong with your rather far-out ideas. To you, it is the *trying* that is important, not the success or failure. To him, it is the end result that matters the most.

You have a great sense of fair play and justice. But he will always ask the question, "Who will profit from this course of action?" or "Who will in the end be helped?" You will get fed up with such a theoretical approach.

However, the picture is not all gloomy. This man has many fine qualities. He will appeal to you on an intellectual level. He is very knowledgeable and terribly patient at explaining things. He will be able to teach you a lot without giving the impression he's a know-it-all.

His advice is likely to be worth following. He has great sympathy for people who have gotten a rough deal. And he is tenacious. No matter how difficult or onerous a job may be, he will always finish it once he has given his word.

He makes a model husband in many ways. He may not be the greatest lover in the world, but he is a faithful man. He is unlikely to get involved in an affair because he always sees the disadvantages of forming an adulterous liaison. With Virgo, the head rules the heart.

You will have to help him overcome his inhibitions in the bedroom. This guy can be rather prudish. It will be up to you to show him that sex can be fun.

He will put you on a pedestal and try to give you everything your heart desires. He is more home-loving than you. He would rather put his feet up and watch a good TV program than go to a party.

He won't be too keen on your having your own set of friends. This man likes to share *everything* with his partner. If you are going to make a success of your life together, it's important that you share a great variety of mutual interests.

Will you be able to remain faithful to a guy who is so cool? Perhaps you'll become so frustrated that you'll go out looking for someone with greater fire and an aura of danger or adventure. These are questions you'll have to consider very carefully before you tie any knots.

All in all, it could be quite a challenge. If you really love this man, you'll be equal to it.

SAGITTARIUS WOMAN—LIBRA MAN

You are likely to hit it off from the word go with fast-thinking, harmony-loving Mr. Libra. You are probably just the kind of woman he is looking for. You are a no-nonsense type and he doesn't want to get involved with a woman who is going to make heavy demands on him. He (like you) prizes his freedom. You will be able to form a marvelous partnership and yet both retain your individuality and independence.

It's quite possible you will have a long courtship with this man. Although you're very much on the same wavelength, neither of you is likely to want to rush into marriage.

You will find you have a congenial partner to accompany you on social outings. He will never try to pressure you.

He knows the right sort of places to take a woman. You will soon realize that he wants to get to know you as a person. Sex is important to him, but he understands that a relationship can't last very long if you don't have more in common than a desire to go to bed together.

He is one hell of a lover. You can be a little shy, so his expertise and abandon may take you aback. Allow yourself to go with him; it will be most important to this man to make you feel fulfilled as a woman. He won't be able to do this if you don't free yourself of your inhibitions.

He feels very much for other people. He would never set out to hurt another human being. Still, he is inclined to be argumentative, and he's not an easy guy to best in an exchange of words. But he'll avoid out-and-out quarrels as much as he can.

This man actually hates confrontations. He feels there is something wrong with a person who sets out to hurt another or resorts to physical violence. Often he will take the easy way out to prevent any kind of a scene.

He has a lot of tact with other people. You will have to watch that habit of saying the first thing that comes into your head. You don't set out to get people's backs up, but you are blunt to the point of rudeness on occasions. You can be a bit of a tomboy. You will have to work at being a little more feminine.

He will like your free and easy attitude. A Libra can never be happy if he feels he is being pressured. Like you, he must believe he is responsible for his own destiny. He can't stand to be dictated to.

Money could be something of a problem. Neither of you is very good at saving. Be sure you put some cash in stocks or bonds, where you can't get at it for a year or two. Otherwise you'll both go crazy one day and blow all your capital on something absolutely pointless.

He's a real gentleman. He knows how to pay a compliment, and will mean it when he does. He will notice when you are wearing something new.

You will enjoy listening to him talk on subjects he specializes in. This man is usually an expert conversationalist. He is capable of making others feel enthusiastic about topics they are normally indifferent about.

It could turn out that you'll have to make most of the important decisions. You don't like this job, but the fact is Mr. Libra finds it almost impossible to decide which fork to take when he comes to a crossroads in life.

Home is important to him, although he does tend to use it as a place to recuperate and restore his energy.

He will work to make your union last. You'll have to be prepared to do the same.

SAGITTARIUS WOMAN—SCORPIO MAN

You will have to forego many of your other interests in life if you're going to get involved with a Scorpio. He's a very interesting, you might say fascinating, man. It's entirely possible you'll feel you're under some sort of spell if you fall for him.

He doesn't exactly expect his woman to be a slave, but he does want to be the number-one interest in her life.

He is a very physical person. There could be a fundamental clash of personalities on sexual matters. His physical urges tend to rule his life. You may find his caveman approach a little overpowering.

There is no way you can dominate this man. You could actually lose your identity in a union with him. He's the sort of guy who could soon make you doubt opinions you have held all your life if they differ in the least way from his own.

He suffers deeply if he has the slightest reason for jealousy. If he sees you talking to another man at a party, he'll always think the guy is out to seduce you.

He isn't big on romantic chatter. To him, actions speak louder than words. Love and hate are very closely linked in his mind. He can also be revengeful if he feels someone has done him wrong. Very often he has few close friends. This is because he has to be boss in most of the relationships he forms.

Of course, a Sagittarius-Scorpio union could work out wonderfully if you are prepared to make this man's happiness your life's work. But remember, no one can ever completely change her nature. There will always be certain fundamental differences between you. You'll have to ask yourself whether your love is the kind that can last and overcome these basic problems.

You are not the type to get serious with other men after marriage. This is a good thing because a Scorpio man is quite capable of resorting to physical violence if he feels betrayed. Scorpio men are often on the smallish side, but they can make mincemeat of guys twice their size when their temper is aroused.

It's unlikely you will have the same tastes in music or art.

You will have to be careful of how the children are brought up. You are both inclined to channel all your interest and emotions into kids. This would be extremely suffocating for any youngster.

Mr. Scorpio will consider the running of the household your domain. He is one of those old-fashioned types who believes a woman's place is in the home, waiting for her man to arrive.

He is an exceptionally hard worker. He also knows how to handle money. He will give you a generous allowance, although he may keep secret exactly how much cash he has in the bank.

This man has almost X-ray vision when it comes to summing others up. He can not only spot a phony, which you're pretty good at yourself, but he can also identify the weaknesses of most individuals. Some of your more fun-loving friends may think he's a bit of a weirdo.

You will be very good for his career. He needs to have his confidence boosted, and you will do this when you think he deserves it. He can get a bit carried away and let success go to his head. You will make sure that he keeps both feet firmly on the ground.

SAGITTARIUS WOMAN— SAGITTARIUS MAN

You will have much in common with a man born under the same Sign. One of the most important things you'll be sharing is a very acute sense of humor, which will help you both when things get a bit abrasive. You will also prefer the same kind of life-style and enjoy the company of the same sort of people. That's a pretty good start.

He is a difficult man to trap, but you are not the type of woman who rushes to the altar. It could be you will know each other quite a while before you finally get around to discussing marriage.

There will be many difficulties to overcome. Neither of you is very good at accepting responsibility or making important decisions. You are both content to drift through life, and this can be very dangerous. He is a talented man, but on occasions needs a kick on the backside. Sometimes he needs a woman who will dominate him. Are you prepared to take on this role?

He doesn't like routine. Neither of you finds it easy to accept the discipline of a nine-to-five job. When you're together, you'll always be able to find a million excuses for not taking a certain course of action. Thus it could be a long time between productive moves.

You will soon realize there's a lot more to this man than he is prepared to let the rest of the world see. Sagittarius people, as you well know, don't wear their hearts on their sleeves. Others often see him as a bit of a rowdy, a life-and-soul-of-the-party type. You know better, though. You know there are hidden depths here. He is afraid of letting his true self be seen. He doesn't lightly trust people with his innermost thoughts.

He has a great feeling for the underdog. He will always go out of his way to help someone less fortunate than himself.

Mr. Sagittarius has to be careful he doesn't overindulge. There is a weak side to his nature. It is dangerous for him to get involved with heavy drinkers or gamblers. He may try to go further than they just to try to prove he is top dog.

You will have to watch the finances. Both of you are pretty useless at money management. Remember that the cash you require to buy all those luxury articles you so enjoy has to be earned. Remember, too, that you have to make provision for such things as income tax and the education of your kids. A live-for-the-moment attitude will make life very difficult as the years take their toll.

He is the faithful type. He will take his marriage vows seriously.

You will have to watch that bluntness. You are both sensitive and inclined to say things in such a way that the other could get hurt. Two people who always speak their minds may end up in Vegas after a couple of weeks together.

He is a bit of a gypsy so there could be problems when you have a family. He may leave you to cope with more than your fair share of parental responsibility.

Mr. Sagittarius will be exceedingly generous with your allowance. He will always want you to look your best. It won't worry him how much you spend on clothes.

Total independence can be a dangerous thing in marriage. You will both have to work hard at taking a more responsible attitude if you're going to stay together.

It will be up to you to make him feel you desire him physically. Unless you make him constantly aware that you want him to make love to you, the sexual side of your relationship could fade away.

SAGITTARIUS WOMAN—CAPRICORN MAN

You are just the outward-looking, no-nonsense type of girl to shake up a Capricorn man. Of all the Signs of the Zodiac, the Goat seems to be more wrapped up in himself, his own emotions and his own feelings, than anybody else.

He's extremely intelligent and a hard worker. His career and success are terribly important to him. He won't settle for second best. He has his eye on the boss's desk.

He wants lots of attention. He likes to be the center of attraction at a party. He will mope and sulk if he is ignored.

Mr. Capricorn may appear from all this to be totally self-sufficient. Don't believe it. Underneath his rather cool exterior, he is a genuine romantic who believes in true love. He's not a man to get casually involved with a woman.

He feels things deeply. He is not a man who dedicates himself to his job because he's trying to shut out the rest of the world. He is intelligent enough to know that if he is happy with what he does for a living, he has a greater chance of making a success of it, and the rest of his life will then fall into place. He knows how important a good wife can be to an ambitious man.

He is very disciplined. He believes in conformity. His tastes and attitudes are usually conservative.

If you want to get through to him, you'll have to be prepared to take the initiative; this is not an easy thing for a Sagittarius woman to do.

He can be a bit of a gossip. You should find there is no difficulty in communicating with him on an intellectual level.

He is very easily hurt. You will have to be on your diplomatic best behavior at all times. When he becomes depressed, it's best to leave him alone. It is practically impossible to reach a Capricorn when he is down in the dumps. He probably will not be able to explain why he gets the blues sometimes.

You are something of a good-time girl. You like meeting other people and going to parties. He is very reserved and usually has only one or two friends. He doesn't find it easy to talk to strangers. He may appear vague and indifferent on first meeting. The truth is he is probably acutely embarrassed.

This man will not be too happy with your attitude toward money because he's extremely security conscious. He's the type who has all sorts of endowment policies and saving schemes to protect him in his old age.

You prefer people who talk their problems out. You may find it terribly frustrating to be involved with a man who is determined to keep so many areas of his life to himself.

One wonders if he has enough to offer to keep you contented for a lifetime. You would not enjoy having to give up so many of your outside interests. He is possessive rather than jealous.

If you meet a Capricorn man who has come to terms with himself, you would have a much better chance of succeeding as a twosome.

It is unlikely he will stray off the straight and narrow. He's not the type to have affairs on the side.

You are basically an optimist, and he tends to be a pessimist: it could be that you will balance each other out rather well. If you are a believer in the attraction of opposites, you could have a happy life together in begging to differ.

In the bedroom, he's one of the most virile guys you'll ever meet.

SAGITTARIUS WOMAN—AQUARIUS MAN

You will probably take an immediate liking to this man. It's quite likely you already have a number of close buddies born under Aquarius because you are both extremely outward-looking Signs. You will hit it off from the start with this truly unconventional person. You will admire him for getting up and doing things while you simply sit around talking about them.

Mr. Aquarius is capable of great deeds of kindness. He is genuinely unselfish. He is prepared to put the needs of others before himself.

Well, this is all very fine in friendship, but how would it work in marriage? You believe very strongly that two people should share everything. You are fond of your home and are not really prepared to share your man with lots of others. The fact is he will have so many interests and so many obligations that you may sometimes wonder where exactly you fit in in the jigsaw puzzle of his life.

You will discover he has a fine mind. If he is in love with you, he'll move heaven and earth to win you. He is extremely forceful when communicating his own ideas, a very persuasive talker who excels at winning people over to his side.

Don't forget that Aquarius is the Sign of friendship, social life, hopes and fears.

He will admire many of the qualities you possess and he does not. He hasn't got much time for weak women. He will think it fantastic the way you can stand on your own two feet when you have to.

You will become terribly frustrated when you see him channeling all that marvelous energy and caring into the outside world and not into the home and all the things that mean so much to you. You will understand his belief in certain causes, but that won't help you to come to terms with his way of life.

He will leave all matters connected with household management to you. He won't even be aware whether or not the house is tidy. He won't notice when you've made new kitchen curtains or put a bunch of freshly picked flowers on the dining-room table.

This man is out to change the world and make it a better place for us all to live in. If you are serious about him and want to keep him for very long, you will have to passionately share his hopes and desires.

Mr. Aquarius is so often ahead of his time. What he is trying to bring about now could well take place in fifty years. Many people label him a revolutionary. That he may be, but he usually believes in peaceful methods for promoting change.

He will allow you all the freedom you want; this could be dangerous because one day you may walk out of the house and never come back. Why? Because you have gotten the feeling he wouldn't really notice if you were there or not.

He is quite likely to change his job a number of times. He doesn't find it easy to obtain satisfaction in his work. He needs to do something with a real purpose behind it.

It is obvious you would have to give up an awful lot in order to make a go of it with the Water Bearer. Don't let's be too pessimistic, though. Your differences could bring you to a greater understanding of what love and sacrifice are really about. And if he looks at it that way too, he'll certainly have found something worth striving for.

SAGITTARIUS WOMAN—PISCES MAN

He's a bit of a will-o'-the-wisp. You will never know when he's likely to appear or disappear. Life with him will be full of surprises. You are a woman who can take change in her stride, so you might be able to put up with the antics of Mr. Pisces.

When you first meet this man, you may feel his head is so high in the clouds he could never get anything together. Actually, he is capable of achieving marvelous results when he puts his mind to it. His enthusiasm knows no bounds.

You will find him difficult to pin down. You will always be discovering something new about his personality. One minute, he will be riding on the crest of a wave, and the next, he'll be overcome by a fit of depression. He can be sentimental to the point of mushiness and ice cold a moment later. Only a foolish person would try to take advantage of his good nature.

He's adroit at clinching business deals in record time. He has the gift of gab. He can talk people around to his way of thinking with seemingly little trouble. He is also a tiny bit crafty.

He is not a weak man, but he does have some trouble keeping up interest in any particular project for very long.

You are a direct person. You usually stick to pretty rigid attitudes. You will find there are many different people contained in one Pisces man.

Your way of rushing about all the time will amaze him. He will wonder why you have to keep so constantly on the go. Perhaps you'll make a good team because he tends to be more a dreamer and producer of new ideas than an activist.

But we have to be honest about Mr. Pisces. If he hasn't got the ball rolling by the time he hits thirty, it's unlikely he'll make the really big time. You will have to give him that extra push. He tends to sit back when he's earned enough loot to keep the wolf from the door for a couple of months.

You must be very careful how you handle him. He can't take brusqueness from the person he loves. His extreme sensitivity may irritate you. He doesn't judge others. He has a live-and-let-live attitude. He is not mean with money. Whatever he earns will be yours if there is something really special you wish to buy.

He will try to get along with your family. He will realize how important the feelings of your loved ones are to you. Even if he is not that keen on your mother, he'll try never to let you know.

If you take the rough with the smooth and decide to make your life with him, you'll certainly never be bored.

He's not exactly a secretive person but he does believe in only letting people know what is good for them. This is the very opposite to your approach. Still, if you hit it off together, he'll always want to please you and you'll get plenty of pleasant surprises.

He is a pushover for kids. They're likely to run all over him. He's a bit of a child at heart and his attempts at playing the role of disciplinarian can be very amusing. He's just too soft, so you'll have to be the one to keep order in the nursery.

He will prefer the evenings when you are alone together most of all. He is a good mixer, but the home is very important to Pisces. He likes to talk about the past and you'll find his recollections very amusing on cold winter's nights in front of the fire. He is blessed with great insight into human nature.

SAGITTARIUS MAN—ARIES WOMAN

To love a man, a Mars girl has to be able to look up to him. You will have to be the sort of guy she can be proud of and whose success she can boast about to her friends.

Miss Aries is the dominant type. She needs to feel she can control her lover. If you are not careful, she'll take you over lock, stock and barrel—or at least, she'll try.

You prize your freedom and individuality so you might not find it appealing to have a woman always saying, "We'll do this" or "We think that." Even in marriage, you insist on retaining your individuality and control over your own destiny. You two could have some fireworks.

Although she'll demand a lot, she'll pay you back twice over. There isn't a more loyal woman in the Zodiac once she's found her dream man.

A woman born under the Sign of the Ram likes to keep on the go. Adventure excites her and she will face up to almost any challenge. The word failure isn't in her vocabulary. You are a bit of a swashbuckler and don't like to keep still for very long. So long as you wish to wander in the same direction, all will be well. The problem is you are something of a loner. She's the jealous type and won't like your going out on your own too much.

This girl is terribly sensitive. That fire in her can soon turn to ice if she discovers you have been two-timing her.

She doesn't generally have a lot of women friends. It's unlikely you'll find her heading the local Junior League or attending hen parties. She prefers the company of men. She's sporting and quite aggressive. It's true she can become too demanding. If she is really gone on you, it's possible you'll begin to feel trapped. She's no good at playing hard to get. Once she's in love, her passion is unquenchable.

She will always play it straight with you. You will admire her honesty and frankness.

She is interested in success—not only for herself, but for her man as well. She is often a career woman. Having so much energy to burn, she's quite capable of running a home and holding down an important job at the same time.

Miss Aries rarely goes for a good-time Charlie. Looks don't matter to her that much. She will be more interested in men who have a special quality. She has a way of seeing through phonies.

You could be the type of man to win her. One thing is certain: you will keep her guessing. It's not good for her to get the upper hand in a relationship, even though this is what she appears to be striving to do.

Never put her down in front of others. She has great pride. Sometimes she is capable of making spiteful or catty remarks, but she really doesn't mean them. Very often she's just trying to be witty.

You will have to admire her guts. Even when she's feeling low, she'll keep plugging away. She's not the type of woman who takes to her bed at the first sign of a chill.

You must keep the passion and romance going in your life together. An Aries woman is a sexy lady. If she is not finding fulfillment in bed, she will get very neurotic.

You are an idealist, a bit of a dreamer. Here is a woman who will believe in your dreams and do all she can to help you realize them.

SAGITTARIUS MAN—TAURUS WOMAN

You'll need to be a mature man to hang on to Miss Taurus. Being a well-adjusted lady, she has no time for games playing. Youthful Mr. Sagittarius likes a good time and is capable of being boisterous, even childish, on occasions. The Bull will not stand for your adolescent ways. If you are determined to win her, you'll just have to grow up.

A Taurus person doesn't readily show what she feels. She is extremely self-contained. She doesn't throw her love around. She is only interested in steady relationships. She's down to earth—you might, in fact, find her a little too slow and deliberate.

She won't judge you because she takes people as they are. If you're not her type, she'll tell you straight out. She's a no-nonsense woman who doesn't like to beat about the bush.

Since her Sign is ruled by Venus, you'll find her a wonderful lover. She's full of passion but all woman.

Miss Taurus has a good brain though she isn't very academic. She has an uncanny knack of being able to sum up people quickly. Don't try to soft-soap her. She'll know if you are really serious in your intentions.

She's a very reliable person. It would upset her greatly to let down someone who was depending on her. If you do marry, you can be sure the lady Bull will stand by you no matter what the crisis.

This woman is not too interested in the hard grind of housework, though she is artistic and enjoys doing artistic things at home. It would be a help if you could afford to get someone in to do the more routine chores. A Taurus lady won't wish to be tied to the kitchen sink. She's a true home lover, but she also wishes to keep up with her outside interests.

Usually she is a great cook who loves to experiment in the kitchen. She will bring her artistic flair to everything she does.

She's slow and deliberate. She takes her time when it comes to making important decisions. More than likely, she will favor a long courtship.

As you get to know her better, you'll realize just how lucky you are. Whenever you feel downcast, you'll be grateful to have your Taurus woman by your side. She's as steady as a rock in times of crisis.

She is much better at money management than you. She knows how to save. You might find it best to leave the budgeting and paying of the regular bills to her.

Don't try to change your Taurus woman. She holds very set opinions. She won't try to alter your views on life, and it would be best not to get involved in arguments on serious subjects.

She is the faithful type. Once she's decided you are her man, she won't be interested in a casual affair. She won't mind your flirting with a pretty girl; she'll realize it's your nature. But woe betide you if you get involved in a heavy love affair. She'll find it hard to forgive you.

The Taurus female loves pretty clothes. That is her one extravagance. She will want to keep up with the latest fashions and look her best at all times.

When the going is tough, she won't moan. This is the sort of woman who is prepared to go out and get a job to keep the home fires burning.

As parents, you should make a good team. You are a bit of a kid yourself, and your Taurus woman is capable of keeping you all in order.

SAGITTARIUS MAN—GEMINI WOMAN

You two are likely to make quite a pair, but you may run into problems if you get deeply involved. You are both outward-looking types who enjoy a comfortable style of living, but neither of you is going to want to sit about keeping the home fires burning.

Miss Gemini finds it hard to take anything—even romance—seriously for very long. She blows hot and cold. One minute, she could be all over you; the next, she'll be switching on her favorite TV program.

You would have to make it your life's work to find the real woman hiding behind the many facades of Gemini. Her Sign is the Twins, so she is rather a split person.

Mercury females are not quite as heartless as they often appear. They have very quick tongues, though, and are capable of making the most cutting remarks. You may feel she is out to tease you. She can't help playing games. Among the things she refuses to take seriously is herself.

Age is an important factor here. There's more chance of settling down with this woman if you have both drunk fully of the cup of life. You are both very curious characters. You want to know what is going on in the outside world, and it takes you a long time to grow up and come to terms with life.

She needs understanding. If you try to lay down the law and restrict her in any way, she'll run a mile.

You will never cease to wonder at the way this woman can suddenly change her moods and personality. One minute, she is the contented housewife happily basting the Sunday roast; the next, she is the life and soul of the party, behaving seductively and dancing with every man in the room. By the way, you'll have to get used to her flirting ways. If you do get married, it's unlikely she'll have an affair, but playing up to the opposite sex is as natural to her as breathing.

She is game for anything. You'll find you become buddies as well as lovers. No matter how far out your suggestions may be for pleasure or entertainment—and you do come up with some weirdies—she will be prepared to have a go. She loves thrills and excitement.

Your Gemini woman adores travel and changes of scenery. She can't stand to be restricted or to stay in one place for very long. She'd rather go by jet than take her time on a luxury liner. She doesn't always know where she's headed, but she sure wants to get there fast.

This female needs a lot of loving. She is quite the little-girl-lost underneath the vivacious image she projects. You only have to think of Marilyn Monroe, who was a Gemini, to get the idea.

You must allow her to keep her individuality after marriage. She will go crazy with boredom if she doesn't have plenty to occupy her mind while you're at work.

This woman is no moaner. She will try to make the best of it when you hit hard times. Even though she can get terribly depressed, she has great faith that better times are around the corner.

The Gemini woman is in her element at a party. You will also find her wonderful at home entertaining. Your boss will like her. She can bring a smile to the face of even the most disenchanted of people.

You'd better face it, this woman is extravagant with money. Not selfish, though, because she likes to spend it on you and the kids. You're not so good at budgeting so you'll have to work something out. Anyway, your Gemini woman is generous to a fault, which will appeal to a guy like you much more than the other extreme.

SAGITTARIUS MAN—CANCER WOMAN

If the love bug bites you and Miss Cancer, you're likely to become a different man. This is the sort of woman who could change your wandering ways and make you want to stay home nights. She's quite a woman. If she loves you, you'll realize what love is all about. The only possible way you can get involved with her is deeply.

She has humor, wit, intelligence and charm. Mind you, she is very changeable. She can break a man's heart. She is capable of playing games with people's emotions.

The Crab does not like to let go. If you are really head over heels in love with her, she'll keep you dangling on a piece of string. She loves to have admirers; they boost her confidence—something she doesn't possess a lot of despite her brave front.

You will find her subject to sudden and unexpected changes of mind. She rarely knows in which direction she's headed. This can be infuriating. She hates to be bossed, yet needs a dominant man. She has great difficulty in recalling what she felt yesterday. That is, until she meets Mr. Right.

You might be too much of a gadabout for her. Basically, she is looking for security. She loves the home.

She has a great way of involving all sorts of people in her problems. Yet when you offer advice, she'll tell you not to interfere.

Money is a subject of unusual interest to her. She would like to have pots of it. She is a great saver and very security conscious. As a bachelor girl, she always makes certain the rent money's there before she goes out and buys a new dress.

She loves others to fight her battles for her. Anyone who takes her side seems to get mixed up in odd skirmishes. She is looking for a knight in shining armor to sweep her off her feet.

When your lunar lady withdraws into her shell, it takes a lot of coaxing to get her to venture out again. You mightn't be prepared to give her all the time she needs on these occasions. It could be a sore point between you.

If you do marry, you'll find the phone bill can reach astronomical sums. The calls to her mother could last hours. Let's hope your mother-in-law lives nearby.

Don't play games with her emotions because if you say you love her, she will believe you. When she gives her love, it is very special. If you were to hurt her deeply, she'd have a lot of trouble getting over it.

You will have to boost her ego constantly. Tell her how beautiful she is and what a wonderful wife she makes at least ten times a day. Keep the romance in your marriage. Take her out to intimate bistros and always give her roses on special occasions.

When things go wrong, she is capable of being the calmest person in the room. In times of great crisis, Cancer folk are often the most level-headed and reliable. There is no end to the sacrifices this woman will make for the people she loves the most.

She will get a wonderful home together for the man lucky enough to win her. She won't mind your having the odd night out with the boys—so long as it's beer and poker, that is!

You couldn't find a better mother for your children. Nothing is too good for her family. You may have to be careful, though, that she doesn't get overprotective with the boys. She's also likely to dish out some rather heavy punishment when the kids get too naughty. She has a very high tolerance of irritation, but when she does lose her temper, she hits out.

SAGITTARIUS MAN—LEO WOMAN

You are both independent types, both fire Signs. One has to ask the question, will the sparks fly in the coming together of Sagittarius and Leo? The major stumbling block to happiness is the fact that you have such widely differing interests.

This woman is capable of applying herself to almost anything. She likes a good time, but can be disciplined when she has to be. You are a great chopper and changer. It could be that once the honeymoon is over, you will grow apart.

Miss Leo is proud, a born leader. She won't take orders from anyone for very long. However, if her long-term happiness is at stake, she will swallow her pride and accept compromise solutions.

You do prize your freedom. This is not the sort of lady who will be content to take a back seat while you hog the limelight. She may get a bit fed up with your rather adolescent behavior.

She is quite a girl. Your friends are likely to fancy her like mad. She will enjoy playing up to them, although it's unlikely she'd go further than flirting. Fortunately you are not the jealous type.

It might be that you can reach some harmonious arrangement. You will certainly have to allow each other plenty of individual freedom.

She may appear to be the gentlest, most feminine creature on the earth, but she can get furious if you make a fool of her.

A good thing to remember when you set out to woo the Lioness is to go armed with lots of presents. Any kitten likes to be spoiled, and this one is no exception. She wants a man to demonstrate his love for her in fairly obvious ways.

Don't ever take her for granted. You love a night out with your buddies—but you'd better get the go-ahead from your Leo woman first. She won't be content to sit patiently at home while you're out painting the town red.

There are many things about you she will adore. She likes a man who has a good sense of humor and is a bit of a joker, which you certainly are. She'll also admire your honesty and candor. She's very straightforward herself.

Don't try to dominate her. Give her freedom of choice. This is an extremely intelligent woman perfectly capable of making up her own mind. She needs outside interests. She has a very inquiring mind. You will be amazed at how well she can apply herself to further educational activities long after her school days are over.

Other women can be pretty catty about her, very often because of jealousy. Her direct, no-nonsense attitude is the envy of many.

She won't give you any more flattery than you deserve. This is not the type of woman who butters a man's ego to get on the right side of him. She has far too much pride for that sort of coyness.

You both have a pretty imaginative attitude toward sex. It is unlikely you will get bored with each other as lovers. You'll find there are many games you can play to keep your physical relationship burning.

She will be a help to you in business. This girl is a definite asset to any man keen to make his mark in the world.

You are both likely to want to wait a while before entertaining the idea of having a family.

SAGITTARIUS MAN—VIRGO WOMAN

Don't believe all you hear about Miss Virgo. She is often portrayed as a shy, reserved woman who is about as passionate as an iceberg. This is not true. All she needs is the right man to help her discover her true nature. You could be that man.

There is so much you could teach each other. You certainly know all about the humor in life and are well equipped to show her that this crazy world doesn't have to be taken seriously *all* the time. She, in turn, would help you settle down. Basically, you are yearning for a secure home, even if you don't want to spend all your free time in it. This is the sort of woman who could supply you with a base from which you could function successfully.

She is shy. When you first begin courting, she will probably blush to the roots at some of the wild antics you get up to in public. Although she may tug at your sleeve and scold you a little, she'll secretly admire your boldness.

Only when she knows she can trust you will she give you her love. She is not prepared to show her true feelings to a man who is here today gone tomorrow.

She finds it hard to admit she is in the wrong. Show her by example rather than by pointing out her mistakes.

This woman is a perfectionist. Anything she takes on she will want to become expert in. You will find her extremely competent. She makes a marvelous secretary or personal assistant to a business tycoon. Time is important to her. She is always punctual.

No sloppy manners when this girl is around, and don't flick your ashes on the carpet. She is very house-proud. Possessions are quite important to her. It isn't that she's mean, but she does treasure articles she has collected over the years. She is quite attached to the past and can get very sentimental.

She can also be a bit of a prude, but this is because she is moral. If someone offends her principles, she's quite capable of cutting that person dead and bearing a grudge for years.

She won't like the idea of your going out on your own too much. She will want to share in your life as much as possible. You might find this a bit too restricting at times.

You are quite a natty dresser when it suits you and this will go down well with Miss Virgo. She will want you to look your best when you take her out. You'll have to restrain your penchant for dressing inappropriately.

Don't try to rush her to the bedroom. This is a woman who likes to take her time about everything, especially something as important as making love. She won't enter into an affair lightly. Casual relationships do not appeal to her.

Your Virgo woman will want to stay faithful to you. As with everything she does, she will aim to make a success of her marriage. Don't try to con her because to her, truth is beauty. It would be better to admit it when you stray. She will respect your honesty if you make a clean breast of things. Your candor is one of your strongest points in her eyes.

Mrs. Virgo knows how to run a home efficiently. Everything will be in its place, including her in the kitchen preparing mouth-watering dishes for you when you arrive home.

You will provide a good balance when the kids come along; she's likely to be fairly strict with them.

SAGITTARIUS MAN—LIBRA WOMAN

This is a woman whose outlook and interests are very similar to your own. You should hit it off right away with this lively, no-nonsense girl.

You like people who are straightforward and don't put on airs. She will depend on you without ever becoming a drag. She is capable of combining a successful career with a happy and contented home life.

Miss Libra is sensible enough to know when to take the lead and when to stay in the background. She would never dream of attempting to usurp your position as head of the household. You can rest assured, though, that she will be able to keep things ticking very smoothly should you ever have to go away on a business trip.

A Libra won't try to curtail your movements. You will never feel trapped or suffocated. She is also capable of keeping the romance and zest in a relationship long after you have celebrated your golden wedding anniversary.

Harmony and balance are terribly important to this woman. She is far more logical than most girls. She will weigh everything twice before definitely making up her mind.

To many people, she may appear argumentative. Not so. It's simply that she wishes to hear every point of view on a particular subject before she decides which side of the fence to come down on.

Libra women, as a rule, are on the petite side and ultrafeminine, which should please you.

Venus girls like to keep active. She is apt to have numerous interests. Apart from her career and family, she is likely to participate in at least one sport and have that blessed knack of being able to show interest in her husband's hobbies and pastimes.

She will never try to wear the pants. She likes her man to be a man.

You must not imagine you can continue your bachelor life if your hitch your star to a Libra woman. She likes a good time, too, and won't want to be left with all the domestic responsibilities while you go out on the town. She can be just as independent as you.

Also, don't forget that Libra is the Sign of partnership and human relationships. Therefore you can imagine how important it will be to a woman born under the seventh Sign of the Zodiac to make a success of her marriage.

More than anything else in the world, she will want you to get to the top in your career. Not only because she knows success means security, but also because she realizes that if you are happy in your job, everything else will fall into place. She's a very intelligent woman behind all that charm and courtesy.

She is likely to favor a very modern house. She will make her kitchen as labor-saving as possible. She won't want to waste her time polishing floors or peeling vegetables when there are machines that will do these things. She will be one of those wives who'll want to invest in a deep-freeze because she knows it saves time and money.

When you get depressed, she will make a fuss over you and cheer you up. A Libra woman will stick by her man through thick and thin.

This woman looks good in anything, but you will find she is happiest in jeans and a floppy sweater (probably one of yours) when she can get away with it.

She makes a dedicated and very understanding mother. You'll be amazed as how well she gets along with her children and their mates.

SAGITTARIUS MAN—SCORPIO WOMAN

You're taking on quite a lot if you decide a Scorpio woman is the one for you. For a start, she isn't easy to get to know. On first meeting, you will be struck by her mysterious qualities. She is certainly a deep person. On her side, she may get the impression that you are a bit superficial. The Pluto lady takes life very seriously. She can be a little too serious—especially about herself.

She prizes her freedom. She can't take being bossed around by anyone. She really likes to be in charge in a relationship.

You don't like confrontations. You are terribly good at deflating people, yet you don't fancy heavy scenes, particularly with people you are emotionally involved with. A Scorpio woman can't abide a close liaison with a man unless there's a certain amount of tension. She likes to feel the adrenalin flowing.

She has nothing but contempt for girls who play wide-eyed and innocent. She can be downright catty about members of her own sex who take advantage of a man's desire to be protector and provider.

Lots of Scorpio girls are tomboys. You won't win her over with fluffy presents or boxes of chocolates.

Life with this woman will not be plain sailing by any means.

Don't ever play around behind her back. If you let her down or make a fool of her in any way, she will never forget it. She can be quite vengeful. It may take her a long time to even the score, but she'll do it in the end. Hell hath no fury like a Scorpio woman scorned.

Miss Scorpio has a disconcerting way of getting what she wants without giving the appearance of trying. If you are her type, she will weave a spell over you without your realizing what is happening. You may think you are the one making the overtures, but don't be so sure.

She's ambitious. She likes to be the leader of the gang. She treasures her individuality and insists on making up her own mind.

It is quite something to have this woman fall for you. You should be flattered if she does because she is very choosy.

She is capable of going to excess because she has no innate mechanism that tells her when to stop. It is extremely dangerous for a Scorpio to get involved in heavy drinking or hard drugs.

Sex is terribly important to her. She has difficulty in coping with life if she is not obtaining sexual satisfaction. She has a lusty appetite in bed. Let's hope you can keep up with her.

She is a great survivor. Although she may get drawn into all sorts of weird scenes because of her inquiring nature, she's likely to come out unscathed. She's pretty secretive and rarely likes to discuss her past. But you'll be surprised at how much she knows about you after your first meeting. She has a knack of making people reveal themselves without realizing what they are doing.

Scorpios love their home. She won't mind being on her own on occasions. Don't take this for granted, though. If you spend too much time out with your buddies, you might return to find she has walked out.

Despite her desire to be free, she is willing to let a man she loves enough make the decisions.

It is also true that of all the females in the Zodiac, a Scorpio woman is often capable of earning more money than her husband. So long as you love her and need her, she won't mind being the breadwinner.

SAGITTARIUS MAN—SAGITTARIUS WOMAN

One thing is certain—you'll know where you

stand with this woman. She's a no-nonsense type. She'll always voice her opinions and speak her mind. Some people find this sort of honesty a little too much to take. After all, how many individuals in this world can face up to the truth?

You two will make quite a pair, though. It's important to have a fair number of mutual interests. When two Sagittarians get together, the relationship won't last long if it is based solely on physical attraction.

The male of the Sagittarius species is usually a little more diplomatic than the female (which is not saying very much). Occasionally she will come out with comments that seem plain brutal. But you must realize she's not out to hurt.

You do need to have your ego boosted from time to time; every man does. She's unlikely to be prepared to do this.

Don't try to boss her around. Never force her into a course of action. This fire lady will dig in her heels and refuse to budge. She simply can't stand to be told what to do.

You will love being in her company. She's always fresh and game for anything. Like you, she gets bored very easily. She loves her home but hates to feel she is a slave to domestic routine.

Miss Sagittarius has a funny attitude toward her man. When she's out in company, she'll try to give the appearance of wearing the trousers. Just watch her making a show and giving the impression she makes all the important decisions. At home, it will be a different story. Basically, she wants a man to lead. She dislikes weakness and has no time for a crybaby looking for a mother.

She doesn't play games. She finds it impossible to conceal her emotions. How she looks is how she feels. Never ask her what she is thinking; if it was worth talking about, she would have said it.

She loves meeting new people and getting out and about. She is wonderfully patient when she has to be. She will rely on her instinct rather than logic in matters of the heart.

Lots of Sagittarius women like to pursue a career after marriage. It is unlikely you'll have any objections to this because she will have no difficulty in combining outside interests with looking after the family.

When she's hooked by a man, she really worships him. She will believe everything you tell her. You will even hear her coming out with your opinions in public as though they were her own. She is very trusting. If the man she loves lets her down, it will take her a long time to get over the pain.

She will not find it easy to forgive you if you go off the rails. She won't object to your flirting; that she will understand. But if you get involved seriously with another woman, she may never feel quite the same about you again.

This woman's love goes deeper than physical passion. You won't find her the most hot-blooded female in the world. Much will depend on you when it comes to lovemaking. She will go for long periods without making love rather than settle for a habitual or half-hearted relationship.

She is great with the kids, but gets a bit bossy with them when they hit their teens.

SAGITTARIUS MAN—CAPRICORN WOMAN

You are a pretty ambitious guy. Many people write you off as little more than a playboy, someone who is only interested in having a good time. This, as you know, is not actually true. But people do make snap judgments. If they bothered to get to know you a little better, they'd realize you are keen to get to the top and win recognition. One person who is likely to understand you right from the start is Miss Capricorn.

This could be just the sort of woman you need. You will get the feeling she knows what she's talking about. There is a feeling of truth to her opinions.

You do need a woman who is capable of being the power behind the scenes. Success is important to this girl. She will always be at your side boosting your confidence when self-doubt inevitably creeps in.

She won't stand for your being lazy, either. There will be no resting on your laurels if you get attached to a Capricorn.

She is a hard worker in her own right. She is also a great survivor. She has loads of ambition. She's capable of giving herself totally to a man. Even though her own career is important to her, she would be prepared to give it up if she felt you needed her around all the time.

She is careful with money. You'll be amazed at how cheaply she can get a meal together.

She is more nervous than you may realize. Though she's able to put on a brave front, she is terribly insecure. Your attitude to life will be a wonderful confidence booster for her.

Miss Capricorn is fascinated by power. She is intensely interested in meeting people who get to the top, not particularly because she wants to use them, but because she's curious to know what makes them tick. In fact, she's very curious about life in general.

Her taste is exquisite. She is wonderful at decorating and furnishing. In many ways, she's quite old-fashioned. She likes things to be done the correct way. She sets great store by charm and good manners. You'll have to watch those boisterous antics of yours, especially when you're out together in public.

Women born where Saturn rules and Mars is exalted are interested in security and wealth. It isn't that she wants the money itself; she desires the power that goes with it.

Always be polite to her family. It's important that you get on with her mother and father. A Capricorn female is very strongly attached to her relatives. She wants to make them feel proud.

She is a true romantic. She's interested in love, not in casual affairs. It may take a bit of time to get to know her well. Don't rush her. She likes to take her time making up her mind.

You will be struck by her great love of music. You'll notice how emotional she can get when listening to her favorite symphony.

Miss Capricorn doesn't mind taking the rough with the smooth. She's prepared to make a sacrifice if it will pay dividends in the future. She will love watching your savings grow. Her ideas on good investments may be better than yours. She'll save you dollars with her shopping.

Her attitude to lovemaking will meet with your approval. She has a vivid imagination in the bedroom.

Allow her to flirt with other men. It's only harmless fun to her. You'll find it interesting to note how many guys fall under her spell.

SAGITTARIUS MAN—AQUARIUS WOMAN

An Aquarius woman is difficult to get to know . . . really know. She can be madly in love with you and still retain her air of detachment.

This is a woman you must never attempt to tie down. She's a freedom lover, but perhaps in a different way than you are.

You tend to be on the lookout for a good time. You enjoy parties and making life a fun experience. Miss Aquarius is quite a different kettle of fish. She's serious—perhaps a little too serious for a Sagittarius man. She believes in causes. She is constantly getting involved with people who need help.

She has an independent streak as wide as yours. She can't stand having anyone lay down the law to her.

Where this union is likely to go wrong is that you do like to have a home to come back to, a home that is comfortable, welcoming and warm. An Aquarius lady will probably be unhappy in the role of dutiful little housewife. She will feel she has far more to offer. And she'll be right.

She gets deeply involved with everyone she meets, and yet you will be hard pushed to find a single person who could say he or she knows her really well.

Money is not that important to her. She's not interested in amassing great wealth.

She's also not given to compromise. She has her principles and she'll stick to them. Miss Aquarius is an idealist.

Remember, this is the Sign of friendship, social interests and aspirations. An Aquarius woman will not stay in one place for long.

If your work is in any way connected with politics or education, she could be the ideal wife. She likes to feel the work her man does is worthwhile. If you believe in the same things and work hard to get your point of view across, she will do everything in her power to assist you.

Your Aquarius woman is not the jealous type. She won't question you about where you've been when you get home late. To her way of thinking, you're mature enough—or should be—to look after yourself.

It's unusual for an Aquarius woman to become involved with another man after marriage. It's not that she won't have her opportunities; she will. It's simply that she won't wish to complicate her life. She's capable of channeling her energies in other directions.

She has very artistic tastes. She will know how to get a home together without spending a great deal of money. Prepare yourself to sit on cushions on the floor rather than a couch.

She doesn't like to borrow or lend. She likes paying her way in this world. She is more inclined to give money to a cause than to an individual.

Her dress sense will be unusual in some way or other. She is unlikely to wear very feminine clothes, though her unconventional style can be most attractive. The way she does her hair is also likely to be extraordinary. In so many ways, she's pretty far-out.

As a mother, she finds it difficult to cope at times. Although capable of getting the whole world together, she's often bewildered by the responsibility of having to look after a tiny baby.

Still, you have several things in common and, with love, could make a success of it.

SAGITTARIUS MAN—PISCES WOMAN

Sweet, dewy-eyed Miss Pisces will be a puzzle to a man like you. She's all woman, there's no doubt about it. She needs protection. And she has more than her fair share of feminine charm, not to say wiles.

Perhaps you are in need of a mate who is a little more independent. You like to play protector, but you also treasure your freedom. This woman may depend on you for everything. She is a great home lover and will find it hard to understand why you want an evening out with the boys. To this woman, marriage is almost a total commitment and undertaking.

She tends to lack confidence, and this is where you will be good for her. Your outward-going personality and sense of fun will help her to lose her self-consciousness.

A Pisces girl likes a man who can take the lead. It will be up to you to make the big decisions. She will want you to be the boss in this union. Only, be warned, she'll be working behind the scenes on you to get the things she wants. She's a great schemer. But if you love her, whatever she sets her mind on will be for you both.

She's a bit of a dreamer. You'll feel she's wandering around with her head in the clouds most of the time. Don't be fooled by her innocent wide-eyed expression. This is a lady who knows what is going on most of the time. Her intuition is amazing.

You will love looking after her, bringing her a cup of coffee in bed and buying her all the pretty things she admires.

She does tend to be unambitious. You could find this lack of drive rather irritating. You like to keep busy. You may find it difficult to understand how she can wander around without appearing to have one thought in that pretty little head of hers.

A Pisces woman can get disillusioned very quickly. She is unlikely to think very much of society and the way it is run. This is one of the reasons she lacks driving force and finds it hard to work up enthusiasm about most things. She finds it easier to commit herself to a person than to commit to a cause.

If you are looking for a woman who will be happy to make you her entire life, then you need not look further.

She's terrific at entertaining. She knows how to make others feel happy. She loves cooking. She will enjoy it when you bring your boss home to dinner.

One of her pleasures in life is making her home comfortable and beautiful. She has an artistic flair and knows a bargain when she sees one.

Pisces people can be taken in by others very easily. They are impressed by powerful personalities, and this is not always good for them. They have some difficulty in distinguishing between good and evil.

She is searching for something, perhaps her true self.

You are both capable of promiscuity, but it's likely you'll want to remain faithful to each other. You'll find there's a special quality about a Pisces woman that helps keep you on the straight and narrow. She appears so defenseless that you could not bear to let her down. The love she offers is far too valuable to put in jeopardy. If you love her truly and don't try to destroy her dreams, she is unlikely to stray.

Sexually, you should be well attuned. You need a partner who is all woman.

SAGITTARIUS' HEALTH

Compared with other Signs, a conspicuous number of you Sagittarius-born people live well into your eighties. You are naturally healthy (unless, of course, there are afflicting influences in the horoscope). You are born with a strong physical constitution—and you certainly need it to keep up the vigorous pace at which you to live.

You are also helped by an extremely optimistic attitude toward life. As a rule, you don't let your problems get you down. You have an enviable way of throwing off worry. You are a great believer in tomorrow. You are more than a good survivor, you are a cheerful, good-natured one. This helps to keep you fit.

You may meet the odd Sagittarius personality who is not like this at all. This type is introspective, even reclusive. Fortunately, he or she is a rarity. Sagittarius is an outward-going, hopeful Sign, and when someone born under it exhibits contrary urges, the result is usually some highly eccentric habits or behavior.

The typical Sagittarius person *needs* constant contact with a wide variety of people and a great deal of physical and mental involvement to keep him or her in good health. Your nervous system is high-strung and keenly adapted to respond to the joy and freedom of outdoor activity. You must keep on the go—visiting, participating, organizing, discussing. Any prolonged curtailment or restraint is likely to lead to some kind of gradual breakdown.

You have above-average resistance to disease. This is not surprising in a Sign known as the great wanderer of the Zodiac. You are very seldom incapacitated with serious illnesses. On the rare occasions when you do have to stay in bed, you soon become distressed and restless because of the enforced inactivity. It's a job to keep you there. Your agitation may have a worse effect on your health than the illness. You feel you'd rather be sick while up and about.

Fresh air is very important to you, and when you're convalescing from an illness, you need loads of it. There should also be no feeling of unnecessary restriction. You have a tremendous aversion to being cooped up—it depresses you, makes you nervous and irritable and impairs your recovery.

Your recuperative powers are exceptional. The strength you show in early youth seems to stay with you well past your middle years. You have the knack of instant restful sleep. Thus you can overcome ordinary fatigue with a few minutes' nap. You often manage to outpace your liveliest associates by sneaking forty winks in the nearest chair.

You are a born sportsman or athlete. You know how to keep yourself in trim. You enjoy games and exercise. But you often don't make the best of your vitality. You have a habit of scattering your energies in ways that produce very little that is worthwhile.

Although you live off your activity, you sometimes tend to push your robust constitution too far. You get carried away with the euphoric feeling that you can go on forever. It is in times of overstrain that you are most liable to get sick. You may suffer from sudden fevers, bouts of delirium and the "cold shivers." Abrupt changes of temperature should be avoided. In your hurry, you are apt to neglect to dress more protectively in wet or cold weather. You are then more vulnerable than other types to flu, colds, sore throats and stiff necks. Your supreme faith in your ability to survive is sometimes foolhardy.

Sagittarius rules the hips, thighs and sciatic nerve. There is also a connection with the chest, lungs, hands, feet and intestines. Among the most common ailments are sciatica, hip injuries and arthritis, rheumatism, indigestion and gout.

Sagittarius people are subject to lameness in various forms. They tend to suffer from accidents affecting their hands, feet or hips. They may dislocate joints. Being impatiently active and rather forgetful, you sometimes get hurt by running into objects and tripping over things.

Although you are basically a very sensible person, there is the risk that you will go to extremes where food and drink are concerned. Sagittarius people are usually not habitual overeaters, but they can become overweight through too much entertaining and rich food. Alcohol may become a problem for the same reasons. Fortunately, your innate desire to keep fit usually makes you cut down or go on a diet when you feel your health is being endangered. You have great willpower when you wholeheartedly put your mind to something.

SAGITTARIUS AT WORK

If you're thinking of taking a job with big money but little scope for meeting people and getting out of the place during the day, forget it. Either you'll be unhappy or you'll soon quit.

And don't think that just because you love freedom and adventure, you would be any happier leading a one-man expedition across the Sahara. It's not that you don't possess the guts, the brains or the stamina. It's that however you earn your living, it must be in the presence of an audience you can relate to. All the money and power in the world are no substitute for acclaim.

So where do you start? You can start as a private secretary or personal assistant to a boss who keeps on the move and who relies on you to handle and organize all his or her engagements. You're wonderful at getting along with others and smoothing over the rough patches in a relationship. You can say "no" in ten different ways without making anyone feel turned down or insulted. You adore travel and would make a splendid courier, guide, companion, ship's steward or flight attendant. You have all the mental equipment to go far in the transportation business. For instance, you possess the concentration and powers of command to captain the biggest commercial jet, though you might find it a bit too exclusive up there on the flight deck and too long between stops.

In choosing a career, you should try to remember that deep inside your personality is an actor or actress clamoring for expression. If you go into the entertainment business, you will have a better than average chance of making the big time because you have the tremendous drive and ambition that, if combined with talent, will take you to the top. Many of the world's leading entertainers were born under your Sign. But if you can find another profession that offers similar opportunities for self-expression, popularity and a bit of glamor, you'll be just as happy.

Take the legal profession, for example. It might sound too dull for a dynamic character like yours. But the fact is no other personality in the Zodiac is more suited to a career in law than Sagittarius. You have a particular gift for profound study and delving to the bottom of things. You can put your finger on the main point of any contention immediately. Your other qualifications are that you sincerely love the truth and are a practicing idealist who sincerely believes in justice for all. You are also disarmingly frank and scrupulously honest.

In the early, somewhat plodding days of a legal career, your natural aptitude and concern for your fellow man will help you endure the tedium. You Sagittarius people often rise to the highest judicial and government positions. Your mature judgments and wise counsel often make you loved and respected leaders. As a type, you have great affinity with the public and always seem accessible to people no matter how great your eminence.

Some of the most brilliant lawyers, judges and politicians were born under your Sign. The higher echelons of these professions satisfy the Sagittarius love of drama, personal attention and dignity of office.

In public positions, the Jupiter-born person is usually respected for the way he or she observes the spirit of the law rather than adheres blindly to the letter of it.

The urge to play a responsible part in human affairs is quite strong in the typical Sagittarius. You would make a successful teacher, lecturer, professor or public speaker. If you are true to type, you do not find study easy unless your interest is sustained by a sense of purpose. But when your reforming instincts are aroused, there is no limit to your powers of concentration and learning. Just remember that once you abandon an activity, it is hard for you to go back to it.

Sagittarius people frequently have many jobs before they settle down. They change careers in midstream. Sometimes they are in their late thirties before they discover what they really want to do with their lives. Much depends on personality development. The earlier you mature, the greater your chances of success. There is usually a "wild" element in the Sagittarius nature, and if your full potential is to be realized, it has to be contained.

Your Sign has close associations with religion, philosophy and higher learning. Sagittarius individuals frequently make a career in the church, where they endeavor to bring about a more enlightened approach to the old traditions. Seldom iconoclasts, they concentrate on achieving progressive reforms. Sagittarius is also associated with advances in medicine and other humanitarian sciences. Few of you can resist supporting some cause or other. When successful, you are frequently philanthropic. Many people born under this Sign head charitable organizations, contribute huge slices of their time and won't even charge expenses.

You have a natural flair for business. You make an excellent partner. Even though you may change jobs in your early years, chances are better than even that you will eventually set up on your own or rise to a position of authority with virtually complete freedom of operation.

As a boss, you are very democratic, you allow everyone to have his or her say—and then do exactly what you think is best. You leave no doubt that the top command is yours. You rule with a firm but relaxed hand. Lower down the ladder, you're prepared to give your executives and managers a very free hand. In fact, you tend to delegate too much; your employees may feel confused by the lack of direction and grumble that you are leaving too much to them.

You are not an easy superior to pin down. You'll give swift, straightforward decisions, but only when you believe they are necessary. Often you're inclined to let things ride when others are pressing for an answer. This is because your remarkable intuition says to hold off. You can be infuriatingly offhand and seem to your subordinates to have missed the point. But chances are, you are right; you just happened to see a little further ahead than they.

Another problem for your workers is they've got to almost make an appointment to see you. Not that you are unapproachable. Just the reverse. You're about the easiest boss in the Zodiac to talk with. But you're seldom around. Either you're catching a plane, going to a meeting, having lunch or off to address the local Rotary Club.

You're basically a kind boss, though sometimes in your haste you can be inconsiderate. No one has to point this out to you because your conscience keeps strict tabs and makes you go out of your way to make amends. Of course, you can be tough, but never unjust. In a personal crisis, your staff members can count on your sympathy and practical assistance; you won't think twice about giving time off, paying a bit of extra money or handing out a loan. You never lose sight for long of the human element in your relationships.

You are friendly and cheerful, but despite your camaraderie, it's unusual for anyone to feel really close to you. There's always an intangible aloofness that draws the line at your personal authority. You are honest and candid with those who work for you, and expect them to be the same with you. You can't stand duplicity. You are not likely to ball out a subordinate in public but you can be privately pretty blunt and hurtful.

As an employee, you're not big on formality. You enjoy breezing around the building, stopping for a chat here and there and hopping out at least three times a week for expense-account lunches with clients. Sometimes you give the impression of being *too* casual. A straitlaced boss may be taken aback by your fresh and outspoken manner, but if he's got any brains, he'll ignore your more zany habits and listen to your suggestions. You've probably earned a reputation for having the most inspired and reliable hunches in the office.

You're lucky, not just for yourself but for those who employ you. Sure, you goof, but even your errors have a funny way of turning out to be advantageous. Your boss may tear you to pieces for forgetting to mail an important estimate, only to discover the next day that the situation has changed and he can quote twice as much.

It's true you're forgetful of little things, but you never forget a business fact or figure.

If you were born between November 23 and December 1, your intellect is sharp and creative. A career in any of the arts, particularly music, may be the answer.

Your business acumen is also first class. You are intent on doing something worthwhile with your life. You possess enough ambition and determination to succeed in any line you choose. You just have to *know* what you want to do. A teaching career may appeal. You have a strong sense of moral rectitude. You are unusually wise and sensitive. You should do well in social administration. You are well adapted to work in partnership or in cooperation with a number of people. You have exceptional foresight and are a born organizer of cooperative ventures.

If you were born between December 2 and December 11, you possess a great deal of dash and daring. All kinds of adventurous occupations will appeal to you. You are apt to make a name for yourself in a military career. You are extremely ambitious and will never allow obstacles to stand in your way. Setbacks only serve to strengthen your resolve.

You should be physically tough, strong and agile. If so, a career as a professional sportsman or sportswoman may be possible.

You should succeed as a civil engineer, preferably on large construction projects. You may also shine in the business or financial world. You are likely to be the kind of operator who makes the quick "killing" by taking the initiative.

You will not be content in a job unless you can employ your pioneering instincts. Be careful not to mistake rashness or recklessness for resolution. You should never ignore the warnings of your intuition when dealing with people. Don't try too hard to please and turn a blind eye to principle.

A career in advertising or selling should offer the activity and challenge you need.

If you were born between December 12 and December 20, you have a pronounced ability to guide and govern others. You should succeed in politics or government. You have the rare ability to inspire confidence in others. Probably you will do best where your success depends on the support of the public. A career in journalism may give you the chance to distinguish yourself.

You are enterprising, creative and have a strong sense of personal pride. You would be wise not to overestimate your capabilities. There is a danger that in whatever position of responsibility you occupy, you will bite off more than you can chew. Beware of people who attempt to take advantage of your good nature.

A career in the entertainment industry may lead you to the success and fame you crave. Chances are, though, you will have to make some sacrifices to gain recognition.

You see the need for social reform. Any effort you make along these lines is likely to lead to public acclaim or endorsement.

You should be successful in publishing, broadcasting, television or public relations. Any literary flair should be developed.

Money

Money slips through your fingers faster than with people born under other Signs. You are an impulsive spender and will probably never be able to save very much out of your wages. However, you have a way of building up assets: you are prone to gamble on get-rich-quick schemes, and some of these invariably pay off. It is unusual for a typical Sagittarius not to be comfortably situated by middle age.

When investing money for later years, you will find solid, conservative concerns more reliable than those offering a speculative element.

You enjoy money by spending it. You are naturally fortunate and somehow manage to get away with a casual—even cavalier—approach to personal finances.

CAPRICORN'S CHARACTER

Well, Capricorn, which are you—a high-climbing, steely nerved, sure-footed mountain Goat? Or a timid, domesticated billy or nanny, happy to be tethered to the same old stake for years because the thought of trying anything new scares you stiff? Quite simply, you've got to be one or the other.

Or it could be, if you are in your teens or very early twenties, that you're still living a fairly hectic life, convincing everyone (except yourself) that you're never going to settle down. If so, it's a brave and admirable performance, but it can't last. It's only a final fling. All genuine Capricorns sooner than later make living a serious business. And when they do, they go the top of whatever they're in—or slide sideways into a comfortable groove where they stay until someone who cares enough gives them a kick in the tail.

It's not easy being born under the Sign of the Goat, even if you are the agile crag-leaping type. No one in the Zodiac is more emotionally cut off or isolated from his or her fellow man. It is almost impossible for you to communicate the extent of your feelings in the accepted ways. You need desperately to be understood, but few people ever comprehend your extreme sensitivity. They get a totally wrong impression. You seem so self-assured, contained, unflappable, competent, detached—an enviable loner. And yet inside, you crave affection, attention, love, recognition, appreciation, respect—to give you that glowing feeling of personal security and acceptance.

Your manner is often the problem. You're a little too stiff with others, reserved, cautious, off-putting, sometimes even brusque. People who would normally reach out to you on first meeting are often deterred by your coolness and obvious lack of response.

It's not your fault. A peculiarity of makeup has destined the Capricorn character for a distinct role in this world. You can't help building an impenetrable wall around yourself to protect your sensitivity. Although strong and fearless in a worldly way, you are terrified of being hurt emotionally. People seldom guess that under that superb self-control is a soft, gentle and vaguely anxious person. You are acutely aware of your inner vulnerability. You know from your childhood and developing years how cruel and demanding the world can be. You have unshakable faith in your ability to cope with it externally (no challenge or trial is beyond your capabilities and endurance, once you've decided to confront it), but emotionally you are straitjacketed, imprisoned by your own defenses. It's tough living on the edge between two worlds. But that's the way life is with Capricorn.

Capricorn is the tenth Sign of the Zodiac, a cardinal Sign, which means it is powerful and outward-going in action, and the individual born under it will get things moving, lead others and work to an end.

Capricorn also represents worldly attainment, fame, honor, prestige, positions of authority, the father, large-scale organizations, public and professional standing—in other words, ambitious drive.

It is not hard to see from this that Capricorn by nature is essentially masculine. It is a good Sign for ambitious men; they are inclined to live for their work and to consider everything else of lesser importance.

For a woman, it is in many ways a difficult Sign. Even in this age of women's lib, few women wish to make worldly attainment their paramount objective, or indeed are in a position to do so. Woman's femininity, the innate grace and intuition of the sex, is cramped and made to feel somewhat ill at ease by the materiality and earthy practicality of Capricorn's primal urges. This certainly does not mean that most Capricorn women have noticeable masculine traits. In fact, many of them are remarkable for their wonderful poise, composure and serene maturity. These women can be ultrafeminine in a sophisticated way. The sheer coolness of their demeanor, superimposed on a tremendously concentrated, cautiously regulated passion, makes them thrillingly explosive material for the man who has the wit and sensitivity to penetrate their facade.

Both Capricorn men and women—but especially men—are surprisingly impulsive at times. It is a contradiction in your nature. In normal circumstances the epitome of self-discipline, you are likely without warning to perform the rashest of acts. These sudden, inexplicable impulses land you in some awful trouble because the rather formal Capricorn nature is not equipped to handle spontaneous or unreasonable behavior. You just don't understand it. When it occurs in you, you are shattered—and secretly ashamed. Capricorn never acts without deliberation. When you don't analyze and use careful judgment, you invariably make mistakes. Maturity for you means learning to examine your impulses as quickly as they arise. You should avoid acting on the spur of the moment, except perhaps sometimes in business.

The strange but very real division between the emotional and rational sides of the Capricorn character has an interesting astrological explanation. The Sign Capricorn represents reason, analysis and judgment. It is intellectuality applied to practical matters in a down-to-earth way. Capricorns are shrewd, sensible, reflective, clever. You possess the unmistakable coldness that accompanies intellectual predominance.

The opposite Sign of the Zodiac is Cancer, which represents the feeling and sentimental side of life, the mothering, protective instinct and all its cherishing emotionality. Whereas Capricorn lives by the mind, Cancer is ruled by the heart. And it is from here, across the Zodiac and deep in the Capricorn subconscious, that come the sudden fanciful impulses that force you to act so uncharacteristically at times. Here, also, is the reservoir of feeling painfully dammed up by your mental nature. The mind can't communicate love and affection. It uses words, symbols and stratagems for the real thing. Love and affection are implicit in the fire of feeling. A Capricorn person in love can usually only manage to express himself or herself adequately through the sex act. You are wonderful at speaking body-to-body intimacy. You are not by nature promiscuous; you need to be in love or to be infatuated to feel real desire. Both Capricorn men and women have a reputation for being nearly insatiable in sex—insatiable in love would be more like it.

Funny, odd things happen to you Capricorns, whether your impulses are to blame or not. You've probably noticed this. You are no stranger to the unusual and even bizarre event. You find yourself innocently involved in peculiar situations. Small events seem to overtake you, causing fierce embarrassment or inconvenience. It may be a case of mistaken identity, the temporary loss of money, car, luggage or a trivial misunderstanding. Confirm this next time you are in a roomful of people; if you can entice fellow Capricorns to talk, you'll hear some very amusing stories.

Take the Goat going home at night with his wages in his wallet when two guys jumped him. He flattened one instantly as the other shouted, "We're police!" Why in the hell, he demanded, had they jumped him? Because he resembled a suspect. And why in the hell, they asked, had he resisted . . .? Etc., etc.

Another Capricorn sitting in a train as it pulled out from a station noticed that the guy who had just gotten off had left his coat in the luggage rack. He grabbed the coat, made a beeline for the window, and as the train went past, shouted, "You left your coat behind," and chucked it into the astounded man's arms. Okay, so you've guessed: it belonged to a guy who was chatting to a buddy in the next compartment.

It's very easy for people to underestimate you until they know you well or observe you in action. You never push yourself forward. You'd rather take a back seat, and from there observe what the opposition is up to. If you are a true Capricorn, you regard every stranger with suspicion, or as a potential obstacle or means to something. You have a cool and calculating mind that does not work with the flashing brilliance of a Gemini, but certainly does outperform most of the other Signs when it comes to meticulous observation and shrewdly accurate analysis. You are always alert to opportunities. You possess a sixth sense for spotting weaknesses in others. And you won't hesitate to play on them if it helps your own cause.

This brings us to a very important home truth about the Capricorn nature. Underneath, it is self-centered and usually intent on the attainment of selfish ends. Now, that's not as bad as it reads. Every type is a bit selfish. Some are even schemingly so, which is definitely not the Capricorn style. The Goat's way is to be on the lookout for the easy path up, and to move in smoothly and quickly—in other words, to use the terrain to best advantage. Frankly, you don't like hard work unless there's something in it for you. Then you're a matchless toiler, the Trojan of the Zodiac.

When the Goat encounters an obstacle in his path, he doesn't waste time on it as some of the other Signs do. Leo, for instance, stays to fight; Taurus laboriously pushes the obstacle aside; Scorpio plots and schemes to obliterate it. You simply choose a good vantage point and jump over it. If the obstacle happens to be a person, your nonchalant indifference to his or her feelings or wishes often earns you the reputation of being unsympathetic and opportunistic.

Responsibility is a key to the Capricorn character. You may run from it for years, especially in youth, until you discover a purpose worth devoting your tremendous energies to. This is invariably a career or life goal, something you feel will give you power, position, prestige and security. You then take responsibility—and never again attempt to dodge it. Often the danger is that you will take too much upon yourself, even to the extent of shouldering other people's burdens as though they were your own.

You are enormously ambitious, but usually in an unobstrusive way. If you are tied to the duties of a housewife, you will assert your ambitious urges through your husband or children. You will never be content to sit back and take it easy for long. You must always be climbing, trying to get above your current circumstances. Mind you, the Goat sticks very much to the mountain he or she is used to. You are rarely tempted to explore greener-looking pastures outside your immediate environment. You strive toward the summit that is attainable from where you are and with the means at your disposal. You are conservative, orthodox. You don't believe in experimentation. You'd rather rely on proven methods. You respect precedent. You understand the value of time and how to utilize it to obtain your ends. Not being an innovator, you don't advocate sudden changes or radical reform. In fact, you look up to the Establishment, even though you may be critical of it. You aim to organize your life along straight and rather narrow lines, which you've probably already fixed. You'll stick to these come what may. And this is a danger.

You are a creature of habit, happiest when performing along familiar lines. You quickly settle into a groove, and the less you venture, the more entrenched you become. Some Capricorns degenerate into dull plodders with rigid, distrustful minds. To others, they are severe, exacting, tyrannical, cruel, bigoted, unfeeling, depressing and pessimistic.

The average Capricorn, however, has a pleasing personality, especially when he or she overcomes a certain timidity. You are charming and diplomatic, probably with a touch of Old World courtesy to your manner. In company you enjoy, you are quite entertaining, thoughtful, modest and anxious to please. No other type is more loyal or faithful to a friend. Though you are difficult to get really close to, once you've extended the hand of friendship, it remains a helping hand in almost any circumstances. Underlying the Capricorn character is a profound seriousness that is reflected in the eyes, even in youth. Sometimes it appears as a touch of sadness belying the haughty aloof confidence you sometimes project.

Individuals born under this Sign have a strong sense of pride. You detest demonstrations of feeling toward you in public. Even affection from your nearest and dearest in the presence of friends makes you uncomfortable. You are acutely sensitive to criticism. You want everyone to think well of you. The thought that people might be talking about you behind your back is torture. You are not a moral coward and won't run from a difficult or embarrassing situation, but you may close up like a clam, ignoring all the sundry, as you go about your duties. You tend to get moody when you feel you're not appreciated. You have a sharp and lacerating tongue when you want to use it.

Though you Capricorns are normally pretty even tempered, that doesn't mean you won't speak your mind. You have set ideas about right and wrong and fair play and justice. What you say usually makes sense, although not everyone will support you. When you are sure of yourself, your personality becomes attractively dynamic. You are as forceful, expressive and aggressive as the occasion requires. Although often terse in conversation, you can be surprisingly eloquent, and very well informed on a favorite subject. You are an excellent protagonist and can be counted on to speak facts. You don't lose your composure easily, and since you are not the type to be distracted by excitement, you shine in emergencies. The greater the pressure, the more you emerge as an obvious leader. Your workmanlike way of attacking problems inspires the faith of others.

You enjoy the role of leader because you love adulation but you are more proud than vain, more self-satisfied than egotistical. You know your own strengths, though you are not so perceptive about your weakness. Perseverance and persistence, you believe, always win in the end. Thus in a crisis, you are likely to underestimate the value of flair, passion, daring—and plan good luck. You only *appear* to take chances; you've usually stacked the deck. It's not that you are dishonest, but that you arrange your moves well in advance. You are seldom caught off balance. Your aim in life is to feel safe and secure. Your way of ensuring this is to gamble on nothing.

You are not only good at giving orders, you are also good at carrying them out. Since you really don't mind being told what to do, you make a conscientious and loyal helper. You see nothing demeaning in serving others diligently and faithfully. Partly this is because of your firm belief that no matter where you begin, you will gradually rise to a position that offers security or power or both. It never occurs to you to question this faith. This is the ultimate end you are interested in. Otherwise there is only the job that has to be done. The idea of immediate reward is not strongly implanted in your nature. In a way, you are a perfect work machine, something like Virgo, built to serve with absolute reliability. But you possess the added advantage of being able to reach the summit of executive power and authority. Your enterprise, resourcefulness and resolution, along with your extraordinary ability to plan, fit you for organizational and commercial empire building. It is not uncommon for Capricorn captains of industry to have started off in the humblest job.

According to astrological tradition, every Sign of the Zodiac has a special function to perform in human evolution. Capricorn's is to demonstrate in worldly terms that a person can rise from the lowest to the highest perfection if he or she is willing to set no other goal.

This explains the Capricorn sense of purpose, your supreme contempt for the possibility of failure. Others are frustrated by time and defeated by obstacles; Capricorn sees these as only a phase of growth before the next advance. To the typical person born under this Sign, only what is impractical is impossible.

If you pause for a moment here and examine your attitudes, you will see that no matter how much your family means to you (that loving influence from Cancer across the way), your work—even if it is the job of rearing children—is the most important single thing in your life. This is not always obvious because Capricorns split their interests into watertight compartments. The biggest and most important is work. The family is seldom allowed to enter this compartment. They are loved and cared for, but you feel no need to involve them. A mature Capricorn will not take a day off from work unless it is absolutely essential; he or she won't be late for work just to drop Johnny off at school—not without kicking up a heck of a row, anyway. Family members are not really welcome to come to the office, and are sometimes discouraged from even phoning. Your work scene is a tightly closed one.

But identification with the family idea is very necessary therapy for work-oriented Capricorn. It is the one thing in this world worth working *for*. Capricorn is able to work purely for personal satisfaction, but working for a family allows him or her to feel needed in an emotional sense. Your family is an extension of yourself, an outlet for your repressed feelings. Thus you serve the family idea with great dedication. If you are a woman, you are better at it because you're softer, more understanding. If you are a man, you eventually become the patriarch who takes full responsibility for your brood. You do your duty without complaining, and you expect to be obeyed. Though you do your level best to show your love, there is always a communication gap. You are kind and giving to those you love, but the walls that divide you from them never melt into real sharing.

The Capricorn mother is wonderful with her children. She teaches them the practical necessities, guides them wisely according to the best precepts, toils for them without considering herself. Her patience is superb. She needs to be loved, and her young children feeling her need and dedication, do love her. They also respect her because they know she'll tell them the truth and do her best to be fair. But ambition is her driving force. As the children grow up, she lives through them, encouraging, organizing, pushing them. As a wife, she will keep urging her husband on in his career, pointing out opportunities, helping him overcome obstacles. Although these women are usually career girls before they marry, they are often quite content to give up their work and obtain their sense of achievement through helping their husbands.

With so much emphasis on unremitting ambition, there is always the danger that the Capricorn person will go to extremes. It is easy for them to become obsessed with a single idea. Given the right circumstances, they are the stuff dictators are made of.

The astrological teaching is that typical Capricorns can never actually reach their ultimate goal without acknowledging a power greater than themselves. It is interesting to note that this Sign rules the knees. According to the old tradition, this means that the self-determining Capricorn must learn to kneel to something higher than the self.

There is another odd fact about this intriguing Sign, which extends from December to January. Christ is said to have been born in Capricorn. And most ancient religions celebrate December 25, when the Sun enters this Sign, with mystical and magical ceremonies. To us, it is the winter solstice. To the ancients, it represented the coming of the Sun god, when the Sun ceased to retreat to the south and began its ascent to the north to conquer winter and the sleeping death it symbolized.

Esoteric Astrology attributes a sense of divine mission to the Capricorn person. You are, indeed, no stranger to isolation. You do not need contact with other people to reassure you and fortify you for the work you must do.

Although you need to be loved and appreciated, you work better undisturbed by others, alone with your own thoughts. If your goal demands it, you can rise above pride, endure incredible hardships, use only bare essentials and resist compromise.

Of course, not every Capricorn person is called upon to display these qualities in day-to-day living. But you do possess them and can call upon them. Though there may be modifying influences in the horoscope, the power to persevere and overcome circumstances when others falter is characteristic of you indomitable people.

The negative type of Capricorn is usually just as singleminded and determined, but lacks humanity. He or she sees only one worthwhile purpose in life, and that is personal gain. These individuals use their power and abilities to exploit their fellow man.

Frequently they are stern and unbending people who have very little time or need for pleasure. Through overwhelmingly selfish and joyless effort, they rise to positions of power where their vices can be inflicted on groups, even whole societies. Capricorn at its worst is both despotic oppressor and miser. It is not surprising that the Tarot card for Capricorn is called "The Devil."

The typical Capricorn character, though, is morally rather idealistic and desires the best for humanity. Sometimes you are secretly hurt and disillusioned at the responses to your good intentions. Fortunately, you understand the advantages of solitude and therefore don't suffer the pangs of loneliness as often as many other Signs. As long as you are absorbed in your career, particularly if it is in the art world or the musical or writing profession (which are most likely to satisfy your expressive urges), you will seldom pine. Yet loneliness can afflict you if you have great talent and have assumed a good deal of responsibilities.

Basically, you Capricorns need a loving soul mate. In the chapter "Capricorn in Love," the possibilities of a romantic linkup between you and all the other Signs are discussed in detail. Briefly, you, more than most people, require a lover who understands your need to pour yourself into a fulfilling occupation. No one is more energetic or joyful than a Capricorn who is happy in both love and work.

As a rule, it is not easy for you to find a compatible partner. For one thing, you are inclined to choose from an intellectual point of view and are guided by preconceived notions rather than your emotions. This is probably a good thing because your feelings are rather unreliable and distort your usually keen perception when aroused.

You are a cautious lover who may never succeed in finding your ideal. But there is a good chance of finding happiness if you are prepared to accept that everyone has faults. It is very important that you don't become overcritical of the person you live with. You may mean well in your efforts to improve him or her, but you can easily give the impression of being nagging.

You are also possessive—which means you will do anything for the person you love except perhaps give him or her sufficient freedom. You are inclined to gradually take a person over. It would be a good thing for you and your partner to mix a lot, to avoid cutting yourselves off too much from others. Fortunately, marriage often inspires you Capricorns; it impels you to get out and do better. A loving and understanding partner can help you break old habits that may have prevented you from making the headway your talents would seem to warrant.

You are a faithful lover once you have given yourself to the idea. But you make a bad enemy. You hold others at a distance until you are quite sure of them. Those who offend you usually regret it and never get a second chance. You have a long and unforgiving memory for insults and disrespect. Still, you are not fanatically vengeful. You are prepared to wait, but won't be put out if you never get the opportunity to even a score.

You Capricorn people generally evince an interest in politics. You are concerned with the broad social scene in as much as it affects your own long-term objectives. You are likely to find relaxation in organizing political and social groups. To others, this may seem a rather demanding and exhausting form of recreation, but to the typical Capricorn person who may be busy all day in an office or on the factory line, such activity allows an outlet for organizational ability.

Once an organization is formed and moving, you are likely to retire into the background from where you will exercise watchful authority. You shine as a power behind the throne. The power game is literally a game to you. You are seldom happy with spare-time activities that simply amuse. You want to be learning, absorbing, even while you play. You enjoy serious reading and music. Only practical hobbies are likely to attract your interest.

You have a way of reversing the aging process. Frequently you appear more mature than contemporaries in your youth. But in middle age, when they carry the creases and lines of responsibility in their faces, you tend to look younger.

In some ways, people born under your Sign are late starters. It often takes you the first three decades of your life to understand your own emotions. It is not unusual to find a Capricorn person—particularly the male who has been inhibited in his early years—discovering after middle age the joys of dancing, cavorting, joining in, having a good time.

You have a keen appreciation of art, which you can often impart to others, especially the younger generation.

It is possible to lose sight of the tremendous contribution that the Capricorn character makes to the affairs of man. You are serious in disposition because you see life in very realistic terms and genuinely want to build a better world. Your self-centeredness, which often provokes criticism, is actually a willingness to accept self-sacrifice as the means toward a greater end.

The ruler of this Sign is Saturn, the planet that overcomes by restriction, limitation and time. You Capricorns stick to your principles and aims. You seem to know instinctively that freedom comes only through discipline, and abundance after limitation.

Capricorn is the Sign at the Midheaven or top of the Zodiac. At its highest, it stands as the model of manhood.

CAPRICORN IN LOVE

YOUR CAPRICORN MAN

You like him? Love him? What sort of person is this man?

He's not an easy man to understand. He's the strong, silent type. In familiar, bright company, he'll probably go along with the fun, but you'll always feel he's holding back something of himself. This reserve gives him an air of mystery that can be quite intriguing to a woman grown tired of life-of-the-party males.

This man knows where he's going. He's ambitious and intends to make a success of his life. He's determined not to allow any emotional involvements to spoil his chances. It's job, position and money first. Love comes second with him.

You may be just the one to change his neat little mind-made priorities. Mr. Capricorn falls just as hard as any other man, but he can't be rushed. Even if he's crazy about you, he won't show it—at least, not until he's sure you won't rebuff him. This man is terrified of being hurt or made a fool of.

And yet he needs to be loved. His whole being is crying out for affection, even though you might never guess it. Usually there were deep family anxieties or disappointments in his childhood, and these are what make him wary. He masks his feelings with iron self-control. Loving him could seem like a one-way street to begin with. But after a while you will discover that inside, he's soft, gentle and more than a little bewildered by his own emotional impotence. Try as he may, he just can't express his feelings adequately. Try a little tenderness. Understand him.

You'll feel deliciously secure in his presence. If he loves you, his body vibes will let you know it. His wooing technique is probably very basic. He's definitely no Latin lover. You could never imagine him as an amorous gallant. He won't sweep you off your feet. But as you get to know him, you'll admire his sincerity, loyalty and fine intellect.

He might be a bit forgetful of the little things that delight a girl's heart when she's being courted. He may forget to open the door for you. He can also be late for dates, especially if you're making a foursome because he gets very self-conscious in company. You'll be amazed at how touchy and fidgety he can be when he's with strangers. His trouble is not an inferiority complex but a communication block. Some Capricorn men have been known to walk out on a dinner party halfway through the meal because the strain of fraternizing was unbearable.

He's really a man's man, the kind who sticks mostly to his oldest cronies. You might have trouble dragging him away from them at times. This is another reason why he'll be late for dates—frequently he gets tied up with the boys.

Capricorn men may be quite heavy drinkers. Alcohol helps to relieve their self-consciousness.

Does this guy have any pluses as a husband? When Mr. Capricorn tells you he loves you, you can be sure he means it. And he'll be true. He's probably less likely to have an affair with another woman than any other type in the Zodiac. And he will not ask you to marry him unless he knows he can provide for you—as well as any kids that come along. He's not the sort of man who enters into marriage lightly.

Young Mr. Capricorn is often a little wild. He gives the impression that he's a great fun lover, always out with the boys and having a good time. But if you look closer, you'll notice he has a deep seriousness that all his bravado can't disguise. This type of young man grows into a very responsible and solid citizen. It's as though he realizes his destined role in maturity and therefore tries to make the most of his youthful days.

In his teens, the Capricorn male usually looks older than his years; in maturity, younger.

Your Capricorn man is definitely going places. If you decide to tag along with him in marriage, you'll find he reaches his goals. He's slow, he's steady, but he's a pretty sure bet.

He has a very strong sexual appetite. It's not

for nothing that his symbol is the Goat. Not usually a very experienced lover, he may be a little heavy-handed and need coaching in a gentler approach. But you can rest assured he's all man. And once committed, he's all yours.

YOUR CAPRICORN WOMAN

You like her? Love her? What sort of woman is Miss Capricorn?

She's looking for love. No matter how reserved and straitlaced she may seem, this woman is aching for affection. But don't think you're going to fool her into having a quickie affair. She's not interested in one-night stands. She wants the real thing. Unless you're serious, it's probably better to forget it. If you did manage to deceive her, you might feel like a swine when you see how terribly hurt she gets.

Miss Capricorn has a pretty good idea of love. She knows exactly the type of man she's looking for. The trouble is, love doesn't always measure up to her mental image. This woman is likely to waste a lot of time in heavy involvements with guys she thinks are right for her but are all wrong. Her mind too often rules her heart.

She believes in idyllic, romantic love. In fact, she's got it all worked out in her mind. She wants her hero to ride up and sweep her off to a faraway motel where they'll occupy separate rooms until the preacher arrives and marries them. You get the idea—she believes in doing things right, she's conventional, she doesn't want sordid or ugly scenes. Her reputation is very important to her.

Unfortunately, she frequently gets involved in sordid or ugly affairs because love does not conform to her calculations. So, she detests casual affairs, but often has them. She doesn't indulge in flirtations herself, but often falls for a man who does. She learns the lessons of love slowly. But in the end, because of her tremendous fortitude and patience—plus her charm—she usually gets the kind of man she wants. Capricorn women frequently marry in their late twenties or early thirties.

Miss Capricorn finds it hard to show how deeply she feels for her man. Because of this, she's often misunderstood. Her reserve makes her seem inaccessible, perhaps even a bit cold. She believes in appearances. She can't bring herself to show her disappointments. She would rather cry herself to sleep than reveal her feelings openly.

She has much to give, this sensitive, affectionate powerhouse of a woman. Often she can express herself in physical love even though her emotions are tongue-tied. She can surrender sexually as she can in no other way—but only to the man she thinks she loves. She loves making love when it's right. She's voracious in her own way. It's practically her only way of giving and receiving affection.

Your Capricorn woman will make a wonderful wife. As a hostess and cook, she's a pearl. She's highly intelligent and will be able to converse on equal terms with your business colleagues. She is a mature type of person with fantastic organizing ability. She loves nothing better than overcoming obstacles. Usually she is career-minded, but would be willing to pour her indefatigable energy and ambition into helping you get to the top. You couldn't have a better supporter by your side. She will see opportunities that you may overlook. Her business sense is terrific. If you allow her to, she can be a real power for good behind your throne. And she'll never try to take over your role as head of the family.

She will be faithful. As long as you love her, she will never have an affair.

The Capricorn woman has a fetish about being liked by everyone. She can't bear the idea that others are saying ill of her. She also needs to feel appreciated by her loved ones. To be happy in marriage, she has to be told constantly how much she is loved. Her self-confidence is very shaky, in spite of her impressive show of cool composure.

She finds the thought of her man going off with another woman excruciating. She is terribly jealous and possessive. If you start playing around, she'll nag you without letup. She doesn't have much regard for other women under the best of circumstances.

If you start dating a Capricorn girl, make sure you are courteous to her mother and father. She loves her family and things will go much smoother if she knows the old folks at home have put their seal of approval on the relationship.

CAPRICORN WOMAN—ARIES MAN

This guy is bursting with ideas and creative energy. Mr. Aries is the type to interest you from the first moment you set eyes on him.

It is quite possible you'll meet in some sort of work situation because you are attracted to the same sort of job. Probably your relationship will begin as a platonic one and deepen. You will be filled with admiration for a man who is so determined to get to the top.

Mind you, he is rather impetuous. The Ram does have a way of rushing in head-first and asking questions afterward. He is a pioneer. Let us hope you share his tendency to go looking for that crock of gold at the end of the rainbow.

You will never make this man your slave. He can't stand to feel trapped or tied down. He will find it very hard to function in suburban life for very long.

He's aggressive. He is prepared to fight for what he wants, and that includes his woman.

He believes in the old-fashioned type of union. He will allow you your uncommunicative moments but won't be too keen on your pursuing outside interests if they alienate you from him.

He loves travel. He's the type to change his job quite a few times.

You will like his aggressive attitude in lovemaking.

You will have to learn to accept the fact that he is a born flirt, chiefly because it boosts his ego and makes him feel good. You must not allow your possessiveness to get the upper hand. The drawback here is that you are likely to get rather tired of his games playing, even if you do realize it's all harmless fun.

Mind you, this fellow doesn't like it if the shoe is on the other foot. He will become really moody if you decide to do your share of flirting.

You're likely to fall out over the best way to handle financial affairs. You will consider it quite shocking the way he throws his cash about.

When you have a row, it's likely to be quite stormy. You are good at controlling your emotions, but when you lose your temper—well, you're a Capricorn woman, so no one has to tell you what happens then.

You will be very good for him because you are more perceptive than he is. If you can get him to take your advice, you'll be able to save him from making a lot of stupid blunders. Perhaps when he realizes how often you are right, he will be prepared to listen to you. Occasionally you will allow him to drag you into ridiculous situations you would not endure with any other guy. You may find it rather stimulating.

If you do get hitched, it might be best for you to keep control of the family budget. Get him to hand over most of his paycheck at the end of the week. In later years, you'll both be very pleased you followed this advice.

If you go off the rails with another man, it's quite likely he'll want to end the relationship. He is not the forgiving type. Unfortunately, he still believes there is one law for men and another for women.

You will be able to help this man get right to the top. Never put a damper on his enthusiasm. Being a Capricorn, though, you would never be tempted to.

CAPRICORN WOMAN—TAURUS MAN

Your family means a great deal to you. You want to make Mom and Dad happy. You have always tried to live up to the expectations of your relatives. Well, dear girl, take home a Taurus male and everyone will be thrilled. This is the type of guy your folks have dreamed you would marry. He is kind, considerate, a home lover and a good provider. He is hard-working and ambitious.

You, too, should be delighted with the Bull. The domestic scene is quite important to you. This guy will love the way you run the house. He will feel he can trust you. He needs to be married to someone he can rely on. Naturally suspicious, he couldn't stand being married to a chick he thinks might be two-timing him while he's out trying to earn the mortgage payments.

He will appreciate your quick wit and dry sense of humor. He will also admire your artistic skills and talents in the kitchen.

You will have to become more romantic. Remember, he is born under a Sign where Venus rules. He loves to talk about love and sex. You will have to get rid of those silly inhibitions.

You will be pleased to discover you have found a man who is so solid and sensible. You are both security-conscious earth Signs.

The pair of you are traditionalists. He resents change. He holds fast to the old values. He prefers to employ methods that have proved themselves over the years.

Never show you may know more about a subject he considers himself an expert on. Occasionally you will have to accept the role of the little woman. It would be fatal for the relationship if you were to show him up, especially in front of his friends or colleagues.

He will enjoy bringing people home to show you off. You will enjoy preparing dinner for his various business associates and mutual friends. He's quite a good businessman and you can expect to be doing a fair bit of entertaining.

You both like a night out, but your happiest evenings will be spent together within your own four walls.

The Bull is a great provider. He will make sure you never go without anything you really need or desire. You are both pretty clever when it comes to handling money. He will appreciate how you cut corners and find bargains when buying the weekly groceries.

He wants his partner to be all woman so he's unlikely to complain when it comes to buying you a new outfit. Your appearance, he thinks, is a reflection on him.

He is a jealous man so you had better remain faithful to him. He is quite capable of doing serious damage if he feels he has been let down.

Mr. Taurus can be a bit bossy, but you are cute enough to let him have his way in areas that you know are really important to him.

He won't be too keen on your continuing with a job after marriage. He's likely to want kids fairly soon.

This man is unlikely to leave you alone in a roomful of other males. He will tend to think of you as one of his possessions. He can't help it. While he loves you, he will always be terrified of losing you.

You will love him more and more the longer you are together. You will always feel protected and secure when he holds you tightly in his arms. He's just that sort of fellow.

CAPRICORN WOMAN— GEMINI MAN

You would have to be in a very special frame of mind to fall for Mr. Gemini because he is not the type you'd be attracted to under normal circumstances. You like to know where you stand with a guy. The sudden changes the Twins are capable of could drive you round the bend.

If you have just got over an unhappy love affair, or if you are feeling fed up with the male sex in general, then our Mercurial friend could fill a certain gap in your life.

You will find he's very easy to speak freely to. He is the type of person you'll feel you can confide your secret thoughts and troubles to.

After starting out on a purely platonic plane with him—a brother-sister type of scene, say—you could find one day he means a little more to you than that. It could be you will fall in love with him.

Certainly there are quite a number of things you will have in common. You are likely to enjoy the sort of places he takes you. The trouble could begin when you start to think in terms of setting up a home. Mr. Gemini is terrified of losing his freedom. When a woman begins to talk about a permanent relationship, he is likely to panic.

A Gemini person rarely knows what he's really looking for in life. He just likes looking. The man born under the Sign of the Twins can easily have as many as half a dozen projects going at the same time.

He finds it very difficult to face up to his responsibilities. You may believe his stories the first couple of times. After a while, you'll begin to lose respect for him.

He finds a one-to-one relationship almost impossible to cope with. He has such an inquiring mind he can't bear to think he is missing out. If there is a party going on, he will try to go, whatever the distance and however tired he may be.

He is also inclined to go to excess with everything connected with pleasure. He doesn't know when to stop. This can be particularly dangerous if he gets involved with drink or drugs.

He's a charming person to be out with if he wants to impress you. Please don't get the idea he's out to fool you. He really doesn't know himself very well and this is probably his biggest problem. He finds it very difficult to hold fast to opinions because he sees two sides to every argument.

You won't find his company very soothing. It's possible your relationship will have to be built on some sort of sadomasochistic foundation if it's going to last for any length of time.

You will certainly be good for him. You will calm him and provide the kind of atmosphere he can unwind in. He may not appear to need much looking after, but he really does need somewhere secure to run to. The question is, will you always be waiting?

As a good friend, you will never tire of seeing his face. But do give the matter plenty of thought before settling down with him in a permanent way. Of course, if you happen to come across a Gemini who has sorted himself out, it's a different story. But how will you ever be sure with this man?

As a rule, he's too juvenile himself to be much of a father. He's kind and gentle and genrous enough, but his restless example is not always the best for youngsters. As a disciplinarian, he's usually only good at shouting—and kids soon have his number.

CAPRICORN WOMAN— CANCER MAN

Poor old Mr. Cancer is a terrible worrier. When things are going really well for him, he will probably be the most worried of all. He lacks confidence. This is the type of guy who very often never realizes his true potential. He finds it difficult to let go. Perhaps you are the woman to make him believe he can get to the top because you are superb at boosting a man's confidence.

He is a complex character, as you'll discover if you become deeply involved. He is highly sensitive and quite intuitive. He is also a bit paranoid. If he sees two people whispering at the other end of a room, he'll be convinced they are talking about him.

He is not all that interested in power. He wants to get to the top all right, and he is a hard worker, having control over other people's destinies does not appeal to him one jot.

You may get the feeling he is afraid to let others get too near him. Even if you are his wife or his lover, he will keep certain areas of his life secret. Basically, he is a shy individual.

He will do his best to understand you. When he loves a woman, it is total. He will certainly try to make your relationship work. One problem may be that he tries too hard.

He will put on a brave front. Often he will hide what he is really thinking by treating important subjects humorously. Just when you think you are getting through to him, he will break off for no apparent reason and beat a hasty retreat into that Cancer shell.

He can be quite hard when his back is up against the wall. He is much more of a survivor than many people give him credit for being.

What are your chances of making a go of marriage? Well, perhaps much better than you imagine. There are quite a number of things you have in common. A great love of the home and family life is one. He feels deeply for his family, and so do you. You will enjoy furnishing and decorating your home together. He will be just as eager as you to have children.

In financial matters, you'll find you are on very much the same wavelength. He can't stand to waste money. He will always do his best to pay the bills on time. He doesn't like to be in debt.

He is terribly kind and considerate toward the fairer sex. You might enjoy making it your life's work to ensure Mr. Cancer makes the best of himself. He does need a person like you around because he has a tendency to give up and settle for second best. Second best has never been good enough for you.

He will constantly need to be reassured that you love him. He needs an enormous amount of love and affection.

Mr. Cancer is quite sentimental and romantic. He will woo you with flowers and presents. He'll keep you entertained, too, with amusing stories about his childhood. He likes to talk to someone he feels at ease with.

He is pretty handy around the house, and what is more, he won't mind if you wish to continue with a career after marriage.

You might find you're in for a long courtship. The Crab always takes his own good time proposing marriage.

CAPRICORN WOMAN—LEO MAN

Mr. Leo could be just the right partner for you. You are well known as a late starter. It is quite possible you won't meet the man of your dreams until you're well past your teens. When you do, you'll be looking for someone to sweep you off your feet. If he fancies you, this guy will do just that. He'll pamper you and put you on a pedestal. In return, he will expect you to provide him with a comfortable and secure home life.

Chances are he is not the type you were thinking of spending the rest of your life with. He has a hypnotic quality, though, so you could fall for him against your better judgment. Have no fears, you won't regret it.

You do need a man who cares. You are the sort of woman who could waste too much time pining for the type of guy who would not be at all good for you.

Mr. Leo *will* be good for you in many ways. He will break down a lot of your preconceived ideas. He will help you to overcome your inhibitions, both physical and mental. You need to feel appreciated. You also need a lot of reassurance. This man will help you grow up and come to terms with yourself. When he is harsh with you, you can be sure it is for your own good. He is an unselfish man.

Once he has decided you are the girl for him, you'll find it exceedingly difficult to retain your composure.

You are ambitious and practical. He won't object to your getting ahead in your career. He will do all he can to make you realize your full potential.

You will be enchanted by his generosity in lovemaking. He is not just a taker. It will be important to him to satisfy you in bed.

He is confident, almost arrogant. He will teach you to believe in yourself. He is seldom rude to people, but he doesn't consider anyone his superior.

He has a way of getting people to jump to it. His whole personality exudes power.

You will have to be prepared to change your ways to a certain extent. You must learn to trust him. You will also have to learn to keep quiet when he loses his temper.

Mr. Leo will always expect you to look your best. He wants his woman to be the envy of every other man in the neighborhood.

He speaks his mind. If you disappoint him in any way, he will let you know it. You could never by any stretch of the imagination call him an introvert. Many people are taken aback by his frankness when they first meet him. When they get to know him better, they wish they could be as honest.

He likes a feminine woman. He will prefer to see you in a fashionable dress than jeans and sweaters.

He will need you by his side when he has a bad day at the office. He requires a woman who is prepared to boost his confidence when it has been damaged.

In many areas, you will have your disagreements. This need not be serious, however. A certain amount of conflict often helps to keep a close relationship alive.

He loves the limelight. Sometimes his antics in company will embarrass a sensitive woman like you.

After the children come along, be sure you don't lavish all your love on them. The King of the Jungle will be mighty hurt if he is given the cold shoulder.

CAPRICORN WOMAN— VIRGO MAN

Whether he is the man of your dreams is by no means certain. One thing is for sure, though: Mr. Virgo is going to consider you his type of woman.

You won't have to date this man too many times before you realize how much you think along the same lines—politically, spiritually and emotionally. He has a fine mind. He has a deep love of art and music. You will enjoy listening to him talk. He is great at expressing himself on pet subjects.

He is a tidy person, both in appearance and about the home. You are both fairly practical.

He is shy. It might take him quite a while to make physical advances.

You will be happy to discover you are involved with a man who keeps his word. If he plucks up the courage to tell you he loves you, you can be pretty sure he means it.

If you do decide to get married it's likely to be a planned occasion rather than an elopement. He's not the type to rush anything so important.

Mr. Virgo does have faults. You may find he's not quite passionate enough. He certainly is not a great romantic, but if you care deeply enough you'll be able to help him become more relaxed in his lovemaking. When you love a man, you are not backward, so you will soon be able to put a bit of fire into him.

He can be terribly fussy. He believes in a place for everything and everything in its place. He also loves to be praised and fussed over. When he has a cold, he'll think it's flu. When he bangs his leg, he'll think its broken. And so on.

The male Virgo tends to marry rather later in life than most men. He is a sticker, though. He will do everything he can to ensure his marriage is a success. He believes in power sharing. He is not a domineering man.

Very often the Virgo man is in some way connected with the world of art or music. He is a bit of an actor. He can also be a showoff. He's not a vain person really, but he's justifiably proud of what he knows.

Mr. Virgo is very conscious of health and hygiene. He's likely to bathe or shower more than once a day. He is proud of his appearance and always likes to look his best.

He is quite happy to share the household chores. He's handy in the kitchen and he doesn't mind doing the shopping.

He has a very logical mind. He loves discussions. He absorbs facts like blotting paper. There are not many people who can get the better of him in an argument. His ruling planet is Mercury, which stands for intellectual power.

You are likely to enjoy the same sort of vacations. You will both be looking for something quite different from your everyday life, a real change—as long as everything is safe and secure at home.

He is blind to his own faults. If you criticize him, even in a helpful, manner he will be terribly hurt and take it as a personal attack. He will always claim you misunderstood his motives. Although quick to spot weaknesses in others, he has difficulty in facing up to his own.

It would be a good idea to have children. He may take a bit of convincing, but once he becomes a father, he'll have no regrets. Unless he has children, he may get too hung up on his own needs and desires.

CAPRICORN WOMAN— LIBRA MAN

Mr. Libra is not too good at living on his own. He needs other people to spark him off. Most of all, he requires a woman to share his dreams and his home. You could be just the girl to fire his imagination. Most women find a man born under this Sign terribly attractive, and you are not likely to be an exception. He is charming, he has a good sense of humor and he knows how to treat a woman.

You will find him hard to resist. If this man takes more than a passing interest in you, you'll probably fall under his spell.

He knows how to play the game called love. He is a bit of a flirt, but a sincere one. He looks for the best in people and will expect you to make allowances for his own faults. If he is a clued-in Libra, he will know himself fairly well and will have no illusions.

You are pretty earthy, quick to sum up a situation and reach a conclusion. As a rule, you have no difficulty making important decisions. These qualities will be a great help to this man because he finds it hard to make up his mind. He is terribly fair and can see both sides of an argument only too well. Result: indecision.

It could be that you won't marry this man since you might be unable to envision yourself as his lifelong partner. There are so many differences you would have to overcome. As you get to know each other really well, you'll realize you are light-years apart. For one thing, he is a social animal. He likes parties and meeting different people. He does not share your love of the home as a snug little unit.

Many people write him off as a good-time Charlie but they are underestimating him. He tries to take a lighthearted view of life, but actually he thinks deeply and the world's problems often weigh on him. Sometimes he gets really depressed. He hates injustice and intolerance.

It is important to you to be a good housewife. You take great pride in your home and want to furnish it nicely and keep it sparkling. It's a pity but Mr. Libra will hardly notice your efforts. Don't expect much praise from him on your domestic virtues. He doesn't consider such things all that important.

He is a bit of a wanderer and you might find this hard to accept. Another thing you will have to come to terms with is his penchant for making eyes at pretty ladies. You're definitely the jealous type and will find this sort of thing most irritating. You'll just have to accept it as a fact of life with a Libra. It is probably all quite harmless. But that's not really the point, is it?

Occasionally he needs a push to get him going. If you are prepared to be the power behind the throne, you could really help him get on in the world, for though he is talented, he is also a bit lazy.

Very often he will appear vague. He can be trusted with your innermost secrets, but he may not understand your innermost feelings.

If you do hitch your star to a Libra man, let's hope you've found a mature one. If he has come to terms with himself and decided what he really wants out of life, all will be well. But Libras need a lot of experience before they are ready to settle down for good.

When it comes to popping the big question, you might have to drop a few hints. As in everything else, he will always find it difficult to take the initiative.

CAPRICORN WOMAN— SCORPIO MAN

There could be something of a clash here. You are certainly taking on a keg of dynamite if you become involved with aggressive and mysterious Mr. Scorpio.

If you do fall under his spell, you'll wonder what has hit you. It is likely to be an experience you will never forget. This union will be all or nothing; there are no half-measures with this man. You will either be so hypnotized by him that you'll be prepared to work day and night to make him happy, or you'll run a mile after he has made his first advances.

He doesn't beat about the bush. If he wants to go to bed with you, you'll be under no illusions. He is quite capable of using the caveman approach and dragging you off to the bedroom. Some girls find this technique rather exciting. It's doubtful whether it would have much appeal for a Capricorn lady.

You will definitely not be able to ignore him. You'll feel the vibes when he enters a room. You will probably find his mere physical presence stimulating, whether you like to admit it or not.

If you do get heavily involved with him, you'll never feel relaxed in his presence. You like a serene life. One wonders if you could live with his moods.

Of course, if he really loves you, he'll worship you. His love will be total. He is a jealous man and a possessive one. He won't be prepared to let you carry on with your own career once you're his wife. He will want to own you body and soul. He is very sensual. You will have to teach him to be a little more gentle and sensitive to your feelings.

He strives for power. Whether in business or in his personal relationships, he wants to get to the top. He is a good provider. He will think the way you run the home quite fantastic. He is not mean, but he is careful with money. He can be a bit secretive, too. He may not be prepared to confide how much he has in the bank.

He can be moody and even downright nasty. You will have to accept that quite a lot of your relationship is going to depend on physical satisfaction.

Your life together will have its distinct ups and downs. It certainly won't be plain sailing. You will have your fights, and they will be fierce, but the making up should be oh so sweet.

He is a straightforward man. You will always know where you stand with a Scorpio. He doesn't have much time for emotion. He can be blunt to the point of sadism.

It is rare for anyone to get the better of him. He is an astute businessman. He's pretty quick to sum people up. He is not really concerned with what others think of him.

Don't tease him. He doesn't have much of a sense of humor about his own weaknesses. He certainly doesn't want his faults pointed out. He also can't stand public demonstrations of any kind. He believes that what goes on between two people is their concern alone.

This man is not a natty dresser. In fact, he's fairly sloppy and out of date. You will have to do your best to smarten him up.

In marriage, you will sometimes feel like packing your bags and going home to Mother. But you will probably stick by him. Such is the power and magnetism of Mr. Scorpio.

CAPRICORN WOMAN—SAGITTARIUS MAN

Mr. Sagittarius is a difficult guy to track down. He is outward-looking, loves to be surrounded by lots of people and hates the idea of settling down to a routine life. Freedom is more important to him than almost anything else. No matter how much he loves a woman, he finds it difficult to cope with a one-to-one relationship for very long. He is always looking for ways to stimulate his imagination. He can't sit still.

He may appear to be one of the luckiest guys around. He gets into such scrapes you wouldn't think he could survive in one piece. He takes his chances, all right, but don't write him off as a fool. Don't forget Jupiter's logic is always at work behind his actions.

Certainly you will get on extremely well on a platonic level. He is a loyal chum who will never let you down. But you may get rather frustrated by his antics if you love him deeply. You could get fed up with sitting around waiting for him to ask you to be his lifelong partner.

If you do marry him, you'll have to adapt to his roaming ways. He is likely to turn up at all hours. That dinner you have so lovingly prepared could be ruined by the time he strolls in through the door. He will wonder what all the fuss is about; such things are not important to him.

So long as you can come to terms with his gypsy ways, it might be okay. Once he feels he can come and go as he pleases, he won't have such a strong desire to keep on the move. This is asking a lot of any woman, though. Don't get the idea he is out chasing other girls all the time. This is unlikely to be true. He just needs to give free rein to his high spirits. He is fascinated by other people. He's also a bit of a showoff and loves to be the center of attention.

You could also call him a gambling man. You won't be too happy about his attitude toward money. He will often take the view that tomorrow will take care of itself. When you have launched a new budget, he will spoil everything by going out and blowing his week's wages.

This man is likely to make many mistakes in his life, but he won't be morbid about them. He is a positive guy who looks to the future rather than over his shoulder to yesterday's sorrows.

You care a great deal about what your family thinks of you and the way you conduct your life. Your mother and father may be rather shocked when you turn up with your Sagittarius boyfriend, for he is not the type to change in order to impress people. He is honest about himself and has a take-me-or-leave-me attitude.

His good points are not always easy to discern. If you are in any sort of trouble and your Sagittarius friend is around, you will soon realize how steady and reliable he can be when it is necessary.

Though he is not a great romantic, he is an imaginative and high-spirited lover. The longer you are together, the more his love for you will grow. He will understand your moods and leave you alone when you wish to work things out for yourself. In many ways, you will find him irresistible. He can seem like a naughty schoolboy when he has been up to one of his pranks. You will forgive him for almost anything—sometimes in spite of yourself.

He is a bit too good-humored on the one hand and too impatient on the other to be a model father. Still, he'll teach the kids honesty and instill in them a love of the truth.

CAPRICORN WOMAN—CAPRICORN MAN

He is a difficult guy to get to know well, but if anyone can get through to him, it's likely to be a girl born under the same Sign. He needs a woman behind him who will boost his confidence and really believe in him.

You are an ambitious woman. Success is very important to you. The reason why this union could be so successful is that you will be content to be the power behind the throne. So long as your man is getting to the top, you will be prepared to make personal sacrifices. Mr. Capricorn could not bear to feel you were in competition with him in any way.

He has quite an ego. You must never try to usurp his position as head of the household.

You will find you are very much on the same wavelength. Your tastes in friends and art and your general likes and dislikes are going to be very similar.

He can be fussy and methodical. Female Capricorns are not quite so set in their ways as the male of the species. You will have to help him to get more fun out of life. Because you are the type of woman he will respect, he will be prepared to take more chances with you than he normally would.

Don't expect to be wooed in a romantic fashion. The Goat finds it difficult to express himself in matters of the heart. You may become impatient with him because he will want a long courtship before he contemplates marriage. He never makes important decisions in a hurry.

He likes his life to be organized. He believes in a place for everything and everything in its place. He will be proud of your tidy ways. He will love the way you organize family life. He will also be exceedingly pleased that he can bring friends home and that you will know how to be the perfect hostess. You are just the type of woman to help him clinch that all-important contract with an influential associate.

Occasionally he will irritate you. You must learn to take a tongue-in-cheek attitude toward his rather set opinions. You may feel he secretly believes women are not quite up to holding down important jobs in business. It would be best not to argue with him about these matters. Just smile inwardly and let him babble on.

You both have a healthy respect for the laws of the land. He is old-fashioned in many ways. He is not all that keen on change.

You could never call him an impulsive person. He will always want to consult with you before altering course in any way.

Mr. Capricorn is likely to be faithful. Oh, he may fancy other women from time to time, but then what man doesn't? Once he has decided to try to make a permanent relationship work, he is unlikely to do anything rash to put it in jeopardy.

He is careful with money, but not mean. He will make sure the future is provided for.

Both of you believe in hard work. You could not stand to be married to a man who was lazy or who lacked ambition.

You must be sure, however, that you don't spend all your life together working hard and worrying about money. It will be up to you to remind him that it's good to let your hair down once in a while and to hit the high spots.

The Capricorn man can get into routine ways very easily. Give him a few surprises to keep him on his toes.

CAPRICORN WOMAN—AQUARIUS MAN

Your friends will think you are out of your mind if you get serious about the Water Bearer. Many people doubt that this union has any chance of getting off the ground. Strangely enough, although you are opposite in so many ways, you could be really good for each other.

One of the main problems here is that you would be alone quite a lot of the time. You are a fairly practical girl; he is quite the opposite. Aquarius people refuse to be ruled by the clock.

When he expounds on the world's problems, you will think he really knows where he is going. The trouble with Mr. Aquarius is that he's a dreamer who is always thinking about utopia. What is more, he's always talking about it (and very lucidly). But when it comes to setting it up, he does get rather lost. Next time you're with him notice that strange faraway look in his eyes.

You will have to keep him neat and in reasonably up-to-date clothes. He doesn't care much about appearance.

The reason you are likely to be so attracted to each other is that you are such different types. It is quite likely you have never known a man quite like him. He will give you a shakeup. You will be forced to reassess your own values and attitudes.

You like a challenge. This could be just the man to excite you.

He could enter your life when you have gone into one of your depressions. When old Saturn has got you down, this is the guy to lift you out of the doldrums. He'll make you stop thinking about yourself and get you doing something for others. He will help you overcome your introverted ways.

Mr. Aquarius doesn't share your great love of the home. He will leave you to cope with all domestic issues. He is unlikely to notice the artistic touches you add to your mutual surroundings.

You will have to get used to the fact that people will constantly be dropping in. Your Aquarius mate collects friends from many different walks of life.

Mr. Aquarius is restless. He can't stay in the same place for two minutes. He doesn't like routine. You will have to be prepared for his sudden changes of plan.

He needs looking after. You will have to keep his schedule straight and make sure he is on time for important appointments.

You tend to save your love for your very close friends and family. He can't help but give himself to everybody.

It might be best if you hold the purse strings because he is not very good with money. If he is convinced a cause is worthy of support, he'll be generous to a ridiculous degree.

He has an agile mind. People born under this Sign are often ahead of their time. They suggest changes that are picked up and used by the rule makers a decade or so later. This, of course, is very frustrating for them.

You will be able to help him become more realistic by showing him that it's not always possible to improve the world until one puts one's own house in order. Aquarius people have great difficulty in accepting their own faults and weaknesses. They don't take easily to permanent relationships. Once this man realizes just how much you need him, though, he may channel most of his love and compassion into looking after you. Then you'll live happily ever after.

CAPRICORN WOMAN—PISCES MAN

This can be a very powerful linkup. Capricorn and Pisces joined together could conquer the world if they make the best use of all the positive aspects of their two personalities. You must both be prepared to take what the other has to offer.

Very often this man appears to dwell in a world far removed from reality. However, his intuitive powers are strong, often remarkable. You should never dismiss his ideas without giving them careful consideration.

When you first come across this guy, you may feel he is a rather weak man, a dreamer who can't get himself organized. This would be a false assumption. He can be very tough when he has to be. He also knows how to get his own way when it matters. Rarely does anyone get the better of him in business.

You are a practical person. If you love and understand him, you'll be able to get him to think again when he gets too carried away with his boundless enthusiasm.

Still waters run deep here. Your Pisces man will always be a mystery to a logical down-to-earth woman like you. However, the fact that you never quite know what makes him tick will keep the relationship going. He is easy to get along with. If he loves you, he will want to include you in all compartments of his life. He won't expect you to make sacrifices he would not be prepared to make himself.

Although he has unlimited energy and loves to get out and about and meet a variety of people from all walks of life, he is, like you, a lover of home comforts. Nothing satisfies him more than to have a quiet evening at home with his woman close to him.

He can also have a very good influence on others. He will help you conquer your dark moments. He doesn't give in to pessimism himself, and his ready wit can turn the most difficult situation into something to be laughed off.

You will have to get used to his vagueness. Sometimes when he is worrying about a problem connected with his job, he will appear to ignore you. You must learn not to bother him when he has important matters to wrestle with.

You will be wonderful for him because he needs an anchor. Unless he has the right person by his side, he tends to drift along with no real purpose in life. He needs someone to work for, to share his worldly possessions with.

He will always be out to better himself. He is not afraid of a challenge. His motto could be, "It's better to try and fail than not to try at all."

He's not much of a handyman. Actually, he's very good at taking things apart, but not too clever when it comes to putting them back together.

He has to have a certain amount of excitement in his life. He likes to travel. You are unlikely to find the Pisces man holding down a boring routine job.

Of course, he has his moments of self-doubt. He will lean on you on occasions. You are the type of woman who takes this as a compliment and a sign of love and trust. Although you appear frail at times, he will realize you have enough strength to pull the two of you through when it becomes necessary.

He is likely to remain faithful. He won't get involved with other women because he wouldn't wish to put his relationship with you in danger.

CAPRICORN MAN—ARIES WOMAN

Miss Aries is fiery and impulsive. She was born under the percussive first Sign of the Zodiac, and she could be a bit too much for you to take. She's direct, straightforward and declines to stand on ceremony.

You tend to go for a woman who is a little more charming and graceful. She could embarrass you when you are out together because she doesn't believe in pulling her punches.

This woman is very wrapped up in herself. When she's in a mood, you'll know all about it.

There could be something of a personality clash here because you both tend to be a bit bossy. Miss Aries may challenge your right to wear the trousers. In marriage, a Capricorn male likes to feel he is in charge. You desire someone who will bring you her problems and solicit your protection. Miss Aries is perfectly capable of looking after herself.

She's also a career girl. Being a Capricorn, you perhaps are looking for a woman who is more of a homemaker. Success is very important to the Ram. She would not be happy playing a background role for very long.

You are a quick thinker, although rather methodical. You may become agitated by this lady's penchant for rushing through everything.

There are a number of things you do have in common. If you are serious about each other, it would be advisable to cultivate the plus side of your relationship. You share a first-class sense of humor. Yours tends to veer toward irony, though. With her, you will have to swallow your pride frequently and learn to laugh at yourself.

You are as stubborn as an old mountain Goat. An Aries woman will be able to teach you a lot if you're prepared to face up to yourself. She certainly will not allow you to harbor false opinions. You will always be able to believe what she says. She may be a dreamer, but she is an incompetent liar. The truth may hurt, but she would rather blurt it out than deceive her man.

An Aries woman has fairly extravagant tastes. You may find you have to constantly remind her just how far your earnings will stretch.

In sex, you will have to play a dominant role. This is an extremely passionate girl who needs to be taken. You could have that happy mixture of aggression and gentleness which she needs to satisfy her.

You will have to accept her neuroses. She's very high-strung and you'll be surprised to discover that in certain areas she lacks confidence.

Aries people have easily recognizable features when they are true to type. Usually they are quite sharply defined. What they are shows in their expressions.

You will admire her resilient qualities. She's capable of bouncing back after a disappointment. She is a fighter and a survivor.

It would be advisable to get to know her really well before contemplating setting up home together. You are a careful man and will have to calm down this woman, who hates to think about things for too long.

She is wonderful in the role of hostess. You will love the way she arranges matters when you bring home friends and business associates. You are unlikely to have any complaints about her cooking, either.

It may be a few years before you decide to have a family because neither of you is prepared to accept such an important responsibility lightly. But once you feel secure, you are likely to want to go ahead. She wants to enjoy her life before settling down completely to domesticity.

CAPRICORN MAN—TAURUS WOMAN

You two should have a great deal in common. A Taurus girl is likely to understand a man like you better than most other Signs of the Zodiac. She is fairly serious-minded, which you like. She is a lover of the home. She takes her time about making important decisions.

You are both earth Signs and have your feet firmly planted on the ground. Neither of you can abide people who constantly change their minds.

You are both subject to moodiness. You also need your private moments. Make sure you respect these needs in each other.

Many people are under the impression that

Taurus individuals are bossy. Let us put it another way: they don't like being pushed around. Taurus people make staunch and reliable friends, but woe betide the person who takes advantage of their generosity. They will never fall for the same trick twice. And they have long memories.

This woman is serious about love and marriage. She is ruled by Venus. She will appreciate the gentleness with which you treat her. If she says she loves you, she certainly means it. When she gives herself, it is invariably for keeps. She is unlikely to get involved in many passing affairs.

You are both fairly artistic types and are likely to enjoy the same kind of art, music and literature.

She cares about possessions and personal treasures just as much as you. The family is also extremely important to you both. From a material point of view, you should be able to set up a cozy little nest egg.

Taurus women have great control over their emotions. It is an extremely rare thing for this lady to make a fool of herself over anyone. She can be hurt as much as anyone, but she's darned if she'll show it. She is capable of concealing her true feelings in just about any situation.

You are both likely to work exceedingly hard at making your marriage work. This is one area of your lives where you would hate to fail.

She has a great love of travel and adventure. You will enjoy your vacations together. You will probably also enjoy showing the slides of your trip abroad and laughing at the shared memories as much as the actual experience. You are both pretty sentimental when it comes to the past.

Miss Taurus loves pretty things. Clothes are important to her. You couldn't call her extravagant, except where fashion is concerned. She can rarely resist buying something that takes her fancy in a boutique window.

You will feel there is a hidden strength in your Taurus woman. This is true.

Neither of you is the sort to go chasing after the opposite sex once you've decided to spend your life together. This is a good thing. She can be a very jealous person if aroused.

It would be wise to leave her to pursue her own interests. If she wants a career after marriage, you should try not to stand in her way even though this may go against your grain.

You may be surprised to discover what a little ball of fire your Taurus girl is in the bedroom. She is far more passionate than you would believe when you meet her socially.

You are likely to spend many happy evenings at home together. She is not the type to waste money on riotous living.

CAPRICORN MAN—GEMINI WOMAN

A number of difficulties would have to be overcome for you two to form a lasting relationship. A personality clash seems inevitable. You both have very different ways of looking at life.

The Gemini woman is one hell of a flirt. She can't help it. Even when the Twins are going steady with a guy, one side of their nature can't resist trying to seduce the attractive guy sitting at the next table. It may not be serious; in all probability, it's perfectly harmless. But it's doubtful whether that knowledge would be enough to allow you to overlook it.

Mr. Capricorn usually knows what he wants out of life. What is more, he has a pretty shrewd idea of how to go about getting it. Not so with Mercury-ruled Gemini. Being a split Sign, these individuals can always see two answers to every riddle that life throws at them. They always have a perfectly good reason for doing or not doing something. Alas, they usually convince themselves that the easiest path is the one to take.

Man or woman, Gemini characters have no time for tradition or conservatism. They admire people who are trying to change the world, even if they themselves do nothing but sit back and cheer the revolution. They are great thinkers but not doers.

Miss Gemini is capable of blowing hot and cold. She doesn't mean to play with a guy's emotions, but that is very often exactly what she ends up doing.

Once this woman thinks she understands something thoroughly, she discards it. She's like the child who excitedly unwraps her birthday presents, examines them with delight and then quickly becomes bored with them.

One could say that the Gemini approach to life is superficial. Of course, this is not the case with the individual who has come to terms with her basic problems. Alas, a mature Gemini is indeed a rare creature to run across.

This girl is capable of being promiscuous, which would put a big dent in your Capricorn ego. It is doubtful you could live with a woman for very long if she didn't make you the only man in her life. Also, Gemini girls find it very hard not to burn the candle at both ends. Could an old stay-at-home like you take the pace?

You do have a certain amount of patience and understanding, and if you love her enough, you may be able to get her to face up to certain facts about herself.

You will find her great fun to date. Perhaps it might be better if you have a whirlwind affair and remain "good friends" when the passion has burned itself out.

Her critical faculty is high. She is pretty good at pinpointing people's weaknesses, and she doesn't pull punches. You may find the way she belts out the truth a little discomforting.

Married Capricorn men beware—you are a steady husband but this is the type of woman you could get heavily involved with. For some reason or other, more girls born under the Sign of Gemini have affairs with married men than any other Sign in the Zodiac.

If you do set up home together, you may find yourself doing more than your fair share of the housework. You like a tidy home and will have your work cut out trying to keep it that way with the Twins about.

CAPRICORN MAN—CANCER WOMAN

Miss Cancer is a woman of passing moods. You will never know which way she is going to turn. She is emotional and high-strung; she is easily hurt; her passions are deep and heavy.

She tends to be ruled by her instincts rather than her intellect. Yours is not such an intuitive approach to life.

She has a laugh that is very contagious. She has a way of cheering up people who are down in the dumps. A Cancer person who is in an optimistic mood is wonderful to be with. But there is another side to the coin—a moodiness that can be very depressing. When Cancer is in this state, it is almost impossible to cheer her up.

She is rather self-centered. She enjoys the spotlight and can't stand seeing someone else become the center of attention. She is a leader, not a follower.

Basically, she lacks confidence. She will never get bored when you're telling her how beautiful she is. Things like birthdays and anniversaries matter a great deal to her.

You are both incurable home lovers. Capricorn men do like to be in control in their relationships, but even you might find it a bit too much to have to be constantly protecting a woman who wants to disappear into her shell every time the going gets rough.

You can be a bit of an actor. That won't get you very far with this woman for a Cancer can see right through a pose. This woman is very quick at summing up people.

Your lady Crab will be pleased to discover that you are a man who keeps his word. She is very trusting and likely to believe anything you tell you. She is hurt by people who let her down.

Although Cancer individuals like to hide away when they are upset, you will never find them running from publicity. People born under this Sign often find themselves in the public eye. Many have musical ability and are involved in the art or entertainment world.

It is extremely rare for a Cancer woman to marry the first man she meets. When she loves, she loves deeply, but she will hold back from taking that walk down the aisle until she is as certain as she can be that it's the real thing.

This woman is a wonderful homemaker. You will love the ways she looks after you. When you come home after a hard day's work, it's likely she'll be waiting to fix you a drink, run your bath and fetch your slippers.

She also makes a marvelous hostess. Therefore, she will be very good for you from a business point of view. She knows how to make strangers to her home feel welcome.

Basically, your Cancer woman needs to be dominated. If you give her too much rope, she will take you over completely. You will have to watch that Capricorn habit of being niggling. She wants a fellow who is masterful. It will be up to you to give her the right sort of guidance and control.

You do like praise and flattery. Well, you won't get too much of that from a woman born under the first water Sign. Your element is earth, and the Cancer woman may tend to swamp you emotionally at times. You will have to do your own ego boosting.

Never take her for granted. She is a romantic. It will be up to you to make sure the romance never goes out of your marriage. Remember, too, that when she cries, her tears are never crocodile tears.

CAPRICORN MAN—LEO WOMAN

You are a pretty arrogant man in many ways but you'll meet your match in Miss Leo. This is a very together lady. She needs quite a bit of taming. Don't forget, you are playing with the biggest cat in the jungle.

Being a Capricorn, you are a man who is fairly careful with money. Not mean exactly, but let us say you know the value of a buck. This sexy kitten will certainly expect you to throw a bit of cash about if you want to win her. She is not really extravagant, but she does have expensive tastes. She likes quality restaurants and will always want to be up with (if not ahead of) the latest fashion.

She wants the best things in life. She is quite prepared to sit at home most evenings so long as when you do go out together, you're not counting the small change to see if you can afford to take her home in a taxi.

You will notice right away that this lass has a commanding air. She expects to be treated like a woman. She will love your Old World manners.

Leo women have some difficulty settling down to a one-to-one relationship. They often get quite heavily involved with a variety of males before they meet Mr. Right.

She is unlikely to have many close female friends. Basically, she prefers the company of men, not just for physical reasons, but also because she feels they are more straightforward.

You will usually find that Leo has many and varied interests. She will have a great thirst for knowledge. Very often she will study new subjects and take courses quite late in life. Leos also make wonderful teachers because they have a built-in desire to impart any useful knowledge they possess to others.

She is quite serious-minded, though it mightn't always show. She certainly has a sense of humor, but it could be too outrageous for your liking on occasions. Still, it's likely you'll have many interests in common.

If she really falls head over heels in love with you, you'll know it. This is not a woman who is backward where her true feelings are concerned.

Miss Leo is very passionate. She will help you lose all your inhibitions in the bedroom. She knows how to turn a man on and keep him turned on. In sex, she has a vivid imagination.

You are quite a home lover. It is fortunate that you're unlikely to have many interests in which she can't be included because you would not last very long together if you continued to lead a bachelor life after marriage.

In many ways, she will be extremely good for you. From a business point of view, this is a terrific woman to have at your side. She is self-reliant and will never lean too heavily on you.

This woman will wish to retain her individuality. Don't try to change her or boss her. You will also need to keep a rein on your fussiness. If her Venus or Mercury is in Virgo, you'll probably find you'll get on better. (This can be established from the tables in the book for her Sign.)

She may want to wait a while before starting a family. It's also likely that she'll want no more than two children. Leos get along exceptionally well with youngsters but they don't want them taking over their whole life.

CAPRICORN MAN—VIRGO WOMAN

This has all the makings of an excellent match. Virgos possess many of the qualities you feel are most important. To begin with, this woman is dependable and sincere. You will always know where you stand with her. She is loyal to her friends.

Miss Virgo is very hygiene-conscious. She's likely to take more showers a day than any other Sign in the Zodiac. She's also the same about her home. She'll probably check the highest ledges and shelves in the house for dust. She likes everything to be in its place. In many ways, as you can see, you have similar attitudes.

Virgo is the second of the earth Signs; you are the third. You both have your feet planted on the ground. In careers, you are both likely to know exactly where you are going.

People born under this Sign where Mercury rules are unlikely to fall deeply in love more than once. This woman is very particular about whom she dates. She probably won't have had many casual affairs.

Miss Virgo can be pretty dogmatic. She usually has firm opinions and is likely to come down on the side of conservatism.

You will have to be pushy on your first couple of dates because she is rather shy. It will be up to you to take her hand and do all the arranging as to where you will eat and what movie you'll see.

You both have a tendency to be prudish but are romantics at heart. Neither of you thinks highly of a smutty joke. Vulgarity has no place in this girl's life.

She is a perfectionist. If she takes on a challenge, she likes to see it through to the best of her ability. There is a strong sense of responsibility here. You will find you have a very faithful and proper wife, one who is unlikely to allow herself to have an affair no matter how tempted she may be. She knows what's most important to her.

Don't give up at the first hurdle if you seem to be getting nowhere fast with Miss Virgo. She isn't the iceberg some people say she is. You will need lots of patience and understanding, though, for she can be very restrained when it comes to showing her emotions.

A Virgo woman will split hairs with you. You may get furious with her when you have an argument. The most irritating thing of all is that in the end she usually proves she was right.

Virgo people are great observers. This woman is an astute judge of people. For this reason, you will find her very useful to you in business. She is also good at entertaining. She knows how to get interesting conversations going between people who are relative strangers. If you are going into business with someone and are not sure if he is trustworthy, take your Virgo lady to meet him. She'll be able to tell you in five minutes flat whether the partnership is a good idea or not.

She will make sure you are always well turned out because she hates to see her man go out with a hole in his trousers or a button missing from his shirt.

Miss Virgo will be enthusiastic about your career. She'll do all she can to help you get to the top. She will realize early on in your relationship how important success is to you. You couldn't have a more able and willing helper.

CAPRICORN MAN—LIBRA WOMAN

You have found a very diplomatic and likeable girl here. Libra women hate to be rude and they hate scenes. This is a girl who can't stand to be alone for long but will do anything to avoid traveling in the rush hour. In many ways, you will find her a mass of contradictions.

Miss Libra is subject to sudden mood changes and bouts of depression. You may think you know her well, but she's full of surprises. It would be foolish to take her for granted.

Though she is usually good-natured and pleasant, it's not easy to live with a Libra. Libras like to be on the move. The idea of an organized suburban life scares them. It is also true to say they want security and the knowledge that they have a nice home to return to.

How would you as a Capricorn cope with this? Well, you do have an analytical mind so you might find all her chopping and changing exasperating. You like to know where you stand with people. You will have to learn to love her for what she is, for you won't last very long if you try to mold her into something else. This is a very determined lady who, although sweetness itself, has a mind of her own.

She is wonderful at coping with people from all walks of life. You may find it difficult to understand how she can fit so easily into any kind of group. The fact is she can accept people for exactly what they are. You could never call a Libra woman a snob.

Don't let anyone tell you that Libra is simply a well-balanced, sweet and gracious lady. She may be that, but it's only half the story. She's got a fiery temper once you stir her up. And she's inclined to be a bit argumentative if you start airing your opinions and trying to lay down the law.

Would you be prepared to accept a wife who wants to retain her individuality after marriage? Very often women born under this Sign are pretty ambitious. She won't be prepared to play second fiddle to you. She feels she has lots more to offer the world than clean floors and well-cooked meals. Certainly she will make a devoted wife because she can combine her household duties with her work, but you will have to accept the fact that she won't be prepared to live through you.

You can be rather jealous. Here you would have to change quite a bit if you want to make a go of it with Miss Libra.

As a rule, these women are very attractive and ultrafeminine. She won't try to take over your role as head of the household. She will do all she can to boost your confidence. She will help you in any way possible to get to the top.

You will be immediately attracted by the warm and natural smile that comes so readily to this girl's lips. She is the friendly type. She has a great sense of humor. She has her wits about her. You'll find her as bright as a new penny piece.

You are a hard and conscientious worker, and these are qualities she will admire. Her tastes are quite extravagant. She will expect you to provide her with a nice home. And she likes her comforts.

She's marvelous at entertaining. She will know how to treat your boss when you bring him home to dinner.

Miss Libra is an extraordinarily good listener and an interesting talker. She can take the floor or she can sit back quietly while others do. She is tact personified.

She makes a gentle and understanding lover and will know instinctively what turns you on. She will gently show you how to take the lead.

CAPRICORN MAN—SCORPIO WOMAN

You can usually recognize a Scorpio girl. Normally, her eyes are green or brown. Looking into them deeply, you will feel you are being drawn into a mysterious whirlpool. You may desire her like mad—she's usually extremely voluptuous—but she'll send a shiver down your spine.

This woman has a very powerful personality. You couldn't imagine her acting coy. She is usually built on the large side. She can outstare anybody. She knows exactly what she is. This is a woman who doesn't put on airs and graces. She will see right through any of your pretensions, too. Forget about playing the Latin lover. She's heard that sort of line before. She's straightforward and would prefer you to be.

Woe betide the man who does manage to pull the wool over her eyes. If she finds she has been taken for a ride, her revenge can be quite frightening. She's that Old Testament "eye for an eye and tooth for a tooth" type.

In many ways, you would appear to be the most unlikely match. Without wishing to give offense, she would simply carry too many guns for you. You do like a peaceful life. This woman *lives* on stimulation. She can't take routine for very long. This is not to say she doesn't like security. She does, but she also likes fireworks.

She is incredibly jealous and possessive, even more so than you. She won't like your keeping your old friends or sticking to your old ways if you do get hitched.

A Scorpio woman can be sitting in a room—even a crowded room—alone and gazing into space, and you'll notice how people keep staring at her. She seems to exude a sort of electricity.

Never ask her opinion or advice if you are merely looking for flattery or ego boosting. But if you are seeking the truth, then go right ahead. She can be brutally honest. It is very important to her to be truthful and to the point.

People born with Pluto and Mars ruling find it extremely hard to control their emotions. You will also find that your Scorpio lady has a deep interest in matters connected with the occult and life after death.

She is a very considerate person in a no-nonsense way. She will do all she can to help someone who is down on his or her luck. She doesn't judge people on their reputations; she takes as she finds. The President could walk into the room, and unless she thought he had something to offer, she wouldn't bother with him.

She's honest about sex and her sensual desires. She needs a virile guy. You're no slouch, but even you may find her a bit too much to take.

This woman is a great survivor. She often becomes involved in hair-raising escapades because of her natural curiosity about life, but, she manages to come through in one piece, as a rule.

She is subject to moods and great fits of depression. One fault is her tendency to blame others when things go wrong for her.

She is often in conflict in her relationships with members of the opposite sex. She wants to be dominated, and yet she's terrified of losing her individuality.

She makes a wonderful mother, but can get a little overly possessive when it comes time for the kids to flex their muscles. This is especially true if she has a son.

CAPRICORN MAN—SAGITTARIUS WOMAN

This liaison could work out extremely well. You may even find that Miss Sagittarius is the girl of your dreams. She will probably possess many of the qualities you admire in a woman. She is straightforward and down-to-earth. You will know where you stand with her at all times.

She has great charm without being sugary, an open manner and a friendly smile. In marriage, a Capricorn man needs a friend as well as a lover. That is exactly what a Sagittarius woman is likely to be.

She is probably a good deal more outward-looking than you, and this is a good thing. You need someone to put that extra fire into you.

She's an ambitious woman, not only for herself, but for her man as well. It will be terribly important to her that you get on well in your career, both for the rewards and because she will realize that your relationship with her will work out better if you are doing well in your job.

She is outspoken. Being a Capricorn, you are a very diplomatic guy. Sometimes she will come out with statements that will make your flesh creep. She doesn't mean to hurt others (you could never call her malicious) but she has a habit of blurting out whatever comes into that pretty little head of hers.

You will appreciate that she had good intentions. You will also admire her for her pluck and courage. She does not give up without a fight and will fight to the end.

Your lady Archer will never lie to you. She may withhold the truth if she feels it is for your good, but if you confront her with a fact, she'll usually come clean. Ask her what she has been doing with her time when you've been out, and you're likely to get a detailed report of her movements right down to whom she met at the supermarket and the price of the weekend roast.

Many girls born under this Sign are the outdoor type. She is likely to be enthusiastic about sports and will do her best to get you out on the tennis court or on a long walk after a heavy Sunday dinner. She looks after herself and often retains a youthful figure long after other women have settled for a corset.

She has loads of energy and likes to keep on the move. She is capable of running a house, looking after you and the kids and holding down a responsible job.

Hard work never bothers her, though dull routine does get on her nerves. And she hates the idea of being tied down to any one job for a lifetime.

You will never come second to her career, but you must never try to boss her around. Don't tell her what to do—ask her. A Capricorn man will possess many qualities that a Sagittarius woman admires. She will love your charm and sense if irony. She also likes a man who holds strong opinions.

Your Jupiter girl may appear lacking in sentiment. This is not so. It is simply that she won't reveal her feelings if she thinks there is any possibility of getting hurt. It will be up to you to show her that you can be trusted and that you'll never let her down.

She's not an extravagant woman but she needs to be shown the true value of money. You may find you are better at budgeting than she is.

CAPRICORN MAN—CAPRICORN WOMAN

This is one of those partnerships between two people born under the same Sign that could actually work. You will certainly have a lot of sympathy and understanding for the problems of your Saturn lady. You could be the founder-members of a club for misunderstood Capricorns.

She is terribly romantic, but she also keeps her feet firmly on the ground. Though she is waiting for her prince charming to come and sweep her off her feet, she is unlikely to be taken in by a guy who is not totally sincere.

She is basically a very correct person. She is also reliable, just like you. She will never let a friend down. If she gives her word, she'll do her best to keep it.

Don't waste her time if you're not serious. But then, it's unlikely that you would. You don't go in for casual affairs any more than she does. What you will find you have in common with a woman born under your Sign is that you're both looking for true love.

Success if very important to her. You may find she is a bit of a career girl when you marry her. Surprisingly enough, though, she is capable of channeling this desire to get to the top into her hopes for you. She is a wonderful person to have by your side. She will give you great confidence and help you to a greater belief in yourself.

When she falls in love with a man, it is total. Then she becomes the most faithful and dependable woman in the world.

As you well know, the Goat is extremely sensitive. You tend to think no one else feels things as much as you. You will have to watch that quick temper and those sudden hurtful statements you sometimes come out with.

Capricorn women have a special beauty that is all their own. You may wonder why she spends so much time looking in the mirror. She's not really vain, she lacks confidence. Don't forget to remind her constantly how much you desire her and how beautiful you think she is.

She doesn't like to make enemies. The Goat gets worried if she feels people don't like her, but puts on a great display of not caring.

Miss Capricorn will not settle for second best. You will make a pretty powerful combination as a married couple. You are both hardworking; your ambition will drive you to the top.

She thinks a great deal of her family. She's likely to be terribly proud of her ancestors. You are apt to have the same sort of friends. Since you are both extremely good conversationalists, you are unlikely to get bored in each other's company.

Whether she comes from a working-class background or Knob Hill, this girl possesses natural refinement.

She will keep your home tidy without appearing to be making any great effort. She is able to cope with routine without making a song and dance of it.

This woman will not give herself to a man unless she feels he is interested in more than her body. She realizes that if a relationship is going to last, it has to be built on something more than physical desire.

She's adroit at handling money. She won't be overly extravagant.

You'll make a wonderful duo as parents. Be sure, though, that neither of you is too strict.

CAPRICORN MAN—AQUARIUS WOMAN

If you have fallen for the Water Bearer, you'd better fasten your seat belt because this woman is likely to give you quite a ride. To be frank, of all the Signs of the Zodiac, an Aquarius woman is the least compatible for an earthy creature like you.

She is a mystery even to herself. It's very unlikely that she is the homemaker you are looking for. Many a night you could find yourself having to prepare your own supper. She is also rather eccentric. A conservative man like you could find it very difficult to adapt to her beatnik ways.

You might find a whirlwind affair rather satisfying. So long as you don't expect too much of each other, all will be well. Her head is so full of crazy notions that you will find it hard to discover what she really wants out of life. The truth is she probably doesn't know herself.

She belongs to everyone and no one. You, on the other hand, are a bit possessive. You don't relish sharing the love of your life with others. She may call you petty and narrow-minded because, by her standards, you are. You, in turn, will be irritated by her elusiveness.

Don't think she will settle down as the years go on. She is unlikely to change and it would be extremely unwise of you to enter into a relationship imagining she will.

What you must realize is that this woman is looking for utopia. She is out to change the world. She is a great believer in making the Earth a better place to live on for future generations. This is a very worthy ambition. But how practical is she in the way she goes about it?

You will have to accept her for what she is because no amount of persuasion will get her to change her attitudes toward life and people.

She is not the suspicious type. She will believe you when you tell her you've been working late at the office. Rarely will she doubt your word about anything.

This woman is likely to have a great many outside interests. And what is more, she's apt to bring them home. You may get rather fed up with the comings and goings of the various oddballs she picks up with.

Be very careful about marriage. Don't walk down the aisle with stars in your eyes. You may think after a couple of dates that you simply cannot live without this girl, but get to know her a little better before you pop the question.

You will find your Aquarius lady knows all about money. Despite her way-out ideas, she knows the value of a dollar.

Possessions, however, mean little to her; they do mean a great deal to you. Likewise with family. She has little respect for past history—for any tradition at all, for that matter.

Miss Aquarius has some difficulty expressing her own deep feelings. You must not try to push her to reveal areas of her personality she wishes to keep to herself.

Perhaps you could make a go of it together. Good luck if you decide to try.

One final word of advice: the quickest way to lose this woman is to show jealousy or possessiveness. You could find this kind of restraint rather difficult.

CAPRICORN MAN—PISCES WOMAN

This could be a pretty interesting combination: you who can be so calm and rational in almost any emergency, and Miss Pisces, whose intuitive powers even you won't be able to shrug off. If the chemistry is right, the meeting of dreamer and realist can be a positive experience.

She possesses qualities that make her the dream girl of most men. She is quite a mixture. For all her vague ways, she has great patience and understanding. If she loves a man, she'll do almost anything to make him happy. This woman can adapt herself to changing circumstances and situations. She's as fluid and as hard to pin down as the water that is her element.

You are a home-loving sort of chap, and so is your water maiden. She is very artistic. She will make your home a place you find irresistible.

She wants her man to be top dog. She will boost you and give you all the confidence you need. She is not too enthusiastic about the drudgery of daily chores, though, so she will want the latest in labor-saving gadgets.

You will have to learn to laugh at life a little more. The two Fishes may find your approach to minor pinpricks rather too serious.

A Pisces girl needs a strong man, someone she can run to when things go wrong. You will enjoy being cast in the role of protector.

She can be a bit of a mixed-up kid. You will get her to understand herself better by helping her to grow up and acknowledge her responsibilities. She's a great actress and her favorite role is little-girl-lost.

The influence of Jupiter is very powerful in a Pisces woman. This gives your lady the optimism and enthusiasm to inspire a man like you with positive and more hopeful attitudes. She will soon wash away those silly doubts and fears.

She sets much store by love and romance and knows how to make a relationship last long into marriage. She will certainly keep you on your toes and will also keep you guessing. You will never know which way Ms. Pisces is going to turn next.

She will bring new friends and interests into your life. Being a highly responsive person, you will welcome the added stimuli.

The guys at the office will adore her because she is a woman through and through. You will be told what a lucky guy you are—as if you needed any reminding.

You need not be worried about other interests keeping her from you. When you get married, you'll become the most important thing in the world to her. You must not be selfish and keep her to yourself, though. This is a woman who can become painfully shy and inhibited if she is not given the chance to meet people and exchange ideas.

She is interested in others. It is important that her curiosity about life be fed. Don't worry, she won't go off the rails if you love her. She's true. You will have to push her into action on occasions. There is a lazy side to her nature.

In lovemaking, she likes to be treated gently. She will want you to dominate her in bed, but she's not looking for you to come swinging in on a rope.

She's great with kids. She'll want them to be able to stand on their own two feet at an early age. She's not too good at disciplining them, though, and is likely to leave that to you.

CAPRICORN'S HEALTH

You, Capricorn, are one of the natural survivors of the Zodiac. There is not much in the way of illness that you can't shake off or come to terms with. Capricorns usually enjoy a long life. The older you are, the younger and more active you seem to be for your age.

You have three main health problems. The first occurs in childhood, when you are likely to be either sickly or weaker than most of your playmates and to catch every minor complaint going around. The resistance of the Capricorn child increases with age. The second problem is you are more liable to psychosomatic illnesses than most other Signs. You are a great worrier and can actually worry yourself sick. Thirdly, you are subject to vague aches and pains, the most pernicious of which are rheumatism and arthritis.

The health troubles of most Capricorns are not the kind that shorten life. They are much more inclined to cause discomfort and irritations that, unfortunately, may drag on.

Capricorn rules the muscles and the bones, particularly the knees. Everything that hardens in the body and protects is under its influence. It gives a tough, wiry constitution that is capable of undergoing tremendous hardship. The symbol of the Sign, of course, is the Goat, a very hardy animal that exists on an austere diet in barren, rocky conditions.

Capricorn individuals often have a food hangup. To put it bluntly, you tend to eat too much. And frequently you choose food that does not agree with you. The Sign has a close connection with the stomach, where there is much nervous activity. Digestive upsets occur through hyperacidity. You are inclined to favor hot or spicy food, which plays havoc with your digestive system.

But your worst health hazard is pessimism and anxiety. These not only affect your appetite but also impair your entire constitution. You are afraid of what the future might bring. Your fears and uncertainties are exaggerated. In all compartments of your life, you tend to look on the gloomy side. You crave security and sometimes seek escape, not only in overeating but also in the excessive intake of alcohol. If this is your problem, you will find it can be reduced by adopting a more optimistic attitude toward life, and by mixing with people who are sunny and outgoing (many of your closest associates tend to be introverted and serious).

It is in the later years, when pessimism and morbidity have become habitual, that the worst effects may be felt. With Capricorn people, abnormal drinking is more likely to be a compensation for mental or physical depression than an addiction.

Capricorn also has an association with the kidneys, and in women, with the ovaries.

Your nervous system is highly developed. You are not the easily unbalanced type who goes to pieces in an emergency. In fact, in time of crisis, no one in the Zodiac apart from Scorpio is better equipped to take charge. Your problem is in coming to terms with *your internal* pressures.

You actually thrive on clearing away obstacles and sorting out tangles in everyday affairs. It is important to your health that you be busily involved with some sort of work or project. You dislike lazing around. You become agitated when you have no responsibilities. Be careful, however, that you don't take on more than your fair share of obligations. Sometimes, because you are so good at coping, others often overburden you. Loved ones are probably the worst offenders.

To avoid sickness, you need plenty of fresh air and outdoor exercise. You have to watch that you don't become so immersed in your work that you neglect to carry out this important regimen.

Capricorn rules the skin, and your Sign frequently suffers from nervous rashes, flushes, allergies, chapped skin and blemishes.

You are more vulnerable than most to the common cold and flu. And unfortunately, in you, these infections tend to linger. Your colds can be quite miserable and more often than not are accompanied by neuralgia.

Your teeth are likely to be either very good or highly troublesome. Some Capricorns never have to have a filling; others are always at the dentist. A lack of calcium—the hardening agent—is usually the cause.

CAPRICORN AT WORK

You are a person who can literally bring order out of chaos. You love to be made responsible for sorting out complicated and complex work problems. You are happy in a job that keeps you occupied hour after hour, so that you give little or no thought to the time of day. You are the complete systems person. Give you a million details, and you'll arrange them in a meaningful form—and delight in every moment you're doing it. You are the specialist of the Zodiac.

Naturally, you make a first-class accountant or bookkeeper. You are thorough, cautious, exact. But you'll rarely remain slaving away in some small-time office and getting nowhere. If you are a typical Capricorn, you can't stay on the same rung of the ladder for long even if you try. Your thoroughness, persistence and dedication to whatever job you undertake guarantees that you'll be noticed and promoted.

If you are not interested in your present job, you're probably rather young and haven't yet decided what you want to do. In these circumstances, you may play around, waste time and appear quite cavalier. But no Sign is more certain to eventually discover a life work than Capricorn.

You would make a fine computer programmer. You have an excellent ear for sound and music and could also be a success in the recording industry. You have a way of spotting problems and inconsistencies in masses of trivia. You can usually improve on any existing procedure.

You have a flair for either financial figuring or the written word. Accoring to your disposition (which will be dictated by other influences in the horoscope), you may succeed in a brokerage or stock-market firm. Otherwise journalism and the writing profession generally may offer opportunities for you to make a name. You could be an excellent media critic, especially in music or art. You may not be so creative yourself, but you certainly have the necessary understanding to criticize objectively and put others on the right track.

The travel industry, particularly if it is connected to multinational concerns, may attract you. You don't mind traveling, so long as you have a secure home base to return to.

You are the type of person who can sort out other people's mistakes; therefore you are often invaluable as a troubleshooter. You can rehabilitate an ailing business concern. You are extremely well fitted for business organization and management. Capricorn people often take over a small department of a business or profession and develop it to perfection. They can walk into an office or factory, and with a few terse questions and shrewd glances, put their finger on the main causes of trouble. They make first-class management consultants.

Your innate respect for authority, combined with your power to rule and manage, may draw you to a career in the armed services. A Capricorn character not only makes an excellent top sergeant, but also a fine, though strict, officer.

Your natural integrity and honesty equips you to handle other people's money. You have an eye for sound investment. You won't be tempted to gamble or speculate unwisely. You can be trusted to make fortunes for others without expecting a share for yourself. You believe that if someone hires you, he is paying for the very best you can do. If you make him a rich man, that's the luck of the game. However, there are very few true Capricorns who don't retire in comfort. The really strong types often become extremely rich and powerful.

As a manager or executive, you tend to gravitate to large concerns where there is security as well as the opportunity to work yourself to the top. It is surprising how many charitable and philanthropic organizations are headed by people born under your Sign. Trustees and patrons are quick to discern your earnest perseverance and ability to get things done.

A career in the sciences is likely to be successful. The Capricorn mind is eminently suited for the detailed analysis and painstaking care and observation so necessary in laboratory work. Astronomy, chemistry, mathematics, education, farming, politics and building all offer the type of responsible and productive employment likely to appeal to you constructive and serious-minded Capricorns.

Government administration, particularly at the top level where there is public and political contact, is also a favorite field of the mature Capricorn. Your unemotional qualities are an exceptional advantage where hard bargaining is required and unpopular decisions must be made or handed down.

In any position, even as an ordinary secretary, clerk, tradesman or general office worker, Capricorn people can be counted on to do more than a fair day's work for their pay.

As a boss, the work and responsibility you can handle are amazing. No work situation or crisis ever seems to overwhelm you. You are always fully in command and capable of giving your troops precise and clear-cut orders. You insist that things be done your way and according to the procedures you have laid down.

You won't tolerate insubordination and any suggestion of personal criticism is unforgivable to you. You know what is going on in every department under your control, and you're aware of exactly where everyone is. You run a tight ship. You delegate responsibilities—in fact, you insist that every subordinate take his or her share of responsibility. However, you accept that the buck stops at your desk.

You can't stand slackers, half-wits or funny boys. You're not above making a wry joke, but you don't encourage levity and banter.

You are stern and a bit forbidding to those who don't know you. Underneath you've got a heart of beaten gold. Your employees may not love you, but they will certainly admire and respect you. You are just too exacting and unremittingly professional to be voted favorite boss of the year.

To your staff, you have something of a parental image. You will listen patiently to their problems and help in any way you can. You'll never rebuff a worker who comes to you for advice or with a personal problem. Where special consideration is deserved, you will give it, whether it be a loan, extra money or time off. Where it is not, you won't. You are a law unto yourself. You are not afraid to say no and offer no explanation. You are strict but just. You feel that when you turn down a request, the person concerned understands why.

You are something of a slave driver, but you never ask anyone to work harder than you are prepared to yourself. It is almost impossible to keep up with you, not because you move around so much, but because you manage to shift such a volume of work. You are usually first in to the office in the morning and last to leave at night. Vacations are not important to you. You take them mostly to keep your family happy.

You don't hand out many compliments. Certainly you're never effusive to those under you. Still, no one could say you are a knocker. You treat your staff like a second family—kindly but never extravagantly.

As an employee, you probably get through more work in a week than anyone else on the payroll. Scorpio has the capacity to keep up, but he's likely to be running upstairs too often to undermine some middle-level manager he doesn't like. Your policy is to live and let live—and to get on with the job.

You are very methodical. Your boss knows you'll always turn up—on time. The morning you don't arrive, you'll probably be dead.

Before you walk through the door, you know exactly what has to be done. You don't bother your boss; you just keep going. Sometimes you work right through your lunch hour without thinking anything of it. Overtime pay? It usually doesn't occur to you. You're not a martyr, though, and you won't allow anyone to exploit you.

You are inclined to be handed the "dirty" jobs, such as handling difficult customers your boss is trying to avoid. You're probably the only person in the office who can listen to a complaint without speaking for twenty minutes and then destroy the whole argument with one searching question.

You also have a way of making others feel uncomfortable by just sitting there.

If you were born between December 21 and December 30, you are extremely strong-willed and self-willed. A less materialistic outlook may make others appreciate you more. You may find it difficult to work in partnership or close association with others because they don't possess the same sense of purpose or take the job as seriously as you do. You will probably do better where you can work free of interruptions.

You are likely to possess unusual mechanical ability or technical skill, depending on other influences in the horoscope. Your commanding personality should equip you for a career as an administrator or an executive, provided you don't allow yourself to become too critical and intolerant. Don't make trouble for yourself; strive to see the other person's point of view. Your powers lie in your stability and tenacity.

If you were born between December 31 and January 9, you are more idealistic and probably suited for a career connected with one of the arts, particularly music. You have emotional receptivity and can gauge public and popular tastes. If you are not equipped to be an artist, perhaps you can be the "brains" behind artists and help to develop or improve their talents and techniques.

A career in medicine or science may also appeal. You have a better chance than most Capricorns of cultivating a friendly and communicative personality, which could help considerably in your career. And don't forget that all work and no play is not a good prescription for your type of Capricorn.

If you were born between January 10 and January 19, you are a bit more changeable and resilient than most others born under your Sign. To make the most of your talents you need to cultivate diplomacy and poise and to study how other people react to words and events. Don't assume too much in your personal relations. Try to be aware of how the other person is feeling; don't be too self-centered in your dealings with associates.

Try to remember that the means doesn't always justify the end. You should be successful in any career requiring intellectual ability. Commerce should also offer the kind of rewards you are looking for.

A career in journalism or nonfiction magazine or book writing may help you to utilize your very keen powers of observation. Travel books may provide the greatest scope.

It is very important for you to study your characteristics and make a realistic evaluation of where your interests lie. Otherwise you could go off on a tangent and make a false start. You may waste some time in your early years.

Money

You are generally careful with money but will spend it on yourself without much concern. You also like your home to be comfortable and your family to be secure and free from money worries. However, you insist that family members spend their allowances wisely. You don't hold with extravagance in any form.

You like to put a little cash away out of everything you earn. You are not likely to spend excessively on clothes. You enjoy a nice vacation when you can get away, and will pay for the best.

If you acquire wealth, you are likely to invest in a large and impressive home and most of the status symbols that go with it. You like to surround yourself with quality possessions because they give you a feeling of success and achievement.

AQUARIUS' CHARACTER

You Aquarius people have been puzzling and confusing the rest of us mortals for thousands of years. Just when we think we've got your number, you invariably manage to shock or astound us. Sometimes you do a complete about-face in conduct or ideas. Other times, odd events seem to pick you up and carry you along helplessly before them. Frequently your presence seems to precipitate surprising or disruptive events for the people who know you.

This is all very strange, for by nature you are one of the most kindly, well-meaning, courteous, friendly, conservative—and certainly the least selfish and aggressive—characters of the Zodiac.

The astrological explanation is very interesting. Your Sign is ruled by Uranus, the planet of drastic change, revolution, upheaval and independence. It is one of the three outer-circle or impersonal planets. Most other people are ruled by one of the six inner planets. Consequently, they can never really understand just how your mind works or the motives behind your actions. You have probably noticed by now that to others you are a bit of a puzzle.

Among the inner planets (remember, yours is an outer one), there are many kinds of revolutionary, aggressive and disintegrating forces at work. These differ from Uranus' by being egotistically ambitious and grasping. Their workings are distinguished by greed, malice, envy, jealousy and the selfish drive for personal power. They are warlike and destructive.

Uranus, on the other hand, is fundamentally constructive. For all the drastic and radical changes it brings, its motives are altruistic. It aims to benefit mankind. Uranus destroys ideas, systems and forms that have become outdated, habitual and deluding. It stands for progress and the discovery of the new. Uranus shocks and surprises. It compels those who cling to old concepts to stand aside—not for the aggrandizement of some power-hungry individual but for the benefit of all humanity, particularly the generations yet unborn. It's not accidental that the ancient name for Uranus was "the Awakener."

So now we know why despite your affable, amiable and sociable disposition you are described as unconventional, unpredictable, erratic and different.

This refined individualism usually shows in the way you dress. You are smart, you have style—but you are somehow offbeat. No real Aquarius ever conforms entirely to a particular fashion. You always manage to put your own distinctive trademark on whatever you wear. Not all of you are hippies or affect far-out styles—but a lot of you do. Aquarius men and women are usually the genuine style setters, the avant-garde of the craziest gear. Tomorrow their ideas may inspire *haute couture.* Even the sartorially humdrum millions are often eventually influenced by the visionary and original spirit of Aquarius. The remarkable blue-denim revolution that swept the world and turned a cowboy fabric into a fantastic fashion success was a typically Aquarius phenomenon. So were the beads, the weird hair styles and most of the other innovations of the past decade that took gutsy independence to wear for the first time in public.

Unlike flashy, flamboyant Leo and a few others, you don't dress to show off or to prove how clever you are. You wear what you wear—offbeat or otherwise—because it's you, and you are different. You aren't bothered by what others think. Not in this regard, anyway.

There are Aquarius individuals whose appearance doesn't make them stand out in a crowd. But take a look at the car they drive. Or their home or apartment. There you'll find something distinctive in the way of color, design, make, decor. Perhaps there's an unusual feature like an exotic swimming pool, bathroom, indoor garden, cocktail bar—somewhere there is a distinctive Aquarius touch.

It's not hard for you to become extreme. You have a disconcerting way of going to exotic lengths in one department of your life while otherwise remaining normal and intact. Although basically you are a very balanced person, other influences in the horoscope can easily tip you off balance. You can even become perverse in the degree to which you are willing to flout convention and demonstrate your refusal to conform.

More eccentrics are born under this Sign than any other. And yet seven out of every ten individuals whose names are recorded in the Hall of Fame were either born under Aquarius or have Aquarius Ascending. There isn't a great deal of difference between genius and eccentricity—often it's only the time it takes for posterity to hand down a judgment.

You are normally diplomatic, thoughtful, sympathetic and tranquil. It is often said that you have fewer objectionable traits than any other Sign. Of course, you have your weaknesses (and we'll be touching on them), but you express moderation in all aspects of your personality. You don't go looking for trouble, you're not excessively ambitious, you don't consider money as important as worthiness and purpose in your work. You tend to see more good than bad in everything. You are studious and philosophical, a wonderful listener—and very hung up on humanity as a whole rather than on individuals. This, indeed, is the key to your character.

If you look at any drawing of the Zodiac, you'll see that the Sign opposite Aquarius is Leo, the "I am" Sign, the most ego-oriented. Leo stimulates the emotions, and people born under it are governed by the heart. They love one individual at a time and want to rule and possess that person exclusively. Aquarius, on the other hand, stimulates the mind; your love nature, instead of centering on individuals, radiates outward in an impersonal and altruistic way.

The result? Your approach to love is intellectual, broad-based, encompassing, nonrestrictive. The absence of physical and emotional emphasis makes you show a coolness and detachment that people born under the more personal inner Signs find very hard to understand.

You may have numerous love affairs, but they are rather casual. Until you settle down, you prefer to play the field and keep your romances brisk and unfettered. You can walk away where others would linger. How Aquarius men and women can expect to get along with love partners of the other Signs is discussed in detail in the chapter "Aquarius in Love." Briefly, your chances of happiness depend on whether or not the other party understands your very mature approach to love. Most of us other mortals may find your love too dispassionate to satisfy our desire to feel wanted. You would give your lover an amount of freedom that he or she may not be able to tolerate. Most people need to feel cherished, even possessed. They sentimentalize the expectations and demands that fetter them and call anything less unromantic and cold. In their blind and thoughtless emotionalism, they often do the opposite to what is good for their loved ones and themselves. Love to the typical Aquarius man or woman is loyalty, caring and trust without bondage. You seldom settle for marriage on any other terms. You believe in the independence and freedom of the person you live with; you insist that love does not seek to own.

The Aquarius attitude is too advanced for most individuals to accept. This is probably why you often marry in your late twenties or early thirties. You choose carefully, and that is wise.

When an Aquarius person finds the right lover, he or she can love quite madly. But the lover need not be someone of the opposite sex, for Aquarius is capable of a love fixation for someone of the same sex that is neither homosexual nor kinky.

Aquarius is so finely balanced between the inner and outer planetary influences that the hard distinctions of sex are not so prominent in your consciousness. The typical Aquarius individual often embodies the finer and more subtle characteristics of the opposite sex. This usually endows you with a light and well-proportioned body that is second in attractiveness only to the Venus-ruled Libra. Aquarius individuals are rarely exceedingly virile or feminine. One might say they express a modification of both sexes.

The Aquarius love nature is very much influenced by the position in the horoscope of Venus, the planet of love and beauty. It is advisable for anyone who is considering forming a permanent relationship with an Aquarius individual to pay close attention to this—and the aspects. Still, the Aquarius reluctance to exaggerate personal feeling in any relationship will be present no matter what the aspects.

People born under this Sign are dreamers and idealists, but are astute enough to know what is attainable now and what is not. You often have a faraway look in your eyes. You are always looking forward to tomorrow and back to now, seldom to yesterday. Your optimism is not the kind that imagines things are going to be *better,* only that things are going to *change*. To your sanguine character, that is improvement enough. Your faith that life provides its own solutions is of the mystical variety.

Often you project your emotions onto unattainable people. You seem to deliberately put the object of your affections out of reach. You are capable of harboring a secret unrequited love for many years.

An Aquarius woman may love her brother with a desperate but unexhibited affection. She may have many affairs and even marry, but no one—including her husband—will ever be able to measure up to her idealized and impossible sibling lover. All other men are second best; none can have her totally. Even her children will be unable to claim the same kind of love from her. In this way, the Aquarius characteristic of personal detachment can actually create a justifying fantasy. Sometimes the emotion is projected onto the image of a fleeting first love or a parent.

Why is the Aquarius character so concerned with groups of people as opposed to individuals? The broad answer to this is that Aquarius is the eleventh House of the Zodiac. This is the House of friendship, of detached and impersonal relationships. It concerns clubs, groups, associates and especially humanitarian and philanthropic enterprises. It represents people who share ideals. It stands for the altruistic in human nature.

Obviously, if one feels his or her destiny is to help humanity as a whole, he or she can't afford to become distracted by a few special cases. To put a small group of friends and family first would be "selfish."

This does not mean that everyone born under Aquarius is preoccupied with sorting out humanity's problems. But it does mean that all of you display an extraordinary interest in other people, more so than any other type in the Zodiac. It is a much more serious and deeper interest than Gemini's, for instance. You have an almost divine inquisitiveness. The desire to know your fellow man is absolutely compelling.

You are always analyzing situations and the people around you. You never cease probing and sounding with well-placed questions, helped by your remarkable intuitive powers. Everyone you meet without exception goes under the microscope. You are sometimes subtle and tactful, sometimes insensitive and embarrassing. You penetrate to the very core of a person's psyche and private feelings.

To those with problems, you are kind and helpful. You have an uncanny flair for calming anxious and worried people. Others naturally go to you for advice. Someone is always popping in for a chat. You have a steadying influence on the mentally disturbed.

But you quickly lose interest in individuals. You don't discard them (you hate to lose a friend), but the urgency goes out of the relationship once you discover what makes the person tick. You then pass on to the next person. This earns you the reputation of being fickle in your friendships. After all, it is irritating for someone to have your concentrated attention, and then to suddenly find himself left out in the cold. You give the flattering impression of being fascinated by the character you are analyzing, and when you pass on to the next suitable case, it's darned disappointing.

You need a lot of friends to keep you going, and you have them. Most of all, you need close associates who have intellect and perception that doesn't pall under your microscopic scrutiny. These are the people you can't help returning to; they are your intimates. There are very few of them in the lives of most Aquarians. It is most important that the person you marry or live with have this profundity or a touch of mystery.

Aquarius is also the House of hopes and wishes. It is amazing how often the dreams of people born under this Sign come true. This includes personal hopes as well as dreams of the future for humanity. It should not be forgotten that as statesmen, scientists and social reformers, they often glimpse (or dream) far ahead of their times. They lay their plans accordingly and work quietly and resolutely toward their goal. Once committed, they are not deterred by disappointments, opposition or time. Often they don't live long enough to see the dream realized.

This visionary power is not just of a practical nature. Aquarius people frequently have weird prophetic dreams. One famous Aquarius was Abraham Lincoln. In a dream shortly before his assassination, he saw himself dead. He dreamed he was wandering around the empty White House hearing sobbing coming from every room. In the East Room, he saw a figure lying in state, guarded by soldiers and surrounded by weeping mourners. When he inquired who was dead, he was told, "the President. He was assassinated."

Lincoln had yet another premonition of his death. The day he was shot he told his Cabinet he had dreamed he was alone in a boat without oars or rudder, "helpless in a boundless ocean." He said he'd had the dream before and each time it presaged a great battle (during the Civil War). "Perhaps in a few hours you'll have some important news, gentlemen," Lincoln said. Five hours later, he was dead.

The Aquarius intuition is nothing less than astounding. You seem to be able to pick knowledge out of the air. You instantly recognize the truth. You possess strong psi and ESP faculties. This abnormally perceptive energy comes from your ruling plant, Uranus. It strikes brilliantly.

Sometimes, though, you get your wires crossed. You scrutinize your inspirational insights too closely and rationalize away all their originality and truth. Then your theories and ideas are not as correct as you believe. If you do get hold of the wrong end of the stick, you make mistakes as you find it hard to take advice.

You should try to remember that your Uranian energy is a subtle electricity—"cold," inspirational, dynamic and different. It makes you seem more energetic than you are. It allows you to know what others are thinking and even to project your own thoughts so that others act the way you wish them to.

You don't have a great memory for details or trivia. You're quite forgetful, in fact. You are the type who goes shopping and forgets to look at the list in your pocket. When it comes to important matters, your power of recall is phenomenal.

You always seem to work in a way that saves unnecessary expenditure of energy. As much as you like to see progress and change, you rarely throw down challenges. You avoid direct confrontations. Violence appalls you. You are neither a physical nor a moral coward, but you strongly believe wisdom and the power of the human mind will solve all problems. You aim to change conditions by discussion and understanding because you believe that as people's ideas change, so does the world. You are an ideological revolutionary, not a terrorist.

In several respects, you are a contradictory character. As much as you like novelty, change and adventure, you have a strong desire for security. You like everything you own to be paid for. You hate borrowing or lending. You'd much prefer to give someone money and let it go at that. You like to know exactly where you stand.

You despise lying, cheating and hedging. You would rather hear the naked truth, no matter how painful. Yet you are capable of twisting the facts a bit to achieve your goals and creating a false impression to protect your friends. You are an instinctive searcher for truth, but sometimes you are inclined to overlook your own deceptions and subtle stratagems, mild and relatively harmless though they may be. You also have an infuriating habit of trying to conceal your motives. Perhaps this is because the element of surprise is so important to you; you desire to keep people guessing right up to the last moment.

You are mule-stubborn at times. You've got your own way of doing things and expressing yourself, and no one, damnit, is going to change you one bit. This is surprising in a character who generally seems so easygoing and tolerant. But tolerance is the point here: you believe every individual should be free to make his own decisions. If he goofs, it's a pity, but liberty, as you see it, includes the right to fail doing your own thing your own way.

It's quite possible you will wake up one morning with a brand-new set of views on life. That they are contrary to opinions you've been espousing for years won't matter to you. You'll put them forward with the same confident certainty with which you advanced the old ones. But what about your old supporters? Well, you feel everyone ought to learn to keep up with the times.

You seldom show your indignation or anger in an unpleasantly aggressive way. You dislike quarrels and would prefer to walk out than to endure a scene. Of course, with that unpredictable Uranian nature of yours, there's always the chance of a sudden blast of temper. On the rare occasions you direct it at someone, it invariably means the friendship is finished.

For such a freewheeling character, you're very fixed in your ideas. You'll listen to other points of view, nod understandingly, even appear to concede a point or two—and walk away with exactly the same opinions as you started with. In a position of power and authority, it is both your strongest and your weakest point that you never doubt your own conclusions. You nonchalantly dismiss or ignore opposition or noncooperation. Fortunately, you are usually concerned with worthwhile reform or righting some injustice, and here you are more often right than your opponents.

However, in your personal decisions, you are not always so reliable. You find it hard to relinquish preconceived notions because you think your own habits and values are so much more valid than the other person's. Even when it comes to bringing up kids, you're likely to be tolerantly amused by the methods other parents use.

It's just about impossible for you to accept or even consider that others might have ideas as good as your own. Frankly, your judgment is usually hopelessly one-eyed when you deliberate from a personal point of view. You should always try to stand back and apply universal principles. Then you will find that the personal looks after itself and that fewer drastic or violent changes are called for.

Despite your love of company and discussion, you frequently have to get off on your own in order to restore your peculiar quality of energy. Without periods of seclusion when you can cogitate and examine your own mind, you become moody, discontented and cranky. You also need a good eight hours' sleep each night.

To be happy, you have to live a life that allows the full development of your potential. Too much of a dull and conventional existence will drive you crazy. You have more than your share of natural talents, but they are inhibited by compromise. Aquarius people often marry dominant types and end up fighting a demoralizing battle of wills.

You have a mind that is easy to train and quick to learn. You need both mental stimulation and discipline. Brilliance without direction and control often appears merely eccentric. You possess the ideal scientific brain. You readily change decisions in the light of new developments. It is not your style to flog a dead horse. You also have an enormous amount of common sense and refuse to close your eyes to facts. Once you know you are beaten or that it is impossible to proceed, like a good general, you retreat.

Basically, every Aquarius person needs a cause. In esoteric Astrology, it is said that each Sign has a special job to do for humanity. Yours is to understand man (hence your inquisitiveness), and then to awaken him to the possibilities of the future. Without involvement in a cause, you usually fail to fulfill your true promise. If you settle for a superficial existence, you will short-circuit your pioneering and original Uranian energy. Sometimes, then, you become a drifter, uncommitted to anything, who excuses your lack of accomplishment by saying that no one wants to listen to you, it's all a waste of time. This type of Aquarius individual is often a dropout. Even the ordinary Aquarius man or woman who can't find a responsive audience for his or her ideas is likely to sink into inertia and pessimism.

If you are frustrated in this way, you can become the victim of your own daydreams. You devote yourself to cataloguing all that is wrong with the world and overlook your own weaknesses and failings. You pursue your ideal in your mind instead of coming down to earth and doing. You become a slogan chanter, a futile theorist, an armchair protester. Because your mind reaches so far out into space, you must learn to keep a firm hold on reality.

You like your home to be attractive and comfortable. In some respects, you have a lust for luxury. This is not a dominant trait, but it appears from time to time. The sense of possession isn't strong in you, but knowing you have the means to obtain what you want is.

You are a great experimenter. Your home is usually filled with gadgets and labor-saving devices. Your home and immediate family mean more to you than many people suspect. You enjoy entertaining and especially having house guests. Numbers don't worry you. You like to give visitors the best you can afford and the free run of your house. In this respect, you are an excellent host or hostess.

You enjoy animated conversation and especially airing your latest ideas. You often gather an odd assortment of friends and acquaintances around you. You are very much aware of people who are down on their luck and will do your best to help them out. Your family is probably used to seeing you arrive home with odd characters to spend the night because they have nowhere else to go. You are egalitarian. You believe the only thing that really counts is what a person is inside. You are not impressed by wealth or position, although you usually number a few well-off and influential people among your friends. You also have friends of different nationalities and with a wide range of religious beliefs. You deliberately cultivate those with diverse interests and backgrounds. Nothing pleases you more than sitting around chatting with people of different cultures. You delight in assessing the truth or falsity of what they believe in. You are quite impartial and unemotional in your judgments. Although you want to know how everyone thinks, you never try to browbeat another into changing his or her views. You usually rely on the intrinsic merit of your arguments.

You often prefer to live in the country or at least where you an have a garden and get close to nature. You're not so fond of changing your residence once you've found the place and environment you like because you like a permanent base from which you can radiate. You also want your family to feel secure, even though you may not care to spend all that much time in the home.

You enjoy vacations, especially when they involve traveling to other countries. If you can afford it, you try to get away once or twice a year.

You have a wonderful way of getting things done without appearing to expend much effort. The secret is you do most of your organizing behind the scenes without fuss and publicity. You generally reveal your hand by playing it.

You love excitement and adventure. You try to find these in your work as well as in your spare-time activities. For amusement, you usually choose odd and stimulating pastimes. You are likely to enjoy flying and dashing around in fast automobiles. In sports, you are more likely to be an eager fan and supporter than a competitor. You love to mingle with crowds, observing reactions and giving imaginary rundowns of different characters. Crowds give you a feeling of security as well as excitement. Some Aquarius types enjoy gambling. At the track or at the gambling tables, it's the swift action and the fervor of the crowd that turn you on.

What about loneliness? One would think that anyone born under the Sign of friendship, associations and commitment to groups would never be lonely. But Aquarius is an idealist, concerned with the basic values of life, rather than personal success and achievement. He stands in the crowd but separate from it. He is virtually alone, alienated by broad aspirations and standards of thinking others can neither comprehend nor accept. According to C. J. Jung, the famous psychiatrist, loneliness is not the result of having no one around; loneliness is being unable to communicate to others the things that are important to you.

Naturally, as a humanitarian with advanced ideas, the typical Aquarius person must expect to experience some form of isolation and sacrifice in his or her attempts to advance the case of progress. Still, *aloneness* is not the same thing as *loneliness.* No one understands this better than the mature Aquarius man or woman whose deepest satisfaction lies in giving his or her mind, energies and devotion totally to something greater than the self.

AQUARIUS IN LOVE

YOUR AQUARIUS MAN

You like him? Love him? What is Mr. Aquarius really like?

Exciting. Dynamic. Confusing. This man could drive any worm-blooded woman crazy. He's terribly attractive and delightfully witty. He knows how to treat a woman, is a wonderful conversationalist, knows all the best places to go and has loads of interesting friends. But he's not much of a lover in the regular sense. And when you really want him, he's seldom around.

Mr. Aquarius is everybody's buddy. He's got extraordinary energy, which he seems to waste like water (his symbol is the Water Bearer, of course) on a wide range of interests and an even wider circle of acquaintances. If only he could pour all that vitality into loving one woman, he'd be fantastic. But he rarely can. You'll have to be a very special kind of woman to hook and hold this man.

He believes in personal freedom and lives it. He's not really the marrying kind. He wants a woman who'll let him come and go as he pleases, who won't make any demands on him whatever! He just can't stand limitations. He wants to be free to think, act and move.

Now, what sort of woman could possibly stand for this? For a start, one who loves him deeply and who understands him. She can't be possessive or jealous (obviously). She'll have to have her own outside interests and do her best to make at least some of them mutual so that she and he can enjoy doing as many things together as possible. Above all, she'll make sure she and her Aquarius lover don't grow too far apart to stay in the same orbit.

Don't get the idea that an Aquarius man can't love a woman insanely. He just has an odd way of showing it. His personal love has to take its place in the rest of his world; it can never be really exclusive. His nature is to spread himself over the widest section of humanity he can possibly cover.

It would be an intolerable contradiction for him to try to live for one person. The marriage of any Aquarius guy who tries to do this is already heading for the rocks. His woman has to be prepared to share him with the big wide world that interests him so much. This doesn't mean he'll get involved in an endless succession of affairs. The whole point, really, is that he's *not* physically oriented.

This man is basically an intellectual being. He loves people for their minds, their ideas. He's terribly curious about how others think. Once he knows what makes a person tick, he's inclined to zoom off to analyze someone else. To keep an Aquarius man interested, you will have to maintain an air of mystery. If you let it all hang out, including swearing your undying love for him, he's likely to run the other way. Demonstrative women threaten his individuality. Declarations of love often seem to him a takeover bid. You have to be extremely subtle with this man.

Mr. Aquarius is frequently impatient with himself but seldom with others. He can listen for hours to people's problems, but he can't sit still alone and unoccupied (except when he slopes off into one of his periodic seclusions). He's got to feel he's doing something worthwhile, that he's helping to give the world a little push in the right direction. Sometimes when events are delayed, he'll explode in a violent temper. It will rarely be directed at another human being. He just hates being unable to control any situation.

As much as you love him, you'll never quite get used to his zany sense of fun. He gets an odd kick out of shocking people by doing the most unexpected things. He might walk down the main street in a top hat, shoes and socks and bathing suit. Why shouldn't I? is his attitude.

Mr. Aquarius is at heart a nonconformist. If he is a strong character he may have the reputation for being a revolutionary or an eccentric. Some of the older, more conservative generation find him a bit too much. You might have some trouble on this score from Mom and Dad if the affair looks serious.

Mr. Aquarius is as straight as a die. He'll always level with you personally. He despises liars and cheats. The more you get to know him, the more you'll appreciate him for what he is.

YOUR AQUARIUS WOMAN

You like her? Love her? What sort of woman is she?

Fun. A bit crazy. Youthful at any age. Yet strangley serious. Almost certainly dedicated to some ideal or other.

Though this girl gives you the impression she has everything under control, she's likely to change her mind without warning. While she believes in something, she believes devoutly and nothing will shake her. But once her excellent judgment tells her she's made a mistake, she'll obliterate the whole thing from her mind—and zip off to something else.

The Aquarius woman believes fervently in tomorrow. Nothing bad today won't be better in the future. This applies to love. She is one of the truest women in the Zodiac. There is no fear of your female Water Bearer planting her jug on another man's table as long as she believes in you.

It would never occur to her to check up on you. Trust is implicit in her particular style of loving. She's not jealous or possessive. She'll believe you're both adult enough to know what you want and what you're doing. But if she learns you are deceiving her, she'll walk out on you because she can't stand a cheat.

Sexually an Aquarius woman is different from all the others. You fiery Latin lovers will have to learn she will not be turned on physically until you've convinced her you've got a bit more brain than passion.

She's the intellectual type. She loves a lively discussion. She's very well informed and knows exactly what's going on in the world, particularly the injustices being inflicted on her fellow man. It will be your mind that attracts her to you first. You'd better start ordering *Time* and *Newsweek*.

Miss Aquarius needs freedom. No man's ever going to tie her down to the bed or the kitchen sink. Oh, she's capable of love affairs, all right. She can be an experimental and imaginative lover. But that's today, or maybe just now. Tomorrow or next minute she'll just want to talk, probably about her idea of the utopia she yearns to see realized on Earth. Until she gives her word to a man, she's a freed lover as well as a flag waving lover of freedom.

She's a dreamer who is basically realistic. She has these great ideas of what the perfect society should be like. But usually Aquarius notions are ahead of the times, and what she envisions today is rejected by most people as wishful thinking. However, the world is likely to adopt her views tomorrow.

She has amazing perseverance. She'll stick to a project with unyielding devotion while she believes in it. But if someone proves to her it is not feasible, she'll admit defeat and retreat—to some other purposeful endeavor.

Would you be able to put up with playing second fiddle over a lifetime to a series of causes and crusades? That's the price you'll have to pay if you marry this extraordinary and often brilliant woman—if she is a true Aquarius. It would be a good idea to check your horoscope against hers in the book for your Sign. For both your sakes, you wouldn't want to make a mistake with this union.

She is a cheerful, good-natured, vivacious female. What she lacks in emotion and sentiment she makes up for in spirituality. She conveys a deep inner sincerity. You would indeed be privileged to live with such a high-minded woman. The success of this union depends on compatibility and your willingness to share her with her outside interests and friends. With all her intense concern for the welfare of the underprivileged and voiceless minorities of this planet, how could you expect a woman like this to pour her love into just one man?

The Aquarius woman knows how to maintain harmony in a marriage. Her home is usually peaceful. She doesn't like domestic arguments. Although she has strong views, she will listen to your point of view. She would never willingly cause another person unhappiness even if it meant suffering herself.

In the right setting, she's a gem.

AQUARIUS WOMAN—ARIES MAN

When you first come across Mr. Aries, you may feel electricity in the air. It's likely you'll get involved in some sort of argument or heated discussion. In many ways, you are opposite types. However, you'll probably find each other attractive because each of you will recognize a personality as strong as your own. You are quite positive in your outlook and admire this in others.

Your girlfriends will probably tell you this liaison will last days rather than weeks. They will tell you it's crazy and can only end in tears. Strangely, you could prove them all wrong.

You can't help but be impressed by the confidence and straightforward manner of this man. He jumps in feet first no matter how delicate the situation. He will never take "no" for an answer. If he is attracted to you, he'll keep calling you until you agree to go out with him.

He is not such a wolf as people think. He has a reputation for trying to get every attractive woman he meets into bed. Actually, he rather enjoys this reputation because it flatters his pride, but it's not the whole truth. When you get to know him well, you'll find he is quite gentle and sensitive. He would bend over backward to help a friend in need.

But he won't accept your ideas on friendship and love. He finds it difficult to become a platonic friend to a woman he has been involved with on a physical plane. He is an all-or-nothing type.

He is likely to get the wrong idea about you in the beginning. He will believe you are much more hung up on the sexual side of the relationship than you are. If you love him, you'll have to teach him to understand you.

In many ways, he is a man's man. He loves a night out with the boys. He is also a sports enthusiast and a very big competitor.

As a husband, Mr. Aries is a good provider. However, his old-fashioned attitude as to where a woman's place is could be unpalatable to you. He will expect your life to center around him. He won't like the idea of your having a job if it's going to affect his life in any way.

He may try to take you over. He will definitely want to influence your attitude toward life. He couldn't stand to live with anybody who did not go along with his views on the world.

This man can easily get caught up in his own whims and fancies. In this way, he's like a little boy with a new toy. He can drop a hobby just as quickly as he picked it up.

He will want to make all the important decisions, and this will not go down very well with you. You are a liberated woman who believes in power sharing.

Mr. Aries is not a great stickler for routine. He won't be unduly bothered if his dinner is not on the table the same time every night.

He can't help flirting, but you'll have no difficulty in accepting this. You'll soon realize it's all harmless fun to the Ram.

If you are one of those Aquarius women who is looking for a virile man to protect you and never allow you to be hurt, you could strike it lucky with Mr. Aries.

When the children come along, he'll take his parental responsibilities seriously.

AQUARIUS WOMAN—TAURUS MAN

Take it easy on the Bull. It would be so simple for a girl like you to slip the rope through the ring on his nose and lead him a merry dance.

He is honest, straightforward and down to earth. He doesn't do things in half-measures. If he loves you, he will soon let you know.

It would appear highly unlikely you could settle down with this man. He is too masculine for you, very old-fashioned in his ways. He plays things by the book and has extremely conservative tastes. You could say he's as straight as they come.

You do like a little mystery in your men. Unfortunately, you will probably be able to read Taurus like a book. On the other hand, you will be such a puzzle to him it will drive him crazy.

It could be you will meet him at a concert or in an art gallery because he is very artistically inclined and so are you. He may see you standing dreamily in front of a masterpiece or sitting with your eyes shut listening to a beautiful piece of music and will be able to convince himself you are the girl of his dreams.

The trouble is he will want to take you over totally. This man is a great provider. He will wish to buy you everything your heart desires. After a while, you could find his love rather suffocating. You do, after all, treasure your freedom.

He could easily sweep you off your feet after you begin going out together. He frequents the best restaurants, is likely to have an elegant car and knows how to entertain in grand style. But after you have started going steady, this sort of life could begin to pall for a woman like you.

You will find your mind wandering while you are in his company. You will be imagining how nice it would be to be sitting around in your old jeans with a few of your hippy-type friends, just having a good laugh. You can survive without a full wallet; he can't.

He has to operate at a fairly slow pace. He doesn't like to take chances and he won't be rushed. Many people may overtake him in business, but he'll probably see them come tumbling down while he continues his climb to the top.

You always go out of your way to help the poor and the underprivileged. So does the Bull. The difference is you'll wish to do it by putting in time helping people in a personal way. This man will wish to do it with his checkbook.

You will get irritated by his attitude toward money. He does tend to believe it's the answer to everything. This is not to say he has no heart. It's just that he would rather help his close family and friends than get involved in great causes.

Mr. Taurus won't be too keen on your having a lot of outside interests. He will expect you to be waiting to throw your arms around him when he comes home from work.

It is obvious you would both have to change a good deal if you married. You would have to be willing to spend a lot of time looking after him. You would also have to be prepared to dress up whenever he took you out. He would feel it was a personal reflection on him if you didn't look fashionable and well put together.

You could probably get him to change to a certain extent. Introduce him to a couple of your more far-out friends. They may help him to understand there is more to life than he realized.

AQUARIUS WOMAN—GEMINI MAN

There are not many men who can sweep an Aquarius girl off her feet, but Mr. Gemini is one of them. You do not generally fall in love at first sight, but here is a man with a strong enough personality to completely bowl you over.

Like you, he is an air Sign. His ruler is Mercury, and this means he's pretty quick-witted. You will love his sense of humor. He will make you aware that you take yourself a little too seriously on occasions.

There are many things you have in common. This is a man who can't stay in one spot for too long. You may think he has ants in his pants. He's got no time for stick-in-the-muds. He will not allow people to impose their morality upon him. He is unwilling to accept rules and regulations that have been passed down from time immemorial. He insists on testing things for himself before he accepts them.

Mr. Gemini will allow you your precious freedom—the freedom to think as you do and to hold your own opinions, as well as freedom of movement—which is very important to you.

He is a persuasive talker; you are a good listener. You are unlikely to encounter a dull moment when you're in his company. He couldn't be called a sentimentalist (neither could you, for that matter), but he does show emotion when he is hurt or let down by someone he believes in.

He will be quite happy to do his fair share of the household chores. He enjoys cooking and is happy to do the cleaning or washing up.

He expects the girl he lives with to be able to take care of herself. He will like your independent streak; in fact, he will encourage you to have your own interests.

There is one danger with an Aquarius-Gemini linkup. You are both so independent-minded that you might pursue so many separate interests that you will grow apart. Be sure you develop enough mutual interests to make a life *together*.

You will have to be the one who ensures a certain amount of stability in the relationship. If this man doesn't have a home to return to where he can relax and feel secure, he could go to pieces. He finds it difficult to hold down a job for very long if his personal life is not running smoothly.

Basically, the Twins need a fairly strong-minded woman behind them to give them an extra push. It's all too easy for this man to sit back in the rocking chair, take a swig from the wine bottle and say, "Why bother with the rat race?"

You are capable of being sensible and showing others the right way to go about things. This guy could even bring out protective instincts you never realized you could feel for a man.

He is even-tempered. He really wants a peaceful life. He will avoid confrontations if he possibly can.

You will have to watch that impetuous streak because he has one, too. Don't make any hasty decisions about the future. You are both capable of being carried along on the wave of the other's enthusiasm.

You will have many common interests. It is possible you'll both be involved in some way in the world of art or entertainment.

It would be advisable to wait a while before starting a family. You both have a lot of living to do before you can comfortably settle down to the many responsibilities of parenthood.

AQUARIUS WOMAN—CANCER MAN

Mr. Cancer would make an excellent business partner for a woman like you. Were you to open a shop together or perhaps some kind of agency—anything to do with buying or selling, in fact—it's likely you would prosper. Your personalities would complement each other in a working relationship. You would probably rush around and organize everything while polite Mr. Cancer would wow the customers.

The possibilities for a deeper relationship are not quite so bright because in your personal lives, you are both looking for very different things in the long run.

This Moon child is a great home lover. He yearns for security and a peaceful life. He is also extremely emotional and high-strung. He is capable of having phases of deep depression. His introverted ways may become unbearable.

He will expect a great deal of you as his wife. He needs a woman who is mother, sister and daughter all rolled into one. He is full of self-doubt and contradictions.

You're always trying to look on the bright side of things. You want to make the world a happier place for everyone. His depressions will depress you. You also have very different attitudes toward home life. Though you like an evening at home once in a while, you do tend to think of your home as a place to relax and recover before venturing out into the world again. The Crab is a veritable hermit, inclined to hide away in his shell and refuse to face reality.

He is careful with money. The reason for this is not meanness but his intense need for security.

He doesn't have much of a sense of humor about himself. Don't tease him or satirize his attitudes and habits. He won't appreciate that sort of joke. Another kind of joke that won't appeal to him is one about his family. He is usually very close to his parents. Blood ties are much more important to him than they are to you.

You will have to put the brakes on your independent ways. He won't be able to cope if you leave him to fend for himself for long stretches.

He will want to spoil you. He makes a gentle and understanding lover. He is probably far more hung up on the sensual side of a relationship than you. He may misunderstand your attitudes to sex and think you are rather cold.

One wonders if his kindness and desire to please you would make up for all the evenings out you are going to have to sacrifice if you do become man and wife.

He is fascinated by water. His idea of a dream holiday is a lazy cruise on a banana boat in the Caribbean. You will probably tell him you'll see him when his boat docks and jet it down to the Bahamas!

Perhaps you would be able to make a go of marriage if you work together. This would ensure enough mutual interests to make it a worthwhile proposition.

You should have some very interesting discussions. This man is quite knowledgeable and discerning. You're pretty fixed in your views, but when you think over what he says, you might be surprised at how often it makes sense.

Mr. Cancer makes a fine father. He will do his best to understand his children.

AQUARIUS WOMAN—LEO MAN

Make sure you know what you're letting yourself in for before you get deeply involved with a Leo. Remember, fire is his element, and that is exactly what you would be playing with. If this man sets his sights on you, you'll find it hard not to be impressed. He will make you feel all woman.

He has a number of drawbacks for an Aquarius woman. He will want you to do more than share his life with him; he'll also want you to accept his standards.

This guy is a born leader. He's King of the Jungle and he knows it. But if you know how to get around him, he can be as amenable as a tabby cat. He might be the last one to admit it, but he's a romantic at heart. He's also a bit of a kid. His taste in movies is likely to run to westerns, and his musical favorites will probably be old-fashioned—Sinatra and Dean Martin.

Girlfriends may feel he is much too dominant a character for a woman like you. They will say you're biting off more than you can chew.

This guy is very hung up on success and will do his darndest to get to the top in his chosen career. He wouldn't dream of accepting a challenging job if he didn't think he could pull if off.

It will be love that brings the two of you together. The question is, will that love endure for a lifetime?

It would be foolhardy to rush down the aisle with a Leo. Give yourself plenty of time to get to know his moods and other aspects of his nature. You might find his pride a bit too much for you to cope with. You may well get bored with buttering up his ego. It would be sad to wake up one day and find you have outgrown him. Once he has shown you everything he knows, you may feel it's time to move on. Remember, you're a woman who wants to experience everything life has to offer.

Without love, a Leo is nothing. He is a one-woman man, but he needs that woman constantly at his side to spur him on. He is no shirker, but he does have to feel he is striving for success for his partner as much as for himself.

Sometimes you will have to act as a cooling influence on his great enthusiasms. He can get carried away by ideas that are not always realistic propositions.

He likes to have his group of admirers. This man will never tire of hearing himself praised.

Next time he's in a real temper with you, suddenly change the subject and tell him how nice his hair is looking or how much you admire that sweater he's wearing. You'll find he soon loses the thread of what he was saying.

He can be a bit of a gambler. He doesn't like for anyone to get the better of him. If he plays poker, he will usually see any raise because he can't endure the thought that someone may be bluffing him out of the pot.

As a lover, he will be wonderful for a woman like you. He is a passionate being. When you are in his arms, you will be swept along by the ardor of his passion. You will soon lose that detached air people sometimes accuse you of having.

You probably won't have a very large family. Leo is happy with a couple of cubs at the outside. He likes to teach his offspring everything he knows (it's a big jungle out there, you know), and two is about all he's got time for.

You are bound to have your rows and differences, but so long as these lead you to want to understand each other better, you could have a happy life together.

AQUARIUS WOMAN—VIRGO MAN

As unlikely as it seems, Mr. Virgo could be just the right man for a woman like you. He is quick-witted—remember, Mercury is his ruler—and you like a man who has speed of thought. He also wishes to do something to help others in this world. He is a strong man with a deep-rooted sense of justice.

You will discover he's not the type to sweep you off your feet. He will take his time wooing you. He will consider it important to get to know you really well before becoming serious. Usually his head rules his heart. You can't help but admire his strength of character and uprightness.

He likes people to be straightforward. If he gives his word he'll try to live up to it.

Virgo people are well known for their great love of music. He is a good talker and can make almost any subject he cares about interesting.

This will not be a madly passionate union. But the love will grow stronger the longer you are around each other.

Despite Virgo's reputation for chastity, lovemaking will not be reserved for Saturday nights only. But this man does realize that a long-term union has to be built on more than purely sexual attraction.

Whatever responsibilities this man takes on, he will see through. He has an extremely strong sense of values and fair play.

He is amazingly quick at summing up people and situations. People often underestimate him. Underneath that charming surface, there is a shrewd mind ticking away. Rarely does anyone put a fast one over on him in business. Sometimes it suits him to allow people to think he is rather slow on the uptake because then they will show their hand first, which is what he wants.

Mr. Virgo can be fussy, and this is where you may differ. He is terribly tidy around the house. He will find it hard to accept the fact that you often leave unwashed dishes in the sink overnight. He will take over chores that are not really his domain rather than see them left undone. He is house-proud, but even more, he is extremely hygiene-conscious.

He also has a puritanical streak. This makes him rather quick to judge others. You will have to help him not to reach such hasty and harsh conclusions. He does have a tendency to believe he is always in the right.

There are many good points about this man. He is as straight as they come. He is unlikely to get involved with another woman after marriage. And he will try to provide all your heart desires.

He knows how to treat a woman. He will be prepared to involve himself in any sensible cause you wish to support. Though he may be a bit slower than you in the way he goes about it, you will find his assistance invaluable.

Mr. Virgo may be a strong critic when you are in the wrong, but you will come to rely on his judgment and it will be a great help to you.

This man is not so good at seeing his own faults. However, he is basically a very modest person, and you'll feel that when he does stick his oar in, he's genuinely trying to help and is not on some sort of ego trip.

He's a bit of a stick-in-the-mud and needs a woman to nudge him out of the same old routine—a woman like you.

He is not all that crazy about having a big family. One or two children are likely to be quite enough for him.

AQUARIUS WOMAN—LIBRA MAN

It won't take you very long to recognize Mr. Libra as a man you could really settle down with. He is extremely charming and won't try to dominate you. As a rule, you don't go for men who try the heavy approach. In fact, it is just possible that here you'll end up doing the chasing for a change.

Libras know instinctively about harmony and balance, understandably; after all, their symbol is the Scales.

You will always be surprised by this man. He will never allow your life together to become dull or in any way routine. He has an inquiring mind and, like you, is always interested in meeting new people and taking on challenges.

He also has a good sense of humor. He makes sure he gets the best out of life. He will try to see the funny side of things.

Sometimes he finds it difficult to make up his mind on a positive course of action. This is because he always sees the merits of more than one point of view.

He is changeable and likes variety, but he is not as superficial as Mr. Gemini; there is more emotional depth to a Libra. His approach to life could be called philosophical.

It may take you quite a while to realize you have fallen for this man. You will probably be drawn to his intellect first. It will be the sort of romance that develops slowly and matures into something rich and lasting.

This guy will not be perturbed by your rather nonconformist attitude. He will listen with interest to your notions about the ideal society. He will take you seriously and attempt to get you to approach things more logically. He will be very good for you in many ways.

You will also be quite influential in his life. Sometimes he gets very depressed with the way the world is going. You could shake him out of his lethargy.

This is a man you will want to impress. He is a real gentleman. He will always pay you a compliment when you are looking your best, it will be sincerely meant. He likes his home but also loves to go out. You'll probably find he knows the best spots to eat in town.

He can be pretty argumentative when he chooses. If someone gets his back up, he won't duck a confrontation. He is an excellent debater. People rarely beat him in an argument.

He will make you face up to yourself. He won't let you get away with sweeping generalizations. He will bring you back to the facts.

You will probably share the same tastes in art. You will also agree on how your home should be decorated and furnished.

Mr. Libra will do everything he can to keep your relationship fresh and interesting. He can't survive for very long without romance in his life. You may both flirt occasionally, but it will be harmless fun. Neither of you is likely to get particularly jealous. In fact, you will be flattered by the number of women attracted to your man.

You would never try to tie him down, and this is why he will keep running back to you. The Libra man is always happier in partnership; a successful love partnership will bring out his best.

AQUARIUS WOMAN—SCORPIO MAN

Here is a man with very positive ideas about what he wants from life. He is direct and determined to get to the top. He is a fighter. Scorpio people won't allow themselves to be dominated. This man always thinks he knows best and can't bear to have his faults pointed out to him.

This will be an all-or-nothing relationship. If you agree with his attitude toward life, all will be well and good. If not, move on. It's no good thinking you will change him because you won't.

Perhaps you will be drawn to him physically because he is a sexy kind of guy. Insist on a long courtship, however. Don't contemplate settling down with a Scorpio until you are pretty sure you thoroughly understand him.

His approach to life is tough. He will probably want to dominate you. He won't like your having friends he doesn't approve of. He will want you to think the same way he does.

He can be very jealous. To a Scorpio, jealousy is very much a part of love. In fact, this man can't really love unless he feels every other guy wants to make it with his woman.

He will want to protect you. If he sees another man give you a wink or try to play footsie with you under the table, he'll be ready to throw a right hook at him.

Mr. Scorpio will put you on a pedestal. He will never stop telling you he loves you. His approach to lovemaking is very elemental. You will have to teach him to be more gentle. At times, you may feel he's a direct descendant of the club-wielding caveman.

He can be unfair in his attitude about personal freedom. He will expect to have his nights out with the boys or his round of golf on weekends, but he will want you to stay home and cook dinner for when he returns. He will want to have his own separate interests, but will expect you to build your entire life around him. He will also not like the idea of your continuing with your job after you marry him.

Mr. Scorpio will show little interest in other people's problems. He feels it is not his worry if someone else is having a rough time. His attitude is that everyone is responsible for the situation he finds himself in.

He can be a bit of a skinflint. You might never know exactly how much he has stashed away. He will always plead poverty and complain that taxes are clobbering him.

He can get pretty hung up about matters connected with life and death. And while he is quick to make moral judgments about others, he tends to ignore his own faults or to excuse them.

He may find you a little cool in bed. But then, very few women can match his ardor in sex. One word of warning: never laugh at him in the bedroom—at his body or his technique—because he'll never forgive you to his dying day.

This man needs to have something to work for, and that something is usually his family. He will want to have kids, lots of them. He makes a good father. He will never tire of playing with his children and entertaining them. He also knows how to be strict. He will make sure they know who is boss. It will be up to you to try to see he doesn't go too far with parental discipline.

AQUARIUS WOMAN—SAGITTARIUS MAN

You will discover you have much in common with easygoing, generous Mr. Sagittarius. He won't try to lay down the law; he is very much an individual and you are sure to have a number of mutual interests.

He finds it difficult to center his concentration on any one subject for long. He can't stand routine. At heart, he is a gypsy. Home is the place where he hangs his hat.

He loves people. He enjoys a good party. He finds it hard to settle down. A Sagittarius man often marries late in life. He is a bit afraid of that band of gold on the third finger of the left hand.

You will probably recognize him by his open features and cheerful disposition. He will always try to make the best of his lot in life.

Like you, he is instinctively on the side of the underdog. He hates injustice.

He's a bit of a showoff. He is also an excellent conversationalist. He enjoys being the center of attraction and he tells a good yarn.

Jupiter's eyes are sparkling and mischievous. He will strike you as a naughty schoolboy. He loves to play pranks. His humor is the send-up variety. He's got no time for snobs and people who pretend to be better than they are.

Even if you only have a whirlwind affair with him, it's something you won't forget.

Don't allow yourself the misconception that he's just a joker or that he doesn't care about the same things as you. But he *does* try to take a positive view of life. He believes in spreading happiness and laughter in order to make the world a more bearable place.

You both seek the good in other people. It's quite likely some of your mutual friends won't be the most praiseworthy types. He will admire your wish to help those in distress.

He can be absolutely outrageous. He has a quick mind and the things he comes out with sometimes make others squirm. He is fast to recognize people's faults and to play on them. He doesn't mince his words.

He's not very good with money. He can be tempted to gamble. Speculation, in fact, may be his biggest weakness. If you marry him, family finances may not always be healthy.

The Archer is a seeker of truth. He speaks his mind. He makes a lot of enemies. People dislike him because they secretly fear he has seen through them.

He will do all he can to make you happy. If you marry, there will probably be certain areas of your lives you won't share with each other. This need not be disastrous because individual freedom is something that you both practice and believe in.

He will put on a brave front but he won't like it if you flirt with other men. These sort of games don't appeal to you anyway.

Mr. Sagittarius will try to give you everything your heart desires. He makes a great fuss over his woman. Apart from being lovers, you will also be good friends, and this can be important in a long-term relationship.

Take your time about starting a family. Make sure you are both ready to settle down first.

When Aquarius and Sagittarius link up, there's an awful lot of living to do.

AQUARIUS WOMAN—CAPRICORN MAN

It takes a lot to break down the barriers this man puts up to protect himself from being hurt by other people, but you could be the woman who wins his heart.

Capricorn likes to have to fight for what he wants. He also likes mysterious women. You will be a puzzle to him. He is a logical man, and will find it difficult to understand your ways or to keep track of you.

You have probably never met a guy like this before. He has great charm and an ironic sort of wit that will appeal to you.

Secretly, he wishes to be admired. He will do everything he can to win your heart.

It could be that he first sets his sights on you when you are going steady with another man. You might not be aware he has more than a passing interest in you for some time. Then you'll realize you've been meeting him for coffee rather a lot, and perhaps he's been taking you to the movies or to various art galleries (he always knows what's going on in town). Suddenly you will discover you have not seen your old boyfriend for quite a while. Mr. Capricorn employs subtle tactics to get through to his woman.

He will be very good for you in a number of ways. He will make sure you don't waste your talents. He is a hard worker himself and he also makes a wonderful teacher. Nothing is too much trouble for him if he loves a person.

He is a little shy when it comes to sex. It might take him a hell of a long time to slip his hand into yours or to give you that first goodnight kiss. He has so much pride he is terrified of a rebuff.

You may feel you never really know every side of the Goat. It can take him quite a while to know himself and what he wants out of life. Many Capricorn men live alone and remain bachelors till quite late in life.

When you start living together, he'll expect to take priority over everything in your life. He won't mind your holding down a job—in fact, he'll like it if you contribute toward the running of the household—but you had better make sure your outside interests don't consume so much of your time that he feels neglected.

At times, you will feel like lighting a rocket under his rocking chair. His ploddish ways could be very irritating to a woman like you.

He's shy about meeting new people. You will discover he has only a handful of what he considers close friends.

You tend to take a different view of life. You look on the brighter side of things. You are always working toward a better tomorrow. He gets depressed easily. There will also be a fundamental difference in the way you approach your various problems. You are an intuitive person; he's a logical one.

Watch out that you don't make any offensive remarks about his family. Capricorn people usually have very close family ties. Let us hope you get on well with his mother.

If he asks you to be his wife, you can be sure he has given the matter careful thought. People born under this Sign rarely do anything on the spur of the moment.

You might be able to combine marriage with a business partnership. Capricorn is an extremely ambitious Sign and this man has a great head on his shoulders for making a few bucks if you can point him in the right direction.

AQUARIUS WOMAN—AQUARIUS MAN

If you have reached a stage in life where you feel true love has passed you by, if you have decided you are probably going to spend the rest of your days living alone, this is the time for a fellow Water Bearer to come into your life. You will immediately feel this is the guy you have been waiting so patiently for. Not all people get along with a person born under their own Sign. Happily there are unlikely to be any great problems with you and a fellow Aquarius.

Although you probably feel you know yourself pretty well, he will be a complete mystery to you. Which is fortunate, since you could not possibly get involved heavily with someone unless he aroused your curiosity.

Neither of you is willing to settle for a routine nine-to-five existence. You will continually make each other sparkle. You are likely to be attracted to the same sort of friends. There will always be people dropping in for coffee and a good, no-holds-barred debate.

You both care a great deal about other people. As a twosome, you will be able to do a great deal to help the underdog.

He would never try to impose rules and regulations on you. Being a freedom lover himself, he will respect your wish to keep your own identity intact.

You can't stand people fussing over you. He would never dream of telling you what you should or should not wear. He will love your hair whichever crazy way you decide to wear it.

If true love is going to bloom, it is essential to both of you to be attracted to each other's mind. Neither of you would last very long in a purely physical liaison.

It could be you just wake up one day and decide to get married. You are both capable of doing things on the spur of the moment. He would be prepared to get hitched to you with only fifty cents in his pocket. If you have decided you can't live without each other, you wouldn't hold back because of lack of funds. You share an optimistic outlook on life.

Mr. Aquarius can be a bit eccentric. He is not out to impress others and is unafraid to speak his mind even if his views aren't popular.

You will share a love of travel. He can't stand to remain in one place too long. He is restless and needs to keep constantly on the move.

The artistic streak is pronounced in the Water Bearer. Many famous people in show business and music and art were born under this Sign.

He will realize it is important to be your friend as well as your lover. This man will love you totally.

Mind you, it won't be a bed of roses. You will have to work very hard to make your marriage succeed. It's not an easy matter for an Aquarius to settle down forever with one person—you or him. The danger here is that you will allow your relationship to become a purely platonic one. Be careful!

He isn't the type to go in for love affairs on the side. Uranus-born people don't like dishonest relationships. If he got involved with somebody else, it would be serious and he would have to tell you all about it.

The way you can make this union work is to try to develop as a *twosome.* Do all you can to ensure you grow together and keep learning from each other.

AQUARIUS WOMAN—PISCES MAN

A Pisces man is quite wrapped up in himself. He will expect you to devote a great deal of your time to looking after him. Some people find Mr. Pisces rather cold. Often he is likened to the two Fishes that are his Sign.

He is interested in anything new and is always trying to improve his mind and his understanding of the world. He can get depressed very easily. He needs to feel loved and wanted.

His feelings are easily hurt. In personal relationships, he often lacks self-confidence. He is an intuitive man who quickly discovers the strong and weak points in other people. He tends to believe in fate and destiny.

He will bring out the protective side of your nature. It is rarely that you feel motherly toward anyone, but you might feel compelled to shelter a Pisces man from outside pressure. He is sensitive. He will be aware of your sudden mood changes.

Mr. Pisces is the type of guy you'll want to confide in because you will feel your secrets will be safe with him.

He will always strive to make you happy. He will work hard to provide all the comforts you require. He has a vivid imagination. He can get carried away by crazy notions. He needs love and is definitely a romantic at heart.

He is a very impressionable person, the type who can get worked up over supernatural stories and horror films. Scenes of violence can have a strong effect on him, even if they are only part of a dramatic story.

He will want your advice on lots of things, from what color shirt he should wear with a certain suit to whether he should think about changing his job. He finds it extremely difficult to make up his own mind.

This Neptune-born man is not aggressive. People born under his Sign are usually gentle creatures. He tries hard not to hurt people's feelings. Of course, another Ascendant or strong influence elsewhere in the horoscope could toughen him up.

He will admire your desire to help people who are not as well off as you are, but he is unlikely to be willing to take an active role in others' affairs himself.

Mr. Pisces often feels guilty about things when he shouldn't. Sometimes he shoulders too many emotional burdens. He can lose the sense of when he is in the right. It will be up to you to constantly reassure him.

He finds it hard to accept responsibility. You must not allow him to take the easy way out. He will do all he can to avoid confrontations.

He is very patient with others. He is a good listener. People often tell their troubles to him.

He may be rather shocked by your unconventional approach to life. He will think you are very daring and brave in the way you dress. He will secretly admire the fact that you don't appear to care what opinions others have of you.

There will be certain areas where you will have to respect each other's privacy. You will have interests and attitudes he could not share.

There is no doubt you'll both have to work hard at this union if it is to last. You will need to take more of an interest in, and show more concern for, a Pisces man than you would for almost any other Sign of the Zodiac.

He's great fun with kids, being something of an overgrown one himself.

AQUARIUS MAN— ARIES WOMAN

You look outside to the world and other people rather than inwardly to the home and acquiring possessions. People born under your Sign are interested in change and progress. You should find you have quite a lot in common with Miss Aries, although she's a much more aggressive type than you.

The Mars-ruled woman is very straightforward and honest. So honest, in fact, that she often makes people cringe. It isn't that she means to be rude or to give offense, but she feels compelled to speak her mind.

You have some difficulty in making a permanent relationship work. It is not always an easy matter for the Water Bearer to give all the love and devotion a partner demands. You will find in this woman an understanding lover. She can be extremely jealous, but she'll try to give you the freedom you need to carry out your ideas.

You are always out to change the world in some way or other. You are much more interested in the future than the past. You will be pleased to note the direct attitude of this woman. You don't get on with devious people. Her frankness and honesty will more than make up for her complete lack of tact and subtlety.

A deep involvement could present certain problems, though. She will try hard to believe in the causes so dear to your heart because she is the sort of lady who puts her man on a pedestal. There will come a time, though, when she'll want you to be more involved in the home and your life together. Will you be able to settle down?

She is quite a career girl. You are one of the few men who will allow her to continue with her career without getting jealous. You will admire your lady Ram's dedication to the tasks she sets for herself and her ability to see them through.

People born under the first Sign of the Zodiac are brave and spontaneous. They love a challenge. She will find you very attractive and will be full of admiration for your deep-felt desire to make the world a better place to live in for future generations.

There are many ways in which you can recognize the Aries woman. Her directness has already been mentioned. When she enters the room, she will seem composed; she is proud and holds her head high. She will look you straight in the eye. She may even take the initiative.

You could learn a great deal from each other. Her attitude to her work could be an inspiration to you. Aquarius people often misdirect their talents. It is all very well to carry the troubles of the world on your shoulders, but occasionally you must put your own house in order.

Aries people can be terribly rash—even stupid on occasions. They can be easily led by others with powerful personalities. Sometimes they don't know when to say "enough."

An Aries woman likes to be treated with tenderness and respect. You are a sensitive man, so there should be no problems here.

Her forceful optimism will get you out of the dumps when you hit one of your low periods. Yes, if you are prepared to get along with her, the Ram will be exceptionally good for you.

When it comes to making love, she is fiery and giving. There is a strong need for physical satisfaction here.

She won't mind your bringing friends home, even if it is pretty late. She enjoys entertaining and you both like meeting people from different walks of life.

She is a good mother, but neither of you takes easily to the burdens of parenthood.

AQUARIUS MAN— TAURUS WOMAN

Love conquers all, or so the saying goes. One wonders if love can bridge the gap between Taurus and Aquarius. At first glance, it must be admitted there does not appear to be much hope here. You are opposites in so many ways. You are an air Sign; Venus-ruled Taurus is an earthy lady.

You have different attitudes to life. This girl is very hung up on security. She wants an organized and peaceful life. She may resent the way you treat your home. She is not terribly interested in meeting strangers. She won't like the idea of your bringing so many people back at all hours of the day and night.

You are a bit of a dreamer, always thinking about the world you want to live in, not the world as it really is. This little lady lives very much in the moment.

The Bull seldom rushes into anything. She knows how to control her emotions. She refuses to be easily led. Once she has made up her mind on a certain course of action, she won't budge.

She is unlikely to have many loves in her life. She is not a fickle person. She is also extremely possessive and won't like the idea of taking second place to one of your causes.

When you first meet her, you'll be impressed by her hidden strength and the calm, steady look in the eyes. She is not easily impressed—nor easily taken in.

Of course, if you do fall head over heels for each other, there's a chance you can make this union work. However, you'll both have to be prepared to make sacrifices and to change your ways. You will discover she's a woman who can't stand to fail at anything, so she will do all in her power to make the marriage not only happy and successful but enduring.

You may find it difficult to get her out of the house. She would much rather have an intimate evening with one or two friends over than go galavanting around town.

She will stick by you through thick and thin. She is a very loyal person. If you are her man, she won't hear a word spoken against you.

Living with a Taurus woman will have a calming effect on you. She will be able to show you it's not always necessary to rush around solving all the world's problems. You will realize that this old planet can take care of itself—at least, occasionally.

She is not a moaner. She won't try that little-girl-lost stuff with you. She is also a healthy creature. Miss Taurus usually has a constitution like . . . well, like a bull!

This little lady can be a bit bossy. You may not be prepared to give up your freedom and toe the line when she wants you to stay home. She won't be prepared to take orders from you, either. She is perfectly capable of packing her bags and leaving if you wave the red flag.

You are both artistically minded people and are likely to share a love of the theater, music and all things beautiful.

She loves to surround herself with pretty things. If you ever catch sight of her bottom drawer, you'll be amazed at all the little goodies she has hoarded away there.

She is a wonderful mother. Nothing is too good for her youngsters. If a child is ill, she will stay by the bedside as long as necessary.

AQUARIUS MAN—GEMINI WOMAN

You will make a zany pair, but in an odd sort of way, you'll be extremely compatible. Both of you will keep the other guessing, that's for sure.

You may never really know where you stand with the Twins. At times, you'll feel you have been affected by double vision. This is a split Sign. People born under it can change their minds at the drop of a hat.

Like you, Gemini enjoys variety. She likes to keep on the go. Without external stimulation, she would go crazy with boredom. You both like meeting people from all walks of life and exchanging ideas.

Of course, if the two of you team up, there could be difficulties. Everybody needs some sort of anchor. You may find yourselves drifting through life.

You will discover you both believe in many of the same causes and ideals. Both of you are staunch defenders of the freedom of the individual. You may have different ways of expressing this conviction, though. You tend to think change results when people band together. Your Mercurial friend believes everyone should be left alone to work out his or her problems.

She gets terribly impatient with people who are set in their ways. She can't abide types who have strongly held opinions, either. This may be a weak spot as far as you're concerned.

You will find she has a striking personality. She usually possesses extraordinary energy.

She can be a bit of a flirt. This is where you will have to exercise some control. It will be up to you to make sure you don't end up just sharing the same house. You are the types who could allow your relationship to drift until it becomes a mockery of all that a marriage is supposed to be.

You might get a little fed up with Miss Gemini's habit of suddenly changing her mind. You will ask her out, she'll agree, then when you go to pick her up, you'll find her apartment full of people she's invited over to dinner on the spur of the moment. There is only one answer: don't ever expect her to live up to her word. It isn't that she doesn't mean what she says at the time. It is simply that she gets carried away by impulse and her own unquenchable enthusiasm.

She is imaginative in lovemaking but does find it hard to stay true to one man. You will have to accept the fact that she likes to provoke male attention any way she can.

It is lucky you are not a jealous guy because you will have to allow this lady her outside interests. She would soon get bored left at home all day while you were out earning the rent. She would far rather hold down a job herself and feel she was contributing something to your life together. You mustn't allow her to feel "lost" in your relationship.

You can both be tricky to live with when you slump into a mood. You will find her a great pal, but it would be wise not to try to dig too deep to discover what makes her tick. She doesn't like people who try to read her mind.

She's not too clever at handling money. Life will be easier together if you take care of the family finances. She can be penny pinching for weeks, then suddenly go out on a spending spree and come home with a bunch of useless articles.

You don't really want a settled life; you enjoy change. Miss Gemini, therefore, could be the woman for you. One thing is certain: there will rarely be a dull moment in this marriage.

AQUARIUS MAN—CANCER WOMAN

Miss Cancer can be an exceedingly moody lady. She is as changeable as her ruler, which is the Moon. She can be very demanding on her partner, perhaps a little too demanding for you.

You are not a great one for remembering such things as birthdays and anniversaries; in fact, they are not all that important to you. Your Cancer woman will be very upset by your apparent indifference to what she considers special occasions.

She is a warm and loving girl, but is not happy unless she's the center of attention. She won't share your interest in politics and people.

When the Crab gets hurt, she scuttles back into her shell. She can be quite secretive. She is very different from you. People sometimes consider you cold because when a love affair is over, you don't appear to have too much difficulty in forgetting your pain and getting on with the other aspects of your life.

This cute little lady is out to capture your heart. She is not particularly interested in casual affairs, though she loves to have admirers. She can also get a kick out of playing one boyfriend off against another (this tactic is unlikely to work effectively with you).

If you really fall madly in love with her, you'll probably have to give her far more attention than you normally would to a woman. You will need to spend a good deal of time encouraging her and doing what you can to boost her confidence. She can be shy and nervous, especially when meeting new people.

A woman born in the fourth House of the Zodiac is a notorious lover of home life. Family is terribly important to her. She's likely to run up a hefty phone bill talking over her problems with Mother. She also has quite a temper. She is possessive, darned possessive.

Miss Cancer certainly likes her domestic comforts, but she'll want to share them with you if you are her man. She won't like waiting patiently for you to come home while the dinner she carefully prepared is burning away in the oven. This woman believes a husband and wife should share everything right down the line.

Cancer women often have to watch their weight. In their teens and early twenties, they can be cutely plump, but later, diet is a problem. They often have a sweet tooth and find it hard to keep their fingers out of the candy box.

If you decide you want to make a permanent home with this Moon child, you'll have to change your ways. Marriage won't work if you have too many outside interests. You must also make sure you get her out of the house occasionally. Sometimes a Cancer female stays in too much for her own good. Make the effort to include her in other areas of your life.

When she is consumed by the blues, it can be a fairly rough passage. She feels things very deeply. Make sure you are around when she needs a sympathetic shoulder to cry on.

She will be careful with your money. She's not known to be extravagant except perhaps when it comes to her wardrobe.

There is no end to the sacrifices Mama Cancer will make for her babies. She is very hung up on motherhood. She is prepared to go to any lengths to ensure her children are all right. It's fortunate you are not a particularly jealous guy. Many a husband has felt resentful toward his children because of the care and devotion showered upon them by a Cancer mother.

AQUARIUS MAN—LEO WOMAN

You must be prepared to fight hard to win Miss Leo because this woman usually has many admirers. She makes a loving and devoted partner. She can be a bit bossy, though, and you might find this side of her nature rather difficult to live with as time goes by.

Like you, she is a freedom lover. It is likely she'll agree with many of your ideas about what is wrong with this planet. Where the difference lies is that Leo people are doers and you do tend to be something of a slogan man.

She is a no-nonsense type. If you can take her criticisms, she'll be very good for you. You have a terribly proud girl here. She would never chase after a man, no matter how much she wanted him. She will expect you to be straightforward. She can't stand a guy who doesn't level with her right down the line.

She has quite a temper. When you first meet, you may get the impression butter wouldn't melt in her mouth. Don't you believe it. Do her an injustice and she will really let fly.

She is a loyal woman. Once she has promised herself to you, it is unlikely she will go off the rails. Mind you, she usually gets her chances: Our Leonine friend is quite a sexy little kitten.

This woman is a born leader. As a kid, she was probably team captain in sports or president of her class. She doesn't like to play second fiddle to others. She considers herself equal to man. Although usually very feminine looking, she is prepared to take on any challenge in work.

Women can be very bitchy about her. She doesn't put on airs. She believes in speaking her mind. Members of her sex are jealous; they are not prepared to be as open and aboveboard about their feelings as she is.

Miss Leo can also be arrogant. Since she is always doing her best to improve her mind, you can't blame her for feeling above other people on occasions. Where some people sit back saying, "Ah, wouldn't it be lovely if . . .," the Leo girl is getting it together and doing something concrete about making her dreams come true.

You would make an interesting combination if you could overcome certain basic differences. There is much to learn from this woman.

The Lioness can be quite a health freak. She's likely to keep herself in good shape physically. She could well have an interest in yoga or some other form of mental-spiritual discipline. She is also likely to be choosy about what she eats. Her diet is apt to be well-balanced and nutritious.

This woman makes a honey of a wife. She is able to combine her domestic duties very successfully with her outside interests. She is the sort of woman you will go home to, not because you feel you have to, but simply because you want to be with her more than any other person.

She knows how to dress, too. You will never see her looking a mess. She looks as chic in a pair of jeans as she does in her finest evening wear.

Count yourself lucky if this lass agrees to share her life with you. You can be sure you have succeeded where many men have failed.

If she loves you, she'll back you all the way. She cares about what goes on in the world as much as you do. Together, you might be able to do something about it.

AQUARIUS MAN—VIRGO WOMAN

Miss Virgo is usually looking for a man who is steady and consistent, who has a calm disposition and is a conservative dresser. Sounds the very opposite of you, doesn't it?

Yes, in many ways you are poles apart. It is likely the sparks will fly when you first meet this woman. Remember that argument you had at a party the other week? It might have been about politics, religion, in fact, any controversial subject. Well, it was probably a Virgo lady you were having verbal fisticuffs with. It's also probable she got through to you in some way; maybe as you were leaving, you casually asked your host for her phone number.

The point about women born under this earth Sign is that they may irritate you, frustrate you, drive you nearly crazy, but most men will want to come back for more.

The more you try to understand her, the less you will, and therefore the more fascinating she will become. Let's face it, half of what romance is all about is discovering what makes the object of your desire tick. Aquarius and Virgo are likely to be a mystery to each other—and mystery is often the foundation for a long-lasting relationship.

This woman strives for perfection. So do you, for that matter, though you seek a different sort of perfection, perhaps, and you definitely have a different way of trying to obtain it. This miss has her feet planted firmly on the ground. She will not involve herself in any sort of cause or protest unless she feels she has a darned good chance of achieving all or most of her objectives.

Certainly you will have to change your ways. She won't want you to go out with you if you turn up in your favorite faded jeans and that old jacket with patches on the elbows. Miss Virgo always looks smart and spruce herself.

This woman is also extremely conscious of hygiene. And she is the type of perfectionist who looks for perfection in a man. This is not the sort of woman who will allow herself to become involved in one casual affair after another.

As a wife, she will be very efficient. It will be a matter of pride to her that her home is well run. You may get a bit annoyed when she constantly vacuums the floor around you and empties the ashtray every time you stub out a cigarette.

As a lover, she's not the most passionate woman. You will have to treat her gently and with loving kindness. The caveman approach won't get you anywhere. She is romantic. It is not easy for her to go to bed with a man unless she is emotionally involved with him.

Sometimes when you get back to your own apartment after an evening out with Miss Virgo you may wonder if it's worth all the trouble. It is possible you'll feel her high standards are just too exacting. After a few days, however, you'll probably be getting out your little black book and calling her up once again.

She is straightforward and honest. She is a seeker of truth. Mind you, this truth seeking stops when it comes to dealing with her own faults. She can't stand to be criticized and finds it easy to make excuses for herself.

If you wish sincerely to make this union work, you are both going to have to change your ways to a very great degree.

AQUARIUS MAN— LIBRA WOMAN

You two should get along famously. There is a great deal you have in common. Your personalities should complement each other because Libra and Aquarius have a natural affinity.

It is possible you will hit it off on first meeting. She has a great sense of humor and, as a rule, is a good conversationalist. She is usually pretty well read on most subjects, and although a feminine type, her logic is a match for most men's.

She will never try to boss you, she will *charm* you. This woman does not get her way by trying to usurp the man's role as head of the household. She will leave it to you to make the important decisions. Still and all, you are bound to feel like consulting her before you make any important changes in the way you handle the domestic scene.

Miss Libra is never likely to do a heavy number on you. She believes in freedom. She will understand why you get caught up in causes and involved in other people's problems. She would never dream of criticizing the manner in which you conduct your own life.

If you decide to make it together, it would be a good idea to allow her the freedom to continue with her career if she wishes to. A woman born under this Sign is usually well able to be both a successful housewife and an outstanding success in her chosen career.

She doesn't like to be on her own for very long. Like you, she enjoys meeting a cross section of people. This girl is no snob. She will be equally at home chatting with the milkman and hobnobbing with high society. Usually the sort of job she chooses involves some kind of power sharing. She gets her ideas from discussing business matters with other people. You could say she epitomizes communication.

A Libra woman is looking for true love. She is a romantic. It is hard for her not to flirt, and you'll have to accept the fact that she has lots of admirers. Don't get jealous, though. If you are her man, she would not put your relationship in jeopardy for an affair on the side. Being an Aquarius, you will be perfectly content to leave all the important decisions concerning the smooth running of the home to her.

Libra people are wonderful at making others feel relaxed. You will love the way she arranges a dinner party. She is always able to create just the right atmosphere for the people you entertain. Just watch how she makes a shy person relax and feel at home.

She won't wish to pry into your business afdoing, and that if you do require her advice, you will have to ask for it.

In a crisis, she is very dependable. This woman keeps her head when others around her are losing theirs.

Your Venus-ruled lady could even turn you into a bit of a stay-at-home. You might discover you enjoy those cozy evenings when it is just the two of you cuddled up in front of the fire.

She is also capable of combining the role of mother and wife. You will never get the feeling you take second place to the kids.

As a mother, she is unbeatable. She seems to

understand children better than anyone else in the Zodiac. She is loving, but not unduly sentimental. The Libra woman is more a friend out to help and guide her children than a parent with a rulebook in one hand and a present in the other.

AQUARIUS MAN—SCORPIO WOMAN

A man born under any Sign of the Zodiac would find Miss Scorpio a very hot number to handle. She could be just a wee bit too passionate and deep for a guy like you. This Pluto-ruled woman is inclined to emotional outbursts and heavy scenes. You don't like to live your life on the knife edge of personal drama.

You will be drawn to her sexually. (Most men are.) Scorpio women are rarely petite. She's likely to be well endowed physically. But remember, it's best to have quite a long courtship if you're contemplating marriage. The dividing line between fierce infatuation and true love is thin.

You will find her a mass of contradictions. She can be a whirlwind of passion or colder than the snow peaks of the Himalayas.

A Scorpio woman is likely to feel just as strongly as you about the injustices of this world. The difference is she'll have another approach. She would much prefer to shelter a person who is down on his or her luck than parade up and down outside the White House protesting what is going on in some faraway country—which is more your style.

You may find her blunt approach to life a little disarming. She speaks her mind and is not too good at hiding her feelings. You won't be able to get this woman to do anything against her will or her principles.

Living with a Scorpio lady will never be an easy ride. You will find when her temper flies, it really flies. The same is true when she gets in one of her dark moods.

Never ask her opinion or advice unless you are prepared to hear the naked truth. Don't go fishing for compliments; you won't get them unless they are felt from the heart.

Mind you, she can be sweetness itself. When this woman loves, there are no half-measures. She will give herself to you completely if you are the right man.

Although she is careful about money, she will give the man she loves everything she owns. Woe betide you if you cross her, though. She is very jealous and she'll avenge herself if you let her down even if it takes her a lifetime.

She doesn't like to show her feelings in front of other people. To her, love is a private affair. It is also true to say she can't stand to have scenes in front of her friends. She might tear your head off at home, but she won't do it in public.

She can be secretive. There are corners of her mind she likes to keep to herself.

She is much more the home-loving type than you are. She won't take too kindly to your coming and going as you please. She will want to share in most departments of your life.

Scorpio has a great interest in religion and all matters concerning the supernatural.

Don't think you will be able to change this woman in marriage. It would be unwise to contemplate a permanent relationship until you're convinced you really do have a great deal in common. You ought to check her horoscope in the appropriate book in this series before making any definite moves. It's better to be sure than live out the rest of your life in regret and misery.

Scorpio women make good mothers. She will be terribly ambitious for her children and will do all she can to get the very best for them.

Don't let us be too hard on this lady. They don't come any better than the best of Scorpio; but the best are rare.

AQUARIUS MAN—SAGITTARIUS WOMAN

Miss Sagittarius will go out of her way to understand you. If she loves you, she will do her level best to adapt to your way of life and live up to your expectations of what a woman should be. No one in the entire Zodiac has more of a sunshine personality than this girl.

Don't get the idea, though, that she is prepared to take orders and be a doormat. Jupiter's pride is here. She will only be prepared to go along with you as long as she feels you are also doing your best to make the relationship work. If she feels you are simply using her, she won't stick around for long.

Although she is hardly a stick-in-the-mud, your wandering and outward-looking ways may not appeal to her over a long period. She will never criticize the way you live your life, but she may not wish to accompany you on all your jaunts. There is a possibility your interests would become splintered and you would grow apart.

People born under this fire Sign are usually sports lovers. Many—though by no means all—love the outdoor life. You will find she has a highly developed sense of competition. This girl can't bear for anyone to get the better of her—be it in a game of tennis or in a discussion of the political situation in Timbuctoo.

She doesn't like to show her emotions. At the end of the biggest love affair in her life, she is likely to laugh it off with her friends and say it was merely a casual affair and she never really cared that much for the guy.

She is a trusting soul and it would be unfair to string her along. Be sure you mean it when you tell her you love her because she will believe you. On the surface, she may not appear jealous, but deep down, she does care desperately about what she considers to be hers—in this case, you. If you do have an affair after you are married, it's unlikely she will ever feel the same about you again.

She's a hard worker who never shirks her responsibilities. Sagittarius women can't stand to fail. She will work hard to make a success of everything she takes on.

She can be a bit clumsy. It's a good thing you don't care all that much about mere objects because the beautiful china Mother gave you won't be unchipped after your Sagittarius woman has washed it a few times.

In conversation, she is likely to put her foot in it. There will be occasions when you will cringe at her "innocent" remarks in company. She's not trying to embarrass people or be rude; it's just her nature to speak her mind. Her intentions are usually good. You will just have to be patient with her and forgive her when she says the wrong thing. But it can be darned annoying when you're trying to impress someone.

Miss Sagittarius is lots of fun. You will never be bored in her company.

She is not bossy, and that's something you are bound to appreciate. She will leave you to make up your own mind when it comes to decisions affecting your career.

Don't try to order her around; like you, she is a great lover of freedom.

The Sagittarius woman is wonderful with kids. Her children will look upon her as a close friend as well as a mother.

AQUARIUS MAN—CAPRICORN WOMAN

Miss Capricorn won't be an easy proposition for a man like you. She is career-conscious and dead set on getting to the top.

She is also a great respecter of authority and tried and trusted methods. Not that you are totally uninterested in getting on in this world or are a lawbreaker. The difference is that whereas this woman often lives by values imposed from outside, you tend to abide by your own particular moral code.

Very many women born under this earth Sign don't marry until quite late in life. They are fairly independent and want to make a name for themselves if they possibly can.

Don't get the impression she is hardhearted. When she falls in love, it strikes deep. She does have a sense of priorities, though. She doesn't waste time on a lot of insignificant affairs.

You should not be misled by the female Goat. She isn't always the calm, steady and reliable creature she appears to be. Though she doesn't easily show her emotions, if she really falls for a man, he will know it.

She is inclined to be a social climber. She is easily impressed by other people's fame and worldly riches. She also has the ability to be a bit of a name dropper.

A Capricorn woman may set out to change the ways of an Aquarius man. She will want you to become far more home loving. For her part, though, she will find it difficult to identify with your causes.

It might irritate you, but you will find that this girl is often instinctively right. There is a Capricorn female behind many a successful man. Ask her advice about an important business matter and she'll probably be able to go to the heart of the difficulty.

You will be impressed on first meeting by her beautiful complexion and refreshing manner. She is also very honest. She will expect you to play it straight with her, and you won't last very long together if you don't.

Her love can come on very strong. You might find it a little overpowering. It would be fair to say she is more physically oriented than you are. The attention she lavishes on a man could suffocate the Water Bearer.

You had better get on well with her family. People born under Capricorn have a great respect for their elders. She'll probably ask her mother's advice on the smallest matters. And if your Saturn woman comes from a poor family, she'll always make sure they are well provided for.

This is a one-guy girl. Once she is really gone on you, she'll stand by you through thick and thin. When your confidence wanes, she'll be the one who picks you up, dusts you off and puts you back on the road to success.

You will have to help her through her depressions, too. She can get really low at times.

Miss Capricorn can get along with all sorts of people. She is a wonderful hostess. When she has a party, it usually goes with a swing. She knows how to mix up her guest list to make an interesting evening.

You will be a great help to her because you're the type of man who can help her overcome her lack of confidence. She can be stubborn but she is not really a nagger. Not unless you deserve it, that is. If you don't want to deserve it, you're going to have to change those perambulating ways of yours.

AQUARIUS MAN—AQUARIUS WOMAN

It can't always be assumed that people born under the same Sign of the Zodiac will get along, but there should be no problem in this case. Miss Aquarius could well be the girl of your dreams. You are likely to think very much along the same lines. You will share many of the same goals.

Like you, this woman loves the company of other people. She also has a strong desire for friendship and brotherly love. You both want to make the world a better place to live in for all.

You like an all-action life, and so does your fellow Water Bearer. Alone, you do reasonably well; together, you could make many of your dreams become reality.

Of course, physical attraction is important in any close liaison, but love is very much a matter of the mind to this girl (as it is to you). She can't give herself to a man unless she feels intellectually attracted to him.

You will find Miss Aquarius has many admirers. She is a fascinating woman, unlike any other you have met. She is pretty choosy. She will take her time selecting a partner.

Aquarius people, as you know, always look for the best in others. Here is a woman who will never admit that any soul is a lost cause. Misguided, yes—but lost, never.

This is the most open-minded and tolerant woman you have ever come across, if she's a typical Aquarius. Like you, she has an independent nature. Neither of you wishes to be suffocated.

You will probably find you share the same views on politics and religion. She will be behind you all the way if you decide to involve yourself deeply in a cause or campaign.

She is free and easy about time. She doesn't like to tie herself down to a set schedule. You will rarely find her working in a routine job. She can't stand the idea of sitting at a typewriter or working on a factory line to make a lot of money for somebody else.

Miss Aquarius is afraid of settling down. She doesn't want to give up her freedom for the domestic life. She is aware that marriage can be a trap. Therefore she might wish to wait a while. You should understand your own Sign well enough to realize this.

She will always give her opinions honestly. This woman does not run with the pack. She makes up her own mind on most issues.

If you only have an affair with an Aquarius woman, you'll probably discover she is the type you want to remain good friends with afterward. Sex will not be all you have in common.

Many women find it hard to get over old affairs and to put their mistakes behind them. This is not so with a woman born where Uranus and Saturn rule. It is the future that fills her mind.

Marriage could be a wonderful thing for you both. You might both change your spots when you get spliced. You will discover there are so many things two can do better than one.

Love should always stay fresh with the two of you. You both enjoy change and variety. You will also find you enjoy the company of the same type of friends.

You will have no problems in putting a few bucks aside. For all your scattiness, you both know the value of money.

AQUARIUS MAN—PISCES WOMAN

Although you're likely to hit it off from the start with this girl, it's advisable to do a great deal of thinking before you make it permanent. You might not be all that good for each other.

Dreamy, introverted Miss Pisces might make life rather complicated for you. This woman needs lots of attention and looking after. You would certainly have to spend far more time at home than you would normally.

She is not all that good at mixing with other people. Large crowds and meeting strangers frighten her. She needs security.

Pisces people are into self-analysis. They do seem to have more strange experiences than people born under the other Signs. You will discover she's always having weird dreams and attempting to work out their deeper meanings. She is warm and all woman, but you might not be prepared to give her all the coddling she needs.

Still, you'll never be bored in her company. Your friends and business colleagues will adore her. People will be constantly reminding you what a lucky guy you are. If Miss Pisces becomes your regular date, you'll get a lot of invitations from your bachelor friends.

You have a wonderful confidence booster in this girl. She will make you feel you can take on the whole world and win. When she loves a man, she'll do everything in her power to make him happy. She'll be quick to recognize your talents; what is more, she'll make sure you exploit them to the best possible advantage.

She will want you to be the pacesetter. A girl whose symbol is the two Fishes needs a man who is capable of making the big decisions. Mind you, she'll challenge your authority from time to time, but probably only to keep you on your toes and to prove to herself that you really care.

A Neptune girl who has been let down by a man in her youth sometimes becomes rather harsh and bitter. If this is the case with your Pisces lover, you'll have to have lots of patience because it will take quite a while to restore her confidence in the male sex.

She is apt to change her mind in the twinkling of an eye. This drives many men crazy. You could be driving along on your way to an expensive restaurant where you've reserved a table. Suddenly Miss Pisces will give you a kiss on the cheek and whisper in your ear that she'd rather be at home alone with you and, so why don't you turn around and go back and finish off that French bread and cheese?

You can leave the domestic arrangements entirely to her. This woman has an artistic touch and is an imaginative cook. She is also content with her own company so long as she knows what time her guy is going to be walking through the door.

Sometimes in order to cover her natural shyness, the Pisces woman will make wisecracks and even hurtful remarks. This is only a defensive tactic to try to stop people from attacking her.

You can be a bit forgetful. You'll have to make a point of noting special days like birthdays and anniversaries, for they are very important to this lady.

She will always look her best when she is out with you. It is a matter of pride to her to look good when under public scrutiny.

She finds it very difficult to mete out discipline. She's a bit soft with her kids.

AQUARIUS' HEALTH

Aquarius people are among the longest-lived types of the Zodiac. You know how to look after your health. You don't necessarily take any special precautions, and you're rarely a faddist, but you live a rather temperate kind of life. As a rule, you don't drink to excess, overeat or abuse your body with drugs and ill-regulated living. Moderation is the key to your physical existence. And it pays off handsomely healthwise.

Your constitution is wiry rather than strong. You are quite willing to engage in physical toil if you have to, but generally speaking, you're not built for prolonged exertion in this way.

Aquarius rules the circulatory system; also the calves and ankles. The shins are a particularly vulnerable part. The ruler of your Sign is Uranus, the planet associated with fractures. Aquarius people are susceptible to leg injuries, especially below the knee. Your love of spectacular and unusual sports exposes you to breaks and sprains.

People born under this Sign often suffer from varicose veins, and in later years, from hardening of the arteries. There is a connection with the heart through the opposite Sign, Leo, and any cardiac problems should be immediately referred to a doctor.

There is also some risk of bladder infections and a connection with the lymphatic system. Sometimes you suffer from poor circulation resulting in swollen legs and ankles, as well as cramps. Of course, there is no reason why the normally healthy Aquarius should have any of these disorders. The point is that if any weakness does occur, it will probably show up there.

You Aquarius-born folk possess a certain waywardness that provokes you into doing things on the spur of the moment. You may suddenly discard your moderate habits and become careless about diet. A particular food or drink is apt to upset your whole system. You have to learn to distinguish what does and does not agree with you to avoid poor functioning of the digestive tract. With moderate living, none of these intestinal problems should arise. It is very much up to the individual.

Good posture is important. Otherwise you may suffer vague pains in the upper region of the back. Aquarius people can't afford to develop a round-shouldered profile. Discomfort will result. An upright posture—but, of course, not an exaggerated West Point stance—should be maintained at all times. The posture of Aquarius children should be observed and corrected by parents. All should be careful when lifting heavy objects.

You have tremendous reserves of nervous energy. It is this rather than physical vitality that keeps you going at such a rate. You are capable of intense effort for fairly long periods, but only when your interest is absorbed. You need an idea or an ideal. When this is absent, you can become bored and restless. To be happy and in good spirits, you must keep occupied with something, you feel is worthwhile.

You need your friends and should take care to be cut off from them. Companionship is like a therapy to you whenever you feel jaded or out of sorts. The typical Aquarius who is denied continual contact with a variety of people of his or her choice is likely to start feeling under par.

Yet you also require very definite periods of seclusion. You need to flop down and relax alone, or to amble off into the woods or by the sea. When the urge to get away from the hustle and bustle comes, you should respond as quickly as possible. Go fishing, walking; commune with nature. This is the way Aquarius is refreshed and the volatile energies of this dynamic Sign restored.

Since you are an intellectual creature, there is always a risk you'll get so involved with your various projects that you will neglect to exercise. For you, exercise and lots of fresh air are essential. The running around you do every day is seldom an adequate substitute. Some sort of deliberate regimen is required to keep your body in proper tone. Yoga, in both its physical and mental forms, is extremely effective for people born under your Sign.

Finally, the Aquarius type is subject to nervous disorders. Frustration may lead to worry and sleeplessness. It is important that you learn to accept the things you can't change. Depression can lead to odd and impetuous conduct that may make life unnecessarily difficult.

AQUARIUS AT WORK

Aquarius is the Sign of genius. A surprising number of people who have made an unforgettable impact on mankind and contributed in real terms to human progress were born at this time of the year. The spark of brilliance is potential in every one of you. Yet unless your efforts are directed along positive lines, you are apt to drift and accomplish very little.

You have a sharp, adaptable and inventive mind. The list of occupations you could succeed in would fill a page. You are capable of doing just about any kind of work you put your mind to, but you will shine most in a career that requires involvement in new and unusual projects. You need to be able to take the lead in some way. You must find a job that gives ample scope for individuality and self-expression. A routine nine-to-five grind will soon bore you stiff.

You are a refined and studious type of person. Many of you have artistic ability. You often possess a particular talent for painting and sketching. You express yourself in uncommon and sometimes surrealistic forms. Your productions are always exciting or provocative. It is rare for an Aquarius artist not to excite comment and discussion. Your work may be trenchantly criticized by those who fail to see the point, but it will seldom be ignored.

Many famous writers and poets were born under your Sign. Your type is also renowned for extraordinary musical ability, both in composing and performing. Your sense of sound and rhythm is very highly developed. You have an innate feeling for orchestration. It is natural for you to produce harmony out of diversity.

The theater and the entertainment profession in general offer splendid opportunities. Here, your strong personal magnetism would help you gain early recognition. Wide popularity usually follows.

Whatever you do, you manage to produce a distinctive effect. As a politician, you are probably without equal. Your genuine concern for the welfare of your fellow citizens and your detached attitude toward personal honors and financial rewards would endear you to the public. Some of you are capable of becoming national heros.

You are inclined to work in fits and starts. This is not necessarily a bad thing. The essence of inspiration is fitfulness. This predilection is one reason why you should avoid a humdrum job where you are expected to perform regularly at a steady pace. What you have to watch is that you don't sit back for too long in between spurts. It is easy for you to procrastinate, to make excuses for not getting started again and to slide into inertia.

Aquarius-born people are natural inventors and innovators. Once they are aware of a problem, they seem to attract the ideal solution to them. Their flashes of inspiration come at the most unexpected times. Archimedes' famous discovery of the displacement principle while sitting in the bath is an example of Aquarius insight. Many people born under this Sign receive their most original ideas during the night. Some of them even sleep with a pencil and paper beside the bed.

You are efficient in any capacity. You are capable of accepting heavy responsibility. You don't like taking orders, but you are excellent at cooperation. You are a very good influence in a group and have a way of making antagonists forget their differences in the interests of the job.

Any kind of experimental work is likely to appeal to you. You are not afraid of physical danger, but you won't take foolish risks. You analyze all propositions and reject those without a reasonable chance of success. You may be hard to follow at times, but you're no fool. Your type is attracted to adventurous kinds of work such as exploration and space and flight research. You could work as a test pilot or astronaut. You are also likely to be successful at scuba diving, electrical engineering, experimental science, and on the social side, rehabilitation of communities and large numbers of people.

You have a scientific mind and are very able in any category that interests you. Whether it's in the biology laboratory or testing the latest nuclear theory, you manage to make your work exciting for yourself. You are happiest in any field when aiding human advancement.

You would make an excellent physician because you have a distinct flair for diagnosis. Your innate ability to create a feeling of trust in others while drawing out their problems could equip you to be a successful psychologist.

Your strong interest in the occult and natural psi and ESP abilities often fits you for the role of investigator in these fields. You may also write or lecture about these subjects.

As a teacher, you are second to none. You quickly establish a rapport with your students, irrespective of their age, and gain their confidence. You would make an excellent college professor; you seldom fail to stimulate interest with your advanced theories and power to visualize. You enjoy working with eager and youthful minds. Children never find you dull because you know how to make a subject enthralling.

If you are a boss, your employees probably know never to try to make you change your mind. Not that you lose your temper; you just listen, nod, agree and go on doing things exactly as before. You expect everyone who works for you to do a good job in his or her own way—as long as it doesn't interfere with your ideas.

You are not a great disciplinarian, but still, you get things done. Your subordinates invariably like and respect you. You have a way of making everyone feel part of a team. You don't like throwing your weight around. In fact, you really see no reason for it most of the time. Besides, you feel a bit silly giving others orders. You believe in treating employees as mature individuals with sufficient common sense to know what is required of them.

You are a great one for springing surprises on your staff. You switch people around, change their tasks without notice and generally dart off on tangents as though reacting to random impulses. It's not really true, though, is it? You always have your plans laid well in advance. It's simply that you don't bother to announce the next move until you make it.

You do, of course, have brilliant Uranian insights that astound and impress everyone. Without them, you mightn't be in so much demand as a boss because, frankly, you lack the air of authority. But the way you can see into the future and come up with an answer—usually when the chips are down—more than compensates. Add this to your gift for analyzing situations and people in two seconds flat, plus your talent for engendering the team spirit, and it's not surprising that quiet and fairly casual Aquarius is often regarded as indispensable.

You don't stick to old methods. You'd rather try new ones. And you're not fussy about how the workers under you dress or wear their hair. Everyone's personal life you consider to be strictly his or her own business. And yours, of course, is sacrosanct.

You have one pet hate: you can't stand dishonesty or deception. With your radarlike intuition, there's not much chance anyone will get away with cheating on the expense account.

As an employee, you are an extremely easy person to get along with. You're a bit forgetful and sometimes don't seem to take the job as seriously as most of your co-workers. You don't horse around or loaf, but you don't seem to exert yourself as much as others. And you're not so worried about impressing the boss or trying to get the last buck in overtime. Yet you get the job done, the boss loves you and he's just given you that raise you didn't bother to put in for!

You work for job satisfaction. That is why you are where you are. You've got a job where you feel you're doing something worthwhile in the broader sense. It offers plenty of variety and opportunities to put your farsighted ideas to work. If not, you'll probably be moving on.

If you were born between January 20 and January 30, you would make an ideal teacher, preacher or educator. You have a particularly magnetic personality and will probably make a name for yourself in connection with the public. You should also succeed in medicine or the arts, especially professional writing.

You are highly idealistic. The danger is you may be content to talk and think about your lofty objectives instead of trying to materialize them. By disseminating your ideas through groups of people, you may manage to awaken others to the changes and improvements you feel are necessary. In this way, you could be very effective.

You are likely to experience more than your share of sudden and unexpected changes. Usually, however, they should work out for the best in the long run.

Marriage is an important influence on your career prospects. You can't afford to live with a person who doesn't understand your brand of individualism and need for personal freedom. With the wrong partner, you will be inhibited and unable to concentrate sufficiently on your goals. You need a mate who shares your altruistic aims. You should be able to feel you are both working together as well as living together.

If you were born between January 31 and February 8, you may find it difficult to stick to one job for long. The life of a roamer may appeal, in which case you could possibly make a living by writing about your travels. You could also be successful as a journalist, especially as a foreign correspondent.

It is very important that you don't become too excitable. Your nervous system is probably unusually high-strung.

You may succeed in a financial career connected with a large institution, or perhaps in broadcasting, airing your views on money problems. Indications are that you will spend a fair amount of money on your general life-style. Artistic pursuits will probably appeal to you strongly but may not provide sufficient income.

If you were born between February 9 and February 18, you will probably favor a career in one of the arts where success seems assured. Some sort of working partnership will probably offer the best opportunities for long-term security. It is important that you work in pleasant surroundings with compatible people.

Physical types of employment may not be a good idea. Aquarius people generally are better suited for intellectually oriented occupations. In your case, there is an added artistic emphasis.

Try not to give in to your emotions. Don't marry unless you are very sure of your partner; an unhappy marriage may kill your artistic urges.

Architecture, interior decorating, landscaping, book publishing, advertising and real estate should all offer opportunities, provided you feel you can make them personally interesting.

Your personality is pleasing and attractive and you should have no trouble in work that involves selling.

Money

Money often runs very quickly through your fingers. You are neither avaricious nor a spendthrift. In fact, money is usually a secondary consideration in the kind of life you lead. But when you have it, you spend it—and not always wisely. Money to you is a means, not an end.

Aquarius people have many financial ups and downs. Cash comes and goes like many other things in your life. Often you see opportunities for increasing income but can't be bothered to make the extra effort. You are inclined to wait around for money to arrive—and frequently you aren't disappointed.

Aquarius individuals, if they become wealthy, usually do so through inventions, discoveries and new ideas.

If happily married, you are more inclined to spend on your home and its comforts.

PISCES' CHARACTER

You Pisces people spend your lives waiting for "the call." Secretly you live for the day when you will be given the opportunity to serve your fellow man in some spectacular, grandiose, even awe-inspiring way of self-sacrifice. Worldly success—even your disdain for it—is never a substitute. No matter how much you manage to serve others or to give them philanthropically, you remain dissatisfied with your efforts. Rich or poor, you wait in the wings for the call that never comes. It's just one of those things you people born under this psychic and mystical Sign have to learn to live with.

Astrologically the explanation is simple. Pisces is the twelfth and last Sign of the Zodiac, the end of the cycle of worldly experience. It is the Sign of sacrificial service, infinite compassion and vicarious suffering. Traditionally, it is the Sign of the advent of the Messiah. It is the most psychic and subtly inspirational of all the Signs. It represents the meeting place of matter and spirit—the plane of emotionality.

No wonder you often get the feeling you are trapped between two worlds. Certainly you have some difficulty coping with this one. You are not quite sure sometimes which is more real—the solid substance of everyday living or the world of your imagination, which seems to reflect reality more meaningfully.

It's all very confusing for you—but imagine how the rest of us feel trying to live with you and understand you! You've got to admit you are very hard to follow, even on your good days. You are so good-hearted, kind, sympathetic, helpful, charming, pleasant to meet; yet dreamy, vague, inconsistent, emotional, sentimental, contradictory and excitable. You are versatile, lightning quick in understanding, methodical, intuitive and artistic; yet timid, shy, self-doubting, impractical and unrealistic.

Have you ever watched a fellow Pisces switch personalities in front of your eyes? Probably not; you wouldn't even notice something unusual was happening. But it's like watching a chameleon change color as it moves to a new background, an impression the observing mind never finds easy to accept let alone pinpoint.

Pisces is the master of disguise, the born exhibitionist—as long as he or she has a mask to hide behind. You can play any role to suit your audience, but which is the real you? We'll never know. You are only your true self in the wings, waiting for the call that never comes. On the world's stage, where you constantly change roles and ceaselessly practice your dramatics, you are never seen without a mask.

Pisces is ruled by Neptune, the second to last planet of the solar system, so far out in space that it is often called "the Hermit." Most people were born under the six inner planets. Neptune's energy is so fine and "unworldly" that ordinary people fail to comprehend how a Pisces person thinks or feels. So we are inclined to call you dreamers, ditherers and impossible idealists when what we mean is we don't understand you.

There *is* a lot in your nature that's exasperating, infuriating and downright perverse. This is not because you don't really understand yourself; you try to have the best of both worlds when it simply can't be done. You can only live in one world—the other has to live in you. When you confuse them, you fail to cope with either and begin to lose your grip on reality.

Which world? Which way? This is the Pisces dilemma. It is represented vividly by the ancient symbol of your Sign, the two Fishes tied together with a ribbon, one swimming upstream, the other downstream.

Everyone knows that fish don't as a rule choose to swim downstream. It is the obvious, easy way—and the most dangerous. Fish require the dynamic stability created by swimming *against* the current, even though they are making no apparent forward progress.

To go with the stream, to turn tail at the first Sign of pressure and to drift blissfully without personal desire or direction, is the temptation of every true Pisces. Yet your destiny, your transcendence of the very forces you are trying to escape, lies in resisting this urge. You want to flee the reality or conflict of life, not life itself. This is not cowardice, or even necessarily weakness. Neither is it laziness (though in less-evolved Pisces individuals, it can come down to that). Because of your extraordinary psychic and spiritual insights, you sincerely, but perhaps unconsciously, question whether the struggle of life is worth it since all results will disappear in the end.

Mature and evolved Pisces people have no doubts on this score. They enjoy their comfort and ease, perhaps even fame, approbation and respect. They are prepared to wade in and hustle for them. But they have no intention of wearing themselves out in the doing. Not on your life. You Pisces people never exert yourselves one tittle more than is absolutely necessary. Now, don't get this wrong. You'll put yourself out no end for others. You genuinely delight in being able to help them. You love to chat, mix, entertain, do favors, arrange, advise, suggest. But concentrated mental or physical effort—no way! You get very bored with that, and frightfully down in the dumps.

Your style is to employ others to do the hard work. You don't use people in the sense that you exploit them. You always pay for services received, whether it be in money, favors, influence or kindness. Your conscience would torture you unbearably if you misused another individual.

But the fact remains that as a typical Pisces pushing your way upstream you are a manipulator of others, a genial fixer, a puller of strings from behind the scenes. You could be called a schemer, except that this word suggests a certain petty maliciousness. You are shrewd, wily and artful, but not in a personally harmful way. You do your best not to hurt others. All you want is for them to dance to your merry tune.

You have some brilliant and original ideas, as well as some pretty zany ones. Ideas are what you trade in; you are one of the best sellers of this commodity in the Zodiac. You plant ideas surreptitiously in the imagination of others and leave them to mature. You also go for the straight hard sell. You talk extravagantly about your schemes. You are glib, garrulous, entertaining, amusing, pleasant to listen to. Your stories are fascinating, spell-weaving. You are rarely short of an appreciative audience because you possess a magnetic quality and your enthusiasm is contagious.

In your effort to sell an idea, you'll buttonhole anyone you feel can be of help—or who will just listen. You are charming, polite, effusive and stoutly determined to get your way while you are riding a particular wave. Then when you have sufficient numbers running around on your behalf, blinded by Pisces moondust, you slump back into your comfortable chair—happy and exhausted. And you dream.

Dreaming (both day- and nighttime varieties) is your favorite pastime. In fact, your main interest in life is seeing if you can make your dreams come true. Most are so impossibly lofty or romantic and exaggerated that they remain only a form of personal entertainment. But you will work very hard to realize any dream with a base in reality.

Now, when we discuss Pisces daydreams we're not talking about vague or indefinable hopes and wishes such as most of us have, but complete life-stirring De Mille epics. You conjure these up with a realism that for you can exceed the intensity and excitement of actual events. It may sound crazy to any other type, but that's the creative power of the almost-divine Neptunian imagination. You could easily spend all your time in this dream world of yours and be perfectly content; half the Pisces population do.

But when you are swimming upstream, something inside insists that you endeavor to materialize your dreams. Okay, actualizing your fantasies is dull by comparison—like seeing a movie a second time. And it involves striving, competing, worrying—all the things you hate. Things never work out as you dreamt they would, either. So it's not surprising that you lose interest terribly quickly in ventures. You want to get them over with. You no sooner start on one than you're thinking about another. You are a restless soul. Boredom is your worst fear. To be happy, you must always have something to look forward to. Routine is a shroud, the harshness of reality a constant disappointment. You work hard to give everything a touch of glamor. And you don't mind fooling yourself because you prefer self-delusion to cold, sterile facts.

The progressive Pisces is a fairly rare Fish. The multitude of the species just manages to keep pace against the flow of the current of life. They depend very much on others. They often attach themselves to stronger personalities who respect them for, among other things, their remarkable intuitive abilities. These range from seeing through a person instantly on first meeting to apprehending the dangers in a certain course of action. These Pisces individuals may not be impressive in practical matters. They are happy and efficient enough working to method where the detail has been worked out and no major decisions have to be made. But when burdened with responsibility, their conduct of affairs may be quite ludicrous. In tandem with the right partner—business or marital—they will often be highly esteemed for their ability to come up with a creative idea just when it's most needed.

The average Pisces person is not very impressive in the conduct of public affairs. He or she is far too inclined to sit back and let things happen until doing nothing becomes the most logical policy. This individual's personal philosophy is that everything comes right in the end. He or she patches up, papers over, compromises—but does it all with such geniality that most people are fooled most of the time. Pisces possesses the most incredible ability to create in the human mind the *illusion* of personal action and acceptable performance when absolutely nothing effective is being done.

As a political leader, the Pisces man or woman can be a formidable figure who appears, to the public, to have everything personally under control even though those who work beside him or her are horrified by the "leader's" insouciance and ambiguity. "Gone Fishing" is the notice that hangs on the door of the ship of state. And yet incredibly, in front of large numbers of people, particularly the public in general, our Pisces friend gets away with it. Opponents who toil and strive conscientiously don't. This amazing cover is the work of the strange Neptunian forces that flow through you unbelievably elusive, evasive and subtly aspiring people.

The many Pisces who drift with the current and live aimless lives are fairly pathetic individuals. Being basically very attractive and likable, they invariably find someone to lean on. As soon as they do, they give up trying completely and sink into a morass of bemused dreaming, introspection or self-pity. They talk about perfection but make no overt effort to achieve it. They are acutely distressed by their own lack of accomplishment, but will avoid at all cost any situation they suspect provides the opportunity to start trying.

A favorite Pisces trick when being sympathetically encouraged toward a positive or creative pursuit is to go along enthusiastically with all the preparations and to balk at the very last minute. Any excuse or device will be used to justify dropping out, including feigning illness, blaming another person and incredible emotional outbursts complete with torrents of tears and hysteria. Negative Pisces men and women are enormously devious when covering up for their lack of performance. It is impossible to pin them down with logic or reason. They desperately surround themselves with red herrings. While insisting that they only want to be truthful, they lie and scheme with astonishing blindness to their own hypocrisy. These individuals project all their fears, fantasies and antipathies onto their "protector" or the one closest to them. The person they love the most they hurt the most, lurching in wild temperamental swings from adoration and gratitude to reproach and despair. These poor Fish, who have yet to learn to cope with their own ambivalent natures, impose tremendous strain on those they live with.

The uncertainty produced by having no direction they can identify with often drives Pisces to drink or drugs. These stimulants, while dissolving their feelings of vulnerability and anxiety, extract a terrible price. After the trip, the person plunges even deeper into depression with nauseating self-pity or self-condemnation. Another form of destructive escape for this type of Pisces is to ride too high emotionally on daydreams. The troughs of despair and despondency have a habit of equaling the peaks of delight.

The one certain and constructive outlet for Pisces' extreme emotionalism is any form of art. It is here that self-expression is most natural to them, and at the same time, deeply satisfying. No Sign has more all-round artistic potential and awareness of the creative elements than Pisces. The astrological explanation is interesting.

It is in Pisces that Venus, the planet of beauty, art and love, is exalted (reaches its strongest point in the Zodiac). Although Venus actually rules Taurus and Libra, the planet's vibrations are more harmoniously in tune with the effluvium of Pisces. Taurus and Libra express *forms* of beauty and love, but the pure Pisces character *is* beauty and love. Pisces would willingly die for love if he or she could only find an object worthy of this sacrifice. Hence, the average Pisces man and woman are notable for their kindness, gentleness and great compassion for any suffering fellow being.

From the artistic point of view, the Venus influence is also much more subtle in the Pisces nature than in the Venus-ruled Signs. Pisces is the perfect menstruum for Venus, and the sublime forces released in the union are the essence of the Sign. Pure Pisces thought or feeling is artistry itself, not just a means for expressing art. Advanced Pisces people possess such a refined appreciation of all that is beautiful and divine that it reaches ecstatic levels and defies overt description or expression. A true Pisces will know exactly what this means.

There is another astrological influence that heightens the sensitivity and natural responsiveness of Pisces. This is the influence of the Moon. The Moon controls the senses and sensibilities, our emotional response to love and beauty. The Moon is exalted in the Venus-ruled Sign of Taurus, and Venus brings this soft, sensuous influence into the Sign of the Fish. The Moon, of course, rules water and the tides, so the association with the watery, intuitive, impressionable, psychic, loving, artistic and changeable Sign of Pisces is extremely significant—and effective.

Pisces individuals excel in poetry, music, dancing and writing. Since you do not possess much capacity for discipline, you frequently fail to learn the necessary techniques. You often show extraordinary aptitude for the arts, but it may not come to much because of your dilettantish approach. However, it is in writing and dancing that you are often most successful. As a writer, the Pisces person is able to draw on his or her profound sensitivity. Pisces' works invariably contain allusions to the beauties of nature and the reality of the intangible soul.

Surprisingly, you have an unusual capacity for bearing physical discomfort and pain, if you feel it is necessary. You have an odd relationship to your body, often regarding it as something separate from your *self*. Normally your body consciousness is not acute, yet when you choose, you can exercise exceptional body control. In dance and yoga, you are able to persist with excruciating exercises and regimens to attain the proper control and expression. Once a Pisces has mastered a physical discipline, his or her movements and actions are sheer grace and poetry, profoundly communicative.

The Pisces person's body (particularly the woman's) is usually distinctive. It is soft, feathery and very appealing, without any spongy fleshiness. It is very female, yielding, receptive, lacking the fiber of impatience and passion. It is not surprising that the Pisces woman is one of the great beauties of the Zodiac when we remember the influence of Venus and the Moon, the two most feminine planets.

And the man? Fortunately, although the man is naturally influenced in temperament by the artistic refinements, his masculine traits come from Mars. Mars is exalted or at its strongest in Capricorn, so the Pisces male has a more solid down-to-earth appearance than the female Fish. He's usually quite strong, more ambitious and better able than the woman to cope with the day-to-day demands of life.

The position in the horoscope of Mars (for men) and Venus (for women) is extremely important for assessing the individual strengths and weaknesses of people born under this Sign. Special note should also be taken of the placement of the Moon.

Both he and she (but especially she) usually have a strikingly young, childlike or "innocent" face that remains so well into maturity. The lines of the face are soft and the complexion rather pale. Despite the geniality of the Sign, the eyes have a wide or sleepy look.

There is a distinct coldness about you people, which you can produce at will. It is guaranteed to stop any unwanted attention or inquisitiveness. The Pisces nature contains a strong desire to preserve personal secrets. The longing to be accepted and liked, however, is almost pathological.

Frequently you are excessively polite, even gushing in your compliments and flattery. This is often a device to cover up for your feelings of inferiority or lack of accomplishment, feelings that are probably not valid. You can even demean yourself to attract sympathy and attention. You deeply resent criticism, even the mildest, especially from loved ones, and will either reply to it caustically or adopt an injured air.

All your problems arise from your extreme sensitivity. You absorb impressions like a sponge. Whereas other types are able to walk confidently through the world, ignorant of the hostile elements surrounding them, you feel the push and pull of these unseen influences. Often confused by them, you start to do one thing, and become aware of a pull to do the opposite. Metaphysically, this is Newton's third law of motion in operation: for every action, there is an opposite reaction; one urge cancels out the other. And poor old Pisces is castigated for doing nothing or not knowing his or her own mind. People who have studied Astrology understand your psyche and sympathize with your dilemma.

You are extremely open to suggestion. Your type is often found on the fringe of movements aimed at bringing about reform or change. You are not the crusading type yourself; such sustained mental and physical application is generally beyond you. But you can and often do respond to a popular call or campaign. You are inclined to believe just about everything you hear. You are easily swayed by colorful and imaginative oratory. You get swept along in a wave of popular emotional response. You are a great follower, rarely a leader or initiator.

One danger is your impulsiveness. You are so impressionable that you tend to react to any stimulus without discrimination. A feeling is often enough to set you on a course of action that may end disastrously before you've realized what you've let yourself in for. You are a sucker for phonies and the hard-luck story. You are inclined to accept people and situations on face value. It seldom occurs to you to doubt or question a story. You have only to hear of another person's plight for your imagination to go to work—usually along the most romantic and unlikely lines.

It takes a long time for you to learn from experience. You often make the same mistakes over and over again. Still, you are a great survivor because of your adaptability. You can fit in just about anywhere. Although you are extremely curious and easily excited, there's not much in this world that shocks you. You accept people and situations as they are. If you don't like them, you leave them alone.

As lovers, the Pisces man and woman are different but have much in common. How both can expect to get along with their opposite numbers in the other Signs is discussed in the chapter "Pisces in Love." Briefly, the Pisces woman lives to be loved. In exchange for love, she will give anything or do anything. But the love she demands is the exceptionally exclusive and intense kind that few men can really manage. Consequently, the Pisces woman rarely finds her ideal and often suffers much disillusionment and disappointment in her love affairs. Impulsive and romantic to an almost absurd degree, she loves an image, a dream. She wants to be the center of her man's life. If she's not, he'll soon hear about it.

This girl actually dreams of fairy godmothers and handsome princes dashing to her rescue, refusing to acknowledge the truth of bitter experience. As a child, the Pisces girl loves to dress up in old-fashioned clothes and to imagine herself a lady among handsome lords and stern knights. In adulthood, when she can no longer masquerade in courtly fashions, she dresses herself in exquisite fantasies. The fashion freedom of recent years has provided Pisces women with wonderful opportunities to affect their fairy-tale visions. Not for them boyish jeans and T-shirts; they prefer dainty, feminine, flowing, stylish gear—long Indian dresses, exotic Eastern creations. The female Fish wants always to be a woman—and for the men in her life to know it.

In lovemaking, the Pisces woman can be so giving, yielding and self-sacrificing that she may seem shatteringly unresponsive. As one man remarked about Pisces girls, "They make me feel a sexual failure." Really, the Pisces woman reflects the capability of the man, his strength to take what he wants. She is no ordinary woman. She's total negative female—all woman, waiting for the positive male element to absorb her absolutely. Several strengthening (or one could say moderating or distorting) influences in the horoscope may create a semblance of passionate involvement. But basically, the typical Pisces woman is the way she is because the "boys" can't bear the aloneness of her lovemaking—she wants a man!

The Pisces man can be a cold fish as a lover. He has an indefinable aloofness. Though he can appear terribly passionate, a woman knows he's holding something back, even if he doesn't know it. He is looking for the right female, and the chances of his finding her are very slim. He is a diligent searcher, though, and usually has many affairs, for his physical-emotional detachment is very attractive. The Ascendant of the man and the position occupied by Mars are extremely important in determining his sexual vigor.

Pisces love is really universal love, not individual or physical. The sexual permissiveness for which people of this Sign are renowned stems from their willingness to give pleasure to another without considering their own needs.

And yet, in mental and emotional relationships, you Pisces men and women are most demanding. You need to be constantly flattered, praised and shown that you are appreciated. Generally you love your home and are intensely proud of your family. You will do anything for your loved ones, and usually spoil and indulge them outrageously. In return, you can never receive sufficient affection or consideration, you often feel neglected or betrayed.

Some of you find solace in the make-believe world of the movies. (You are also avid television viewers.) Others of you turn to religion and philanthropy. All of you usually possess a deep interest in the occult. You love delving into mysteries and are frequently found at seances. Some of you are natural mediums for psychic phenomena. Your ESP abilities give you considerable prominence and success in this field. However, most Pisces are suspect as objective investigators because their vivid imagination gets in the way and makes exaggeration difficult to avoid.

And loneliness? No type feels the pangs of loneliness more fiercely or more frequently than Pisces. And yet you constantly cut yourself off from people, withdrawing into moody or profound silences.

This is the basic contradiction in your character, which is more dual in some aspects than even Gemini, the Sign of the Twins. You love parties, large gatherings and masses of attention. But the artist, the poet and the mystic in you demand periodic solitude and seclusion. The private world where none may intrude often beckons you at the height of delicious excitement.

The reason you hate to be alone is that you fear you will slip into the bottomless abyss you feel is always waiting to receive you. But you possess a built-in mechanism, which when the danger point of solitude is approaching, usually projects you once again into the crowd of friends and new acquaintances you need so much.

You Pisces people often have very real and disturbing dreams. These can be precognitive, and sometimes extremely frightening. Remember that your planet, Neptune, is the great deceiver. Just as you enjoy manufacturing realistic daydreams, so the process continues at night. You can actually terrify yourself with your own creations.

If you are ever in doubt about whether an apparition or dream is real or not, scrutinize it, don't look away. Illusion always fades under a dispassionate gaze. If it's real, you will be stuck with it anyway, as will the rest of us—which can't be all that bad, can it?

PISCES IN LOVE

YOUR PISCES MAN

You like him? Love him? What sort of a fellow is he?

Dreamy. Gentle. Kind. Generous. A born romantic, a most sensitive lover.

You'll never have to worry about this guy remembering your birthday and other special occasions. He'll always have a lovely gift for you, beautifully wrapped—and it won't be something you *needed*, it will be an item you've secretly admired or wouldn't dare be extravagant enough to buy for yourself.

This man understands women. You don't have to tell him what you feel or what you like. He has extraordinary intuition. He tunes in to emotions, especially those of the woman he loves. You'll be amazed at how much he knows about you after your first meeting. He will have summed you up in the first few minutes. If he shows he's attracted to you, it's a sure sign you're his type of woman. And this means you'll find him a charming, witty, courteous and delightful person to be with.

But there is a problem if you're contemplating a permanent relationship with a Pisces man—or there could be if you get involved with the wrong one. Just as his symbol is two Fishes, so he comes in two types. Fish Number One spends most of his time swimming in a dream world. He sometimes mistakes it for reality. He's filled with all the best intentions and has got some of the brightest and most original ideas you've ever heard. He can talk for hours about what he's *going* to do. He'll hold you spellbound with his vivid imagination and his powers of description.

But will his plans ever come to anything? Chances are they won't. He's a lovely guy. Likable, sweet-tempered, not a harsh word for anyone. But he's darned slow at getting started at anything. He always has a good reason for procrastinating. He likes things to happen in their own good time. He doesn't want to initiate. He's frightened of pressure and responsibility. He's terrified of failing.

The other Fish is an upstream swimmer. He's also a dreamer, but one who can't wait to put his ideas into action. He loves excitement. He can't stick at any one thing for very long. But he does get things moving and always manages to coax others into running around on his behalf. You'll have to watch out with this guy because he has a way of involving people in his projects and then disappearing on urgent business. As his girlfriend or wife, you might find yourself toiling in a series of nets the Fish has managed to slip through.

You must never let the romance go out of your relationship. He will certainly do all in his power to keep it in. As much as he loves getting out and mixing, he'll prefer quiet evenings at home with you, cuddled up by the fire. He has an artistic temperament. He loves comfortable and harmonious surroundings. His home is very important to him.

It is very unlikely that an affair with this man will come to anything if you are a dominant, bossy type of female. He can't stand being told what to do. He doesn't like to be cross-examined, either. He's independent, an individualist.

Despite his gentleness and sensitivity, he is not weak. He won't be pushed around or bullied. If anyone tries to take advantage of his good nature, he will soon display the spikes that are hidden along his backbone.

This man will stick by you through thick and thin. If he believes in you, he will trust you all the way. He has very few prejudices. He won't attempt to judge you. He will only want to understand you.

If you decide to make it permanent with a Pisces man, you'll be delighted with his gestures of love, the kind that may not occur to other men. He will think of the little things that mean so much to a woman.

This man *needs* a woman. On his own, he

tends to feel unfulfilled and settle into a habitual sort of existence. He has much to offer. He needs someone to work and succeed for. With the right woman by his side, he has the enterprise, wit and energy to get to the top. He must have an incentive greater than power and acquisition. Your love and faithfulness will provide it.

YOUR PISCES WOMAN

You like her? Love her? What sort of woman is she?

Feminine. Exquisitely feminine. Soft. Gentle. Delectable. A sheer delight for any man to love.

This girl is *not* a women's libber. Nothing affronts her more than the idea of being independent of her man. She wants him to be the boss. She can't be happy if he's not masterful. She wants him to protect her and care for her—to love her . . . divinely!

She is the greatest romantic in the Zodiac. Love to her, as the poet said, is not a thing apart—it is her whole existence. Don't play around with this girl by pretending you're serious if you're not. If she falls for you, the question will be, can you stand such an intensity of devotion? Are you really up to being worshipped?

She's no fool. In fact, she's remarkably perceptive. She can read men like books. But sometimes she ignores what her sixth sense tells her and falls for the wrong type, probably because in some way or other he has measured up to the dream of her lover she's had since childhood.

This woman spends a lot of her time in dreamland. Usually she has manufactured a romantic image of her life-to-be well before she turns sixteen. It's all in her head—including her version of the Sir Galahad who's going to rescue her, provide her with a beautiful home and cherish her forever. So it's obvious why she gets herself into some terrible romantic messes.

The trouble is as soon as she spots a guy who might look good on a white charger—and she likes the emotional feel of him—she assumes the rest. She puts him on her mental pedestal and kneels at his feet. She listens for hours (assuming he's told her he loves her) while he talks about himself. Those beautiful compelling eyes of hers open wide with wonder and admiration. She serves him absolutely. She does exactly what she's told. When he's away, she waits patiently and placidly till he returns. She prepares little surprises in the way of food and drinks.

Even in the smallest of apartments, the Pisces girl achieves an unmistakable charm and elegance. Her furnishings are fine and in the best of taste. There are always one or two very small vases of fresh-cut flowers, probably some tiny or delicate wildflowers picked with loving care by those dainty Pisces hands.

This girl breathes and exudes a subtle refinement. While you love her, she's the most adaptable creature on earth. The whole of society can come crashing down around her, and she'll quietly and unobtrusively pick her way through the debris until she's at your side. Situations that would drive another woman mad she floats through with marvelous tranquility. So what's the catch?

Disillusionment. Very few guys can live up to Miss Pisces' dream image of her lover. She will do all in her power to make a man fit her ideal, but sooner or later the scales start to fall from her eyes and she sees him for what he is—just a man. Miss Pisces is really searching for a male god.

When she's disappointed in love, she retreats further and further into her dreams. Few men can stand the vacuumous isolation this implies.

If you are unfaithful to her, she will be absolutely shattered and will never really forgive you. Things will never be the same again, no matter what promises are exchanged. If she doesn't walk out, it will be because she can't be bothered to. When crushed or disappointed, she takes the easy way. She rarely resists. She floats, drifts and disappears into herself.

When things are going smoothly, she loses her cool from time to time. But her temper is seldom furious and is certainly short-lived.

She can be irritated by responsibility and pressure. Then she becomes cranky and sarcastic. She may be scornful of her man for not protecting her from ordinary problems.

If you're a weak man, forget her. Miss Pisces is a prize that goes only to the strong.

PISCES WOMAN—ARIES MAN

You can't help but be impressed by this man's enthusiasm for life. He seems to take great joy from the very fact that he is alive. He will be good for you in a number of ways. You have a tendency to escape into your dream world; Mr. Aries is a realist.

There is bound to be a certain amount of friction in this particular zodiacal linkup. But you like excitement in your life. He will find you difficult to understand. You will either both end up completely disillusioned or be fascinated and keep coming back for more.

Mr. Aries will want to protect you. You like a masterful kind of guy, and the Ram certainly fits that description.

He is the no-nonsense type. He won't take your moods seriously. He will tell you to cheer up and involve yourself in something that takes your mind off your problems.

There are many things that will atrract you to him. He is a stable person and an active one. He is also a hard worker. And he always comes out with what is on his mind.

He can be overpowering. You may get the feeling he is taking you over. You are a woman who prizes her individuality and freedom to think as you choose.

From the start, he will be magnetically drawn to you. So long as he channels his dominating and sometimes aggressive ways into his work, all will be well but if he tries to take over in areas you consider your domain, there will be trouble.

If this man falls for you, he will be prepared to fight off all comers to win your love. He has tenacity.

He is a physical type of man. His straightforward style of lovemaking will appeal to you.

He is ambitious. His work means a lot to him. He is prepared to work all hours to get to the top. He will also take on another job if he has to in order to provide you with the things you want.

He is not a subtle type so don't try to play games with him. Be careful with other men. He could easily misunderstand and think you were flirting with them.

As a rule, your Aries man prefers the company of his own sex to womenfolk. If you are his mate, he will love being with you, of course, but he will still want to have his all-male evenings. At a party, you are often likely to find Mr. Aries singing the old school song with his buddies over in the corner of the room.

Sometimes he will shock you. He can get bored very easily. He's likely to come home one day and tell you he has quit that nice secure job he's been holding down (pension and all) to go into business with a friend. Sure, he's a steady guy, but he won't settle for routine forever.

You will have to let him make the big decisions—or at least let him *think* he is making the big decisions.

You love your home; he will love the way you run it. You also like having a man around you can make a fuss over. He's a bit of a gadget fanatic. He goes for the latest in everything. He'll want to change his car every year if he can afford to do so.

You will have to accept his bragging and boasting. Being a perceptive person, you'll be able to see right through him when he struts around trying to impress others. You would not wish to hurt his feelings, though.

He can't help thinking he can conquer almost any woman he meets. You'll probably smile to yourself when you see him winking at a pretty girl—especially if he thinks you haven't noticed. But being a Pisces woman, you don't miss much.

PISCES WOMAN—TAURUS MAN

This union has all the hallmarks of being a truly perfect love match. In many ways, you are opposite types, but your personalities should complement each other. In Mr. Taurus, you could discover you have met your dream man.

There are not many guys who can totally satisfy a woman born under the last Sign of the Zodiac. You are a mysterious person. Very often your moods control you. You can't help the way you react to people and situations.

The Bull will give you all the strength you need in a partner without trying to change you. He will love you because you are so feminine. He is quite old-fashioned in his ways and he will treat you with love and respect.

You will always feel secure when he's around. He will protect you if the going gets rough. He will do all he can to make sure you are not upset or slighted by others.

He can be jealous and possessive, but you'll be able to accept this. To you, it will be proof of his love and faithfulness. You look for fidelity in a close relationship. It is unlikely he would go off the rails.

Being an earth Sign, he has both feet planted firmly on the ground. He will accept your advice when he thinks it's worth following, but he will always take practical matters into consideration before he acts.

You will always be provided for. Mr. Taurus would never let his woman want. He is not afraid of hard work. He would consider taking almost any job in order to keep his head above water.

Once the Bull gives his word, he sticks to it. He doesn't fall in love easily. If he does whisper those three little words, you can bet your bottom dollar he's on the up and up.

He is ambitious. He wants to have authority over others. The reason for this is he doesn't like to take orders. You admire a man who strives to make his mark in the world. It is unlikely you would last very long with a guy who is afraid to stand up for himself.

Mr. Taurus will try to provide you with all the little luxuries you need in order to feel happy and contented. Like you, he regards his home as terribly important. He will leave all the decorating and furnishing to you, since he considers that very much the woman's domain.

Naturally you will have your fights. But then, what couple doesn't? He has a flaming temper, yet he doesn't bear a grudge for long. He is careful with money but is never likely to begrudge you the cash for a new dress because he will always want you to look your best. You will enjoy going out together. He usually knows the best restaurants and the latest "in" clubs to visit.

You will always know where you stand with the Bull because he is not very good at concealing his true feelings. He might have been a bit wild in his youth, but it's amazing how quickly this man settles down when he finds what he wants.

Your chopping and changing will infuriate him, and this is something you'll have to watch. He insists on planning ahead. Try not to say yes to arrangements he wishes to make unless you are absolutely sure you'll stick by your word. He can't bear to be let down or made to look a fool in front of others.

One final word of warning: don't contradict him in front of his pals. If he gets his facts wrong, point it out to him in a gentle way when you're alone together.

You will consider yourself a lucky woman if a Taurus man has gone overboard for you.

PISCES WOMAN—GEMINI MAN

Life with a Gemini mate will always be interesting. That's one thing you can be sure of. You will get on well from the start. It's likely you'll be drawn to each other's minds. The intellectual attraction will probably precede the physical one. You will have a good deal in common.

You both have a vivid imagination. You will find him fascinating in many ways. He's a good talker and has lots of charm. He can be rather unreliable, though, getting carried away with a hobby or interest, and then suddenly dropping it. The trouble is he also does this with people. He can be self-centered. He likes to get his own way and can't stand to be bossed.

If you do fall under his spell, beware. He doesn't mean to do it, but Mr. Gemini is a great user of people. He takes everything he can get from them. He has an inquiring mind and is the sort of guy you will want to confide in. You will find yourself letting out secrets you would never dream of telling another soul.

As a friend, or perhaps even as a lover, you will find him charming. But one wonders how long you would last in a permanent arrangement. He would probably give you much cause for concern. He might even break your heart.

You will never know what time of the day or night he'll turn up. Many a dinner lovingly prepared could be spoiled. When he goes cold on someone, he doesn't stay around to offer explanations. In fact, you can't see him for Mercurial dust.

But you are perceptive, and if anyone can keep this man coming back for more, it's a woman born under the Sign of the two Fishes. The Twins will never get bored so long as there is an element of mystery surrounding the person he is involved with. Still waters run deep with you. He will never quite know where he stands.

You could show him what true love is all about. A Gemini man is always searching for it, but rarely finds it. He is in love with the *idea* of love, and thus expects too much.

He can't stand to be dominated. You will have to let him go his own way in the hope he will choose a path you wish to follow.

He is a terrible flirt. You will have to ask yourself whether you can live with a guy who has such a roving eye. Don't forget you can be extremely jealous when aroused.

He tends to live for the moment. You like to have someone around to protect you. The problem is that he needs a lot of looking after.

You are a home-loving creature. Would you be prepared to sacrifice a good part of your domestic life to keep pace with Mercurial Gemini? This union could work out well if you are one of these rare Pisces women who can go on living her own life and keeping up with her own interests after marriage. Your best chance with a man born under this Sign is to meet him when he has had a good deal of experience and enough time to get his priorities right.

Mr. Gemini is generous to a fault. It would be a good idea for you to have some control over the bank account.

He is quite emotional. Your tears and laughter will always have a greater effect on him than your words.

PISCES WOMAN—CANCER MAN

Romance will be in the air when Cancer and Pisces get together. He could be the ideal man for a woman like you. He will understand you so well and he is one of the few men who will be able to adjust to your moods. Like you, he is a water Sign. His ruler is the changeable Moon.

You will never feel pressured by this man. He believes in the gentle art of persuasion.

Certain difficulties will have to be overcome, of course, and it would be best if you face them squarely in the early days of your liaison. You could have a negative effect on each other. In a Cancer-Pisces union, there will always be a good reason for *not* doing something.

You both love your home. Like you, he needs a place where he will feel secure. The Crab is a sensitive creature, and it takes quite a lot to coax him out of his shell. He is terrified of getting hurt. The idea of meeting new people can be frightening to him.

He does his best to be steady. He is the kind of man who is always interested in improving his mind. You will be able to bring out the very best in him. He needs something really worthwhile to work for. Security is vital to him.

Still, you do need a man you feel is in control of the overall situation. One wonders if Mr. Cancer would be able to play such a masterful role.

The physical side of your life together should pose no problems. In fact, he should make an ideal lover. He has imagination and understanding. His moods in bed can change. He will know when you want him to be gentle and when you want him to be aggressive. He picks up other people's vibrations immediately.

On the negative side, you are very similar. You both tend to escape to a fantasy world. You also enlarge situations and make much more of your problems than is warranted.

Around the home is where you two will be happiest. There will be many nights when you will lock the door and take the phone off the hook. A Cancer man is usually domesticated. He won't need to be told to take his shoes off at the front door. He will be as house-proud as you.

He will also be willing to take on his fair share of the chores. Often he is an extremely good cook. And he won't object to your continuing with a career after marriage, if that is what you want. He is a trusting person. He would only get jealous if you got involved deeply with another guy.

He enjoys entertaining. You will get a kick out of giving little cocktail and supper parties.

He will exert a lot of power over you without your always realizing it. You'll find yourself putting his needs and desires before your own.

You must try not to take each other too seriously. You both have a tendency to look on the bad side of things. Make sure you preserve the humor in your relationship.

If you really love him and are prepared to give as much as you expect, this union could work out well.

He makes a super dad. He will bring up the children to respect their elders and to do the right thing. You'll have to make sure he doesn't put too much emphasis on traditional values.

PISCES WOMAN—LEO MAN

Chances are you will be drawn to a man born under Leo from the first time you clap eyes on him. He has so many of the qualities you admire and respect. He is a born leader and a bit of a showoff. You like a guy who is not afraid to voice his opinions.

Our Leonine friend is always looking for an audience. He has very strong ideas about almost everything. Some women find him too hot to handle, but not you.

He will want to dominate you and even try to change you in some ways. He won't realize you can read him like a book. You will be perfectly happy to let him rant and roar from the mountaintop. You will smile in a dreamy sort of way. and in time get him to follow plans he'll think are his but which you've decided on long ago.

He can't help putting on a show for people. Leo seems to think he is on stage all the time. If he can't be the center of attention, he'll leave the party or fall asleep in the most comfortable chair in the room.

You admire a man who seems to know where he is going. You can rely on Leo to make the big decisions without flinching. He is not the sort to panic in a crisis.

He is security-conscious. He also has quite a temper and is a jealous man. If you are his woman, he won't stand for any games playing. Mind you, he does like to pay attention to pretty girls himself, but this is nothing to be worried about. He just likes an occasional reminder that he's still considered desirable by members of the opposite sex.

He's got amazing tenacity. If he decides you are the girl for him, he won't give up the pursuit with much ease.

He will love the way you organize the home. He will work hard to ensure that you have the best of everything.

He is careful with money but will never be miserly with you. You will only have to ask for a new dress, and he'll do his best to get it for you.

Mr. Leo is possessive. He won't be too happy if you want to work after marriage. You'd also better forget about keeping up with the pals you had when you were single. He won't want you to have a life apart from the one you share with him.

People born under this Sign have fairly logical minds. A Leo man will make a good teacher. If he is interested in a person, and if he thinks he has a special talent, Leo will show infinite patience in helping that person fulfill himself.

He can't bear to remain idle for very long. He doesn't like to be bossed, either. He won't stick to any job where his every move is subject to a higher authority.

The typical Leo enjoys a good party. He will be happy to spend a number of evenings quietly at home with you, but occasionally that old wanderlust will surge up and he'll have to have a fling on his own.

He will expect to be the number-one interest in your life; fortunately, you are the sort of woman who can give that much attention to the man she loves.

He can't stand criticism. Be careful how you tell him he is in the wrong, even if it is for his own good.

Never puncture his pride. He doesn't like to be ridiculed. You will always be able to win him over when you want to.

He is a disciplined man. He's straightforward, too. If he gives you his word, he will do all in his power to live up to it.

PISCES WOMAN—VIRGO MAN

Life with Virgo won't be a crash-bang romance from beginning to end, but you could do a lot worse than settle for such a stable and dependable kind of fellow. The sort of love this man has to offer is enduring. He may not be a fireball, but he won't let you down.

He is a logical man who works everything out in advance. Only rarely will he act impulsively. He wants to do everything the "right" way. He is a great respecter of the law. In many ways, you could call him old-fashioned. He actually resents change. You will notice by the way he dresses and the sort of restaurants and clubs he frequents that he is a traditionalist.

He might have some difficulty coping with your fluctuating moods. Temperamentally, you are poles apart. But he is patient, and if he loves you, he will do his best to understand your sudden fits of depression.

This relationship could start off quietly. It is possible you will meet a number of times before he asks you for a date. A Virgo man never does anything in a hurry. The sort of love that exists between you is likely to grow over time.

Never try to rush him. He likes to make up his own mind.

He's a bit of a fussbudget. He will love the way you run the home. He likes his comforts. He can also be extremely particular about food.

You don't mean to be hurtful but you can't help playing games with men who admire you. Be careful you never hurt this guy. He will take everything you tell him seriously.

Don't get the idea he is a fool because he has a quick and analytical mind. He can soon sum up people. Remember, Mercury is his ruler.

He's careful with money and is usually a good businessman. You can be sure he'll make the best possible use of his talents.

You may wonder how long you'll have to wait before he puts his arm around you at the movies or tells you he loves you. He *is* rather shy. It may take him quite a while to pluck up the courage because he is frightened of being rebuffed by you.

He is a good son to his parents. He will try to live up to their expectations. There is a strong sense of responsibility here.

He will try to protect you. In fact, you could find him a little too protective for your liking. You like to have a strong shoulder to rest your head on, but you do like the freedom to think and act for yourself.

You will certainly respect him. If you do get married, he is unlikely to give you any reason to be jealous.

On the physical side, he may find it rather hard to take the lead. You will have to be gentle with him and help him overcome his inhibitions.

You make an ideal parent combination. You are a bit of a child at heart and will give the kids all the fun they need; your Virgo husband will be sensible with them. He will bring them up with a strong sense of responsibility and justice.

To be honest, you may get bored with this man at times. He lacks the fire and aggression you look for in a man. But you would be wise to hang on when the going gets rough. If this man loves you, you will never find another one more devoted.

PISCES WOMAN—LIBRA MAN

You will certainly be on a similar wavelength with charming Mr. Libra. He is great fun to be with. He is a good conversationalist and a humane person. He can't stand to see people being taken advantage of.

One wonders, however, if he would be strong enough to handle a girl like you. His symbol is the Scales, and he often has difficulty making up his mind because he can always see both sides of an argument. You do like to be involved with a guy who seems to know where he's going.

He is curious about life. He likes to meet new people and is prone to accept any kind of challenge. He is also fond of travel.

Mr. Libra is a great diplomat. He knows how to pay a compliment. He would never do anything that would hurt or upset you. He will help you overcome your shyness because he has a fantastic ability to make others feel relaxed. He will help you gain confidence in yourself.

You both like beautiful surroundings. The home is likely to be special to the two of you. He can be rather extravagant with money. That wonderful sense of balance he is usually able to maintain often flies out the window when he sees something his heart desires in a shop window.

You will be fascinated by his mind. He is usually pretty good with anything mechanical. You will find you have a partner who is quite handy. It will not be necessary to call in a professional for minor repair work.

If this union is going to be successful, it is important that you have a strong sense of direction. One of the dangers in this liaison is that you both have a tendency to drift.

A guy born where Venus rules is bound to be romantic. He can't help but admire beautiful women. You can be possessive and like to know where you stand with a man. One wonders if you could live with someone who has so much to give so many people.

You could get into financial trouble. You like to be made a fuss of and, as pointed out earlier, he does have a tendency to throw his money about freely.

Sexually, you will be in total harmony. A Libra is one of those rare men who knows instinctively how to make a woman happy in bed, He will understand your imaginative mind. He will be willing to play a role in your fantasies.

He can be rather vague, especially about time. If he gets involved in an interesting conversation or carried away with a project he is working on, there's no telling what time he'll be home.

Don't try to boss him. His element is air and he can't bear to feel tied down in any way.

You will learn a lot from a Libra. He will be able to interest you in almost any subject he enjoys. He transmits to other people his passion for what he holds dear.

Mr. Libra won't object when you withdraw into your own little dream world. He will understand your wish to have your private moments. He needs to spend a certain amount of time on his own, too.

You may not be able to help getting jealous on occasions. On the whole, though, you have every chance of making a happy and successful life together.

When the children come along, you will make a wonderful parent combination. You will instill in them an appreciation of all things beautiful. Your man will teach them how to cope with the world.

PISCES WOMAN–SCORPIO MAN

You are one of the few women who might be able to understand a Scorpio guy. He is difficult to get to know. A lot of women are frightened off by first impressions. He gives off vibes of aggressiveness and insensitivity. But that's only half the story. With your intuition, you will soon realize he is bluffing to hide his sensitivity.

You are both spell-weavers. If you become involved, it could be magic.

Remember, your element is water; so is his. Thus you are likely to agree about many things in life. You will find he shares your interest in the mysterious.

He makes a good husband, although a possessive one. This should not bother you since you like to be involved with a man who cares deeply.

Occasionally he will assume a false dignity, and this is a side of his nature that won't appeal to you. However, you must try to understand why he strikes poses. He is likely to be an excellent businessman, and therefore knows only too well that a certain amount of bluff and bravado are necessary to get to the top.

You will have to put up with his strutting. He needs to be constantly reassured. You will have to listen time and again to his stories of how well he did in the office that day.

He's the jealous type. He'll pick a fight with a guy twice his size if he catches him making a pass at you.

Sex is terribly important to him. You will find this man is a passionate lover. The fire of his desire will stimulate you on a mental as well as a physical plane. As you get to know each other better, you'll discover it's more than physical attraction that drew you together.

You will know how to look after him. Instinctively, you will realize when he needs quiet. You will soon get to understand his many moods. He will need to use you to let off steam, for you will be most sympathetic and loving toward him.

He is capable of standing up for his rights. Mr. Scorpio is a good worker, but he doesn't like to be bossed around.

He has a mighty temper. Don't laugh at him. He can't stand to be made fun of.

There are dangers. One is that he likes to give the impression he's a better man than he is. He also makes harsh moral judgments about others when, in all honesty, he himself is not entirely blameless. The truth is important to you. You will find it difficult to live with a man who tries to fool other people while in reality he is only kidding himself.

His intensity could grow on you. You may suddenly wake up one day and decide you can't live without him. You would probably be willing to stand for far more from him than you would from most other men.

Home is an important place to you both, but you must make sure you get out and about a lot. He will want his evenings out with the boys. Build up a group of friends you both like so he won't become a loner.

He makes a smashing dad. He will be ambitious for his children. He can be a bit heavy-handed with the discipline, though. Still, you will be able to supply all the gentleness and affection he finds it so difficult to show.

PISCES WOMAN—SAGITTARIUS MAN

You will think you have struck it lucky when you come across gay, debonair, dashing Mr. Sagittarius. He is the life and soul of the party, always on the go. You will find there is never a dull moment when the Archer is about.

There are certain drawbacks to shacking up with him, though. One, he finds it difficult to settle down. He is terrified of losing his freedom. He likes to keep moving. Two, you are probably looking for a man with a little more depth. He is a bit afraid of getting deeply involved.

You are a home-loving girl. His restless ways could put you on edge. He has difficulty in making up his mind. He doesn't like to make plans.

Sagittarius people make wonderful friends. They never let a pal down in a crisis. Should you find yourself deep in despair, it's quite possible you would turn to a Sagittarius man for advice and comfort.

Many people label this guy a good-time Charlie and nothing more. This is not so. He cares deeply about the world, but doesn't like to show his emotions. Underneath all the bravado is a very private man.

He won't allow you to lead a settled life. He will want a constant change of scene. You won't have many cozy evenings in front of the fire.

You will always have the feeling there are certain areas of his life you can never be a part of. It is unlikely you will ever get to know all of him. He prefers his nights out with the boys to evenings with mixed company. If you are his woman, he will love and protect you, but he's not the type to derive much pleasure from an evening with other couples.

He's sporty and likes the outdoor life. Although he can go to extremes and debauch himself, he usually makes up for it by keeping fit through participation in one sport or another.

He needs a lot of looking after, even mothering. Chances are he was not very close to his family. You might feel he is looking for a mother substitute. Is that a role you would be happy playing? It seems doubtful.

He needs a strong woman behind him. You are strong, but perhaps yours is a different kind of strength than what he requires.

Although he likes his freedom, he is not always fair where the gentle sex is concerned. He can be unreasonably demanding. You will become annoyed by his attitude that he always knows what's best for you.

This could be a successful union, provided you go along with his ideas about the world and how it should be changed. He will never do anything, of course, but he *is* a good talker. If you accept his statements for their entertainment value, all will be well.

A lot will depend on how much you admire him. Life won't be dull when he's around, that's for sure. The trouble is he may not be around when you need him most.

Take your time in courtship. It could be disastrous if you rush into marriage before getting to know him really well.

When kids come along, you could see amazing changes take place. Mr. Sagittarius loves his offspring. He might channel all his enthusiasm for life into helping them along.

PISCES WOMAN—CAPRICORN MAN

A Capricorn-Pisces linkup is a union of two pretty powerful personalities. If you can accept each other for exactly what you are, you'll find your relationship is a balanced one. To be frank, though, you are in many ways opposite types.

To begin with, you approach life from a different premise. Your approach is intuitive; his is logical. You will have a lot of fun arguing various philosophical points. But you must ask yourself the question, can two people who differ so greatly make a lifelong partnership work?

He won't be in a hurry to get married. He is a cautious person. The Goat is an observer of life. He tries to learn from other people's experiences. Since he has seen so many marriages disintegrate, he is extremely cautious about taking the plunge himself. This is another area where you differ. Your attitude is that one has to experience everything first-hand. You may get the idea he is frightened to live his life to the full.

He will also have a preconceived idea of what his future wife should be like and a mental picture of the perfect marriage. Reality is never like our dreams; you should know—you live in the world of imagination quite a lot of the time yourself. He would certainly have to make some changes in his life-style for this union to endure.

Mr. Capricorn can't stand scenes. He may get embarrassed when you speak your mind. He is often more interested in making a good impression than in seeking the truth.

Perhaps one of the main problems you will have to solve derives from your very different attitude toward people. Basically, he wants to be liked. He would never dream of saying anything that would hurt or upset another person. He believes in charming manners and in conformity. He will keep his opinions to himself in order to avoid a blazing row. You are the opposite. You like to speak your mind and are not interested in nice manners and polite handshakes. You want to know where people are at and your perception usually tells you pretty quickly.

On the credit side, he is a good provider. He will give you a beautiful home. He will pamper you. He can be tight with money, but not when it comes to home furnishing and decoration. He will consider such things an investment. You aren't likely to catch him in expensive restaurants or fancy nightclubs, though. He would consider such outings a waste of money.

He's an industrious worker. His job is usually very important to him. He is prepared to work at it all hours if he deems it necessary. He's not a great believer in natural talent. He thinks you have to work hard and acqurie knowledge to get on in this world.

A Capricorn man often marries rather late in life. He's a fussy bachelor and can get very set in his ways. He's a creature of habit.

Together, though, you could go far. If your relationship is a business one as well as marital, you'll find it easier. Combine his determination to get to the top with your gentleness and deep understanding, and you have a first-rate team.

He's likely to want a small family. You might find very young children a source of irritation to him.

PISCES WOMAN—AQUARIUS MAN

You will probably desire this man right from the start. People find it difficult to get to know you; this time the shoe will be on the other foot.

It might take him forever to realize you are attracted to him. As a rule, he doesn't enter into relationships with love on his mind. He is an outward-looking person. He will be attracted to you on an intellectual level first.

He has lots of friends but very few close ones. He spreads himself about. He is giving.

You will find him unselfish. He would take in every stray dog and cat in the neighborhood if he could possibly house them. You are a patient woman, but this is the one man who could drive you into a jealous rage.

He is very caught up in the future. He's always thinking about tomorrow's world. He's a bit of an idealist. You know what people *really* are; he sees the best in them and tends to overlook the negative points.

It is not an easy matter to keep the passion burning with this man. He has so many different interests. You really need a man who is willing to center his life around you. Would you be be happy when you see Mr. Aquarius getting involved in so many other causes?

Another drawback is that he won't make the major decisions when you want him to. When you are crying out for him to take control and guide your life together, he's likely to tell you that you are an individual and he does not intend to dictate to you.

You will click in bed. On an erotic plane, there should be no problems. It will be when you are in each other's arms at night that you'll know you are the number-one person in his life. He may not talk much about romance, but you'll find him a passionate lover. Perhaps he will come to understand you better through your lovemaking. He may eventually realize just how much you need him.

The sort of job he chooses is likely to be one of public service. He is too idealistic to settle for working just to make money. He'd probably be prepared to settle for a lower salary if he felt he was doing something worthwhile. This is one thing you are both likely to agree upon.

He finds it hard to reveal his true feelings. You will have to be patient with him. Show him you love him. Tell him to put down his placard and stop shouting slogans. Get him to think for himself and to stop identifying with other people.

He is trustworthy. He will always keep his word. He doesn't switch and change like the other air Signs, Libra and Gemini.

He won't find it easy to cope with your moods. Uusally he will say the wrong thing, telling you to snap out of it and think of people who are not as well off as you are.

Perhaps you can make him into more of a home-loving bird. He has little interest in possessions. You will have to make it clear from the start exactly what you want out of life and how you need to be treated. He can be so preoccupied that he won't notice what is written all over your face.

Try to get as many mutual interests going as possible. Make sure you share the same friends and the same hobbies. Don't allow him to cut his life up into various little compartments.

PISCES WOMAN—PISCES MAN

On face value, this coming together with your own Sign would appear to be doomed from the word go. How can two dreamers, to romantics, two people who have such difficulty in facing reality, possibly make out in this rough-and-tumble world. Well, very nicely thank you. You will confound the critics and cope.

Your chums may warn you off from the start. Friends of yours who take an interest in the stars may say you both need a stronger character to steer you. But you are always coming up with surprises, so others should not try to put you in a pigeonhole.

Of course, you will have a great deal in common. You will understand the moods of this man and be able to identify with them. You will know instinctively when he wants to talk his problems out and when he wants time to meditate alone.

He's got loads of energy. He is also ambitious. Very often people born under the Sign of the two Fishes do artistic work. He doesn't take too well to the humdrum nine-to-five existence that so many come to accept as their lot.

He's got a quick mind and a ready wit. He is also a kind man, but one who is quick to perceive the strengths and weaknesses of others. He makes a good employer because he knows how to get the very best from people without strong-arm tactics.

This will not be a limited liaison. A Pisces-Pisces linkup will embrace all facets of a man-woman relationship. You will find you are attracted to him intellectually as well as physically. Growing older will mean growing fonder. You will always want to do your best for him; he will try never to let you down.

A stranger type of woman might be very bad for him. He's a sensitive human being and will do anything to avoid a violent confrontation. A weaker woman would give him no incentive to work or aim for anything in life.

You are both terrible worriers. He seems to *have* to have a problem. If he has no cause for anxiety, he will worry about why he has nothing to worry about.

He is a romantic, but not in a mushy way. He will do his level best to keep the love you share alive. He's full of little surprises. Special days like birthdays and wedding anniversaries will not be forgotten. They will probably mean as much to him as they do to you.

There could be financial problems in this liaison because he is not that good at handling money. The female side of this Sign is usually better at looking after financial matters.

Fortunately, he is not petty, for you could not bear to live with a small-minded person. Beware you don't escape at the same time to that fantasy world you both tend to take refuge in. Be sure one of you keeps your feet on the ground at all times.

You will understand that he doesn't like to be questioned. When he decides on a certain course of action, accept his word.

Occasionally you will get each other down. You are both emotional people. Sometimes he will experience your dependence on him as a strain. Just give him all the love you've got and he will realize you are someone worth working for.

You are both in love with the idea of love. Never, never let romance go out of your life.

PISCES MAN—ARIES WOMAN

This is an interesting combination because you are different types in so many ways. But the advantages could well outweigh the disadvantages.

You have here a woman who is quite a powerhouse. She could be the driving force in your life. An Aries woman is prepared to take risks you would never dream of. At times, you don't assert yourself when you should. The lady Ram will make sure you stand up for your rights.

Perhaps she is not quite as feminine as you like your women to be. Mind you, she is far more sensitive than most people give her credit for. You will be perceptive enough to realize that a great deal of her brashness is an attempt to hide her true feelings from others.

She is very ambitious and will want you to get on in the world. If you do decide to take her for a wife, she will be prepared to make any sacrifice asked of her if it helps you to get to the top.

Miss Aries does not like to be bossed around. A man who tries to take her over body and soul will not last very long. She has a quick temper. Her emotions are easily aroused.

You will be so good for her in many ways. She will find you something of a puzzle. You will be able to show her a new way of experiencing life. You will also be able to awaken spiritual understanding in her.

In marriage, she might well be under the impression that she is making all the important decisions, whereas, in fact, you will be guiding the union along without any fuss or bother.

You both find it difficult to stay put. It is also true that although you both enjoy traveling, you like to have a base to operate from.

This little lady likes her home comforts and gets a great deal of enjoyment from the domestic scene. Motherhood also appeals to her. An Aries woman needs to have children at some point in her life because of her deep-rooted desire to provide and protect.

Don't try to fight her. Go along with her ideas and suggestions. If she feels someone is trying to dominate her, she'll meet him head on. You are a man who can sit easy on life. You will soon find she is *asking* for your opinions!

At times, you may find the pace she sets makes you neurotic. She is a high-strung girl with a lot of energy, the self-starting kind. It will amaze you how much activity she can cram into one day.

When you first meet her, you might be rather taken aback by her aggression. If you attract her, she'll come on strong. In fact, she might be the one who asks *you* out.

Never point out when she's in the wrong. The Ram can't stand an I-told-you-so attitude.

The physical side of your relationship is likely to be exciting. You will be the sort of man to satisfy her. She likes a gentle but virile lover.

She will want to share in every department of your life. She will encourage you to bring your friends home. She will be willing to write business letters for you and to support you in any way she can.

An Aries woman likes to experience everything life has to offer. She is likely to have had quite a few boyfriends before deciding to settle down. She is a brave woman and never shrinks from a challenge. She would rather try and fail than not try at all.

Miss Aries is sympathetic and understanding. You will feel you can share your innermost secrets and doubts with her.

PISCES MAN—TAURUS WOMAN

You should hit it off from the start with steady, reliable, down-to-earth Miss Taurus because she will have so many of the qualities you have been searching for in a woman. She is sensible as well as passionate. Romance is very important to her. She will admire you for your sensitivity and understanding.

She is a person who can't stand to be bossed. If a man tries to dominate this girl, he will never win her.

Venus-ruled Miss Taurus is a great homemaker. She loves the domestic scene. She will be quite happy to take care of family life while you go out to earn the money. She will be a good confidence booster, as well. When you get into a self-doubting mood, she will know instinctively how to get you thinking positively again.

She can be a little dogmatic and you might find she sometimes lacks imagination. She will find it difficult to go along with your whimsical plans for the future. But a Taurus lady can give you the firmness you need. She can be the anchor that keeps you secure when the sea of life tosses you about.

You might get the wrong impression when you first meet her, thinking her a selfish woman who cares only about herself. This is not true. You will be surprised at many of the good deeds she has done for others (she's not the type to brag about these things).

You will have to make sure this becomes a power-sharing relationship, because in marriage, this woman can dominate if she's allowed to. She will even begin to tell you how to run your business if you let her. You must make it clear from the start that there are certain areas of your life where you have to be in total command. When you put it this way, she'll understand you and respect your strength.

Miss Taurus is full of optimism. She reaches important decisions in a logical way. She also has very firm likes and dislikes. She is conservative by nature and resents change.

She won't decide anything in a hurry. She is unlikely to agree to marriage after a whirlwind courtship. Even if she is smitten by love at first sight, she'll take her time before agreeing to walk down the aisle with you.

This woman takes people for what they are. Though she is not impressed by wealth and position, she usually moves in these circles.

Possessions are quite important to her. She loves pretty things. She's a hoarder who finds it difficult to throw anything away, whether it's an outdated dress or the teddy bear she's cuddled since she was three months old.

With Venus ruling her, you would expect her lovemaking to be passionate; you won't have any complaints in this area of your life.

She is the type of woman who is prepared to work hard to make her marriage a success. She doesn't like to fail at anything.

It is likely your Taurus woman will remain loyal to you through good times as well as bad. If the going gets tough, she will be prepared to go out and get a job to bring more money into the family treasury.

She is a patient and understanding mother. She's not as easygoing as you are with kids, but she'll probably be better for them in a way because she wants the very best for her children. She'll be quite tolerant, though, of the way you spoil them.

PISCES MAN—GEMINI WOMAN

You two would undoubtedly have a lot of fun together, but whether you would be happy married to each other is questionable. You appear to be two rather unstable characters; each of you needs a steadying hand that probably neither of you will be able to provide. A whirlwind affair would definitely be an experience neither of you would forget in a hurry.

A woman born under the Sign of the Twins has as much difficulty as you in making up her mind. If you suggest marriage, she might say "yes" not only because she loves you but because you asked her!

She wants to experience everything in life. Her willingness to try anything once can lead her into some rather strange situations. She tends to live for the moment. This is all very well to a point, but tomorrow can't always be relied upon to take care of itself without a little help from the rest of us mortals.

Gemini girls can't help flirting because they love to be admired and flattered. You might get hurt by such carryings on. You like to know where you stand with a woman. After all, it's hard enough for you to cope with your own sudden changes of mood let alone hers!

Mercury-ruled Gemini has itchy feet. It is difficult for her to stay in one place for very long. she always thinks the grass is greener on the other side of the fence.

You would not be able to boss this woman around even if you wanted to. She can't stand being told what to do. She will rebel against anyone or anything that tries to exert authority over her. She is a lover of freedom, though she may not always know what to do with it.

She can be irresponsible and is easily carried away by the enthusiasm of others.

In love, she blows hot and cold. One moment, she will be the sexiest woman you have ever come across. The next, she'll seem colder than the ice cream in the freezer.

Friends are very important to people born under this Sign. She won't be prepared to forget her old chums after marriage. She'll want to keep up with people she has known all her life. Her relatives will also be in the picture. It is unlikely she will accept the role of the little woman who remains forever in the background.

You would be wise to allow her to keep her job after marriage. So long as she feels there are no restrictions being placed on her, she'll always run back to you. You don't need to play games with a Gemini; but it is important that you never let her take you for granted. Since you are a mysterious sort of man, just by being your natural self, you will keep her guessing.

She is usually quite artistic. You will probably discover she has a talent for painting or writing. She certainly has a vivid imagination.

Don't try to change her. She needs gentleness and understanding. This girl is a romantic at heart, but don't keep asking her if she loves you. She doesn't like weakness in a man. Even though she can't stand to be dominated, she wants to think you are in control of your life together.

It might be a good idea to wait a while before you start a family. The responsibility of parenthood is not something to be taken lightly in a Pisces-Gemini union.

PISCES MAN—CANCER WOMAN

There is no doubt about it—you'll probably have more in common with Miss Cancer than with any other Sign in the Zodiac. You will certainly understand each other's moods and pain.

She is not an easy woman to get to know.

Many people are fooled by their first impression of her. She can seem so outward-going and confident. Less perceptive people than you might think she is well organized and doesn't have a care in the world. But she can drive many guys crazy. After falling madly in love with her, they suddenly discover just what they've gotten involved with. It's lovely, but it's not easy.

She's a deep person. You are both water Signs, remember, and she is ruled by the changeable Moon.

You will have to sort out who is going to be the leader. It had better be you. If you wish to keep this woman, you're going to have to adopt a more aggressive role than you usually like to play. She will test you. Basically, she wants to be dominated, but she will fight you every step of the way to see if you're capable of doing it.

You will need a good deal of patience to deal with her moods. You can talk and talk her problems over with her, but it is likely to have very little effect.

Like the Crab, Miss Cancer needs a secure and watertight home to which she can withdraw when the outside world gets too much for her. She can't stand to be on her own for very long. She needs someone she feels she can turn to when she gets down in the dumps.

You will have many interests in common. It's likely you will enjoy the same sort of friends. You both need your quiet moments. There will be many evenings when you will be contented to stay at home and enjoy each other's company. Then, suddenly, you will decide you are getting in a rut and want to hit the town. Let's hope you and your Cancer mate are well enough attuned to be overtaken by this urge at the same time. You probably will, because when a man is involved with a Moon maiden, he can't help but be influenced by her moods.

You are quite a faithful type of guy, which is a good thing because a Cancer woman feels shattered if she is betrayed by her man. She is a trusting soul. If you tell her you love her, she will believe it.

You're both romantic types. Never allow the romance to go out of your relationship. Remember dates like her birthday.

She doesn't have a great sense of humor about herself. Be very careful, too, of making jokes about her family.

She has an inquiring mind. She admires people with special talents. She wants to find out as much as she can about life. She will want you to be her teacher as well as her lover.

Spoil her with presents. She loves surprises. She will never take you for granted.

Miss Cancer is a good cook, as a rule. She will know how to run things at home. She is prepared to make almost any sacrifice for the man she loves. She will give up her career if she feels it will make you happy.

Your friends and business associates will love her. She has no problems in mixing with people from all walks of life.

As a mother, she is second to none. She has lots of love and understanding for her children.

PISCES MAN—LEO WOMAN

These two Signs are often attracted to each other. You will find Miss Leo is the sort of woman who could make your dreams come true. Many aspects of her character will complement many aspects of yours.

In many ways, she is your opposite. She is someone you'll really want to prove yourself to. She has high ideals. You will find her passionate, competitive and aggressive.

Success is important to her. She believes in the old adage that if a job is worth doing, it's worth doing well.

You will have to get used to the idea that she likes to be admired by other men. If she is yours, you will understand her well enough to realize it's not serious. In fact, you may feel flattered at the attention lavished on her by members of your own sex. Other guys will certainly be envious if you have a Leo wife.

She is the no-nonsense type. She will want you to be a man and stand on your own two feet. Strong as she is, she'll not allow any guy to hide behind her petticoats.

Your approach to life is quite different from hers. She is a logical person. You are a more intuitive one.

You will both have to be prepared to give a little ground. Since you are such opposites types, it would not do at all if either of you were to ride roughshod over the wishes of the other.

A Leo woman is likely to be the leader of her pack. She doesn't like to play second fiddle to anyone, male or female.

She will expect you to stretch yourself to the very limits of your talent. She won't be happy with a man who is prepared to sit back and let the world pass him by. This is not because she is ambitious or eager to be terribly rich, but because she knows you won't be happy unless you are fulfilling yourself.

You may find other girls making catty remarks about your Leo woman—out of jealousy. She doesn't need to become a militant women's libber to show her freedom. She is quite capable of looking after herself without resorting to a group to back her up.

You could find yourself digging pretty deep into your pocket when you are wooing this woman because she has expensive tastes. You will probably find yourself eating in chic restaurants and sitting in the best seats at the theater.

She also likes to look her best at all times, so providing her with a wardrobe can be an expensive business. It shouldn't bother you, though, because you'll want your little lady to look her best.

In bed, she has a fiery passion. As her lover, she will keep you on your toes.

You are an unselfish man, and this is a good thing because a Leo can't stand to be neglected. For all her strength of character, she needs to feel wanted and loved. You are likely to put her wishes and desires before your own, and this expansive attitude will not pass unnoticed.

She does not play about with her man's emotions. She has integrity.

If you have an important business deal to clinch, take your Leo friend along. She has a way of talking to men that relaxes them and puts them in a good mood. She can make anyone she converses with feel important.

You will both want a family, but it's unlikely you'll want a large one.

PISCES MAN—VIRGO WOMAN

Are you the type of Pisces male who wants a woman who'll always be there when you need her? Someone dependable whose moods don't fluctuate like your own? Then Miss Virgo may be the woman you should share your life with.

Virgo people are hard-working and diligent. This woman may fall for you against her better judgment. Certainly she will find you to be a bit on the mysterious side.

Romance is not something she gets caught up in lightly. It is highly unusual for a Virgo woman to get deeply involved with a great number of men during her life. She is selective and particular. She could be just the woman to help you retain the balance you need in life.

It might take you quite a while to get to know her well. She will want to understand what makes you tick before she contemplates going to bed with you.

You will be surprised at her fantastic memory for faces and places. If you do decide to make a life together, she'll come up with little memories about your courting days that you had long forgotten. Her mind is something of a filing cabinet. People born under this Sign make very good secretaries.

You had better keep on your toes with her. If you are late from the office a few nights running, you'll need to have your facts right.

Be sure your appearance is always neat and immaculate. A Virgo girl will take it as a personal insult if you don't dress up when you take her out on the town.

Don't expect her to be madly passionate. She can be romantic and very affectionate, but you must not rush her. This woman often needs a considerable amount of petting to get in the mood for making love.

Another thing: you must watch that you don't embarrass her in public. She can't bear scenes in front of friends. She might turn her cheek to you if you try to kiss her good night at the bus stop. She will consider your love a very private thing.

You will have to learn to be a bit tidier around the house because this woman gets irritated by any kind of mess. Her constant tidying up can get on some people's nerves.

She is excellent with finances and very good at sticking to a budget. She is fairly security conscious. She will want to put as much aside as she can for that proverbial rainy day. There is a tendency here to worry unnecessarily. She can magnify minor pinpricks out of all proportion. You have a keen wit. Use it to help your Virgo woman to stop taking herself so seriously.

She prefers quiet evenings with one or two friends to lavish parties. She loves good conversation. She also gets great pleasure from debating subjects with people whose opinions differ greatly from her own. She has a very agile mind. Don't forget that Mercury is her ruler.

The past is important to her. She is quite sentimental. She doesn't welcome change. She prefers the old ways and the old traditions.

As your wife, she will be faithful. If this union is to work, you must not become involved with another woman, even on a casual basis. People born under this earth Sign find it difficult to forgive even one mistake.

Don't let her become too identified with the domestic scene. Be sure you get her to go to office parties or to visit friends on weekends.

PISCES MAN—LIBRA WOMAN

You make a fine duo. Miss Libra is the sort of woman you'll strike it lucky with on first meeting because you will have so much in common. Your love for each other will be something really special. It will endure after the flames of passion become fitful.

She is a lively girl. She is also unselfish. She will therefore want the very best for you. She will make sure nothing hinders you in achieving your objectives in life.

You love feminine women; you will have no complaints with a girl whose ruler is Venus. Like you, she is a romantic. She won't settle for a mundane union.

She will work hard to make sure your marriage endures, but there will be certain dangers you should be aware of. This girl needs a strong partner, a person who can make the big decisions when necessary. Sometimes she has considerable difficulty making up her mind on a definite course of action. Very often she finds two possibilities equally appealing. You, too, can be a ditherer. You will have to give the lead and direct the course of your life together.

Libra loves to be surrounded by beautiful people and objects. A woman born under this Sign is usually attracted to the sensitive man.

She is interested in everything and everyone. She is perceptive and quick to sum up others' stengths and weaknesses.

Most of the time she is extremely good at money management. She will budget carefully. She knows a bargain when she sees one. Occasionally, however, her excellent judgment will fly out the window and she'll go on a spending spree. Something could catch her eye—usually something pretty to wear. Once she has started spending, she doesn't know when to stop. In this sort of mood, she could dent your reserves.

Men will find her attractive, and a lot of them will fall for her. You are not the jealous type, but even you are likely to get worried when you see how quickly she gathers male admirers around her.

Miss Libra is a sensible woman. She will stop you from going off into your own little world without ever killing your dreams. She is sensitive to the feelings of others. She would never do anything to hurt you intentionally.

If you do decide to get spliced, you'll probably think you did all the chasing and that it was your idea to settle down together. On reflection, however, you may discover it was the other way around. Libra women usually know the man they want to marry as soon as they set eyes on him.

She will want to keep up with her outside interests after marriage. But don't worry; she would never allow her work to interfere with your life together.

Making love to a Libra woman is never likely to lose its excitement. You will know instinctively how to satisfy each other.

A sense of justice and fair play is very pronounced here. You will find she is always on the side of the underdog and the person who has gotten a bad deal.

You will have no complaint about her when it comes to looking after domestic matters. She will love preparing special surprises for you in the kitchen. She's an excellent cook.

This woman is very comfortable with children. She will probably want several of them.

PISCES MAN— SCORPIO WOMAN

This will be an all-or-nothing relationship. You will either get caught up immediately in the passion of this woman, or will drop her completely after a couple of meetings.

She is direct to the point of hurting. She speaks her mind and never pulls her punches. You might find she is a bit too much to handle. She will certainly find you a mystery.

You are without doubt the two most romantic people in the Zodiac. The only difference is that Scorpio can get disillusioned if badly hurt or let down. Surprisingly, you are better equipped to take bad love affairs without damage to your attitude toward love.

There are very few men who at one time or another have not been physically drawn to the Scorpio woman. She is very sexy. She can also be moody. She doesn't go overboard for sentimental love. She prefers a man who plays it completely straight with her.

She is the jealous type. If you are going steady together, don't flirt with other women. She would give you a black eye and think nothing of scratching out the other girl's.

She will always be honest with you. When she thinks you have achieved something really worthwhile, she'll praise you to the skies. Mind you, she can be extremely critical when she doesn't approve. Her bluntness could be rather wounding to a sensitive creature like you.

You will need to be exceedingly patient with this woman. She can get into terrible moods and fits of depression. Be careful about criticizing her. She can't stand to have her mistakes pointed out; she is usually well aware of them anyway.

Sex is a driving force in her life. It is important to her to have a good physical relationship with a man. If her love life is going well, everything else usually falls into place.

Never show her up in front of other people.

She can't stand to have scenes in public. You both have a good imagination and will probably find you share the same sense of humor.

You are likely to have many mutual interests. Both of you are fascinated by the mysterious and the unknown. You are both water Signs, and this does make you rather introspective and at times unwilling to reveal your true feelings.

You had better be the faithful type of Pisces male, because if you two-time this woman, it's unlikely she will forgive you and welcome you back with open arms. Once her trust is betrayed, she'll probably never believe in you totally again.

Life with this woman will have its ups and downs, but it will never be dull. She can be rather self-centered. You will discover she is well able to take care of her own interests.

You are unlikely to tire of her in the bedroom. She knows how to win and keep a man.

A Scorpio woman will want to make a comfortable home for herself. She won't wish to stay in all the time, but she does like to have somewhere secure to retreat to when she periodically shuts herself off from the outside world.

You both enjoy a good party and meeting new and interesting people. But you'll be happiest having romantic evenings alone together.

PISCES MAN— SAGITTARIUS WOMAN

Miss Sagittarius is likely to find a man like you extremely attractive. For one thing, you won't put a lot of pressure on her. She can't stand to be bossed around or told what to do. She has a mind of her own. She has to make her own decisions, even if this means making a lot of mistakes. She is the sort of woman you have to accept for what she is. Don't try to change her; it simply isn't possible.

She will be attracted by your gentleness and understanding. She will also appreciate your quick mind and your wit. She is an optimistic person and can't bear being too long in the company of people who have a depressing or negative effect on her.

If you wish to make this liaison work, you'll have to take responsibility for the finances, as well as for running the household and arranging vacations and the like. Miss Sagittarius is not a good organizer. She learns best by example—let's call it the gentle art of persuasion, at which you are a past master.

It's amazing that a woman so sensitive to criticism can be so blunt with others. Some people may call the remarks she comes out with downright cruel. She will have you wriggling with embarrassment when she tells the couple you like so much exactly what is wrong with their marriage. She doesn't mean to be hurtful. It's simply the most natural thing for her to speak her mind.

Miss Sagittarius likes to keep on the move. She finds it hard to settle down and accept the routine of domestic life.

You are a patient person. In fact, patience is one of your strong points. You are going to need it when you get involved with a Jupiter-ruled girl. She's a butterfingers, very clumsy, always breaking things. That lovely tea set handed down from Grandmother won't last very long when she starts doing the washing up.

This woman is extremely loyal. If you win her, she is likely to stick by you through thick and thin. Although she likes her comforts, love is far more important to her than these or money. She is prepared to make all sorts of sacrifices for people she cares about. She will put her loved ones before herself every time.

She does have a tendency to rush through life. She finds it difficult to relax and settle. She is nervous and rather worried about what other people think of her. She wishes to please, to make a good impression and to be liked.

This woman will always make the best of whatever situation she finds herself in. She is no moaner. Whether you end up in a one-room apartment or a palace, she'll do all in her power to make it a good home.

She's a one-man woman. She won't go off and have an affair unless you two-time her. If that happens, she might well take up with another guy just to get even.

Miss Sagittarius usually keeps her emotions well under control, but if she does lose her temper, brother, watch out! Don't forget this woman was born under a fire Sign; she can really let rip when aroused.

Love between Pisces and Sagittarius is likely to grow slowly. But after a few years together, you'll wonder how you ever lived without her.

Your love life should not give you any cause for complaint. It will be up to you to make sure that romance never dies.

PISCES MAN— CAPRICORN WOMAN

This will be a powerful combination. Here is a woman who usually knows what she wants out of life. You are a man who usually gets what your heart desires, once you've worked out exactly what that is. If you are both on the right wavelength, there should be no stopping you.

Miss Capricorn can be reserved. Many people find her difficult to get to know, but you should not. She will warm to your gentle personality. She loves sensitive people. She will also be aware that you care very much about other people's feelings.

Some say this woman is frigid. Not so. The fact is she is shy and not always willing to reveal her true feelings for fear of being hurt. Many guys don't know how to treat her. She doesn't go for the he-man, physical approach. She's very sexy, sure. But she'll want to know what is going on in your mind before she shows any interest in taking the relationship further.

You are both home lovers. You will find you have much in common. A Capricorn girl is both a good talker and a good listener. She will understand when you wish to pour out your heart, and she will also come up with good, unprejudiced advice. She is able to look beyond her own feelings and attitudes and see what would be best for her man.

She will admire the fact that you are ambitious. She will help you to channel that ambition positively.

Miss Capricorn is subject to unaccountable changes of mind. You will be able to understand this because, as a Pisces, you often appear to act totally out of character to people who think they know you well.

Success is important to her. She will want you to get on in the world. Although she appreciates the value of money, this will not be her motivating force in life.

She has a great need to be in the swim of things. She loves meeting interesting people. She makes a good hostess. You will enjoy bringing your friends and business associates home to meet her.

If you do decide to get married, your Capricorn woman will do all in her power to ensure that the union is successful. She may be tempted, but she'll try hard to be faithful as long as she knows you are playing it straight with her.

She needs to be taken care of. A Capricorn woman wants a man who can look after her. She will give you everything she has to offer in return. But she'll want you to be the provider and to make the important decisions. You may feel a little frightened at taking on so much responsibility for another human being. This is certainly the type of liaison you should enter into with much care.

Don't string her along. The lady Goat only wants to know about true love. Don't neglect her, either. She won't be happy if you leave her at home to enjoy weekend outings with the boys.

She likes to keep on the go. She has an inquiring mind and is always interested in learning a new art or craft.

You find it easy to get along with all sorts of people. This will be an advantage with your Capricorn mate. It will be important to her that you like her friends because she is a very loyal person and will wish to retain them after marriage.

Let's also hope you get on well with Mom and Dad. She is usually close to her family and has a great respect for tradition and the law.

PISCES MAN—AQUARIUS WOMAN

Miss Aquarius is the sort of woman you will understand. You are one of the lucky ones because few people do comprehend her. She is sympathetic and humane. She is out to change the world and make it a better place for all its inhabitants. Many label her a muddleheaded idealist. Her ideas are certainly progressive.

This will be a complicated relationship because you are both a bit scatterbrained in your own style. She will have some difficulty understanding your dreaminess. You are a loving person. You are deeply interested in your relationships with family and close friends. This girl is deeply interested in social relationships and in changing the system.

Miss Aquarius has little regard for rules and regulations. She might not have fully worked out what she wishes to replace the present system with, but she definitely wants to give it a good shakeup while she's deciding.

She has an independent nature. She likes to stand on her own two feet and fight her own battles. She may also try to organize you.

It would be pointless to think in terms of a permanent relationship if you are drawn together solely by physical attraction. To have a chance of a happy life together, you would have to be on the same mental plane.

Aquarius is always striving after perfection. She has high ideals and would never settle for second best.

There will never be a dull moment in your life when you're dating the Water Bearer. No matter how attracted you are to her, it would be advisable to make this a long courtship. Get to know her really well before you contemplate getting married.

There is certainly magic in the air when this

woman is about. Aquarius seems to have some sort of magnetic influence on nearly every Sign of the Zodiac, and Pisces is no exception.

She won't be willing to stay at home and deal with the household drudgeries while you go out to do the breadwinning. She is an independent woman. She feels she has more to offer the world than scrubbing the floors and washing some guy's underwear.

You could call her an eccentric in some ways. One of the first things you will notice is her far-out clothes. She dresses to please herself not to suit the occasion.

She is not the jealous type. She would never question you if you were late from the office. Do it two or three nights running, and she may want to know what's happening out of interest. She's a very curious person.

Miss Aquarius is likely to get quite a few proposals of marriage. Men are often attracted to her against their better judgment.

Aquarius is the child of the future. This woman will work tirelessly for charity or for a political party if she thinks this is the way to improve social conditions. It's strange, but a lot of what she works so hard to achieve comes about years later. You could say she is a woman who is ahead of her time.

She is an adventurer. She wants to know all about life.

You will only be successful if you don't try to force your opinions on each other. Children could be very important in this union; they may help you to understand each other better.

PISCES MAN—PISCES WOMAN

This should be a remarkable pairing. When Pisces man and Pisces woman get together, it could be the biggest romantic linkup since Romeo and Juliet. It is rare for the woman and man born under the same Sign to be so suited. A woman ruled by Jupiter and Neptune will be determined to make a success of anything she takes on.

She is intuitive, often psychic. You will be quite amazed at how she can read your mind. Sometimes she will surprise you by giving voice to what you were thinking.

Never underestimate her. Certainly she is dreamy and fey, but she knows what is going on around her. She has an uncanny way of summing up people very quickly.

You, being born under the same Sign, will be in tune with her sudden mood changes. She needs to have a man around who will protect her, someone she can look up to. You will find she draws out the best in you.

She can get neurotic because her vivid imagination builds up insignificant little incidents into matters of great importance.

Her emotional requirements are great. She can't live on one level for very long. Occasionally she will rush into an early marriage; this often works out disastrously. In her search for someone to look after her and love her, she doesn't always exercise discretion.

Pisces, as you well know, is the Sign of whose symbol is two Fishes swimming in opposite directions. Your woman is carried along by the ebb and flow of the river of life. Her moods tend to come in waves rather than spasms.

Occasionally she will infuriate you. Her sudden changes of mind can be impossible to keep up with. You will have to guard against her having a negative effect on you.

With a Pisces woman on your arm, you will be envied by many men. She will flirt, but not to make you jealous; just sisterly and sweet.

She's the type of woman you will want to work hard for because you will realize you have something very precious to look after.

You will have a head start over your competitors. Guys born under other Signs will find her hard to fathom. You will see much of yourself reflected in the way she carries on.

One danger is that the two of you tend to confuse your dreams with reality. The dividing line between the two is very thin with a couple who can so easily believe in myths and get swept along by the music of words.

You will need to get her to accept more responsibility for herself and her own actions. She does have a habit of blaming others for her own shortcomings.

Once she has decided you are the man for her, she won't seriously look at another man. A Pisces woman always tries hard to live up to what she believes in. She would not feel happy being involved with two men at the same time.

You will never get bored in her company. This is one person you'll not tire of easily.

She will love and respect you. She will be grateful to you for not trying to tie her down or cross-examine her.

You will both want to have at least a couple of kids. It will be up to you to see that they receive sufficient discipline. With you two old softies as Mom and Dad, they'll get more than their share of love. But don't forget it is possible to be cruel by being excessively indulgent.

PISCES' HEALTH

You Pisces men and women have an uncanny ability to control your health mentally. So long as your attitude remains positive, you should rarely be ill. If you do pick up an infection, then, you throw it off quickly. The trouble is you frequently suffer from bouts of depression and these lower your will to resist and leave you very vulnerable to any disease that's going around.

Generally, your constitution is stronger than it appears. When in one of your emotional "highs," you have great powers of endurance. It's as though you can rise, body and soul, to any occasion when you feel destiny is involved (not an unfamiliar feeling for you). But in the normal course of events, your metabolism is weaker and less dynamic than that of most other Signs.

You run out of pep very quickly. It is often difficult for your type to get going in the mornings. The position of Mars in the horoscope will give a good indication of the amount of vitality available to you.

Pisces are the most suggestible people in the Zodiac. When you are sick, it is very important that you have a doctor with an optimistic and encouraging manner. If you are assured you are making progress by someone in authority or one whose opinion you respect, you invariably show immediate improvement. This is something to bear in mind where Pisces children are concerned. Parents should remember they are easily convinced. The Fishes, both young and mature, are so impressionable they can even hypnotize themselves.

Pisces rules the feet. It is amazing how many people born under this Sign actually have some kind of foot trouble or lameness. You have to be careful of sitting around in damp shoes or socks because it is very easy for you to catch colds and chills through the feet. Pneumonia is not an uncommon complication. Pisces is closely associated with the lungs. Your physical resistance falls very quickly when you are exposed to wet or damp conditions. You should avoid living in low-lying localities.

You are apt to suffer from pains, swelling and rheumatism. Gout is a characteristic disease. Other common disorders are weak ankles, fallen arches, problems affecting the toes and especially bunions. The hip joints are also susceptible.

Frequently your eyes are weak. You may find it necessary to wear sunglasses even when there is no great degree of glare. It is advisable to have regular eye examinations.

Pisces people have to watch their diet. Your type tends to suffer from overindulgence in food or drink. You are not really gluttonous, but you do enjoy the good life and like to share everything with your friends, including some of their more immoderate appetites.

You are a bit inclined to overestimate your powers of resistance and endurance. You are apt to get carried away emotionally and drive your body to the breaking point, particularly where pleasure and excitement are concerned.

You are fond of all kinds of sensuous, mental and emotional stimulation. You get bored quickly when there's nothing to entertain you.

There is always a danger that Pisces individuals will become addicted to drink or drugs. And once you develop a habit, you find it exceedingly difficult to break it. Often you don't see any reason for making the effort to get back to normal. What *is* normal? you may ask. A typical Pisces attitude in these circumstances can be "I'm going to die anyway sooner or later, so why worry?" This is not as morbid as it sounds. You strange but profoundly perceptive individuals often have spiritual insights that remove fear of death.

You need to get outdoors as often as possible. Fresh air and plenty of exercise that doesn't tire you is essential for good health. You also require periods of quiet and seclusion.

One of your least understood needs is to have someone to whom you can confide your dreams and hopes. These well up in you day and night, and if not released verbally, can become congested, causing moodiness and excessive introspection. Talking is a simple therapy for Pisces' uptightness.

You must endeavor to control a tendency to worry too much. Emotional strain is very bad for your health. Concern for family and friends can lead to sleeplessness, loss of appetite and ennui.

PISCES AT WORK

No Sign works more conscientiously, imaginatively or with a greater sense of duty than Pisces—once you've found the right occupation. Finding it is not easy.

The young Pisces starting out to make a living often feels like a fish out of water. Why does he or she feel so unhappy in a job others seem to take in their stride? And especially after being assured "it's a first-class opportunity" or "it's a secure and interesting position."

You are indeed interested in security—but not at any price. You require interesting work—but your idea of "interesting" can be rather eccentric.

To be happy in your work, you should never have to contend with sordid conditions or harsh and aggressive associates. You should rely on first impressions rather than dismissing them. Your extreme sensitivity will let you know immediately when conditions or people are incompatible. Don't compromise. Don't imagine things will get better. Your natural enthusiasm and urge to look on the bright side can be painfully misleading.

You need work that makes full use of your creative ideas. You will shine in a job dealing with the public or one that requires you to be in constant contact with groups representing a variety of interests. Your soaring imagination can solve just about any problem as long as you recognize the need to keep at least one foot on the ground. Remember, though, your idealism can get out of hand. You often require the restraining influence of another liberal but more down-to-earth personality.

You should succeed as an author, dramatist, poet or advertising copy writer. You should also have a flair for design—fashion or industrial. You possess a fine appreciation of color, textures and structure. The appearance of different woods often fascinates Pisces people; they make gifted and painstaking restorers of furniture and antiques. You may also be interested in interior decoration, ceramics, tapestries and unusual lighting effects.

As an actor or actress, you would be in your element. Your extraordinary range of emotional response enables you to identify with any character. You project your feelings with subtlety and force; you don't so much sway an audience as penetrate people's hearts with a lasting, charismatic effect. You are likely to be long remembered or secretly idolized.

Once your interest is aroused, you have great determination. Otherwise you tend to switch your attention from one new idea to another. Scientific inquiry—provided it is along unusual, new or exciting lines—can offer great scope for your particular talents. Medical research, psychiatry and detective work may also satisfy your penchant for solving mysteries.

As a business person, Pisces possesses considerable flair. But it is essential for you concentrate your fertile imagination on definite goals. It is tempting for people born under your Sign to suddenly change direction on the strength of a new idea or whim and to neglect or forget about the more solid, bread-and-butter side of the business. You are the type who can be engaged in two businesses at the same time. But it requires strong personal discipline to avoid spreading yourself too thinly.

You are especially suited for all types of agency work and for meeting the fast-moving demands of the service industries. You are at your best when solving problems for others, but you do need to be protected from pressure and harsh demands. You will always do your best—no one need be concerned on that score—but you are not up to coping emotionally with failure that affects others. Basically, you are better as number two.

However, as a self-employed individual, you are usually very successful. When you are working for yourself, you can choose the way you wish to operate. You then look after yourself and accept the necessary responsibilities. You are extremely good at getting along with others and you make sure that what you promise you can perform. You should succeed in public relations, politics or any kind of social work.

You have a particular aptitude for helping those who are sick—mentally or physically. Your understanding, patience and placid manner make you an exceptionally fine nurse. You have great sympathy for anyone in distress; you are able to tune in intuitively to their problems and offer comforting advice. Your presence is often enough to make a sick person feel better.

The arts will probably strongly appeal to you. If you do not have artistic talent yourself, you could succeed as a publisher, connoisseur, critic, librarian, gallery manager or lecturer. You are a born teacher. You also make a wonder bartender because you listen with interest and attention to other people's stories. You can tell a good yarn yourself, and with the encouragement of an appreciative audience may go on for hours!

You are methodical and good at details, if the subject interests you. If it doesn't, your attention will wander. You prefer to follow standard procedures rather than interrupt the flow of work by pausing to make decisions.

You are naturally equipped to make a name for yourself in the restaurant and food business. Your approach to food is artistic. You would make a splendid creative chef. But you'd be unhappy cooking for pedestrian tastes or having to do menial tasks. As a restaurateur, your refined tastes in decor and presentation would attract an appreciative clientele. You should also do well in the food-merchandising industry because you have a sixth sense for assessing just what the public really wants.

As a boss, you are likely to be a bit too relaxed and lenient. You don't like throwing your weight around. You are prepared to leave others to their own devices. You'd rather accept someone's excuse than call him or her on the carpet. You are not an empire builder because you are not after power. You love glory, but not if it means wielding a big stick or competing on other people's terms. Frankly, the executive positions you would be happy in are pretty limited.

You are much more suited to lone enterprise or the leadership of a team where your authority derives from the others' respect for your abilities. In these circumstances, you could be a famous figure, the head of a charitable organization, the president, patron or secretary of a national trust or a top political appointee. You don't like the rough and tumble of elective politics, so in this field you're inclined to stay quietly in the background, ensuring that your qualifications are widely known but waiting for the party or the people to discover they need you (with a little help from your friends). You are always a guest, never a gate crasher.

Travel is one of your favorite pastimes. If you happen to be an employer, much of your time will be spent in other cities or traveling to other countries. Many Pisces are to be found working in the travel industry, though a lot of them don't enjoy flying. You like to keep those Pisces feet close to the ground (or near the water).

The Pisces boss, when provoked enough, can be extremely brusque or caustic. Your anger or displeasure is short-lived once your point has been made. You have a gift for choosing just the right words when issuing a rebuke. Afterward, you'll go out of your way to be kind. You're hard-headed and shrewd, but never petty.

As an employee, the Pisces person just needs to find the right niche. If you can't seem to discover it, you should think seriously about striking out on your own.

If you were born between February 19 and February 29, you are likely to be changeable and unpredictable. You will probably do best having an agency or service organization of your own. Your sensitivity and psychic faculties will be helpful, but be sure your ideas are realistic. If you can get yourself established before, say, the age of thirty, you could go on to make a fortune. You are fairly lucky and will probably amaze others by your ability to land on your feet.

You may suffer from bouts of negative thinking. Try to sit these periods out without hasty reactions. Your ideas are likely to be absolutely different when the positive side of your nature begins to reassert itself.

It is not wise for you to gamble. Be cautious about taking financial risks. You will have enough ups and downs without looking for them. You are inventive and artistic. Overall, you have the intelligence and organizational skill to build a good future for yourself.

If you were born between March 1 and March 10, you are likely to make a career out of writing, publishing, teaching or dealing in antiques. You could climb to the top of one of the branches of medicine. You have a strong desire to help humanity, and if you can express this in your career, you have a good chance of gaining public recognition.

You may find it difficult to stick to one job at the outset. Be sure you choose an occupation that appeals to you emotionally—not just mentally. You may have to overcome feelings of insecurity that have no basis in fact. Be sure you make the effort and don't sink back into apathy. Once you have overcome your unwarranted anxieties, you should never look back.

It is very important for you not to judge yourself too harshly.

If you were born between March 11 and March 20, you have more energy than most Pisces individuals. Once you decide on a career, you should have no trouble applying yourself and making the most of your opportunities. You are more constructive and positive than those born earlier in your Sign.

Try to avoid being unnecessarily secretive. You may have to watch your temper. You have an intensity of thought, feeling and expression that should be developed along positive lines. You probably possess a flair for psychiatry and all kinds of investigative work, including studies connected with the occult. You may be able to write or talk about these subjects professionally.

MONEY

You are an impulsive spender, yet basically conservative in your habits. You desire money mainly to preserve your independence. The personal power it brings is secondary. If you amass a fortune, you will use it to bring happiness to others rather than to lord it over them.

You are also apprehensive about insecurity in old age. You would hate to have to accept charity from anyone.

You like to save and usually manage to keep adding to your assets. But while any spare cash is around, there's a danger it will suddenly vaporize—on a spending spree, a good time or some relative who is temporarily down on his or her luck. Loved ones have a way of separating you from your money.

You enjoy comfort and easy living. You are often extravagant where family members are concerned. You are also liberal in entertaining friends and business associates. Frequently, you can't work out where your money has gone.

You need to stick to definite financial goals. Otherwise cash will literally run through your fingers. When you have a target to work toward, your excellent methodical qualities come to the fore. You have no trouble making personal sacrifices to reach your objectives. In fact, you enjoy this kind of challenge and treat it something like a game. The Pisces housewife who has something worthwhile to aim for is a little gem at running the family budget. But she is easily discouraged, especially when others in the household take advantage of her conscientious efforts.

You are likely to be lucky with money. You are not the type to be broke for long. Try to avoid straight-out gambling and remember to hedge your bets when investing.

BUSINESS PARTNERS

The following guide to business partners for all the Signs is based on the position of the Sun, the most powerful influence in the horoscope. Most people conform to the solar influence. However, variations do take place as a result of the position of the other planets at the time of birth.

For a closer examination of a business partner's character, it is advisable to study his or her personal horoscope, which is available for every Sign in *AstroAnalysis*. All you need to know is the person's date of birth. You can then Astro-Analyze your partner and determine his or her basic characteristics. Some Signs are naturally more and less compatible with others; you can get a better idea of how you'll hit it off with a partner by checking the Compatibility Guide in *AstroAnalysis*. (Grosset & Dunlap, 1976.)

YOUR ARIES BUSINESS PARTNER

Teaming up with the Aries person can be a risky business. You will need to understand the type very well to make the partnership work. Much will depend on the restraint you are able to impose without making the Aries feel he or she is being restricted or dictated to.

The Aries partner has much to offer. But there are also quite a few minuses. To begin with, he is a born leader, so he'll want to take charge or feel that he is really the driving force behind the firm. At the outset, he will acknowledge your position as an equal partner and have every intention of keeping to it. But when the action starts, he won't be able to help make decisions on his own. This is one of his greatest faults. He'll assume he knows the best way to deal with a situation, and even if you're in the office across the hall, nine times out of ten, it won't even enter his head to consult with you.

Aries are frightfully impatient. They can't wait to tie things up. To confer with someone else seems to them an unnecessary waste of time. Sometimes their judgment is excellent—they can pull off the most impressive coups, following a decision through with a dash and speed that leave their rivals and competitors hopelessly outdistanced. Other times, using the same technique, Aries make colossal blunders. You will need to get some meaningful assurances from your partner right from the start that he won't act unilaterally in important matters. At the same time, you will have to be careful not to inhibit him too much. His spontaneity is probably his greatest gift, so be cautious how you handle him. He will break up the partnership immediately if he suspects you are trying to give him orders. Despite his faults, the Aries has much inventiveness and resourcefulness to contribute. He just needs that gently restraining hand on his shoulder to prevent him in his eagerness from being rash and impulsive.

Aries is a straight shooter, a person who will never go behind your back. And you won't catch his hand in the cash register, either.

The Aries partner is a person of great energy. He or she is extremely active in all that is going on and is the one to handle the difficult out-front jobs where boldness, courage, fearlessness and originality are required. But your partner is not the best person—in fact, he's probably one of the worst—to cope with a situation requiring tact and diplomacy. Aries are too outspoken and confident of their own simple solutions to the world's problems to reassure a sophisticated and hesitant client.

Aries impress most people with their dynamic energy, quick, intuitive intellect and optimistic and positive approach. But they are a bit reckless, careless, too willing to take a chance, and should not be expected to handle the detail work in a partnership because they very quickly tire of concentrated mental effort. Best at responding to stimulus rather than trying to produce it themselves, Aries have a great deal of initiative yet lack persistence. They are quite good at carrying out instructions but have the infuriating habit of "improving" on them. They like to put their imprimatur on things, as though this alone makes an action worthy of their participation. If in discussions you can give way to your partner on matters that aren't essential to your plans, you will find that he or she works with much greater enthusiasm. And there is no doubt that an Aries person will put immense energy and unlimited time into anything he or she undertakes.

Remember, Aries are very self-willed, quite aggressive and frequently headstrong. Your partner is probably one of the most ambitious types you will ever meet. If you oppose him directly, he will fight you to the last breath (opposition excites him to greater effort). He is fairly fixed in his ideas, but can lose interest in projects very quickly, particularly if they require much hard work apart from the expenditure of energy.

If you run one side of the business and Aries the other, he won't have a great amount of sympathy for your problems. *His* will be the most urgent and important, even though the success of the business is supposed to be a mutual aim. He wants to succeed first in what he is personally doing; the group or partnership objective always remains secondary.

Aries expect to finish a job without much trouble. If complications occur, especially delays and drawn-out discussions about minor points, your partner is likely to walk off in disgust and leave you to sort things out.

It is not in Aries' nature to reflect or do much homework before starting on a project because they prefer to play it by ear. Their great knack is for manufacturing expedients to deal with the exigencies of the moment. As forward-looking planners, they lack depth of vision and are likely to fall into the same old traps—in different trappings—over and over again.

When delicate business negotiations are in progress, you would be wise to try to arrange to do the letter writing yourself. The Aries partner has a habit of being curt and assertive in correspondence. If there are two ways of expressing the same thought, he or she will unwittingly choose the blunter or, in other words, the one more likely to offend.

The Aries is a stickler for conventional behavior where business and partners are concerned, and will expect you to conform. He is rather blind to the fact that his own impatience and impulsiveness often involve him in what amounts to unorthodox methods and actions. He can have quite a volatile temper, which may explode over the simplest issue. But you'll seldom find him holding a grudge. He is inclined to keep to old and proven methods, updating them here and there with a dash of inspiration.

Aries is quite imaginative, though practical, in everyday affairs. Sometimes he gets the facts and his own viewpoint so mixed up he may seem to misrepresent a position.

If you happen to get caught up with the passive or negative type of Aries, you'd better forget a partnership altogether. He's a sad lot. And unless you've seen his birth certificate, you'd never spot him for one of these energetic and very decisive people. This character can't make up his own mind, isn't at all sure of what he's doing, and when he does act, it is usually too late. He spends his time worrying about the outcome when he should be following through.

YOUR TAURUS BUSINESS PARTNER

The Taurus man or woman more often than not makes a fine business partner. If you link up with this person, you will have a lot going for you. But if your aim is to make a quick buck from fly-by-night schemes or any form of risk taking, you'd better look for another buddy.

Taurus is the zodiacal Sign that refers to possessions and money. The Taurus has a natural flair for accumulating both. He or she possesses a very sound business head and is often the solid banker, the clever citizen, extremely good at making money for other people. If you give a Taurus a dollar to invest, in a few years he will hand you back fifty—less expenses, of course. He is not likely to make you any spectacular profits off his own initiative. He is a steady, persevering plodder who makes his fortune by sheer dogged effort, and usually with a bit of luck just when it is needed most.

You'll have to watch that your partnership does not become a rather dull affair. If you leave running the operation to your Taurus associate, you'll discover everything settling deeper and deeper into a pattern. You might have a fine money-making machine, but the boredom will send some of the more adventurous Signs up the wall. Your partner is no experimenter. Taureans loathe taking chances. They play every card by the book, always with an anxious eye to safeguarding their security.

You will have to be the brains of the outfit. You can leave all the tedious organizing and implementing to this tireless and dependable person. If you two hit it off together personally and you are prepared to make a few concessions, you can form an unshakable combination with a Taurus.

The Taurean is intelligent, but not intellectual. He or she is a very conservative, down-to-earth person. You will find you are able to discuss your ideas and problems in an adult way, and your partner's great good common sense and very practical approach will help keep your more imaginative schemes on the rails. When it comes to making expansive moves or undertaking any project that requires a bit of a risk, you will have to handle this person with kid gloves—and be ready to answer some very searching questions. Taureans hate change. But even more, they resist disturbing their resources. They don't care how much time and effort they put in, but when it comes to spending their own money or mortgaging their hard-earned assets, they will dig in their toes. And what big toes the zodiacal Bull has! It will take a sound case, as well as some very persuasive talk, to enlist your partner's cooperation.

The obstinacy of these people can be truly incredible. They are rather slow to grasp an idea. You may think at times you are talking to a brick wall for all the comprehension they show. But when they do catch on, and a proposition appeals to them, they really go for it. They put the objective up there on their mental horizon and head toward it with astounding dedication and one-eyed purposefulness. Once they've decided on a course, nothing will make them deviate from it. Virtually every consideration thereafter is referred to that particular aim. Their amazing stubbornness works the same way. If they decide they don't like your idea, that's the end of it. They won't come around. You'll have to find a way to deal with this extraordinary trait, which can often blind a Taurus person to his own obvious good. And, of course, in a partnership, it can spell stormy weather.

Similarly, you'll find your partner very fixed in his ways and not too keen to learn new ones. The mental effort seems to tire him. Perhaps it bores him. He likes to be physically and psychologically comfortable, undisturbed, at rest. By sticking to routine and going about their job in a methodical and habitual way, Taureans achieve a soothing peace and contentment. They are always in great danger of going into a waking sleep, of wrapping themselves in a cocoon of comfort and regulated doings and virtually disappearing from the creative scene when needed.

You'll find it necessary to give your partner a shake now and again. How to do this without undermining the association will depend a lot on your personal relationship. But there is a way of reaching Taureans and getting them to sit up and take notice, and this is through their feelings. Their sensibilities are far more acutely developed than their intellectual processes. They feel things continuously that never reach the level of their conscious mind. It's a sort of inner self-sufficiency. If their feelings are not penetrated so that they feel emotionally involved with what's going on, Taureans remain unmoved and uncommitted. This is why others often regard them as mentally sluggish. It is also why Taurus children are slow to learn from an intellectually top-heavy education system. Your business partner is no exception.

Taureans are emotionally attached to everything they own, and this includes their loved ones. Any proposition they feel endangers these they will probably turn down. They are moved by art and beauty and are quick to respond to nature. A day out in the country can resensitize them emotionally, especially if they have sunk into the habit of town or city life, which actually doesn't suit them. Too much movement around them is upsetting and makes them heap more protective layers around themselves. Taurus is an earth Sign and these people are inclined to bury themselves digging for material treasures.

Your Taurus partner is honest and loyal. He won't touch you personally for a penny and will be most scrupulous in keeping accounts correct and up to date. But since he does enjoy the good life, his expenses may be very high for entertainment, clothes and especially food. He is very good at making influential friends and usually moves freely with a natural self-assurance among the affluent.

These men and women are kind and gentle. Just as they're not easy to get started on a project, they're not easy to provoke to anger. They are certainly one of the least temperamental Signs of the Zodiac. They exude patience and self-control. But there is a limit to their restraint. Under sufficient goading, they are capable of breaking out into an irrational fury that can be physically dangerous to the person it's directed at.

The negative type of Taurus is not as bad for business as some of the other unevolved characters—at least he'll grab every penny he can and stash it away with the ardor of the traditional miser. But you will probably find this partner's grasping and heavy materialistic ways just too much. This weaker type may be so downright lazy, stodgy, self-indulgent and stubborn about even the simplest matters that you'll willingly leave him down in the basement counting out his gold.

YOUR GEMINI BUSINESS PARTNER

At first meeting, the Gemini man or woman may seem the ideal person to co-opt as a business partner. But be careful, for all is not as it seems.

These people can adapt to just about any situation. They have the happy knack of being able to provide any conversationalist with just the audience he wants. If you're talking business, Gemini will show intense interest and an amazing grasp of what you're saying. His replies will be everything you want to hear. And when it comes to discussing a partnership, you couldn't wish for a more understanding mind, one that seems to see things exactly as you do. Well . . . that's now. In five minutes, it may all be different. Gemini will have changed his tune and be agreeing with a contrary point of view or indulging in the sort of tantrum that would appall any partner.

A partnership with this elusive, Mercurial Sign can work, but it is a iffy proposition. Much will depend on you. If you can handle this bright and clever chameleon character, you could have yourself a winner. *If!*

Geminis are changeable and unpredictable. They find it difficult to keep at one thing for long. But while they are engaged in something that appeals to them, they are exceedingly deft, competent and quite often just plain brilliant.

Your Gemini partner will be unbeatable when you are meeting or entertaining clients. Amiable, often suave, intensely communicative and possessing a sophisticated sense of humor, he or she can discuss practically any topic. Instinctively these people know just where to put the emphasis if the task is to convince a difficult client. They have a flair for making strangers feel like old friends and putting clients at their ease. Even the standoffish types soon wilt before the charm, wit and affability of these extremely pleasant and outgoing people.

Since Gemini is a mental creature—intellectual, logical, reasonable—you can count on this partner to come up with a constant succession of bright ideas. All you have to do is point him or her at a problem and, quick as a flash, you'll have an answer and (probably a good solution). A challenge that tests their ingenuity and mental powers is what these people enjoy most. So, if you are an individual who likes to deal with the bread-and-butter side of the business, there is no better type to leave the ideas and public relations to than Mr. or Ms. Gemini.

They are very perceptive and discerning people. If anyone is going to put anything over on anyone in a business deal, it will be your Gemini partner and not the other way around. Not that he'll double-cross you; he knows where his bread is buttered. If you're a good bet, he'll be keen and honest. But in the whiz-biz he's handy to have around because he can detect a lie or a fishy story with the first "ahem." Gemini is the zodiacal Sign of mental activity, the raw nerve ends that are pulsing with information waiting to be communicated. The brain processes are so highly strung here that the mind and body are extremely restless. Gemini people operate on a nervous energy that needs positive direction or it is likely to go haywire. They require a steadying hand, but certainly not a constraining one. You'll have to handle your Gemini partner literally without touching him. Since he understands completely an appeal to reason and logic, he'll be the first to appreciate your argument or to catch on to what you're driving at. He'll cooperate all the way and work very hard to please you. But you mustn't try to hem him in. He's the type who wants to come and go as he pleases. You'll never find him sitting beside you from nine till five pouring over accounts or writing tedious reports. He'll do those things—and about 50 others as well during a normal day. He's extremely good with figures and writing. But he's not going to take over one aspect of the partnership and make it his routine. He'll pull his weight, but the load must be in numerous small parcels.

You can call your Gemini partner up at any time of the night to solve a problem. Chances are, if he's had a hard day, he'll have been out "relaxing" with lots of friends or amid the bright lights. He has amazing energy and the more active he keeps, the less rest he seems to need. He recharges his batteries through continual human contact.

If there's any heavy manual work to do, you'd better not count on Gemini. These people's bodies are built for speed, not labor. Physical toil soon depletes their vitality and makes them unnaturally depressed and morose. They're very capable with their hands, though, and even if they haven't learned to type, they can knock out a presentable letter on the office machine in very short order.

Your partner will be a great asset as a go-between or middleman. He'll rap with the bank manager, tick a slow payer off (preferably over the telephone) with stinging expertise while giving you a puckish wink, make the most plausible excuses for late deliveries and do his darndest (with a great amount of success) to keep everyone happy from the biggest client down to the messenger boy.

Gemini men and women are not really combative. They prefer to circumvent trouble and tend to compromise or reason their way out of things without looking for the source of the trouble. Although able administrators, they are likely to upset their employees by treating them as numbers and being generally unsympathetic. Geminis can become irritable when things aren't going well and fuss around the office in an ineffectual way.

If your Gemini partner hasn't got much of a head for business, it's not filled with criticism or malice either. If you have an argument, he won't be the one to hold a grudge. Neither will he nag you or try to shout you down. He believes passionately in freedom of speech—so if you have the occasion to tell him a few home truths, he'll respect your right to do so.

By taking on a Gemini partner, you'll be doing him or her a good turn because these people need the stability that a sober and understanding partner can provide. Their numerous outstanding talents will be fair exchange.

Gemini's creative mind sometimes makes it difficult for him to stick to a decision once he's made one. No sooner does he make up his mind than he discerns other possibilities. He lives in his head and is constantly outdistancing himself. With an intellect that works like lightning and seldom stops, he is continually revising and dissecting his own thoughts. He's really in business more for the mental stimulus than for the profit.

The negative Gemini type should be written off as a partner because he's likely to be devious and a bit of a con man, living for the moment on what he can get away with rather than what he can earn. This person doesn't know his own mind from one minute to the next—is unreliable, lacks continuity and quite often is heartless.

YOUR CANCER BUSINESS PARTNER

The developed Cancer person has a natural flair for business. He or she understands finance, has a superb sense of timing and seems to find a constructive release for gnawing ambitions in the business world. But as a partner whom you must be able to work and cooperate with personally, Cancer is not ideal.

These men and women are rather moody. You may feel you don't know where you stand with your partner from one day to the next. Cancerians can be effusive and communicative, and then turn sullen or introverted. They can disturb the atmosphere of the office. If they have been offended at home or crossed in a love affair, they won't shake off their despondency quickly. Like the Crab, which is their zodiacal symbol, they are all soft and fleshy inside, nothing like what their crusty exterior suggests. They hurt easily and retreat very quickly into their shells.

Your Cancer partner will soon display his business acumen. He may not have a lot to say on occasions, but you would be well advised to be guided by him when he recommends a course. Cancerians do not, as a rule, make idle proposals or suggest moves they have not thought or "felt" through thoroughly. These people are highly intuitive and rely more on the communications of their inner feelings than on their intellectual processes. They often "know" things, though if you question them logically, their conclusions may seem unreasonably based.

You will discover that your business partner is extremely persistent. He does not expect to attain his objectives with the same speed that others do, but has an extraordinary tenacity that allows him to hang on even when everything seems to be crashing down around him. As long as he maintains faith in what he is doing, he will not give up. The Cancer business person is a master of the war of attrition. He prefers to concoct a good corrosive plan and to wear the opposition away with it, often without their even knowing a battle is on. He is a silent worker, a takeover specialist who bides his time, *quietly* buys up company stock until suddenly he's got control. He is not deterred by setbacks or rebuffs. Even when all his work has been negated, he carries on, building up again as though nothing had happened.

It is your Cancer partner's nature to remain in the background as much as he can. He doesn't like participating in overt action or making a scene about things. For you two to get along, you'll have to tolerate his rather old-fashioned methods, for he won't change. You might say: If he gets results, why should he? A good point. He's pretty fixed in his habits. And he has a great respect for precedent. He sincerely believes the "good old days" were preferable. If you're a modern whiz kid embued with novel ideas, don't expect him to share your enthusiasm. Even modern furniture goes against the Cancer grain. And as for discotheque decor—if this is your choice—you'll definitely need separate offices. His office will be relaxingly redolent of some past period, comfortable, homely and liberally sprinkled with relics, souvenirs and the like.

Despite their natural reserve, Cancer people are surprisingly ambitious. They need to succeed and enjoy being looked up to. Cancer will cooperate with you as a business partner as long as he feels you can help him get where he wants to go. Otherwise, he'll judge you as a person, and you'll soon know from his moods and responses whether he likes you or not.

The danger with a Cancer partner is that he is too quickly contented with his lot. If everything is going along okay, why rock the boat? Well, without some new activity, the boat may very well start rocking on its own. It will be in your interest to take the initiative, to see that business keeps moving. Cancer often needs a kick in the backside—if you can get him off it long enough to do it!

To mention a few other debits, the Cancer business partner can be indecisive. He's not the sort to take along to a client meeting where everyone is expecting mind-blowing ideas because he can be terribly ponderous and give the impression of missing the message when he's under fire. What he's actually doing is feeling his way, taking everything in and preparing to digest it afterward in the snug isolation of his office or home. He'll give you an answer tomorrow or the day after (and it will probably be a good one), but just now, he'd like to be the hell out of here! Cancers hate being pressured, can't stand the big heat or the spotlight. They are feeling creatures, remember, and feeling surfaces more slowly than bright ideas or palliatives. When your partner does make a suggestion, it won't be superficial. The trouble is that by the time he comes up with it, the client may have gone elsewhere.

Having a Cancer partner around makes some people feel a bit dusty because these people are usually preoccupied with the past. They clutter the office with bric-a-brac and pieces of junk. They never seem to throw anything away. They are romantic, idealistic, sentimental and easily hurt. They have exalted ideas about themselves and may lead you to believe their function in life is far more profound than the prosaic business role. If you offend your Crablike partner, he'll scurry into his familiar crevice and may become morbid. When he doesn't get the attention he feels is due him, he will be restless, touchy and probably irritable.

Cancer is economical and cautious. He won't want to spend the partnership's money except perhaps on a library of good old books and a few tasteful antiques. You'll get along much better with him if you share his views on the essential aspects of life and are able to dish out some approval and praise from time to time. If he thinks you think well of him, he'll try much harder. Although he may say he wants to be let alone, he tends to flounder when left to his own devices. You should tactfully keep him on course.

Cancer is quite hospitable, especially when entertaining at home. He or she can often cook a meal that will impress the most fastidious client. These people have an excellent memory and a good sense of the dramatic, which help to make them quiet but pleasing hosts. They like to chat with amiable company and will move around to find it. Quite often they are very well informed. They would rather entertain clients at home than take them out.

Cancer tends to imagine slights where none exist or were intended. These people are thin-skinned characters. Once they've been affronted, like the elephant, they never forget. They're not malicious or vengeful, but they'll never let the offender get close to them again.

The negative Cancer person might be all right as a silent partner, but in an active capacity, his moods, indecisiveness, complaints and unprogressive attitude make him a crustacean delicacy you can well do without.

YOUR LEO BUSINESS PARTNER

You'd better face it from the word go: your Leo partner is not going to take a secondary role. He'll work alongside you, give your partnership all he's got, but at the first sign of any high-handedness on your part, there will be a showdown. He's a good partner, but if anyone is going to take over, it will be him. That's his attitude, anyway.

In Leo, you have the most complete and balanced representative of all the Signs. These men and women are big-hearted, strong willed and reliable. They possess tremendous energy for work—when they really get involved in a project, there is a danger that they will literally work themselves to death. They don't seem to realize their own limitations, physical or mental (perhaps they just refuse to acknowledge them). But if you can learn to handle Leo, you can point your partner in just about any direction and he or she will return you more than your money's worth.

The first move to guarantee a successful partnership is to concede Leo sufficient control from the start. You won't regret this, for while you're engaged in your side of the business, you can be sure his side is being handled capably and conscientiously. But see that he *stays* on his side of the fence. In Lionlike fashion, he's apt to leap across and start lording it over your territory. Leo is trustworthy and more inclined to choose the noble way than the surreptitious. As a rule, he is too proud and cognizant of his own dignity to stoop to mean and dishonest actions. But if he believes he is right and acting according to his rather idealistic principles, he will stick to his guns come what may and regardless of what others think of him.

Your partner is a good contact man and you would be wise to use him in this capacity. His personality is usually impressive, his disposition positive and optimistic. People tend to respect him. Personally, he's a bristly character and not so easy to get along with. But when he's turning on the charm—say, as the public relations part of the outfit—he's a likable and popular figure. Toward you, his partner, he will develop an infuriating I-told-you-so habit. Leo men and women imagine themselves to be oracles, and when things turn out the way they thought they would, they'll draw your attention to it every time. They are know-it-alls in many ways, who love to be right and want everyone to be aware of it. What you would let slide, they tend to make big news of. It's the petty side of their nature.

Leo is basically a showman. He is addicted to the big flourish, the exaggerated gesture. Nothing delights him more than the roar of admiration from an audience. To make this Lion purr and literally eat out of your hand, all you have to do is show him you appreciate his efforts and keep the compliments coming. He's a bit of a fool where flattery is concerned. But you should have no reason to be insincere in acknowledging his willingness and conscientiousness.

Your Leo partner is not so well suited to routine, detailed work. Being born leaders, Leo people need to feel they are directing matters. They can be very happy and productive in creative work that allows a broad scope. They are solid idea types who are often drawn to literary work or the entertainment industry. Their sense of the dramatic is highly developed. If allowed to go too far, though, they can be embarrassing show-offs and nauseating boasters.

In dealing with clients, you will find your Leo partner quickly wins their trust and confidence. Although his manner is dominant and forceful, his sincerity is seldom questioned. He hardly ever attempts a venture unless his heart is in it because it is essential for him to believe in what he is doing. He doesn't like selling spurious goods or ideas. Sometimes he identifies so completely with what he's doing that to criticize it is to criticize him. And Leos do not enjoy criticism. In fact, they can't believe it! They are so self-assured that when they hear a complaint about themselves, they dismiss it as a misunderstanding on the other party's part.

You'll find your partner excitable and quite irritable at times. He will flare up without warning and say exactly what he thinks. He will then go on as though nothing had happened. If you take umbrage, he is likely to be hurt, although there is little risk he will hold a grudge. Leos consider malice and revenge beneath them, but they are capable of maintaining a clear-meaning aloof distance which is difficult to penetrate.

Leos are first-class organizers and enjoy taking a chance or two, though usually they will be pretty sure of their ground before risking money or reputation. Capable enough with finances, they may seem extravagant on occasions, especially when it comes to entertainment or amusement. Usually, though, they have a little put away for emergencies or know exactly how far their resources can be stretched. Worrying about the morning coffee money is not these people's style; they like to think and talk in big round figures.

Your Leo partner will want to expand the business as quickly as possible. He's not in it so much for the money as for the opportunities to direct and control. He may show some impatience, which can develop into recklessness if not wisely monitored. Being generous and fond of display and keeping up a good front, he may also overspend on unnecessary items at a time when budgetary restraint is necessary.

Leo's head for business in the art of wheeling and dealing is not so good. These men and women are not as shrewd in this department as they think—in fact, they are rather easy to see through. Their capacity is very much dependent on their interest. Only when their imagination is vividly excited do they go on to succeed. Half-measures and incomplete commitments leave them languid and yawning.

You'll discover your Leo partner is able to sum up or generalize a situation with a few bold verbal brushmarks. He or she can discard details that, although essential, may obscure the human interest and even the beauty of some arrangement. Leo can present a picture that is not only informative but also satisfying. Being somewhat mystically inclined because of the Sun's lordship of this Sign, Leo often catches sight of the wood and not the trees.

If your partner gets bossy or domineering, you'll just have to have it out. Generally speaking, the advanced Leo type is easy to reason with and will see the error of his or her ways. Don't try to lecture a Leo; handle him. If he disagrees with your observations, you can bet your life it is because he has examined them against his own experience. But if pride prevents him from acknowledging that you were correct, once he sees your point, he will endeavor to change.

In adversity, your Leo partner tends to become downcast. He can fight the drawn-out battle only so long. Here, a sympathetic and understanding partner with a few right words of encouragement can restore his heart. Otherwise, alone, he will use his last energy to force a fight to the death.

The undeveloped Leo is too loud-mouthed, brash, reckless, dogmatic and overweaning for any business partner to tolerate for long.

YOUR VIRGO BUSINESS PARTNER

Here is a steady, reliable partner who will work hard with great patience. You won't have to worry about this man or woman trying to steal the limelight or attempting to take over. Virgos are rather shy and retiring and would prefer that you take the public bows while they concentrate on getting the books and the business generally in better running order.

This doesn't mean your Virgo partner is antisocial. Far from it. These individuals like being with people they know, and enjoy meeting others in familiar circumstances. They are intensely chatty. It's only the unfamiliar face or situation that puts them off. They enjoy moving around and visiting old friends and clients. They are intelligent and good conversationalists.

You'll find your Virgo buddy extremely cooperative. He will make helpful suggestions and do much to improve the business in practical ways. But he will never try to force issues or impose his will. He does *not* want to lead. He is best suited for a secondary role, for implementing orders, for serving others. Don't worry about offending him when a menial job comes up and everyone else happens to have suddenly vanished; this is what he enjoys. You couldn't find a more willing or dependable person to look after the detail and routine side of the partnership. He'll absorb himself in this with obvious, though restrained, delight. He is painstaking and meticulous and will work all day—without looking over his shoulder to discover what, if anything, you are doing.

Virgo is a progressive thinker, but strictly in the practical sense. His ideas seldom rise to greatness. But once you get going together, you may wonder how you ever managed to cope before without his novel ideas. He has a knack for evolving specialized ways of handling work. If you've got a logjam in the office or *on* the factory floor, your Virgo partner is the one to solve it. He's what you might call a budding expert at all sorts of production-line work. What others may regard as tiresome detail or statistical euthanasia, he revels in, and will arrange facts with exacting discrimination into an acceptable and proper order. He strives for efficiency in himself and everything around him, and he is not afraid to get down on his hands and knees and scrub the floor, if that's the job that has to be done. Virgos are modest and unassuming, frequently humble. Their egos are not affronted by tasks others may regard as below their station.

This does not mean you can bully or ride roughshod over your Virgo partner. You wouldn't want to do this anyway to anyone so obliging and lacking in airs and graces. But if you try it, you will soon realize your partner is very sensitive about the dignity he or she retains, little though it may be.

Your partner's main fault is that he is extremely critical, quite unnecessarily so at times. His mind is always discriminating, observing things and actions that to him are out of order. If your behavior doesn't come up to scratch, he'll tell you so with outrageous frankness and frequently unerring accuracy. This is not a malicious or destructive trait in Virgo. It is an attempt to be helpful, to allow you (or anyone in his company) to distinguish in yourself what needs to be rectified. But it's a very vexing habit all the same. The gems that dart from the mouths of these people—especially when you are entertaining important clients—are likely to bring on an attack of apoplexy. But still, Virgo's criticisms do not offend as easily or as deeply as those that come from more egotistical types.

Your Virgo associate is very good with money. He or she is quite capable of taking over the financial side of the business and keeping accurate accounts, though you must prevent this partner from putting too much emphasis on economizing and constricting all ambitious projects. Virgo can drive a hard bargain and is just the person to handle final negotiations. He enjoys taking the mickey out of smart-alecky or more lofty minds in these deals. Being a rather cold and unsympathetic person, he can show great control and dispassion at these times and hold out to the last minute. But in normal business affairs, your Virgo partner is hampered by a lack of understanding of how irrational human beings can be. His approach is purely intellectual, so he is apt to miss the vital subtleties of response that distinguish normal business relations from horse trading.

Virgos are a bit straitlaced and narrow-minded, or appear to be. They *know* what is right and wrong, rather than feel it. It was all implanted in their heads in their early years, and their moral code is like a reference book that rarely undergoes any change. Actually, they are less concerned with morals than with propriety. Being unemotional themselves and often lacking the fire of enthusiasm, they don't have much experience of the passionate side of life.

They are perfectionists whose striving for this impossible ideal is reflected in every aspect of their nature. That's why Virgos are prepared to labor at just about any job. Someone's got to do it, to make a perfect world. It's an unconscious motivation, of course. And some less earthy and practical Signs may argue that these people should seek the perfection more in themselves. But thank goodness, Virgo is Virgo. He wants everything to be working in its right place, and he's prepared to do more than talk about it.

Your partner may be a terrible fusspot around the office: putting things back after they've been deliberately moved, tidying up his desk a dozen times a day, restacking the phone books almost before you've finished looking at them. He is never satisfied, complains ceaselessly and lives on a nervous energy that requires his constant application to some task or duty.

Despite his small number of faults, you'll find your Virgo partner a very easy person to get along with, personally. He doesn't pretend to be what he isn't and doesn't expect a great amount out of life in the way of material rewards. He is almost embarrassingly obliging at times and is prepared to try out just about any idea that is new and novel. You can't ask for much more than that! But if you are a Sagittarius, Pisces or Gemini, you may find him a bit too detailed, and almost facelessly dull.

The negative type of Virgo will seldom want to become a partner but will prefer to work as an employee, either among numerous other employees or in an inferior position where he can follow instructions precisely and be as persnickety and fault-finding as he wishes, knowing that he will not be endangering his job.

YOUR LIBRA BUSINESS PARTNER

In the Libra person, you have the ideal partner. Libra is the Sign of partnership, symbolized by the balanced Scales of justice. So you can't go far wrong taking Libra as an associate because his or her whole makeup is adapted to cooperation. Libras are the most composed, rational and temperate people of all the Signs.

Librans love to be successful. They will do all in their power to achieve the objectives mutually agreed upon. They enjoy the good things of life that usually accompany success and are very aware of the power of money to make the going easy. Your Libra associate will make all the sacrifices necessary in the early stages while the firm is being established. But when the money is there, you can expect your partner to spend his or her share of it—and perhaps a bit more. Librans enjoy luxury and would rather have a gracious home, an elegantly furnished office and a first-rate wardrobe than money in the bank.

Your business finances will be in competent hands as a rule if that side is left to your partner. Librans are extremely good with figures, and when responsible for budgeting, their judgment is usually remarkably accurate. But if the character is not developed, the individual's mathematical ability and love of what money can buy may lead to juggling the books. But one thing is certain: any embezzlement will be done well—and very neatly.

Librans are rather conservative and definitely not revolutionaries. Rarely enterprising themselves, they will support advanced and unusual schemes with shrewdness and ingenuity. You will find a Libra partner a great asset to a business connected with one of the learned professions, the arts or a beautifying pursuit. Objects these people handle or produce must be finely worked or contain materials of pleasing grain or texture. To give their best, they require clean, harmonious and, if possible, beautiful surroundings. This may sound a bit much, but in vulgar or squalid conditions, Libra quickly wilts and becomes unhappy and nervous. He is then likely to retreat inside himself and become moody and unproductive. It is not unusual for a Libra person forced to work in ugly or uncongenial surroundings to become physically ill. Even if your partner is not consciously aware of this propensity, it will be in the business's interest to see that he or she is not forced to perform in these conditions by you or by the needs of a client.

Libra is a charming person to be associated with. He will never intrude or try to dominate you. He will certainly influence you in the direction he feels you should take—at this he is really brilliant—but it will not be by pushing or arguing. Libra uses gentle and subtle persuasion. His tactic is to sow the seed of an idea in your mind and then quietly nurture it with suggestion. By the time you implement it, you will believe it was your own creation. Libra will just smile knowling to himself and never mention it again.

Librans are difficult people to fight or to pin down. They are suave, immensely tactful and equipped with every attribute to please. They will not dispute with you on your own ground. They tend to regard their partners as a means of gaining their own ends. They genuinely want their partners to be content, for to wish otherwise would be to go against themselves. They know their destiny lies in partnership, that this is their psychological niche. And they won't leave you—unless they find a better partner.

Libra men and women believe passionately in freedom and equality. They demand these qualities for themselves and insist on them for others. This is one area where you may find your partner surprisingly singly aggressive and ready for open conflict, if necessary. He is a champion of the underdog and may put up a vehement defense for any employee he feels is being unfairly treated by the firm or his co-workers.

But as a rule, your Libra partner will do his best to avoid an argument or any unpleasantness. He is an excellent person to entertain clients, the essence of diplomacy and genteel hosting. He speaks and writes in a pleasing way and is one of the most plausible types you will ever meet. Underneath his poise and composure is a very active mind. He is highly intellectual and analytical and is gifted at understanding a problem very quickly. Since Librans are not emotional, they seldom allow their feelings to influence their judgments. Therefore, in business, they have the advantage of being able to take a dispassionate view of a situation. You will find your associate's advice extremely helpful and objective, especially when passions are aroused.

Your Libra partner will never upstage you. He will always see that you receive your rightful recognition and respect, even when you are absent. Because he does not want to be associated with anyone about whom others might harbor a bad opinion, while he remains your associate, he will never try to undercut your confidence or dispute your competence. He will aim to create an aura of agreement and harmony around the partnership. If he sees faults—which he will—and is unable to rectify them, he will ignore them and proceed as though they didn't exist.

One of the problems with Librans is that they are often indecisive. They are at their best when responding rather than initiating. In the course of trying to reach a decision, they are inclined to see so many alternatives that the moment for action passes. This can be exasperating to you as a partner. Another thing you have to be alert for is the tendency of the Libran to drift. He loses direction quickly by relating to other events going on around him and needs to be gently pulled back on course. Librans are fairly curious-minded; they are very content to be eternal sightseers quietly absorbing the changing scene without paying much attention to where they are going. Being smooth talkers, the weaker types are likely to camouflage their innate lack of purpose with a convincing spiel that contains nothing more than diplomatic platitudes, admirable intentions and questionable "facts."

Librans also tend to sit on the fence in discussions, bending this way and that according to the direction in which the wind of opinion seems to be blowing. They will support contending views in the space of a few minutes, as though the object is to restore harmony rather than to batter out a workable solution. Their basic urge is to please everyone at the same time!

Their unwillingness to say "no" often gives the impression that they are easily led. They *can* be manipulated by difficult employees, who may take advantage of the Libran preference for using persuasion rather than disciplinary action. In a partnership, however, this agreeable and amiable characteristic has obvious advantages.

A negative type of Libra partner is still likely to be a better bet than some other Signs, even though he or she will be indecisive, changeable, frivolous and lazy. If you can balance these shortcomings, much may come of the association.

YOUR SCORPIO BUSINESS PARTNER

Forget Scorpio as a business partner. Well . . . almost. These people do have some tremendous qualities such as unlimited patience, superhuman endurance and a passionate drive to get at the truth. But the scalding nature of their temperament makes them almost unthinkable candidates for partnership. Fortunately, the Scorpio character is rarely met in its pure state; the type is normally modified by the positions of the other planets in the horoscope. It's fair to say that *any* modification of this extreme Sign has to be an improvement. Perhaps the partner you have in mind is a suitably toned-down version. You can ascertain this from the Yellow Tables found in the Scorpio book of *AstroAnalysis.* (Grosset & Dunlap, 1976.)

The first thing that strikes you about Scorpio men and women is their penetrative intelligence. They go straight to the heart of the matter with an economy of words and astonishing accuracy. You won't even get around to a discussion with your prospective Scorpio partner if he doesn't think you're very bright. Unless, of course, he has an ulterior motive. In which case, he will mentally note all your weak spots with terrifying insight, butter you up and prepare to dispose of you to his advantage.

But let us say he sees the partnership as desirable and you as a reasonably acceptable representative of the human race. He will want to get down to business immediately and be told exactly what preparations have been made, the objectives and the market potential. Here is where you'll need to have done your homework, for Scorpio has an uncanny gift of assessing the chances of success and failure for an enterprise. He can look years ahead and see future developments, anticipate trends. And he'll analyze your scheme on the spot with computerlike precision—and with about the same type of emotional involvement. If the plan is any good, he'll probably appreciate the possibilities better than you—at least the long-term ones. This, you must admit, makes Scorpio an exceptionally handy business partner.

Next, you'll be impressed by Scorpio's thoroughness. This guy or lady never goes off half-cocked. Everything is worked out, analyzed, schemed beforehand—particularly the strengths and weaknesses of the personalities involved. The shrewdness of the Scorpio mind is almost inconceivable. It quite easily degenerates into the Machiavellian doctrine that any means, however unscrupulous, may be justifiably employed to achieve a desired end. This tendency can be carried to diabolical lengths. But let's assume your partner is a modified type. To outwit your rivals, you couldn't have the assistance of a more fertiley cunning and relentless mind.

Your Scorpio partner's incredible power of persistence may even weary you. He never, ever gives up. Whereas the Taurus partner will perservere with great plodding determination, your Scorpio buddy will keep up such a high-pitched scream of pressure that the opposition will usually give up, give in, compromise or surrender in some way just to escape the perpetual nerve-pinching pain. Scorpio himself is quite unaffected by the exertion and tension involved in maintaining such pressure. He can keep it up for years. And he hasn't got a weak stomach, either, if you're in the rackets and it comes to a bit of physical torture. He has such a massive and enduring constitutional strength that to win he will literally press on to the point of his own destruction—which is normally far beyond any other individual's. Out of *all* this emerges Scorpio's reputation for dependability. He doesn't accept challenges lightly; he dismisses fools; he manipulates and struggles to the death. Such a temperament, if nothing else, has to be dependable.

Well, that's about it for the pluses.

On the debit side, Scorpios are exceedingly obstinate. Their amazing willpower makes them unbending psychological beings. They keep their attitudes intact in separate watertight compartments so there is no overlapping. Scorpio people know exactly what is in each department of their mind, but have little idea of what they add up to as a whole. If they did, they would be more tolerant, more forgiving, more failing, more human. As it is, they respond from fixed opinions. One opinion may oppose another, but since the mind can have only one conscious thought at a time, no serious conflict arises. Scorpios will defend their conflicting views with implacable severity, which is aimed at destroying an antagonist rather than considering the logic of the argument. If you, as Scorpio's partner, dare to point out his inconsistency, he will erupt into a vituperative rage—and perhaps create another secret, seething department in his mind with your name written on it!

Scorpios can be cruel and vengeful enemeis. And yet, by the strange quirks of opposites that distinguish this Sign, they are capable of devoting themselves with the same tireless, repressed passion to a loved one, work or a cause. You take a lottery ticket when you select Scorpio—the odds are against you, but someone wins somewhere every draw.

Scorpio will expect you to work as hard as he does. If you—or members of your staff—try to keep pace with him or emulate him, you will probably endanger your health.

He is no diplomat. He believes in going directly to the point. He'll tell you, or perhaps even your top client, a raw-boned home truth without the slightest regard for personal feelings. He is contemptuous of displays of emotion and expects everyone to be as dispassionate as he is on the surface. Inside he twists and creaks with personal dissatisfaction and repressed desire. He wants desperately to rise above himself, but is not sure how to do this except by suppressing one or more of his emotions.

Scorpio finds it difficult to adapt to new conditions. Once you've fixed your mutual aims, he'll want to go on, come what may. He's the old-fashioned type who'd rather let his business disintegrate under him than change his methods. You may wish to take advantage of a profitable year and enjoy an extra holiday—but not Scorpio. His mind will be fixed on the agreed future objective; there must be not letup until it is achieved. If he feels his position may be weakened by his absence, he won't take a holiday, for years if necessary. And if he's dying, he'll still come to the office and put in a full day's work.

Your partner loves power. It is this desire that drives him. His thirst for it is unquenchable. He is a budding tyrant with a stormtrooper's baton in his kit bag. His moral consciousness has no outside reference. His own opinion is what is right. Sometimes the Sign produces the ennobled human being; in that case, this doctrine works wonderfully. But in the lesser Scorpio mortal, it is his own selfish purposes that count. Financially, this may lead to fiddling and recklessness on a ruinous scale. Although your partner possesses great personal magnetism, he is unlikely to be a favorite among your clientele. He is a type who attracts or repels people violently—a dubious credential for any business partner.

YOUR SAGITTARIUS BUSINESS PARTNER

Sagittarius has much to offer as a business partner. If you manage to link up with one of the highly developed types, you've really got it made. These people have incredible breadth of vision, which they can apply in practical ways. They are highly intelligent, extremely active and temperamentally equipped to handle the largest business enterprises. The bigger the scheme, the better Sagittarius performs.

Needless to say, your Sagittarius partner is not going to take to a partnership that involves him in a lot of petty detail or small transactions and fiddling correspondence. He doesn't get the decimal point easily. He's definitely no clerk.

Sagittarians are marvelously adaptable. They can succeed solo or in double harness. They like people and people take to them, though they do not form deep attachments. To a Sagittarius, buddies are to talk to and share adventures with, not feelings. You, as his partner, will enjoy his cheery, outgoing sociability, though you may never feel really close to him. He's just not built that way. He literally loves the whole wide world and longs to serve it in his way. He doesn't find the individual such a reliable proposition. Your Sagittarius partner will always be looking ahead, beyond the current scene that occupies and captivates most people.

He is an inordinately lucky person—which is lucky for you. You will be surprised at how often he lands on his feet when the mat is pulled from under him. This probably accounts for his unbounded optimism. Even when he loses out, he immediately looks to the future with the same, almost naive expectation of success as before. As a consequence, he is inclined to take too many chances—and for stakes that are far too big for comfort. He needs a wise, restraining hand. Wise, because he won't tolerate being ordered about. But he will submit to tactful treatment and listen to advice. However, when the temptation to take a chance is high, you won't want to leave him to his own devices for too long.

In normal financial business matters, the Sagittarian judgment is most reliable. You will find your partner's approach impersonal and balanced because he is swift to discern the advantages and disadvantages of a situation. It is when he gets the feel of personal adventure—often the opportunity to be a rover or to experience new situations—that he seems to become emotionally involved and lose his perspective. As a result, your Sagittarius partner is likely to enjoy a plunge on the horses or a session at the gambling tables. Once the gambling bug bites him, he is very difficult to reason with—until either he loses disastrously or has lived it up with his winnings. He'll squander all his ready cash on a night out because money doesn't mean that much to him. Sagittarius, in fact, is the original big spender. Easy come, easy go is his attitude. The ruler of his Sign is Jupiter, the jovial and luckiest planet of them all. So your partner's faith and confidence in his continuing good fortune are not hard to understand.

Novel and way-out business ventures have an odd attraction for him. Although definitely no fool, he frequently gets mixed up with people whose ideas normally would not be considered a safe business bet. For instance, he might decide with great enthusiasm to back an invention that no one really wants. It is the *idea* that impresses him rather its practical uses. He's often a sucker for fly-by-night projects and may be left holding the baby (with you as assistant nursemaid). But if the preliminaries drag on, he'll lose interest very quickly and turn his attention to another new gimmick. These distractions are usually secondary to the mainstream of business activity, so it's not all that bad.

Naturally, some of the people Sagittarius attracts are not sterling characters. Since he is not a suspicious or critical person, he is likely to be deceived. Reputations can be damaged through such associations and it could be in your interests to keep an eye on this aspect of the partnership.

Sagittarius is extremely energetic. He works hard, plays hard and lives hard. You will need tons of vitality to keep up with him. He can scatter his energies, running from project to project and not getting a great amount done in any particular area. But he is a colorful and likable character and his sense of the dramatic gives him style. He usually possesses a tremendous sense of fun and humor, and in any social situation, you'll find him surrounded by an appreciative audience. You can leave the entertaining to him any time and be sure he'll keep your guests happy and amused. He is an expansive, generous and innovative host.

Your partner will be a valuable asset at business conferences. He is skilled at getting a point across, enjoys a verbal dual and has a flair of repartee. He is also clever at cross-examination. With a few words he can expose the merits or demerits of a proposition. His intuition is quite extraordinary at times. He senses weak spots in his antagonists immediately. In an undeveloped Sagittarius, this ability expresses itself as a bluntness that can be offensive. The natural frankness of the type is refreshing, but it does require a modifying emotional concern for other people's feelings.

In business transactions, impatience is likely to force your Sagittarius partner to jump the gun. He often finds it difficult to wait while necessary preliminaries are concluded and his hastiness may ruin delicate negotiations. His confidence in his own ability to be tactful—which is generally warranted—can convince him he is persuading others when he is not. A negative response the next day is apt to prove the point occasionally.

Promises, promises . . . this is another Sagittarian fault that may reveal itself quite early in your association. Your partner, in his enthusiasm, often promises results that are far beyond his capabilities or the potential of the venture. Explaining to disappointed clients or trying to match promises with performance can be a frustrating and annoying business.

Despite his shortcomings, which are not all that important to a successful partnership, Sagittarius will not try to throw his share of the responsibilities back onto you. He will handle his side of the business energetically and efficiently. He is not a fusser. He is an understanding person and will amaze you on occasions with the soundness and sagacity of his counsel.

From a health point of view, you should know it is of the utmost importance for your partner to get enough exercise. Although he is constantly on the move, he usually requires a sport or regular exercise to keep his body toned up and his liver in good order.

The undeveloped Sagittarius will be restless, talkative and highly imaginative. The freedom he insists on may be to do as he wishes. He is likely to be boisterous and an out-and-out gambler.

YOUR CAPRICORN BUSINESS PARTNER

There are two distinct types of Capricorn people, whose zodiacal symbol is the Goat. One type is contented to be tethered to a stick in the ground, provide domestic milk with machinelike regularity and wander around in circles thinking he's going places. The other is a self-centered and deliberate mountain Goat who might not stray too far from his favorite peak, but at least is always climbing toward the summit.

A business partner with the imagination and aspirations of the Capricorn milk machine is guaranteed to sour the association in no time, but the active mountain Goat variety is a different proposition.

The mature Capricorn person is a mighty solid type. He's honest, practical, persevering, cautious and probably has a better grasp of business and the commercial setup in general than any other Sign in the Zodiac. Sagittarius might be exceptional in breadth of vision, but Capricorn has the capacity to administer and understand a worldwide conglomerate while knowing essentially what is going on in any department!

His ability to grasp the practical intricacies of a mammoth business operation is incomparable. Now, coming down from those giddy heights to your partnership, there are bound to be some problems. For a start, your Capricorn associate will want to have the last word. A departmentalized mind capable of exercising centralized control on a huge scale is going to insist on a good deal of authority for itself. And chances are, a severe or rigid discipline will be required to maintain it.

Capricorn is extremely conservative and patient. Although one of the most ambitious types of the Zodiac, he or she doesn't believe in new-fangled methods of getting to the top. Capricorn's faith is in what has been tried and proven in the past. Why experiment? The old way is safe and sure. And if you're prepared to work hard enough and long enough, you'll make it, says Capricorn.

Well, he'll certainly work hard with unremitting dedication—and he'll expect you to do the same, the old slave driver. If you're looking for plaudits because you've put in 12 hours straight, forget it. That sort of exertion is routine to Mr. or Ms. Capricorn. These people might not believe in shortcut tactics, but they do think time is precious, and once they have begun a task, they won't allow one minute to be wasted. Yet to get Capricorn started can be a job in itself. He's inclined to circle and hover, sizing up the situation carefully to protect himself from surprises.

Capricorn prefers steady advancement to spectacular gains. He's suspicious of anything that doesn't follow a pattern. Actually, he is uneasy until he settles into a routine, so the first thing you'll find him doing is reducing the work to familiar forms, methods, procedures and routines—an obsession of his you might be tempted to describe as organized drudgery or mind-pinching tedium. Still, someone's got to attend to details and ensure accuracy, so you could be onto a good thing with a Capricorn partner.

You'll need to be the public relations part of the outfit, though. This guy or lady takes life too seriously to put much store in the sociable side of business. Pleasure, as most other people know it, is not that important to the Goat perched on a rugged outcrop—work is the thing. With Capricorn's single-track nature, there's not much chance of producing stereo sounds out of this partnership unless you can provide the stylus. You'll probably need to get out and about regularly, anyway, as relief from this stern and uncompromising influence.

Whether or not a partnership with Capricorn works out depends on your personal attitude. Your associate is really not built for double harness, as you've no doubt gathered. He's got enormous business sense, but his disposition is austere and intense, and all the business capability in the world doesn't add up to much if two people can't hit it off together as partners.

Capricorn people won't waste pennies. But they might be a bit foolish with the dollars. They know exactly how much is left in the morning coffee tin. If your partner is in charge of accounts, there'll be no errors. These men and women are meticulous in everything they do. They would rather stick to the letter of the law than take a chance on the spirit. They accept the limitations of their environment—their task, as they see it, is to do the best they can with what's at their disposal. Besides, it's less trouble that way . . . and a darn sight less risky. Capricorns like to be looked up to, regarded as dependable, steady and persevering. Others may want to be remembered for more human qualities, but not these people. Needless to say, they take to responsibility like a duck to water. Extra business burdens or problems never daunt them. They just knuckle down, and with amazing methodical grace, proceed step by step toward the conclusion they know lies at the end of all relentless effort. They don't conceptualize the end; they concentrate on the means.

Old Capricorn's only fear is loss of security, psychological or material. He finds comforting reassurance in the respect that others show him. He will never commit an act that might bring him into public disrepute if it can be helped. Not being a particularly warm person himself, he tends to underestimate the potency of feelings in others and their effect on hitherto fixed situations. He is thrown off balance by sudden changes, becomes unsure of himself, edgy, until he can settle down again into routine. He works and saves for the future. The strain of modern living never gets him down, no matter how hard it presses him. He doesn't develop "nerves." He often displays a surprising sense of humor that allows him to laugh at himself, even in company. You mustn't, but he can! It's a fair enough concession for an otherwise painfully self-conscious type of person.

Your partner is rarely generous. Fair, but not spontaneous. In dealing with employees, he will pay them exactly what has been agreed to—and they can forget about bonuses. But he will sometimes take up a fight on behalf of someone he feels has a rightful grievance. Time and effort he will give unsparingly, but money and resources he likes to keep for himself and his dependants.

With a Capricorn partner, most of the good ideas and original thinking will have to come from you because he is too conventional and careful to be inventive or creative. But he is highly resourceful and adroit when it comes to materialistic dealings. Although he may be unable to visualize an end in itself because he is basically a self-centered individual, he knows every moment precisely where he is and the direction in which he is heading. That direction is *always* toward his own best interests. As long as your own interests lie in the same quarter, you should prosper as a partnership. But remember, like the mountain Goat, he really prefers to climb alone—the pickings might be too sparse for two.

With only a little bit more hardening, a Capricorn partner can be dogmatic, tyrannical, mean, hard—and just about impossible for a normal human being to stay teamed up with.

YOUR AQUARIUS BUSINESS PARTNER

Aquarius people make good partners. Their calm and moderate ways help balance out just about any other zodiacal type. This partnership should be able to build a reputation for solid and sensible performance. But mind you, Aquarius is no ball of fire. He's not very good in a fight or in trying to cope with emergencies. He comes into his own *after* the battle, healing the rifts and handling everyday affairs with extraordinarily good common sense and practical wisdom. If you can handle the crises—and for a business to succeed there can't be too many of these—your Aquarius partner will look after the rest, admirably.

Aquarians are not troublemakers. Dissension of any kind disturbs them. They won't quarrel and they have a natural discretion that steers them around awkward situations. Good-natured, friendly types, they would rather talk things over in a calm and civilized way than pommel you with their point of view.

It is a fact that the Water-Bearer doesn't usually possess any special flair for business. (Perhaps that's oil in his jug and he's too busy pouring it over troubled waters.) But each of his characteristics can be useful to a partnership in one way or another, more so than most of the other Signs. The Aquarian is a sort of composite person with a little bit of good from all other types. **Check the Compatibility Guide (*Astro-Analysis*, Grosset & Dunlap, 1976); some Signs find Aquarius just a little too much of a good thing to be in harness with.**

His or her mind is not that quick in action. But it is very broad in its attitudes, tolerant and receptive. And the Aquarian power to receive flashes of inspiration about new trends and desirable improvements is quite remarkable. Aquarius has a lot of the gentleness of Libra and the vision of Sagittarius, and is progressive in a very special way. This man or woman will never try to upset the established order to introduce new ideas. Aquarius would rather put them before you—or society—and allow you to judge their merits for yourself. This is an evolutionary rather than a revolutionary character. Generally, the Water-Bearer's insights are so obviously beneficial that they are quickly adopted into the system, and this is a quality you will find particularly helpful in your Aquarius partner. If you pay attention to his or her suggestions, your business should prosper along modern and efficient lines.

With money, your buddy is completely trustworthy. In a personal sense, Aquarius can be extravagant, but you won't find him spending beyond his means and dipping into the till for the deficit. He's not so interested in accumulating money, although he will work diligently enough to earn it. He won't appreciate penny-pinching methods where the business is concerned; he'll want it to advance, and he's realistic enough to know that you must keep up a presentable image and spend money to make money. If he doesn't approve of some expenditure, you can bet your life he's had a brainstorm about where the money can be used to greater advantage. It will pay you to listen to him.

Don't be put off by a certain coldness in your partner's makeup. Aquarians are not excitable or emotive, but they are tremendously optimistic—to the extent that they will let things slide. On occasions, Aquarians will be greatly enthused and determined to show what they can do. But if you're looking for dash and bubbling fervor, you're not going to get it here. There are few or no extremes in the Water-Bearer's nature. Basically, he or she is built for bigger things than our usual daily aspirations allow. (This is something we will all come to appreciate now that the world has entered the 2000-year Aquarian Age.) Aquarians are intellectual beings, equipped to deal with the problems of humanity rather than with those of the individual. Although they have intense inner feelings, they rarely show them in individual cases. These people are not sentimentalists, though they are very kind and sincere. Just don't expect emotionalism.

Your Aquarius partner won't make any special demands on you. He will respect your independence as a person and expect you to return the consideration. One thing you will find pleasing is his habit of anticipating the likes and dislikes of people he comes into contact with. This is a great asset in a partnership when it comes to close dealings with clients.

There are many people who admire the Aquarius trait of maintaining an impassive front in all situations. This apparent unflappability often masks tumultuous feelings. Aquarius is the Sign of friends, so your partner's congenial and amiable nature will attract a wide variety of acquaintances. His conversation is usually on a fairly high plane. He won't gossip about you or your friends or break any confidences. But don't expect him to show any fanatical zeal either when the partnership agrees to implement one of your really bright ideas. If he goes along with it, you can be certain it makes good sense. That may have to be enough.

You'll find your Aquarius buddy is quite conventional in moral outlook. His ideas of freedom and progress seldom include any watering down of the golden rules. He enjoys traveling and working and living in new surroundings, but he is upset and confused by sudden changes, which seem to be forced on him more often than on most other Signs.

To get the best out of your partner, you must understand he is an idealist. Any suggestion of crooked dealings or exploitation of others will meet with his instant disapproval. He won't compromise with his conscience. In fact, the more your business leans toward some form of acceptable public service or worthwhile objectives in humanitarian terms, the more you will appreciate the talents he has to offer.

Aquarians are splendid mediators and can be counted on to mend differences and alleviate friction. They have a sensible word for everyone. Of course, we don't always want the proper advice but rather some form of partisanship—and Aquarius is a bit too advanced intellectually to play that emotional game. So, nice placid person that your partner is, you might find him at times too adaptable and lacking in definite response.

He may also seem a bit hesitant or uncertain if you are pushing him for a decision. He's got a mind that understands a situation from all angles, and that sort of comprehension often cancels out the desire to act.

You may never be able to get a decision out of the backward-type Aquarius. His or her life is lived on the premise that if you don't do anything, you can't possibly make a mistake—which is probably the biggest mistake of all!

YOUR PISCES BUSINESS PARTNER

Pisces people can make excellent partners, but only if you are lucky—or astute—enough to select one of the developed types. Any lesser Fish will slip through your fingers every time you try to catch him or pin him down. No Sign is more talented, pleasing and sympathetic. And none is more infuriatingly indecisive, vague and impressionable.

Assuming your partner is at the right end of the yardstick, you have here a person with extraordinary insight and intuition. He or she has an incredible knack for making the right decision at exactly the right time. But you're not going to get the answers when *you* want them because the Pisces doesn't work that way. In fact, when pressured, he tends to go to pieces. His method is to wait, his patience when working "his way" is unequaled. To his business associates, what he is doing may seem like ineffectual muddling,

It has been said that the Pisces makes a better sleeping partner than an active one. This is largely because in the hustle and bustle of the commercial system, the Pisces' insouciance seems out of place. In business, when we're worried or intense, we usually expect our associates to show similar concern. Pisces won't. Although no mean actor when he wants to be, he is incapable of this basic betrayal of his own inner workings. His attitude has been called "escapism," among other uncomplimentary things, but it's really a matter of faith in himself and proper timing. If you understand and appreciate this trait in your partner, you will be able to make a success of your association.

Not that Pisces is not a worrier. He very definitely is whenever things are not going the way *he* thinks they should. This may not coincide with your view of things, so you will need to remember that though Pisces works at a different level, he is just as intent as you are on advancing your mutual interests. Once you fully understand this, you'll be able to appreciate this extremely sensitive, perceptive and creative character.

The partnership finances, though, would be better left in other hands. Pisces is a bit of a contradiction when it comes to handling money. He is generous but careless, saving but extravagant. He spends without getting a great deal of value for the money. He is also a sucker for a hard-luck story. His sympathetic nature makes him dig into his pocket to help—without considering the sacrifices it might mean for others, such as his dependants or partners. It's just too risky to allow Pisces to handle partnership funds, though he wouldn't deliberately rob you of a single cent and is extremely good at managing when funds are short because he can make the pennies go a long way. But anything he manages to save is likely to be dissipated in one impulsive action. In good times, he is a profuse and indiscriminate spender.

Your Pisces partner is a very kind and trusting person. At the same time, he doesn't miss much. So, he is a superb judge of character, yet extremely tolerant and forgiving of the failings of human nature. He will know all your shortcomings, and yet won't nag you about them or even bother to mention inconsistencies others would make an issue of. He won't try to overshadow or dominate you. He is retiring, often shy, and prefers to work in the background. He has a way of literally dreaming up schemes and manipulating people and events to make his dreams come true! Linked with a harmoniously balanced and active partner, he can be an acceptable power behind the throne.

If he accepts you as his business partner, he will never blame you for what goes wrong and will stand by you through thick and thin. Neither will he allow others to run you down in his presence. If you are active and dynamic honestly, he will help make your work easier and more effective, even though it inconveniences him.

The Fish is essentially lazy and doesn't relate easily to the world of physical action. It would rather drift with the tide and gets its kicks from an emotional dream world of its own making. But once it senses a really stimulating enterprise—say, your exciting new partnership—it will swim against the current toward the objectives with great resourcefulness and determination. The secret, of course, is that Pisces has to be excited by a project to be induced to start swimming; only then can he show his special skills and talents. He tends to favor artistic pursuits and the professions, especially writing and publishing.

Your partner will be popular with the business's employees. He may be too indulgent of them at times, for he has a deep feeling for people in an inferior position, even though they may not be deprived or exploited in any way. He will often give in to them when a sterner course is indicated. However, through his caring, he attracts a loyalty that often produces better work results and less labor dissension.

Pisces enjoys the good life and sometimes gets carried away with the glamour of a situation, losing sight of the realties. His judgment may be more unreliable when he is confronted with an opportunity for self-indulgence. Pisces feels that if he must live in this world, then he ought to have the best of it—physical comfort, respect, admiration and harmonious surroundings.

Although naturally reserved, Pisces are social creatures who enjoy the passing parade rather than lead it. In the company of familiar people whom they like, they often discard their inhibitions temporarily to reveal the fun-loving and extroverted person underneath. When your partner attends a business conference or lunch, you'd better check that he doesn't leave his briefcase or papers behind; since he's usually thinking (you might say benignly scheming) and is a bit absentminded. His impressionable nature is very easily disturbed by the presence of rigid and uncompromising personalities. He can't stand the exacting, standover type, who, in turn, is irritated by his vagueness and tries to pin him down. He can be surprisingly obstinate, and if forced to work in uncongenial surroundings or with incompatible people, will become moody and manage to make everyone aware of his unhappiness.

The Fish is capable of reaching unfathomable depths of creative understanding, but is rather badly equipped to withstand pressure. A partnership that corrects this serious imbalance can be a winner!

FRIENDS

The following descriptions of the various Signs as friends are based on the position of the Sun, the most powerful influence in the horoscope. Most people conform to the solar influence. However, variations do take place because of the position of the other planets at the time of birth. For a closer examination of a friend's character, it is advisable to study the individual's personal horoscope, which is available for every Sign in *AstroAnalysis*, (Grosset & Dunlap, 1976.) All you need to know is the person's date of birth.

Since some Signs are naturally more and less compatible with others, you can get a better idea of how you'll hit it off with a friend by referring to the Compatibility Guide.

ARIES AS A FRIEND

The Aries person enjoys friendship, but it has to be largely on his or her terms. Aries people are too self-willed and organizing to fit everybody's notion of the ideal buddy. Yet their closest companions think they're really great—they love the male and female Ram's way of getting things moving and stirring up the entertainment. After all, it does suit some people to have a personal master of ceremonies around—and anyone with an Aries pal will agree that that just about sums up the favorite role of these very active and decisive individuals.

Aries are always eager to meet new faces. They need them. It's suicide for Aries people to try to cut themselves off from the mainstream of life that is people. They temper their mental and emotional mettle on relationships and require contact with the widest range of personalities to bring out the best in themselves. Mixing with others also instills in them the need for restraint and consideration, not their strongest points.

Aries quickly become part of a group. But no matter how enthusiastic and communicative they may appear, they hold a little bit of themselves back. They don't give that part away on casual acquaintance. True friendship means a great deal to them, and they are selective and discriminating in this regard. Which is one reason why they usually don't have many close friends. Another is that they have some very fixed opinions, which they propound and defend passionately. Close relationships can't always stand the strain of their fierce, combative verbal outbursts. They're too quick on the jaw. After a smashing start, people go cold on them. Aries individuals, as a rule, don't hold grudges, and they don't try to get even (there's no malice in them). When a relationship doesn't work out, they just wheel away, Ramlike, and charge off in another direction.

In company, people born under this Sign are very entertaining. They've got that audacious boyish or girlish impulsiveness, which sometimes comes very close to naiveté. They're a little bit unbelievable, amusingly impertinent, refreshing. What they'll say or do next is anybody's guess. This, of course, makes them exciting characters to be with—for some people. When they want to, they can mix easily with the most sophisticated company. But only for a time. The two types pretty quickly tire of each other.

Aries people are constantly on the alert in social circles for an appreciative ear, someone who laughs or applauds one of their clever, humorous or insightful remarks. They are then spurred on to outdo themselves, and before they know it they have corralled a mate (audience) for the evening.

They are staunchly loyal to close friends and generous to a fault. If a buddy is in trouble, they won't waste time spouting sympathetic platitudes. They'll bound into instant action, set on doing something practical to help. Without a single reservation, these spontaneous people will dig into their pocket or purse or run around organizing whatever they think is necessary to relieve a situation.

Being extremely idealistic, they have a habit of seeing others as they are not. Given the right emotional stimulus, they project their deeper longings onto individuals and pursue friendship with a vigor that frequently ends in disillusionment—and shock—when the truth is finally revealed to them.

As much as Aries enjoy and need numbers of people at times, they prefer mainly the company of a few close and trusted comrades who understand them and appreciate the sincerity that underlies their self-assertive nature.

They also require brief periods of seclusion.

TAURUS AS A FRIEND

No one makes a more faithful friend than dear, loyal Taurus. It's true Taureans do not excite great inspiration—what they offer is solid, sympathetic, warmhearted companionship. They satisfy where the need is greatest. And what is more desirable in a friend?

Taurus can also be a hatful of fun. But usually these men and women are quiet and reserved to begin with. They truly value friendship and don't offer theirs haphazardly.

Taurus individuals frequently have friends in the higher echelons of society where money and position count. They may not be wealthy or powerful themselves, but they are accepted by the affluent and influential and take their place among them naturally without awkwardness.

One side of the Taurean character that appeals to others is an innate appreciation of the artistic side of life. Your Taurus friend may not be a Michelangelo or Hemingway or possess any special knowledge, but his or her affinity with most that is creative, harmonious and beautiful seldom fails to come through.

Even though they may work hard all day in an office, Taureans are almost sure to have a creative outlet that they share with special friends at night or on weekends. This may be anything ranging from handicrafts to entertaining (Taurus usually love giving dinner parties). Most of them are quite capable of preparing a small banquet with Cordon Bleu expertise and flourish. And what is more, they—especially Ms. Taurus—will manage to emerge from the kitchen unruffled, impeccably dressed and at ease.

Friends enjoy visiting a Taurus home because these people are wonderful hosts and hostesses. They can also be counted on to have very pleasant accommodations, if they can manage it, with a garden or in a rural setting. But very definitely their home will be nicely furnished and comfortable, with as many touches of luxury as they can afford.

They are a little hesitant and unsure when it comes to making friends. They don't think of themselves as great conversationalists and they're never quite sure how to break the ice. They are inclined to hold off making contact and to wait for events to dictate the action. Taureans prefer not to take the initiative. None of that bumptious bouncing up to strangers for these people. Their fraternizing methods are subdued and dignified.

It is not unusual for Taurus to become close personal friends with the boss and other superiors and their families. They may visit each other's homes and carry on a friendship for years without ever disturbing the workday relations. These people have intuitive tact; they never give those in important positions the impression that they will take advantage of the friendship. They themselves are easily put off by presumptuous behavior, and when they make up their minds to end a relationship, there are no two ways about it. When Taureans lose faith in a person, they obliterate that person from their thinking.

Taurus' closest friends are those who share their love of beautiful things. This includes a distinct penchant for rambling in the great outdoors.

They are inclined, however, to settle too comfortably into a niche among special buddies and to gradually lose their spontaneity. They get caught up in the same old conversations and habitual recreations. They don't like changing friends and sometimes fail to keep their relationships alive and vital. It pays Taurus to circulate and bring new companions into the fold every now and again.

And the friends of Taurus should be careful that they, too, don't get into a rut.

GEMINI AS A FRIEND

Gemini people love having loads of friends—but as few deep attachments as possible. To them, friendship is for fun, kicks and mental stimulation, but no obligations, please. They don't want to be pinned down to what they said last week. Geminis are likely to say anything in the excitement of a racy moment, and they expect their friends to understand this. Not that they're illogical, not by any means. They can make logic out of just about any nonsense, so quick and shrewd are their reasoning powers. But, try to tie a Gemini down to something he or she said yesterday? You have to be joking.

The strange thing is that the real friends of these Peter Pan characters *do* understand them. And they don't find them unreliable because they accept them for what they are—very likable, entertaining, optimistic, helpful, intelligent bundles of (mostly) good-humored energy.

Gemini probably has more telephone numbers of pals in his or her head than most other people keep in their address books. These men and women have a memory for facts and figures that is as remarkable as their ability to strike up casual acquaintanceships. Their friends are usually spread over a vast area. When Geminis visit a town where they're not known, you can bet that by the time they leave, they'll have a dozen new addresses memorized. These Mercurial individuals make enough friends for two people—which is probably why Gemini's symbol is the Twins.

The Geminian doesn't stick to one type of friend like some other Signs. He or she chooses buddies from all walks of life. They're just as likely to include a couple of tramps as the governor himself. Gemini must have various personalities to bounce off his ideas. And the more types he can gather together at one time, the happier he is. He or she can handle two or three conversations simultaneously—and do two jobs or have two or three love affairs going at the same time.

Geminis love novelty. Their minds are intensely keen and curious. They get bored very quickly, especially with ponderous types who take themselves and life too seriously. They can enjoy a good laugh with or at these people, but only so long as they're entertained or collecting interesting information. Otherwise, these children of Mercury are off to the next unexpected meeting. For anyone who tries to tag along, it can be a very tiring threesome.

They love to argue but not at the emotional level. Sometimes they rub people the wrong way at first meetings because they are quite capable of taking an opposite point of view just for the sake of exercising their formidable intellect at another's expense.

These Mercurial characters may seem inconsistent, flighty and frivolous, and some may regard them as insincere, but none of their friends will ever call them dull. They are the nerve end of any party or gathering.

In social circles, they sail along famously. They can adapt to just about any situation and keep up a patter of well-informed or inconsequential talk, depending on what's required. They sprinkle their conversation with amusing anecdotes. At repartee, they are down-right brilliant. They have a wonderful knack of changing their personality to fit the mood of the room.

Geminis' closest buddies are intellectual types who can discuss the more abstract subjects that interest them—and who don't object to being called up at the oddest hours simply for a chat!

CANCER AS A FRIEND

Cancer people enjoy having a few loyal intimates. They like to feel they are of service to these pals, and that they enjoy their respect and esteem in return. They choose their friends more by feeling than by intellectual discrimination. If the person "feels" right to a Cancer, it is almost certain he or she will enjoy the same interests or hold similar views. The point is that these June–July-born men and women are almost inspirational in their sensitivity to other people's vibes.

They have such a fine rapport with their closest buddies that it is often not necessary for them to speak at all for hours at a time. They literally absorb the presence of their friends in a way that transcends the normal idea of communication. But they do enjoy chatting with different acquaintances and can be surprisingly loquacious as well as interesting.

Cancers are moody characters, and can be very irritating to people who don't know them very well. They are seldom the same person from one day to the next. Their temperament fluctuates according to where they are and whom they're with, and sometimes even with the weather! However, the male and female Crab are far deeper individuals than they appear to be, and their real friends appreciate this and love them for what they are.

The intensity of a close Cancer friendship can be a bit claustrophobic. Although wonderfully sympathetic and helpful, the Cancer individual tends to be overprotective, too solicitous of his or her friend's welfare. The object of this solicitude sometimes feels he is being taken over, that his individual expression is being stifled. When Cancers are trying most to give, they are likely to be excessively demanding. These very sensitive people have a great need for affection. They often end up being hurt when their friends decide it's time to disentangle themselves and take a break.

Although Cancers are not vain or egotistical, they do possess considerable personal pride, which means they have to be appreciated and constantly assured of their worth and value.

This is not difficult because they are rather lovable characters. Still, they're touchy and easily offended and will sometimes sulk or sink into sullen silence when they aren't getting enough attention. It is excruciating to them to sense that their friends are underrating them. They know, in a humble kind of way, exactly what they are worth.

Friends and acquaintances have a habit of confiding in Cancer. The Crab often shares more secrets than all of his or her companions put together, but would never think of divulging another's private affairs even in the most intimate exchange of confidences. It is this kind of loyalty and understanding, together with an aura of high-minded seriousness, that make even casual acquaintances tell Cancer intimate details and seek advice. The Crab has a great deal of patience and good old common sense.

Cancers intensely dislike arguments and discord. They'd much rather give in to a friend or walk quietly away than engage in a stand-up, knock-down fight. Mixing with aggressive and rowdy people literally upsets their stomachs and can make them ill.

Many people don't realize just how sensitive these gentle Moon children are because they manage to conceal their emotions under a calm and confident exterior.

LEO AS A FRIEND

The problem with Leo friends is they're likely to be *too* generous and giving. They often deny their buddies the satisfaction of feeling friendship is a two-way affair. This is not so much related to the things money can buy. Leo's friendship is not as smothering as Cancer's can be. It's just apt to be overwhelming!

Of course, we're talking about the developed Leonine character. The immature type is too bossy and brash to hold friends for long. But even the openhanded and magnanimous Leo often has to realize it's possible to kill or at least mar a friendship with overdoses of well-intended goodwill. This is likely to include handing out good advice. Neither the Lion nor the Lioness can resist giving his or her opinion whether it has been asked for or not.

Make no mistake, though, Leos are true and tried friends. And they usually manage to attract companions who are also generous and kind. This is indeed fortunate because these are the only people with whom they can have any reasonably good kind of relationship.

These proud and usually commanding characters demand a great deal of respect, applause and loyalty from their pals. Worldly gifts are nothing to them in comparison. Anyone who's not something of an admirer won't be calling a Leo "friend" for long.

Leos really believe all that talk about being King of the Jungle. They tend to gather around them friends who are their intellectual equals but emotionally dependent on them. They enjoy holding court, giving good advice here, solving someone's problems there. When they can smile on their friends and feel like big mommy or daddy, they are happy. In adversity, although they are unlikely to admit it, they need their buddies desperately.

If you're a friend of a Leo, you probably enjoy showing off a bit too. You have probably noticed that this intensely competitive character will stay in his or her seat as long as you are not getting all the attention. If that happens, you can bet the Lion will think up something to steal the spotlight.

Leo people are rather fixed and one-pointed in their ideas and aspirations. They therefore find restless types with many interests fascinating but vaguely unsettling. These comrades disturb Leo's enormous self-assurance that he's on the right track, and force him to examine his goals and wishes more closely. He usually recovers his equilibrium (which means his self-confidence) fairly quickly, but for a time he may be confused. Friends like this actually do Leo a service by breaking down some of his rigid ideas and shaking his complacency. He needs to learn he can't be right *all* the time.

Leo people can get mixed up in dubious company and often their friends have to extricate them. They are not great judges of character at first meeting. They may fall for flattery and insincere gestures, particularly if these have a touch of glamour. In this way, so-called friends and casual acquaintances manage to penetrate their guard and make chumps of them. Oddly, they are seldom offended by people who try to get favors out of them by phony compliments.

Both the Leo man and woman have strong personal magnetism and make loads of friends. Many of their buddies are apt to be prominent in government and community circles. Some of their friendships last a lifetime. They like to entertain their pals at home as well as at popular night spots.

Leo usually establishes one or two lasting

friendships with people from abroad.

Come what may, neither the Lion nor the Lioness will ever let a friend down.

VIRGO AS A FRIEND

Virgos are not the easiest people to get close to. They may say they have many friends, but others are more likely to call these acquaintances. It's not so simple for people born under the Sign of the Virgin to understand the profundity of real friendship, the emotional and sympathetic link that can't be put into words. Virgos make friends largely at the intellectual level; the relationship has to make sense to them. Their personal alliances generally lack resilience.

This is not to say that these practical people don't have numerous friends they can phone, visit and call upon for help at any time—and vice versa. But they are very choosy and don't encourage friends who want to share intimate details because they resent all kinds of intrusion. They don't intrude on others and they expect the same consideration. Virgo people enjoy good healthy relationships where there is open discussion of mutual interests. Their private affairs they consider sacrosanct. Only to an unusually compatible person of tried and trusted integrity will they confide. Here again, they don't go looking for this type of person with whom to share their most intimate secrets.

You are most likely to find a Virgo friend among a group of people who share one of the many interests of these intelligent and discerning individuals. They are reserved and a little apprehensive at first meeting. They prefer to stay in the background until they get their bearings—which usually means a pretty acute summing up of everyone present.

Although quiet personalities, Virgos are certainly not dummies. In discussions, their shrewd and scholastic mind allows them to see the practicalities of a proposition in a flash. They speak up and people listen, for it is obvious they are being constructive even though critical.

People with similar interests usually take a liking to Virgos. They might be a bit severe in their outspokenness, but they are refreshingly honest. In fact, honesty is one of their most impressive characteristics. People always know where they stand with them. They are both conscientious and idealistic.

Frequently, however, Virgo individuals break with their friends over differences of opinion. Whereas other types may be able to ignore a divergence of fundamental views with a fast friend, Virgo men and women can't—as a rule. For as long as possible, they will tolerate such a situation, but eventually their own nature compels them to force a showdown. They must get to the bottom of things. Their minds insist on a logical analysis. It's the principle that counts. And so friendship, that indefinable thing, too often flies out the window.

Some of Virgo's closest friends are met through sporting and outdoor activities. They are not the rough-and-tumble type, but are keenly aware of the need to keep fit through exercise and plenty of fresh air. Most of their buddies share their absorbing interest in diet and food.

When Virgos do choose a pal, they are scrupulously honest in the relationship. They won't tolerate another person talking behind their friend's back. They will always come out into the open and confront you if they have any grievances. They are honorable people and can be depended on to do the correct thing.

LIBRA AS A FRIEND

Librans need to belong. Friendship is as essential to them as breathing. But their alliances often seem much more intimate than is actually the case. Librans don't, as a rule, form deep, soul-stirring friendships. The agony and the ecstacy are usually missing. Friendship to them is a dignified and entertaining way of ensuring they are seldom alone or isolated.

Libra is the Sign of partnership. And as far as Librans are concerned, there's no essential difference between a marriage and a fraternal partnership. The reason for this is they are idealists, not sensualists. To them, a lover is first a friend.

Librans seldom give themselves entirely in any liaison. Always they hold a vital bit in reserve which gives them an appearance of slight formality, the discretion that says: "Not too close, please." This discretion, with their other positive attributes, makes them interesting and desirable companions; nothing is quite so irresistible as that which entices but gently demurs.

Librans are charming, easygoing, polite and terribly diplomatic. They want everyone they meet to love them, to want them as a friend—everyone, that is, except bullying, aggressive, course types, who literally make them ill if they are forced to remain in their company for any length of time.

Libra, as most people know, is ruled by Venus, the planet of love, beauty and harmony, and these are the essential qualities that Librans look for in all their relationships. Wherever they work, live or play, they gravitate toward that which is artistic, elegant and pleasing. Their favorite companions are those who are skilled in the creative or fine arts or who have an appreciation or specialized knowledge of them. Libran people themselves are often talented in these ways and may go into partnerships with friends as color consultants, interior decorators, designers, hair stylists and other occupations connected with beauty and beautifying.

They love entertaining, dressing up and visiting friends in their homes. Their manner as guest or host is gracious and amusing. Often their friends are among the most influential and socially prominent people in town.

Libra friends will do all they can to bring new and interesting people into their circle. Often they are responsible for making romantic matches for others. They delight in seeing people enjoying themselves.

These mentally active and self-expressive individuals are a bit moody and unpredictable. Sometimes when their guard is down, they become critical, sharp and quick to anger. However, they recover their balance quickly. After all, their symbol is the Scales.

They have a fiery sense of dignity and justice. Any companion who unfairly attacks an underdog in their presence can expect a stinging rebuke. Libra men and women believe wholeheartedly in the brotherhood of man. But when it comes to actually doing something about it, they're frequently missing, because, as a rule, they are too fond of comfort and ease to embrace unnecessary effort.

These individuals are delightful companions, but they do have a way of using their friends to get what they want out of life.

SCORPIO AS A FRIEND

Scorpio people can be the most demanding friends of all. They are basically loners, they won't share their feelings and they want everything their way. They expect their friends to be as intense about their interests as they are. If not, they're out. A Scorpio doesn't have a friend around unless he or she has something to give.

As harsh as this sounds, it's the key to the extraordinary personality of the pure Scorpio type. Fortunately, the pure type is always modified by other factors in the horoscope, although the essential framework remains.

It is not easy for Scorpio to attract true friends because he and she doesn't have a great need for them. And what is not needed, normally becomes expendable under stress.

But Scorpio generally does have a compulsive desire to satisfy the sex drive, which is intensely strong in him or her. This drive in this remarkable Sign may go to the opposite extreme and propel Scorpio, still alone, to the self-denying heights of mystical experience. But usually the Scorpio man or woman directs libidinal energies in one way or another into love. So he or she *needs* a lover, and will serve or treat that person according to that need.

So what is it that Scorpio needs in a friend? An echo of his or her own idea, a sounding board, a captive audience? The problem is, Scorpio's friends usually need Scorpio, and this places them in a most unenviable position.

The Scorpio personality is intensely magnetic to some people; to others, it is exceptionally repulsive. Those who are attracted frequently have great feelings of love and devotion, which the Scorpio person probably does not require. To remain in his company, they must indulge this generally selfish, tyrannical, vindictive, suspicious, scheming, stubborn and quite often cruel and violent personality.

But, of course, there are always exceptions, produced by positive and favorable influences elsewhere in the chart. These more developed Scorpio types—when not emotionally aroused—are staunch and sympathetic friends. They will work and fight courageously on behalf of a comrade. Weaker companions often draw inspiration and strength from their dauntless determination and patience.

However, when a Scorpio person encourages a friendship, it usually means he has an ulterior motive. For instance, he is likely to be a personal friend of his boss. He has an astonishing gift for weighing situations and seeing who will come out on top—and therefore is the best person to cultivate—in a future power struggle. His ability for intrigue is unmatched by any other zodiacal type, for there is no limit to his perfidy and wily patience when self-interest is involved.

The Scorpio person can passionately and devotedly serve a cause or a person he or she loves—and be just as violent in his or her hatred or loathing of either.

Scorpio seldom gives an opinion unless it's asked for, and doesn't accept the views of others without investigation.

If friendship is understood to be based on trust and sharing, Scorpio friendships do not have a lot going for them.

Ask Scorpio, for he or she has that chilling, detached honesty that would probably agree.

SAGITTARIUS AS A FRIEND

Sagittarius people are wonderful companions. Lighthearted, witty and extremely intelligent, they make and attract friends from all levels of society. They have a passion for experimenting with life, for traveling as widely and as often as possible—and people enjoy the adventure of tagging along with them for a time. There's seldom a dull moment when these good-humored individuals are around. They adore novelty and jump from experience to experience with a lust for living that may leave less strenuous types bewildered and breathless.

Yet they can be intensely serious. Their love of fun, uncomplicated manner and tendency to clown constitute only one-half of their nature. This half has undeniable appeal and makes Sagittarius one of the most popular of the zodiacal types. But these people are deeply interested in the problems of their fellow man and will support all kinds of projects aimed at making his life easier and freer.

The Sagittarian's closest companions are usually like him- or herself. They never tie each other down—the link is pure comradeship. Sagittarians manage to divide their time without conflict between the serious and lighter sides of existence. Their energy and enthusiasm are exuberantly boundless.

The above characteristics describe the positive and mature type of person born under this Sign. The negative type manages to distort the higher qualities into odd but still recognizable shapes. For a start, he or she is a boisterous kind of individual who lives mainly for a good time and attracts shallow, showy friends of similar temperament. Negative Sagittarians also eat and drink excessively, make promises they have no intention of honoring, can't resist gambling and usually are chronically in debt. Because of their innate magnetism, these people can be a bad influence on others. Their levity and contempt for responsibility may appear glamorous; the young, especially, may admire and imitate their swashbuckling freedom.

Even the higher types of this Sign need occasionally to restrain their exuberance and impulsiveness where pleasure is concerned. The party life and all forms of revelry can be irresistible. Even the serious, high-minded and respected Sagittarius, a pillar of his community or the business world, can suddenly break out and land himself and his friends in embarrassing and ridiculous situations that are impossible to explain in the light of day.

Although the Sagittarian's breezy manner may suggest unconcern for what others think of him, his conscience pricks him painfully and he will always try to make amends in some way.

These people are generous and sincere friends. Their intimates respect their outspoken honesty and high ideals regarding the treatment of others. They love their freedom and independence and will never, even in a position of judicial power, deprive another of his liberty without deep soul-searching.

Sagittarians try to give their friends the benefit of their experience by taking a personal interest in their problems and endeavoring to offer solutions. Their hospitality, kindness and openhandedness with money is usually legendary among their intimates.

CAPRICORN AS A FRIEND

People born under Capricorn do not have many intimate friends. Their main interest is their work. When that's done for the day, they do enjoy relaxing with someone who understands that any discussion of personal affairs must be initiated by Capricorn. Their friends are mostly casual types who don't expect any exchange of intimacies.

Capricorns are capable of making fast friendships, and in those rare instances, they are as staunch and loyal as any one type in the Zodiac. But the individual Goat's fraternity club has a very restricted membership, and members don't meet that often. It's enough for these characters to know there's someone in this world they can discuss their troubles with—if the necessity ever arises. This gives them the feeling of security that is so essential to their happiness and well-being. It isn't the actual exercising of this option that matters, for deep, confiding friendship is something Capricorn holds in reserve—or in his mind—and probably never needs to make use of.

So it's on with the surface show. These people are easily entertained: a quiet chat, a few drinks, listening to music, watching TV or discussing business and current affairs will often satisfy them. They are not romantic types with social aspirations and they're not addicted to pleasure. All they really want is a temporary break from their main concern, which, as they mature, is to get as far ahead as they can in their job or career, and if possible to make a name for themselves.

Their closest friends and all those who love them realize they are supersensitive. They may appear solid, stable and practical, but, deep inside, they are aquiver with diffidence, uncertainty and vague, indefinable fears.

On first meeting, Capricorns appear to many to be standoffish and cold. This is frequently a pose they affect to compensate for their uneasiness. They are so determined that no one shall hurt their feelings that they won't give others the chance to rebuff or slight them by making overt moves of friendship. Their emotions are generally tucked safely away where nobody can get at them.

The real friends of Capricorn men and women are those who care enough to patiently and affectionately penetrate to the real person. There is no doubt that this protective veneer begins growing on Capricorn people early in life. Their childhood is frequently sad or disorganized, which teaches them to be wary of so-called close relationships.

They sometimes appear distrustful and suspicious when others extend a friendly hand. It's not that they don't want to grasp it; but they worry about the price that must be paid in pain if one fails the other. They are deep and serious people, these Capricorns.

A Capricorn person who allows his or her fears to dominate becomes withdrawn and uncommunicative. The process can start very early, sometimes in the middle of the happy and fun-loving teens. This person is often critical and builds up a repressed passion, which expresses itself in instant and violent dislikes.

All in all, the odds are against Capricorn being a very satisfactory friend for most people.

AQUARIUS AS A FRIEND

Aquarius friendship is of the highest order. It gives what might be called soul satisfaction, and for those who get close to these likable individuals, it is often a source of inspiration. This is not surprising because Aquarius is the Sign that rules friendship, associations and commitments to groups. In other words, Aquarius can make the ideal buddy.

These people are neither jealous nor possessive. In fact, the clinging-vine type of person who looks for some form of exclusiveness in a friendship will be bitterly disappointed here. Aquarians are attached to the ideal of comradeship, its intrinsic freedom and lack of demand, and not so much to the individual. They make more successful friends than lovers or marriage partners, as a rule. Marriage tends to confine and restrict when their whole nature craves variety of intellectual experience through different companions.

None of this means they are supertypes who don't need warmth and affection. In fact, they are idealists, and their aloneness is often the result of having standards of thought and behavior that don't conform to those of the crowd. Yet they seem to possess a built-in loadstone that attracts others to them, even if only for a short time.

These people are genuinely interested in human relationships. Although not so intense and possessive as most others, they are tremendously aware of the deeper aspect of friendship. They know it's not just a convenient way to fill up a few pleasant hours. There's a dignity to their friendship, which they always manage to preserve and endow with meaningful significance. Both sides retain their individuality in an Aquarius friendship.

The friends of Aquarius are usually intellectually serious types who agree with their somewhat advanced ideas about social reform and making life easier for the masses. Those who advance the course of progress are seldom social butterflies. Their views usually separate them and their closest pals from the ordinary run-of-the-mill people.

In some cases, these people even earn a reputation as radicals and revolutionaries. Occasionally, little bands of Aquarians and their friends strike out and refuse to join the Establishment. They may live a bohemian-type existence to underline their refusal to conform to comfortable, accepted standards, which they regard as outdated and socially inhibiting. They may dress differently. In some cases, their overzealous identification with a cause may lead to serious clashes with authority.

But generally, Aquarians are reasonable individuals who are extremely just and generous to their friends. They have a fine sense of give and take. And their inventiveness and brilliant intellects often elevate the minds of their companions and bring out the best in those people.

The true Aquarius—because of his or her intelligence—is very selective in the choice of intimates but is never a snob.

PISCES AS A FRIEND

Pisces people are always looking for the perfect friend; naturally, they are frequently disillusioned. Their problem is they have an ideal of friendship that often is beyond the capacity of any human being to fulfill. They expect too much. When they don't get the impossible, they tend to lose active interest in that particular person. Not that they would ever "disown" someone they have called a friend. They are aware of their irrational expectations, and in any case, possess a superb sense of loyalty. They simply push those who "fail" them gently to the back of their mind and keep on searching for the impossible.

Love and friendship are not easy for the Pisces person to maintain in separate compartments. It's too often both together or nothing.

They loathe being alone—and yet, they must have periods of seclusion. This is one of the qualities of their nature that new acquaintances are apt to find confusing.

They enjoy stimulating company and can work themselves into a near-frenzy of excitement. Yet, the next day, they may be withdrawn, almost self-reproachful, unable to face those with whom they have shared such fun and comradeship. This disturbing emotional turbulence is a subjective experience only the Piscean is really familiar with. So when the phone or doorbell rings, they answer and are able to respond naturally and charmingly—though quietly—to their friend. There is much of the instant actor or actress in these strange and gentle people.

Pisceans sometimes choose their friends unwisely. They get carried away with their enthusiasm for contact and sharing. They start sympathizing and confiding before they know where they are, or more importantly, before they've bothered to assess the caliber of their companions. In personal relationships, they tend to think things will improve, even when experience has taught them just the opposite.

A Pisces' friends are almost certain to be artistically inclined. They just can't tolerate heavy or coarse company. They themselves are highly and prolifically artistic. Although they may not be accomplished in any of the arts as such, they have a way of inspiring those who are.

There are not many Pisceans who have not poured their sensitive feelings into writing poems at some time or other. But it will be a very dear friend indeed, as a rule, who has the privilege of reading them because poems will be quickly destroyed by these oddly self-critical people.

Pisces individuals have a great gift for making those around them happy—except when they are trying to turn a friendship into a romance in their own imagination. Then they may be cloying and just too, too obliging and loving.

These people are wonderful at entertaining and making their friends feel deliciously at home. Pleasing others pleases Pisces most.

PARENTS

The following descriptions of the various Signs as parents are based on the position of the Sun, the most powerful influence in the horoscope. Most people conform to the solar influence. However, variations do occur because of the placement of the other planets at the time of birth. And, of course, the birth Sign of the child will also be an important consideration.

For a closer examination of these factors, it is advisable to study the individual parent's and child's horoscopes, which are available for every Sign in *AstroAnalysis.* All you need to know is the person's date of birth. Since some Signs are naturally more and less compatible with others, you can get a better idea of how parents and children will hit it off by referring to the Compatibility Guide. (*AstroAnalysis,* Grosset & Dunlap, 1976.)

THE ARIES PARENT

The Aries parent is kind, generous and fairly strict. The Aries woman often makes a better parent than the Aries man. Neither is particularly sympathetic or understanding; Aries people have difficulty seeing things through a child's eyes, possibly because they want too much to be proud of their offspring.

But the Aries woman takes parenting very much to heart. She's determined to bring up her children the way she thinks is right, even if it kills her—or drives her neighbors crazy, which is more likely.

Aries mothers have some very advanced ideas about child rearing. Their methods are often unconventional. They believe in teaching their youngsters initiative from the outset. And that may include permitting the three-year-old pride of the household to toddle over and pour himself a cup of coffee from Aunt Nellie's best bone-china set. Or to get busy with a pair of scissors or a crayon, perhaps on the wallpaper, while mother's attention is elsewhere. Not that Mrs. Aries is irresponsible. Far from it. But one freedom is likely to lead to another in the child's eyes, and she is impelled to go along with it. Still, it's the child that counts with her, and you've got to admire the way she tries to prepare him to cope with the practical side of life without putting a stranglehold on his self-expression.

The Aries dad is somewhat different. He's also progressive, extremely proud of his offspring and wants the very best for them. But he won't allow kids to take over his whole life the way some fathers do. They occupy a very special place in his affections and he'll see they never want for any material things. But he's a busy man, and although he'll do his best to satisfy their emotional needs, he's not particularly good at it—consciously anyway. But children usually love him and they do delight in the way he'll do things they enjoy on the spur of the moment.

The Aries father tends to become impatient and irritable under the constant demands of his children. Both parents believe that experience is a great teacher. If the child has to burn himself to learn not to touch the hot stove, then the attitude is, okay, let's let him get on with it. Mother is the softer and more efficient parent of the two. But they're both wonderful examples to the growing child of initiative and independence.

The birth Sign of the child, of course, will have a large bearing on the success of the individual Aries parent.

THE TAURUS PARENT

Taurus men and women adore their children and make them the center of family life. But these loving and affectionate people are far too wise in normal circumstances to put the children before their mate. In fact, this question just doesn't arise with them. They manage in a wonderfully sensible way to make the family a unit. And the youngsters usually grow up with a keen respect for the virtues of family life based on their Taurus parent's example. These children often go on to make happy marriages themselves.

It's not surprising, therefore, that Taurus is frequently considered to be the ideal mom or dad. These people are kind-hearted and sympathetic personalities with a deep, intuitive understanding of those they love. As homemakers, they are generally considered to be without peer as a rule.

Because of their sensitive nature, they are conscious at all times of the emotional impact that unpleasant scenes and quarreling have on children. They have their marital disagreements, of course, but would rather lose an argument—or eat humble pie for a while—than disturb the tranquillity of the home.

Their views on child rearing are rather conventional. They believe generally in the old-fashioned way—teaching children good manners, good behavior and good morals right from the start. Freedom and independence, they feel, are qualities of character natural to children who feel loved and secure. If they are given correct values—and who, asks the Taurus parent, would argue against goodness and kindness as the golden rule?—then youngsters will have a firm foundation on which to build for themselves.

One of the secrets of the Taurean's success as a parent is that he or she loves home life; the domestic routine is never a bore, as it is to several other zodiacal types. Home, to these people, is not just a place to sleep and eat—it's a place to live in with as much comfort, elegance and harmony as is humanly possible.

Taurus parents are acutely aware of surroundings and the importance of environment on a child's development. They prefer to make their home in a suburb well away from the city, or ideally in the country.

Taureans have a strong protective instinct. They are among the last people to seek a divorce because they fear it would unsettle the children. They will endure considerable personal hardship for the sake of a growing family.

The birth Sign of the child, of course, will have a large bearing on the success of the individual Taurus parent.

THE GEMINI PARENT

Parenthood is not an easy role for a typical Gemini man or woman. Their temperament and outlook are generally too youthful and adaptable to impart the solid direction and psychological security so necessary for a developing personality. Children who compare Gemini's example of restless activity and nervous excitement with conventional ideas of steady citizenship may become confused and uncertain of themselves.

The Gemini mother is likely to make a better fist of it than the Gemini dad. These versatile women are inclined to carry on with an outside activity after marriage, but when the children come along, they will probably realize they can't manage both. Or can they? There's no telling with ingenious, energetic Gemini. These women, although appearing domestically slack at times, loathe untidiness and are very fussy about how their home is run. What they would prefer is to have someone else do the housekeeping while they get out and on with their other interests.

Both parents love their children, but they're not prepared to make them their whole life. To do so, they feel, would be to give the youngsters a wrong impression of what living is all about.They are deeply interested in their children's intellectual development. They don't believe they should have second-hand ideas and values stuffed into them. They believe in free speech, free thought and independence—and this is what they try to teach their offspring. After all, that's what democracy is about, isn't it?

Geminis put a lot more thought than emotion into their relationships with Children. Critics may say they show a deficiency of heart. They tend to reason with them rather than try to "feel" with them. Emotionally, the Twins and their children may be miles apart.

The Gemini father is very quickly bored by the routine of family life. He's inclined to go out as often as possible, and may even seek an occupation that requires him to spend odd days away from home. However, he has a great deal of affection for his children as well as his home base. He is apt to rush in after a short absence in a flurry of expectation and excitement, stimulating everyone (especially the youngsters) to fever pitch.

The Gemini father may at times be unduly strict. He is likely to put on a display of irate authority to cover up his own feelings of uncertainty and insecurity.

Both Gemini parents find, as a rule, that they are able to guide their children more effectively by creating a restful atmosphere in the home.

The birth Sign of the child, of course, will have a large bearing on the success of the individual Gemini parent.

THE CANCER PARENT

A person born under Cancer often feels he or she is the best mom or dad in the world. Cancers do have some remarkably fine parental qualities (some even say that Cancer is the personification of motherhood), yet they are at the opposite extreme to Gemini: Cancer is all heart or feeling and not enough reason.

Both Cancer parents love their children in a

most possessive, effusive and sentimental way. They are determined to nourish and protect them—and often succeed in almost suffocating them with affection in the process.

The Cancer parent is completely devoted to home and family. Every other activity is incidental to this one great absorbing idea. While the children are growing up, they receive every consideration. Nothing is too much trouble; no desired object is denied them while there is any money available.

The Cancer mom and dad are of much the same temperament. But since this is a mothering Sign, the characteristcs generally fit the woman better than the man. He's moody, changeable, sentimental and and often oblivious to the exacting demands he makes on his family in exchange for his devotion to them. If you call him selfish, he will be flabbergasted, then highly indignant—and reel off incontrovertible evidence of all the sacrifices he's made for his family over the years. Yet his family might feel that despite his loving kindness, he has cheated them emotionally—that the price he has extorted in sympathy, approval and recognition of his virtues down the years was just not worth it. His fussiness around the home, insistence on accepted forms of behavior and corrective criticism may make the children nervous and self-conscious paragons. He can't seem to see beyond his own feelings of devotion and worthiness.

The Cancer mother will indulge and coddle her children with doting kindness, and then punish them with undue severity when they are naughty. Her moods change abruptly with irritation. Then this woman, who normally serves her children day in and day out and regards it as a privilege, will flare into a near-hysterical outburst. The children are often left bewildered and puzzled by this adult inconsistency.

Cancer parents need to exercise more reasoning and control over their fluctuating emotions if they are to balance their love with wisdom.

The birth Sign of the child, of course, will have a large bearing on the success of the individual Cancer parent.

THE LEO PARENT

Leo, as most people know, is the Sign of children, so it is to be expected that both the man and woman make fairly good parents.

They are exceedingly ambitious for their offspring. They want them to succeed in everything they attempt and are prepared to ensure that they enjoy every possible advantage. They won't take the initiative from their youngsters, but they will let them know they expect big things from them.

The success of these tactics depends to a great degree on the character of the child. If some of the zodiacal types are driven too hard or too much is expected of them, their development will probably be impaired or they will become resentful of the parent in later years.

Fortunately, Leo is also the Sign of deep love. The parent's ambitions for the children are usually tempered with profound affection and understanding. A typical Leo won't push a child beyond safe limits. Leo's style is more showmanship than shovemanship.

Children, whatever their Sign, can't help but be aware of the strength and loving concern of these parents. They will frequently indulge their offspring with extravagance, yet usually manage to attach some sort of condition that encourages a responsible attitude toward life. Despite their strong desire to be able to show off their youngsters to others, when it comes down to fundamentals, they want what is best for each child.

Leo parents (particularly dad) are likely to run the home as though it were their own private kingdom. Unless they receive homage and attention from their family, they are apt to become silent and sulky or stride off in a huff. This is more a device for drawing attention to the ingratitude of loved ones (who really should know better!) than moodiness or brooding. Once the acknowledgments are forthcoming, the whole household smiles again.

When Leo parents feel a visitor or friend is receiving more attention and admiration than they are from their offspring, they'll sometimes do ridiculous things to go one better. Junior may enjoy this, but the effects of such egocentric contests on his outlook are hard to gauge.

Leo parents have a habit of going from one extreme to another with their children; they either lavish too much attention on them or demand too much.

The birth Sign of the child, of course, will have a large bearing on the success of the individual Leo parent.

THE VIRGO PARENT

Virgo men and women make first-class parents, although their mates may have to see to the emotional development of the children because this side of child rearing is not one of Virgo's strong points.

These parents are practical, neat and orderly. They teach their children admirably how to cope with the problems of everyday life. They are especially mindful of diet and careful to instill in youngsters the necessity for cleanliness and good hygiene.

The Virgo mother instructs her youngsters from an early age in the virtues of good manners, tidy appearance and moral behavior. She doesn't believe in waste and makes sure that the children, both boys and girls, do their share of the chores around the house and learn to be methodical.

Sometimes she's a bit tight with the purse-strings where small personal luxuries are concerned. Occasionally, though, she is unexpectedly indulgent, particularly when she feels the child has earned a treat. Her youngsters never want for necessities, and they always have good, nutritious food to eat.

Both Mr. and Mrs. Virgo encourage their children right from the start to save for a rainy day. They are not social climbers nor particularly ambitious for themselves, but they do with all their heart want to see their children get a good start in life. They are very much aware of the benefits of a good education and will themselves help with lessons at home. They can grasp a subject very quickly from a textbook and have a knack for explaining things in clear, concise, and logical concepts.

Both Virgo parents want their children to stand on their own two feet, and will do everything possible to encourage this. However, they are apt to overlook a child's emotional needs because they feel the practical side is more important in the youngster's development. It is not easy for them to demonstrate love and affection. Although highly sensitive within themselves, they find it very difficult to show their real feelings. Although they love and care deeply for their offspring, a child may miss the warmth of cuddling and close physical contact.

The Virgo mom and dad both have a strong tendency to nag children. They may also be very possessive and fail to extend the freedom of choice in play that other children normally enjoy.

The birth Sign of the child, of course, will have a large bearing on the success of the individual Virgo parent.

THE LIBRA PARENT

Librans make excellent parents, probably the best of all the zodiacal types. They have an affinity with children that shines through their relationships in many delightful ways. They love to play with them. As the youngsters grow up, they genuinely enjoy having them and their young friends around. They help with the entertainment and can join in games and conversation without appearing to be intruding.

Basically, Libran men and women treat children with the same consideration and regard for dignity that they extend to their own many friends. They are gentle and patient; persuasive rather than pushy. They know instinctively what is right for a child, but would rather guide him to choose for himself than put an object into his hands with a ready-made explanation.

Because Librans are very fair, they won't allow themselves to inflict their own hangups and prejudices on a developing mind; nor do they permit others to intrude in this way. They can be surprisingly adamant and forceful if an adult—whatever his position—attempts to bully or tyrannize a child. Although they are the last people to go looking for a fight, they are the first to resist injustice in any form.

The Libra parent loves beauty and harmony and will do all in his or her power to awaken similar feelings in the children. Librans endeavor to interest their children early in one of the arts—say music or painting—believing that this will aid their higher development and enable them to mix with creative and socially refined people. They are not snobs by any means, but they do appreciate sophistication and culture, so they can't help but endeavor to educate their children along many of these same lines.

Librans have a way of making instruction interesting for children. And children do their best to please them. These individuals make loving and affectionate parents, but not stupid ones. They don't spoil their young ones by over-indulging them in material possessions or waiting on them hand and foot. They believe in moderation in all things. Gushing sentiment and insincere platitudes cut no ice with them.

Having an independent and spontaneous nature themselves, they endeavor to see that these qualities are not inhibited in the young personality. They will never attempt to hold back or delay progress out of jealousy.

The birth Sign of the child, of course, will have a large bearing on the success of the individual Libra parent.

THE SCORPIO PARENT

The Scorpio parent usually runs a tight family ship. Oh, these moms and dads are generous enough, keenly solicitous of the physical and moral welfare of their children and intent on providing a good home for them with every modern convenience. No one could say they aren't deeply devoted, but they are rarely capable of appreciating the child's point of view. Everything must be as they divine it. The result is often a rigid and unyielding discipline that cramps the child's style.

Scorpio is one of the clearest-thinking, nononsense Signs of the Zodiac. It seems a pity these men and women can't always humanize their gift for dealing with realities when it comes to child rearing.

Their function as parents is to help form an integrated personality through which the reality of the youngster's character can unfold. But too often the Scorpio parent's stern methods of discipline disintegrate the child's personality. The child's main concern, then, is to obey—it is, after all, his or her best means of defense. The personality such a child presents to the family may have no relationship at all to his or her inner state. Some children of Scorpio parents wait only for the day when they can quit the rigorous regimen of their home. Others may be so intimidated that they grow up repressed and cowardly.

The Scorpio dad is often the worse offender of the two parents. He frequently runs his home like an old feudal baron, insisting that his wife as well as his children follow his instructions to the letter. The overbearing and tyrannical methods that he often employs to become a successful businessman are imposed on his household.

The Scorpio mother is a great homemaker and she idolizes her children. As long as she is in love with her husband, all is relatively well. But if the marriage breaks up or if she falls in love with another man, she will usually follow the dictates of her passionate nature. Although the children's material needs will be looked after in every respect, their psychological development may be seriously impaired.

Both parents are likely to suffer from inordinate and irrational jealousy, which may intensify their urge to restrict their child's personal freedom.

The birth Sign of the child, of course, will have a great bearing on the success of the individual Scorpio parent.

THE SAGITTARIUS PARENT

The Sagittarius man is usually too in love with his own freedom to make a really good father. He's a great sport, a fine companion and a real man's man. But when it comes to supervising children, he's usually a dead loss. He gets impatient with his own family. He wants to be out and about, roaming and sharing his ideas and comradeship with the rest of humanity.

The Sagittarius mother is a much more stable and settled character as far as the home and parenthood are concerned. She has a deep inner wisdom and a lot of common sense, which allow her to bring up her children in a balanced way. She also believes in freedom, but is more inclined to regard it as a state of mind than as the absence of any physical restriction; she teaches her children accordingly.

Both parents are intellectual types, have a broad outlook and are usually well informed on world affairs. They are also likely to approach religion from a philosophic rather than dogmatic angle, and to encourage their children to be tolerant of the opinions of others but to make decisions for themselves.

Both mother and father are splendid influences from a moral point of view. Although sometimes bluntly outspoken, their frankness and honesty are among their finest attributes. They are also good-hearted, kind and generous, but not foolishly so (except dad sometimes when he's out with the boys).

The children of Sagittarius parents will probably be more at ease confiding their personal problems to their mother. Dad, although just as capable of giving sound and helpful advice, may become a little uneasy when intimate matters are discussed. He prefers to stay clear—if possible—of emotional problems concerning his family. He feels more comfortable if his wife deals with them and lets him know the happy result when it's all over! Both parents will see that their youngsters take an early interest in sports and get plenty of exercise and fresh air. With a Sagittarius parent, a child is almost sure to develop great affection for animals of all kinds.

The birth Sign of the youngster, of course, will have a great bearing on the success of the individual Sagittarius parent.

THE CAPRICORN PARENT

The personality of the Capricorn parent ranges between two extremes. On the one hand, these people may be too indulgent with their children. On the other, they may be unduly stern, demanding and forbidding.

The Capricorn woman, especially, finds motherhood an outlet for her often cruelly repressed emotions. Capricorn is nowhere near as self-sufficient as the individuals born under this Sign usually manage to convey.

Generally speaking, Capricorn parents do have a deep love for their children and regard them as necessary to complete a marriage. The parents' own childhood is often memorable for its unstable conditions, particularly in the relationship between their mother and father. They tend to retain vivid emotional impressions of any unhappiness suffered in those days and endeavor to protect their own children from such similar and painful experiences.

However, the less mature Capricorn parent, especially dad, may have been so bitterly affected by his past that he is unsympathetic and intolerant of his own children. He is likely to impose rules that restrict normal pleasures and emphasize responsibility and duty. He may justify his harshness by saying it is for the children's own good. This parent may feel he enjoys the respect of his children, when in fact they fear him and in later years may detest him.

The Capricorn mother is frequently very ambitious for her offspring. She will see that they are always well dressed when going out, but may not worry so much when they're around the house. She will tend to nag continually, trying to improve their speech, their manners and their behavior. Her object is to make them more socially acceptable and popular. She will take a close interest in their education and insist on homework (as well as chores about the house) being done.

Both parents may be possessive or jealous. Those who spoil and indulge their own youngsters may find that they are irritated by other people's children.

Capricorn mothers and fathers will instruct their children to be careful with money, although they themselves may be quite unwise in their spending habits.

The birth Sign of the child, of course, will have a large bearing on the success of the individual Capricorn parent.

THE AQUARIUS PARENT

Aquarius men and women make wise and mature parents. They are intent on allowing the child to develop as himself or herself and not as a carbon copy of either mom or dad.

Aquarius is the Sign that rules brotherhood and understanding, and Aquarius parents base their relationships with their children on these qualities. Although intensely devoted to them, they keep their emotional distance. The child is never stifled or confused by displays of jealousy or the inconsistencies of sickly sentimentality.

The Aquarius mother and father both encourage their youngsters to be intellectually fearless, to question rather than blindly accept the opinions of others. The children are taught to be keen and considerate rather than purely competitive. These people desire their children to succeed as much as any parent, but they put less emphasis on materialistic values and egocentric pride. The Aquarius parent likes first to think of his or her child as a successful human being.

Aquarians are gentle and reasonable with children. They endeavor at all times to awaken the youngster's interest so that he feels he is making his own way under their sympathetic and helpful supervision.

Both are exceedingly independent, with strong ideals and humanitarian feelings. Their views on child rearing are often well ahead of the times, and may be criticized by conventional members of the family. But they are firm in their beliefs and will not allow in-laws or other relatives to interfere.

When it comes to discipline, both parents are likely to have an enlightened and original approach. They are usually most reluctant to resort to corporal punishment. They find it difficult to rebuke children who are too young to heed an appeal to reason. They are sometimes accused of being permissive by stalwarts of the old school.

The Aquarius mother will usually manage to dress her children in a distinctive way. She will encourage them to be honest and not to compromise with their conscience. The child with an Aquarian parent will be brought up with a high regard for loyalty to family and friends.

The birth Sign of the youngster, of course, will have a large bearing on the success of the individual Aquarian parent.

THE PISCES PARENT

Pisces mothers and fathers are both gentle and loving—but it's debatable whether they are really up to coping with the practical demands of their parenthood.

No one derives more pleasure from their children than these parents. They wait on their charges hand and foot, listen sympathetically to their small talk and problems, welcome their friends and spoil them in every way.

The problem is they are reluctant to face up to the often unpleasant and disagreeable side of parenthood—training and discipline. The child is frequently so indulged that unless the other parent is strong and determined, the child will grow up thoroughly spoiled and unreasonably demanding in his or her personal relationships.

However, there is a saving grace. These people do all in their power to encourage their children to be socially acceptable. It is extremely important to Pisces' own happiness and contentment that their offspring be liked by others.

So although they may adroitly sidestep the nasty and serious business of disciplining youngsters, they will use their splendid gifts of persuasion to inculcate the social graces—correcting speech, manners, deportment and so forth at every opportunity.

Both the Pisces mother and father are inclined to crack emotionally under pressure in the home or in disharmonious surroundings. Trying to cope with intractable young children or willful teenagers is apt to send them screaming for the door—or the bar.

Pisces parents usually imagine they are good parents—and they are more than half right. But for the sake of their mate, as well as for their children, it will pay them to learn to be a little less softhearted and permissive.

There is no doubt that the children of Pisces have a rare opportunity to be associated with spiritually uplifting influences. Also, their parents' fondness for all that is artistic and aesthetically pleasing can have a most beneficial effect on children's developing personalities.

If tangible direction is lacking, there is certainly no absence of love, affection and a subtle appreciation of beauty and graciousness in the home of a Pisces parent.

The birth Sign of the child, of course, will have a great bearing on the success of the individual Pisces parent.

CHILDREN

The following descriptions of children born under the various Signs are based on the position of the Sun, the most powerful influence in the horoscope. Most individuals conform to the solar influence. However, variations do occur because of the placement of the other planets at the time of birth. And, of course, the birth Signs of the parents will also be reflected in the child's conditioning.

For a closer examination of these factors, it is advisable to study the individual child's and the parents' horoscopes, which are available for every Sign in *AstroAnalysis*. All you need to know is the person's date of birth.

Since some Signs are naturally more and less compatible with others, you can obtain a further idea of how children and parents will hit it off by referring to the Compatibility Guide. (*Astro-Analysis*, Grosset & Dunlap, 1976.)

THE ARIES CHILD

The Aries child is extremely bright (sometimes brilliant) and usually very advanced for his or her age.

Too much applause and reference to the child's precocity by admiring adults is likely to make him strive to outdo himself and overexcite his nervous system. This could result in sleeplessness, supersensitivity and an overcritical approach to his playmates and later all his associates. The Aries child is high-strung and needs to be intelligently quieted. His mind is so alert to the possibilities for action in his environment that he finds it difficult to concentrate on one thing for very long. He begins new interests with great enthusiasm, but usually veers off well before they are finished. Sometimes it is because he has discovered the challenge is within his capabilities and so loses interest in it. But if a toy or game is beyond him, he will petulantly turn his back on it—or perhaps break it or throw it away. He should be taught to apply himself to finish what he starts. The chances of success will be greater in an atmosphere where he feels there is due recognition of the importance of what he is doing.

From the start, these youngsters should be taught the advantages of slowing down without inhibiting their spontaneity. Their excited, sudden movements are apt to lead to more than their share of accidents. They will usually be recovering from a bruise, scald or cut somewhere on their body. It is terribly important for Aries boys and girls to be physically active; it helps to work off the excess nervous energy that subtracts from their powers of concentration. But they need to learn the value of deliberate, measured movement as against unrestrained hustle and bustle; their parents should inculcate in them a sense of grace of rhythm, which their impulsive actions seldom allow.

Sports are good for the Aries child and he or she is usually proficient at them. It is wise to have children coached from an early age so that they express themselves with style and expertise. Abounding energy and desire to succeed will prevent them from becoming performing cogs in a wheel. Either they'll get to the top of the team or they'll quit and try another activity until they make their mark.

In none of his activities should the Aries child be encouraged to show off. If restraint or discipline is required, it should be exercised tactfully so it won't injure the youngster's pride. Aries is a fiercely proud Sign, and this is the key to the nobility that can readily be developed in this character.

It is important that this type of child be allowed to discover things for himself and not constantly be told what to do. He likes to experiment. Too much supervision and interference make him resentful. He learns from making mistakes. He might make the same mistake more than once (which can be rather exasperating for a parent), but this is his style. He packs a lot of experience into his life. He is attracted by the challenge rather than by the end result.

The Aries child often reveals creative talents quite early. These should be nurtured and developed as soon as they appear, without stressing the competitive angle.

One of the main problems is an overactive imagination. Young Aries should be taught not to exaggerate and to learn to describe objects and events as they really are, not as he or she fancies them to be.

THE TAURUS CHILD

Taurus is usually a lovely child, both to look at and in disposition. But he has some very definite characteristics that are not immediately discernible. These need to be understood, especially by his teachers, for him to develop in a normal, balanced way.

Above everything else, young Taureans need love and affection. They are deeply sensitive and unsure of themselves inside. They often give the appearance of being wonderfully self-assured, but this is to compensate for their uncertainty, which can amount almost to an inferiority complex at times.

Taureans are not intellectual beings, essentially. They live on their feelings, which need to be constantly stimulated by the demonstration and knowledge that they are loved and appreciated. You can't just tell a Taurus child that you love him or her. You have to show it in physical terms by cuddling and petting—or with caring actions. If you don't do this, the child will become more and more indifferent, and as he gets older, will turn to sensual self-indulgence as a substitute for the loving stimulation he missed as a child. Failing this, Taurus may become increasingly stolid, and, in maturity, a rather dull and uninteresting person.

Young Taurus has exceptional willpower, which may, at times, reveal itself as a fearful obstinacy. If he digs in his toes, no argument or threat will shake him. He can be absolutely unreasonable. Again, only an appeal to his emotional self is apt to make him relent. Should he ever lose his temper, it could be a devastatingly memorable occasion.

He is an extremely modest child and tends to underrate his own abilities. He should not be criticized to make him "do better" because criticism will only make him feel more inferior and then, perhaps, defiantly overconfident and prone to making silly mistakes. He responds much better to praise and encouragement.

Taurus children are not studious types. Normal education methods don't work so well with them. To learn, it is vital that they have their feelings aroused so they can take a genuine interest in the subject. These boys and girls need to relate to topics through their senses; if they're to learn about nature, they must examine the specimen, touch it, smell it. With arithmetic and other abstract subjects, the teacher must find a way of exciting them into participation with demonstrations, models. The failure to realize this often leads to branding the Taurus child a slow learner, when he is, in fact, nothing of the sort.

Friendship and playmates are very important to Taurean youngsters. If they can't mix with children they like, they will slow down physically and mentally, and may easily become lazy and indifferent. Having a great love of pleasure (because it helps them learn to be intellectual creatures), they might choose companions who teach them bad habits.

Properly handled and encouraged, the Taurus child quickly puts aside his timidity and becomes a friendly and congenial little person. He is likely to be artistic with his hands and any sign of this should be cultivated.

THE GEMINI CHILD

Gemini children are usually filled with restless, nervous energy. It comes from their minds, which are like delicately tuned electronic instruments. They simply can't keep still, mentally or physically. They must be constantly engaged in something that interests them. Parents and teachers may find this an exhausting business, mainly because these lovable little imps lose interest more quickly than most children. And when that happens, and no one's around, their capacity for mischief is almost unbelievable!

Young Gemini is an exceedingly bright child. He or she learns instantaneously and has an alert, inquiring mind that demands to know the reason behind everything that catches his or her attention.

As often as practical, Gemini children should be answered factually and not put off because the question happens to be irrelevant. This is the way they absorb, and every fact goes into their formidable memory, where it will be recalled as soon as it's required. In a very short time, you can teach a Gemini child practically anything.

He may not be physically strong in his early years because his whole system is under the continual tension of febrile nervous activity. As his body adapts to this, he will get stronger, until finally, in maturity, his health will be dictated largely by his state of mind. Just as Gemini can stage remarkable recoveries when new and novel interests appear, so he can become listless when assailed by boredom and depression.

The pure Gemini child needs plenty of exercise, but usually not in the form of rough and strenuous sports. His lithe, agile body and quick actions enable him to excel in games requiring thought and technique rather than brute strength and endurance.

It is especially necessary for these boys and girls to get as much sleep and rest as possible. But this is usually easier said than arranged. At bedtime, the aim should be to avoid excitement that stimulates the imagination. Stories and television shows should be carefully selected. Horror movies and the like are almost certain to cause nightmares and extreme anxiety. The child may be afraid of the dark well into his or her teens.

Gemini youngsters frequently exaggerate and tell outrageous lies—with remarkable plausibility. Their imagination is so active and vidid that they live out adventures and dramas in their heads and can't (or would rather not) separate fiction from reality.

They make excellent actors, able to mimic sounds and reproduce the characteristics of people they observe. Sometimes these children suffer from a slight speech impediment—the brain is too fast for the vocal equipment. But with patience and understanding, this can be overcome. Otherwise, the Gemini child is usually well advanced in his speech and comprehension. He may be a terrible chatterbox, though.

A child of this Sign is more intellectual than sentimental and may sometimes be slow at showing love and affection.

THE CANCER CHILD

The Cancer child looks for love and a placid existence. These boys and girls are extremely sensitive and timid. Even though they crave to make friends, their retiring nature renders it difficult to make the first move. They do not enjoy being alone; they need to feel they belong. A Cancer child will cling tenaciously to anyone who loves him. The most difficult parental task is to push this sensitive little creature gently forward into the world.

Although the Cancer child is not necessarily the smartest or brightest of children, he possesses innate talents that a sensible upbringing will help make manifest. The tendency for late development makes the formative years extremely important for them.

Young Cancer responds remarkably to adults who show they have faith in him. For those who love him, he will do almost anything. A responsive and understanding parent or teacher will try to arouse his interest in games and activities that he can confidently share with other children. He should not be left to feel lonely. The object is to coax the child out, to make him more independent and outspoken. It is best to encourage him to do as much as possible for himself and let him feel he is actually achieving results. These should be praised and appreciated.

Cancer children are splendidly conscientious when they have been entrusted with a task. Psychologically, the reason for this is they are in constant need of approbation and learn quickly that one way of guaranteeing this is to do a job assiduously.

These children are not studious and intellectual, although they may become so in adulthood. They learn through their feelings. Unless they are very clearly associated with sensation, concepts and ideas confuse them. They need to smell a flower, to sing a song, to taste a piece of fruit if they are going to be taught about these things. You can't assume that a Cancer child has got the idea of a subject from a verbal description—which would suffice for most other children. Cancer is the Sign of the senses and intuition, so the child's intellectual development depends on *emotional* understanding. Once a parent or teacher manages to arouse an absorbing interest in him, the Cancer child may apply himself to this subject for the rest of his life. Great artistic and creative careers may be begun with the right treatment of these finely balanced little people.

Otherwise, the younger person of this Sign is tempted to become introverted and live off his own emotions—moody, changeable and lethargic.

Being exceedingly sensitive, the Cancer child is easily discouraged and takes criticism much to heart. Worry may upset his stomach. He is also apt to suffer from colds and chills. His health in his earlier years may be indifferent. He may pick at his food and cry more than most youngsters.

Cancer children are usually competent at making handicrafts. In later years, they often show an extraordinary flair for business coupled with an intensely ambitious spirit.

THE LEO CHILD

The Leo child has a vast amount of vital and mental energy at his or her disposal. It is important for parents and teachers to see that this is directed along positive lines. This youngster, because of his forceful determination, is apt to find that success comes fairly readily. He may get so carried away with applause and admiration that he overlooks the value of accomplishment itself.

Young Leo has a natural gift for leadership and will assert this as his or her right in the presence of other youngsters. The problem is a tendency to become domineering, to throw his weight around unnecessarily, show off and generally bore everyone within earshot with his boasting. In some cases, little Leo becomes "little Caesar" and exhibits a distinct love of power, which may be harmless in a child but is an objectionable quality in an adult.

The Leo child is an active and lovable little person. Quite apart from the early "ego flexing," there is a dignity and nobility to his nature. His unquestionable courage becomes obvious early. Although as disobedient as any child, he will seldom resort to mean and spiteful actions. He or she will probably only have to be told once that it is dishonest to tell tales. This child's sense of loyalty is ingrained and at times may be carried to absurd lengths.

Leos are deeply affectionate children, and despite their love of display and applause, are keenly sensitive. Their intuition is often remarkable. They have a great sense of pride and yet are quick to forget and forgive. Once they make up their minds to do something, they are unswervingly determined.

A Leo child often acts impulsively, especially where pleasure is concerned, finding it very difficult to turn down an opportunity to enjoy himself. When playing, he is likely to lose all sense of time and arrive home at nine o'clock at night for his evening meal. He has a love of the great outdoors and is likely to acquit himself well at all kinds of sports.

Young Leo, although enjoying his periods of seclusion, will usually be found among groups and clubs where he can demonstrate his organizing ability and powers of leadership.

Parents of the Leo teenager should endeavor to have him trained in any profession or line of work he shows an interest in. He has a great capacity for learning, not by gathering and memorizing information but by inquiring and understanding its significance. He is never really satisfied unless he comprehends the reason for an action or instruction. A natural commander of men and women in the making, Leo will never be a shallow echo of another person's caprices.

The Leo youngster has a deep-seated ambition to get to the top even though he or she may not understand this inner drive. This child's considerable energies and diverse talents work better harnessed in a definite direction, whether in the arts, literature, politics, journalism, science or executive management.

Young Leo also benefits from a good example. Conversely, he or she should not be allowed to fall into bad company.

THE VIRGO CHILD

Virgo children are worriers. They take the smallest disappointments very seriously. They want to be liked, and yet have an unfortunate way of upsetting others by being unduly critical and faultfinding. A Virgo child is often exasperated and discouraged by other people's negative reactions to his or her good intentions, and by his or her own frustrated desire to please.

Young Virgo needs to be taught to accent the positive side of his or her nature. Although reserved and modest, these children are naturally optimistic and progressive. They are also keenly intelligent. But the slightest antagonism and adversity tend to deflate them. They live on their nerves to a great extent. They are continually analyzing other people's motives and endeavoring to find a rationale for everything. The sheer impossibility of satisfying this desire explains their basic problem.

The Virgo child loves order and method. Once these are established at home or in school, he or she will settle down emotionally and seldom be any trouble. But in a disorganized system where people are uncertain, Virgo becomes disoriented. That's why it's often a traumatic experience for a Virgo child—or a Virgo adult for that matter—to move to a new home, school or job. One astrologer has even claimed you can cause great agitation in a Virgo cat by relocating its saucer!

Schoolwork itself, however, is seldom much of a problem for the Virgo youngster. Along with Gemini, he is one of the easiest types in the Zodiac to teach. He has an inquiring and logical mind, which is always trying to make practical sense out of the information received. Naturally, school lessons make sense to these boys and girls. They often take a special interest in science and mathematics. They are also quite inventive and enjoy devising new methods of doing things.

Young Virgo makes friends cautiously. He's not a sentimental or emotional character and prefers to judge people on their actions and achievements rather than their words. He is an idealist and at heart a perfectionist who wants to see everything in its proper place and logical order. When he discerns that a person is not being honest with himself or true to his type (his intellectual acuity is first rate), he will say so, not with the desire to hurt, but to help. This trait is naturally often misinterpreted, and his playmates may resent his remarks and attitude and ostracize him for them.

The Virgo child needs a good education so that he doesn't feel inferior to others. He doesn't, as a rule, enjoy close physical contact—in fact, he may feel that cuddling and caressing are unnecessary and embarrassing. His finer feelings have to be handled delicately and with understanding to prevent fussiness and queasiness from becoming fixed in his character.

Virgo children are apt to be faddish about certain foods and instantly dislike some kinds. They may refuse to eat in a place they feel is dirty, although they are unable to give a conscious reason for this attitude.

These children are very quick to learn about cleanliness and hygiene, but the subjects should not be overemphasized.

THE LIBRA CHILD

The Libra child is a delicate flower because he or she is a meeting point of intellect and emotion and these two don't integrate easily. The child is usually very intelligent and bright but unsure of how to handle his or her feelings.

Libras crave love yet are reserved and shy about reaching out for it. Consequently, they may cling and yet be unable to give in return. They are constantly weighing up what to do in their relationships, which way to go, what is best. The result is they don't appear to have much initiative, and unless guided and directed by an understanding parent or teacher, may grow up unable to make positive use of their many potential talents.

Young Libras don't seem to have much willpower, mainly for the reasons given above. They become excited by an idea, plunge into action with enthusiasm—and then lose interest and look around for something new. If they can't find something special, they may lapse into apathy. These children have very little urge to develop their capabilities; ambition is something they have to learn. They prefer to depend on others without exerting themselves. They need to develop the habit of working along methodical lines—games and hobbies can be used for this. If their interest is not maintained—by the parent acting as a sort of partner—they will quickly get into mischief.

The wise parent of a Libra youngster will realize right from the start that his or her child is artistically inclined and that a harsh, uncongenial, severe or ugly environment will inhibit natural expression. In such an environment, the child is likely to become highly nervous and a constant problem for the parent. But once the innate Libran love of beauty and harmony is acknowledged and cultivated, the prospects of steady development and accomplishment are much improved. For these reasons, it is advisable for the parent to observe the child's proclivities in the formative years and coax him along in the right direction.

A Libra child is much more likely to become a successful dancer, actor, singer, writer, painter, interior decorator, architect or beauty specialist than shine in a cutthroat commercial occupation.

Moodiness and jealousy are often a problem. These children want desperately to be liked, but their attitude often suggests indifference to their playmates. They may be happy and gay one moment, and inexplicably depressed and silent the next. The more they are left alone, the more temperamental and introspective they become. If this is allowed to continue, the child may grow up with few friends and unreasonable possessiveness may cause great unhappiness in his or her future love life.

Libran children are usually well formed and attractive. They have a magnetic appeal that makes other childrren want to be with them, but they seem unable to maintain the initial attraction. This confuses them. The parents' task is to teach the Libra child, with love and understanding, to integrate his or her emotional and mental activities and express them in unselfish ways such as in art and social endeavors.

THE SCORPIO CHILD

The Scorpio child is a tight concentration of intense energy and the direction of his or her development will depend largely on the influence parents or guardians bring to bear.

Young Scorpio is particularly strong-willed. He or she also possesses abundant capabilities that bode success in future life as a surgeon, dentist, psychiatrist, scientist, occult investigator, researcher, lawyer, detective or military person.

If you can interest this youngster in constructive and productive activities, there is not much he or she is incapable of achieving. Once this child fixes a goal, he will pursue it relentlessly. And his capacity for hard work and endurance is unequaled by any of the other Sign of the Zodiac.

The problem is that Scorpio can go from one extreme to the other; that is, he or she can be very good and very bad. If early training is neglected or haphazard, or if the child happens to fall into bad company, he may grow up to be a selfish and tyrannical adult.

Young Scorpio has a keen and penetrating mind and cannot long be entertained by frivolous and pointless games and pastimes. At every stage, Scorpios enjoy grappling with sturdy problems that are not so easy for others of their age or experience to solve. Everything they attempt, they do with zest and relish—provided they are genuinely interested.

Schoolwork comes easy to Scorpio children. Trouble occurs when they can't find sufficiently satisfying outlets for their tremendous vitality.

It is wise for the parents of a Scorpio child to be honest and straightforward with him or her from the beginning because these children possess an almost mystical ability to detect lies and attempts to deceive them. Also, the negative side of a Scorpio nature is less likely to assert itself in an atmosphere of frank and open commitment. The habitual faults of the Scorpio character include brooding resentment, secretiveness and jealousy. These have less opportunity to fester in a young personality used to candid and truthful parents.

Young Scorpio is fiercely independent but surprisingly tractable if handled with subtlety and sensitivity. He or she resents being ordered about, and may react violently and willfully to this sort of treatment. Parents who reason with their Scorpio children and deal with them in an adult fashion will get the best results.

The shrewdness and comprehension of these youngsters may develop into an infuriating air of superiority when they are with less mentally acute adults. Their self-confidence is enormous. Their vanty is a weak spot.

The Scorpio child is sometimes so bent on getting his own way that when opposed by young playmates, he may resort to underhanded methods. He can be vindictive, and in extreme cases, exact cruel reprisals. If the negative qualities are strong in these boys and girls, they may plot revenge while pretending to be sorry.

THE SAGITTARIUS CHILD

The Sagittarius child is not a fast developer. He or she is cheerful, trusting, optimistic and a very congenial little person to have around, if you can tolerate some changeable and unpredictable ways. Sagittarius sometimes retains these childlike qualities well into adulthood, and in some cases, for his entrie life. His trust and faith in humanity is one of his most admirable traits. Yet, as many parents are pained to find out, this faith is often violated and imposed upon.

Still, not to worry—little Sagittarius certainly doesn't. He loves to play, to roam far afield, to visit people, to go on "adventures." These boys and girls are too interested in being on the move and experiencing life as it actually is to have much time for reading and study. However, they are mentally eager, bright and quick to learn, though lacking in concentration.

Sagittarius is passionately fond of animals. If he can get hold of a horse and ride it on his explorations and adventures, he is in his element. The parents of a Sagittarius child can expect to have around the house a menagerie of pets on which their youngster will lavish considerable affection. He may sometimes in his haste forget to feed the animals and afterward cry inconsolably with remorse. He is so genuine in his affection and sincere in his intentions that it is not wise to make a fuss over this kind of neglect.

Young Sagittarius tends to think everyone is good. He himself is truthful, spontaneous and honest. He doesn't have a selfish or vindictive bone in his body. He has to be taught, though, that there is such a thing as deceit and that he must practice putting his inherently good judgment to full use.

The Sagittarius child is not possessive. Emotionally, he or she loves to have a home, family (and pets) to return to. But these children can't stand the thought of being tied down to a confined or regimented existence. Their sense of freedom is essential to their continued and broadening development.

Here, a parent must exercise great care, striking a balance between the child's need to be restrained and taught responsibility and his or her fundamental urge to learn. The most effective way of securing this child's cooperation and interest, as well as this objective, is to treat him or her like a buddy and not try to dictate. Sagittarius is built for companionship and affection rather than for possessive love. He makes one of the finest friends of all.

Young Sagittarius *has* to be guided toward a more responsible attitude to life. He thinks he can look after himself, but rarely can unless his parents have managed to cultivate in him the judgment that curbs impatience, restlessness, recklessness, extravagance and all that goes with a personality trying to throw off authority and its controls.

When it comes to a career, the Sagittarius youth is ambitious and resourceful. But he is inclined to jump from one job to another because he just can't stand the tedium of waiting for normal advancement.

THE CAPRICORN CHILD

The Capricorn child is often far too serious for his or her own good. And frequently, it is the fault of one of the parents. This child needs mature but cheerful and happy handling that makes a point of *not* overstressing duty, responsibility and restriction. There are enough of these sobering elements in the Capricorn temperament already. Exaggeration will only create further problems for the youngster as he or she grows up.

Young Capricorn needs a great deal of praise and affection. These boys and girls often feel afraid and deeply dissatisfied with themselves. Criticism wounds them deeply, not because they resent it, but because they unwittingly believe it to be true. Obviously, these little people require a very special parental technique to help them develop a balanced and buoyant personality.

Never nag this child. Criticism should be leveled so that the positive alternative appears as the ideal solution. Every effort to instruct should be made optimistically and encouragingly.

With this Sign, the positions of the other planets in the child's horoscope are extremely important. If there are sunnier and more easygoing influences such as Jupiter in Leo, Sagittarius or Aries, the youngster's disposition will be correspondingly less grave. These other planetary configurations can be checked out in Capricorn, *AstroAnalysis.* (Grosset & Dunlap, 1976.)

The true Capricorn child is very self-conscious. He wants to make friends, but is uneasy in the presence of others, especially strangers. Being withdrawn and a rather solitary figure, he doesn't attract the usual number of playmates. Without friends to help draw him out, he is inclined to become distrustful and wary of personal relationships, thus isolating himself even more.

Young Capricorn is very good at schoolwork and a willing little helper around the house. He enjoys running errands and completing small tasks for elders who display trust in him. He is extremely conscientious and wants to please. He usually enjoys study and reading and has a great capacity for sorting out detail and cataloging data. He is well suited for all kinds of hobbies connected with sciences such as chemistry, biology, astronomy, and the like where he can apply his considerable reasoning abilities.

The longer his education can be continued, the better, especially from the social angle. He needs to be in the company of people his own age to help overcome his shyness.

As Capricorn has a distinct talent for practical pursuits, he or she will generally feel more confident with an education along these lines rather than one that is strictly academic.

People of this Sign are born leaders and vaultingly ambitious. When young Capricorn does get around to organizing young friends, he or she is enterprising and frequently bossy.

THE AQUARIUS CHILD

The Aquarian child is often precocious in a shy and rather retiring way. Juvenile pastimes and games don't hold his or her interest for as long in the formative years as they do other children's. Aquarians "grow up" mentally very quickly and often prefer the company of elders "when they should be out playing." Sometimes they are called "old-fashioned" because of their adult ways, but these are only a reflection of the advanced understanding of life which is peculiar to Aquarius.

The Aquarius child is naturally affectionate and very obedient if parents or teachers are reasonable. He or she enjoys a position of trust and is particular about honoring obligations. The cooperation of these children can't be secured by threat or force. They are highly intellectual and demand to know from a very early age why they should or should not do certain things.

The most effective parental policy is to treat an Aquarian youngster as a mental equal, to confide in him or her and encourage confidences in return—in other words, to regard the child as an intelligent companion.

Although young Aquarius is a loving child with a sweet and kind disposition, he is noticeably impersonal in the way he shows affection. He doesn't cling to people in sentimental ways and is more likely to be adult and friendly.

These boys and girls are not great students and need to be encouraged and helped with their schoolwork. They find routine book learning and formal concentration arduous. Their independent minds tend to reject attempts to condition their thinking. However, if they can be convinced that education is a means to a personally desirable end, they will apply themselves and work conscientiously. They need to know there is progressive development for them in whatever they tackle. To accumulate indiscriminate knowledge is just not their style.

The Aquarian child is uniquely lacking in self-centered drive. Basically, he or she wants to be of use to the community. Material possessions are not all that important, and over the years this indifference becomes more and more evident. A strong humanitarian tendency is apt to appear. Finally, Aquarians will probably choose a career in science or medicine, one connected with large welfare projects or social reform where they can satisfy their urge to serve on a wide scale. They are not so concerned with the individual as they are with the masses, which accounts for their sometimes detached attitude.

Young Aquarius often has a great love of animals. Here, he or she begins to demonstrate a deep protective instinct.

This child sometimes has the potential of brilliance—even genius—but not necessarily in conventional forms. His or her inclinations need to be closely observed so that any unusual aptitude can be cultivated and guided.

THE PISCES CHILD

The true Pisces child is very intelligent but emotionally unstable. He or she is born believing that everything and everyone are good. Thus Pisces' life seems to be a progression of disillusionment.

Faced with an unacceptable reality, Pisces children retreat into a dream world where all is as perfect as they originally thought. The problem for the parent is to coax these little people back without smashing their dreams, to teach them it's not so bad after all and that every human being has within them the power to cope.

These children are essentially artistic and often show a talent for dancing, painting, music and writing—especially poetry. They are terribly self-conscious and need to be encouraged at every step with love, praise and admiration.

They are very critical of their own efforts and never seem to reach the standard of perfection their nature calls for. In despair, they will tear up what they've written or drawn, even though by normal standards it might be excellent. Or, more likely as they grow up, they will decide not to try at all anymore, that indolence is better than the pain of failure.

Young Pisces have no confidence in their own ability. They are great actors and can put on a show of indifference and self-assurance, for a short time. But then they are likely to go away on their own and cry until they sink into the delicious world of their own vivid imaginings. These boys and girls are generally timid, shy, secretive and very loving. But they also possess a strong spiritual quality.

A Pisces child has to be taught that harsh self-judgment is damaging to his or her attempts to be productive and expressive. These boys and girls must be led to understand that they are highly artistic, and that even their compassion for others (stronger in them than in any other Sign) is an act of love and creation—sublime artistry—that most others are not capable of. On the practical side, they must learn to allow those who are competent to judge their efforts to do so, since no one will be as cruelly critical of their work as they are themselves.

These boys and girls must be given a sense of proportion so that they understand every success means "failure" for someone. The important thing is to instill in the child a desire to perform, and especially to complete, for the sake of the work itself, without encouraging a competitive spirit or even acknowledging that it is necessary.